THE NEW ILLUSTRATED
ENCYCLOPEDIA OF
MOTORCYCLES

THE NEW ILLUSTRATED ENCYCLOPEDIA OF
MOTORCYCLES

EDITED BY ERWIN TRAGATSCH

Revised and updated by Kevin Ash

CHARTWELL
BOOKS, INC.

Published by Chartwell Books
A Division of Book Sales Inc.
114 Northfield Avenue
Edison, New Jersey 08837
USA

ISBN 0-7858-1163-X

QUMEOMB

This book is produced by

Quantum Publishing
A division of Quarto Publishing PLC
The Old Brewery
6 Blundell Street
London N7 9BH

Project Manager : Joyce Bentley
Designer : Stephen Croucher / Earl Neish
Editor : Alex Revell

Printed in Indonesia by APP Printing Pte Ltd
Manufactured in Singapore by United Graphics Pte Ltd

Quantum Publishing would like to thank the following for providing pictures used in this book:
Kevin Ash, Motor Cycle News and Richard Rosenthal

CONTENTS

INTRODUCTION

Throughout my last decade as a motorcycle journalist there has been one utterly invaluable reference work to which I've regularly needed to refer: The Illustrated Encyclopedia of Motorcycles. This dauntingly comprehensive book which aimed to include every motorcycle manufacturer in history was originally created, then updated, by Erwin Tragatsch. Tragatsch not only worked in the motorcycle trade and industry (for companies including Triumph as well as building his own machines in his Czech workshop) he also raced and wrote for the press, so saw and understood all sides of motorcycling as well as building up a vast range of contacts, placing him in a unique position to be able to see through such an apparently impossible task.

It therefore came as a great honor and privilege to be asked to revise and update The Tragatsch, as the encyclopedia is universally called, and produce this latest version. The task was enormous, partly because so much has happened in the fascinating world of motorcycles in the last decade or so, and partly because it was decided that the time was right to substantially increase the size, from 320 pages to a huge 560 pages!

The task was more than I could possibly have hoped to achieve alone, so I was extremely fortunate to be able to call on the help of some of the best motorcycle journalists in the business, each specialists in particular aspects of motorcycling. Former Bike magazine editor, TT lap record holder, highly successful endurance racer and current racing journalist Mat Oxley's input into the road race histories of many factories is both comprehensive and authoritative, while former Classic Bike and Motor Cycle News archivist Richard Rosenthal never ceases to surprise me with his detailed knowledge of marques and machines which, without people of his rare ilk, would be long forgotten. Mac McDiarmid, another ex-editor of Bike and now a highly respected freelance, combines a unique combination of historical and technical knowledge with an endearing appetite for beer and cigarettes, while who else but the former editor of Dirt Bike Rider, Mike Greenough, could have written so much,

so accurately, about the off-road forays of the motorcycle factories? Scooters haven't been left out - the disdain in which some less enlightened motorcyclists hold them ignores their enormous contribution to two-wheeled history, so Martin 'Sticky' Round of Scootering magazine ensured this wasn't overlooked with his knowledgeable and substantial input, and I was pleased to have the help of a new young journalist, Indi Archdale, in some lengthy research and writing.

My own input has covered many areas, but focused on the more recent histories of the current motorcycle factories, and it's here that the biggest additions have been made. Of course this is partly because they have spent the last 10 years adding to the history this encyclopedia aims to cover, but in addition I hope that in paying much more attention to manufacturers and machines which are still around, the appeal of The Tragatsch will be extended to newer and younger motorcyclists, who then might be tempted to read more of the intriguing history of motorcycling.

Such is the respect for The Tragatsch, many of the current motorcycle factories around the world, from Japan to Germany, Italy to the United States, proved more than merely helpful, being positively encouraging, especially in supplying pictures, including some rare and valuable ones from their archives.

A special thank you too must go to Motor Cycle News, which opened up its own compeling archive to me for a selection of photographs and brochures. My only complaint is that the place is so fascinating, I spent far too many hours just browsing when I should have been working!

The result is by far the most comprehensive record in existence of motorcycling's rich history, with a work which I am sure will prove as invaluable to scholars, professionals and enthusiasts as the earlier editions have to me.

Just as important, I do hope it will prove quite simply to be a good, enjoyable read.

Kevin Ash

Kevin Ash on a Ducati 916 at Misaro race track, Italy

THE PIONEER YEARS

In the second half of the 19th century, both in Europe and in the USA, there were a good many attempts to build a practical steam bicycle. None was truly successful. Reducing engine and steam systems to a manageable size and weight almost inevitably compromised power output and reliability, but the real drawback was the speed with which any steam engine used its water. Topping-up the boiler feed water tank every ten or 15 miles was hardly convenient, or indeed always possible, while carrying a reserve supply was no answer at all as it was far too heavy and bulky. Few people did more to further the cause of the light steam-powered vehicle than the famous Count de Dion, yet his first sight of a very early gasoline-engined car was enough to convince him that here lay the future. For all his success with steam up to then, he turned immediately to the internal combustion engine.

The internal combustion engine itself then went through a period of considerable development and refinement. The earliest gas engines had no compression stroke and so were extremely inefficient. Etienne Lenoir's commercially successful workshop engine of 1860 drew in gas and air for half of one stroke, when it was ignited and the subsequent expansion provided what power there was. Exhaust took place on the return stroke. The engine was 'double acting' - ignition took place on both sides of the piston. The four-stroke cycle of induction, compression, expansion and exhaust, proposed by French railway engineer Alphonse Beau de Rochas in 1862, was first attempted - and patented - by Nikolaus Otto of the Deutz gas engine works in Germany in 1876. Nine years later, Otto's one-time colleagues, Gottlieb Daimler and Paul Maybach, tested a liquid-fuelled four-stroke engine in a two wheeled chassis they called

Even during the boom period of the 1920s, BMW had adopted a typically methodical production system

the 'Einspur'. Often spoken of as the world's first motorcycle, the Einspur was intended to test only the engine, but in practice it was a remarkably well thought out and practical vehicle for its time.

Daimler's engine was astonishingly well suited to automotive use. Light and self-contained, it was of 270cc swept volume, with the flywheel assembly enclosed in a cast aluminum crankcase and a fan-cooled, cast iron cylinder and cylinder head. The inlet valve opened automatically, while the exhaust valve was pushrod operated from a camtrack in the face of one of the flywheels. The 'benzene' (gasoline) fuel was vaporised by passing air over its surface in a carburetor. Mistrusting electrical ignition, the inventors used a 'hot tube' of platinum, heated externally by a gasoline-fuelled burner. The engine ran at the then remarkable speed of 800rpm and produced something like half a horsepower.

That Europe was indeed ready for the automotive engine in 1885 is shown by the almost simultaneous appearance of gasoline engined tricars from Karl Benz in Germany and Edward Butler in England. Of the two, Butler's was in its later, developed form far the more sophisticated, but repressive British traffic laws, not repealed until 1896, prevented it ever reaching commercial production. Butler's engine was fitted with rotary valves, a sort of primitive 'magneto' (actually dependent on the generation of static electricity rather than magnetic flux) and a spray carburetor rather than a surface vaporiser. Butler's patent on the carburetor prevented later inventors from obtaining a monopoly.

Count Albert De Dion and his partner Georges Bouton of the firm of De Dion Bouton probably did as much - and more - than anyone else to further the cause of the early motorcycle. In the 1890s they concentrated on gasoline engined tricycles rather than two wheelers, but their single-cylinder engine was suitable for both. In 1897 De Dion Bouton offered these engines for general sale, thus enabling scores of experimenters to copy - and improve upon - the remarkably successful machine popularised by the Werner brothers. As a result, the De Dion engine was copied - with and without acknowledgement - and made under licence all over the world. In its early form, the De Dion was of 70mm x 70mm bore and stroke, giving 270cc, which was very soon uprated to 86mm x 86mm and 500cc. As an indication of the De Dion's outstanding penetration of the market, it was significant enough at the time for these engine dimensions to be chosen by Britain's newly formed Auto Cycle Club in 1903, when it came to standardise capacity classes for competition.

The engine was entirely conventional with air cooling, an automatic inlet valve, surface carburetor and battery and coil ignition. However, it set new standards in precision engineering and provided a benchmark for power and reliability by which all other contemporary engines were judged. Needless to say it soon had many rivals, of which the Belgian Minerva and the French Clement were the most popular, while inventors were quick to improve on the basic concept. As early as

The advanced Rudge multi had variable gear ratios, a multi-plate clutch and an inlet over the exhaust valve engine

Germany's Hildebrand & Wolfmüller, the worlds first production motorcycle, was powered by a massive 1488cc twin cylinder engine

The elegant Czech-built Laurin & Klement single cylinder B-D of 1903

1898 in Britain, Coventry's Percy Riley, later to become a famous car maker, built an engine with a mechanically operated inlet valve, and went on to develop (and patent) 'overlap' valve timing. There were spray carburettors in profusion, one of the best of which was the British Amac of 1903. The hated and unreliable battery and coil ignition system was gradually superseded by the magneto, perfected through the work of Frederick Simms in England and Robert Bosch in Stuttgart in collaboration, first as a low-tension system and then in 1902, as a high-tension one with rotating armature. As a result of Bosch's developments, high-tension magnetos almost became a German monopoly, which led to some practical difficulties on the outbreak of the First World War in 1914.

Early development of the motorcycle seemed to progress best when it was left to the instincts of practical men - gifted amateurs and superior blacksmiths, rather than formal engineers. This is no doubt an over-simplification, but certainly the purpose-designed Hildebrand and Wolfmuller Motorrad of 1894 was a failure, as was the equally impressive four-cylinder motorcycle designed by Colonel Holden - later to design the Brooklands race track - a few years later. Both employed direct drive via exposed connecting rods to crank axles on the rear spindle, which naturally severely limited engine speed and flywheel effect. The Motorrad had a large capacity of 1490cc and made about 2hp at 380rpm, enough for a top speed of about 25mph. But the bulk, weight and complication hindered performance so much that it was put to shame by the Werner brothers' crude Motocyclette.

From time to time, engineers of other disciplines took a look at contemporary motorcycles and decided they could do better. In 1908 for instance, T. W. Badgery of the James Cycle Co commissioned a design from the respected consulting engineer P. L. Renouf, which became the sensation of that year's London Motor Cycle Show. The 'Safety James' had a tubular chassis constructed along car lines, with hub-center steering, quickly detachable wheels on single sided stub axles and internal expanding brakes front and rear. It had a 500cc single-cylinder side valve engine of James' own make and belt drive with an engine-pulley clutch. Sadly it was a monumental flop, and the James company rapidly turned to more orthodox designs. The public response to the four-cylinder air-cooled 680cc Wilkinson TAC and later the 850cc water-cooled TMC models was also disappointing. For 1910 and 1912, these offered truly advanced and luxurious specifications, but failed to sell in viable numbers.

It seemed as if motorcycle design had to advance a small step at a time, not too precipitately and never too boldly. To be sure, Alfred Scott's radical two-stroke twin of 1909 (or 1908 if you include six prototypes built by Jowett Brothers for development) found a market, but never a large one, even after Scott's TT wins in 1912 and 1913. And, in retrospect, the wonder is that the Scott sold at all, for not only was the two-stroke engine virtually unheard of, this one was a twin and was partly, and very soon fully, water-cooled. The straight-tube triangulated frame and the cylindrical fuel tank embracing the saddle tube must also have looked very strange to the typical motorcyclist of 1909.

One of the Scott's most striking features was that it had a kickstarter - the first ever offered - and so the engine could be started at rest and the machine moved off by engaging the lower of two 'gears' - actually two separate primary chains driving two sprockets on a countershaft with expanding clutches. The kickstart apart, there was nothing new about this machine. P & M, for one, had long since offered such a transmission, as had many of the large V-twin 'tricars' that were popular between about 1904 and 1909. What riders were demanding around the same time as the Scott made its appearance was a `free engine' or clutch, and it was a big selling point for Triumph when it fitted a multi-plate clutch in the rear hub in 1909. There were, even then, numerous proprietary clutches, usually incorporated in a special belt pulley.

Sprung front forks started to become really popular in about 1907. Again, many were proprietary fittings designed for use on older machines, although, for example, Quadrant had had such a front fork since 1903, while Rex had fitted them as standard since 1906.

Some of the early designs of forks look downright dangerous to modern eyes, and probably were - but it was the Scott of 1909 which had probably the best design of all with

The first Daimler and Maybach two-wheeler

The De Dion Bouton three-wheeler

*T.Tessier on an English BAT
in 1903, on which he broke various
speed records*

*Road conditions contrasted infavourably with
those of the track in the early days.*

a true telescopic action. The famous Druid front fork, with parallel lever action controlled by coil springs first appeared in 1906, and became very popular -almost standard fitment on British bikes and in successively modified form, setting a fashion that was to last for 30 odd years and more.

Spring frames were the subject of many an invention in the early years, although very few of them had much merit. Curiously, those that enjoyed a certain success, such as the BAT,

the Zenette and the much later Edmund, were not really spring frames at all, but sprung sub-frames, whereby the saddle and footrests were isolated together from road shocks. Such systems did absolutely nothing to help to keep the rear wheel in contact with the road.

Lighting remained an afterthought. Few people rode at night in any case, and very few motorcycles were sold with lights of any sort. At first, cycle oil lamps were used, and sturdier versions than the fragile first ones were soon

made. But from an early date, acetylene gas lighting became available and was soon accepted as the standard. It might have been messy and demanded considerable looking after, but it was comparatively reliable and cheap.

As for brakes, these were considered unimportant for a very long time. Even so meticulous an engineer as Alfred Scott could at that time see no further than a cycle type stirrup at the front, and a shoe bearing on the

THOSE MAGNIFICENT MEN ON THEIR CYCLING MACHINES

The von Sauerbronn-Davis velocipede of 1883 was powered by a steam engine fired by

As if the early designs weren't dangerous enough already... this Anzani of 1906 featured propellor power!

The 1887 Millet prototype had a radial engine similar to those used in aircraft

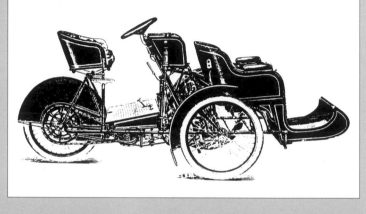

Look, no pedals! An ordinary bicycle gets a shove from an auxillary engine, Italy 1893

'Luxurious high-powered, all-weather car-ette' was the description of the twin engined Quadrant, made in Britain in 1905

Every possible engine position was being tried at the turn of the century. (1) Werner in 1899 to drive the front wheel, Enfield the rear. (2) Singer in the front hub, (3) British Excelsior, (4) Phelon & Moore, (5) Hildebrand and Wolfmüller, (6) Beeston, (7) Ormonde, (8) Singer, (9) Humber

inside of a drum formed in the rear chain sprocket. Front brakes were in any case regarded as mere 'bobby dodgers' (fitted simply to satisfy legal requirements) and not to be used, first because they damaged the paint and plating of the front rim, and also because of the firm conviction that front brakes were dangerous. This fallacious belief still lingers even today, with some motorcyclists preferring to rely on the rear alone for fear of locking up the front and falling off.

Varying gear ratios proved a fruitful field for inventors in those early years. The 'adjustable pulley' was an early development, usually sold as a proprietary item and a not terribly satisfactory one at that. Early competition riders would carry two belts - one for use on the level, with the pulley flanges screwed close together to give a high ratio. When a hill had to be climbed, the pulley flanges were screwed apart and a slightly shorter belt fitted. The once famous Zenith Gradua and Rudge Multi systems were extensions of this idea. These took mechanical control of the driving pulley and, in the case of Zenith, automatically extended or shortened the wheelbase of the motorcycle to keep the belt taut. The Rudge Multi's rear pulley flanges moved in and out as the engine pulley did the opposite.

Quite a few simple two-speed epicyclic

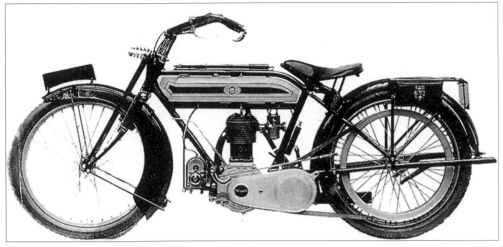

1910 Scott 450cc twin cylinder, two-stroke with water cooled heads bult by Alfred Scott

The sturdy Triumph Model H nicknamed 'The Trusty' has an unbeatable 550 side-valve engine and its three-speed Sturmey Archer countershaft gearbox

gears - notably from NSU - made an early appearance, and eventually migrated to the rear hub in bicycle fashion. Such three-speed Armstong hubs featured strongly in the results of the 1911 Junior TT, held for the first time on the Mountain circuit in the Isle of Man. But the Indians, which finished 1-2-3 in the Senior race that year, used countershaft gearboxes, and these made a big impression. Development of such gearboxes was rapid, and their wide acceptance really dated from the use by the Triumph company of the superb Sturmey-Archer gearbox and clutch in its late veteran masterpiece, the 550cc Model H, famed for its use by despatch riders in the war years between 1914 and 1918.

Throughout this era, the side-valve engine reigned supreme. The ohv layout occasionally appeared for racing, but showed no great superiority. The theoretical advantages of overhead valves were, with compression ratios

An acetylene headlight set, gas is generated in the cannister and fed to a burner in the headlight

of about 4:1, more apparent than real, and valve steels being so poor then, the ohv layout was widely mistrusted for its threat of mechanical carnage from a 'dropped' valve. Pistons were universally of cast iron, although racing pistons were painstakingly (and expensively) machined from steel.

Ball and roller bearings were coming into use, especially for racing, but phosphor bronze bushes were still widely used, almost always

1905 International Coupe winner Václav Vondich on a CCR

lubricated by 'spit and hope' total loss systems. These depended upon a simple hand-operated pump transferring oil into the crankcase, where it was distributed by 'splash'.

Two major companies, JAP (founded in 1903) and Precision dominated the engine scene as far as Britain was concerned. Although Precision did not start making engines until 1910, its products rapidly gained a good reputation. The Stevens brothers of Wolverhampton had made engines of various sizes before settling for producing the 350cc AJS motorcycle, while Dalton & Wade, Blumfeld, and half a dozen others long forgotten, also competed for a place. Of imported engines, the MAG, made by Motosacoche of Geneva, was by far and away the most successful.

Nor were these engines long stroke designs as commonly thought now, but were mostly square (with equal bore and stroke) or nearly so in their configuration. Towards the end of the period, small capacity V-twins became popular and did well in competitions.

The `Lightweight' - 250cc - class was barely established before 1914. By that year the weak and feeble machines, little more than motorised bicycles that had struggled for a foothold in 1900, had become sturdy, powerful and reliable motorcycles that in the words of a contemporary writer, had `attained a state very close to perfection'. Such complacency invites mockery, but there is no doubt that, looking back a mere 14 or 15 years, there was some excuse for it. The motorcycle even then had come a very long way. Few people realised how much further it still had to travel on the road to `perfection'.

Ludwig Opel with a 2³/₄ Opel motorcycle on army manoevres in 1905

THE FIRST WORLD WAR

Working on the family vegetable plot, Madame Metevier stiffened as she heard the even engine beat of an approaching motorcycle. Rounding the bend at the bottom of the hill the dispatch rider rode into view. Sensing their mother's relief at the sight of an Allied uniform, the children ran and waved at the rider. As his bike climbed the hill into the village Private Bedford could only nod in acknowledgement, needing both hands on the handlebars to guide his bucking Triumph along the cart tracks.

Ten minutes later the dispatch rider entered the village square, bounced across the cobbles and halted in front of a large hotel. Having

14

stopped the engine and heaved the machine onto its rear stand, Bedford dashed into the local HQ and handed over a package wrapped in a canvas bag to the duty Sergeant. Outside, steam and heat shimmered from the cooling

Triumph as wet mud dried on the hot exhaust pipe and thick black oil dripped from the engine. Back in the morning sun, the young rider was able to enjoy a quick smoke before stroking the bike into life with the kick starter and heading towards the coast.

A typical scene, repeated millions of times throughout the Great War by forces using motorcycle dispatch riders - abbreviated to DR - for messenger duties. But the first attempts to use motorcycles for military purposes had been tried almost two decades earlier, in 1899, when both Britain and Germany toyed with powered two wheelers as weapon carriers.

During the early days of the twentieth century, powered vehicles were developed and refined, becoming more reliable and powerful. A minority of military personnel realised the potential of the motorcycle within the armed forces. Unfortunately, the improved reliability gave the small handful of soldiers lucky enough to ride bikes an excess of freedom of movement which was unwelcome to the commanding officers. Another hiccup for the acceptance of the military motorcycle.

In Britain, a motley assortment of motorised bicycles was bought for individual regiments, often by senior or commanding officers with private means. The Simms Motor Carriage was one of the first examples of the use of a motorcycle-type machine by the British army. Although a four wheeler, the Simms was of motorcycle-type design. With a .303 Maxim machine gun mounted ahead of the rider, the armed vehicle was tried without success in the Boer War and quickly disappeared from favour.

German forces found that a party of armed motorcycles could ride on ahead of their advancing troops and occupy enemy territory until the main regiment arrived by foot. But the unreliability of primitive machines, compounded by the need for the riders to stop and dismount to fire the mounted gun, encouraged the Germans to put the experiment on hold.

The cavalry looked on, first in amusement and then horror, as the popularity of the military motorcycle gained momentum. Early pioneer machines were no match for a skilled horseman, but as development advanced the cavalry officers became increasingly worried about their future careers, deriding and belittling the motorcycle at every opportunity.

By 1910 the advantages of the motorcycle were demonstrated regularly at military

maneuvres and they were beginning to be adopted by forces throughout the world. Although the military motorcyclist did occasionally see action in a fighting role, he usually served as a messenger or policeman. The majority of machines used by the forces were generally identical to those bought for everyday use by civilians, but the development of bikes for specialised roles became more commonplace.

Seeing the possibility of extra sales, a number of manufacturers vied with each other for the potentially lucrative Government orders, especially as the war clouds built up. Notably: Scott, Triumph, Douglas, BSA, Sunbeam and Phelon & Moore locked in battle with each other for firm orders. On the European mainland the German-built NSUs, Belgian FNs and Austrian Puch models found favour. The USA makers, Indian and Harley Davidson, were an obvious choice for the Americans, who were already using the big V twins, along with other models, for police and civil duties.

Following the murder of Archduke Franz Ferdinand at Sarajevo, Austria attacked Serbia in July 1914. Russia supported Serbia, while Germany backed Austria. War was then declared on France, and the invasion of Belgium drew Great Britain into the war. Later, Turkey and Bulgaria sided with Germany and Austria. Due to their central geographical position these four formed the Central Powers; France, Russia, Great Britain, Belgium and Serbia were members of a group called the Allies. The war lasted nearly $4\frac{1}{2}$ years and up to 30,000,000 men were under arms at any one time. Loss of

American machine gun carriage, for towing behind motorcycle outfit on light vehicle

Two-stroke twin cylinder Scott outfit with Vickers machine gun, pose for the camera

A 1000cc Indian outfit with machine gun.

life was immense, as was the expenditure in money and weapons. The main theaters of war were the Western Front, where France and Great Britain confronted Germany, and the Eastern Front, where Russia was confronted by Germany and Austria. Other theaters included the Gallipoli Peninsula and Mesopotamia.

Both the Central Powers and the Allies were served by motorcycle mounted dispatch riders in all the theaters of war as well as in their home countries. An almost unbelievable variety of machines carried battle instructions, letters from home, equipment, spare parts, carrier pigeons in baskets and thousands of other items small enough to fit onto a motorcycle.

Although Europe had been heading to war for some years, before the outbreak of war no one had estimated the large volume of equipment and resources that a prolonged war would consume. Preparations were inadequate and countries scraped and struggled to adequately equip their fighting men. Although even the most die-hard cavalry supporters realised that motor cycles were more suited to the battlefield than horses, the military did not have enough machines at the outbreak of WW1. Civilian motor cycles were pressed into service to supplement the existing models owned by the forces. With thousands of motorcyclists volunteering for military service to ensure the lines of communication between the battlefield and the command post were kept open, the dispatch rider at last began to make his mark as a valuable tool of war.

Many dispatch riders were motorcycle

enthusiasts before the outbreak of war, sometimes bringing their civilian machine with them when they signed up. Although often dated, these extra motor cycles supplemented the limited numbers in service with the military forces. As the war progressed the DRs were joined by riders pulled from the ranks, who underwent instruction on machine control and route finding at military training centres. Today, bikers are used to all-weather riding suits, full face helmets, heated undershirts, and a battery of boots and gloves for every occasion. The pre-WW1 motor cyclist made do with thick clothing worn in many layers, horse riding or workman-type boots, and stiff leather gloves, while the best head protection money could buy was a cap, beret or hat. The development of crash helmets as we know them was not thought of in those early days. The winter rider often made use of fisherman-type oilskins, a cape, goggles, and leather gloves with water proof overmitts.

Roads comprised of crushed rolled stone, often severely rutted by horse drawn and steam driven vehicles, while minor country lanes were either grass or mud tracks covered in horse droppings. Little wonder the intrepid pre-WW1 riders stopped regularly en-route to rest and maintain their machines. Major British cities had wood board let into the road surface in parts, or cobbles and tram tracks. Cobbles were the order of the day for many European cities. Not much fun on two wheels in wet or icy conditions. Motorcycle engines needed oiling by the rider using a tank mounted hand pump

The Coventry, England factory of Triumph supplied 30,000 Model H motorcycles to the allied forces for dispatch-rider duties

During World War 1, motorcycles were pressed into many roles. Here the 4000cc Indian Powerplus acts as a stretch bearer for feeding the wounded away from the front line.

every few miles, the oil dripping onto the crankshaft. Tires were inflated to rock hard pressure to keep them on the rim and lighting was by acetylene gas, similar to that used by miners.

The military dispatch rider used service uniform as his motorcycle riding kit, supplemented with greatcoats. In an effort to keep warm in winter, the DRs stuffed torn up blankets, rags and paper into their uniform as crude insulation, huddling around fires between runs or simply stopping to warm their hands on

the hot engines of their machines. All desperate stuff.

The lack of adequate safety equipment may seem extremely dangerous, but motor cycles of the period were light, often weighing less than 100kg, with a cruising speed of under 40mph, so in the event of a crash impact speeds were less than on today's roads. However, the DRs contended with dire road conditions, angry horses and more mud than we can ever imagine.

Many dispatch riders were able to carry out their own maintenance and roadside repairs. Punctures from horseshoe nails were commonplace and broken or stretched drive belts were fixed in moments. Most DR bases had general vehicle and equipment repair depots, some with men and an area set aside solely for motorcycle maintenance.

Although the conditions of service on many European fronts were dire, the DRs considered themselves amongst the élite, with freedom of

A Beeston Quao gun carriage demonstrated on Richmond Common in 1899 by the maker F.R. SIM

"I am really satisfied with my 'Douglas,' and have done over 6,000 kilometres and never a stop. My machine is still as efficient as in November. Every day my engine is the admiration of many people. Bravo, for 'Douglas'!"

One of a series of postcards printed by the Bristol factory depicting Douglas dispatch riders

travel while carrying out their duties and avoiding the hand to hand fighting of the trenches. However, the hazards were plentiful. As it was for all front line troops, shellfire was a constant threat, but for the DR it carried the added dangers of newly-cratered roads - difficult to see in the dark - and telephone wires, brought down across the roads by shellfire, often at neck height, felled many a rider. In the brief periods of open warfare, when the stalemate of the trenches had been temporarily

broken, a lone DR was an easy target for an advancing enemy who wanted to capture working machines to supplement the stock of their own DRs, rather than live riders. But even while carrying out more mundane duties the constant risk of riding frail motor cycles on rough roads at flat out speeds of 40-45mph accounted for many injuries. The comradeship amongst the military bike riders was strong, many taking great risks to assist their fellow servicemen.

But of what real use were military motor cycles? By the outbreak of WW1 the sidecar machine gun carrier was common. The Yorkshire firm of Scott built an outfit which, due to the use of special ammunition clips, permitted the gunner to fire the weapon while

the outfit was on the move. The thought of firing a machine gun while the motor- cycle combination was travelling across rough terrain must have sent shivers down the spines of the commanding officers and the idea was not adopted for general use. A moving motorcycle with gun ablaze would have been as much danger to the home troops as the enemy.

At the outbreak of war the Vickers Ordnance Company approached Alfred Scott and his Bradford based company to build a more conventional machine gun carrying sidecar outfit. Powered by Scott's own 486cc water cooled two-stroke twin, with an unconventional foot operated two-speed gear system, the outfits proved maneuvrable and attracted a following amongst riders and gunners. The Scott-armed outfits usually operated in units of three as detailed for the following Clyno machines.

Other gun-armed outfits, such as the Clyno-Vickers set up, gained popularity and were used in considerable numbers. The Clyno-Vickers comprised a water-cooled, belt fed, .303 Vickers machine gun mounted on the sidecar of a 5-6HP Clyno outfit. The gunner fired while stationary and the Clyno combinations operated in units of three: one with an armour plated sidecar and the Vickers machine gun, the second, armour plated but unarmed, and the third without armour for carrying back-up stocks of ammunition.

These Wolverhampton-built Clyno gun ships were part of the British Motor Machine Gun Corps which was formed at the outbreak of WW1. Quite an up market machine, the 5-6HP Clyno offered over 50mph in solo trim, all chain drive, a decent rear internal expanding rear brake and a strong three-speed hand change gearbox. Well over 2,000 Clynos were supplied to the British forces and a number to the Russian armed forces, including 1,500 larger 8HP models powered by V-twin JAP engines

British gunners prepare for action. Vickers machine guns mounted on Czyno 'V'
twin outfits which the Triumph mounted dispatch rider takes shelter

in place of Cylnoís own unit.

Although the Simms Motor Carriage was the first recorded example of a gun mounted on a motorcycle-like vehicle - albeit with four wheels - the Germans made successful inroads into this development with guns mounted on both solo and sidecar outfits. So it is no surprise that the Neckersulmer factory of NSU built a 7-9HP V-twin model for the Central Powers' war effort.

This powerful German machine, capable of holding 60mph with ease in solo trim, was offered with a sidecar platform onto which a removable machine gun was mounted. Again, like the British versions, the NSU gun ships operated in small units of twos and threes, attempting to gain prime attack positions to support the infantry advance or to attack isolated Allied positions.

In WW1 days no small Jeep-like overland vehicles were available for the high speed transport of senior or specialist personnel. Motor- cycle sidecar outfits fulfilled this role. The Douglas 4HP ably served in this role for both the British and Allied forces, joined in 1917 by the American Harley-Davidson and Indian model 61s with chairs hitched to them.

The Douglas 4HP model B was a smooth-running quiet machine which enabled it to creep close to enemy positions undetected. It was powered by Douglas's own 595cc horizontally opposed twin cylinder side valve engine driving through a three-speed gearbox and a V-belt to the back wheel. An easy starter and reliable in service, the model B's Achilles heel was its brakes; just adequate in solo trim, but poor when the bike was coupled to a sidecar, relying on a stirrup, cycle-type front brake - which did little more than scrape the mud off the wheel rim - and a foot operated belt rim back brake. Stopping apart, the 4HP Douglas combination was popular with most who drove it, and a

number survive in preservation today in testament to a good workhorse.

Although the majority of military motor cycles were used by the army, the Royal Flying Corps (RFC) - forerunner of today's Royal Air Force (RAF) - made use of bikes, primarily for messenger and personnel transport. The RFC usually rode P & M machines, built by the Yorkshire based firm of Phelon and Moore.

Like the Scott, the P & M bucked traditional design. The engine formed part of the frame by replacing the headstock down tube. Although fitted with a two-speed gear system, involving two primary chains and a selective clutch, the P & M was equally happy solo or with a factory made single-seat sidecar fitted. A quality, versatile machine, which suited the RFC's needs perfectly. In 1923 the company brought out the Panther, which in the early thirties was nicknamed 'The Big Pussy from Cleckheaton'.

The motorcycle sidecar outfit lent itself to a number of specialist roles in specific theaters of the war. Radio transmitters - in their infancy during WW1 - were mounted in the sidecar for use in the field. The Medical Corps made use of a number of adapted outfits, especially Sunbeams, for field ambulance duties. Quicker than the horse and cart, but pity the injured soldier who endured a speedy trip across rough terrain!

Although the sidecar outfit made useful contributions to both the Allies' and Central Powers' war efforts, the majority of military motor cycles were used in solo form, being ideal for ease of transport to their specific theater of war. Maneuvrable in the field, but equally at home in London, Berlin or the other major cities of Europe.

Surprisingly, the two most popular bikes - the Triumph model H and the Douglas model V - used by the Allies and built in large numbers,

were so opposite in design and ride qualities. Yet both gained many lifetime admirers, as they still do today amongst the preservation enthusiasts.

Built at the Coventry factory founded by Siegfried Bettamann, later joined by fellow German Mauritz Schulte, the Triumph model H -nicknamed 'The Trusty' - was renowned worldwide for itís reliability and ease of starting. The Trusty had its faults, including the Triumph designed rocking action front fork and the retention of belt drive which is prone to slipping and breakage, especially in the wet.The heart of the model H was its dependable single cylinder 550cc SV engine with heavy flywheels. Depress the kick starter, spin the flywheels and the motor could not fail to start. No speedster, with a top speed of 45mph, the Trusty would slog up impossible gradients with the drive belt slapping on the road, through glutinous mud, yet could cruise at its near maximum speed. Frugal in its consumption of precious fuel resources, the Triumph just kept going and going and going. Triumphís own double barrel-carburetor worked well in hot or cold conditions; the primitive brakes were adequate for a light

machine, the three speed gearbox made maximum use of the engine's power and even the suspect front fork was controllable. The girder front fork pivoted at the bottom of the headstock and was controlled by a spring located near the top of the headstock. Unfortunately, the action gets carried away on rough ground and each movement of the fork alters the bike's wheelbase. Great! The DRs moderated the fork action by fitting a leather strap around the spring, limiting movement - a dodge which is used by the many proud riders of preserved Trusties today. Over 30,000 Triumph model H machines were built for military use in WW1. Looks can deceive. The Trusty looks a strong machine but the equally popular Douglas model V appears frail and delicate. The sort of bike which was ideal for popping down to the shops on but best avoided for long trips. Technically the Dougie was probably the least advanced of the purpose-made military bikes. Lacking a clutch, fitted with a simple two-speed gearbox, exposed chain primary drive, V belt final drive and no kick starter, the 35mph horizontally opposed 348cc SV Douglas twin had little going for it. But like

a sound tool it worked well despite outward appearance. Engage low gear, flood the carburetor, set the control levers and paddle away and the model V snuffles into life within yards. Hit 10 mph, squeeze the valve lift lever and knock the tram handle-like gear lever into high gear and the bike quietly whisks along. Survivors of the model today, and there are plenty of them, perform in a similar effortless manner.

The Dougie's fans claim that when the going got tough the rider simply picked the machine up, tucked it under an arm and carried the bike out of trouble. An impossible feat for a Trusty, they claimed. Well, hmmm.....possibly, but the bike weighs 90kg, which is heavy enough, and the Triumph model H is only 5kg heavier. The Bristol-based Douglas factory supplied over 25,000 machines to the British and Allied armed forces. While machines for the Allied war effort rolled off the Triumph and Douglas production lines in an endless stream, other British marques were adding their support: including BSA, Sunbeam, Rudge, Ariel, James, Norton, New Imperial, Royal Enfield, Rover and Premier. During November 1916 the Ministry of Supply

A photo to send home. An orderly group of Douglas mounted dispatch riders await orders on the beach in the Dardanelles. The troops were given photos like this to send home and assure family all was well

banned the production of motor cycles for civilian use. Bike assembly at factories like Rudge Whitworth stopped almost overnight and efforts were concentrated on ammunition production.

Although Herstal, the Belgian-based factory of La Fabrique Nationale d'Armes de Guerre, did not build many machines for military use during WW1 - concentrating efforts on arms production - many of the shaft drive inline four cylinder models, designed by Paul Kelcom, and the lighter 285cc singles, were in use with the Belgian army at the outbreak of hostilities. Given a quick lick of appropriate service paint, they were widely used in Northern Europe.

The Swedish factory of Husqvarna, Eysink from Holland, Bianchi and Frera of Italy, and Peugeot and Terrot of France round off the list of major players of motorcycle production for the Allies on mainland Europe. But in 1917 the

A variety of motorcycle outfits undergoing military trials. Machines include BSA, Royal Enfield and Indian

USA joined the Allies in the struggle, bringing with them boat loads of bikes, predominately model 61 Indians, Excelsiors and Harley-Davidsons. American bike and car manufacturers measure cubic capacity in cubic inches — the model 61 is equivalent to approx. 1000cc — hence all three companies called their bikes the model 61. Strong and powerful sums up the Harley-Davidson 987cc V-twin, of which almost 15,000 each of solo and sidecar variants were made for the American military during the war years. All chain drive, three speed gearbox, a Schebler carburetor and mechanically operated inlet over exhaust valve design, ensured this big 160kg bike could easily hit 60mph solo and 50mph with a sidecar. Typically for American bikes of the period the Harley has no front wheel brake, but two independently operating brakes on the rear wheel.

The Hendee-Indian factory was another big supplier of machines to the American forces during WW1, with the 61 and the Powerplus. Both powerful 998cc V-twins, suitable for high speed solo work, but again, a quick sidecar machine too. Although a smaller player as far as the American military is concerned, 2,600 Chicago built Excelsior 997cc V-twins were supplied during the war. A superbike of its day, albeit painted in army drab for military work, the big Excelsior hit an easy 75mph, but stopping was hazardous with brakes again fitted only to the back wheel.

The potential for military orders always throws up one or two oddballs. The offerings of the Militaire Auto Company of Cleveland, Ohio are unusual. The first offering in 1912 was a slow, heavy 480cc single cylinder machine with a pressed steel car chassis, wooden artillery wheels, a steering wheel and small outrigger wheels to allow use of a reverse gear. Hot on the heels of this baby followed a 1306cc inline four cylinder powered model of similar design, capable of 35mph. Weighing a staggering 360kg with sidecar, a few were shipped over to France where they immediately sank into the mud.

German dispatch rider with his 4¹/₂ Wanderer 'V' twin poses for the camera

The Central Powers used motor cycles for dispatch work and as armed sidecars, but to a much smaller extent than the Allies. Produced by a handful of factories, notably NSU and Wanderer from Germany and the Austrian Puch company.

Despite the NSU factory being converted to arms production, it built three main models for the military during WW1. A lightweight 190cc four-stroke single, a rapid and maneuvrable 499cc V-twin, both for dispatch duties, and the 7-9HP V-twin used solo and as an armed outfit. All the NSU models were reliable, handled well in the field and were well liked by their riders.

Wanderer, a factory noted for the high quality of its pre-WW1 civilian machines, built both single cylinder and V-twin four-stroke solos for the German military. Lucky was the soldier who served the war on a Wanderer; the machines

Ready for colonial action. BSA single and rider with pith helmet

were of advanced design and the engines were responsive for the enthusiast rider. The Austrian Puch firm produced two small capacity basic but well made models for the Austrian forces.

The armed forces used a variety of other marques, often requisitioned for military service. Sometimes these were painted in service colours, but more often ridden in civilian trim until they dropped.

Odd machines were built for specific needs or to suit the ideas of enthusiastic commanding officers who sometimes financed these 'specials' themselves.

THE WAR HAS ENDED, WHAT NOW?

Throughout the war the military of both the Allies and the Central Powers had continued placing orders for further motor cycles from the makers. At the end of hostilities the armed

Dispatch riders enjoying a break from the pounding of their none-to-comfortable seats.

forces were left with large numbers of machines. Some were very old and of obsolete design, others worn or damaged, others simply excess to peacetime requirements.

From a manufacturing point of view many pre-WW1 factories could not restart motorcycle production immediately the conflict had ended. Machine design had evolved through the war years, and the expectations of the new peacetime rider were greater than in pre-WW1 days. Motorcycle factories which had produced arms and equipment throughout the war, not bikes, had to redesign their models and in many cases retrain staff in new manufacturing techniques.

On the other side of the fence, the serviceman of WW1 had experienced, for the first time, travel away from his home town or county while serving his country. An experience he was unwilling to give up easily. For some, the freedom offered by a motorcycle offered a form of escape from the return to humdrum life.

Armed with their demob gratuities, many enthusiasts were flocking to the dealers' shops, desperate to buy a motorcycle. In fact for some, any motorcycle would do. The few new models available quickly sold, elderly pre-WW1 bikes were snapped up, and a rash of poorly made lightweights and feeble motor scooters hit the market. Prices rose, but some dealers were offering ex-service machines, the supply of which helped satiate public demand for personal transport.

Redundant military motor cycles in all states of repair, from the unused to the mortar damaged, were assembled at points across Europe for inclusion in dispersal sales. Some returned to the manufacturers, others to dealers, and opportunistic individuals snapped up the rest. Machines were either returned to running condition and repainted as appropriate, others were broken for spare parts. Once overhauled, usable models were sold to eager ex-servicemen. As the bike factories swung into production again, with new ranges of machines, the demand for secondhand machines dropped, along with prices.

Motorcycle design progressed rapidly during the post WW1 period. All chain drive, electric lights, twist grip throttle control, and even electric lighting replaced acetylene sets. But for years many riders commuted to work, toured and visited friends, riding Trusties, Dougies and large American V-twins. The great days of freedom.

THE AMERICAN STORY

A steam-powered bicycle built by Sylvanus Roper in 1870 is still preserved in the Smithsonian Museum in Washington DC, but the real involvement of the USA in the story of the motorcycle dates from the importation of a De Dion tricycle in 1898 by Hiram Maxim who was at the time - among his many other activities - consulting engineer to Colonel A. A. Pope's Columbia bicycle manufacturing concern. As a result, in 1900 Columbia was the first company to offer a motorcycle for sale in the country; within months, it had a dozen competitors, none of whom offered much more than the crudest of specifications.

In early 1901, however, the Indian, designed by Springfield bicycle maker, George M. Hendee and toolmaker Oscar Hedstrom, made its first appearance. Its strengthened bicycle frame, retaining the pedalling gear, incorporated the single-cylinder engine as part of the seat

tube, and thus inclined rearwards. It had an automatic inlet valve and an ingenious spray carburetor of Hedstrom's own design, but the engine, although designed by Hedstrom, was made by the Thor Manufacturing Co, as were all Indian engines until 1905.

From the start, Indian used chain drive to the rear wheel as did most of its rivals. Curiously, one of the few makes to use belt drive - and to persist with it until 1912 (and return to it in modern times) - was the Harley-Davidson, first produced for sale in 1904. Although Indian sales were modest at first - 143 machines in 1902 - success came quickly after good showings in early endurance events, and Hendee and Hedstrom pursued a policy of innovation and improvement. In 1907, when sales were in the thousands, a V-twin engine of 600cc was introduced, built by Indian itself, with the 'Hedstrom motor' cast into the crankcase. One

such machine, with twistgrip throttle control and a sprung front fork, was shipped to Britain, where it took part in the ACC's 1000-mile trial, winning a gold medal. Indian was already extremely alive to the possibilities of export to Europe, and especially to Britain.

In 1909, expatriate American W. H. Wells was made British concessionaire, and entered himself and George Lee Evans in the Senior TT in the Isle of Man. Sensationally, Evans led the race for half its distance, finishing a close second to Matchless rider Harry Collier. In 1910, Indian introduced a two-speed countershaft gearbox and clutch - already successful at home in pure speed events on board tracks, it now provided Wells' English agency with racing machines that competed with spectacular success at Brooklands. And for the 1911 Senior TT, run for the first time on the famous Mountain circuit, Indian visited in force, with George

Riders await the starter's signal for the 1908 Isle of Man TT: the 15 3/4 mile St Johns course, went via Ballacraine, Kirk Michael and Peel. J. Marshall averaged 40.4 mph on his 'works' Triumph to win the single cylinder class

Hendee himself, Oscar Hedstrom, ace rider Jake de Rosier, and a full complement of machinery and race mechanics. It meant to win -and win it did, with its British riders taking the first three places. In 1912, Indian's sales reached 20,000.

Not that Indian had it entirely its own way in America in the first decade of the new century. In racing, and especially in board track racing, it had serious rivals in Excelsior, Merkel and Cyclone. Harley-Davidson, who made its first V-twin in 1909, did not race itself but was happy to advertise the success of private owners. By about 1912, there were at least 30 well-established makes that almost had the status of household names in US motorcycle manufacturing.

By that time a pattern had been established. Roads that were atrocious by European standards demanded sturdier frames. Front

forks were usually of the bottom link pattern and again very robust, twistgrips were common for controls, with the throttle usually on the left, and piano wires were used rather than the Bowden cable that was ubiquitous in Europe.

Brakes were, if anything, ahead of those in Europe, a popular system being a contracting band and expanding shoes using the same drum on the rear wheel. Similarly, American carburetors, such as the Holley, Schebler and Hedstrom, were definitely ahead of their European counterparts. Much attention was paid to comfort, with large and elaborately suspended saddles and sturdy metal footboards. Spring frames were not common, but when offered, as by Pope, they were of sound design. Europeans found American controls difficult. Like the throttle the gears were also controlled by the left hand and often, even the clutch - this might have a lever alongside the left side of the fuel tank as well as a foot pedal, also on the left.

Lighting and electrical equipment was generally excellent. The US manufacturers did not make the mistake of depending on Germany for magnetos, and offered electric lighting as standard, long before it was thought of in Europe. Indian, indeed, scored a notable 'first' in 1914 with the all electric 'Hendee special' featuring electric starting! Although this innovation was a failure, costing the company a good deal of money, it illustrated Indian's forward-looking attitude.

As early as 1914, however, economic forces were at work that could not be denied. Quite a few of the pioneer names had already disappeared in the face of determined marketing by Indian, Harley-Davidson and Excelsior. Now the appearance of incredibly cheap cars, such as Ford's Model T, was to eat into the sales of motorcycles, so it was no coincidence that, between 1915 and 1918, such respected companies as Pope, Yale, Iver Johnson, Cyclone, Thor and Peerless ceased production, along with many others. Of those 'household names' a mere half dozen survived into the 1920s and only Indian, Harley-Davidson and Excelsior lasted out the decade.

Excelsior - sold in Europe as 'the American

Harry Reed was in the saddle of his DOT for over 4 hours to win the 1908 twin cylinder class

X' - had sprung from Ignatz Schwin's bicycle manufacturing company in Chicago in 1908 and during the war years had absorbed the Detroit-built four cylinder in-line Henderson, which Excelsior was to sell in vastly improved form post war. In-line fours, indeed, became something of a cult in the USA. They had their origin in the Pierce Arrow of 1909, a free-hand copy of an imported Belgian FN. The Pierce lasted just long enough to inspire the Henderson, first made in 1912. Post-war, the Henderson brothers left Excelsior to make the Ace, which, when Bill Henderson was killed in a road accident, passed in due course to Indian. As the Indian Four, it remained in production until the USA entered WW2 in 1941.

The USA's other highly respected in-line four was the Cleveland, made from 1925 to 1929. All of these were extremely powerful and luxurious motorcycles with tireless performance. As much as anything, they exemplified a general US trend in the 1920s towards a super sporting performance that no car - cheap or otherwise - could provide. With a power-to-weight ratio at least three times better than that of a powerful car, US V-twins and fours were used in large numbers by the police, the armed forces and, to a lesser extent, by public utilities. They also sold to sporting enthusiasts, the V-twins forming the backbone of Class C Amateur racing in the 1930s. The demands of off-road competition, hill climbing, and long distances on the vastly improved roads of that era resulted in motorcycles that, to European eyes, soon became almost grotesquely over-engineered.Excelsior had

For many years the Indian typified by this 1930s V twin was America's leading marque

dropped out of contention in 1931 to concentrate on bicycles and, for most of the 1930s, Indian and Harley-Davidson were on a fairly equal footing in almost every respect. There was one vital difference, however. George Hendee had retired from his Indian company in 1916. Harley-Davidson remained firmly in the hands of the families which had started it back in the pioneer days of the 1900s.

The 1930s saw a general stagnation in design, actively encouraged by Class C competition which limited amateur racing to side-valve engines of 750cc. An afterthought in the regulations allowed overhead-valve engines of 500cc, although this remained academic until Canadian rider Billy Matthews won the 1941 Daytona 200 mile race on a Norton International! The overwhelming popularity of British motorcycles in the USA after WW2 was a phenomenon that the local industry could never have foreseen. Harley-Davidson regrouped, and bought out the Italian Aermacchi company at the end of the 1950s. Indian, however, tried to meet the invasion head on with a totally new European-type range, the so-called 'Torque' models, the 220cc (later 250cc) and 440cc (later 500cc) single-cylinder Arrow and vertical twin Scout. A 1000cc in-line four was also planned.

At this point, the British company J. Brockhouse & Co provided a massive capital injection that gave it control, not only of the Indian Sales Corporation, but of manufacturing at Springfield. Losses on the Torque range forced Brockhouse to suspend manufacture in 1953 and subsequent 'Indians' sold in America were thinly-disguised British models. Indian's long and honourable Springfield manufacturing

Small town America 1910. A Sunday morning gathering of enthusiasts in Nebraska, on a 150 mile jaunt

history was over, but the heritage that took so much effort to attain lead to years of sometimes messy fighting for the rights to use the name.

Harley-Davidson took a different view of the US market. Arguing that, although lightweights might be popular, there would always be sales for the traditionally rugged style of native motorcycle, it re-designed and updated its big V-twins and elevated ownership into something of a cult. It also tried to use its Italian connection to satisfy the considerable demand for cheaper and lighter models with at least an American name, but in practice this had the effect of

detracting from Harley's image, while the machines themselves were generally not as good as the Japanese competition. Increasingly strict exhaust emissions legislation was heralding the end of the two-stroke in many American states, especially California, the Aermacchi connection was severed in the late 1970s.

With the home opposition gone and no foreign manufacturers really competing directly, Harley had it easy in the US, and sales trebled during the 1970s, despite porr quality and very old-fashioned designs. Harley received a jolt at

This Harley-Davidson typifies the American dream of the 1930s: hand gear shift, foot boards and giant pan saddle

Historic border-crossing. An American Harley-Davidson crosses into Germany in 1918

the beginning of the 1980s when the Japanese sales war led to the dumping of cheap machines on the American market, and Harley sales started to suffer badly.

Controlling company AMF agreed to a management buy-out, after successfully lobbying the US government to impose strict import tariffs on foreign machines, and Harley found a new direction. A new engine, the Evo, was developed, quality improved, and with motorcycles increasingly becoming leisure items, sales increased.

By the end of the 1990s, interest in motorcycling was becoming so strong again, conditions were becoming right for new concerns to try and enter the market. The giant snowmobile manufacturer Polaris introduced its first ever motorcycle, the Victory, wranglings with the Indian title were sorted and a handful of machines was built as a precursor to greater sales, the name Excelsior-Henderson is due to make its debut. All of these machines and a large proportion of Japanese ones are still imitations of the basic Harley-Davidson look - laid back and lazy V-twin engine with classic American styling, a massive influence on modern motorcycling.

Sales in the US at the end of the 1990s are still very low compared with the almost 1 million machines sold annually two decades before, and over the previous 20 years a large proportion of them have been for off-road machines, there being plenty of opportunity in America's wide open spaces for making good use motocross and enduro bikes. But road bikes are making a come-back, and in particular, despite all the competition and its imitations, Harley-Davidson is still doing the best of all in its home market, taking more than 50 per cent of motorcycle sales.

THE 1920S AND 1930S...
THE GOLDEN AGE

Golden ages become so only in retrospect, so no doubt motorcyclists everywhere grumbled just as much about their grievances in the years between the wars as they ever did before, or have done since. Those years, however, definitely saw enormous changes for the better, both in the economic circumstances of the average enthusiast - this was the first time ordinary wage earners found themselves able to afford to buy and run a motorcycle - and in the way motorcycles were designed.

If the average motorcycle of 1939 is compared with that of 1919, the typical enthusiast would marvel not so much at the differences but at the improvements. Side valves had given way to overhead versions, which were also fully enclosed and quietened by a copious circulation of oil that, as a bonus, carried away excessive heat from the cylinder head. The lubrication systems themselves were vastly improved, with instead of the arbitrary injection of oil by a simple hand-operated pump, automatic engine-driven pumps circulating it to every vital part, then returning it to the oil tank. Dubious three-speed gearboxes with clumsy hand changes had given way to foolproof four-speed varieties, operated by a foot pedal. Brakes had improved beyond belief. So had tires, now wired onto the rims rather than held on by air pressure alone - no longer did a deflated tire roll off the rim in lethal fashion. Final drive belts had been replaced by chains, and even the cheapest lightweight two-stroke had electric lighting, usually with a battery and automatic control that ensured correct charging by the built-in dynamo.

The motorcycle of 1939, therefore, was an altogether more practical affair than its 1919 ancestor. It was easier to clean, too, with extensive use of durable chromium plating in place of nickel (which, unless laboriously polished, dulled to a dirty grey within weeks). Performance had been transformed as well. Between the first post-war Senior TT of 1920 and that of 1939, the speed had risen from the 51.48mph of Tommy de la Hay's side-valve Sunbeam to the staggering 89.38mph of Georg Meier's supercharged dohc BMW twin.

Such was the universal appeal of motorcycling in these years that, despite local influences and accidents that shaped the designs of one nation's industry along different lines to those of another, progress was constant, in Europe at any rate.

That the same was not true of the USA was not entirely the fault of the US motorcycle industry. In fact, the best American motorcycles of 1919 were considerably in advance of most of their European contemporaries. Pre war, the US industry had already standardised the use of countershaft gearboxes, while in Europe, flimsy epicyclic hub gears had been all the rage. Similarly, the

The unorthodox 5 cylinder Megola was raced by Toni Bauhofer and reached speeds up to 140 km/h.

Above: George Broughon (on the left) with a business associate and staff member outside his factory in 1927

Left:
"Lawrence of Arabia" on one of the eight Brought Superior he then owned

US had moved over to chain drive, while Europe stuck to the belt. The motorcycles themselves were handsome, powerful and robustly made. The factories were superbly equipped, taking advantage of the most up-to-date production methods, which meant that US machines could be shipped across the Atlantic and still sell at competitive prices. They did so in sufficient quantities to panic the British and European domestic industries into demanding that tariff barriers should be erected to halt this penetration, and laws were duly passed. For all their vision and efficiency, US manufacturers were abruptly denied access to an export market that had become vital to them, because cheap cars, a menace before the war, now threatened the very existence of the domestic American motorcycle.

The industry shrank and retrenched, with many of the companies that had survived until now disappearing. The 'big three' - Indian, Harley-Davidson and Excelsior (maker of big V-twins as well as the superb Henderson four) - were forced to depend on what export markets were left to them, on sales to the police, the armed forces, public utilities and sportsmen. Excelsior stopped manufacture in the face of the depression in 1931, leaving Indian and Harley-Davidson to fight out their bitter rivalry.

The USA's vanishing motorcycle industry was saved in the 1930s by the introduction of Class C Amateur racing, whose regulations specified that little more than basically standard production machines with 750cc side-valve engines should be used. Events comprised a strange mix of road racing, enduro runs, TT racing, flat track and speedway. TT racing was on a dirt surface, with gradients plus left and right turns. Flat track was on loose-surfaced oval tracks of up to half a mile, while speedway racing took place on longer tracks with steeply banked turns.

Class C was an instant success. After 1937, when Daytona Beach became its focal point, a genuine revival of interest in motorcycles and motorcycling resulted. On the other hand, however, the somewhat restrictive formula and the need for one motorcycle to fulfil so many functions led to stagnation and moved the US motorcycle far away from the concepts of European design.

There was another facet of the US scene, particularly in urban California, that is often forgotten. This was the motor scooter, which cropped up over and over again in the years between the wars. It was one such scooter, an American Autoped, owned by a prominent English member of parliament, that found its way into an article in early 1919 in the Daily News and started a craze in Britain that amounted to a mania.

The newspaper was swamped with letters, literally by the sackful. A rumour that one London store had Autopeds in stock saw people queuing half way down Oxford Street. The interest spilled over into the motorcycle magazines, although the editorial staff showed little enthusiasm. Every week saw dozens of projected designs, most of them crude and impractical. Many small and under-capitalised firms were set up to build scooters and a few staggered into production, by which time the mania had subsided. This left concerns such as ABC Skootamota, Kenilworth and Autoglider high and dry. No wonder that British manufacturers hesitated when Italian and German scooters appeared on the market 30 odd years later. Curiously, although the craze for scooters did not reach the same height in Germany, it lasted longer, and DKW made scooters that at least sold in reasonable numbers. Expatriate Danish engineer J. S. Rasmussen had founded his DKW company at Zschopau near Chemnitz in Saxony to build steam lorries - Dampe Kraft Wagen - but quickly switched after 1919 to making clip-on auxiliary engines for bicycles, scooters and ultra lightweight motorcycles, all powered by simple two-stroke engines designed by Herman Weber. These engines were also widely sold in Germany to other makers. Although DKW did make larger machines, favourable tax concessions meant that the vast majority were of 200cc and less.

The post-war years saw a short-lived craze for the scooter.

Quality from BMW in the 1930s. oil damped telescopic front fork, quiet smooth horizontal flat twin engine and shaft drive make this the first high speed motorcycle

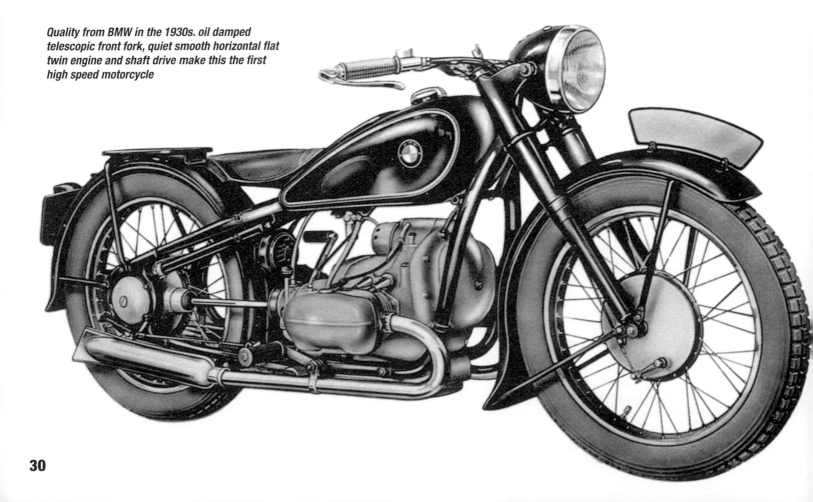

Bert le Vack, here with his Zenith racer, broke the world speed record in 1929

Somehow, the company managed to survive the appalling hyper-inflation of 1923 that killed off so many other concerns, and indeed flourished mightily. It began racing in the 175cc and later 250cc classes with Hugo Ruppe-designed engines, utilising his patented Ladepumpe charging piston below the crankcase. Soon these 'blown' DKWs demanded water-cooling to cope with their power. They were extremely successful in road racing and in the long-distance hill climbs so popular in Germany. However, in grand prix racing they were not really a match for the British four-strokes, or for that matter the Austrian Puchs, which used a split-single two-stroke engine, also pump-charged.

So soundly was DKW beaten by Puch in the 1930 and 1931 seasons that it called in designer Arnold Zoller, who laid out split-single racing engines - still using the charging piston - that were gradually developed into the most powerful two-strokes that the world had ever seen. As a result, DKW won the 250cc European championship in 1934, 1935 and 1938 and both the 250cc and 350cc championships in 1939. Perhaps its finest racing achievement was Ewald Kluge's 1938 Lightweight TT win at over 80mph, a result that convinced even the most sceptical.

Germany's other most celebrated and successful motorcycle between the wars was the BMW, first seen at the Paris Salon of 1923. Originally a wartime aircraft engine maker, BMW had embarked on a number of enterprises before starting to manufacture a proprietary flat twin motorcycle engine. It then decided to make a motorcycle of its own, with shaft drive, so that a transverse engine layout and unit gearbox were natural features to incorporate. Like DKW, BMW raced from an early date with great success and adopted supercharging wholeheartedly. Rider Ernst Herne held the world speed record no less than six times in the 1930s, and BMW won the 500cc European championship of 1938, and in 1939 riders Georg Meier and Jock West finished first and second in the Senior TT.

Innovative and superbly crafted, the big BMW bikes were very expensive as befitted what were probably the best motorcycles in the world in those years. It did make smaller, somewhat less expensive single-cylinder models of between 200cc and 400cc - still with shaft drive - but exclusivity was BMW's trademark. Next to Britain's, the German industry between the wars was probably the busiest in Europe, despite economically troubled times. Strangely, many firms, by no

Built for the average Frenchman, this 100cc pedal start velomteur is more rugged than looks imply. Forerunner of the 'moped'

means obscure concerns, used British engines, gearboxes and other proprietary components. To some extent, this was a tribute to the efficiency of the British industry and its resulting low prices, but it also reflected the esteem in which British motorcycles were held on the continent. JAP, Blackburne, Sturmey-Archer (Raleigh) and Python (Rudge) engines were widely used, as were the Bradshaw oil-cooled engine and the remarkable Barr & Stroud sleeve valve. It was a considerable loss to Britain when Adolf Hitler came to power and put an end to this widespread dependence on imported components. No less was it a source of embarrassment to those German firms left high and dry.

As in Germany, France saw an upsurge of interest in motorcycling immediately after WW1 and a number of imaginative and advanced designs were produced. Aircraft maker Blériot and engine manufacturer Gnome et Rhône both saw the mass production of motorcycles as the solution for factories suddenly made idle. The former showed interesting vertical twins, while the latter chose to build the British ABC under licence. However, French enthusiasm was short-lived and although the native industry tried hard to keep up with the latest technological developments, this soon became little more than a prestige exercise at the annual Paris Salon. What did sell, and in numbers that kept the industry alive if not exactly flourishing, was the 100cc Velomoteur that needed no tax and which could be ridden

Top left:A superb 750cc in line, four cylinder ohc Motobécane built in uint with gearbox. Final drive is by shaft

Below left: A rocket-powered motorcycle was tested by Fritz von Opel in 1928. The machine was basically a 496cc Opel Motoclub ohv production model with rockets strapped to the back. Soon after this short-lived experiment, Opel stopped making motocycles.

reputation in racing and in the International Six Days Trial, why the Italians made no attempt to export is hard to understand. Perhaps it was because, as in Germany, taxation encouraged smaller engines, so many of those exquisite Italian ohc models were of 250cc and below.

Without doubt, however, it was the British industry that dominated European motorcycling between the wars. To some extent, this was because it enjoyed a virtually 'captive' colonial export market, particularly in Australia, but there was naturally more to it than that. The concentration of diverse skills and experience in the British Midlands, the intense competition between not only motorcycle manufacturers, but also the makers of proprietary equipment all had their influences.

Although British design was conservative, this might have been no bad thing - evolution is better than revolution, as history seems to show. In addition, many British designers were only too aware of the strange story of the post-war ABC. This wonder motorcycle, with its 400cc ohv flat twin engine set transversely across the frame, unit construction car-type gearbox with gate change by hand lever, self-damping leaf-spring suspension fore and aft, internal expanding brakes, ingenious frame design and electric lighting with built-in dynamo, embodied everything that a motorcyclist could wish for, including generous weather protection.

Designed by the young Granville Bradshaw, the ABC truly appeared to be 10 or even 20 years ahead of its time when it was revealed in prototype form early in 1919. The machine was to be made by the Sopwith aviation and engineering company in a purpose-equipped factory, with a production target of 10,000 a year, but despite the brilliance of the overall concept and Sopwith's money, the ABC was a damaging fiasco. It took 15 months to reach production, only for Sopwith to go into voluntary liquidation after fewer than 2,500 motorcycles had been made. A disappointed British public turned to the next best, which might not be all that much ahead of the times, but which did at least live up to the maker's claims and reputation.Such British marques as Sunbeam, Norton, AJS, Scott, BSA and Triumph sold worldwide. British bikes won the TT year after year and European grand prix races as well. Britain's dominance of the market extended beyond the super-sports sector into other areas as well. There were plenty of companies using the 270cc Villiers two-stroke engine, or the small side-valve engines made by JAP and Blackburne. As in

without even the formality of a driving licence.

Nor was there the sporting interest in France that so sustained motorcycling in Germany. The French Grand Prix turned into an ill-supported and even worse attended farce. The magnificent racing complex built at Montlhery, 20 miles from Paris, never paid its way, although the 1.7-mile banked track was popular for record breaking. Yet, strangely, the 'speed week' at Arpajon, held on a narrow tree-lined stretch of road with a four mile undulating straight, attracted entrants from all over Europe, while the Bol d'Or, an extraordinary 24-hour race with no change of rider, that started in 1924 on a public road circuit in the forest of St Germain near Paris, survived in this format for the next 15 years. The first race was won by a 500cc ohv Sunbeam, victory in it remaining a British preserve, which makes its survival all the more surprising.

Italy was a late comer to motorcycle manufacture but, as the 1920s wore on, made up for it in full measure. Garelli and Moto

Guzzi joined Gilera and Frera as sporting makers, as did Benelli and Bianchi. Italian designers were early and enthusiastic advocates of ohv and ohc engines and the use of light aluminum alloy components and soon developed a sense of style that they have never lost.

Racing - especially long-distance open road racing from town to town - became an Italian institution. With the supercharged Rondine - later Gilera - the Italians could justly have claimed to have begun the trend towards four-cylinder racing machines. Dorino Serafini's European title on the 500cc Gilera in 1939 was a taste of things to come. Moto Guzzi first raced in the TT in 1926, and in 1935 was rewarded when Stanley Woods won both Lightweight and Senior races, and in 1937 on a Moto Guzzi Omobono Tenni won the Lightweight TT - the first foreign rider ever to win a TT.

Yet, for all their excellence and sporting pedigree, Italian motorcycles were virtually unknown elsewhere in Europe. Given their

Germany, there were many 'manufacturers' who fabricated little themselves, instead assembling their motorcycles almost entirely from bought-in components. This could be an expensive method, especially for the smaller firms who could not bargain quantity against prices, as could a larger company such as OK Supreme. Many small firms and quite a few larger ones were under-capitalised, so did not survive the depression of the early 1930s. Some, however, flourished. New Imperial, for instance, began to make its own engines in the mid-1920s and went on to introduce its own range of unit construction engines and gearboxes and its own cantilever spring frames in the 1930s. Vincent HRD became its own engine maker in the 1930s, as did Excelsior with the famous Manxman ohc engines, which it took over when Blackburne stopped making motorcycle engines.

The king of the assemblers was the incomparable George Brough, who, working from his small Nottingham factory, advertised his Brough Superiors as 'The Rolls Royce of motorcycles'. Brough always insisted on the best, was his own head tester and rode his

own machinery in trials and speed events with great success.Brough Superiors really were hand-made. Having ordered one and paid a deposit, customers were encouraged to visit the factory several times to check on progress.

On each visit they were expected to pay a further installment, a procedure that on the one hand made the eventual settling of a the final bill less painful, and, on the other, gave Brough a healthy cash flow.

Most of Brough's machines used big V-twin JAP (and in later years Matchless) engines, although he built several show stoppers - a transverse engined V-twin, a narrow angle V-four and an in-line air-cooled in-line four - it is doubtful he had any serious intention of making any of them. However, he did make a dozen or so sidecar outfits with an 800cc water-cooled Austin Seven engine, gearbox and shaft drive and twin rear wheels on either side of the final drive unit. Unfortunately, the outbreak of war in 1939 stopped the development of another model that Brough certainly intended to make. This was the ill-fated 1000cc transverse flat four Golden Dream, with contra-rotating crankshafts, unit

gearbox and shaft drive. It had been the sensation of the 1938 Motorcycle Show.

If the 1920s were the years of development, the 1930s were those of consolidation. The depression of the early 1930s that eliminated many small companies - and brought changes of ownership to several larger ones - only confirmed the conviction that sales depended upon value for money. The resilience of the motorcycle industry was quite remarkable. The years between the wars culminated in the birth of not so much a new motorcycle, but a new style of motorcycle - Edward Turner's 500cc Triumph twin. Although nothing new technically, the Speed Twin and its super sports version, the Tiger 100, opened up a whole new avenue - it was exciting, fast and affordable. To have been young and able to buy a Triumph Twin in 1937 must have been exciting indeed! Little did those lucky few realise what lay ahead not so far in the future. But that is the way of the world, and we cannot blame those who experienced those days - and indeed those who only read about them - from regarding the years between the wars as a Golden Age.

Riders in the German Six-Day race of 1927 pose with their Standard machines. This standard marque was a quality German bike

THE SECOND WORLD WAR

Although Germany moved into Czechoslovakia in March 1939, it wasn't until the invasion of Poland on 1 September 1939 that the war which was to engulf much of the world was triggered. The armies, navies and air forces had weapons of massive destructive power compared to those used two decades earlier, but once again the motorcycle played a major role in the war.

Films and novels often portray the image of the British despatch rider as a lone Tommy picking his way across war-ravaged countryside on a BSA M20 just minutes in front of a coldly efficient, advancing Panzer tank division, avoiding land mines, fallen trees and the odd sniper to reach Command HQ in the nick of time with a package of vital instructions that change the course of the war.

The Germans might be seen as a convoy of BMW R75s powering a course through thick Flanders mud in driving sleet, with armed passengers ready to riddle the enemy with bullet holes and effect another successful hit and run raid.

Reality or pure fantasy in the name of entertainment? A certain mystique does surround the wartime role of the despatch rider, and some DRs, as they were known, did perform acts of heroism. But in the main solo riders were used well behind the battle lines, acting as links in the communication networks, for police work, or in a shepherding role. Most motorcycle outfit crews hated their vulnerability and would have been happier in armoured four wheelers, but, as in WW1, motorcycles again served their countries well.

BETWEEN THE WARS

The military forces of WW1 had been the biggest customers the motorcycle industry had ever known. Factories streamlined production, model choice was often limited to one or two machines and unnecessary frills and accessories were dropped. Reliability and volume were the two key words dominating production strategies.

The Great War also offered the first opportunity to test machines on a large scale, often over long periods of service, and development progressed fast as a result. In turn, the riders, when returning to civilian life, expected a higher standard of reliability, combined with more design sophistication. The single-speed veteran machine with gas lights, an excess of control levers and hand-pump oiling, which needed to be either pedalled or pushed into life, was too crude for the 1920s enthusiast.

So the twenties became a period of design advancement for civilian machines. Hand-change gearboxes with a kick start facility were universally expected. New engines incorporated mechanical pump oiling, although many makers still fitted a hand pump too, as some customers distrusted this new-fangled technology and felt secure in the knowledge they could still lubricate the engine by hand! Throttle control levers were replaced by the rotating drum type twistgrip in universal use today, while reliable electrical generators were produced which banished acetylene lighting to the dark ages (where many had been stranding their riders up to then anyway). The majority of manufacturers stuck with magneto ignition throughout the inter-war period as the unit proved reliable over high mileages. Battery-powered coil ignition was usually reserved for economically built lightweights, and didn't spread to other machines until much later.

By the late 1920s, overhead valve (ohv) engines powered both sports and quality touring machines, while the sidevalve (sv) layout was reserved for motorcycles destined for years of hard, reliable work or purely economy models. Along with these advances came an increase in average machine weight, a typical quality touring machine of 1930 weighing twice as much as the WW1 Triumph Model H.

But some examples of technological progress occasionally took years before becoming accepted practice. Experienced WW1 despatch riders would bend the hand change gear levers on their Trusties enabling them to hook the gear lever up or down with their foot to change gear, a jury-rigged device which was hit and miss, with changes from first to third gear in a single movement being all too easy, but it did enable the DR to keep both hands on the handlebars.

It took until 1929 for the first commercial positive stop foot change gearbox to appear, produced by Velocette, although it was soon followed by most other European manufacturers. The system enables the rider to change up or down one gear at a time with each foot movement, and is used on all modern machines.

A British Military official photograph. The instructor explains to the female trainees how a headlight blackout mask works while the cat looks longingly at the 'out of bounds' door.

British experimental gun attatchment on a Norton

The Germans tried out portable scooters for their paratroops

The NSU HK 101 Kettenkrad tracked vehicles

During this period of fertile development much work was carried out in Europe to perfect the design of the ideal military motorcycle. Some ideas were clearly misplaced, such as the French army's fully tracked, armoured, machine-gun-carrying 500cc monster weighing over 1300lb (590kg). In Britain, Triumph and OEC among others secured ministry funding to develop half track machines where the rear wheel is replaced by a continuous tank-type track running over two powered wheels. Although more practical, this idea too was destined to collect dust in the factory store.

Bourne, a small and almost unknown British factory, developed successful sidecar wheel drive for the first time. It enabled the drive to the sidecar wheel to be engaged or disengaged at will by the rider. Designed for motorcycle trials, a sport from which the design was then banned (as happens to many radical advances), it had a major impact on military outfits used in WW2. For example, the Belgian FN factory incorporated sidecar wheel drive for its 1000cc flat twin M/12 personnel carrier.

The Germans took the idea on board and built a range of outfits with twin rear wheel drive. Offered as a simple motorcycle combination for personnel transport, they weighed a more modest 530lb (240kg) But some of the fully armed and armoured BMW and Zündapp machines weighed over 2000lb (900kg) ready to roll, a far cry from the nimble WW1 belt-drive single cylinder despatch machines.

In America, Excelsior, Indian and Harley-Davidson built outfits which were popular among WW1 servicemen, and in solo trim these powerful bikes were a favorite with the lucky British DRs who were issued with one. But many US factories went to the wall during the Great Depression of the 1920s and 1930s and the survivors were slow to develop military machines, with the threat of war appearing to be less than in Europe, while Willys had begun building the Jeep, which performed most tasks in warfare a bike could, only better.

Meanwhile, the Spanish Civil War gave the German Wehrmacht - which along with the Italians sided with the Nationalists - a chance to sample first hand the excellence of Belgian and French military motorcycles which were in use by the warring factions. This once again brought home to the German military the value of an all-terrain vehicle - they had no Jeep, while the VW Kübelwagen wasn't yet in production, so design of the motorcycle combination with sidecar wheel drive was honed to their idea of perfection.

THE AXIS POWERS

After WW1 the Austro-Hungarian empire was broken up into several smaller states: Austria, Czechoslovakia, Hungary and Yugoslavia. Less than 20 years later the Austrians and Czechs found themselves part of Hitler's new German Empire.

Austrian cycle maker Puch built its first production motorcycles in 1903, going on to become a leading world authority on two-stroke design, especially the split single type. Puch combined with Austro-Daimler and

Spotted at a post-World War II demonstration in Germany. The NSU-Kettenkrad is powered by a 1.5 litre Opel engine. These half track/half motorcycle vehicles were ideal for rough terrain during the war

Steyr, forming a powerful company. In 1938 it became part of the German war effort, production was increased and the factory built bikes for the Wehrmacht until bombed in 1942. Although the Puch factory had built a flat four-cylinder sidevalve model along similar lines to the Zündapp flat four, production of this model stopped in 1938 and the factory's war production concentrated on its two-stroke designs, which in military guise became known for their rugged reliability. The unorthodox split single design comprises two cylinders and pistons sharing a V-shaped connecting rod, which gives asymmetric timing of the transfer and exhaust ports. As the combustion chamber fires the two pistons down the barrels, the ports open and the gaseous fuel mixture is forced from the charge cylinder into the combustion cylinder, while the spent gases are purged into the exhaust pipe. The system keeps the spent and fresh gases apart and proved highly successful in competition for both Puch and the German

DKW factory, which employed a similar idea for its racing machines.

Under the German Schell program for rationalisation the Puch factory was limited to producing 125cc and 250cc two-stroke machines for military use, although some 200cc two-stroke and 800cc four-stroke models were pressed into service. Restrictions were later relaxed and Puch was also permitted to build 350cc split single two-strokes.

You can't keep a good man down and the Czechs proved this more than once in the military field. Early Czech-built military machines were dull plodders, but in the early 1920s events took an upward turn for military machinery - the officer in charge of equipping the army with bikes was a fan of motorcycle racing. Instead of steady military sidevalves, orders were placed with predominantly British factories for sports and competition type bikes, including the powerful Brough Superior SS100 models. An indiscretion brought the

Czech army competition sponsorship to an end in 1929, but not before the enlightened racing officer had enjoyed many victories astride his "sponsor's" Nottingham-built Brough. Good fun while it lasted.

As European unrest increased during the 1930s, the Czechoslovakian military replaced its racers with reliable, sturdy, home-built models from makers like Jawa and Itar, with a sprinkling of imported BSA and Indian V-twins, but sadly no more Brough Superiors. Jawa, the best known Czech factory, was allowed to repair only German machines during WW2, but in a building on the factory site company personnel developed a 250cc single-cylinder two-stroke, built in unit with the gearbox. The German security personnel never found the

Khaki painted, black out masks, ample pannier bags and a rock-hard seat are all standard kit for this military 350cc ohv single

machine and the new bike formed the basis for all post WW2 Jawa production. During the 1930s the Nazi party worked and schemed to make Germany a world super power. Apart from subsidising exports and promoting all forms of pro-German publicity, including motor and motorcycle sport, the country was also equipping its military forces in readiness to deal with any who stood in the country's way. Industrial production was modernised and the population learnt many new skills. Low priced, lightweight motorcycles were mass produced, giving affordable transport to everyone. As a result the masses became skilled riders and mechanics, very important for a country heading for war and needing drivers, bike riders and vehicle repair personnel for the war effort.

German industry was completely rationalised in 1938 by Colonel (later General) Oberst von Schell, who was charged with preparing the country's industry for war. Model ranges were reduced, companies closed or put onto other types of work and components standardised. Motorcycle factories were instructed precisely which types of machines they could build and where to source parts. Design work was strictly controlled.

Thus, at the outbreak of WW2, Germany was more prepared than any other country, and the motorcycle had a precise, planned role to play within this war machine. Yet despite all this preparation, German military machines switched from one trend to another, and the Germans started the war with a range of two-stroke and four-stroke single cylinder models from 125cc to 800cc, the bigger machines also being used for sidecar work, the sidecar wheel of some BMW and Zündapp combinations being powered.

Some bizarre armoured outfits and gun

ships were created. NSU built what was probably the weirdest motorcycle of WW2, the Kettenkraftrad, a small, tracked personnel carrier with motorcycle front forks and handlebar steering. Powered by an Opel 1478cc ohv four-cylinder water-cooled car engine, the Kettenkraftrad, coded HK100, might have looked odd but it was certainly practical. The driver controlled the vehicle with car-type controls, although the handlebars were fitted with a motorcycle-style twistgrip throttle. This soon took over many motorcycle outfit tasks as it was able to carry two seated passengers and others perched on the body work, as well as tow trailers or other vehicles, and cover rough terrain. In 1944, as Germany struggled against the onslaught of the Allied forces on many fronts, along with relentless bombing at home, production of many military motorcycles almost stopped, precious resources being turned elsewhere as demand for motorcycles fell away. The expensive BMW and Zündapp combinations with sidecar wheel drive were being replaced by the cheaper and more practical military VW Kübelwagen, while the radio displaced the despatch rider for many communication duties. In the dying months of the war Germany built only DKW 125cc and 350cc models.

Although BMW, DKW, Zündapp and NSU were the major players in the military bike market for the German forces, there were other suppliers. Ardie built 125cc and 200cc twin-port two-stroke singles, TWN supplied a range of two-stroke solo machines and dallied with the design of a 125cc airborne scooter (which was never produced) and Victoria concentrated on the production of the KR35WH, a 342cc long-stroke, ohv single for the Wehrmacht. Of all the countries involved in

the Second World War, the approach of the Italians to military motorcycles was the most unusual. The land of design flair, and passion for motor vehicles was still holding major road races for cars and motorcycles during the war, the last motorcycle event being held in Genoa in the summer of 1940. Despite the war raging across Europe, works machinery lined up, including a Moto Guzzi and supercharged Gilera.

Although the Italian forces did use some mundane sidevalve machines, other bikes were much more exotic, with some lucky Italian riders kitted out with Benelli 250cc or 500cc machines. The overhead camshaft (ohc) design was similar to that of the Benelli which was raced to victory by Ted Mellors in the 1939 IoM Lightweight TT, at an average speed of 74.25mph! Although the Moto Guzzi military range was designed solely for forces use, the bikes still showed some of the design flair we associate with the Italians. They were often equipped, for example, with twin silencers fitted to a single exhaust pipe and a laid down engine to help handling by keeping the center of gravity low. Both Gilera and Moto Guzzi supplied three-wheelers for military use, as well as conventional motorcycles. In both cases the motorcycle rear wheel and frame was replaced by a platform-like frame, an axle and two wheels. Showing much less evidence of rationalisation in Italy than Germany, the Gilera Gigante VT three-wheeler was offered with a choice of 500cc and 600cc engines with either sidevalve or overhead valve options. The Moto Guzzi three-wheeler, of similar design to the Gilera, was based on the 500cc single-cylinder Alce model, and again offered with many engine and other options.

As well as building models fitted with sidecars, the Italian factories also offered

Fold up Weldbike which was dropped by parachutte to the advancing British paratroops

Harley Davidson mounted military policemen chats to collegues

Stripped for action when the going is hot

German BMW R75 ohv horizontally opposed twin with shaft drive

armed versions. Even solo bikes were fitted with armour to protect the gunner and a machine gun, but these bikes, unsurprisingly, were top heavy and difficult to ride. Bianchi assembled a workmanlike 500cc single for military use and, like the British and German forces, Italy too considered the possibility of parachuting lightweight machines to the forces on the ground. With small scooter-type wheels, a single-cylinder 125cc two-stroke engine and an all-chain operated two-speed gear system with a double reduction facility, the Volugrafo Aeromoto was capable of speeds up to 40mph, exciting performance for the rider sitting on a bike no larger than the more recent and familiar Honda Monkey bike. Unusually, the mini-bike was offered with an option of twin front and rear wheels, allowing it to stand upright without a stand or support. The Volugrafo Aeromoto's scooter-like appearance has many similarities to the post WW2 Lambretta and Vespa machines.

The Japanese motorcycle industry was in decline during the 1920s but the military build-up of the 1930s saved it. Most Japanese bikes of the period were copies of either European or American designs and some were very crudely built. The Rikuo Harley-Davidsons built under licence became the machine of choice for the Japanese Imperial Army. The factory made over 18,000 for the military, fitted with either 1200cc or 750cc sidevalve V-twin engines.

THE ALLIED FORCES

Only three firms built bikes for the Belgian Army, all based in Herstallez-Liege, despite the country supporting many motorcycle factories during the inter-war period. After occupation by German forces the factories were staffed with forced Belgian labour.

Gillet built large 708cc two-stroke twin machines, mostly used for sidecar work. The four-speed gearbox, with a single reverse gear option, was built in unit with the engine, and the sidecar wheel drive was taken by shaft from the bike's back wheel. Unlike Gillet, Sarolea built four-stroke machines for military use, the smaller 350cc models in solo form, while the larger 600cc versions were often coupled to sidecars.

Like the British manufacturer BSA, FN (Fabrique Nationale d'Armes de Guerre) was an armament manufacturer which also built motorcycles. Famed for many years for its shaft drive, in-line four-cylinder machines, FN built a 992cc, horizontally opposed twin-cylinder sidevalve combination with shaft drive

1940-42 Royal Enfield model WD/C 346 side-valve single cylinder machine built in large numbers by the Redditch factory for the allied forces

to both the rear and sidecar wheels. The German forces were so impressed with the traction of the Belgian twin rear wheel drive models, in both the Spanish Civil War and Flanders mud, that BMW and Zündapp were ordered to build outfits with sidecar wheel drive.

In Denmark, vacuum cleaner firm Fisker and Nielsen of Copenhagen built only 12,000 Nimbus machines in the bike's entire production run from 1919 to 1959. All had four-cylinder car-type engines fitted in line with the frame. The Nimbus was ideal for military use because of its smooth running, shaft drive and sturdy pressed steel frame. The Danish forces bought the machine in small numbers, but made them last. On 9 April 1940 the German forces overran Denmark in a single day and began using the Danish military Nimbus motorcycles.

The British military was very fond of its motorcycles, and with England still a world leader in bike manufacture it built more military models than any other country. With the clouds of war gathering, the War Office issued new contracts for the supply of military machines as early as 1937, with new military specifications coming into being a year later. Even so, once WW2 started the supply of military motorcycles fell far short of demand. To cope with this the authorities impounded just about anything and everything that moved on two wheels, from both factories and dealers. A quick coat of khaki paint and the bikes were ridden off to war.

The specification of purpose-built British military bikes remained almost unaltered, except in minor detail, until near the end of the war, when a call for an easy-to-ride lightweight

twin-cylinder sidevalve was made. Douglas, BSA and Triumph all built prototypes but only the Triumph TRW went into production. This continued to be sold after the war, mainly overseas and to the RAF.

BSA M20, Matchless G3L, Norton 16H and Big Four, Velocette MDD/MAF, Ariel, Triumph and Royal Enfield sidevalve and overhead valve models satisfied most military needs for four-stroke models. Machines like the BSA M20 and Matchless G3L were supplied in batches of up to 17,000 at a time. Costs and quality were pared: tank knee grips, footrest and handlebar rubbers were considered luxuries so were left off!

Although many of the sidevalve machines, like Norton's 16H and Big Four, along with BSA's M20, were considered slow and heavy, their engines were so understressed they were able to withstand the abuse of a whole battalion of ham fisted riders. But it was the overhead valve 350cc single-cylinder models of Ariel, Matchless, Triumph and Royal Enfield which were the favorite mounts of many DRs. Once the Matchless factory replaced the G3L's girder front fork with telescopic units early in the war the bike became one of the best all round despatch rider machines in use.

With more motorcycles and despatch riders than any other country, rivalry among the riders was intense. Highly unofficial races took place, while some of the riders of the overhead valve models considered themselves the élite.

Where many other forces used the motorcycle in fighting situations, British machines were used primarily for messenger and transport purposes, both at home and abroad, although small numbers of sidecar outfits were armed and some DRs carried

hand guns and rifles.

As the war progressed, British military authorities began to see the need for featherweight bikes. Excelsior built the 98cc single speed Welbike, which was intended for parachute drops alongside soldiers into or near battle zones and occupied territory. Just under 4000 Welbikes, each of which could fit complete into a parachute tube, were built, but in practise the machine was underpowered and many were sold to overseas countries at the end of the war.

The James ML (Military Lightweight) and the Royal Enfield WD/RE, both 125cc two-stroke lightweights, were a better option than the Welbike, and a number of MLs and REs found themselves thrown out of airplanes, wearing nothing more than a parachute, to provide transport for troops on the ground. The Villiers-powered James ML, and the WD/RE with its Royal Enfield engine, were built and used in significant numbers in the last years of the war.

The British authorities set up DR training schools, and a lucky few were taught to ride by well known competition riders or racers such as TT winner Freddie Frith. Motorcycles, like all equipment, needed maintenance and the REME (Royal Electrical and Mechanical Engineers) straightened frames, fettled engines, endlessly rewired bikes and assembled the new machines, which often arrived in kit form from the factories.

Wisbech-born Fred Fowler typified the REME mechanic. Trained as a motor engineer in pre-WW2 days, Fred reported for his first day's duty at a workshop 'somewhere in England' on a Monday. The sergeant presented Private Fowler with a new BSA M20 in kit form and left him to assemble it as part of

US H-D 45 WLAs with sub machine gun holster

British mortar attatchment

German Army BMW R35

Indian soldier reclining on a 350cc ohv Matchless G3/L

his REME training. By mid-morning on Tuesday, Fred was riding the BSA around the REME yard under the watchful gaze of his boss. Fred was sent home for the rest of the week, 'training' passed with flying colours, and began REME work in earnest the following Monday, fitting parts, welding, and spraying gallons of khaki paint onto all forms of military equipment, including motorcycles.

On the other side of the Channel, Terrot, Monet et Goyon, Peugeot and Motobecane were being used by the French forces in capacities from 100cc to 1000cc. With two- and four-stroke engines, the designs varied from the simple pedal-start model to heavyweight flat and V-twin machines. Gnome et Rhône and René Gillet predominantly built well-made twin-cylinder sidecar models.

In May 1940 Germany marched through the Low Countries into France. The following month, Italy sided with Germany and an armistice in France took place. Split in two, occupied France had to work for German forces while the Free French were under Vichy government control. By the autumn of 1942 all of France was under German control and the French military motorcycles were pressed into

use by the Wehrmacht.

Russian forces had far fewer home-grown models to draw on, and limited facilities to build more in quantity. The TIS-AM-600 was loosely based on the 1920s BSA Sloper, while Moskva and others, such as the Leningrad-built L-300 two-stroke single, were crude and basic, but mostly reliable. At first the Russian forces were supplied by the Allies with Ariel, Matchless, Norton and Velocette machines from Britain and later the USA supplied Russia with almost 30,000 V-twin motorcycles.

America furnished Allied forces with large numbers of machines, before joining the war itself after the Japanese attack on Pearl Harbor. Although heavy and with foot clutch and hand gear change, many European riders took to the big Indian and Harley-Davidson V-twins because they were strong and could hold high speeds for long periods.

Vast numbers of these conventional - to the American enthusiast - bikes were shipped over to Europe, many returning to civilian use after the end of the fighting. Harley-Davidson did break with American convention by producing a flat twin model, the XA, but it was not a success and further development was halted as the supply of Jeeps to US forces increased.

Although Harley-Davidson and Indian V-twins were used in volume by the Allied forces, America also produced two oddballs for the war effort, the Cushman scooter for parachute drops and the even more bizarre Simplex Servicycle. The Cushman's 125cc two-stroke engine with overhung, ported crankshaft acting as an inlet port was odd, and so was transmission with its belt primary and final drives. But in other respects, the centrifugal clutch and simplicity of controls could be considered a forerunner of the modern twist-and-go scooter, although the spindly cycle-type frame and large diameter wheels did a good job of disguising this!

Many civilian machines were commandeered for American military use and run until they dropped.

Although not directly involved, both Sweden

and Switzerland continued to build machines in their native factories for their own forces during the war.

THE END OF THE ROAD

Although the motorcycle entered WW2 as a significant player, its role diminished as the war progressed. The Willys Jeep and the VW Kübelwagen all-terrain vehicle more than ably replaced the sidecar outfit for personnel transport and were cheaper to make than the complex twin rear wheel drive outfits. In addition, the increasing use of radio reduced the need for bike-mounted messengers. Increasingly the role of the motorcycle was downgraded.

Just as at the end of WW1, the military had large stocks of unwanted machines in all conditions when hostilities ceased in 1945. Once again civilians needed cheap transport, while the factories had been flat out for the war effort and had no stocks of new civilian machines for the demob-happy serviceman with Government gratuity in his pocket. The military either sold machines to dealers for refurbishment or the bikes were collected at sites throughout the country for auction. Civilian industry and transport were again kick-started into life.

Those accustomed to the fast pre-war sports models or quality tourers found the ex-DR machines slow and basic, but they were better than nothing and basic tuning gave them a little more go. Many machines ended up serving their owners for years, and were still running into the 1960s, after being resold time and again as low priced transport bargains by dealers. In the UK, the Matchless G3L especially lent itself to conversion into a capable competition mount for the trials or scrambles rider, while enterprising small Italian factories grafted sprung rear ends onto rigid British models for their home market.

Post WW1 history had repeated itself as far as motorcycles were concerned, along with so many other aspects of the two great conflicts.

Common Military Motorcycles and Three-Wheelers of WW2

IoE Inlet over exhast valve   **OHC** Overhead camshaft   **OHV** Overhead valve   **Split** Split single design   **SV** Side valve   **TS** Two-stroke

Marque	Model	Cyl	CC	Bore mm	Stroke mm	2/4 stroke	BHP	Country
Ardie	RBZ	1	193	61	66	TS	7	D
Ariel	W/NG	1	346	72	85	OHV	17	GB
Bianchi	500	1	496	82	94	SV	9	I
Benelli	250	1	247	67	70	OHC	NA	I
Benelli	500	1	494	85	87	OHC	NA	I
BMW	R35	1	342	72	84	OHV	14	D
BMW	R61	2	600	70	78	SV	18	D
BMW	R71	2	745	78	78	SV	22	D
BMW	R75	2	745	78	78	OHV	26	D
BSA	B30	1	348	72	82.5	OHV	15	GB
BSA	C10	1	249	63	80	SV	NA	GB
BSA	M20	1	496	82	94	SV	13	GB
Condor	A-1000	2	997	82	94	IoE	NA	CH
DKW	NZ 350	1	346	72	85	TS	12	D
DKW	RT 125	1	123	52	58	TS	5	D
Excelsior	Welbike	1	98	50	50	TS	2	GB
FN	Model 12	2	992	90	78	SV	22	B
FN	Tricar T3	2	992	90	78	SV	22	B
Gilera	LTE	1	499	84	90	SV	10	I
Gilera	Marte	1	499	84	90	SV	14	I
Gnome et Rhone	AX2	2	804	80	80	SV	18	F
Gnome et Rhone	750 Armee	2	721	80	72	OHV	15	F
Harley-Davidson	74 cu in	2	1205	86.9	101.6	SV	33	USA
Harley-Davidson	WLA	2	741	69.8	96.9	SV	23	USA
Harley-Davidson	XA	2	739	77.8	77.8	SV	23	USA
Indian	340B	2	1204	82.5	112.7	SV	30	U
Indian	741-A	2	492	63.5	77.7	SV	15	U
Indian	741-B	2	744	73	88.9	SV	24	U
James	ML	1	122	50	62	TS	6.5	G
Matchless	G3L	1	347	69	93	OHV	16	G
Meguro Rikuo		2	1200	NA	NA	SV	28	J
Monark	M-42-SV	1	495	79	101	SV	15	S
Monark	M-42-OHV	1	495	79	101	OHV	20	S
Moskva	(M)72	2	745	78	78	SV	22	SU

Marque Model	Cyl	CC	Bore mm	Stroke mm	2/4 stroke	BHP	Country
to Guzzi GTS	1	499	88	82	IoE	13	I
to Guzzi Alce	1	499	88	82	IoE	13	I
bus Model 750	4	746	60	66	OHC	22	DK
J HK 100 Kettenkraftrad	4	1478	80	74	OHV	36	D
J 125ZBD	1	122	50	62	TS	5	D
J 251OSL	1	241	64	75	OHV	10	D
J 601OSL	1	562	85	99	OHV	24	D
ton 16H	1	490	79	100	SV	13	GB
ton Big four	1	633	82	120	SV	15	GB
ch GS-350	1	349	48	83	TS	13	A
			55	83			
ch 125T	1	125	2x38	55	TS	NA	A
ch 250S4	1	248	2x45	78	TS	10.5	A
yal eld C	1	346	70	90	SV	10	GB
yal ield CO	1	346	70	90	OHV	15	GB
yal ield RE	1	126	54	55	TS	4.5	GB
olea Military	2	873	88	80	SV	20	B

Marque Model	Cyl	CC	Bore mm	Stroke mm	2/4 stroke	BHP	Country
Simplex Servi-cycle	1	125	NA	NA	TS	4	USA
Terrot HDA	1	346	70	90	SV	9	F
Terrot RDA	1	498	84	90	SV	12	F
Terrot VAAT	2	746	70	79	SV	18	F
TIZ-AM 600	1	595	85	105	SV	15	SU
Triumph 3HW	1	343	70	89	OHV	17	GB
Triumph 3SW	1	343	70	89	SV	12	GB
TWN BD250	1	248	2x45	78	TS	11	D
Velocette MDD	1	349	68	96	OHV	14	GB
Velocette MAF	1	349	68	96	OHV	14	GB
Victoria KR-9	2	497	60	88	SV	15	D
Volugrafo Aermoto	1	125	NA	NA	TS	NA	I
Zundapp DB200	1	198	60	70	TS	7	D
Zundapp K-500-W	2	498	69	66.6	SV	16	D
Zundapp K800	4	804	62	66.6	SV	22	D
Zundapp KS-750-W	2	751	75	85	OHV	26	D

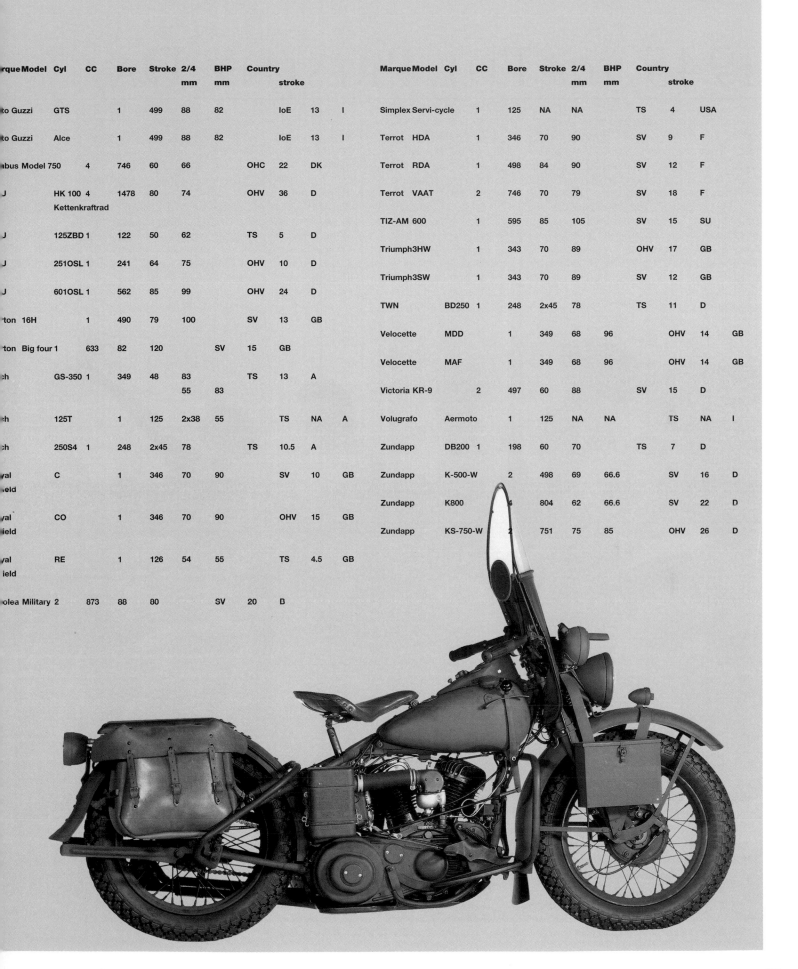

1945 TO THE PRESENT DAY

During the six years of WW2, British manufacturers supplied more than 420,000 motorcycles to the armed forces. A quarter of these were built by BSA at its Small Heath, Birmingham, factory. This meant the factories' production capacity was considerable, yet its main market all but evaporated on the arrival of peace.

Fuel was in short supply in many countries after the end of the war in Europe, generating a big demand for economical transport. The British Government, for example, launched a gasoline rationing scheme on June 1 1945,

permitting the use of motor vehicles for private use for the first time since 1939. Owners of small machines could buy two gallons (9 litres) of commercial grade 'pool' gasoline per month, while a larger bike was allowed three gallons (13.5 litres). Owners of tiny 98cc and 125cc models were squeezing out hundreds of miles to the gallon with frugal use of the twistgrip, which was not much fun, but at least it was transport, still something of a luxury in any form.

Perhaps surprisingly, motorcycle sport restarted almost immediately, in the UK with a Motorcycling Club (MCC) event at Wrotham

Park in June 1945, while in Ulster pre-war stars Rex McCandless, Ernie Lyons and Artie Bell returned to their winning ways at an Ulster MCC grass track meeting. A full house packed the first post-WW2 speedway meeting at the New Cross, London stadium on June 27 and the Ards MCC started road racing again in Ireland with a meeting at Bangor, Co. Down. Many other European countries returned to motorcycles for sport, pleasure and essential transport in a similar way.

Many motorcycle factories rapidly returned to peacetime motorcycle production, eager to

A 1961 press release photograph taken in Hyde Park, London by the German firm NSU, L-R Prima, Max, Quickly and Superfox. Girls are from the Central School of Speech and Drama

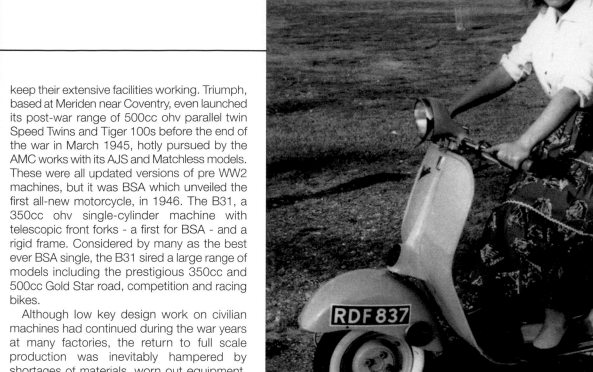

The attractive Italian Vespa 125cc of 1956 made an ideal town runabout

keep their extensive facilities working. Triumph, based at Meriden near Coventry, even launched its post-war range of 500cc ohv parallel twin Speed Twins and Tiger 100s before the end of the war in March 1945, hotly pursued by the AMC works with its AJS and Matchless models. These were all updated versions of pre WW2 machines, but it was BSA which unveiled the first all-new motorcycle, in 1946. The B31, a 350cc ohv single-cylinder machine with telescopic front forks - a first for BSA - and a rigid frame. Considered by many as the best ever BSA single, the B31 sired a large range of models including the prestigious 350cc and 500cc Gold Star road, competition and racing bikes.

Although low key design work on civilian machines had continued during the war years at many factories, the return to full scale production was inevitably hampered by shortages of materials, worn out equipment, damaged premises and a lack of skilled staff. So the British motorcycle industry, despite its huge potential capacity, was simply unable to meet the demand for new bikes. Consequently, just as happened after WW1, many ex-service machines were overhauled and sold while the prices of secondhand pre-war models soared.

While the bigger factories were designing and building new models the smaller concerns weren't idle either. Vincent uprated its 998cc V-twin Series A into the Series B Rapide and the then blisteringly fast Black Shadow with its famous 150mph speedometer. Velocette brought out the LE (Little Engine), a sophisticated machine with a water-cooled, horizontally opposed twin-cylinder side-valve engine housed in a pressed steel frame with shaft final drive. Nicknamed the 'Noddy bike' this kept the local police mobile for more than two decades. Villiers continued with production of its proprietary two-stroke engines, powering a rash of lightweights from firms like Ambassador, Tandon, Norman and James. A handful of tiny firms were trying their own ideas too, EMC with a 350cc split single two-stroke and Wooler with horizontally opposed four-cylinder models.

Elsewhere in Europe the motorcycle industry faced a similar situation - the same demand and the same problems - as their UK counterparts, but none had it more difficult than the Germans. The Allied Control Commission, set up to oversee most of German industry to ensure no fighting equipment would be produced, made many restrictions including a ban on German factories building motorcycles. As a result, companies such as BMW were

reduced to making cycle parts and cooking pans. By early 1946 the BMW and NSU plants were used to maintain American service vehicles, and still the trade in pots and pans continued.

Eventually the Allied Control Commission began to relax its regulation of transport, so BMW started building complete bicycles as well as assembling a limited number of 247cc ohv single-cylinder R23s from stocks of pre-war parts. The first all-new BMW rolled through the factory gates in 1948, a 247cc model R24, in effect a redesign of the R23. The first post-war twin didn't appear until 1950, and even this, the ohv horizontally opposed 494cc R51/2, was a redesign of the pre-war R51.

The dismantling of much of German heavy industry in 1945 meant many other companies fared as badly or worse than BMW, but somehow NSU managed to build a small number of Quick motorcycles as well as Kettenkraftrads and bicycles during the immediate post-war period. However, the DKW RT125 - a lightweight which gave the Wehrmacht sterling service during the war - was the most significant of all German bikes of the time, despite its small size and low performance, as it became the most copied machine of all time, inspiring a host of imitators including the BSA Bantam, Yamaha YA1, Harley-Davidson Hummer, and Moska 125, as

well as a range of East German MZ models.

Although Italian industry was not so severely tied as the Germans, they had problems of their own, and to help meet demand became adept at re-engineering ex-WD machines. Rear suspension, better lighting and dual seats were grafted onto ex-service bikes and a few side-valve models like the BSA M20 even gained ohv conversions.

In the USA, Harley-Davidson returned immediately to civilian machines, although the once great Indian factory headed for oblivion with its modular engine designs all based on a 220cc single, a far cry from the Indian Scouts and Big Chiefs of pre-war days.

But it was in one of the vanquished countries that stirrings began which would eventually change the face of motorcycling beyond recognition. In Hamamatsu, Japan, a 40 year-old engineer and inventor called Soichiro Honda sold his piston ring company, and after dabbling with other ideas, bought 500 war surplus tiny two-stroke stationary engines. In October 1946 he took over a small shed in the city center and began fitting the little engines to cycles. The transport hungry Japanese public snapped up the machines, inspiring Honda to make his own engines. In September 1948, Honda established the Honda Motor Company Ltd, and the phenomenal growth of the Japanese motorcycle industry started.

The 150cc Barton Major two-stroke was "easily handled" by women riders claimed BSA in 1954

Sales of motorcycles boomed throughout the world in response to three distinct factors. Primarily the need was for cheap utility transport, generating a huge selection of basic models for commuters and larger machines for the family man who would attach a sidecar to his bike. But even from the early post-war days sportsmen and tourers wanted to get straight back onto two wheels, and the seeds of motorcycling as a leisure pursuit were sown.

Feeble attempts at scooter design and production had been made throughout motorcycle history, aiming at producing user-friendly two-wheeled transport, but when Italian firms Vespa in April 1946 and Lambretta in October 1947 launched well-made, stylish and brilliantly designed scooters the public fell for them instantly, launching a whole new breed of machine which reached an entirely new customer.

At the economy end of the market manufacturers had gone back to pioneer ideas and built small 'clip on' engine units for attachment to bicycles. Usually less than 50cc, basic, cheap and mostly two-strokes, these cycles buzzed about the streets of Europe powered by names such as Cyclemaster, Trojan Mini-Motor, Berini, VAP and dozens more. One of these was Ducati, although this particular company bucked the two-stroke trend when it took over production of the Cucciolo (little pup), a sophisticated pull-rod ohv four-stroke two-speeder. This humble machine was Ducati's first ever motorcycle.

As the 1940s gave way to the next decade Britain remained a world leader in motorcycle design and manufacture. Seeing the sales potential of speed and power in an increasingly affluent society, Edward Turner designed faster and bigger vertical twin cylinder Triumphs, while BSA, Norton, AJS, Ariel, Matchless, Norton and Royal Enfield all launched their own variations on the theme. This was the last major advance in road bike engine design of the old British industry, ultimately stifling it with its restrictions and limitations. Even the stopgap BSA/Triumph triples of 1968 were effectively one and a half twins.

Even so, Norton moved machine handling onto a new level of excellence with the introduction of the all-welded duplex cradle frame designed by the McCandless brothers of Belfast. So good was this new frame that its adoption enabled the Norton works singles with engines of pre-war design to hold their own against the powerful and exotic Italian Gilera fours for a year or two longer, thanks purely to the superior handling. When works rider and TT winner Harold Daniel took a Norton single housed in the new frame round the IoM TT course for the first time, he returned to the pits grinning from ear to ear, announcing the bike was like riding a featherbed. The name stuck, and the featherbed frame was used on an increasing number of Norton road-going models throughout the 1950s. It was a long time before any other manufacturer could match the handling of the new Norton frame, and so superior was it that at the end of the decade and throughout the sixties, many motorcyclists went to the trouble of transplanting engines from other machines into Norton frames. Most popular were Triumph's excellent twins, and so common were the transplants that many thought, and still believe, that the resulting Tritons were a make in their own right.

In Germany too, as the 1950s pushed aside pre-war austerity, production increased and model ranges expanded. The majority of machines followed typical German practice: well engineered, good standard of finish, long lasting and with high cruising speed potential - often the bikes were capable of being ridden flat out continuously, although top speeds were low compared to the British sports bikes. The influence of the country's infrastructure and culture was as clear here as in Britain, German machines being well-suited to long distances and the high speed autobahns.

But it was NSU which proved the most radical, signing an agreement with Lambretta to build German-framed, Italian-powered scooters, before going on to develop the sophisticated strap-driven ohc range of models, with engines housed in pressed steel spine frames. Soichiro Honda was so impressed with NSU at the 1954 TT which he attended, he took a particularly close look at the range-topping Max and Super Max machines to help him formulate his own design ideas.

While France and Belgium continued to manufacture well-built utility models and tourers, the Italians pursued a path forged by their passion for motor vehicles and racing. In addition to their stylish scooters for the fashion conscious, the country manufactured scores of highly attractive lightweights such as the 70mph Rumi Junior Gentleman of 1955, a 125cc two-stroke twin, and the MV Agusta 125cc single-

1971 Triumph Trident 750cc tripleo. The BSA equivalent was called the Rocket Three

cylinder Turismo Rapido. These were little gems of motorcycles, and many of the larger machines from Moto Guzzi and Gilera were just as good, sometimes styled with all the flair of a leading fashion house.

Across the Atlantic, Harley-Davidson continued to thrive with a range of traditional V-twins - perfect for American roads - and DKW-based lightweights and scooters. But the Indian story went from bad to worse: the company bought the manufacturing rights to a range of modular upright engines comprising a 220cc single, 440cc twin and an 880cc four from the Torque Manufacturing Company of Connecticut. The V-twins were dropped and new models were built around the single and twins which were uprated to 250cc and 500cc. The four never went into production. The Americans hated them and the company was reduced to becoming no more than a British bike importer and dealership before eventually closing. The Indian name has since been used on a number of different models by various companies claiming ownership.

Soichiro Honda remained unnoticed by the rest of the world - and why should it have been any different? - when he visited the 1954 IoM TT races. He was disappointed to realise his company's racers could not yet compete on the world stage, but things would change. Japan in the mid-1950s was suffering a crippling recession and many of the 55 Japanese motorcycle manufacturers folded, but Honda had invested heavily in sophisticated engineering equipment from Switzerland, Germany and the USA, and managed to weather the storm by building dependable lightweights in vast numbers and selling them for a modest profit.

In 1953 NSU launched its two-speed 49cc two-stroke Quickly, manufacturing 9120 in the first year and well in excess of a million before production stopped in 1967. Although not the first true moped - a word derived from motorized pedal cycle - it was the first to gain major sales success, and within a few years the moped wiped cyclemotors, autocycles and some lightweight motorcycles from the dealer's

shops for ever. But even this paled almost into insignificance in comparison to a little Honda. In 1958 the company launched the most successful commuter machine ever, the Super Cub, which sired a range of 50-90cc step-thru's. Half moped and half scooter, the model not only survives today, it is thriving, having reached a whole new motorcycle-buying public, and is now the best selling motor vehicle in history, with more than 21 million units being produced.

The 1950s saw the whole picture of motorcycling change. Road and race speeds increased, underlined in the UK when "works" Gilera road racer, Scotsman Bob McIntyre posted the first over-100mph lap at the Isle of Man TT, then the world's premier event. Competition riding, land speed record events, speedway and motorcycling in general thrived. Famous motorcycle clubs like the '59' were formed, haunts like the London's Ace Café or Jack's Hill on the old A1 attracted big crowds every night, with motorcycling dividing into sub-cultures which often did not mix well. In Britain,

Triumph factory press release photograph with 350cc 3TAi in foreground while the couple are posing on a 1959 Tiger Cub 199cc T20

and only in Britain, these polarised into stylishly dressed scooter-mounted mods and leather-clad rockers who rode and lived for their bikes, speed, racing on the roads and their café culture. The Triton was the weapon of choice, at least when riding: it was a clash of styles which culminated in sometimes vicious fighting at popular seaside resorts in the mid-1960s.

In the United States, motorcycles became associated with violent and outlaw gangs, culminating in the Hell's Angels (formed by Vietnam war veterans) to the point where 'biker' almost became a generic term for thug. America's dominance of the film and then television industries helped to propagate this around the world to those places where it wasn't already happening locally, and motorcycling was done a great deal of harm, especially as the Hell's Angels' influence extended worldwide. The ill feeling and prejudice towards bikers was strong for more than two decades, and indeed its influence is still much in evidence today, although with some irony the current turnaround of motorcycle sales can be partly credited to riders after some association with this very anti-social image.

German makers were so uncomfortable with the way motorcycling appeared to be going, many began looking at alternatives. NSU investigated new ideas involving car production (its come-uppance as far as motorcyclists are concerned being the disastrous rotary-engined model Ro80).

Meanwhile, Italy continued down its own inimitable, soulful path undeflected, while mismanagement, unrealistic shareholder profits

and a lack of investment in new design was hampering the British bike industry, along with a belief in its own invulnerability. Triumph boss Edward Turner summed up the situation when he stated that British companies were no longer making machines in a style the young man of the day wanted, but as a man of enormous influence in many ways he was as guilty as his contemporaries.

Over in Japan the picture was changing too, but in an entirely converse way, with for example major investment in quality automatic machine tools enabling Honda to build machines to a much higher degree of engineering precision than ever before. Honda entered a works team for the first time in the 1959 IoM TT, its best result being sixth place in the 125cc class for Taniguchi. Nearly there, and Soichiro Honda learnt two important lessons: his bikes needed more power and his team riders needed European track experience.

Just two years later Honda won its first two TTs, and Australian Tom Phillis and Englishman Mike Hailwood won a world championship apiece on Honda racers. The buying public took note, and began to demand Honda motorcycles. Not to be left out, musical instrument maker Yamaha and textile machinery builder Suzuki, which had established bike production in the early 1950s, took little time to realise the sales potential of racing success, and the newcomers soon started to rob the established companies of podium finishes. Shortly after, late starter Kawasaki joined in - it had waited until 1962 to build its first complete bikes, doing so to increase the profile of this

enormous heavy engineering company.

Gradually through the 1960s one European manufacturer after another stopped motorcycle production or went bankrupt. Amalgamation with similar or complementary companies halted the decline for some, but only temporarily, as entrenched attitudes prevented the established players from moving on as rapidly as their customers. Mostly their products simply weren't good enough, spares back up was poor, standards of finish mediocre and they needed too much maintenance. In addition, the cessation of production at the Villiers engine plant along with the collapse of the parent company had a domino effect, ending bike production for many small firms, as with no more engines they could build no more bikes. Others looked to Europe for Sachs, Puch and Zündapp engine units, which enabled them to struggle on for a few more years, but in the face of what boiled down to better products, the outcome was inevitable.

Complacency had set in because initially the Japanese factories only built small capacity models, albeit in very large numbers. Honda for example exported almost 340,000 machines in one year, but still these weren't seen as threat to the 'real' motorcycle industry. Yet the majority of European firms hadn't made that level of volume in total since WW2. The sceptics still felt the Japanese invasion would be a five minute wonder, holding the (inaccurate) view that build quality was poor, materials were sub-standard and the high revving engines would blow themselves apart within months.

As if it would help, the Japanese factories were accused of being mere imitators. In their early days they were to varying degrees, but only in the basis of their designs. Where they moved standards on were in the increasingly important values of build quality and consistency, and by setting new levels of manufacturing excellence. Engineering and machining were better than the industry had ever seen before, reliability reached new heights and servicing was simpler with longer intervals. Add to this their style and imagination, like a breath of fresh air lined up against the same old British twins, and it's easy to see why motorcyclists converted to Japanese bikes in droves.

Yet many big bike riders in Britain still favoured the instant, low rev power of the big twins, and many buyers' attitudes were almost as conservative as the manufacturers'. Norton brought out the Commando, the fastest production British twin ever, BSA soldiered on with the A65 range and Triumph eventually

The KH250 was the smallest in Kawaski's range of fearsome two-stroke triples and the tamest

enlarged its 650 twin into the 750cc T140 Bonneville series at the start of the 1970s, and sales remained competitive to some extent.

The BSA/Triumph group had even unveiled its new triple in 1968, after five years of development work. Although still a pushrod design, the 750cc T150 and later T160 models were powerful, smooth running and quite well finished. But the BSA Rocket Three and Triumph Trident were built as stopgap models to counter the Japanese invasion, and they were simply too little, too late. The BSA factory at Small Heath, Birmingham finally folded in 1972, leaving just Triumph and Norton as the last of the big British companies. The Triumph T160 was launched in 1975, but stayed in production for just two years.

Even so, the triple proved a useful engine for road racing machine builders, the famous Triumph-based Slippery Sam (now on display at the National Motorcycle Museum near Birmingham, UK) won five TTs, and BSA and Triumph triples enjoyed many race successes

The Honda CB750 Four, glamourous yet reliable

throughout Europe and America. Contemporary motorcycle press testers were unimpressed by reliability, finish and gasoline consumption, but few could argue with the performance, as when they went, they went well. Many of the problems lay as much with the ancient manufacturing equipment as the design.

The German firm BMW weathered the storm by sticking to a policy of building high quality but expensive twins, capable of clocking up very high mileages with only basic maintenance requirements. Harley-Davidson, like BMW, continued to cater for its specific niche market with antiquated but very durable V-twins, while Italian makers continued to excite, Ducati with its quick singles and bevel-drive V-twins, MV Agusta with the exotic, Benelli with stylish multi-cylinder models and Moto Guzzi with a range of shaft drive V-twins.

Until 1968, big capacity Japanese machines such as the Meguro and Kawasaki W1 were based on British designs, while others aped Harley-Davidson's V-twins, but at the 1968 Tokyo show Honda launched the first of the modern generation of superbikes, the CB750, which was to be ready for the 1969 season. The 67bhp 736cc in-line four with a top speed of 120mph should have sent shivers down the spines of the remaining European factories, but they were still so complacent nothing of worth was done to counter the threat, the factories convincing themselves the Hondas were too flashy or fragile to catch on. Instead, the big Hondas lasted longer than any of the competition, in both senses.

Kawasaki, Yamaha and Kawasaki soon followed with superbikes of their own.

Kawasaki's Z1 moved the game on again in 1973, catching out even the fast-moving Japanese opposition, let alone the struggling Europeans. The 900cc transverse four-cylinder four-stroke's 134mph top speed was nothing short of awesome to a motorcycling public used to British twins incapable of a sustained 100mph without self-destructing, helping to forge the image Kawasaki was creating of itself as producer of the fastest, most exciting motorcycles - its two-stroke 500cc and 750cc triples, the H1 and H2, already had wild reputations.

Yet the strength of the Japanese went beyond their engineering and design. The marketing targeted new customers, such as the enormously successful "You meet the nicest people on a Honda" campaign, turning the tide slowly but surely away from the gang warfare image that built up in the 1960s, and to fulfil the needs of the new audience the Japanese filled their glossy brochures with complete ranges of bikes from basic commuters to tourers to headline grabbing flagship sports machines. Of the big four who remained by the 1970s, only Kawasaki has held back from producing a machine for every category of motorcycle, preferring not to make scooters, mopeds and the like in order to engender its image as the enthusiasts' marque.

The Italians were left behind as much as the British by the Oriental advances, but stricter import controls and peculiarly Italian laws which made it much harder for a company to go bust than in the UK helped to keep the industry alive, if gasping at times. Moto Guzzi then Benelli were taken under the wing of the De Tomaso

The best selling vehicle, two wheels or four, ever made is the Honda Cub and its variants. More than 26 million have been built and sold

automotive empire, enjoying the cash but suffering from a lack of direction. MV Agusta lost its way too, following the death of its founder Count Agusta, while Ducati was kept going as a state-owned company.

A lack of meaningful investment meant the Italians were also unable to keep up with the Japanese directly, selling their machines instead on their handling superiority, style and rather ironically, their higher prices, which lent the machines something of an exotic and hence desirable status. In truth, the quality generally was poor, the high cost coming through manufacturing inefficiency.

Both the Germans and Americans stuck grimly to what they knew best (boxer twins and V-twins respectively), Harley-Davidson being supported at the end of the 1970s by strict import taxes on foreign machines, relegating itself from mainstream producer to niche player, albeit with strong followings which at least assured its continued existence.

With the closure of Triumph in the mid-1970s, the once dominant British industry finally died away completely, leaving the Japanese only one another to compete with. Yamaha took up the two-stroke banner, advancing this previously scorned engine beyond recognition by refining European inventions such as the Schnärle loop and coming up with its own, such as the reed inlet valve. Specific power values increased massively, and the two-stroke did the unthinkable by taking over at the very highest

level, in grand prix racing. MV Agusta raced its last four-stroke in 500cc grands prix in 1976, but amazingly, and against the tide of technology, Honda took up the four-stroke banner, declaring it would build no two-strokes. This seemed to be motivated mostly by opposition to its greatest rival Yamaha, and what was at first healthy competition degenerated into what the Japanese themselves were referring to as a war by the end of the 1970s and into the early 1980s.

On the race tracks Honda poured seemingly endless funds into its fabulously exotic four-stroke racer, the NR500 (cruelly dubbed the 'Never Ready' in several quarters due to the many delays before its debut). The bike featured oval pistons with two conrods and eight valves per cylinder in an attempt to reach two-stroke power levels, but these were never achieved and the bike was a failure.

Meanwhile, the showrooms were being filled with wider and wider ranges of models at increasingly rapid rates, new machines superseding older ones sometimes at six month intervals, as Yamaha declared its intention of taking over from Honda as the world's number one motorcycle manufacturer.

Reputations were damaged at several levels, with customers almost as unhappy at the instant obsolescence of their bikes as their unexpected unreliability and under-development. This battle of the giants was cripplingly expensive, and it's thought came

close to bringing Yamaha's motorcycle division down altogether, but a dramatic peace treaty was agreed in 1982 when the factory bosses met and signed an agreement in neutral territory - the Kawasaki factory at Akashi.

The damage spread beyond Japan, as the acceleration of bike production and new model introduction led to major 'dumping' of bikes at very low prices, primarily in the United States, which responded with protectionist policies imposing severe taxes on all foreign imports.

At the same time, and entirely unconnected, the motorcycle markets of the world had begun a major metamorphosis was to lead first to crisis, then a revival, which is only now just beginning. Sales in 1980 were at an all time high, with the total output of the western world reaching around six million machines. But people were becoming wealthier and advances in car manufacturing technology meant four wheels were simultaneously becoming cheaper, with the inevitable result that two wheels were being abandoned as cheap transport in favor of higher status and often more practical small cars. At the same time, accident statistics were so bad that a groundswell of bad feeling against motorcycles was resurging, fired up by tabloid press reports of motorcycles massacring the country's youth. The decline of the motorcycle as a utility vehicle had begun.

This, at least, was the situation in the West (which includes Japan as part of that economic sphere). Behind the almost closed doors of

Ducati's move to V-twin power helped carve out a sports bike niche which it has filled, and led, for the last three decades

China, the situation was not dissimilar to Europe in the two decades after WW2, where shortages of materials, poor road conditions and a desperate need for mobility from the huge population led to the creation of giant, state-owned motorcycle factories, which produced mainly older Japanese designs of small, utility machines in their millions. Some engines were bought directly from Japan, some assembled from parts while others were simply copied. In India too vast numbers of basic, utility machines were supplying the voracious home market, with so few being exported the rest of the world had little idea some of the world's largest motorcycle factories even existed, and certainly they couldn't name them.

A handful of these machines were reaching the West by the end of the 1980s, but poor build quality and the old designs meant sales would never challenge the established players. At the same time, by the end of the 1980s demand for utility machines had plummeted, sales in the UK for example dropping from 320,000 units in 1980 to less than 45,000 by 1993. Western output had halved to 3 million machines, and the prospects for the industry were looking bleak.

But a new trend was becoming clear. The sales proportions of enthusiast and leisure machines were climbing, as the motorcycle returned to favor among the fashion conscious, as well as older riders keen to revisit a 'lost youth'. Custom-styled machines proliferated and became more varied, Kawasaki began a trend of retro machines with its Zephyrs, which borrowed styling cues from the original Z1, sports bikes became so fast and proficient they were grabbing headlines outside the specialist

press, and for the excitement potential rather than danger, minor niche bikes suddenly became individualistic, and traffic-clogged city centres became an excuse or reason to buy two wheels and bypass the jams.

In the UK in 1986, Triumph was revived by building magnate John Bloor. With some irony, the now fledgling British company took to stripping Japanese bikes to see how things were done, and bought technology from Kawasaki, a complete reversal of the situation some 30 years before. By starting from scratch, Triumph was also able to fit out its factory with the very latest in production technology, setting it ahead of the Japanese in this respect while it learnt how to make motorcycles all over again.

In Italy, Moto Guzzi struggled through the 1980s with little investment in its ancient Mandello factory, surviving, just, on sales which fell to just 5000 machines a year. A proposed move in 1998 to a brand new factory was scotched by worker resistance and management in-fighting, so for the moment Moto Guzzi looks destined to continue to tread the backwaters of the industry.

In contrast, Ducati's fortunes turned around dramatically when it was bought and revived by Cagiva, then sold again in 1996 to an American finance company, the Texas Pacific Group. The beautiful 916 V-twin became a milestone machine, even more for its looks than its all-conquering race success in the new World Superbike series, and the company is now growing rapidly.

BMW in the early eighties saw the dominance of the four-cylinder engine and jumped on the bandwagon in its own individual way with the K-Series, and even planned to phase out boxer

twins altogether. Production did stop for a brief period in 1986, but this was a move against the direction motorcycling was taking - the outcry from customers was considerable, production restarted and work began on a new generation of boxer.

What BMW had discovered was that motorcyclists had started to look for more than performance from their machines, which were reaching the stage of having more than enough anyway. In addition, riders wanted identifiable character and individuality, something the Germans' boxer twins had in abundance compared with the fours. They needed uprating, certainly, but in this climate not replacing.

Japanese sports bikes kept leaping forward technologically, first with the Kawasaki GPZ900R of 1984, then the Yamaha FZR1000, then the Honda Fireblade and now most recently with the Yamaha R1. The advances have been as much in rider useability as outright performance, which has broadened the appeal of many machines immensely.

Today's motorcycle market is populated by the widest variety of machines we have ever seen, with all conceivable tastes being catered for, and growth in some countries is extraordinarily fast. In others it seems likely to follow suit shortly. In Britain, growth has averaged more than 30 per cent annually since 1994, although the biggest sales rises have been of scooters, suggesting a return to utility use - primarily as traffic beaters - but as an addition to other vehicles rather than substitute for them as two-wheelers once were.

Happily, the future for motorcycling is now as bright as it has been for very many years.

THE CHINESE INDUSTRY

Few westerners are aware that China even has a significant motorcycle industry, let alone realise that it is not Japan but China which produces far more motorcycles and scooters than any other country in the world, currently outputting more than 10 million machines annually.

Only a small proportion of these machines is exported, mostly to other far eastern markets, although a handful does find its way to the west. As these are low numbers of small capacity utility machines of poor build quality, they offer little clue as to the giant capacities of the factories which produce them.

These machines are entirely typical of the entire Chinese output, which is dedicated solely to providing cheap, mass transport, with not even a nod towards motorcycling as a leisure pursuit, let alone a competitive sport.

The history of the Chinese industry is also entirely different to the story of motorcycling in the west, reflecting the vice-like central control on the economy of the communist regime as opposed to the market forces we're more familiar with. 100 years ago when the first European and American pioneers were busy creating all manner of weird and wonderful designs in the quest for the optimum solution to powering a two-wheeler, China was still a relatively primitive and fragmented country comprising mainly peasants eking out subsistence lives from the land - motorcycles were unthinkable and unthought of luxuries of no relevance.

It wasn't until after the Second World War that China's industry was sufficiently developed (and organized, thanks to government controls) for both a need for motorcycles to arise and the capability of satisfying that need to be in place. This led to the first of two distinct stages in the development of motorcycle production in China, the first of which lasted up until the end of the 1970s, and which saw motorcycles being produced almost entirely for the military or other government organizations and remaining relatively small scale.

In 1950 the Chinese army declared its requirement for motorcycles to the government, so the PLA Beijing Number 6 Automotive Works was assigned the task of producing something suitable. Development of a new machine from scratch was well beyond its capabilities, so after studying various western machines it was decided to copy the German Zündapp Z500, and in July 1951 the first five machines were built, bearing the badge 'Jing Gang Shan'. These worked

The Qjiang QJ 125 is typical of current Chinese production – a copy of an old Japanese design with low q[...]

well enough for the bike to be put into full mass production, and by the end of 1954, 4248 motorcycles were produced.

Production stopped in 1955 when the factory was incorporated into the new Beijing Number 1 Automotive Accessory Factory, but nevertheless the Jing Gang Shan marked the beginning of what is now the world's largest motorcycle industry.

The army's need for motorcycles had not diminished, so two aeronautics subsidiary factories, the Hongdu Machinery Plant and the Xing Jiang Machinery Plant, were given over to the production of more motorcycles, this time copies of the Soviet M-72 boxer twin, in turn a copy of a pre-war BMW. In December 1957 a version with a sidecar also went into production.

Further factories turned to motorcycle production, still entirely for the military in various roles, and began producing copies of Czech Jawa 250cc and 50cc two-stroke machines.

It wasn't until 1970 that any moves were made to supply machines to other organizations. Then it was the post office which put in a request for motorcycles to the central government, to motorise and speed up its delivery service, so more than 10 regional factories were assigned to produce basic 250cc two-stroke twins for this purpose. Again, these were copies of other designs, but by now China was producing machines of 50cc, 250cc and 750cc and could claim to have a proper motorcycle industry, albeit a relatively small one.

MIGs are built in the former MIG aircraft factory

Copy of pre-war BMW still being built

For the next 10 years the industry continued along the same lines, with demand being determined by various government organizations and production being allocated either centrally or locally to various factories which could just as easily have been producing a whole range of other products, all according to centralised planning.

Private demand up to this point was negligible, not because people did not need personal mobility, but because this did not fit in with the communist philosophy. There was anyway nowhere near enough capacity to meet any greater need.

By 1980 there were 24 motorcycle manufacturers producing a total of just 49,000 machines, an amount similar to BMW alone in the west, let alone the 6 million or so the Japanese were producing at the time.

In 1981 that all changed, and the Chinese motorcycle industry entered its second phase. This was due to government reform and a policy of greater openness and contact with the outside world, and in particular, the application of some capitalist values. In the next three 'Five Year Plans' with which central government drove the whole of the Chinese industry, targets were set to meet the demand for personal mobility through market forces alone, with no funding being allocated to motorcycle production other than the profits attained from selling machines to customers.

Yet so huge is the country that by 1997 there were more than 2000 different listed models of Chinese motorcycles (although many were very similar), with output increasing substantially every year. The vast majority are from 50cc to 125cc, with 250cc models following and then a relatively few larger machines, such as the 750cc boxer twin BMW-derived machines.

Once the market's true potential was unleashed the growth of the industry was staggering. From that original annual output of 49,000 machines, by 1996 the output of 100cc machines alone reached 2.399 million! Total production reached an astonishing 9.5 million machines, and it is still on the increase.

Despite the vast size of the industry, the majority of machines are either copied from foreign designs or built in collaboration with or under license from Japanese manufacturers. The nature of Chinese industry still means large profits in the western sense are frowned upon or are simply not made possible due to government price controls, so investment in new designs and technology is very restricted. But many western manufacturers have seen the enormous potential of the Chinese market and made moves to become involved, usually through collaborative agreements with local companies. All four Japanese manufacturers operate joint ventures in China, as do Cagiva and Piaggio, while Aprilia is also looking at similar ventures.

In the immediate future China is purely an area of enormous opportunity rather than a threat to western companies, and it will remain that way while the basic economic and political infrastructure stays more or less as it is. But should market freedoms increase much further, along with public wealth, then the Chinese motorcycle industry will be in a position to develop its own designs, and eventually produce motorcycles aimed at leisure markets rather than utility ones.

That time might never happen, and if it does it is probably a long way off, but should it come to pass then the sheer size of the Chinese industry will make it a serious threat to established concerns.

It seems unlikely to the point of being laughable at the moment. Just as the Japanese industry was in the 1960s...

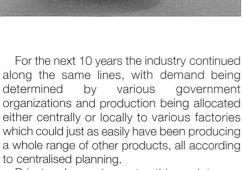

GREAT DESIGNERS

Perhaps the first really famous design, if only because it was so bold, was Paul Kelecom's in-line four-cylinder FN of 1904. The first model was only 400cc and had no clutch or gears, but it was rapidly enlarged and improved, gaining a clutch and gears, and as well as selling extensively in its native Belgium, it was exported to the UK and America. The first American 'in-line-four', the Pierce Arrow, was an acknowledged copy of an imported FN and started a tradition that embraced Henderson, ACE, Excelsior, Cleveland and Indian. Kelecom's FN 4, latterly of 750cc and with chain final drive, was still in production in 1926, having extended its influence across the Atlantic. In England, Alfred Scott as good as re-invented the Day-cycle (crankcase compression) two-stroke engine, developing it over several years into a small twin suitable for a motorcycle. First offered for sale in 1909, the 'two speed, two cylinder, two stroke' Scott was a design of remarkable integrity that sold steadily until the end of the 1920s, and amazingly, the engine layout lasted into the 1960s.

The air-cooled single-cylinder Levis two-stroke, designed by Howard (Bob) Newey and the Butterfield half-brothers, was the first downright practical and uncomplicated light weight. It first appeared in 1911, became enormously successful and was the basis of Levis two-strokes until 1939. It was also very widely imitated and made under license. The German Zündapp company paid it the ultimate compliment in 1921 by copying it down to the smallest detail, without acknowledgement. It subsequently copied Levis model changes year by year until 1926!

No such plagiarism was involved in the Velocette two-stroke of 1913, designed by Percy Goodman. Velocette continued to make excellent two-strokes until the Second World War. Goodman also designed the glorious overhead camshaft K series of Velocettes, which first appeared in 1925, and later, the 'high camshaft' series of MOV, MAC and MSS, of 250cc, 350cc and 500cc. The 500cc Velocette 'Thruxton' was still in production in 1970, an astonishing run of 37 years.

Other long-lived designs include the horizontal single-cylinder layout of Carlo Guzzi's Moto Guzzi of 1921, Alberto Garelli's side-by-side split-single two-stroke of 1933 and Giovanni Marcellino's fore-and-aft split single Puch (with asymmetrical port timings) that stayed in production in one model or another from 1923 until the late 1960s.

However, very rarely is a design really and truly 'original', most being developments of earlier designs or at least inspired by them. Edward Turner for example is sometimes credited with having invented the even-firing vertical twin with his Triumph Speed Twin of 1937. But of course there had been dozens of such twins before this, while Triumph itself had been making the 650cc Val Page-designed 6/1 twin since 1933, and even that was probably inspired by Herman Reeb designs Horex in Germany had launched a year earlier

George William Patchet (left) of McEvoy, FN and Jawa and Walter William Moore of Douglas, Norton and NSU.

Pioneer Max Friz made aircraft engines, then the first BMW motorcycle.

Jack Williams, chief development engineer on the AJS 7R, with son-in-law Tom Herron of Yamaha.

as 600cc and 800cc ohc models for sidecar use. The difference with Turner's 1937 design was not that it was in any way radical, but that it was compact, simple to produce, offered excellent all-round performance and was stylish, setting a trend that many others would follow. Development of Turner's design in its various incarnations lasted for more than 40 years.

Even so, Turner had earlier been responsible for another design that really did show originality, the 500cc overhead camshaft Ariel Square Four that was the sensation of the 1930 Motor Cycle Show. Its unique cylinder layout and coupled contra-rotating crankshafts were never copied in its lifetime, even though its production life spanned nearly thirty years. Its capacity was raised to 600cc and then, after a complete redesign, to 1000cc. Brilliant designer as he was, Turner proved an even greater success as a manager at Triumph, where his career was legendary.

Nothing like so flamboyant as Turner, although equally deserving of being remembered as a designer, was Val Page, who joined JAP in 1914 and after the war revitalised its range of engines before leaving in 1925 to join Ariel. Page laid down a series of designs that put Ariel on a par with any other manufacturer of the time. He helped Turner with the square four and then went to Triumph. There, he designed the 250cc, 350cc and 500cc range of ohv singles later restyled by Turner as the Tiger 70, Tiger 80 and Tiger 90 models, as well as designing the 650cc 6/1 twin. In 1936, Page moved to BSA, where again he drew up a range of eminently modern single cylinder engines including the original M23 Gold Star. He moved back to Ariel in 1939 where his last design for it was the brilliant fully-enclosed 250cc twin-cylinder Ariel Leader two-stroke and its sporting version, the Arrow. Very few designers in any country can have been so prolific and successful.

In 1919, J. S. Rasmussen's DKW factory in Saxony set Germany on the road to supremacy in the manufacture of two strokes between the wars. Original designs by Hugo

Fabio Taglioni designed the Ducati desmodromic valve gear in the early 1960s. The system is still in use.

Ruppe were developed and then superseded by those of Herman Weber. In 1931, the Swiss-born designer Arnold Zoller was called in to develop split-single DKW racing machines with water cooling and piston-pump assisted (blown) induction. With patient development by August Prussing, the 'blown' DKW became insuperable in the 250cc class in European road racing in the 1930s.

Unlike Puch, whose Marcellino-designed and developed racers had inspired DKW to call in Arnold Zoller, DKW did not sell split-single two-strokes for road use. Instead, it became the first in the world to market flat-top piston two-strokes, using the Schnürle patents. Herman Weber was again the designer. His RT125 of 1937 set entirely new standards of two-stroke performance but its extraordinary claim to fame was that its design was copied post war by BSA for its 125cc Bantam, by Harley-Davidson, by JLO, by Yamaha, Suzuki, Kawasaki and by at least another half a dozen firms in Russia and Eastern Europe. It even formed the basis of post war DKW and MZ racing machinery when Germany was re-admitted to international competition. Under the control of race chief Walter Kaaden, MZ went on to develop the first two-strokes to equal and then to surpass the specific power

outputs of four-stroke engines. Today's all conquering racing two-strokes all derive from Kaaden's work at MZ.

Walter Moore designed a 500cc ohc racing engine for Norton, which won the 1927 Senior TT on its first outing. Thereafter, though, it proved disappointing, so when Moore left to join NSU in Germany and to design a similar engine for the German company, Norton's Joe Craig breathed over young Arthur Carroll's shoulder as he designed a new engine for 1931, with which Tim Hunt that year did the double, winning both Junior and Senior TTs. So was born the Manx Norton, which in the next 18 seasons was to win 28 TTs, not to mention uncounted grand prix races and a myriad successes in the hands of private owners right into the 1960s and even beyond.

In post-war Italy, Giulio Carcano attained legendary stature with his designs and development for the Moto Guzzi racing team between 1948 and 1957, his masterpiece being the celebrated 500cc V8. But one Moto Guzzi design of that era, the 500cc in-line water-cooled four-cylinder with shaft drive, raced in 1953 and 1954, was designed not by Carcano, but by Carlo Giannini. He, together with Pietro Remor, had been involved long before the war with the four-cylinder design that became the water-cooled supercharged Rondine, later taken over by Gilera for the 1937 season.

Post-war, Remor was to design first the 1947 air-cooled 500cc four-cylinder Gilera, and then in 1950, the very similar four-cylinder MV. Credit for developing the Gilera must go to Franco Pasoni, and that for the MV to Arturo Magni. Remor left MV in 1953 and joined the obscure company Motom. But between 1958 and 1974, MV won the 500cc world championship no less than 17 times.

A man who achieved legendary status within the Italian motorcycle industry was Ducati's Fabio Taglioni, the man responsible for designing the only mass produced desmodromic valve system used by any manufacturer. Taglioni's singles followed by his 90 degree V-twins took Ducati to the forefront

of racing, yet it was a protégé of Taglioni, Massimo Bordi, who furthered the cause by designing the liquid-cooled, fuel-injected eight valve V-twins which started out as the 851 and were developed to power the 916, a bike which has dominated World Superbike racing even in the face of massive competition from all four Japanese factories.

The 916 itself was the product of another Italian great.

Massimo Tamburini was a founder of Bimota where he already proved his talent with such excellent machines as the DB1 (which saved the company from extinction) but working at Cagiva's Research Center in San Marino Tamburini created the 916, a bike whose style has been enormously influential since it was first seen in 1993. This was no swan song though - Tamburini went on to design the MV Agusta F4 of 1999, a bike hailed in many quarters as the most beautiful motorcycle ever made.

In Japan, the culture of teamwork over the individual means that many machines are more the work of groups of people rather than individuals, but some have nevertheless shone out. Kawasaki's Ben Inamura stunned the world with his Z1 of 1973, often called the first true superbike, yet he merely underlined his talent by producing the GPZ900R a decade later, a machine which set totally new standards for big capacity sports motorcycles and which continued in production for another 15 years (truly astonishing in the modern climate of continuous development). Inamura was also responsible for the ZX-9R Ninja unveiled in 1993. Although this was not a milestone machine like his previous designs was still known for its outstanding power, and which gave Inamura the unique distinction of designing three major 900cc fours each a decade apart.

The next big sports bike to significantly move on the genre was the Honda CBR900RR Fireblade, the work of

Above: Designer Joe Craig supervises a Manx Norton engine test. He was the architect of Norton's racing success.

Below left; Remora (left) with Gilera

Tadao Baba, who made it his mission to produce a machine with the power of a one liter bike yet the weight and handling of a 600. This he undoubtedly achieved, as every manufacturer since has used the Fireblade as the benchmark for its own designs. Baba in fact was also involved at a lesser level in the design of the original Honda CB750.

The Yamaha YZF1000-R1 is the machine which finally had the beating of the Fireblade, but this and the equally brilliant YZF600-R6 are both the work of Kunihiko Miwa, whose nickname within the factory shows another quality so often needed by designers. He's referred to as 'Mr No Compromise' which on the face of it suggests his designs are particularly single-minded. They are, but that's not the whole story: Miwa accepts no compromises in the whole design process, from marketing to the processes of design and from those who work with and for him.

It takes a special type of person to create a great motorcycle - he not only needs extraordinary engineering talent, originality and vision, just as the important is the doggedness and character to see it through.

THE CLASSIC BIKES THROUGH THE DECADES

No four-cylinder motorcycle has achieved such pre-eminence in its own time as the Henderson. It provided riders in the early years of motorcycling with simple starting, smoothness, silence, oil tightness, reliability and generous power to a degree unmatched elsewhere. The model shown here is that of 1912, the first year of production.

The original 7hp model was soon further developed, with a multi-speed gearbox, improved power and more robust construction. Sales rose accordingly and the model achieved greater popularity than any comparable machine in the United States. Finally, Ignaz Schwinn's Excelsior Company bought the firm in 1917, initially retaining the services of founders William and Tom Hender-

son. After that, the Henderson Big Four also incorporated the name Excelsior on the tank. Two years later, William and Tom Henderson left Excelsior, unhappy with the new business arrangement.

William founded his own motorcycle company, under the name of Ace. He was soon manufacturing an Ace four and challenging the Henderson's reputation for quality. After many successful years Ace ran into financial troubles and was bought by Indian.

The name of Scott stands out in the history of the motorcycle. Alfred Scott was an inventor and engine designer who played a leading role in the development of the two-stroke. Scott built his first motorized bicycle in Yorkshire as early as 1898, even then using a twin-cylinder two-stroke. The engine was fitted to a heavy pedal-cycle with transmission by friction roller. By 1903, he had built a machine with power to the rear wheel and a year later Scott was granted British patent rights on a two-stroke vertical twin engine.

Scott's first true production motorcycle was manufactured in 1908. Its engine was built to Scott's design by the nearby Jowett car factory, another Yorkshire concern famous in automotive history. This 333cc engine had a bore and stroke of 58 x 63mm, and the entire unit weighed only 169kg (371lb). The cylinder heads were water-cooled through a thermosiphon system, but the barrels were air-cooled. By 1914, Scott had settled on a basic design for his machines and was using a wholly water-cooled engine. This two-speed machine had standard gear ratios of 3:1 and 4:1, and the unusual open frame design which came to characterise the marque. This type of frame was popular with women motorcyclists, whose dignity it helped preserve. Telescopic front forks were used from the outset and a disk-valve induction and exhaust system was introduced at an early stage. Other machines could match the Scott's 55mph top speed, but none of its contemporaries offered the same handling qualities. It was this characteristic in particular which afforded Scott such great racing success.

Alfred Scott left the company after the First World War and died in 1923: within four or five years the marque had lost much of its shine. Production since a takeover in 1950 was limited to small-scale revivals. The Scott shown here is a 486cc model specially reconstructed for vintage racing.

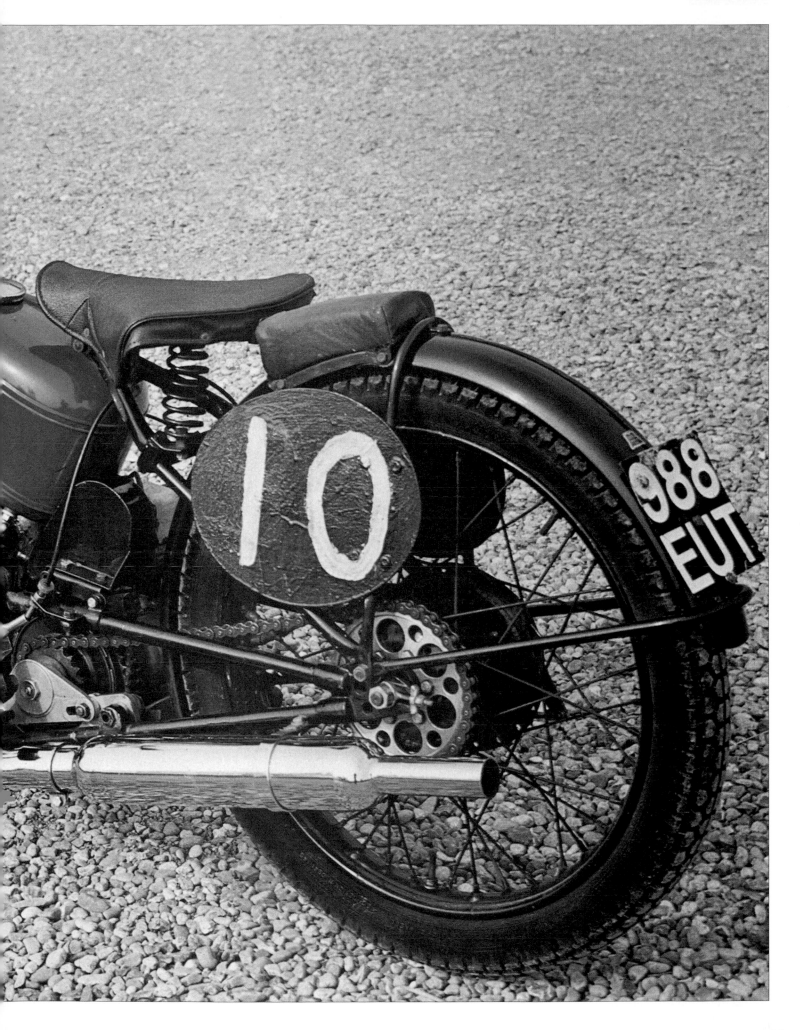

Indian was without doubt one of the foremost names in the development of the modern motorcycle. In 1905, the factory became one of the first to put a V-twin into commercial manufacture. The first V engine was little more than a doubling up of two Indian 1.75 hp singles, but improved and enlarged versions soon followed. These ultimately provided the basis for the very advanced motorcycles produced under the aegis of the factory's founder, George Hendee, and the great designer Oskar Hedstrøm. After they had left the company, Charlie Gustafson became Indian's chief designer in 1915. He established the side-valve style of engine which became a tradition of the factory and the American motorcycle industry generally. His greatest machine was the

7hp, 998 cc Power Plus shown here. This sophisticated and speedy motorcycle included such advanced equipment as leaf-spring suspended pivoted fork rear suspension, all chain drive, electric lighting, electric starting and a proper kick-start.

Indian

As the original William Brough motorcycle company entered the last year of its life, son George's rival firm launched the most famous machine to bear the family name. The Brough Superior SS100, introduced in 1925 was more popular than any other prestige sports roadster before or since. The SS100, shown here, was an overhead-valve V-twin. It became one of the two mainstays of Brough Superior's 19-year production period, along with its predecessor, the SS80 side-valve V-twin. As with all engines of its type, the side-valve twin was less durable at speed than the ohv. The `100' and `80' model designations referred to the machines' guaranteed top speed. Brough Superior was also known for a proliferation of multi-cylindered exotica. The machines were largely assembled from proprietary components, with the engines being principally JAP or Matchless units, and even the famous Castle forks were originally a Harley-Davidson design. This philosophy eventually proved to be the Achilles' heel of Brough Superior. The company tried unsuccessfully to develop its own power units, while the cost of buying-in specially-manufactured engines in small quantities proved to be crippling. The company stopped motorcycle production in 1940.

Brough Superior

Douglas

Although Douglas did sometimes use other engine layouts, the marque was always known for its horizontally-opposed twins. Today, Douglas is usually remembered for its post-war series of transverse-engined 350cc machines, but these were only made in the company's last seven years. In its earlier days, and for more than three decades, Douglas found its fame and fortune in exceptionally well-designed twins with fore-and-aft cylinders.

The success of these machines owed much to the work of the company's chief development rider, Freddie Dixon, during the middle and late 1920s, but fate also played a part. When the Douglas EW series of 350cc sv racers began to find the competition tough, Douglas had planned a new ohc model, but a fire at the works destroyed the blueprints and set back the company's work. The new engine was abandoned and the company chose instead to breathe new life into its old ohv twins, with considerable development work by Dixon. By happy chance, these machines proved most successful in the newly-arrived sport of speedway. Some of their success was due to a freak of design which led to the frame flexing helpfully during broadsliding, but its achievements on the cinder track boosted all aspects of Douglas's reputation. During this period, the classic Douglas machine was the model FW, which was produced in 500cc and 600cc versions. The road-racing version is shown here. The road-racing models were capable of 90mph and 95mph respectively. In 1929 alone, 1300 machines were sold.

Sunbeam

The Sunbeam Model 90, shown in its traditional black and gold livery, is probably the finest example of British single-cylinder engineering. It combined simple, proven design solutions with a meticulous finish.

The machine was conceived in 1923 as a sports roadster and successfully adapted as a works racer. It was produced in both 350cc and 500cc ohv versions. Production standards dropped after the factory was bought in 1930 by ICI (Imperial Chemical Industries). Sunbeam was later owned by Associated Motorcycles and BSA.

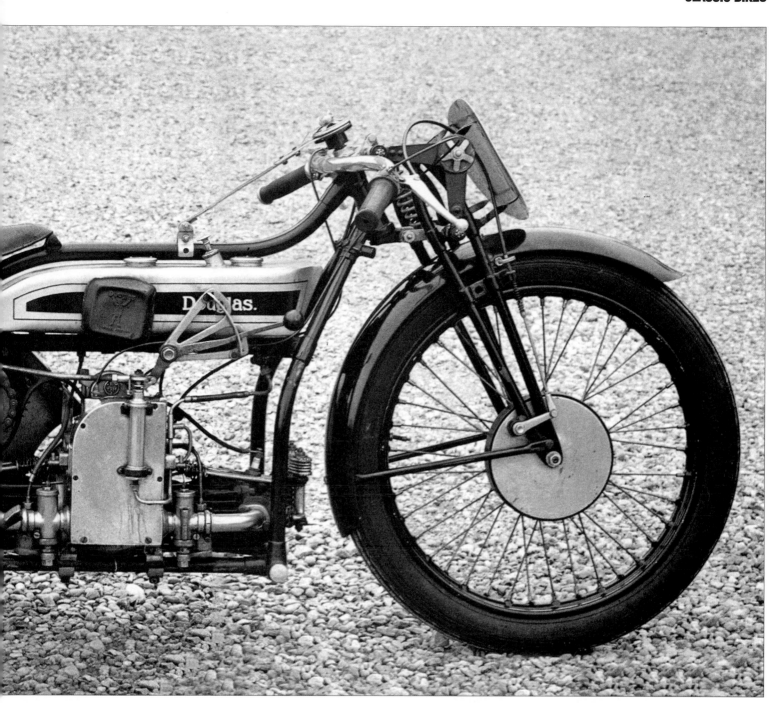

Rudge

Some of the best British production bikes were replicas of their makers' works racing models. A fine example was the 1929 Rudge-Whitworth Ulster, which came from a factory famous for its advanced approach. The machine was introduced to celebrate Graham Walker's win in the Ulster Grand Prix and it proved to be exceptionally fast and reliable. It had a four-speed, positive-stop, foot-change gearbox, dry sump lubrication with a mechanical pump and a four-valve cylinder head in a pentroof combustion chamber.

The British Excelsior company is remembered with affection for a 250cc single which was popularly known as the 'Mechanical Marvel', but this four-valve ohv machine suffered from its own complexity. Undaunted, Excelsior continued along the same development path with an improved four-valver, the famous Manxman, shown here. This machine had a single overhead camshaft with each inlet valve fed by its own Amal RN carburetor. The bronze head, as shown, improved thermal efficiency in the days before aluminum had come into common use. The Manxman shown is a 250, but a 350 was also produced. Valve gear and carburetor tuning still proved "...very pernickety" according to Excelsior's managing director Eric Walker, and in 1938 the firm introduced two-valve engines. These were equally fast, but wholly reliable. They had sprung frames, and proved so successful that they continued to be raced in private hands into the early 1950s.

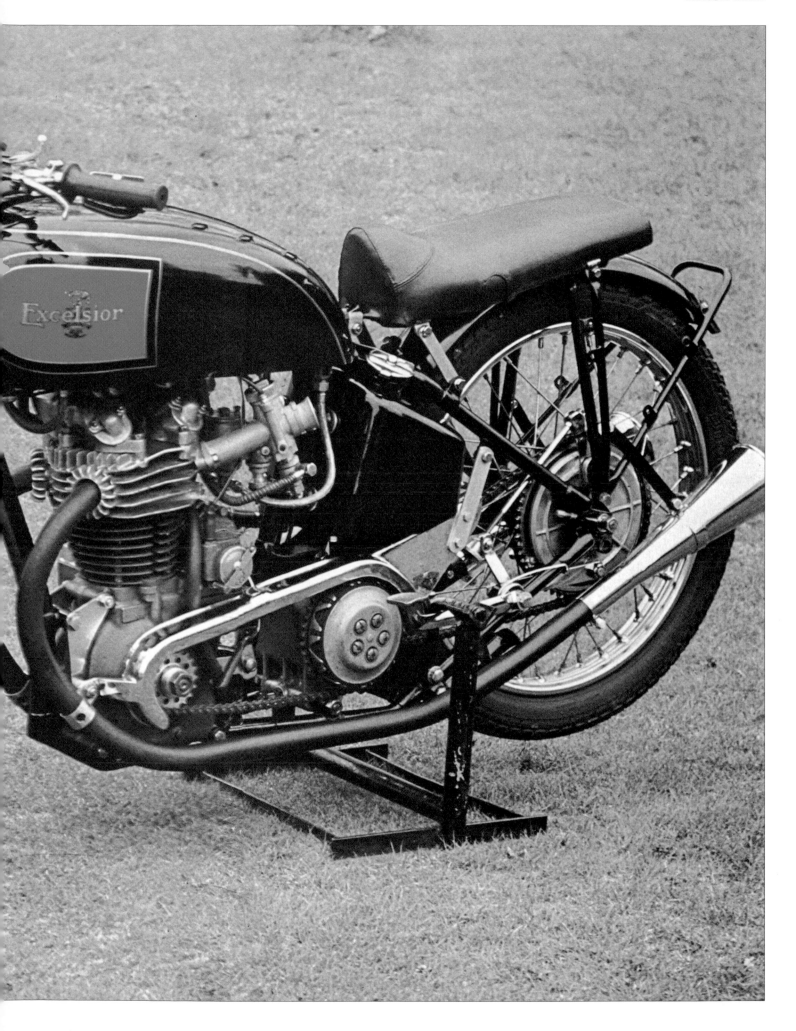

Velocette

Other single-cylinder machines might have exemplified a particular aspect of engineering or performance, but those produced by Velocette demonstrated the full range of attributes. This was best illustrated by the KTT, a racing replica of the factory's own grand prix machinery, which was also notable as the first model to sport the Velocette-perfected foot gearchange system. This was an ohc single of 350cc, sold with a guaranteed top speed of 85mph. As an option, Velocette offered a 100mph model sporting a 9:1 compression ratio for running on alcohol-based fuel. The range ran from the 1929 Mk I illustrated here to the 1949 Mk VIII. In 1956, Velocette demonstrated its skills with a quite different range of well-remembered singles. These were ohv sports roadsters. First came the 499cc Venom, shown above, with square (86 x 86mm) engine dimensions, then the smaller 349cc Viper. The Venom engine developed 36bhp at 6,200rpm, giving the machine a top speed of 95mph. After 12 and 24-hour records had been set at Montlhèry, a highly-tuned version was produced as a clubman racer. This was the Thruxton (far right), which had a top speed of approximately 120mph.

For most of its life the BSA marque was known primarily for singles of simple and inexpensive design, made for everyday transport. The motorcycles in the small picture are examples: a 250cc machine from 1925 (background) and the 1928 Sloper. In later years, the same qualities of durability and reliability were show-cased in a much more exotic motorcycle, the Gold Star. No clubman racer since has enjoyed the success or reputation of the Goldie. The range was produced in trials, motocross (then called scramble), touring and racing versions, and a 1959 model of the latter is shown here. The 500cc engine developed up to 40 bhp at just over 7,000 rpm, driving through a close ratio gearbox. Top speed was around 120 mph in full clubman trim.

There are many reasons for celebrating the famous marque founded by Howard R. Davies (hence its original name, HRD) and bought shortly afterwards by Philip Vincent. Mostly it's still known for its exceptionally advanced engineering - often 20 years ahead of its time or more - although the marque is also remembered for its spree of high speed achievements during the 1950s. It's said these sporting feats were the inspiration for the unusually large and ambitious 150mph speedo which was fitted to Vincent motorcycles. Factory and private riders captured national and world speed and sprint records by the handful on the competition model of the period, the Black Lightning. One unsupercharged Black Lightning achieved a speed of 185.15 mph in the hands of Russell Wright, a New Zealander, in 1955. Sadly, this was also the last year of full production. The firm went out of business in a blaze of glory with

the announcement of the semi-streamlined Series D models, but few were made. In design, the Series D machines were the natural successors to the Series C Rapides, which had been launched in 1949, with 50-degree, 998cc V-twin engines. The Series C standard touring machine had a top speed of approximately 110 mph and its sporting counterpart, the Black Shadow (shown here), went on to 120 mph, reaching 56mph in only six seconds on the way. These machines were in turn developed from the Series A Rapides, which were launched in 1937, had 47-degree engines and a web of external pipes.

Ariel was in every sense an historic British marque. Established in 1898, the firm exhibited all the characteristics of British motorcycle manufacture. The products were well made, even sporty, but initially of conventional design. In 1929, a much more sophisticated machine made a considerable break with tradition. This was a 500cc four with a highly-unusual square cylinder configuration and single overhead camshaft. This distinctive engine layout became so identifiable with the marque that the nickname 'Squariel' passed into the language of motorcycling.

Like the later Triumph Speed Twin, another pace-setting machine, the Square Four was designed by Edward Turner. It had an all ball-and-roller bearing engine and horizontally-split crankcase. In 1931, the engine was bored out from 51mm to 56mm, increasing capacity to 600cc. Although some modest success was achieved in competition, such as the Bickel brothers' supercharged 111.42mph lap at Brooklands in 1934, the machine was really a sports tourer. In 1936, Ariel launched a 1,000cc Square Four of all new engine design.

This model had a pushrod power-unit, with plain bearings and it also utilised a unique trailing-link rear suspension system. It remained in production in various roadster forms until the late 1950s, by which time it boasted four individual exhaust pipe ports and an all-aluminum engine. The 1956 luxury roadster shown here developed 42bhp at 5,800rpm, providing a top speed of 105mph. It had a bore and stroke of 65mm x 75mm. The machine's kerb-weight was 225kg (495lb).

TRIUMPH

Triumph will always be associated with the vertical-twin engine layout. This classic design was introduced in 1938 as the 498cc Speed Twin, the forerunner of many famous motorcycles. A memorable example was the larger Thunderbird (above), introduced in 1949. This 649cc tourer produced 34bhp at 6,000rpm on a compression ratio of 7:1. Three standard models averaged 101.06mph between them for 500 miles at Montlhèry.

The Bonneville was the most sporting and best known Triumph twin however, providing leading performance in a relatively affordable package, along with good looks, and in the later versions at least, good handling.

A break with the vertical twin layout came in the 1960s with the transverse three-cylinder Trident (left). The T160 had a 740cc engine of 67mm x 70 mm bore and stroke, producing 58bhp at 7,250rpm to reach a top speed of around 120mph. the most famous Trident was the version raced to great success by Percy Tait and many others, a machine which became known as 'Slippery Sam' after its habit of spraying oil over its rear tire!

A Trident with styling by American Craig Vetter became a landmark machine in its own right. The X75 Hurricane had swooping bodywork which merged the fuel tank with the sidepanels, a look since copied by almost every other motorcycle manufacturer.

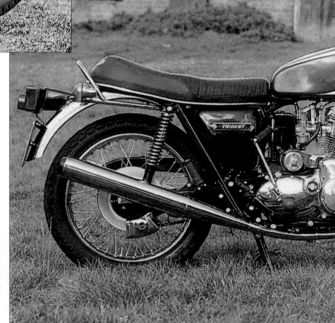

Norton

It was the great racing success of the Norton marque which created the need for an improved frame in the 1940s. The need was met by the McCandless brothers' Featherbed frame, which in turn influenced motorcycle design almost everywhere. After being introduced on the Manx racers, the Featherbed frame was modified for road use in the existing 497cc tourer, which became the Dominator in 1952. The example shown above is a Manx, built in 1958.

Ten years after its launch, the Dominator had grown to 647cc, giving a maximum speed of 112mph. In 1965, Norton launched the 745cc Atlas, but a more significant development came two years later. The same engine was fitted, with rubber mountings, into a new duplex frame with unique 'Isolastic' rubber mountings isolating the swingarm and engine from the rest of the bike, to keep vibration from the rider. This new model, the Commando, was subsequently increased in size to 828cc. With a top speed of 120 mph, the Commando (bottom) was the most powerful road-going Norton ever produced, and was the fastest production bike of its time.

HARLEY– DAVIDSON

The Harley-Davidson Electra Glide is probably the most famous motorcycle model of all. The first model had its origins in the SV 74 twin of 1922, although its more recent and direct ancestor is the first ohv 1200 of 1941. These early machines displayed the familiar styling features of most American motorcycles: leading link front forks, solid rear wheel mounting, pan saddles, footboards, high, wide handlebars and the unmistakable Harley V-twin engine, all of which add together to give exceptional low cruising speed comfort. Over the years the range of Glides has been modernized and added to, but the essential concept has remained the same. In 1949, the Hydra Glide was introduced with a telescopic front fork, while the next model, with swingarm rear suspension, was the Duo Glide of 1959. With the addition of a starter motor in 1965 came the name Electra Glide. Since then, the bike was generally only modified gradually, adopting cast alloy wheels for example, and numerous Japanese components such as forks and carburetor. Most significant was the fitment of the then-new Evolution engine in 1984, followed by a fuel-injected version of the same in 1998, by which time the Electra Glide was sporting many luxuries usually only associated with cars, such as cruise control, on-board sound system and so on.

The Electra-Glide is one of the heaviest mass produced motorcycles ever built, weighing 800lb fully equipped, and the latest machine also carries one of the longest names, as the Harley-Davidson Electra Glide Ultra Classic FLHTCUI! The 45 degree, 1207cc V-twin of the model shown had hydraulically-activated pushrods and produced 62bhp at 5,200 rpm with 70ft.lb of torque at 4,000rpm.

In 1989 Harley-Davidson introduced the oddly-named Fat Boy, but there was no questioning the bike's success. Its Softail frame (a sprung rear subframe designed to look like the old solid frames of the 1950s and earlier) and classically good-looking styling, enhanced by solid aluminum wheels and expanses of chrome, encompassed everything that was appealing about this sometimes anachronistic marque, and became one of its top sellers. For the year 2000, the Fat Boy has been fitted with an all-new Twin Cam 88 engine of 1449cc, using for the first time in Harley's history a balance shaft to smooth out the vibration. The frame and most other components are also new, although the bike looks almost identical to its predecessors, confirming that it is this Harley look and image which is the company's strongest attribute today.

The MV Agusta 750S America was exotic for several reasons, many of which boiled down to its very high price and limited availability. But it was also one of the very best looking machines to have been produced for many years, and most significant of all, it was a direct development of MV Agusta's mighty four-cylinder grand prix racing machines, suitably adapted for road use. MV Agusta had resisted making road-going sports machines, which might have reflected its race bikes, for many years, Count Domenico Agusta worrying that these might end up on race tracks in private hands, perhaps not do so well and so dilute the image of all-conquering success which he held so dearly. Thus the anticipation which preceded the arrival of the 750S was enormous.

These factors endowed the bike with its very special status (MV Agusta being the most successful grand prix racing company in history) although the reality was perhaps a little disappointing. The bikes were quick, certainly, although no more so than the upcoming Japanese fours, while the handling (due to the excessive unsprung weight of the shaft final drive) was not in the same league as the high standards set by other Italian machines of the time. Even so, the 789cc dohc motor produced a useful 75bhp, enough for a top speed of around 130mph, and the bike attracted a huge amount of attention wherever it went.

The real MV Agusta classics were of course the race bikes themselves. Pictured is the 497cc four-cylinder machine which took Englishman John Surtees to his first 500 World Championship for MV, before he went on to win another six world titles with the Italian company. The bike's distinctive 53mm x 56.4mm dohc engine produced 56bhp at 10,500rpm.

By the mid-1970s Laverda had already established for itself a reputation as a manufacturer of high quality, high performance machines, but it was the British importer Slater Brothers which was responsible for the creation of the decade's most desirable, overtly masculine and, not to be forgotten, fastest motorcycle.

The Jota used a version of the 981cc, dohc three-cylinder engine first used in the 3C of 1973, tuned with high compression pistons, hotter camshafts and a very free-flowing (for which read, noisy) exhaust system, the result of this being an output of 90bhp with a top speed of 143mph. This made the Jota the fastest production motorcycle in 1976 when it was launched, quicker even than Kawasaki's high performance fours, and it was an instant it with production racers of the time as well as sports road riders. But achieving good results on the race tracks didn't come easy: the Jota's power was matched by at best wayward handling, which if anything only added to the bike's image as a beast of a motorcycle which only the best could tame.

After the first model various changes were made, although as these tended to soften the bike's image it's the first machines which are now considered the most desirable. The crankshaft configuration for example was changed from the unusual 180 degree throws to a more conventional 120 degree set-up, which reduced vibration considerably, while a half fairing was later added. Increasingly stringent emissions laws saw the Jota evolve into the RGS and RGA models, which were quieter and generally more friendly to the rest of the world, but the high prices ensured sales remained low, and Laverda went into receivership in 1987, before its low key revival several years later.

DUCATI

The Ducati SS (Super Sport) range was inspired by Paul Smart's famous victory at the Imola 200 in 1972 on a race version one of the firm's new V-twin desmos. The first road bike was the 750SS, and in 1975 this was enlarged to 864cc for the 900SS, which produced 79bhp and had a top speed of just over 130mph. The bike's great rival was the Moto Guzzi Le Mans, but the Ducati's superior handling ensured it was far more successful on race tracks, although its more complex and demanding engine made it a more committed buy for the road rider.

The bike was known for its very stable handling (still a Ducati trademark) as well as powerful and torquey engine, but like many other classic machines, it combined its dynamic abilities with exceptional looks, in this case a pared down, lean and overtly mechanical style which underlined its single-minded focus on speed and performance. The most famous example of this machine is undoubtedly the fully-faired 900SS raced by Mike Hailwood to Senior victory in the 1978 Isle of Man TT races (after he had been retired from motorcycle competition for an amazing

11 years). Although the factory helped very little in the preparation of this machine, which was almost entirely the work of Steve Wynne, in 1979 a Hailwood Replica version of the 900SS was introduced alongside the original model, sporting its Castrol color scheme.

Unlike Moto Guzzi, Ducati managed to keep its V-twins at the forefront of motorcycle performance, if not always in speed then certainly in handling, although the new eight-valve, liquid-cooled models designed by Massimo Bordi were quick even by contemporary standards. But it was the Ducati 916 (right) which really made a major impact, first for its breathtaking styling when it was displayed at the Milan Show in 1993, then for its devastating performance.

The look was the work of Massimo Tamburini, originally a founder of Bimota, whose underseat exhausts, single-sided swingarm and wide, low headlights have since been copied extensively. The frame design too was Tamburini's, and this extended the Ducati tradition of exceptional handling with the bike dominating the World Superbike race series ever since. Even the engine, although only a twin, offered performance very close to that of the definitive Honda Fireblade. Since the first 916 the changes have been relatively few, the most significant being the uprating of the engine to 996cc at the end of 1998 (inset).

A very different Ducati which appeared a year before the 916 also headed for classic status. The M900 Monster was the work of Argentinian designer Miguel Angel Galuzzi, and its aggressive, original look has also been imitated by many others. In addition, for Ducati it was a very canny machine to produce as most of the bike's components were already in existence, such as the 888 frame and 900SS engine. The Monster has since appeared in many other variations, with capacities of 600cc and 750cc, and has become something of a cult machine around the world.

vespa

The Vespa was a pivotal machine in providing cheap transport to the general public, offering the low costs of two-wheelers with unheard of convenience and cleanliness thanks to its enclosed bodywork, spare wheel and open frame making access far easier than on conventional motorcycles. Its originality was the result of using aircraft engineer Corradino d'Ascanio, who approached the problem of designing a two-wheeled machine with none of a traditional motorcycle designer's preconceptions, hence the Vespa's unique steel monocoque chassis, for example.

Like many classics, the Vespa's status has been proved by the test of time - more than 50 years after its debut it is still in production.

Two closely related Moto Guzzis have proved to be truly outstanding machines of their time. The V7 Sport was created from the 757cc V7 and sold in 1972 as a limited edition special produced to homologate racing versions. With its distinctive lime green fuel tank and red frame (Telaio Rosso in Italian, which became the bike's nickname) designed by Lino Tonti, the V7 Sport was immediately going to do well if only for its gorgeous looks. The first version featured a lightweight chrome-molybdenum frame and hand-built internals, and some 200 were made, but even the later

production versions performed extremely well, with a top speed of more than 125mph (faster even than the Honda CB750 and Kawasaki H2), so its performance matched its style. At the time Moto Guzzi had been in some financial difficulties, and it's the V7 Sport which is credited with saving the factory from extinction.

Only four years later, Moto Guzzi extended its sports bike credentials with another classic, the Mk 1 Le Mans. This featured an engine derived from the V7, but with a capacity increase to 844cc and a power output of 71bhp at 7,300rpm, enough for a top speed of close to 130mph. Two things were special about the Le Mans, even aside from its state-of-the-art performance. First, it matched its exceptional speed with everyday usability, needing only simple maintenance and being perfectly capable of civilised low speed riding as well as much sportier stuff. Secondly, it was another Moto Guzzi with quite exceptional looks, the long, low profile being beautifully enhanced by the blood-red and black paint scheme. The Le Mans line ended as late as 1991, but none of the later models managed to capture the purity of purpose which was the essence of the original.

MOTO GUZZI

BMW's R32 of 1923 (above) was not its first motorcycle, but it was by far the most successful of those early years. But what really singles it out is that the success went way beyond the immediate one of sales and profits, with the R32 defining a concept which BMW was to follow for the rest of the century and still does today.

The R32's boxer twin engine has since become a trademark of the Bavarian manufacturer, but the bike's intelligent, contemporary design, reliability and high build quality are also equally associated with the marque. The R32 featured a 494cc boxer engine with transverse cylinders, shaft drive and unitary three-speed gearbox, all housed in a double triangular frame. More than 3000 were made from 1923 to 1926.

Many worthy boxer twins followed, but another great was surely the R90S of 1973, (top right) a really fine looking machine with its smoked effect paintwork. The styling was the work of Hans Muth, the first stylist employed by BMW. The tuned 898cc engine produced 67bhp, enough for a top speed of 125mph, which matched superbikes of the day, and competition versions won many races including the production race at the Isle of Man TT and at Daytona. This was the last BMW capable of such feats, and considered by many to be BMW's only true sports bike.

The R90S was the basis for one the great sports touring bikes, the R100RS, (right) famous for its enormous mile-eating ability in exceptional comfort as well as its sophisticated good looks. The RS was a top selling machine for more than 10 years and ensured BMW's profitability throughout the late 1970s and early 1980s, when the company decided to phase out the twins in favor of its K-Series fours and triples. This was soon seen as a serious mistake, and the old boxers were reintroduced while a new generation of twins was being designed.

HONDA

As probably the most prolific of all manufacturers, there's some inevitability in several classic motorcycles wearing the Honda badge. But this leading Japanese company sells its machines in great numbers for the very reason they are also often exceptionally good motorcycles, so any list of classics will always contain a great number of Hondas.

The one machine which set Honda off on the path to greatness as a company was the humble Cub, originally called the C100 Super Cub at its debut in 1963. The bike and the accompanying marketing ca~e as the engine ensured millions took to two wheels who might otherwise never have wished to do so. This was not a motorcycle in the enthusiast sense, but cheap, economical and sensible transport for the masses. The bike's reliability became legendary, its utility indispensable, and today it is now the best selling motor vehicle ever, with more than 26 million examples being sold, accounting for more than a quarter of Honda's total production.

Many more Honda classics have followed. The company's glorious race bikes of the 1960s established its reputation as a serious technological leader, although it's often overlooked that Honda's current two-stroke V-four racer as ridden by Australian Mick Doohan to five world championships is the greatest of all. The NSR500 has completely dominated the 500cc class in GPs for much of the 1990s, and on the rare occasions when Doohan has been out of the running, almost inevitably there is another NSR500 rider at the top of the podium.

Honda advanced the cause of high performance street bikes long before the NSR500 with its glamorous yet also highly accomplished CB750 of 1969. Its four exhaust pipes, disk brakes and four-cylinder, overhead camshaft engine had many proclaiming it would be unreliable and wouldn't catch on. They were utterly wrong as the beautifully built CB750 came to redefine big capacity sports machines.

Honda managed a similar task in 1993 when it introduced the Fireblade, a bike which combined the power of contemporary one-liter machines with the agility, weight and handling of 600s, showing the rest of the world that this was the best way forward. It took many years for the opposition to catch on, then catch up, with only the Yamaha YZF1000-R1 of 1998 finally getting the better of the 'Blade.

But Honda hasn't always built in-line fours to power its bigger bikes. During the 1980s its initially notoriously unreliable VF range of V-fours was transformed into the exceptional VFR750, the best sports tourer of the late 1980s and for most of the 1990s, while a racing variant, the RC30, was another all-time great racing machine, winning championships around the world including in endurance and world superbikes.

YAMAHA

Yamaha's RD350LC (top) took a generation of street racers to the streets, combining its adrenaline-pumping screamer of a two-stroke engine with fresh and appealing styling, plus handling and agility which at the time was good enough to beat bikes three times its size on race tracks. The bike's image as something of a hooligan's machine was very much a part of its image and attraction, and it managed to upset many upright citizens as it wheelied past them in the high streets of Europe followed by a haze of two-stroke smoke.

Yamaha's sports bike prowess has constantly been a theme in its history, exemplified by the FZR1000EXUP of 1988 (above) which offered superb handling with 160mph performance. The EXUP, as it was universally known, was one of many sports bikes in Yamaha's family of 'Genesis' twin spar aluminum framed machines powered by its four-cylinder, liquid-cooled engines with their distinctive forward-slanted cylinders (for better weight distribution) and five-valves per cylinder.

The EXUP was eventually displaced by the Honda Fireblade as the top sports bike, but Yamaha hit back in 1998 with the astonishing YZF1000-R1 (right) in 1998, a bike which combined the incredibly low weight of 177kg with a 148bhp power output. The handling was more like a race bike's, the brakes phenomenal, yet the engine was well-endowed with low rev torque and the machine perfectly usable in everyday riding. At the time

of writing, this is still the sports bike which sets the standards of the day.

The R1 and other Yamaha fours are closely related to the company's FZR750R (or OW-O1 in Yamaha's internal code designation) (top center)limited edition supersports machine, designed to homologate the racing versions. It's this which after some development finally had the beating of the Honda RC30, and which took a World Superbike title for American Scott Russell.

In an entirely different vein is the Yamaha V-Max, (top right) a bike claimed to be the hardest accelerating production motorcycle in the world at its launch in 1984, something few disputed. The 1200cc V-four engine's immense power and torque was one attraction, but more so was the V-Max's mean street rod looks, styled for Yamaha in California, home of the genre. So right was the bike that 15 years later this 140bhp machine is still in production with no significant changes from the original.

SUZUKI

Suzuki was a late entry into four-stroke production, and even then the company modeled its new GS750 of 1977 very closely on the Kawasaki Z1. But if these were bad signs, the reality was quite different, as the GS proved to be an exceptionally good machine with unusually good handling. Better still was the GS1000 which followed the next year, considered thea first Japanese superbike to feature handling which really matched the immense power of its engine, and as such it was something of a milestone in the history of superbikes.

From the eight-valve GS machines the 16-valve GSX series was developed, although some were very heavy, few particularly attractive and the handling was not always as good as the GS1000. An exception was the dramatic GSX1100S Katana, styled by Target Design in Europe in a futuristic, aggressive look which ensured front pages for Suzuki around the world. It was perhaps too much for its time as the 145mph Suzuki actually sold rather poorly, although since its introduction in 1982 it has become something of a cult machine, and various styling features have since been copied by many others.

Suzuki's GSX-R750 however has sold in huge numbers since the first version of 1985, gaining itself a reputation as a something of a tearaway's machine in much the same mould as the Yamaha RD350LC. The bike's performance has matched the image, with a howling high revving motor that has always been at or near the top of the 750cc class, with agile and sometimes too-flighty handling that has made it a perfect track tool as well as very rapid road machine.

K Kawasaki

Kawasaki has prided itself on producing the best and most powerful engines in modern motorcycling, and for many years has also featured the world's fastest production bike in its stable. The reputation for speed really started with the 1969 H1 three-cylinder two-stroke, followed by the 750cc H2 version, which gained a fearsome reputation for barely controllable power with frightening handling (both of which were subject to some exaggeration, it has to be said)As two-strokes fell out of favor, so Kawasaki turned to the four-cylinder four-stroke, although Honda pre-empted Kawasaki's own planned 750 with the CB750. Designer Ben Inamura went back to the drawing board and came up with the 903cc Z1, since hailed as the first Japanese superbike for it then-staggering performance (well-matched with the glamour of disk front brake, plenty of chrome and four exhaust pipes).

This handsome bike was not only fast, it spawned a line of four-cylinder Kawasakis that built a reputation for extraordinary reliability as well as power which continued for many years.

Then in 1984 Kawasaki - and Inamura - did it again, this time with the 16-valve, liquid-cooled GPZ900R, a bike that redefined what a sports machine should be capable of with its 155mph performance and precise handling.

So good was the 900R that production continued for another 13 years, long after several 'successor' machines were discontinued. But one of its descendants, the 1052cc ZZ-R1100, upheld the company's speed image from 1990 until 1997 as the fastest production bike in the world, capable of an amazing 173mph.

THE SPEED
<u>RECORDS</u>

THE SPEED RECORDS

"Speed, it seems to me, provides the one genuinely modern pleasure."

Aldous Huxley, 1894-1963.

Mankind was obsessed with speed long before the development of the motor vehicle, but it is only since its appearance that he has been able to truly indulge the passion to travel fast. The need to move from one place to another as fast as possible is an explanation for this desire, but it's an incomplete one. Speed so often is the goal in itself, the challenge of achieving higher speeds than before and the sheer exhilaration

and danger of attemping it being enough on their own for men and women to risk their lives purely to travel faster than anyone else. This drive to stretch the bounds of human ingenuity and determination has been a measure of progress of the internal combustion engine, whose invention saw the birth of an era in which man has been able to achieve speeds beyond the comprehension of previous generations.

The history of land speed records dates back to more than a century ago. The first record was set in 1898 by Count Gaston de Chasseloup-Laubat of Paris, France. His single run through a measured kilometer took 57 seconds; an average speed of 39.24mph.

The sole purpose of his run was to prove that his automobiles worked well. However, he unwittingly started a challenge which captured the imagination of millions, but it has tempted only a select few to take on the challenge - many of these have given their lives as a result.

The first official world land speed record for the motorcycle was established on April 14, 1920, at Daytona, USA, by Ernie Walker, riding a 994cc Indian V-twin. The motorcycle was sufficiently reliable by this time to realistically achieve such a feat, and new records were being set regularly in the period up to the outbreak of the Second World War. Indeed, the 1930s were great years for the record breakers. Bert le Vack set a record in 1929 on

Germany's Ernst Henne used a series of BMWs between 1929 and 1937, including the supercharged 746cc machine.

a 998cc JAP-engined Brough-Superior, but less than a month later Ernst Henne of Germany set a new record on a 733cc BMW, near Munich, and a fight began to win it. Claude Temple had by now retired from competition, but continued to design motorcycles aimed at winning speed records. In 1930, a new record was set by Joe Wright at Arpajon, riding a Temple-OEC with a supercharged 996cc JAP V-twin engine. Within one month, Henne and his BMW had reclaimed the record.

Joe Wright's next intention was to bring the record back to England before the start of the Olympia motorcycle show in November 1930. He went to Cork in Ireland with the Temple-OEC and a Zenith with an almost identical engine. His first run on the Temple-OEC was so fast that the only photographer present left the scene, eager to dispatch the picture to his agency. Technical trouble prevented the OEC from completing the return run, but a successful attempt was made on the Zenith.

Left: Joe Wright on a JAP-engined OEC

When the Olympia show opened, OEC proudly exhibited a machine labelled "the fastest machine in the world". There had been no photograph of the Zenith, and OEC must have been aware that it was not its machine which broke the record. However, J.A. Prestwich (JAP) reasoned that the engines were almost identical anyway, and furthermore, it was JAP which sponsored the attempt. OEC gave it improved sales publicity, while the Zenith factory was experiencing financial difficulties. It took a while for the controversy to die down. In 1932, 1934, 1935 and 1936, Ernst Henne continued to break his own records. Then in 1937, Eric Fernihough, a lone Englishman who bought and tuned his own machines, broke the record at Gyon, Hungary.

He used Brough-Superior cycle parts, powered by a 996cc supercharged JAP motor. In that same year the record was broken again, this time at Brescia, Italy, by Piero Taruffi, riding a 492cc supercharged, water-cooled Gilera four. Eric Fernihough was tragically killed during a 1938 attempt, when his machine went into a violent wobble at around 180mph.

There were no new records from then until 1951, when William Herz achieved 180mph at Ingolstadt, near Munich in Germany, riding a 499cc NSU. In 1955 Russel Wright set a new record riding a tuned 998cc Vincent-HRD, near Christchurch, New Zealand. In 1956 William Herz was sent to the USA by the German NSU factory: the new venue was Bonneville, where the salt flats permitted higher speeds than anywhere in Europe. Herz had two record breaking machines, one of which was a 499cc supercharged dohc twin in a streamlined shell. At Bonneville he reached 211.4mph, with Johnny Allen marginally ahead at 214.5mph. Allen's machine was powered by a 650cc Triumph twin engine, but his US record was not ratified.

In 1962, Bill Johnson reached 224.57mph on a 649cc Triumph. Robert Leppan's "projectile" was powered by two similar engines, which enabled him to reach 245.6mph at Bonneville in 1966. This record was held for four years until September 17, 1970, when Don Vesco stole the limelight with his 700cc streamliner. The twin 350cc Yamaha engines enabled Vesco to set the record at 251.924mph, making him the first person to ride a motorcycle at speeds in excess of 250mph. However, Calvin Rayborn ensured

that Vesco did not rest on his laurels. Rayborn's 1480cc Harley-Davidson reached 254.84mph, and he then went on to break his own record at 265.49mph.

This record stood until 1975, when Don Vesco reached 302.94mph on his improved 1496cc Yamaha-powered streamliner, named "Silverbird". Vesco had lengthened his machine by 40 inches and replaced the 350cc engines with two Yamaha TZ750 road racing engines. "Silverbird" made Vesco the first motorcyclist to exceed 300mph. Three years later, he went on to break his own record riding a new 2030cc streamliner called "Lightning Bolt I". This was powered by a pair of modified 1015cc Kawasaki Z900 engines. On August 25, 1978, Vesco and "Lightning Bolt I" set the record at 318.598mph. On September 27, 1978, during Bonneville Speed Week, Vesco turned the fastest speed of the meet, including cars, at 333.17mph. However, on this run, a chunk of rubber sheared off the rear tire, causing Vesco to shut off before the end of the measured mile. Consequently, this record was never officially recognised. In October 1978, "Silverbird" crashed. Most of the streamliner was destroyed, but miraculously Vesco sustained no serious injuries. In 1999 he held a total of 18 motorcycle records and five automotive records. He held the motorcycle land speed record of 318.598mph for 19 years. On November 5, 1997, at Bonneville, Vesco's record was finally broken by Jim Feuling, who achieved the fastest speed ever recorded for a motorcycle on his way to capturing two AMA (American Motorcycle Association) and two LSA (Land Speed Authority) world speed records in his single-engine Harley-Davidson streamliner.

A spectacular new attempt was made by Englishman Richard "Rocket Man" Brown in 1998. Brown believed he could top the previous record by at least 100mph on the 4.2 mile track at Pendine Beach, South Wales, with his unique 26ft long rocket bike called Maximum Impulse, but in the end the venue proved unsuitable. Even so, with Brown claiming the machine is capable of more than 500mph thanks to the 6000bhp produced by its three hybrid rocket engines, the record looks as if it will shortly be broken once again.

One thing is for certain. Whatever the record, and whoever holds it, it will always represent no more than a target to be beaten by the next contender. The higher the speed, the bigger the challenge and the greater the risk. And that will make the desire to go one better all the stronger.

Joe Pejrali on the record breaking Ocean Sand bike in 1965

George Roeder with his record breaking "Sprint " in 1965

Don Vesco with turbo-charged Yamaha in 1975

Bob leppon and his triumph powered Gyronaut above.

Richard Brown

The 26ft long rocket bike, "Maximum Impulse"

THE FASTEST MEN ON TWO WHEELS

Year Course	Driver	Motorcycle	ccm	kph	mph
1920 Daytona (USA)	Ernie Walker	Indian	994	167.670	104.12
1923 Arpajon (F)	F. F.W. Dixon	Harley-Davidson	989	171.502	106.50
1923 Brooklands (GB)	Claude Temple	British-Anzani	996	174.580	108.41
1924 Arpajon (F)	Bert le Vack	Brough Superior	998	182.780	113.50
1924 Arpajon (F)	Bert Le Vack	Brough Superior	998	191.590	118.98
1926 Arpajon (F)	Claude Temple	OEC-Temple	996	195.330	121.30
1928 Arpajon (F)	O. M. Baldwin	Zenith-JAP	996	200.560	124.55
1929 Arpajon (F)	Bert Le Vack	Brough-Superior	998	207.330	128.75
1929 Munich (Ger)	Ernst Henne	BMW	735	216.590	134.50
1930 Arpajon (F)	Joe Wright	OEC-Temple	994	220.990	137.23
1930 Ingolstadt (Ger)	Ernst Henne	BMW	735	221.540	137.58
1930 Cork (Irl)	Joe Wright	Zenith-JAP	998	242.590	150.65
1932 Tat (H)	Ernst Henne	BMW	735	244.400	151.77
1934 Gyon (H)	Ernst Henne	BMW	735	246.069	152.81
1935 Frankfurt (Ger)	Ernst Henne	BMW	735	256.046	159.01
1936 Frankfurt (Ger)	Ernst Henne	BMW	495	272.006	168.92
1937 Gyon (H)	Eric Fernihough	Brough-Superior	995	273.244	169.68
1937 Brescia (I)	Piero Tarffi	Gilera	492	274.181	170.27
1937 Frankfurt (Ger)	Ernst Henne	BMW	495	279.503	173.57
1951 Ingolstadt (Ger)	Wilhelm Herz	NSU	499	290.322	180.29
1955 Christchurch (NZ)	Russell Wright	Vincent-HRD	998	297.640	184.83
1956 Bonneville (USA)	Wilhelm Herz	NSU	347	304.356	189.00
1956 Bonneville (USA)	Wilhelm Herz	NSU	499	338.092	211.40
1962 Bonneville (USA)	Bill Johnson	Triumph	649	361.410	224.57
1966 Bonneville (USA)	Bob Leppan	Triumph Spec.	1298	395.280	245.60
1970 Bonneville (USA)	Don Vesco	Yamaha	700	405.25	251.66
1970 Bonneville (USA)	Cal Rayborn	Harley-Davidson	1480	410.37	254.84
1970 Bonneville (USA)	Cal Rayborn	Harley-Davidson	1480	426.40	265.49
1975 Bonneville (USA)	Don Vesco	Yamaha	1496	487.80	302.928
1978 Bonneville (USA)	Don Vesco	Kawasaki Turbo	2030	509.757	318.598
1997 Bonneville (USA)	Jim Feuling	Harley-Davidson	3000	534.800	332.103

A-Z

OF THE
WORLD'S
MOTORCYCLES

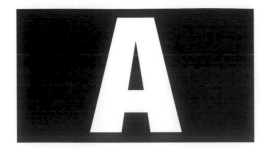

ABAKO • Germany 1923–1925

Small 129cc single-cylinder machines with Abako's own two-stroke deflector-type three-port engines, two and three-speed Sturmey-Archer gearboxes and chain drive to the rear wheel.

ABBOTSFORD • England 1919–1920

Scooter-like lightweights with 1.5hp ohv power units. Limited production.

ABC • England 1913–1914

Designed by Granville Bradshaw for the All British (Engine) Company, this 496cc ioe flat twin was the first motorcycle created by Bradshaw. Some of these engines were supplied to W. Brough.

1914–1919 The reorganized ABC Motors Ltd, originally based at Brooklands, Byfleet, moved to Walton-on-Thames and produced mainly war supplies and motorcycle engines for the military.

1920–1922 Another reorganisation took place at Walton-on-Thames, with production centred around spare parts and the development of new designs, but there were no new motorcycles put on the market. Bradshaw's policy was to sell his designs to other manufacturing concerns.

ABC • England 1919–1922

This was the best known ABC, built by The Sopwith Aviation & Engineering Co. Ltd at Kingston-on-Thames, a company which built aircraft during the war and which afterwards took over Bradshaw's newest creation. This was a transverse-mounted 398cc flat twin with ohv, 4-speed gearbox, all chain drive, spring frame and forks, automatic lubrication etc. Often regarded as the predecessor of the first BMW, the Sopwith-ABC was an advanced but underdeveloped design when Sopwith put it on the market. The valve gear was unreliable, the lubrication bad and although it could sell more than it was able to produce, the ABC failed and by 1921 Sopwith was in liquidation, mainly because failures of the design led to too many guarantee claims. The price for the Standard Model was £98, the Lucas Dynamo Model was offered at £118.

ABC • France 1920–1924

Made under licence from Sopwith by a branch factory of the French Gnome & Rhone aero-engine and motorcycle company, the French ABC lasted longer than the English original. A Captain Bartlett, who headed the production in France, used modified cylinder heads for his machines and supplied in addition to the 348cc ABC a 493cc machine. Together with Naas, he competed in races and other sporting events with great success.

ABC Skootamota • England 1919–22

Granville Bradshaw designed and Gilbert Campling made and sold this scooter, with effectively half an ABC industrial engine driving the rear wheel by chain. It featured a tubular welded frame and no suspension. The best of a bad bunch.

ABC • England 1920–1924

Built by J. Barwell at Birmingham, this ABC had no connection with Bradshaw's ABC designs. It was an assembled machine with proprietary 296cc and later 247cc Villiers two-stroke engines.

ABC • Germany 1922–1925

Another, but little known ABC built in Berlin. The engine was a deflector-type 149cc two-stroke of the company's own design and manufacture.

ABENDSONNE • Germany 1933–1934

Designed by Georg Weissbinder, who coupled two 98cc Villiers engines together. Few of these machines were made.

ABERDALE • England 1946–1959

London-built 48cc autocycles and lightweight motorcycles with 98cc and 123cc Villiers and Sachs two-stroke power units. Bown, another manufacturer of such machines, took over Aberdale production in 1959.

ABE-STAR • Japan 1951–1959

One of many Japanese motorcycle factories of the 1950s. The top model was a 148cc four-stroke with the company's own ohv engine.

ABINGDON • England 1903–1925

Early models had MMC, Minerva Kerry and Fafnir engines. Later ones used Abingdon's own 3.5hp singles and 5-6hp V-twins. After 1918 the range consisted of 348cc singles, 496cc and 796cc V-twins with Abingdon sv engines. A 624cc single was built for a short period. The producer, Abingdon-King-Dick, a well-known tool factory at Birmingham, after 1925 renamed the machines AKD and concentrated on singles up to 346cc. Abingdon motorcycles were of sturdy design and many were sold in the colonies.

ABJ • England 1950–1954

Lightweights with 48cc, 98cc and 123cc Villiers two-stroke engines, made by a bicycle factory. The 48cc Auto-Minor was sold for £41 15s.

398 ABC (ohv flat twin) 1921

ABRA • Italy 1923–1927

Assembled motorcycles with German 146cc DKW two-stroke engines. From 1924 onwards also used its own 132cc engines. Small production.

ACCOSSATO • Italy 1976–

Manufacturer of 49cc, 79cc, and 124cc motocross, trial and enduro two-strokes with Minarelli and Hiro engines.

ACE • America 1919–1929

William `Bill' Henderson sold his famous four-cylinder Henderson design in 1917 to the Chicago-based Schwinn company and in 1919 founded the ACE Motor Corporation in Philadelphia. There he once more built four-cylinder air-cooled in-line unit-design motorcycles with 1168cc, later 1229cc and 1266cc engines. He was killed in 1922 in an accident while testing a new model and another famous designer, Arthur Lemon, took over design and development. All engines had ioe valves, light-alloy pistons and Schebler carburettors. The engines developed between 20 and 25bhp. In 1927 Indian took over the ACE, which ran into commercial difficulties, and moved production to Springfield, Massachusetts. It was renamed Indian 4 after 1929.

ACHILLES • Czechoslovakia 1906–1912

Built by a bicycle factory in what is now the Czech Republic, Achilles motorcycles had 3.5hp single-cylinder and 5hp V-twin proprietary engines made by Fafnir and Zeus.

ACHILLES • Germany 1953–1957

Scooter-like machines with 98cc and 123cc Sachs engines and also sporting 48cc mopeds. The same company built motorcycles in the Austro-Hungarian Empire before WW1. When it closed down in 1957 in Germany, the English Norman motorcycle factory bought the production equipment.

ACMA • France 1948–early 1960s

Licensed production of Italian 123cc, 147cc and 173cc Vespa scooters. The factory was at Fourchambault.

ACME • England 1902–1922

Built motorcycles with 2hp Minerva and 2.5hp Automoto engines. After 1918, 293cc JAP engines and its own 348cc sv singles and 997cc sv V-twins were put into production. In 1922 Acme amalgamated with Rex at Coventry, forming Rex-Acme motorcycles, which became famous when Walter Handley won races on Blackburne-engined racing models. See also Rex-Acme.

1299cc Ace (ioe in-line four) 1923

293cc Acme (sv-JAP) 1922

ADER • France 1901–1906

Pioneer manufacturer which also built cars. Motorcycles built by Clément Ader had 2hp single-cylinder and transverse-mounted V-twin 4hp engines.

ADLER • Germany 1901–1957

Originally a bicycle maker, which first fitted De Dion engines, then made its own singles and twins until 1907, when the concern switched from bikes to cars. In 1949 motorcycle production resumed with the superb 100cc (later 125cc) M series two-strokes. An advanced and luxurious 200cc and 250cc two-stroke twin range was soon developed - later copied in Japan by Yamaha and Suzuki. The final Adler offering was the Junior scooter which was not a great success, although the water-cooled RS250 racer, developed by privateer Helmut Hallmeier, did well in German events. Adler eventually abandoned motorcycles to become a highly successful maker of typewriters and office equipment.

ADLY • Taiwan 1985–

Trading name used in Europe for scooters and mopeds manufactured by Her Chee.

ADMA • Germany 1924–1926

Interesting 169cc two-strokes with internal fly-wheels. Own design, limited production.

ADONIS • France 1949–1952

Small Vap-engined 48cc and 75cc scooters of simple design.

ADRIA • Germany 1912–1928

Sturdy sv singles of 276cc, 282cc, 294cc and 346cc capacity. Adria also built proprietary engines for cars and boats, but motorcycle manufacture was on a limited scale only.

ADS • Belgium 1949–1954

Small assembler of 98cc machines with Sachs and Ilo two-stroke engines.

246cc Adler (two-stroke twin) 1953

ADVANCE • England 1906–1912

Once a well-known make with own 3hp, 3.5hp and V-twin 6hp power units. Compared to other makes of that period, Advance motorcycles had very low frames.

AEL • England 1919–1924

A motorcycle and accessories dealer in Coventry which fitted various 147cc to 348cc proprietary engines made by Villiers, JAP and Blackburne. The frames were probably built by Hobart in Coventry.

AEOLUS • England 1903–1905

Interesting 492cc single-cylinder design with shaft drive to the rear wheel. Production was on a limited scale.

AEOLUS • England 1914–1916

Had no connection with the first London-made Aeolus. This Aeolus was fitted with its own 269cc two-stroke engines. The company—Bowns Ltd—produced Bown lightweight machines after 1945.

AER • England 1938–1940

Scott motorcycle specialist A. E. Reynolds produced from 1927 onwards modified 498cc and 598cc Scott machines, called Reynolds Special. In the late 1930s, modern 246cc single-cylinder and 346cc vertical twin two-strokes of his own design and manufacture came into being. WW2 stopped production.

AERO • Japan 1925–1927

Single cylinder 633cc and 250cc motorcycles built by Narazo Shamazu who had built NS machines before WW1.

AERO-CAPRONI • Italy 1948–1964

Once a famous aircraft factory at Trento, after the war Aero-Caproni built motorcycles of its own design with 73cc, 124cc and 148cc ohv and partly face-cam ohc engines. Some had tubular, others pressed steel frames. 48cc machines were also built and there was a 149cc model with a transverse-mounted ohv flat-twin unit-design engine in a pressed steel frame. This model produced 7·5bhp at 6000rpm and had a 60mph top speed. Small two-stroke models assembled by Aero Caproni (Capriolo) had NSU engines.

AERMACCHI • Italy 1950–1978

Famous aircraft manufacturer Aermacchi made a scooter before, in 1956, it launched Alfredo Bianchi's all-enclosed Chimera with a horizontal single-cylinder ohv 175cc engine and unit four-speed gearbox. The Chimera did not sell well and the engine was enlarged to 250cc for a more

346cc AER (two-stroke twin) 1953

conventional sports model, which did well in production racing. Later came genuine racing machines of first 250cc, then 350cc, which, though outclassed at Grand Prix level, enjoyed great success in racing throughout Europe until about 1970. Aermacchi riders won the 1966 Lightweight Manx Grand Prix, the Junior race in 1967, 1970 and 1972 and finished second in the Junior TT in 1969 and 1970. After a takeover in 1960 by America's Harley-Davidson, Aermacchi also made a line of lightweights directed at the US market, including the 150cc Breeza scooter which was a very unlikely wearer of the Harley-Davidson badge. In the early 1970s, two-strokes for both the road and racing appeared, with famous Italian rider Renzo Pasolini riding the racing versions in the 250cc and 350cc classes. He was tragically killed in the accident at Monza in 1973 that also claimed Finnish rider Jarno Saarinen.

Although the road machines still sold freely in the US, they eventually fell victim to the anti-pollution legislation that outlawed two-strokes there. By the late 1970s, Harley-Davidson had re-established the big V-twins in the US market.

In July 1978, Harley-Davidson had seen no future in its small two-stroke development and sold the Aermacchi factory at Varese to Claudio and Gianfranco Castiglioni, who started a new company on the site called Cagiva. Initially the Harley-Davidson two-strokes were simply rebadged as Cagivas, but the company soon developed its own machines, and went on to take over and save Ducati, as well as reviving the MV Agusta marque. So although the Aermacchi name no longer exists, it has played an important role in Italian motorcycle history.

AEROS • Czechoslovakia 1927–1929

Designed by Franz Brezina, the Aeros had a BMW-like frame with a leaf spring fork and German 347cc and 497cc Küchen three-valve ohc proprietary single-cylinder engines.

AETOS • Italy 1912–1914

Produced one model only, a 492cc V-twin 3·5hp machine.

AFW • Germany 1923–1925

Limited manufacture of 246cc ohv machines with engines supplied by the Bielefeld-based Hansa factory.

AGF • France 1948–1956

Well-known as a producer of scooters and motorcycles with 123cc and 173cc Ydral proprietary engines.

AGON • Germany 1924–1928

The Benninger-designed machines had different engines, including the 197cc Paqué, 346cc Bradshaw, 498cc Kèchen and JAP units from 173cc to 996cc. The 746cc and 996cc JAP engined Agons were V twins.

AGRATI • Italy 1958–

Agrati made bicycle frames and, post war, mopeds and scooters, including the 50cc to 150cc Capri scooter range. The engines were supplied by Garelli to whom Agrati supplied frames in turn. In 1961 the two companies were merged to their mutual benefit. See also Garelli.

AGS • The Netherlands 1971–

Motocross machines with 123cc two-stroke engines supplied by Sachs, Puch, Zündapp and other makers.

AIGLON • France 1908–1953

Zurcher, Minerva, Mirus, Peugeot, AMC, FMC and others supplied engines for many years to Aiglon. Debarelle's last models had 123cc and 174cc ohv AMC engines and FMC-built 248cc two-strokes.

AIKOKU • Japan c1934

Lightweight 50cc machines built by Tetsuji Makita with Meguro gearboxes and sv engines made by JAC and HMS.

175cc Aermacchi Chimera (horizontal ohv single) 1956

AJS • England 1911–1969

The Stevens brothers, Harry, George, Jack and Joe, experimented with petrol engines as early as 1897 at their father's engineering works in Wolverhampton. They went on to make excellent air- and water-cooled engines for early motorcycles, tricars and light four wheelers. In 1909, using Jack's initials, (Albert John Stevens), they formed the AJS company and in 1914 entered the Junior TT with 350cc side valve engine bikes with all chain drive, two-speed gearboxes and two-speed 'overdrive'. Riders Eric and Cyril Williams finished 1-2, Eric Williams setting the fastest lap time at more than 47mph. With a new trend-setting ohv machine, Cyril Williams won the 1920 Junior, and in 1921 Eric Williams and H R Davies again scored 1-2. Sensationally, Davies went on to win the Senior race - on his 350cc AJS.

In 1922 came yet another 1-2 in the Junior TT, but there was no further TT victory for AJS until 1930, when Jimmy Guthrie sprang a surprise in the Lightweight class. For 1926, AJS introduced chain-driven ohc racers and, throughout the 1920s, was renowned for its excellent sports models, including the celebrated ohv 350cc 'Big Port'.

However, the Stevens brothers over-reached themselves with ventures into cars, trucks, buses and even radios, and had to sell out to the Collier brothers, makers of Matchless motorcycles, in 1931. As Associated Motor Cycles Ltd (AMC), the Matchless and AJS ranges were rationalised in the 1930s, but AMC continued to make the ohc sports and racing AJS models. It also showed an ohc V-four at Olympia in 1935, which appeared as a 'blown' 500cc racer in 1936, but without success. It reappeared again with water-cooling in 1938, but, although this version was blisteringly fast, its handling was atrocious. Walter Rusk lapped at 100mph on one in the 1939 Ulster Grand Prix before retiring.

Post-war, AJS launched new 350cc and 500cc singles, with 'Teledraulic' front forks and soon with swinging arm rear suspension. The concern also offered up-to-date 500cc vertical twins, followed by 550cc, 600cc and 650cc versions, notable for their use of a three-bearing crankshaft. AJS also raced a brand new horizontal engined parallel twin - the dohc 500cc 'Porcupine' - on which Les Graham won the first 500cc World Championship in 1948. The next year, he had all but won the 1949 Senior TT when his magneto broke two minutes from the chequered flag! The factory continued racing the Porcupines until 1954 with considerable success. Although it also raced the single-cylinder 350cc chain driven ohc 7R (Rod Colman winning the 1954 Junior on a special three-valve version), this machine won its fame in the hands of scores of private owners and was the mainstay of the Junior class in Europe for many years. AJS riders won the Junior Manx Grand Prix ten times between 1950 and 1965. In trials and motocross, 350cc and 500cc AJS machines performed as well as any others, and although often considered conservative in retrospect, the post-war AJS models exactly suited the taste and temper of the times, selling for export as freely as they did at home.

Despite new lightweight 250cc and 350cc models for 1958, AMC sales declined in the 1960s and so did profits, largely due to bad management. The company collapsed in 1967 and was sold to Manganese Bronze Holdings. It attempted to keep alive the name AJS on Villiers-engined motocross machines, but finally gave up to concentrate on another AMC make, Norton. So ended nearly 60 years of a world famous marque. Celebrated riders associated with AJS as well as those mentioned include: Jimmy Simpson, Walter Handley, Frank Longman, Bert Denly, Jock West, Hugh Viney, George Rowley, Bob McIntyre and Alistair King. Although production of AJS largely ceased in 1967, two-strokes based on the Villiers Starmaker engine were made for some years.

498cc AJS H10 1927

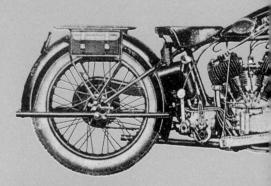

996cc AJS (sv V-twin) 1930

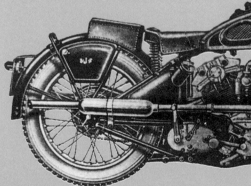

496cc AJS (ohc V-four prototype) 1935

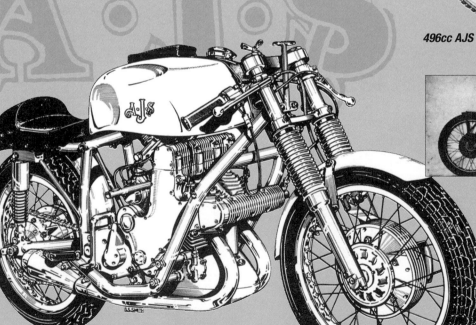

498cc AJS Porcupine (ohc twin) 1947

495cc AJS (supercharged ohc V-four) 1936

348cc AJS 'Boy Racer' (ohc) 1948

348cc AJS (3 ohc 3-valve works racer) 1953

678cc AJW (ohv JAP) 1929

490cc AJW (ohv JAP) 1952

173cc AKD Sport (ohv) 1929

AIM • Italy 1974–

Producer of sports machines, especially motocross versions with 49cc and 124cc Franco Morini two-stroke engines.

AIROLITE • England 1921–1923

Lightweight machines with 110cc Simplex two-stroke engines.

AJAX • England 1923–1924

Cheaply assembled machines with open frames. These housed 147cc, 247cc and 269cc Villiers two-stroke and 346cc Blackburne sv engines.

AJR • Scotland 1925–1926

One of the few Scottish makes, A. J. Robertson of Edinburgh built machines which housed 346cc and 490cc single-cylinder ohv engines made by JAP in London. Robertson rode them in many sporting events.

AJW • England 1926–1977

Designed by A. J. Wheaton as a machine to compete with Brough-Superior motorcycles, the AJW had at first big V-twin sv and ohv JAP and British-Anzani engines of 678cc and 996cc capacity. Beautifully made, with saddle tanks and a very low saddle position, Sturmey-Archer gearboxes, Pilgrim oil-pumps, Binks and Amal carburetters, they were expensive. So AJW produced smaller models with 172cc and 247cc Villiers engines. During the 1930s, most AJW machines had 496cc single-cylinder ohv power units made by Python (Rudge), JAP and Stevens (the Stevens brothers, former owners of the AJS factory). After 1945 the reorganized AJW factory, now owned by J. O. Ball, built

beautiful 498cc vertical twins with JAP sv engines. Limited production of these engines forced AJW to stop manufacture of these machines. Assisted by Ball's son Alan, only 49cc mopeds with Sachs and Franco Morini engines appeared on the market until AJW folded in 1977.

AKD • England 1926–1933

Successor to Abingdon motorcycles. The factory still exists as manufacturer of tools. The range of models included 147cc, 173cc and 198cc ohv singles and 298cc and 346cc sv singles of AKD's own design and manufacture. 173cc supersports models raced successfully around 1930.

AKKENS • England 1919–1922

Made by a small company, Akkens motorcycles had 292cc Union two-stroke engines with deflector-type pistons.

ALATO • Italy 1923–1925

Made by the Gosio brothers at Turin, Alato machines had its own 131cc two-stroke engines.

ALBA • Germany 1919–1924

A good four-stroke machine with 198cc and 247cc sv engines. The last model was a unit-design 249cc ohv version. Alba at Stettin (now Poland), owned by Alfred Baruch, also built delivery three-wheelers and supplied motorcycle engines to other factories including Huy and Teco. Although it stopped motorcycle manufacture in the mid-1920s, a company headed by Alfred Baruch's son Manfred supplied spares until the mid-1930s.

ALBERT • Germany 1922–1924

During the hyper-inflation period in Germany built 183cc two-strokes with its own engines, in limited quantities.

ALBERTUS • Germany 1922–1924

Was the original manufacturer of motorcycles with the Julius Löwy-designed crude-oil two-stroke engines of 113cc, 142cc and 176cc. While the engines were made at the Königsberg works, complete Albertus motorcycles came from Achern in Badonia.

ALCYON • France 1902–late 1960s

Once a leading motorcycle producer. Over the years bought other French makes including Labor, Thomann, Amor and Olympique. In pre-1914 days built potent V-twins and vertical twins, and when Alcyon competed in 1912 in the Isle of Man TT races, it had 348cc ohv singles with two inlet valves and two exhaust valves. These engines were designed by Zurcher. Between the wars, most Alcyon models had 98cc

249cc Alba (ohv) 1924

142cc Albertus (two-stroke crude oil) 1922

to 248cc two-stroke and 173cc to 498cc four-stroke sv and ohv engines. Some bigger versions already had shaft drive around 1930, and some had pressed-steel frames. 173cc Alcyon racing models, ridden by Joly and Lemasson, won many races in the late 1920s and early 1930s. After 1945 Alcyon produced two- and four-strokes up to 248cc with AMC, Zurcher, Vap and other engines and concentrated on 48cc mopeds and similar designs.

ALDBERT • Italy 1953–1959

Well-designed typical Italian machines with 49cc to 173cc two-stroke and 173cc to 246cc four-stroke ohv engines. The Razzo model had a 174cc 60mm x 61mm bore/stroke ohv unit-design, four-speed gearbox and a 93mph top speed.

ALDIMI • Belgium 1953–1956

Produced its own Sarolera-engined 200cc scooter before building Piatti scooters under licence.

ALECTO • England 1919–1924

Had its own 295cc and 345cc two-stroke deflector-type three-port engines and belt drive to the rear wheel. An all-chain 345cc model was made 1923–1924. It had 76mm bore and 76mm stroke.

ALERT • England 1903–1906

Made by Smith & Molesworth at Coventry, these machines had 2.35hp, 2.75hp and 3.25hp Sarolea engines.

ALEU • Spain 1953–1956

Conventional design with 198cc and 247cc two stroke engines of Spanish manufacture.

ALFA • Germany 1925–1928

Designed by the former BMW chief development engineer Alexander von Falkenhausen, the Alfa used a 172cc Villiers engine. Some later models had bigger ones including a 344cc vertical twin.

ALFA • Italy 1923–1926

Assembled machines with English 170cc ohv Norman and 346cc ohv Bradshaw and Blackburne engines. Limited production.

ALFA-GNOM • Austria 1926–1928

Made by Franz & Anton Rumpler, also the manufacturer of FAR motorcycles, the 598cc Alfa-Gnom had a single-cylinder ohc engine.

ALGE • Germany 1923–1931

Produced 173cc to 498cc single-cylinder sv and ohv machines of conventional design and also utility three-wheelers with motorcycle engines. Owned by Alfred Geissler, from 1928 onwards Alge also fitted 173cc and 347cc Villiers engines and 497cc sv Blackburne engines.

ALIPRANDI • Italy 1925–1930

Beautiful 123cc and 173cc machines with Swiss Moser ohv engines. Other models made by the Aliprandi brothers had 173cc to 498cc sv and ohv power units by JAP and Sturmey-Archer.

ALKO • Austria 1927–1930

Assembled motorcycles with sv and ohv JAP and MAG engines, with capacities from 490cc to 996cc. The last ones were V-twins.

ALLDAYS • England 1903–1915

As early as 1898 built De Dion-engined three wheelers, later cars and motorcycles. These had its own 499cc single-cylinder and 539cc V-twin sv engines. Concentrated afterwards on Allon motorcycles.

ALLEGRO • Switzerland 1925–early 1960s

Well-known make which won many races in the 175cc class with Marcel Bourquin and the manufacturer Arnold Grandjean in the saddle. These machines had 172cc Villiers Brooklands two-stroke racing engines. In 1929 Grandjean built a 344cc racer for his own use in races, which had two such engines coupled together in tandem. Production versions had engines up to 348cc, supplied by Villiers, MAG and Sturmey-Archer. Allegro supplied mopeds in later years.

ALLON • England 1915–1924

Already mentioned with Alldays, the Allon housed its own 292cc deflector-type two-stroke engine. The second model, supplied 1923-1924, had a 346cc sv engine made by JAP.

ALLRIGHT • Germany 1901–1927

Known in England as Vindec-Special and VS, the Allright was also sold in other countries under the Tiger and Roland trademark. Early models had Belgian Kelecom, Minerva and FN, from 1905 onwards German Fafnir engines and Belgian Truffault forks and swinging arms. In 1922 the German Cito works amalgamated with Allright, with the result that Allright also produced the famous KG (Krieger-Gnädig) motorcycle. This was a 503cc, later 498cc ohv unit-design single with shaft drive to the rear wheel. The range also included 149cc two-strokes of the company's design and 248cc to 996cc sv and ohv JAP engines. Some models had MAG and Blackburne engines. All were of orthodox English design and also had many English components. In the mid-1920s, chief designer Rudi Albert modified the 1919 KG design, which now received a horizontal shaft to the rear wheel and also the improved ohv engine. Allright motorcycle production stopped when it decided to concentrate on the manufacture of Tiger forks, hubs and other accessories. Paul Henkel, a former KG technician, took over the production of these machines until his death in 1932. Among successful Allright and Allright-KG riders were Zündorf, Soenius, Ehrlenbruch, Kniebecke, Roggenbuck, Fast, and Karsch.

ALLSTATE • Austria 1953–1963

This is the name of Austrian Puch, Italian Vespa and American Cushman machines sold in the USA from about 1953 by Sears-Roebuck of Chicago through its nationwide branches. Allstate is a Sears trademark, also applied to car parts, insurance and so on.

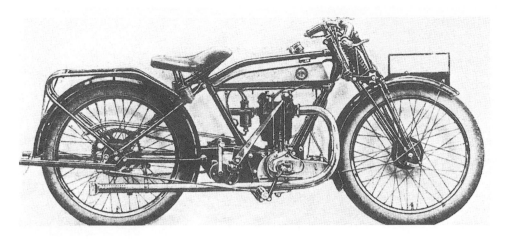

346cc Allright (ohv JAP) 1924

ALMA • France 1949–1959

Producer of mopeds, scooters and lightweight machines from 49cc to 149cc with its own engines and also proprietary engines made by Le Paulin and Ydral.

ALMORA • Germany 1924–1925

Interesting but not very successful design. Used Julius Löwy-developed 113cc, 138cc and 176cc two-stroke engines which ran on crude oil after they had been 'hotted up' on petrol. They failed because they didn't develop enough power and proved unreliable.

ALP • English 1912–1917

Was originally an English branch of the Swiss Moto-Rêve motorcycle factory. Produced models with 3hp and 3.5hp V-twins, vertical twin-cylinder engines and as a bread-and-butter model a 199cc machine with an English Precision proprietary engine. The last Alp had a 348cc two-stroke engine.

ALPHONSE THOMANN • France 1908–1923

Once a well-known make, and not the same as Thomann. Main production concentrated around 98cc to 173cc two-strokes.

ALPINO • Italy 1948–1962

Typical Italian post-war machines from 48cc to 174cc with two- and four-stroke ohv engines. 48cc models broke world records with Tamarozzi, Pennati, Pasini and Sozzani.

ALTA • Wales 1968–1971

Trials models with 50cc, 80cc and 125cc Suzuki engines, made by the son of Geoffrey Taylor, famous for his pre- and post-war Alta Sports and racing cars.

ALTEA • Italy 1939–1941

Designed by former MAS boss Alberico Seilig for the famous Max Türkheimer motorcycle company at Milan, the modern Altea had a 198cc unit-design engine with vertical overhead valves among its interesting features. Türkheimer, since 1897 Ariel importer and once even shareholder of the English Ariel works, also built Astra motorcycles.

ALTENA • Holland 1900–1906

Dutch Pioneer from Heemstede-Harlem, fitted De Dion and own engines of 2hp and 3hp.

ALTER • France 1955–1956

Small French manufacturer of 49cc machines with various two-stroke engines.

ALWIN • England 1920

Shaft drive 1¾hp two-stroke scooter built by pram maker, Alwin Manufacturing Co., Teddington, London.

AMAG • Germany 1924–1925

Another small producer of lightweight machines. These had 149cc Bekamo two-stroke engines which used a pumping cylinder in the crankcase.

AMAZONAS • Brazil 1980–1986

Huge, massively heavy machines powered by 1600cc VW Beetle flat-four car engines.

AMBAG • Germany 1923

Fitted 155cc Gruhn sv single-cylinder engines into its own frames.

AMBASSADOR • England 1947–1964

Owned by ex-motorcycle, car and motor-boat racing driver Kaye Don, the Ascot-based company was also importer of German Zündapp motorcycles and American Pontiac cars. All Ambassador motorcycles and scooters housed 147cc to 248cc two-stroke Villiers engines. When he retired in 1964, everything connected with Ambassador manufacture was sold to the DMW factory.

AMBROSINI • Italy 1951–1953

Built the Freccia Azzura scooter powered by a 150cc Sachs engine.

AMC • USA 1912–1915

There was no connection between the Allied Motor Corporation of Chicago and either Associated Motor Cycles Ltd of London or the French AMC proprietary engine concern. The American AMC was a typically sturdy big V-twin with a 980cc ioe engine and bottom-link front forks.

AMERICAN • America 1911–1914

It is possible that this make was identical with the above AMC, although the address reads American Motorcycle Co. of Chicago. Manufacture consisted of a 550cc, 4hp single.

AMERICAN • America 1978–1979

Used on ohv 748cc vertical twin power unit, designed by the former Triumph (Coventry) technician Jack Wilkes.

AMERICAN-X • America 1910–1930

Made by Ignaz Schwinn's Excelsior Company at Chicago, this was really a 996cc Excelsior ioe V-twin, exported to England. As there was already an English Excelsior factory, the American product was renamed American-X.

AMI • Germany 1921–1925

A 49cc ohv engine for bicycles designed by Heinrich Hillebrand, late of Hillebrand & Wolfmüller motorcycle-pioneering fame. A similar engine was made by the Columbus engine factory (later Horex) and called Gnom. Both had to be fitted in front of the pedalling gear. This started a fight between Ami and Gnom which lasted a long time in the courts.

AMI • Switzerland 1950–1954

Designed by Jaroslav Frei, former boss of the Czech Jawa factory, the Ami was a scooter with 98cc and later 123cc two-stroke engines.

AMMON • Germany 1923–1925

Interesting frame design, which consisted partly of tubes and partly of pressed steel. Used various proprietary engines which included DKW, Baumi and Bekamo two-strokes and the 123cc Paqué ohv engine.

AMO • Germany 1921–1924

Simple design of 146cc two-stroke lightweight machines.

AMR • Italy 1979–

Specialises in motocross, trial and enduro machines with German Sachs two-stroke engines from 123 to 400cc.

AMO • Germany 1950–1954

Mopeds with own 48cc two-stroke engines made by Westendarp & Pieper, a company which built TX motorcycles in the mid-1920s. The factory was at Berlin.

AMS • Spain 1954–1965

Assembled two-stroke motorcycles with 124cc, 198cc and 247cc Hispano-Villiers engines. It also built 248cc vertical twins.

ANCILOTTI • Italy 1967–1985

Maker of motocross, enduro and trials models, using Sachs, Hiro and Franco Morini engines of 50cc and 125cc. Later produced a 246cc model. Well thought of in its day, but production ceased in 1985.

ANCORA • Italy 1923–1939

For many years used 147cc to 347cc Villiers engines and won many races during the late 1920s when the late Raffaele Alberti rode a 172cc Brooklands Villiers-engined Ancora in competitions. Umberto Dei bought the factory in the early 1930s and built 60cc, 74cc and 98cc models. After 1945 Dei supplied more lightweights, this time with the Garelli-built 39cc Mosquito bicycle engine.

ANDREES • Germany 1923–1929

Assembled good machines with oil-cooled 346cc and 496cc flat twin Bradshaw engines and after 1925 also used proprietary units made by MAG and Blackburne. These included 346cc single-cylinder and 498cc and 598cc V-twin MAG motors with ioe valves. Among successful Andrees riders were Heinz Kürten and Franz Sieder. The end came in 1929, when H. W. Andrees built a new factory for the mass-production of 198cc single-cylinder two-stroke motorcycles and engines. The commercial depression of that period finished his ambitions.

ANGLIAN • England 1903–1912

Anglian, of Beccles, Suffolk, made motorcycles and forecars with De Dion and, later, other proprietary engines. Featured two speeds and chain drive. Well regarded and successful in early long distance trials.

ANGLO-DANE • Denmark 1912–1914

Built in Copenhagen by Fredricksen Motors, the Anglo-Dane was made from English components and with different engines of JAP and Villiers manufacture. Production was on a limited scale.

ANKER • Germany 1949–1958

A once-famous German bicycle factory which built Ilo and Sachs-engined two-stroke mopeds and motorcycles from 48cc to 244cc. Afterwards it concentrated on business machines including cash registers, but closed down early in 1976. The motorcycle production was transferred in 1952 to a branch factory at Paderborn. The main works was at Bielefeld.

ANTOINE • Belgium 1900–1910

A pioneer company which first fitted Kelecom engines and afterward produced 3hp, 3.5hp and 4hp singles and 4.5hp and 5hp V-twins. It also supplied engines to other motorcycle manufacturers. Other Antoine products included car and aero engines.

APACHE • America 1907–1911

Made by Brown & Beck at Denver, Colorado, the Apache had a rearward-facing 597cc single-cylinder ioe engine of its own manufacture.

APEX • Germany 1925–1926

Assembled sporting machines at Cologne with 247cc and 347cc ohv Blackburne single-cylinder engines. The production was on a small scale.

API • India 1955–1987

Versions of the 150cc and 175cc Lambretta scooter produced in Bombay.

APOLLO • Sweden 1951–1992

Now part of the Volvo-controlled MCB group, Apollo motorcycles used among others 123cc Villiers and 198cc Zèndapp engines. Production in the 1980s then concentrated on 49cc mopeds.

AQUILA • Italy 1927–1935

The Turin-built Aquila was originally a 174cc two-stroke and later ohv machine. Made by a small company, during the 1930s it used English Rudge-built Python 248cc, 348cc and 498cc four-valve, single-cylinder ohv engines. Other models had the 497cc Küchen sv single-cylinder and the Italian OBM engine.

124cc Ancilotti (two-stroke Sachs) 1974

AQUILA • Italy 1953–1958

The Rome-built Aquila had no connection with the older machine of the same name. The range of models included 48cc, 123cc and 158cc two-strokes and 98cc and 174cc ohv four-strokes of sound design and finish.

ARAB • England 1923-1926

Simple lightweight machines with 147cc Villiers engines.

ARBINET • France 1927-1934

Used exclusively its own two-stroke engines of 98cc, 173cc, 198cc, 347cc and 497cc capacity in conventional frames.

ARC • Spain 1954-1956

Hispano-Villiers-engined 123cc two-strokes of simple design.

ARCO • Germany 1922–1931

Water-cooled 248cc and 348cc ohv single-cylinder machines and from 1929 onwards also a water-cooled 498cc ohc single formed the range of Speyer/Rhine-built Arco models. From 1927 onwards, the make was owned by an Amsterdam finance group.

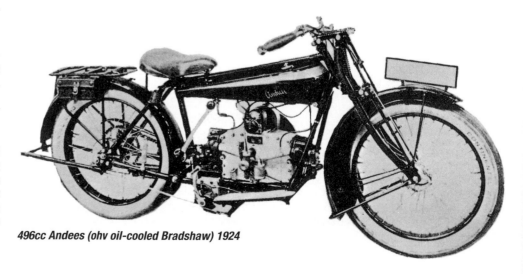

496cc Andees (ohv oil-cooled Bradshaw) 1924

APRILIA • Italy 1975–

Aprilia was founded in 1968 to produce bicycles on a small scale, but the passion of the founder's son, Ivano Beggio, was for motorcycles, and in 1970 he built himself a trials bike with which to enter competitions. In 1975 Aprilia began making its own production motorcycles.

These were so successful that in 1980 Aprilia committed itself fully to motorcycle production alone, making mainly trials and motocross machines for the home market.

In 1990 Aprilia turned its attention to foreign markets, concentrating initially on Europe. At the same time it produced its first scooter, the Amico, the first in a line of scooters which now includes the executive Leonardo, futuristic Area 51 and retro-styled Scarabeo.

In 1992 the credibility of Aprilia was underlined by an agreement with BMW to assemble the Germans' F650 single at the Italian Noale factory. Many elements of the design of the BMW were also shared with Aprilia's own Pegaso trail bike, introduced in 1993 and comprehensively updated as the Pegaso 3 in 1997, although it was still recognisably an individual Aprilia product - for example, the use of five valves in the single-cylinder engine was unique.

Another notable Aprilia was the Moto 6.5, introduced in 1995. Styled by famous designer Philippe Starck, the

49cc Aprilia RS50 (two-stroke single) 1999

bike attracted plenty of interest but flopped in the showrooms.

Aprilia commenced its Grand Prix programme - which went on to give it real credibility and world recognition - in 1985, with a home-built 250, powered by a tandem-

249cc Aprilia RS250 (two-stroke twin Suzuki) 1998

649cc Aprilia Moto 6.5 (dohc single) 1995

twin Rotax motor and ridden by Loris Reggiani, who brought the firm its first GP win at Misano two years later. Reggiani stayed with Aprilia pretty much for the rest of his career, which ended in the late nineties, and his skills as a development rider were of great use to the Noale factory.

Gradually Aprilia's GP engines became more its own than Rotax's, and by the time Alessandro Gramigni won the factory's first world title in 1992, in the 125 class, the machines could rightly be called Aprilias. Though the bikes were initially notoriously unreliable, owner Ivano Beggio oversaw his factory race operation with pragmatism and generosity and step by step the machines became a dominant force in the 125 and 250 world championships. Beggio wasn't slow to capitalise on racetrack success, manufacturing a whole array of replica sports bikes and scooters for the street. Within the space of a few years Aprilia had became almost as well known as long-established Italian marques like Ducati.

652cc Aprilia Pegaso 3 (dohc 5-valve single) 1997

998cc Aprilia RSV Mille (dohc V-twin) 1999

Charismatic Italian Max Biaggi was the man who really put the marque on the map, riding Aprilia's super-fast RSV250 to three consecutive 250 world championships from 1994 to 1996, roundly defeating rival factory efforts from Honda and Yamaha. Kazuto Sakata added the 1994 125 crown to the factory's list of successes and the Japanese repeated the feat in 1998, when Loris Capirossi also won the 250 title on his RSV250.

In 1994 Aprilia became the first factory in two decades to enter a twin-cylinder machine in 500 GPs. The theory was that the bike's higher corner speed would allow it to compete with faster four-cylinder machines around the modern generation of tight, twisty GP circuits. The RSV twin started life as a 400 and was gradually bored and stroked to just under 500cc. By 1999, however, it had failed to do better than a third-place finish at the 1997 Dutch GP. Aprilia continues to be the lone believer in disc valve induction, a system long championed by the factory's chief race engineer, Dutchman Jan Witteveen. Rival factories involved in GP racing prefer reed valve induction for the system's more friendly power characteristics. Witteveen meanwhile uses electronics to calm his engines' vicious power delivery, without compromising their superior top-end power.

However, the road bike sold on the back of the GP successes, the RS250 two-stroke sports twin, used reed valves, as the engine was sourced from Suzuki's RGV250 road bike, although as with Rotax units the Italians made several modifications of their own.

The same applied to the smaller 125cc sports bikes, such as the AF1 Replica of 1988, which evolved through the Futura AF1 and Europa AF1 of 1991 to the RS125 of 1993, Europe's most successful sports 125.

In 1998 Aprilia entered the highly competitive big capacity sports bike market with the introduction of the V-twin RSV Mille, the 1000cc 60-degree V-twin engine being designed in collaboration with Rotax of Austria (like the Pegaso), although mostly an Aprilia effort.

A limited edition, high specification version, the RSV Mille SP, was introduced in 1999 to homologate the company's World Superbike machines, due to compete the same year alongside the company's Grand Prix efforts.

The RSV marks the first major step for the company in its declared aim of producing models in every market sector, to compete directly with the dominant Japanese. It is currently the fastest growing scooter manufacturer in Italy, threatening the giant Piaggio's position as market leader, so has the technical and financial foundation to do just that.

346cc Aco (ohv water-cooled) 1927

499cc Aco (ohv water-cooled) 1929

ARDEA • Italy 1928–1933

A Moto Guzzi-like design with a flat single-cylinder 173cc and later also 248cc ioe and ohv engines. Competed successfully in trials with Silvio Vailati, Virginio Fieschi and Bruno Martelli.

ARDEN • England 1912–1920

Small but versatile company which built small cars and also motorcycles with 269cc two-stroke Villiers as well as its own engines. These were also supplied to other producers, including Priory.

ARDENT • France 1950–1957

Mini-scooters and motorcycles with 49cc and 64cc Vap and Le Paulin engines.

ARDIE • Germany 1919–1958

Founded by ex-Premier technician Arno Dietrich, the first Ardie machines had Ardie's own 305cc and 348cc two-stroke deflector-type engines. After 1925 Ardie - owned by the Bendit family since Dietrich's fatal accident in 1922 - exclusively used JAP engines of 246cc to 996cc. Best seller was the 490cc single-cylinder sv machine, but there were even V-twins of 45hp, and 55hp ohv JAP racing engines. Frames made from duralumin were used in the early 1930s. Bark, Küchen, Sturmey-Archer and Sachs afterwards

305cc Ardie (two-stroke) 1924

supplied engines up to 598cc to Ardie. Tubular frames were used again and in 1938 Richard Küchen designed an interesting 348cc V-twin ohv machine with the engine transversely mounted. It never made quantity production. After the war, designer Noack created new crossflow two-strokes with flat pistons from 124cc to 346cc. The last ones were vertical twins. The Nuremberg factory was at that time owned by the Barthel-controlled Dürkopp works at Bielefeld. Ardie was successful in races during the 1920s and early 1930s. Besides the Thumshim team—Hans, Konrad and Georg—it had excellent riders in Franz Islinger, Karl Dobberkau, Gerd in der Elst, Josef Schörg and Karl Dobler and won many events, including TT races in Austria and Hungary.

ARDITO • Italy 1951–1954

A small producer with a big production programme of various two-strokes from 48cc to 98cc and ohv four-strokes from 123cc to 173cc.

ARGENTRE • France 1927–1932

Assembled machines with many English components. Built 247cc and 347cc two-strokes with its own engines and also 348cc sv and ohv models with JAP engines.

ARGEO • Germany 1924–1927

Berlin-built two-strokes with its own 198cc and 246cc deflector-type engines.

ARGUL • Germany 1923–1926

Limited production of two-strokes from 146cc to 198cc with engines supplied by DKW and Bubi and of four-stroke machines with Alba power units.

ARGYLE • England c1913

Limited production of JAP-powered motorcycles at Birkenhead.

ARGYLL • England c1913

Small production of JAP-powered machines built at Stoke, Coventry.

ARI • Germany 1924–1925

Another small producer of 146cc two-stroke motorcycles with DKW engines.

ARIEL • England 1902–1970

See panel

ARIEL • Australia c1920

JAP-engined machines built by the Ariel Cycle and Motor Works of Footscray, Victoria.

ARISTOS • Germany 1923–1924

Designed by Johannes Pässler, the 614cc Aristos was a very unorthodox machine with a water-cooled flat twin sv engine. The Mars-like frame was made of welded steel plates and allowed a low seat position. The Berlin-based company never developed this machine to the full. This led to more reorganisations and also to two more trade names for the Aristos inside of three years: Menos and Sterna. The differences between the three makes were small; they included, besides different tank transfers, the colour and the lfork design.

ARLEN NESS • America 1960–

Manufacturer of custom motorcycles in California, probably the best known and most innovative in the world.

ARLIGUE • France 1950–1953

Small assembler of motorcycles with AMC and Ydral proprietary engines from 98cc to 248cc.

ARIEL • England 1902–1970

Built De Dion-engined three-wheelers at Birmingham in 1898 and four years later began the manufacture of motorcycles with 3.5hp single-cylinder White & Poppe engines. In later years, Ariel built them under license. When the 1914 war broke out, the Ariel range consisted of 498cc sv singles and 998cc ioe V-twins. Other models had 348cc and 669cc V-twin power units, which were superseded by 794cc V-twins. In 1921 a 586cc single with 86.4mm bore and 100mm stroke came on the market, followed in 1922 by a 664cc single with 92mm bore and 100mm stroke. Another new model was a MAG-engined 992cc V-twin which was sold for £125 solo and £160 with sidecar. The price for the 499cc sv single was then £95. By 1924 the Ariel range consisted of a 247cc

sv Blackburne-engined machine, 498cc sv and ohv models and a 993cc ioe V-twin.

Ariel, then owned by Jack Sangster, in 1927 took on the young technician Edward Turner. Chief designer was Val Page, who designed new 498cc ohv and 557cc sv singles, which proved to be bestsellers. In charge of publicity was Vic Mole, and of competitions the famous Harold Perrey. New 248cc and 348cc machines appeared soon afterwards and 1931 saw the introduction of the well-known 498cc Square Four, with the four air-cooled cylinders set in a square formation and the ohv gear operated by a chain-driven camshaft. This machine was designed by Edward Turner. Redesigned Square Fours of 596cc and 996cc followed during the 1930s, and also models with forward inclined engines (slopers) and some very nice sports models, the 248cc, 348cc

and 498cc ohv Red Hunter range. The big sv single was now 598cc and on the big Square Fours the ohc valve gear was superseded by pushrods.

In 1936 Edward Turner left to become boss of Triumph in Coventry, after Jack Sangster bought that factory. During the war, many 347cc ohv Ariel machines were used by the Forces. Main Ariel production after the war concentrated around 347cc and 497cc ohv Red Hunter singles including competition models, 498cc ohv vertical twins, a 598cc sv single and the 997cc Square Four. This machine sold in 1952 for £287 10s. At the other end of the scale, the 197cc Colt, an ohv single selling for £134, came into production and also the twin-cylinder Huntmaster range, including 646cc ohv versions. Jack Sangster, also head of BSA at Birmingham since the early fifties, moved Ariel nearer to Armoury Road. Many BSA

557cc Ariel (sv) 1929

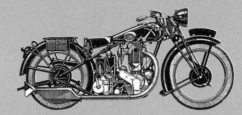

497cc Ariel (ohc) 1930

498cc Ariel Square Four (ohc) 1931

Ariel square four advertising poster of 1931

and Ariel parts were identical. Edward Turner moved from Meriden (Triumph) to Armoury Road (BSA). He was also responsible for Ariel - which eventually moved from Selly Oak (Birmingham) into the BSA factory - and created in the early 1960s the 49cc Pixie, an ohv single, which did not gain much fame. In contrast, the famous 247cc vertical twin two-strokes, the Leader and the Arrow which were designed once more by Val Page, proved to be excellent machines. A 197cc version was the last real Ariel machine to be built. By 1970 the name Ariel was unfortunately no more on a two-wheel machine. All that are left are memories of success in trials and of famous trials riders, including Harold Perrey, Fred Povey, Ted Ray, Ron Langston and the famous Sammy Miller.

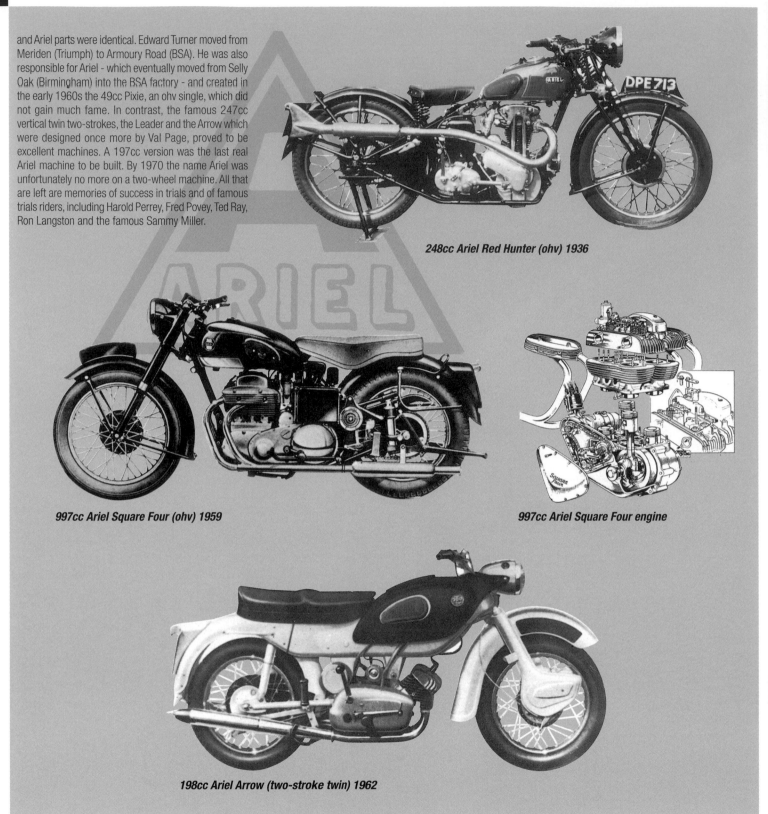

248cc Ariel Red Hunter (ohv) 1936

997cc Ariel Square Four (ohv) 1959

997cc Ariel Square Four engine

198cc Ariel Arrow (two-stroke twin) 1962

ARMAC • America 1911–1913

Produced 14 different models with its own 4hp single-cylinder and 7hp V-twin engines.

ARMIS • English 1920–1923

Well-made machines with 269cc Precision two-stroke, 293cc and 348cc JAP, 346cc and 538cc Blackburne and 654cc V-twin ioe MAG engines.

ARMOR • France 1910–1934

Once a popular make and since the 1920s part of Alcyon. Produced two-strokes from 98cc and four-strokes from 173cc upwards. These included 498cc ohv and ohc unit-design singles, some with shaft-drive to the rear wheel.

ARMSTRONG • England 1902–1905

Assembled machines with 211cc Minerva engines and frames supplied by Chater-Lea.

ARMSTRONG • England 1913–1914

Only a single model with a 269cc Villiers engine was made before WW1 stopped manufacture.

ARMSTRONG • England 1980–1987

An industrial group, which took over CCM and Cotton. Produced mainly competition machines with Rotax engines, and four-strokes for the British army.

Arlen Ness Antiqueness 1998

ARNO • England 1906–1914

Coventry-made machines with 249cc, 348cc and 498cc sv engines. Limited production.

ARROW • England 1913–1917

Birmingham-built 211cc two-stroke machines with engines supplied by Levis and Precision.

ARROW • America 1909–1914

Lightweight motorcycles with 1hp engines of own manufacture.

ASAHI • Japan 1953–1965

Old arms factory which already built in 1909 prototypes of motorcycles. When they went into quantity production in 1953, most models had 123cc and 173cc two-stroke engines of own design and manufacture.

ASB • Germany 1953–1954

Limited production of 50cc mopeds and a scooter with a 50cc Zündapp motor mounted over the front wheel.

ASCOT • England 1905–1906

Assembler of motorcycles with Minerva and Antoine engines.

ASCOT-PULLIN • England 1928–1930

Cyril Pullin's most advanced motorcycle design, the 498cc Ascot-Pullin, was built at Letchworth. It had 82mm bore, 94mm stroke, a flat single-cylinder ohv engine with aluminum pistons, dry-sump lubrication, 3-speed gearbox,

fully enclosed chains, hydraulically operated brakes, quickly detachable and interchangeable wheels, handlebars of pressed steel with a range of built-in instruments, leg-shields, windscreen etc. Despite the comparatively low price of £75, the Ascot-Pullin failed to gain much popularity.

ASD • Australia c1913

Assembled motorcycles in limited numbers using English-built Precision engines.

ASHFORD • England 1905

Assembled machines with 3.5hp engines supplied by Minerva and Fafnir.

ASL • England 1907–1915

A company formed to publicise and exploit Professor Archibald Sharpe's pneumatic suspension units - hence Air Springs Ltd. Used mainly single-cylinder and V-twin JAP engines in large luxurious frames with air springing fore and aft. A very clever idea and well made machines, but before their time.

ASPES • Italy 1967–1982

Though Aspes used Franco Morini and Minarelli engines in some of its machines, it mainly relied on its own 125cc two-stroke unit, with five- and six-speed gearbox. The RCC Moto Cross and Juma sports road bike (the later capable of 85mph) both used this engine, while a full road race version was also offered in the late 1970s. The 125cc Aspes motocross model was particularly popular in Britain in schoolboy motocross.

ASSO • Italy 1927–1931

Sporting lightweights with own 174cc unit-design ohv engines.

ASTER • France 1898–1910

Originally a producer of proprietary engines during the pioneering period, Aster also built three-wheelers, cars and motorcycles. Most Aster engines had horizontally-split crankcases made of bronze. One of the most popular models was a 355cc single, which was also supplied to the Orient motorcycle factory in the USA.

ASTON • England 1923–1924

Was a 142cc two-stroke machine not unlike the Atlas. It had a deflector-type three-port engine with outside flywheel and was supplied with one, two and three-speed gearboxes and belt drive. Only the last versions could be supplied with belt-cum-chain drive.

ASTORIA • Germany 1923–1925

Built 289cc two-stroke machines on a limited scale. Nestoria, another Nuremberg factory, took over Astoria when it ran into difficulties.

ASTORIA • Italy 1950–1957

Designed and produced by ex-racer Virginio Fieschi, Astoria of Milano built nice two-strokes and ohv singles from 124 to 246cc. The range also included a fast 174cc production racer with an ohc engine of own manufacture.

ASTRA • Germany 1923–1925

The first Astra had 293cc Bosch-Douglas flat twin engines;

Arlen Ness 'Aluminess' 1998

614cc Aristos (sv flat twin, water-cooled) 1929

496cc ASL (sv JAP) 1909

from 1924 onwards Astra also fitted 348cc and 490cc (496cc) sv and ohv JAP and Blackburne single-cylinder engines into low frames. Ernst Henne, who later broke world records for BMW, in 1924–1925 rode an Astra

machine with a 348cc ohv Blackburne engine. SMW at Munich built the Bosch-Douglas flat twins under license.

ASTRA • Italy 1931–1951

A famous former Italian motorcycle importer, Max Türkheimer & Co. at Milan was since 1898 closely connected with Components Ltd. (Ariel) at Birmingham and shareholder of Charles Sangster's company. This arrangement continued when Jack Sangster took over from his father. Türkheimer used many Ariel-made parts, especially frames, for his Astra machines; many 248cc and 498cc Astra sv and ohv singles used Ariel engine parts. Other models were 123cc, 174cc and 220cc. In pre-1914 days, Otav and other motorcycles were also made by the Türkheimer group.

ASTRAL • France 1919–1923

Concentrated on 98cc and 122cc two-strokes and was part of the Austral group which was in turn part of the Alcyon combine.

ATALA • Italy 1925–1934

An assembled machine which used mainly English components. Among them were the 174cc to 496cc sv and ohv engines made by JAP and Blackburne. Atala is currently a trading name owned and still used by the Cessare Rizzato company.

ATALA • Italy 1954–

Accessory manufacturer which also built 50cc, 70cc 100cc and 125cc mopeds and lightweights with its own two-stroke engines. Also made scooters. Production was considerable, but spasmodic.

ATLANTA-DUO • England 1935–1937

Made by OEC at Portsmouth, Hants., these machines had duplex steering, rear springing, foot boards, leg-shields and a low position (19 inches from ground) and Dunloppilo seats for two. The JAP engines used were 248cc and 490cc ohv singles and 746cc sv V-twins.

ATLANTIC • France 1929–1932

Limited manufacture of 98cc two-strokes and 347cc and 497cc ohv and ohc engines made by Chaise, Blackburne and other suppliers of proprietary engines. At a Paris show, Atlantic exhibited a motorcycle equipped with a fully enclosed engine.

492cc Italian Astra (ohv) 1939

248cc German Atlas (two-stroke) 1925

142cc English Atlas (two-stroke) 1924

ATLANTIC • Germany 1923–1925

Small producer of 193cc sv single-cylinder motorcycles with engines supplied by the former Hansa factory at Bielefeld.

ATLANTIK • Germany 1925–1926

Built 173cc two-stroke machines on a limited scale.

ATLANTIS • Germany 1926–1932

Made by a small company, the first models had its own 348cc and 398cc single-cylinder two-stroke engines. From 1927 onwards, 497cc ohc Kèchen, 498cc sv JAP, 598cc sv Blackburne and 498cc, 746cc and 990cc ioe MAG engines came into production. All MAG engines were V-twins.

ATLAS • England 1913–1914

A small company which used 492cc JAP and 496cc sv single-cylinder Blumfield proprietary engines.

ATLAS • England 1922–1925

Birmingham-built 142cc two-stroke of simple design with forward-facing carburetor and belt drive to the rear wheel. Used one and two-speed gearboxes. Price with 2-speed gearbox: £30/9.

ATLAS • Germany 1924–1929

Fitted own 248cc and 348cc single-cylinder two-stroke engines. Designer/manufacturer Schleif rode these machines with success in hill-climbs.

ATTOLINI • Italy 1920–1923

Equipped with rear suspension, the Attolini housed a 269cc Villiers two-stroke engine.

AUGUSTA • Italy 1924–1931

Designed by Angelo Blatto, the Augusta was launched with an advanced 350cc overhead camshaft engine. Later models had 125cc and 175cc engines still with overhead camshafts. Earned a sporting reputation, being fast, but they were also unreliable. Like many small companies, probably lacked the resources to develop a design advanced for its day.

AURORA • England 1902–1907

Used a variety of proprietary engines from 2.25hp to 3.25hp. Engine suppliers included MMC, Coronet, Whitley, Coventry-built Condor and other makes.

AURORA • Isle of Man 1919–1921

Built in Douglas—the Aurora was a machine with a 318cc two-stroke engine made by Dalm. The other Isle of Man-built motorcycle was the Peters.

AURORA • New Zealand 1913–?

Manufactured in England by E. A. Radnall & Co, maker of the Radco motorcycle using its own 211cc two-stroke engine. Sold as the Aurora in New Zealand by T. W. Vickery Ltd., Invercargill, New Zealand.

AUSTEN • England 1903–1906

Small assembler who fitted 2.25hp Kelecom engines, among others.

AUSTRAL • France 1908–1932

Old established factory. For many years produced 211cc two-strokes, and after 1918 ones with 246cc capacity. The range also included machines with 246cc and 346cc sv and ohv JAP and Zurcher engines. Austral was also part of the Alcyon group of companies.

AUSTRIA • Austria 1903–1907

Was one of the first producers of a bolt-on bicycle engine. Designed by Josef Mezera, it produced 0.8hp. His son Rudolf Mezera was with the Austro-Motorette factory during the 1920s and also raced in the Austrian TT of 1926.

AUSTRIA • Austria 1930–1933

The Lamperts-owned Austria motorcycle factory - housed in the former DSH works at Trautmannsdorf - built 246cc and 347cc machines with frames made from duralumin and built by Ardie in Nuremberg. The range of engines included water-cooled and air-cooled Villiers, as well as the 347cc sv single made by Sturmey-Archer in Nottingham. Designer at the Austria factory was Hauler.

AUSTRIA-ALPHA • Austria 1933–1952

Formerly with the Werner-MAG factory and a successful racing motorcyclist, Josef V. Illichmann designed first various racing machines including a 248cc narrow-angle ohc V-twin and a 498cc ohv single. After the war he built mainly models with 248cc double-piston Puch two-stroke engines and 244cc Ilo vertical twin two-strokes. Afterwards he concentrated on the manufacture of foot gearchanges, rear suspensions, full-width hubs, forks and other parts.

AUSTRO-ILO • Austria 1938

Only a few of these 120cc Ilo-engined two-strokes had been built when Hitler occupied Austria and stopped this company from further manufacture of motorcycles.

AUSTRO-MOTORETTE • Austria 1924–1927

Built first 82cc two-stroke bicycle engines, afterwards Karl Schüber-designed 144cc vertical-twin two-stroke motorcycles. Interesting were the 173cc Austro-Motorette racing machines of 1926 with vertical-twin double-ohc engines, raced in the Austrian TT by Rudolf Mezera and Ladislaus Hajos-Hihalom. They proved very fast, but did not finish.

347cc Austria (two-stroke Villiers) 1931

144cc Austro-Motorette (two-stroke twin) 1927

490cc Austro Omega (ohv JAP) 1932

198cc Autinag (two-stroke) 1925

AUSTRO-OMEGA • Austria 1932–1939

Superbly finished and well made 348cc, 490cc and 746cc machines with sv and ohv JAP engines and other English components. A few racing models had 348cc Sturmey-Archer ohv power units. Ridden by Hermann Deimel, Rudi Hunger and Franz Behrendt, they won many races. Martin Schneeweiss used in 1934-1935 a JAP-engined 498cc Austro-Omega ohv racing single.

AUTINAG • Germany 1924–1925

Limited production of 127cc and 198cc two-strokes and of a MAG-engined 496cc single-cylinder machine with ioe valves.

AUTO-BI • America 1902–1912

Produced motorcycles and scooter-like machines with enclosed engines. Supplier of engines with 1.5hp and 2.5hp was E. R. Thomas.

AUTO-BIT • Japan 1952–1962

Produced 249cc single-cylinder machines on typical English lines.

AUTO-ELL • Germany 1924–1926

Designed by racing motorcyclist Max Ell, these lightweight machines had 142cc Grade two-stroke power units.

AUTO-FAUTEUIL • France 1902–1906

Cyclecar manufacturer of Blois, Loir-et-Cher which occasionally supplemented car production by building batches of motorcycles. Models included the 430cc two-speed water-cooled Auto-Fauteuil (motor armchair) introduced within a year of the firm commencing trade, and a similar machine using a 350cc four-stroke engine.

AUTOFLUG • Germany 1921–1923

Scooter-like machines with a long wheelbase and small wheels, designed by Egon Weitzel for a former aircraft manufacturer. The normal Auto-flug motorcycle had identical 129cc and 146cc Bekamo engines to the scooter-like machines. The Ruppe-designed Bekamo engine was a two-stroke with a pumping cylinder in the bottom of the crankcase.

AUTOGLIDER • England 1919–1922

Another scooter-like machine with a 292cc Union two-stroke engine above the small front wheel.

AUTOMOTO • France 1901–1962

A pioneer make which built for many years very sturdy - and quite heavy - motorcycles with engines up to 499cc. Used engines made by Zurcher, Chaise, JAP, Villiers; after 1945 mainly AMC ohv engines up to 248cc. Never regarded as a very sporty machine, the Automoto of pre-1939 days was a typical 'farmers machine' of great durability. During the concentration of the French motorcycle industry, Automoto joined the Peugeot group, which already included the Terrot-Magnat Debon combine.

AUTOPED • America 1915–1921

Once a well-known scooter with a 155cc four-stroke engine above the small front wheel. Krupp in Germany and CAS in Czechoslovakia built the Autoped under license.

AUTOSCO • England 1920–1921

Another early scooter, which failed to become popular. The engine was 180cc.

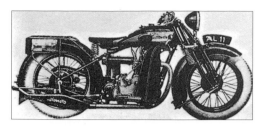

490cc Automoto (ohv Chaise) 1929

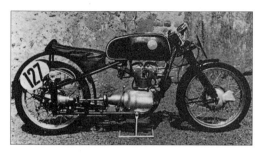

248cc AWO (dohc twin) 1953

122cc Autoflug (two-stroke Bekamo) 1922

AVADA • The Netherlands 1953–late 1950s

Small moped manufacturer which used 49cc two-stroke engines.

AVELLO • Spain 1976–1987

Lightweights from 49cc to 79cc built by a branch factory of the big Austrian Puch works.

AVENIR • Belgium 1956–1974

Another mofa and moped manufacturer which built two-strokes of 49cc capacity.

AVIS-CELER • Germany 1925–1931

Hanover-based Avis-Celer built machines with Villiers engines from 172cc to 346cc and - from 1928 onwards - also bigger models with 347cc and 497cc ioe and ohv single-cylinder MAG engines. Leading rider was Hermann Wiedemann, whose 248cc, 348cc and 498cc racing versions housed engines made by JAP.

AVON • England 1919–1920

Limited production of motorcycles with 347cc Villiers single-cylinder two-stroke engines.

AWD • Germany 1921–1959

AWD & Wurring motorcycles used such proprietary engines as DKW, Blackburne, JAP, Küchen, Sachs, Villiers and Ilo over the years. Pre-war, August Wurring was known for building special racing motorcycles to order. In post-war years, a similar operation was again set up, using proprietary engines of between 100cc and 250cc. The last models made use of a 250cc twin Ilo two-stroke engine.

AWO • East Germany 1949–1957

Built at the former Simson-Supra car factory at Suhl in Thuringia, the AWO was a 246cc single-cylinder ohv machine with unit-design engine and shaft drive to the rear wheel. Special works racing models had 248cc vertical twin-cylinder single and dohc power units with chain, bevel and gear-driven ohc and also single-cylinder engines with overhead camshafts. During the 1950s, the name changed to Simson.

AYRES-LEYLAND • England 1920

Flat twins with 688cc Coventry Victor sv engine, own gearbox and spring frame.

AZA • Czechoslovakia 1924–1926

Lightweight machines with 147cc engines. The same Prague factory also built the big 996cc JAP-engined MC V-twin machines.

AZZARITI • Italy 1933–1934

Designed by Vincenzo Azzariti, these 173cc and 348cc ohc machines had twin-cylinder engines, some of which had desmodromic valve gear, in which the valve is opened by a cam and then closed by another cam, rather than by a spring.

496cc AWD (sv Columbus) 1936

B

BAC • England 1951–1953

The Gazelle, made by this Blackpool-based aircraft company, was one of the first British scooters after WW2. It was supplied with 98cc and 123cc Villiers engines. The BAC lightweight motorcycle also used the 98cc Villiers engine.

BADGER • America 1920–1921

Unconventional design with the 163cc four-stroke engine built into the rear wheel.

BAF • Czechoslovakia 1927–1930

Designed by B. A. Frisek, the Prague-built BAF motorcycles had Bekamo two-stroke 173cc and 246cc 'pumping-piston' engines, 346cc ohv Kühne and 496cc Chaise unit-design ohc single-cylinder engines.

BAIER • Germany 1924–1930

One of the many two-stroke motorcycle factories which existed during the 1920s in Berlin. The first models were 173cc, 198cc and 248cc singles with some unit-design engines. From 1927 onwards the only model in production, a design by Willy and Karl Baier, was a 492cc two-piston single-cylinder machine with a BMW-like triangular frame.

BAILEUL • France 1904–1910

Small producer which fitted Peugeot and Buchet engines into its machines.

BAJAJ • India 1960–

Bajaj was formed in 1960 to produce Italian Lambretta scooters under license, but grew to become the largest manufacturer of two-wheelers in India, and one of the

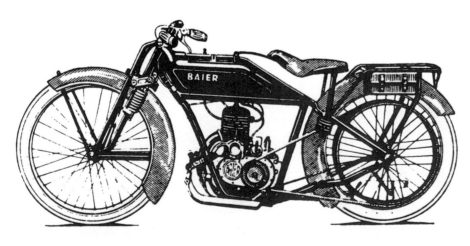

249cc Baier (two-stroke) 1925

world's biggest. Today the company employs around 17,000 people. Bajaj began exporting lightweight motorcycles into Europe at the end of the 1980s, first under the Chetak name as 124cc and 148cc scooters, based on the Italian Vespa and also originally built under license from Piaggio. Over four million Chetaks have now been produced. Bajaj badged machines followed, and the company currently produces a wide range of small motorcycles and scooters, some developed by Bajaj, others under license from western and Japanese manufacturers and in collaboration with Kawasaki and Cagiva..

BAKER • England 1927–30

Frank Baker worked for the American firm Cleveland before making Precision proprietary engines in Britain. After the crash of the post-WW2 Beardmore Precision company, Baker designed stylish Villiers-engined lightweights of 150cc-250cc, the 175cc 'racer' being especially popular. The company was taken over by James in 1930.

BAKKER • Netherlands, 1973–

Nico Bakker has specialised in producing frames and complete bikes for racing, plus specialist road bikes or frame kits for road bikes. He is noted for his innovative engineering, which has resulted in the hub-centre steered QCS and QCS2 machines of the late 1980s and early 1990s, as well as much behind the scenes consultancy work for Laverda, BMW and others.

BALALUWA • Germany 1924–1925

The Balaluwa was a 346cc ohv single-cylinder machine of very advanced design. Like other German factories of that period, it probably had insufficient finances to carry on.

BALKAN • Bulgaria 1958–1975

Built Jawa-like 246cc single-cylinder two-strokes and concentrated afterward on various models - including mopeds - with 49cc and 73cc two-stroke engines of its own manufacture.

BAM • Germany 1933–1937

The 'Germany' in this case refers mainly to the name BAM. Reason for BAM 'production' was Adolf Hitler, who made import of foreign motorcycles nearly impossible. The Belgian FN works had an assembly plant at Aachen and a sales office at Berlin; as it was not able to send its own motorcycles via Aachen to Germany, it created a new name which stood for 'Berlin-Aachener-Motorradwerke'. Apart from the name, everything was original FN. The range included 198cc two-stroke singles, 346cc sv and 497cc sv and ohv models. This arrangement satisfied the Hitler Government.

BAMAR • Germany 1923–1925

Assembler of lightweight motorcycles with 149cc and 198cc engines made by DKW, Gruhn, Baumi, Alba and other engine suppliers. Limited production.

BAMBER • England c1903–1905

Cycle maker R. Bamber of Southport claimed to have a 40 man motorcycle department repairing machines and building single- and twin-cylinder Bamber models.

BAMO • Germany 1923–1925

Another small German make. Used 148cc and 173cc DKW proprietary engines.

BANGOR • America 1937–1939

Built a basic scooter using a Clinton engine.

BANSHEE • England 1921–1924

Produced machines with 269cc Villiers engines and was among the first to fit the 347cc Barr & Stroud sleeve-valve engine. Other models had oil-cooled 346cc Bradshaw and 347cc and 497cc Blackburne sv and ohv engines.

746cc Bayern (ioe V-twin MAG) 1926

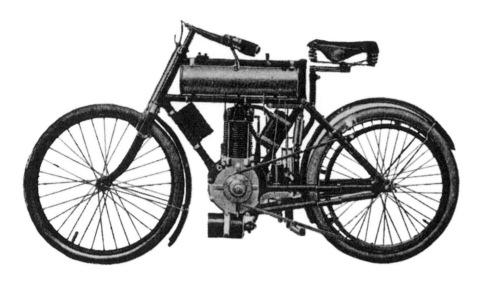

8½hp BAT (single) 1903

BAT • England 1902–1926

Designed by the famous pioneer competition rider T.H. Tessier and made by his family firm. BAT ('Best after test') was an early user of single-cylinder and V-twin JAP engines, with a range of capacities from 500cc to 1000cc. The BATs featured a magneto at petrol tank level driven by bevels and shaft and also a spring sub-frame, often mistakenly called a 'spring frame'. Very sporting.

BARDONE • Italy 1938–1939

Once a well-known producer of delivery three-wheelers, Bardone also built heavy 499cc motorcycles with its own unit-design ohv single-cylinder engines.

BARIGO • France 1991–

Produces single-cylinder, Rotax-powered sports bikes with the French-inspired supermoto styling features of long travel suspension and wide handlebars, plus a sports-touring machine, the Onixa, based on the same twin spar aluminum frame and 600cc engine.

BARNES • England 1904

A little-known make which fitted various proprietary engines, including the MMC and 211cc Minerva.

BARNSON-VILLIERS • England 1923

Just six machines were built by the Wokingham garage owner A. C. Barnes Jnr. The 2½hp model was powered by a 247cc Villiers single-cylinder two-stroke. A 3 ½hp version was also on offer.

BARON • England 1920–1921

Concentrated on assembling motorcycles with 292cc Union and 348cc Blackburne sv engines.

BARRY • Czechoslovakia 1932–1939

The first models were 248cc ohv racing singles, designed by Friedrich Drkosch. A 98cc two-stroke of up-to-date design was ready for production when WW2 broke out.

BARTALI • Italy 1953–1961

Named after a famous bicycle racer, Gino Bartali, these good-looking motorcycles had 48cc, 124cc and 158cc two-stroke and 123cc, 174cc and 198cc ohv engines. The 158cc Marziano was a sports model.

BARTER • England 1902–1905

Unusual single-cylinder machines with rear-wheel drive taken directly from the camshafts. The designer W. J. Barter afterwards created the Fairy (Fee) motorcycles with flat-twin engines which were the forerunners of Douglas machines.

BARTISCH • Austria 1925–1929

In 1925 Franz Bartisch designed a 348cc single-cylinder machine with chain-driven ohc and in 1928 added a 498cc model with bevel-driven ohc. This machine had no outside oil pipes and was of very clean design. Lack of finance prevented the manufacture of large numbers of these excellent machines.

BASIL • England c1911

JAP-engined machines built by the W. B. Payne Cycle Works, Harlesden, London.

BASTERT • Germany 1949–1955

A well-known company in its time which produced Sachs and Ilo-engined motorcycles from 49cc to 247cc and also various mopeds and scooters.

BATAVUS • Holland 1911–

Factory known for 49cc mofas, mopeds and lightweight motorcycles which also produced in earlier years motorcycles up to 198cc with Ilo, Villiers and Sachs engines. Now produces mainly bicycles, but still in production with 49cc mopeds.

BAUDO • Italy 1920–1928

Produced at Turin JAP-engined V-twins of 474cc, 668cc and 972cc. After 1924 the range included models with 248cc Train engines (two-strokes), 348cc Barr & Stroud sleeve-valve singles, 173cc Moser ohv motors and also JAP-engined versions of 173cc, 246cc and 346cc.

BAUER • Germany 1936–1954

Well-known bicycle factory. Produced in pre-1939 days mopeds with 74cc and 98cc Sachs engines, after 1945 motorcycles with 123cc, 147cc and 173cc Sachs and Ilo two-strokes. A new 247cc machine, introduced in 1952, led to technical and subsequent commercial difficulties. This machine had an ohv single-cylinder engine with the carburetor in front and the exhaust valve on the rear of the engine. This arrangement led to overheating and a comparatively low output. Bauer carried on bicycle production, but withdrew completely from the manufacture of motorcycles in 1954.

BAUGHAN • England 1930–1936

Built by an experienced trials man who later as ACU official was in charge of big trials including the International. Most Baughan machines were made for cross-country events and its sidecars had their own drive. The engines used were 247cc 347cc and 497cc sv and ohv Blackburne.

BAYERLAND • Germany 1924–1930

A 996cc V-twin with a JAP ohv racing engine, ridden by Sepp Giggenbach, won the Grand Prix of Europe in 1927 in the 1000cc class. Bayerland machines had 248cc, 348cc and 490cc sv and ohv JAP engines. Designer of Bayerland motorcycles was Anton Bayerlein.

BAYERN • Germany 1923–1926

The first models had 293cc Bosch-Douglas flat twin engines, built under license by SMW of Stockdorf, near Munich. After 1924 new versions with 498cc, 746cc and 988cc V-twin MAG engines came into being. The production of these machines was not large.

BAYLEY-FLYER • America 1914–1917

Very unorthodox design with a flat 3.5hp twin-cylinder engine, shaft drive, automatic gear change and hand starter. Despite these features, not many Bayley-Flyers reached the market.

BB • Germany 1923–1925

Assembled machines with 197cc Alba sv single-cylinder engines.

BB • Italy 1925–1927

Small 123cc two-strokes with a horizontal cylinder. Designer-manufacturer of these nice lightweights was Ugo Bocchi.

BCR • France 1923–1930

BCR designer Raynal's motorcycles were among the first to use rear springing. It was also a manufacturer of Poinard machines. Most models had 98cc and 174cc two-stroke engines, others were fitted with sv and ohv JAP engines of 248cc, 348cc and 498cc.

BD • Czechoslovakia 1927–1929

Superb J. F. Koch-designed 490cc unit-design ohc touring-sport single-cylinder machines, made by the Breitfeld-Dank machine factory at Prague. When Praga, the well-known car maker, took over this factory, it continued

490cc BD (dohc) 1928

the manufacture of motorcycles under the Praga trademark. Koch also joined Praga.

BEAM • America 1946–1947

Manufactured the primitive Doodlebug scooter using either Briggs and Stratton or Clinton engines.

BEARDMORE PRECISION • England 1921–1924

Giant Scottish industrial group Beardmore (ships, locomotives, cars, aircraft engines) took over Frank Baker's Precision company to produce an advanced, but ugly, motorcycle with leaf springing fore and aft, integral petrol tank and band brakes. The marque generally used Precision engines, though one model was fitted with the sleeve-valve Barr & Stroud. Beardmore itself built a disastrous ohc engine with twin carburetors for the 1924 Junior TT. In the event 250cc engines with leaf valve springs were hastily substituted, but failed. Beardmore then closed the operation.

346cc Beardmore Precision (sleeve valve B&S) 1923

BEAUFORT • England 1923–1926

Producer of Argson invalid three-wheelers, Beaufort also produced a 170cc single-cylinder two-stroke motorcycle.

BEAU-IDEAL • England 1905–1906

Assembled motorcycles with Clement, Minerva and JAP engines.

BEAUMONT • England 1921–1922

Designed by Monty Beaumont, these machines had 269cc Wall two-stroke engines and also 348cc Blackburne sv motors. Beaumont became better known in the 1940s when he designed the ill-fated Kendall `people-car' with a three-cylinder radial engine.

BE-BE • Germany 1923–1927

Small 117cc two-stroke made by a small iron-producing company.

BECCARIA • Italy 1925–1928

Motorcycles assembled mainly from English components. These included 346cc Villiers and 348cc sv and ohv Blackburne engines.

BECKER • Germany 1903–1906

Limited production of machines with its own and Fafnir single-cylinder and V-twin engines.

BECO • Germany 1923–1925

Motorcycle assembler which fitted 149cc DKW two-stroke proprietary engines into simple frames of own production.

BEESTON • England 1898–1910

Owned by the motor pioneer Harry John Lawson, Beeston was one of the oldest makes in the trade. It produced three-wheelers, motorcycles and cars at and around Coventry in different factories. Beeston motorcycles had strengthened bicycle frames and the 1.75hp engine housed between the pedalling gear and the rear wheel. The engine was of De Dion design, of which H. J. Lawson had all patent and production rights for England. The capacity of the engine used in Beeston motorcycles was 346cc.

BEFAG • Germany 1922–1924

Used the Julius Löwy-designed 113cc and 176cc crude-oil engines in conventional frames.

BEHAG • Germany 1924–1926

Simple design with open frames. Fitted own 218cc two-stroke and JAP engines of 348cc and 490cc with side-valves.

BEKAMO • Germany 1922–1925

Famous two-stroke machines with a pumping piston at the bottom of the crankcase. Designed by Hugo Ruppe, the first models had wooden frames, from 1923 onwards they had orthodox tubular frames. The powerful 129cc engines won many races and were also sold to other motorcycle producers as proprietary power units. Other factories produced Bekamo engines under license. Among them were Windhoff, MFZ, Eichler, TX and Böhme. Leading Bekamo riders were Sepp Thevis, Max Hucke, Paul Lüdtke, Karl Jurisch, Kurt Pohle, Gerhard Ahrens, Otto Heller and others.

BEKAMO • Czechoslovakia 1923–1930

The first Czechoslovakian Bekamo machines were made at the Berlin Bekamo works. For tax reasons they had the two-stroke pumping-piston engines reduced to 124cc and

1¾hp Beeston (De Dion engine) 1897

173cc Czech Bekamo (two-stroke) 1927

129cc German Bekamo (two-stroke) 1924

while the German factory still used wooden frames, the Czechoslovakian Bekamo works at Rumburk fitted these power units into equally unorthodox TX frames. These had a top tube of 8-inch diameter which acted as the petrol/oil tank. The Rumburk factory was until 1925 an assembly plant for Bekamo machines supplied to Czechoslovakia, but when the German factory at Berlin closed down, everything was transferred to Rumburk. A 174cc model was added in 1927 and in 1929 a 248cc Bekamo with an orthodox tubular frame, made at the Aeros factory, came into being. Leading riders on Czechoslovakian Bekamos were Heller, Franz Olbrich and Josef Kosinka.

BELL • Australia 1911–1912

JAP-engined machines built by A. E. Bell Cycle & Motor Works, Woodside, South Australia.

BELMONDO • Italy 1945–1948

Maker of the 98cc Sachs-powered Velta scooter.

BENOTTO • Italy 1953–1957

One of the many small factories of the 1950s, Benotto

fitted German Ilo two-strokes from 48cc to 198cc and also ohv engines to 198cc.

BENELLI • Italy 1917–

See panel overleaf

BERCLEY • Belgium 1905–1909

Designed by Gustave Kindermann, the Bercley was one of the first vertical twins in quantity production. The sv engine had 616cc and was of advanced design.

BERESA • Germany 1923–1925

Produced motorcycles with 198cc sv engines on a limited scale.

BERGFEX • Germany 1904–1909

Berlin-built single and V-twin machines with its own and also with Aachen-built Fafnir proprietary engines.

BERGO • Germany 1924

Assembled machines with 145cc DKW two-stroke power units.

BERINI • The Netherlands late 1950s

Well-known manufacturer of mopeds etc. with 49cc two-stroke rotary-valve engines.

BERLIN • East Germany 1958–1965

Scooter, equipped with 148cc MZ two-stroke engines.

BERINGER • France 1989

Currently best known for its aftermarket brake systems, especially six-piston calipers for supersports machines, but in 1989 the company produced its own street-styled bodywork for the Honda XR600 trail bike and made other modifications (including the fitment of its own brakes) and briefly sold the bike as the Mustang.

616cc Bercley (sv twin) 1905

600cc Beringer Mustang (ohc single Honda) 1989

BENELLI • Italy 1917–

Benelli was founded in Pesaro as an engineering workshop in 1911 by widow Teresa Benelli as an occupation for her sons Giuseppe, Giovanni, Francesco, Filippo, Domenico and Antonio (known as Tonino). Originally the workshop was dedicated to repairing and making spares for cars and motorcycles.

The first Benelli engine was a 75cc two-stroke designed in 1917 for a motorcycle, although the first complete machine didn't appear until 1921, powered by a 98cc version of the first engine. By 1923 Tonino had taken up racing on Benellis and showed exceptional

talent. His development ability led to the production of the superb 173cc racing two-stroke in 1927, while road-going 124cc two-strokes and 174cc ohv four-strokes were being produced simultaneously.

The racing continued before the war, the most famous victory being that of Englishman Ted Mellors on a 250 Benelli in the Lightweight TT at the Isle of Man. Supercharged bikes, including a supercharged, liquid-cooled four, were built in 1939 but the outbreak of hostilities prevented development, while Tonino was killed in a road accident at this time.

The factory was destroyed during the war, but the Benellis kept going and quantity production resumed in

1949, although Guiseppe Benelli left to form his own marque, Motobi.

Racing continued with Dario Ambrosini taking the world 250cc title on his Benelli four-stroke single in 1950, and during the sixties the great Tarquinio Provini and Renzo Pasolini had many successes on Benellis. After that, with the Japanese losing interest, Kel Carruthers took the world title on a 250cc Benelli four in 1969. A variety of road bikes was leaving the Pesaro factory at the same time, mostly smaller machines of 49cc to 174cc, both two- and four-strokes, but the pressure of competition from Japan proved too much, and in 1971 Benelli was sold to the Argentinian

498cc Benelli (ohv single) 1936

248cc Benelli (ohv single) 1939

605cc Benelli (ohc four Sport) 1982

350cc Benelli GP machine raced by Mike Hailwood

entrepreneur Alejandro De Tomaso, who also bought Moto Guzzi a year later. His autocratic leadership and poor understanding of the motorcycle market failed to restore Benelli to its former glory.

Some glamorous Honda-based road bikes were produced, drawing on Benelli's multi-cylinder heritage.

The dramatic-looking six-cylinder 750 Sei of 1975 had six silencers on each side, but proved no faster than contemporary fours, and was unreliable and expensive. The 900cc version which followed was better, but still didn't sell well. A more sensible four-cylinder 605cc machine, the 654, was expensive compared to the Japanese opposition without offering any obvious advantages, and this was the story with the rest of Benelli's range during the seventies and eighties, such as the little 231cc Quattro four-cylinder and small two-stroke twins.

231cc Benelli (two-stroke twin) 1977

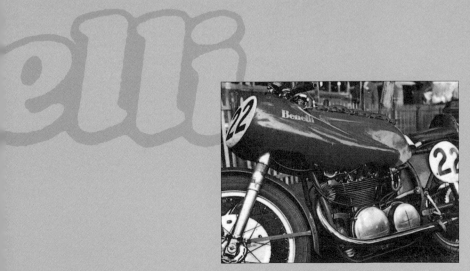

248cc Benelli racer (dohe) 1952

Despite the transfer to a state-of-the-art factory in Pesaro in 1981, the company faded from De Tomaso's portfolio, and the right to the name (but nothing else) was bought in 1989 by forward-thinking Pesaro businessman Giancarlo Selci.

Benelli then went into hibernation until an agreement between Gattelone semi-works Ducati World Superbike team owner Andrea Merloni and Selci was arranged in May 1996.

Merloni's family owned the former Benelli factory in Pesaro, which had been turned over to the production of various white goods, but it has been returned to two-wheeler manufacture.

Currently Benelli makes the very successful 491 scooter as well as the K2 with 50cc Minarelli engines, and various 101cc, 125cc and 250cc scooters powered by Yamaha motors.

On the basis of the scooters' success, in 1997 Merloni declared his intent to create an entire range of motorcycles with the intention of gaining a significant proportion of the European motorcycle market by the year 2000. In 1999 he announced the first of the new

49cc Benelli K2 (two-stroke Minarelli) 1999

generation of Benelli motorcycles, the 900cc three-cylinder Tornado, which will almost certainly provide the basis for a World Superbike racer.

With Merloni's determination, experience and package of investors behind Benelli, the future for this famous but once defunct name is looking much brighter.

900cc Benelli Tornado prototy

49cc Benelli 491 (two-stroke Minarelli) 1998

...ale) 1999

906cc Benelli (ohc 900 Sei) 1982

49cc Beta Quadra (two-stroke Minarelli) 1998

BERNARDET • France 1930–1934

Chaise and Train proprietary engines from 98cc to 498cc drove these machines, which were in limited production.

BERNARDET • France 1949–1957

Another business founded and owned by the three Bernardet brothers - René, Robert and Roger - produced exclusively scooters, which in the 1950s were among the leaders in France. They had 123cc and 246cc Ydral two-stroke engines.

BERNASSE • France 1905

Single-cylinder direct belt drive machine with unusual for the period rubber suspension. Built in Toucy.

BERNEG • Italy 1954–1961

Beautiful small 159cc and 174cc vertical-twin machines, designed by Alfonso Drusiani. They had their own ohc engines and were built to the highest standards.

BERO • Germany 1924–1925

Lightweight machines with 145cc DKW two-stroke engines. Limited production.

BERTIN • France 1955–1958

Manufacturer of small machines with 49cc engines.

BERWICK • England 1929–1930

The only English make which fitted shaft drive to the rear wheel at that time. The engines used were 246cc and 346cc single-cylinder Villiers.

BETA • Italy 1904–

Beta is one of Italy's longest-established motorcycle manufacturers, producing a varied selection of machines throughout this century, including since the Second World War two- and four-stroke road bikes of 125cc to 350cc capacities, as well as smaller scooters. In recent times Beta has become very successful in the World Trials Championships, winning a total of six titles.

Known as a pioneer of advanced technology, the company, based at Rignano sull'Arno near Florence since 1972, won its first crown in 1987 with Spaniard Jordi Tarres, who went on to become the main development rider for the first water-cooled, perimeter-framed 250cc Beta, which set the technological benchmark in 1990. Tarres took a total of four world crowns, and in 1997 and 1998 Englishman Doug Lampkin brought the factory two more titles in World Trials and a further two in the World Indoor Championship. Lampkin's machine, the Techno, uses Beta's own 247cc liquid-cooled motor, cast aluminum perimeter-style frame that incorporates the fuel tank, disc brakes front and rear, inverted Paioli front forks and tubeless tyres, all innovations on this type of machine.

The company also currently produces the Ark and Quadra 50cc scooters, Eikon scooter in 50cc, 125cc and 150cc capacities, plus Jonathon and Euro four-stroke single-cylinder custom motorcycles of 125cc and 350cc respectively. Beta's more recent 50cc scooters are powered by Minarelli engines, while the latest 125cc and 150cc machines use Taiwanese Kymco four-stroke motors.

124cc Beta Jonathon (ohc Kymco) 1999

385cc Binks (sv four) 1905

123cc Bismarck (two-stroke) 1953

BEUKER • Germany 1921–1929

Two-stroke machines with 145cc, 173cc, 198cc, 231cc and 246cc engines of own design and manufacture. The Beuker engines were of the deflector-type and had three ports.

BEZDEZ • Czechoslovakia 1923–1926

Produced bicycle engines and also complete machines with these 145cc sv power units.

BH • Spain 1956–1960

Small moped manufacturer, which used 49cc two-stroke engines.

B & H • England 1923

Engine producer which also built 996cc V-twin sv machines on a limited scale and for a limited period. These machines were made at the once-famous Napier Works.

BIANCHI • Italy 1897–1967

See panel

BIMOTA • Italy 1973–

See panel

BICHRONE • France 1902–1907

One of the first producers of motorcycles with two-stroke engines of 2.25hp, 2.50hp and 2.75hp, also supplied to other factories.

BIM • Japan 1956–1961

Was one of the small Japanese factories which built BMW-like sv twin machines without great commercial or sporting successes. Models included 248cc, 348cc, 498cc and 598cc machines.

BIMM • Italy 1972–1980

Younger Italian producer of trials and motocross machines with 49cc and 123cc Minarelli two-stroke engines.

BIMOFA • Germany 1922–1925

Designed by Gustav Kunstmann, German Bimofa 1.8hp and 2.5hp machines had sv engines made by Hansa.

BINKS • England 1903–1906

Charles Binks, who later became famous as a producer of carburetors, was one of the pioneers of four-cylinder

493cc Bison (sv flat twin BMW) 1925

motorcycle manufacture. His 'fours' had air-cooled in-line engines of 385cc. Some models had them transverse mounted.

BINZ • Germany 1954–1958

Simple scooter with 49cc Sachs and Ilo engines.

BIRCH • England 1901–1905

The first Birch was already made in 1901. The designer J. J. Birch of Nuneaton near Coventry, had the single cylinder built into the rear wheel. This design was sold to the Coventry Singer Company. The conventional Birch motorcycles had a triangular frame, which included a built-in crankcase and bottom bracket casting. Bradbury built such machines under Birch license. Birch engines were of 2hp, 2.5hp and 3.5hp. All had direct belt drive to the rear wheel.

BIRMA • France 1949–late 1950s

Lightweight machines of 98cc with Aubier-Dunne two-stroke engines.

BISMARCK • Germany 1904–1956

Produced big V-twins up to 1300cc with engines supplied by Minerva, Anzani and Fafnir. Around 1908 it stopped motorcycle manufacture and resumed in 1931 with motorised bicycles of 75cc and 98cc. After 1945 Emil Fischer designed well-made two-stroke motorcycles of 98cc, 147cc and 173cc capacity. Sachs and Ilo supplied the engines.

BIANCHI • Italy 1897–1967

Edoardo Bianchi was one of the great pioneers in Italy. His first motorised bicycle was made in 1897, his first car in 1900. By 1903 he fitted engines in the centres of strengthened bicycle frames; by 1905 he used Truffault leading-link forks and by 1910 a superb 498cc single made Bianchi a very successful make. A 650cc V-twin was built in 1916 and in 1920 enlarged to 741cc. A smaller, 598cc V-twin came into production in 1921 and there was also a new all chain-drive 498cc single. It was followed in 1923 by a 348cc sv single and two V-twin models with 498cc and 598cc; in 1924 by 173cc ohv single-cylinder machines. 1925 saw the introduction of the 348cc ohv single and of the famous 348cc double ohc works racing machines designed by Bianchi chief engineer Albino Baldi. Ridden by Tazio Nuvolari, Amilcare Moretti, Mario Ghersi, Karl Kodric, Gino Zanchetta, Luigi Arcangeli and others, these Bianchi `doubleknockers' were until 1931 the most successful Italian racing 350s. In addition, they were probably the fastest of their kind

in the world. Bianchi also built during the 1930s Baldi-designed 498cc single-cylinder ohc racing machines. Ridden by Giordano Aldrighetti, Aldo Pigorini, Terzo Bandini, Dorino Serafini, Guido Cerato, Alberto Ascari and others, they too were successful. A new 1938-built 498cc four-cylinder double-ohc machine with supercharger was never fully developed. After 1945 Bianchi returned to racing with 123cc and 248cc single-cylinder ohc machines, and—during the late 1950s—with new 248cc and 348cc twin-cylinder double-ohc models, designed by Colombo and Tonti. Among the riders was Ernesto Brambilla and there were also a few bored-out models for the 500cc class. Production versions of Bianchi machines included many 49cc, 122cc and 173cc two-strokes and also the Tonale, with its own 173cc ohc engine, which had the camshaft driven by chain. Some 49cc two-strokes had engines built under Puch license. Bianchi had given up car manufacture many years ago and it was a sad day in 1967 when this once great company also stopped the production of motorcycles.

348cc Bianchi Racer (dohc) 1925

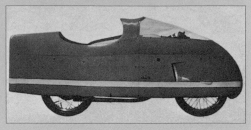

500cc Bianchi, early 1950s

173cc Bianchi Sportster (ohc) 1962

173cc Bianchi (ohv Sport) 1939

BISMARCK • Germany 1921–1923

Yet another small German company which used this trademark for small bicycle attachment engines and afterwards for 148cc 1.5hp single-cylinder sv machines.

BISON • Austria 1924–1926

Designed by Oskar Hacker, who later became chief designer of the Austro-Daimler car factory, Bison motorcycles always had flat twin-cylinder engines. Among them were the 293cc Bosch-Douglas, the 493cc BMW and the Coventry-built 678cc Coventry-Victor. Limited production.

BITRI • The Netherlands 1955–1960

Small producer of scooters with 147cc engines.

BJR • Spain 1953–early 1960s

Produced 123cc and 174cc machines with two-stroke engines.

BLACKBURNE • England 1908–1921

Cecil and Alick Burney were pioneers of the British motorcycle industry. Originally connected with Geoffrey de Havilland, they designed engines, later complete motorcycles of 3.5hp and 4hp (singles) and 8hp (twins). They eventually left the company and concentrated on the

manufacture of proprietary power units. In 1921 Osborn Engineering Company (OEC) took over the manufacture of Blackburne motorcycles.

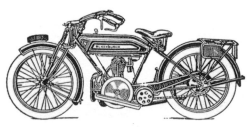

448cc Blackburne (sv) 1921

BIMOTA • Italy 1973–

Bimota was founded in Rimini on Italy's Adriatic coast by three men who made their living designing and fabricating ducting for air conditioning systems. The company name came from the first two letters of their surnames - Bianchi, Morri and Tamburini. Massimo Tamburini left Bimota during the eighties, joined the Cagiva Ducati group and went on to create one of the most influential machines of the last twenty years, the Ducati 916, following that up, after Ducati was sold off, with the arguably even more beautiful MV Agusta F4.

Bimota has concentrated on producing high quality chassis powered by proprietary engines, lightly modified, first from Japan and later, Ducati and BMW. It was a formula which worked extremely well at first, as 1970's Japanese motorcycles had the best engines, but their frame and suspension technology lagged behind.

Bimota's first bike was the HB1, an off-the-shelf racing machine. The H signified the Honda engine (a 750cc four), the B was for Bimota and the 1 was because this was the first Honda engine Bimota had used. The terminology is still in place today, so you can tell from the name SB8 for example that this is the eighth Suzuki-engined model made by Bimota.

Bimota had built the HB1 because the founders' interest in motorcycle racing had already led them first to modify production frames for themselves, then other competitors, until they were inspired to create complete frames of their own.

Because of the big demand it was only a short step to fitting an engine themselves, rather than leaving this to their customers, although it wasn't until 1977 that the company produced its first purpose-built road going machine, the SB2. This used Suzuki's four-cylinder GS750 motor producing 75bhp. The frame was a tubular

steel lattice construction, which wrapped so comprehensively around the engine that it was designed to separate into halves, so the motor could be removed for maintenance. Its 130mph top speed immediately guaranteed the SB2 exotic status in 1977, but it was the bike's exceptional handling which really justified its existence.

The Italians' superlative handling was a constant theme as further bikes followed, such as the 998cc KB1 (with a Kawasaki four) of 1978, the Yamaha FZ750 powered YB4 of 1983 and the 1100cc SB4 in 1984.

The YB4 was developed from the aluminum beam-framed machine on which Italian Virginio Ferrari won the 1987 World Formula One championship (the predecessor to World Superbikes), while before that Bimota's race bikes had been winning global limelight in the late seventies, when American Randy Mamola raced Bimota-framed Yamaha TZs in GPs. The company went on to

906cc Bimota Tesi (dohc V-twin Ducati) 1990

749cc Bimota SB2 (dohc four) 1977

1047cc Bimota SB6R (dohc four) 1997

accumulate five 250 and 350cc Grand Prix world titles with Johnny Cecotto and Yamaha power, plus Walter Villa with a Harley engine. A sixth came in 1980 from South African Jon Ekerold, again with a Yamaha TZ engine in Bimota's frame.

Three years later Bimota unleashed its Tesi racer, a radical Honda-powered machine employing hydraulically controlled hub-center steering. But Ferrari's FZ750 Bimota marked a return to more conventional technology and success with it, while the following year Davide Tardozzi came within a handful of points of winning the inaugural World Superbike title on a fuel-injected development of the same bike.

Bimota was therefore proving its credibility and gaining knowledge out on the tracks at the highest level, but even with engines such as the 1100cc four cylinder Honda unit in the HB3 of 1983, Bimota's road bike advantage was gradually eroded by the great advances in Japanese frame design.

It was therefore rather ironical that the machine credited with saving the financially strapped company in 1985 was powered by another Italian engine - the DB1 used the 649cc Ducati Pantah motor. The bike sold because of its beautiful and innovative appearance (fully enclosed bodywork) as much as its precise handling, showing Bimota that it should focus on other values beyond handling.

The message was perhaps misunderstood though. Bimota decided to distinguish itself from mass-produced machines with very advanced technology, and embarked on a project to create a road-going machine with hub-center steering in place of conventional telescopic forks, based on the Tesi racer but with mechanical rather than hydraulic steering. The Tesi, introduced in 1990, was the brainchild of Bimota's engineering chief Pierluigi Marconi (the man behind the DB1) whose initial work on the project was actually his thesis while at university - Tesi is Italian for thesis.

Many of the theoretical advantages of hub-center steering are undoubtedly attractive, but in the Tesi at least these were not enough to offset the loss of feedback from the front tire to the rider, and Bimota couldn't completely eliminate bump-steer, where the front wheel would steer slightly as the swingarm moved through the full extent of its travel.

The development of the Tesi proved very expensive, something reflected in its very high price (more than ú20,000 in 1990 when it was introduced). But because it offered little extra over conventional machines, sales were poor.

Other machines have fared better, especially the Yamaha FZR1000-powered models, the YB8, Tuatara, Furano and Dieci (dating from 1989 to 1991) and later the Suzuki GSX-R1100-powered SB6 and SB6R, and another Ducati-driven Bimota, the DB2. Less successful was the Supermono and Bimota's sole experiment with non-race replica machines, the outlandishly styled Mantra of 1996, product of commissioned French designer Sacha Lakic.

Throughout this period Bimota continued its high tech policy, and had been developing its own engine, a two-stroke V-twin, designed initially for Grand Prix racing. This was hailed as the world's first direct injection two-stroke (although a direct injection two-stroke car was produced in Germany in the fifties, and Bimota was also beaten to it by Mercury with a marine engine), but the power was inadequate for Grand Prix success and the project evolved into the V-Due, a lightweight yet very powerful road bike. The bike should have been called the BB1, but that name had already been earmarked for the BMW F650-powered single which preceded the V-Due by two years. Oddly, the BMW machine eventually came to be known as the Supermono and the long-awaited BB1 moniker was never used.

The V-Due's development was inadequate, cost being the major hurdle, and even the final versions which reached customers did not work properly. By the summer of 1998 Bimota was once again having serious financial problems, due mostly to the development, then recall and rectification costs caused by the V-Due. These only

499cc Bimota V-Due (two-stroke V-twin) 1998

998cc Bimota SB8R (dohc V-twin Suzuki) 1999

seemed to have been solved in the short term by an investment package amounting to £2.4 million, put in place in late 1998 by former Laverda investor Francesco Tognon. This will keep Bimota going for a while, but it might even take a rethink of its basic philosophy for Bimota to survive in the long term, as cutting edge technology these days is very expensive and Bimota only

998cc Bimota Mantra (dohc V-twin Suzuki) 1999

174cc Bleha (two-stroke) 1924

498cc Blériot (sv twin) 1920

BLACKFORD • England 1902–1904

Designed by Frank Blackford, these machines had 211cc Minerva engines.

BLACK-PRINCE • England 1919–1920

E. W. Cameron's design was more a black sheep than a prince. It had a 497cc flat-twin two-stroke engine with one plug only and a pressed steel frame with rear suspension. It is unlikely that this engine was ever fully developed. When Cameron closed down, the production concentrated on a more orthodox model with a tubular frame and 292cc Union two-stroke engine.

BLEHA • Germany 1923–1926

Not a big factory, which fitted 247cc DKW two-stroke and 247cc sv engines of own design and manufacture.

BLÉRIOT • France 1920–1923

There was a certain similarity between Sopwith in England and Blériot. Both aircraft factories turned to motorcycle production after WW1, Sopwith with the ABC, Blériot with 498cc vertical twins. Blériot's were built with sv and with ohv, but proved to be a failure, like the ABC, because they were not fully developed.

BLOTTO • France 1951–1955

Limited production of two-stroke machines with proprietary engines from 123cc to 348cc.

BLUMFIELD • England 1908–1914

T. W. Blumfield became the creator of Blumfield motorcycles and engines. Some versions had water-cooled engines and competed in TT races.

BM • Italy 1950-1972

Mario Bonviccini used Ilo and Franco Morini two-stroke engines of between 125cc and 175cc to launch his range, but soon devised his own superb ohc engines of 50cc, 65cc and 125cc. A dohc racer was produced in 1956, while later machines included a range of nicely styled 80cc two-strokes, for the road and also for off-road riding.

BM • Italy 1928–1931

Meldi's BM motorcycles, built in limited numbers, had 490cc single-cylinder sv and ohv JAP engines.

BMA • Italy 1978–

Small manufacturer of competition machines with 124cc and 248cc two-stroke engines.

BMG • Hungary 1939–1944

Lightweight machines with BMG's own 98cc two-stroke engines.

BMI • Holland 1934–1938

Bilthovense Metaalwaren Industrie built 3500 basic 80cc lightweights designed by Mr Beyerman. The BMI four-stroke engine had an automatic inlet valve.

48cc BM (dohc) 1956

BMP • Italy 1920–1925

Two-stroke machines with BMP's own 240cc engines and four-speed gearboxes.

BMW • Germany 1923–

See panel

BNF • Germany 1903–1907

Bielefeld based, the company mainly produced machines with 2.75hp single and 3.5hp V-twin Fafnir engines.

BOCK & HOLLÄNDER • Austria 1905–1911

Produced in 1898 four-wheeled vehicles with engines, afterwards a real car, the Regent. On the motorcycle side, 3.5hp and 6hp machines with V-twin engines came into being. When WAF - a car factory - took over Bock & Holländer at Vienna, no more motorcycles were built.

BODO • Germany 1924–1925

Small assembler which used 147cc DKW two-stroke engines.

BOGE • Germany 1923–1927

The well-known manufacturer of shock-absorbers built 246cc and 346cc sv machines with its own engines; a very successful 246cc Boge had an ohv Blackburne single-cylinder engine and was ridden in races by Curt Wemhüner.

a small company - production levels are no more than 1500 bikes a year.

However, Bimota's staff are confident about the future, having recently introduced the well-received the Suzuki TL1000-powered SB8R, with plans for a 1300cc Suzuki Hayabusa-powered machine, which should be capable of close to 200mph.

BMW • Germany 1923–

The Bayerische Motoren Werke (Bavarian Motor Works) was formed in 1917 from an aircraft company called BFW (Bavarian Aircraft Works), itself the product of an amalgamation between the Rapp Motorenwerke and a company founded by Gustav Otto, who invented the four-stroke engine.

After the First World War, with aircraft production in Germany banned by the allies, BMW (whose blue and white roundel badge represents a spinning propeller) turned to other projects including the production of a proprietary motorcycle engine, the 500cc side-valve flat twin M2B15 unit. This was supplied to Victoria, SMW, SDB, Bison and other smaller companies, and also fitted to the Helios which BMW made in its own factory for another company in 1921 and 1922.

Chief designer Max Friz saw it could be improved and in 1923 designed the now-classic boxer twin motor along with the rest of a complete motorcycle, the R32. Until 1984, BMW continued to produce only boxer twins and single-cylinder engines (effectively being one cylinder from a twin mounted vertically), while all of its bikes have had shaft drive, like the R32, until the F650 of 1994.

In 1924 Rudolf Schleicher developed the R37, with an ohv engine. The R32 had 8.5 bhp; the new model had

16 bhp at 4000 rpm and won many races. In 1925 the first BMW single was built; this was the R39, with an ohv engine having 248cc and 6.5bhp at 4000rpm.

While maintaining the basic design concept, development led to more sophisticated and faster machines. All BMWs built to 1929 - except the R39 which was dropped in 1927 - had half-litre sv and ohv engines. The first 733cc model, the R62, came into production in 1929. It was identical to the smaller models except for the bigger engine; a bigger ohv model was the R63. Soon BMW also introduced the 733cc sv and ohv engines in pressed steel frames. A new ohv 198cc single-cylinder in a pressed steel frame was built in 1931. 248cc, 298cc, 348cc and 398cc singles followed, up to the R27, built from 1960 to 1967. From 1935 BMW dropped pressed steel frames on most models and reverted to tubular frames.

By 1935 BMW had also dropped leaf spring forks; new models had telescopic forks. The first BMW with rear suspension was the R51 of 1938, a sporty model with a 496cc ohv twin. The similar R61 had a new 598cc sv with 18bhp at 4800rpm; an ohv version, the R66, had 30 bhp at 5700 rpm. From 1941 the R75, with a 746cc ohv engine, had a sidecar drive and no fewer than ten gears: four road-going, four cross-country and two reverse. It was built for the armed forces. After the war,

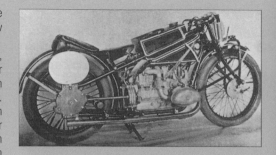

733cc BMW racer (ohv supercharged flat twin) 1929

198cc BMW R2 (ohv flat twin) 1931

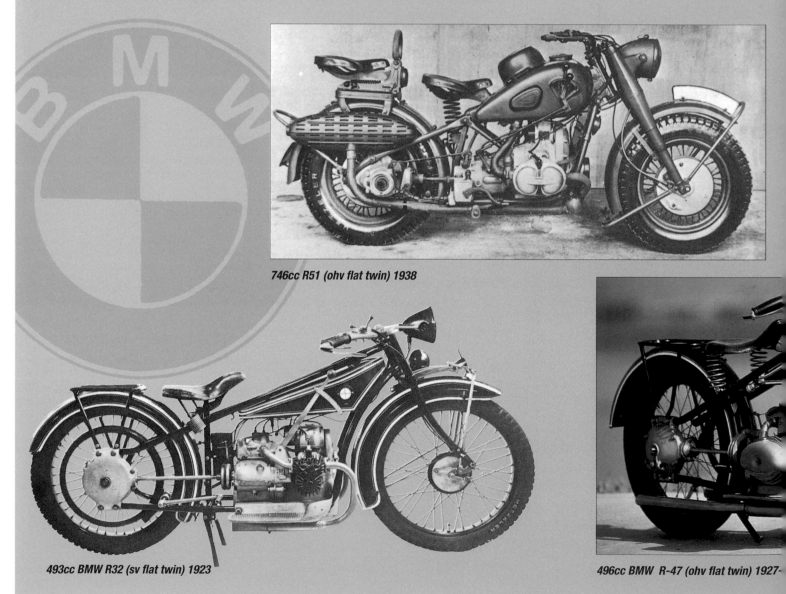

746cc R51 (ohv flat twin) 1938

493cc BMW R32 (sv flat twin) 1923

496cc BMW R-47 (ohv flat twin) 1927–

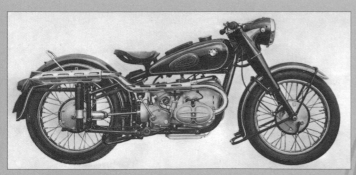

596cc BMW R168 (ohv flat twin) 1955

246cc BMW R25(ohv flat twin) 1950

496cc BMW racer (ohc flat twin) 1954

496cc BMW R51 (ohv flat twin) 1938

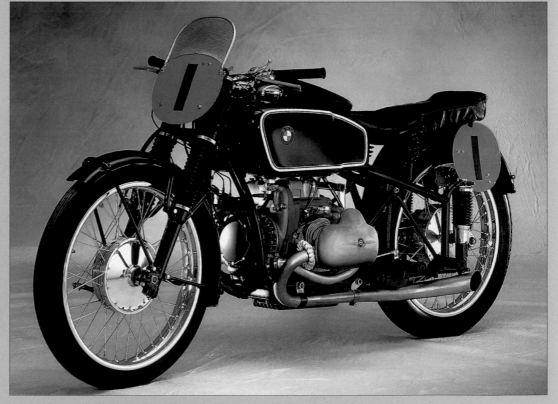

499cc BMW Kompressor (ohv flat twin supercharge) c. 1949

the first new model was the R24, a single ohv with 12 bhp at 5600 rpm, introduced in 1949. The first new twin appeared in 1950; the R51/2 had a 496cc ohv with 24 bhp at 5800 rpm. A similar 598cc came into production in 1951; this was the R67, mainly a sidecar machine with 26 bhp.

By 1954, all BMWs had telescopic forks, tubular frames and plunger rear suspension. Then the R50 and R60 arrived, with 498cc and 598cc ohv twins and using swinging arms at the rear with Earles front forks.

A new range was introduced in 1969: the R50/5, R60/5 and R75/5 had new frames, telescopic forks and ohv engines of 498cc, 598cc and 746cc with 32bhp, 40bhp and 50bhp. A new 898cc with 60 bhp at 6500 rpm was first sold in 1974; this was the R90/6. A sports version with 67 bhp at 7000 rpm was called R90S, but after only two years in production all 898cc models were superseded in late 1976 by new 980cc ohv models with slightly more softly tuned twins. The R100RT and the R100RS with their 980cc 70 bhp engines became the flagships of the BMW range, selling alongside a standard R100 version with 67 bhp and the 797cc R80G/S with 50 bhp. This proved a very significant machine, going on to win several Paris-Dakar rallies and spawning a whole new category of large capacity off-road motorcycles. Further down the range, the factory produced two 650cc models, the R65 and R65LS also with 50 bhp, and the 473cc R45 in two guises.

The docile nature of the road bikes gave little hint at BMW's considerable track and record successes. Ernst Henne set many speed records on supercharged BMW twins, produced from 1928, while the first foreign rider ever to win the Isle of Man TT was Georg Meier in the 1939 Senior on a supercharged BMW 500 twin.

The racing effort continued after the war, with works rider Walter Zeller coming second in the 1956 world championship and BMW boxers dominating sidecar racing between 1954 and 1974 (19 out of 21 world championships fell to BMW power). Other successful riders included Toni Bauhofer, Karl Stegmann, Jock West, Otto Ley, Josef Stelzer, Ludwig Kraus, Walter Zeller, Willi Noll, Willi Faust, Helmuth Fath, Dickie Dale, Fritz Scheidegger, Florian Camathias, and Gerold Klinger.

Meanwhile, in 1974 the R90S, for all its competence and subsequent classic status, also signalled BMW's submission to the Japanese in the battle for more horsepower and speed, as it was no match for the contemporary Far Eastern superbikes. Its handling was also less accomplished and overtly sporting as the Italian bikes which set the standards of the day, the R90S instead selling on its quality, comfort, smoothness and reliability. It needed to be all of these as the BMW cost double the price of a Honda CB750.

In 1976 the R90S evolved into the R100S, but the company's new flagship arrived at the same time, the R100RS, destined to become another classic for its combination of superb weather protection with high performance.

The Germans' capacity for innovation, so often overlooked, brought about the introduction of the R80G/S in 1981, its off-road design with big boxer twin engine looking like a bizarre aberration. Instead, it spawned a whole series of similar machines from most of the other manufacturers and has since become another classic.

599cc BMW R60/6 (ohv flat twin) 1974

798cc BMW R80 G/S (ohv flat twin) 1980

473cc BMW R45 (ohv flat twin) 1980

980cc BMW R100RS(ohv flat twin) 1982

987cc BMW K 100 (dohc four) 1983–89

987cc BMW K1 (dohc four) 1983

Even so, by the end of the seventies the Germans looked like capitulating in the face of falling boxer twin sales, due to the inherent superiority of the four-cylinder engine in terms of power and torque output, and they began designing their own four-cylinder power unit plus a triple based on it. It was planned to phase out the boxer twins altogether, and indeed an entirely new design team headed by Stefan Pechernegg was brought in to work on the fours.

The new K-series bikes were certainly innovative in many respects. The four fuel-injected and liquid-cooled cylinders were arranged longitudinally and on their side, as much to differentiate them from transverse Japanese fours as for any engineering advantages - BMW couldn't compete in sheer power, so being different was extremely important. While this facilitated the use of shaft drive (with the crankshaft rotating parallel to the drive shaft) it was difficult slotting the engine into the motorcycle without increasing the wheelbase excessively. So to keep the motor as short as possible an unfashionable long-stroke design was used, reducing the cylinder bore diameters and hence shortening the

engine. The width of the motor also had to be minimised, achieved by using shorter than ideal conrods. These two features compromised both the power of the engine and its smoothness.

The first of these bikes, the 987cc K100 of 1984, in addition had several reliability and build quality problems which took BMW more than a year to sort out. Even so, the strength of the brand name was so great that the company's good reputation was barely affected.

In 1985, the 750cc K75 was introduced, similar to the K100 but with one less cylinder—this proved smoother and many riders preferred it despite the capacity deficit.

The sales performance of the K-series was not bad, but it wasn't as good as BMW had hoped, and in addition opposition to the announcement that the boxer twins would be phased out was vehement. Production stopped for a while in 1986, then resumed.

Oddly, throughout this time, the company's reputation for ultra-conservative design was not borne out by reality – in practice BMW has been one of the most innovative companies of the eighties and nineties, even if the results

848cc BMW R850R (high cam flat twin)1997

652cc BMW F650ST (dohc single) 1998

1085cc BMW R1100 RS (high cam flat twin) 1993

1085cc BMW R1100GS (high cam flat twin) 1994

haven't always been to everyone's taste. The highly streamlined K1 for example, powered by a 16-valve version of the 987cc K-series four, was garishly-colored right down to the painted gearbox and drive shaft cases, with a giant front fender and bulky bodywork. The K1 featured ABS brakes, already introduced on the K100 for the first time on any production motorcycle.

BMW began work on an entirely new boxer engine, unveiled in 1993 as the R1100RS sports tourer. Despite the traditional engine configuration, the bike was more innovative than ever, featuring a unique wishbone-braced telescopic fork front end (called Telelever), single-sided swingarm/shaft drive, ABS brakes, fuel-injection and chain-driven high cams, positioned alongside the valves.

The following year BMW's innovation spread to its production method. It introduced a single-cylinder bike (its first ever machine with chain drive), developed in conjunction with Italian company Aprilia and Austrian engine manufacturer Rotax, and assembled at the Italian factory in Noale near Venice, from components sourced entirely from outside suppliers. The versatile F650 worked well and sales surprised even BMW.

A variety of boxer twins were developed from the R1100RS, including the R1100RT tourer, R1100GS big trail bike, uprated in mid-1999 to 1150cc, R1100R roadster and then another first for BMW, in 1997 the R1200C cruiser. Naturally, it avoided cloning most cruisers' Harley-Davidson looks for something more original, but although it was exceptionally stable, for some its suspension was unnecessarily harsh.

In 1998, the R1100S reintroduced the S suffix and won much praise for its exceptional stability and high engine torque, while in 1999 the luxury tourer K1200LT was introduced with an astonishing array of features including CD player and reverse gear, while the innovation continues with the C1 scooter, complete with roof and various crash safety features.

1171cc BMW K1200RS (dohc four) 1998

1085cc BMW R1100S (high cam flat twin) 1998

125cc BMW C1 (twostroke cingle) 1999

603cc Bohmerland (ohv single) 1927

BÖHME • Germany 1925–1930

Designed by two-stroke expert Martin Böhme, these watercooled 123cc, 129cc, 173cc and 246cc single-cylinder machines had also Dunelt-like double-diameter pistons and horizontal cylinders. .

BÖHMERLAND • Czechoslovakia 1925–1939

Very unconventional motorcycles which were also supplied with the name Cechie instead of Böhmerland on the tank. Designed by Albin Liebisch, they had a very long wheelbase, a very strong frame and fork and disc wheels made of alluminium. Some extra-long models had three 'officially permitted' seats and two petrol tanks, mounted on each side of the rear wheel. There was also a racing model with a shorter wheelbase, which was used in hill climbs. All models had the ohv single-cylinder 598cc Liebisch engine and even the last machines made just before WW2 had engines with open pushrods and valve-gears - not dissimilar to the ones designed in 1925 by Liebisch. A new 348cc two-stroke single-cylinder Böhmerland with a lighter but still unconventional frame was built in 1938. As a result of the war, only a few were made.

BOLIDE • France 1902–1910

Made at Pantin, these machines had own 1.5hp power units.

BOND • England 1949–1962

The first Bond product was a 98cc Minibike with a pressed steel frame. More orthodox motorcycles with

246cc Boge (sv) 1924

tubular frames had 98cc and 123cc Villiers and 123cc JAP two-stroke engines. From 1958, the fibreglass P1 to P4 scooters were the last two-wheelers to carry the Bond Badge.

BONVICINI • Italy 1956–1963

Produced lightweight step-thrus and scooters using engines of various makes.

BOOTH • England 1901–1903

London-built motorcycles with 2.75hp, 3.50hp and 4hp engines made by De Dion and Minerva.

BORD • England 1902–1906

Another London-built machine with a 1.5hp engine.

BORGH • Italy 1951–1963

Assembler of lightweight machines with 38cc Mosquito and 49cc Ducati Cucciolo engines. The 123cc Olympia had a BSA Bantam two-stroke engine.

598cc Böhmerland Touring (ohv single) 1927

129cc Böhme (two-stroke) 1925

BORGO • Italy 1906–1926

Once a famous factory, founded by A. B. Borgo and his brother Carlo. Built fast 497cc singles with ioe valves, and afterwards singles with 453cc, 493cc, 693cc and even 827cc. Another Borgo - Edmondo Michele - designed bicycle engines and built at his Turin factory in 1915 a 996cc V-twin with belt drive to the rear wheel. A 477cc ohv V-twin was built in 1921. It revved up to 6000rpm. With four-valve heads, these machines won many events. The last Moto-Borgo was a 496cc V-twin with ohv and a

4300cc Boss Hoss V6 (ohv Chevrolet) 1997

two-speed gearbox in unit with the engine. It had chain drive and a very low saddle position. The top speed was around 80 mph. After 1926 Borgo concentrated mainly on making pistons.

BORHAM • England 1902–1905

Minerva 2hp and 2.5hp engines were fitted to these primitive machines.

BOSS HOSS • America 1992–

Boss Hoss was founded by Monte Warne in Dyersburg, Tennessee, in response to overwhelming interest in a 5.7 litre Chevrolet car-engined motorcycle he'd built and taken to Daytona in 1991. At first Boss Hoss produced mainly frame kits designed to accept the V-eight, with just a few complete bikes, but Warne is steadily increasing the production of complete machines and now exporting to Europe on a small scale. Production is running at about 250 bikes per year. In 1997 Boss Hoss produced its second model, the 4.3 litre V6, also Chevrolet powered, and an automatic version of both bikes the same year.

The V8 is available in 200bhp, 350bhp ZZ4 and 450bhp Turbo versions.

5700cc Boss Hoss V8 (ohv Chevrolet) 1997

BOUCHET • France 1902–1905

Not much is known about these machines, which used acetylene instead of petrol.

BOUGERY • France 1896–1902

One of the first French makes. The engine was mounted between the pedalling gear and the rear wheel.

BOUNDS-JAP • England 1909–1912

Assembled motorcycles with 345cc single-cylinder and 492cc V-twin JAP proprietary engines.

BOVY • Belgium c1906–1932

Albert Bovy built transport vehicles in 1902 and also cars in limited numbers. His motorcycles were of typical English

design and of sturdy appearance. They had 98cc to 996cc proprietary engines made by JAP, MAG, Python, Blackburne, Aubier-Dunne and others

BOWDEN • England 1902–1905

Frank Bowden, who eventually became Sir Frank, fitted 2hp and 2.5hp engines made by FN and also by his own works into his motorcycles. He was also the founder of the Raleigh-Sturmey-Archer Company at Nottingham.

BOWN • England 1922–1924

Small assembler of machines with 147cc Villiers and 248cc and 348cc JAP and Blackburne engines.

BOWN • England 1950–1958

Originally known under the Aberdale trade mark, Bown autocycles were built in different versions with 98cc Villiers engines. Motorcycles made by this company had 98cc and 123cc Villiers engines, but from 1955 onward manufacture concentrated around 49cc Sachs-engined mopeds.

BPR • Switzerland 1929–1932

Founded by former Moto-Rêve and Motosacoche employees - Buratti, Ponti and Roch - BPR fitted 347cc and 497cc single-cylinder Moser and Motosacoche engines into well-made frames. It had also a branch in France.

BPS • France 1973–1978

Producer of trials and motocross machines with engines of 49cc to 123cc supplied by Franco-Morini, Sachs, Aspes and Minarelli. Good and successful design.

BRAAK • Germany 1923–1925

Assembled machines with 129cc and 198cc Heilo and Namapo engines with frames which were supplied by Gruhn of Berlin.

BRADBURY • England 1901–1925

Once a leading British motorcycle factory at Oldham. Built under Birch patent, the first single-cylinder models had 2hp and 2.5hp. When WW1 broke out, the range of models included 554cc singles, 749cc V-twins and 499cc flat twin versions. Improved machines followed after the war and before Bradbury stopped cycle production, there was a 349cc sv single.

BRAITHWAITE • England c1920–1924

Built alongside Lake Windermere in moderate numbers, often with engines made by W. E. Brough (father of George Brough) of Nottingham.

BRAND • Germany 1925–1930

Small factory which built two-stroke machines with flat single-cylinder Bekamo-licenced engines of 123cc, 147cc

123cc Brand (two-stroke Bekamo) 1923

497cc Brondoit (ohv MAG) 1928

and 173cc. These Hugo Ruppe designed engines had a pumping cylinder at the bottom of the crankcase.

BRAVIS • Germany 1924–1926

A famous German rider, Franz Seelos of Munich, rode these 148cc two-strokes and 293cc flat-twins with Bosch-Douglas licenced engines successfully in many events, mainly in the Bavarian part of Germany.

BEDA • Italy 1946–1951

Like Macchi and Caproni, Breda was originally a leading aircraft factory. After the war the firm built motorised bicycles with its own 65cc two-stroke engine.

BRÉE • Austria 1902–1904

Of French origin, Théodor Brée built at Vienna lightweight machines with 1.5hp single-cylinder, two-stroke engines of his own design and manufacture.

555cc Bradbury (sv) 1914

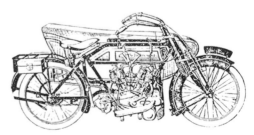

788cc Bradbury (sv V-twin) 1921

1000cc Britten V1000, (dohc V-twin) 1995

BRENNABOR • Germany 1902–1940

There were two periods when the firm built motorcycles. The first was until 1912, when it fitted 3.5hp, 4hp and 6hp engines of Zedel, Fafnir and of its own manufacture into sturdy frames. Afterwards it concentrated on bicycles and cars, but when it stopped car manufacture in 1933, production at the Brandenburg/Havel factory included motorised bicycles with 73cc and 98cc Sachs and Ilo engines.

BRETON • France 1952–1954

Limited production of 70cc Lavalette-powered Babymoto scooters.

BREUIL • France 1903–1908

Fitted different proprietary engines from 4hp to 6hp into its own frames. The engines were mainly Peugeot, Aster and Zurcher.

BRIDGESTONE • Japan 1952–early 1970s

Was part of the famous Bridgestone tire factory and commenced manufacture of motorised two-wheelers with 49cc two-stroke mopeds. Later it built first class motorcycles, mainly 98cc singles and 173cc, 247cc and 348cc vertical twins; all two-strokes with rotary-disc engines of its own manufacture. Among the models were many special versions for the USA market, which was of great importance for Bridgestone as it was not interested

in the home market because of the opposition of Honda, Yamaha, Suzuki and Kawasaki, which were among the best customers of Bridgestone tyres. To keep such big tire customers, Bridgestone decided eventually to pull out of the manufacture of motorcycles.

BRILANT-ALCYON • Czechoslovakia 1932

Built by a well-known bicycle factory - Fuchs & Co. at Zuckmantel - the Brilant-Alcyon (Alcyon license) had a 98cc two-stroke engine and was intended to become a 'people's motorcycle'. Only a few of these machines were made.

BRILLANT • France 1903–1904

Small assembler of motorcycles which used Peugeot and Zurcher engines.

BRITAX • England 1954–1956

Produced mini-scooters with 48cc Ducati ohv engines and was also the first in England to build 49cc racing machines, called Hurricane. They were powered by Ducati Cucciolo ohv engines. Britax is still a leading producer of accessories.

BRITISH-RADIAL • England 1920–1922

Interesting and unorthodox motorcycles with 369cc three-cylinder radial sv engines, designed by J. E. Manes. The engines were made by C. B. Redrup; Chater-Lea supplied

the frames. The 120 degree three had a vaned outside flywheel, detachable heads, enclosed valves etc. Production was on a limited scale.

BRITISH-STANDARD • England 1919–1923

A wide range of 147cc to 548cc engines made by Villiers, TDC, JAP, Bradshaw, Blackburne and Barr & Stroud, powered these 'perfectly standard' motorcycles.

BRITTEN • New Zealand 1990–

John Britten began building roadracing motorcycles in the late 1980s, initially powered by air-cooled V-twin Denco engines, manufactured in New Zealand for sidecar speedway.

An engineer by trade, Britten realised he would need a different engine if his machine was to succeed on tarmac, so he built his own, a water-cooled, fuel-injected 60 degree V-twin. He housed the motor in a radical minimal chassis, running girder-type front forks.

The 165bhp V1000 became the bike to beat in Battle of the Twins racing during the 1990s, winning multiple successes at Daytona and other venues. Britten built a handful of bikes for sale and though he tragically died of cancer in 1995, Britten Motorcycles is still a going concern.

BRM • Italy 1955–1957

Produced small 48cc two-stroke machines and had no connection with the once famous British BRM racing car firm at Bourne.

BROUGH SUPERIOR • England 1921–1940

Known as the 'Rolls-Royce among motorcycles', Brough Superior motorcycles were built regardless of costs by George Brough, son of W. E. Brough. He was a famous technician and since his youth a very successful competitor in sporting events, first with his father's Brough machines, then with his own Brough Superiors, which were mainly built with V-twin engines. These included models with 678cc, 746cc, 980cc, 996cc and 1150cc engines, made by JAP, MAG and Matchless; in some cases especially for Brough Superior, in other cases with special parts for this make. There was also a 498cc ohv V-twin with a JAP engine in 1930 and in 1932 a 796cc in-line four with a water-cooled and modified Austin car engine. This model, destined for sidecar work, had two rear wheels, which were only a few inches apart and fitted in the center. Most famous were George Brough's SS100 ohv and SS80 sv V-twins and there were also many interesting one-off prototypes, ie machines which never came into quantity production. These included air-cooled 996cc V-fours, air-cooled 990cc in-line fours and also the famous Dream of 1938, which had a transverse-mounted flat four-cylinder 996cc engine and shaft drive. It was not yet fully developed when the war broke out. Brough intended to produce motorcycles again after 1945, but as there were no suitable engines available, he eventually had to give up. Famous Brough Superior personalities included Harold 'Oily' Karslake, works manager Icke Webb and T. E. Lawrence of Arabia, who owned seven BS machines during the years. Among the leading racing men were Brough himself, Eric Fernihough, Freddy Dixon, E. C. E. Baragwanath, Bert le Vack, Joe Wright, Eddy Meyer, Kpt. Vladimir Kucka, Ernst Zündorf, Otokar Weinhara, Bob Berry and Lucky Schmied.

998cc Brough Superior SS100 (ohv) 1938

998cc Brough Superior SS100 (ohv V-twin Matchless) 1938

1150cc Brough Superior 11-50 (sv V-twin) 1938

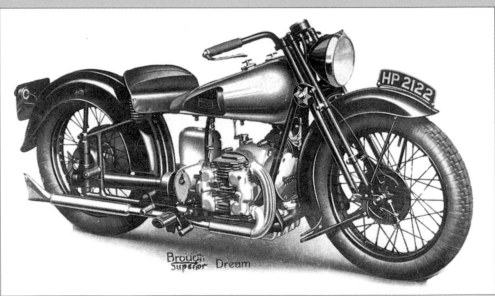

996cc Brough Superior Dream (ohv boxer four) 1938

998cc Brough Superior SS100 (ohv V-twin Matchless) 1938

The New "11-50 SPECIAL" (1935)

PRICE.

Completely equipped as Specification.

11-50 SPECIAL RIGID FRAME MODEL, complete with Special Lucas Magdyno - Lighting Set and Lucas Altette Horn,

£118

11-50 SPECIAL SPRING FRAME MODEL, complete with Special Lucas Magdyno Lighting Set and Lucas Altette Horn,

£128

EXTRAS.

	£ s. d.		£ s. d.
Rear Wheel Driven Speedometer	3 10 0	Wheels as above, also with Chromium Hubs and Brake Drums per pair	3 0 0
Large Dial Speedometer (5in.)	5 10 0		
Carrier	1 0 0	Racing Type Screen fitted to Forks	10 6
Folding Pillion Footrests	12 6	Interchangeable and Instantly	
Aluminium Number Plates	17 6	Detachable Wheels per pair	7 0 0
Propstand	1 5 0	Spare Wheel, with Tyre	3 19 0
Legshields	1 5 0	Large Alpine Bags, with Valises, per pair	2 0 0
Chromium Plated Mudguards, with Black Centres (Solo)	3 10 0		
Chromium Plated Mudguards, with Black Centres (Combination)	5 0 0	Safety Bumpers	2 5 0
		"Castle" Forks for 11-50 (Recommended when machine required Solo.)	5 0 0
Wheels, with Chromium Rims and Black Centres per pair	1 10 0		
Positive Foot Change	1 10 0	Rev. Counter	3 10 0

GEORGE BROUGH

Motor Cycle Designer Manufacturer : Rider

BS

1150cc Brough Superior 11-50 Special (sv V-twin) 1935

BROCKHOUSE • England 1948–1955

Famous engineering company and one time producer of 98cc Corgi Mini-scooters which could be folded up. Eventually bought the Indian motorcycle factory at Springfield, Massachusetts in the USA and produced for them at the English factory the 248cc Indian Brave, which had its own sv single-cylinder unit-design engine. Some other firms, including OEC and DOT, fitted it also into their frames. Brockhouse afterwards sold Indian to Associated Motor Cycles Ltd. in London.

BRONDOIT • Belgium 1924–1929

Paul de Bussy's Brondoit (Brondoit-Herstal) factory produced 248cc and 348cc two-stroke machines with outside flywheel engines and also from 1928 onward a sporting 498cc model with the Swiss single-cylinder double-port ohv engine, made by MAG (Motosacoche).

BROUGH • England 1908–1926

This was the machine designed and built by W. E. Brough, George Brough's father. The range consisted first of singles and V-twins, but soon William Brough became a flat-twin devotee. With Granville Bradshaw on friendly terms, he used first Bradshaw's 496cc ABC engines, afterwards his own 496cc ohv and 692cc as well as 810cc sv engines. All were flat twins, a design which was not favoured by his son George Brough, who eventually left his father's works and founded his own motorcycle factory at Haydn Road, Nottingham in 1921.

BROUGH SUPERIOR • England 1921–1940

See panel

BROWN • England 1902–1919

Brown motorcycles had 348cc and 498cc single-cylinder and 498cc V-twin sv engines. After 1919 they used the name Vindec, but had no connection with the former German Allright motorcycles of the same name, Vindec-Special (VS). These names were used by Allright only for machines exported to England.

BROWN-BICAR • England (USA) 1907–1913

Equipped with 3hp single-cylinder and 5hp V-twin engines, the Brown-Bicar was an unusual motorcycle design with enclosed engine. It was also built in the USA under license, but was not a commercial success.

BRUNEAU • France 1903–1910

The first versions had Zedel proprietary engines, but around 1905 Bruneau built 498cc vertical-twin machines of its own design. They were among the first vertical-twins ever made.

BSA • England 1906–1971

See panel

B & S • Germany 1925–1930

Identical to Brand two-stroke machines with 123cc, 147cc and 173cc pumping cylinder Bekamo engines. The B & S stood for Brand & Söhne of Berlin.

BUBI • Germany 1921–1924

Small bicycle producer who built 1.5hp two-stroke engines into strengthened bicycle frames.

BUCHER • Italy 1911–1920

Known also as Bucher-Zeda, the once prominent factory built singles and V-twin cylinder machines of 342cc, 499cc and 568cc with its own ohv engines.

BSA • England 1906–1971

Years before BSA (Birmingham Small Arms) produced complete motorcycles, it supplied most British and foreign factories with cycle parts of the highest caliber. The first complete machines were motorized bicycles. Afterwards, single-cylinder sv models with its own engines were built. These were 498cc (85mm x 88mm bore/stroke, 3·5hp) and 555cc (85mm x 98mm bore/stroke, 4.5hp) designs. The first sv V-twin had 770cc and was built in 1921. The following year another V-twin of 986cc made its first appearance. Other models built during the 1920s and early 1930s included the famous round-tank 249cc version, 349cc sv and ohv singles and similar 498cc models. There were also 174cc two-strokes, and in the late 1920s 493cc singles including the famous Slopers with sv and especially ohv engines. The 1930 range included 249cc sv and 249cc double-port ohv singles, 349cc sv and ohv singles and also 493cc versions with (as always) BSA's own sv and ohv power units. Most models were supplied with vertical or inclined engines, the ohv versions with one or, if required, two exhaust pipes. The V-twins had 770cc and 986cc engines. The 174cc two-stroke was superseded by a 149cc ohv single during the 1930s. Other models in these pre-war days had 249cc sv and ohv and similar 348cc and 499cc single-cylinder engines. Then came 498cc and 748cc ohv V-twins and a 595cc sv single. The prices in 1936: 149cc ohv £31.7s.6d., 499cc sv £56.10s., 748cc ohv V-twin £75 and the same for the

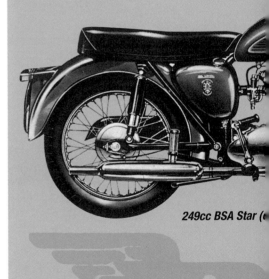

249cc BSA Star (

497cc Brough (ohv flat twin) 1919

246cc BSA Roundtank(sv) 1924

497cc BSA Sloper (ohv) 1928

493cc BSA (sv) 1929

493cc BSA Empire Star (ohv) 1938

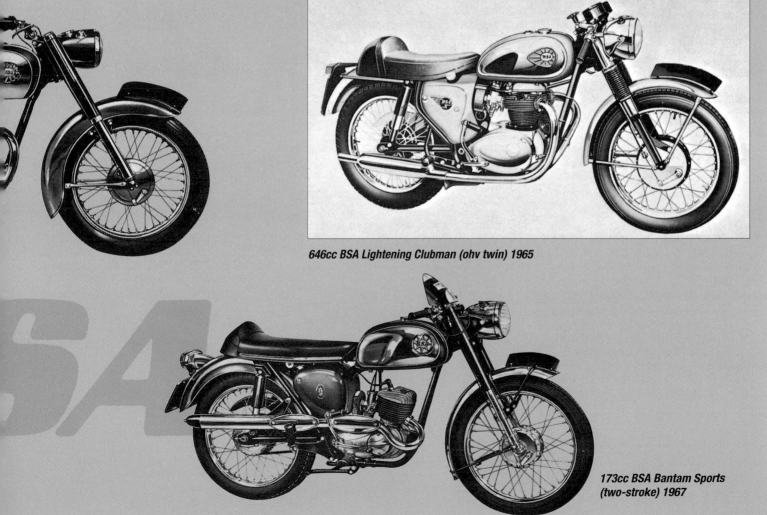

646cc BSA Lightening Clubman (ohv twin) 1965

173cc BSA Bantam Sports
(two-stroke) 1967

986cc sv V-twin. Although BSA never competed officially in races, in the late 1930s it produced very sporting singles. Walter Handley won a Gold Star in June 1937 at Brooklands (riding a tuned 493cc ohv Empire Star), an award made to all riders who lapped the track at over 100 mph. This led in 1938 to the first 'Gold Star' BSA model, which—also with a 348cc engine - was built for many years and after WW2 was one of the most popular sports machines ever built in England, especially among clubmen, as these machines were not only fast and reliable, but also comparatively cheap and of simple design. Among many other events, they won clubman's TT races and also showed great reliability and high speeds in the 'pure' TT events. New 123cc, 148cc and 174cc two-stroke singles, the Bantam models, were introduced after the war, in which 493cc sv singles were among the leading machines of the Forces. Like so many similar machines, the Bantam was a copy of the DKW RT 125, the design effectively taken as a 'spoil of war'.

Among the post-war BSA models were the single-cylinder 249cc and 343cc ohv Star versions, new 497cc and 646cc vertical ohv twins and also different single-cylinder trials and scrambles models. During the late 1960s it produced the 441cc single-cylinder Victor and twin-cylinder Royal Star versions with 499cc (65·5mm x 74mm bore/stroke) engines as well as 654cc (75mm x 74mm bore/stroke) twins, which included the Thunderbolt, Lightning, Hornet and Spitfire models. In the early 1970s BSA produced 173cc Bantam two-strokes, 247cc and 441cc Starfires and Shooting Stars with ohv single-cylinder engines, 654cc Thunderbolt ohv twins, the very popular 654cc Lightning ohv twin and the Firebird, a 654cc twin-cylinder 55 bhp scrambler. New was the 740cc Rocket, a three-cylinder ohv machine with a transverse mounted engine. This machine produced 58bhp at 7250rpm and had a top speed of over 120mph. Later models had 64bhp at 7500rpm. In addition, there was also a new Gold Star, the 500SS, with a 499cc single-cylinder ohv engine. Once England's leading motorcycle factory, BSA ceased production in 1972.

The BSA workforce continued making Triumph T150 and T160 triples for the next three years, under the new ownership of Norton Villiers Triumph, a consortium part-funded by the British government. Eventually though, NVT went into receivership and the Small Heath factory was first closed then demolished.

The story continued however, as around a dozen former NVT staff reformed the company at Shenstone, aiming to finish development and produce the Wankel rotary-powered machine which had been worked on by BSA/Triumph's research and development department. The name was changed to Norton Motors but the group still controlled the BSA name as well as other old British marques, and many hundreds of Yamaha-engined 125cc and 175cc trail bikes were built for the growing African market for dependable small capacity semi off-road machines, all sold with the BSA badge which was still known and trusted in many African countries.

499cc BSA Gold Star Clubmans (ohv single) 1960

BSA

In 1979 two NVT staff, Bertie Goodman (formerly of Velocette) and Bill Colquhoun, formed an independant BSA Company to allow Norton Motors to concentrate on Nortons, and moved to a new site in Coventry from where they supplied military machines, based on Canadian Bombadiers, to the British military.

In 1990 BSA combined with Andover Norton International (a company set up to maintain spares supply for old Norton twins) to form the BSA Group, which imported MZ motorcycles from Germany as well as still supplying BSA Bushmans to Africa. In 1994 the company was bought by Regal Engineering, which has recently unveiled a new model called the BSA SR, featuring Gold Star type styling and a Yamaha single cylinder engine.

This should not be seen as a precursor to a return as dramatic as Triumph's.

198cc BSA Bushman (ohc single Yamaha) 1998

398cc BSA Gold SR (ohc single Yamaha) 1999

BUCHET • France 1900–1911

Better known as producer of proprietary engines and cars, Buchet also built motorcycles in limited numbers and even some unusual three-wheelers; one - a racing version in 1903 - had a vertical twin-cylinder engine of 4245cc.

BÜCKER • Germany 1922–1958

Was a leading assembler of motorcycles from 98cc to 996cc in Germany. The proprietary engines used included the makes Cockerell, Rinne, Columbus, MAG, JAP, Blackburne and Bark. After 1945 all Bücker machines had Ilo or Sachs two-stroke engines, including 244cc twin-cylinder versions. In the late 1940s, a pre-war 248cc Bücker with an ohv JAP engine, ridden by Friedl Schön, won the 250cc road-race championship of Germany.

BUELL • America 1985–

See panel

BULLDOG • England 1920

Small assembler of orthodox lightweight machines. Used 269cc Villiers two-stroke engines.

BULLO • Germany 1924–1926

Unconventional electric motorcycle made at Bremen. The power unit was mounted in the steering center and supplied via a 120-Ah-Battery 0.7hp. Only a limited number were built.

BÜLOW • Germany 1923–1925

Produced 2hp, 2.5hp and 3hp machines with own two-stroke engines.

BULTACO • Spain 1958–

See panel

244cc Bücker (two-stroke Ilotwin) 1953

BUELL • America 1985–

Former Harley-Davidson engineer Erik Buell built his first machine in 1985, the RR1000, to combine his twin passions for racing and Harley-Davidsons - the bike was powered by a tuned Harley V-twin engine. This was followed other racers, then in 1989 the RR1200, Buell's first road-going model.

Buell maintained close links with the Harley factory at Milwaukee, which in turn saw an opportunity to move into the sports bike market without any danger of diluting the strength of the Harley-Davidson badge, exclusively linked to American custom-styled machines. As a result, in 1993 the Buell Motorcycle Company was founded in East Troy, 30 miles from Milwaukee, as a collaboration between Harley-Davidson, which owns 49 per cent, and Erik Buell.

The engines are built by Harley but incorporate from the production line the many modifications designed in by Erik Buell to achieve major power increases compared with the originals.

Buell motorcycles have consistently featured several unique or distinctive characteristics, including tubular steel trellis frames, rear shock absorbers slung beneath the engines and a clever rubber mounting system for the engine to isolate its vibration from the rider.

The first bike from East Troy was the S2 Thunderbolt, and the model range then expanded to include Lightning, White Lightning and Cyclone models by 1999, all sports or sports-touring machines with highly individual looks and tuned 1200cc Harley-Davidson engines. Current production levels are around 4500 machines annually, but Buell is concentrating on expanding into many new markets worldwide.

1203cc Buell White Lightning (ohv v-twin H-D) 1998

1203cc Buell S3T Thunderbolt (ohv v-twin H-D) 1998

1203cc Buell M2 Cyclone (ohv v-twin H-D) 1998

BULTACO • Spain 1958–

Founded by Francesco X. Bulto, previously co-founder of Montesa, and early on, successful in Spanish racing. Later, modestly successful in Grands Prix, but better known for its sales of 125cc, 250cc and later 350cc racers to private owners. Later still, Bultaco turned successfully to motocross and especially to trials, enlisting help from Sammy Miller who became the premier trials rider. Bultaco two-strokes sold well in the USA as road and trail bikes in the 1960s and 1970s, but sales declined with new clean air laws. Bultaco turned to 50cc road racing in 1976 and won the world title four times between then and 1981. The factory also won the first World Trials Championship in 1975 with Englishman Martin Lampkin, and went on to claim a further four World Trials titles until pulling out of top-level competition in 1980. However, the company was in financial trouble by then and, despite government intervention and talks of merger with Montesa and Ossa, failed in the mid-1980s.

The Bultaco name was then bought in 1998 from the Bulto family by a conglomerate including French Scorpa owner Marc Tessier and former Gas-Gas technician Andre Codina, and it has just re-entered the market with a new trials machine after more than 12 years.

The first liquid-cooled 250cc Sherco machines, a progression of the original Sherpa name, rolled off the French production line in December 1998 and the new factory is campaigning its first World Championship season in 1999 with Spain's David Cobos.

49cc Bultaco Labito (two-stroke single) 1999

244cc Bultaco Metralla (two-stroke) 1971

BURFORD • England 1914–1915

The war prevented any larger production of these 496cc single-cylinder sv and 269cc two-stroke Villiers-engined machines.

BURGERS-ENR • The Netherlands 1897–1961

Once a leading Dutch make which for a long period fitted engines of its own design; afterwards 497cc Blackburne single-cylinder and 676cc JAP V-twin engines. There was also a 246cc two-stroke with the Vitesse engine.

BURKHARDTIA • Germany 1904–1908

Early two-stroke machines with 165cc single-cylinder and 244cc twin-cylinder engines, made by the famous Grade works at Magdeburg. The twin-cylinder versions had vertical cylinders.

BURNEY • England 1923–1925

Designed by Cecil Burney, formerly of Burney & Blackburne fame, these 497cc machines had Burney's own sv engines with an outside flywheel. Captain Baldwin, the well-known rider, was commercially connected with this make. Burney also built a very limited number of 679cc sv V-twins.

BUSI • Italy 1950–1953

Sporting two-stroke machines of typical Italian design. The range included 123cc, 160cc, 173cc and 198cc versions.

BUSSE • Germany 1922–1926

Well-designed and sturdy machines with 143cc Grade and 147cc and 173cc DKW two-stroke proprietary engines. There was also a 198cc model with the ohv Paqué engine and other versions with power units of its own design and manufacture.

BUYDENS • Belgium 1950–1955

Produced two-stroke machines with Ydral and Sachs engines from 123cc to 248cc. The production was on a limited scale.

BV • Czechoslovakia 1923–1930

Made by a small factory, the BV - Balzer & Vemola - was fitted with the company's own engines. These included 173cc two-strokes, 346cc and 746cc sv, as well as 496cc ohv versions. The biggest model was a V-twin. Julius Vemola himself raced a 496cc single with ohc in 1925.

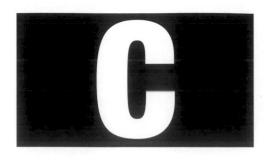

C

C & G • England c1920s–early1930s

JAP-powered motorcycles built by Clifton and De Guerin, Bath.

CABRERA • Italy 1979–1986

Produced on a small scale 124cc and 158cc two-stroke trials machines.

CABTON • Japan 1954–1961

Was a leading manufacturer. The machines, built much on typical English lines, were 123cc to 246cc two-strokes and - mainly - ohv vertical-twins from 248cc to 648cc.

CAESAR • England 1922–1923

Small assembler of lightweights with 269cc Villiers two-stroke engines.

CAGIVA • Italy 1979–

See panel on this page

CALCOTT • England 1910–1915

Built by a well-known car factory at Coventry. White & Poppe proprietary engines of 292cc and also its own 249cc and 292cc singles powered these machines.

CALTHORPE • England 1911–1939

Founded by George Hands, Calthorpe had a very mixed story with many ups and even more downs, but it built some very nice machines at reasonable prices. The first machines had 211cc two-stroke engines, others four-stroke Precision and JAP power units. During the 1920s, various 147cc to 498cc single-cylinder Villiers, JAP and Blackburne engines powered Calthorpes. From 1925 onward, new 348cc ohv and 498cc ohc single-cylinder models of its own manufacture came into being. From 1929, the Ivory range of new 348cc ohv machines, later also 248cc and 498cc versions - all with ohv double-port engines - headed Calthorpe production. Prices were comparatively low and just before the Birmingham factory closed down in 1938, official prices for the fully equipped machines were as follows: 248cc £47, 348cc £52 10s. and 498cc £54 10s. When the receiver sold the works, Bruce Douglas of Bristol, who was a nephew of the founder of the Douglas motorcycle factory and who owned a firm producing parts for aircraft engines, bought the Calthorpe production equipment and moved it to Bristol. There he built new models with 347cc and 497cc ohv Matchless single-cylinder engines. Only a few were finished when the war broke out. After 1945 he did not return to motorcycle manufacture and eventually sold the equipment to the DMW factory. Calthorpe was never a leading producer of successful racing machines, but had some successes with Stanley Gill and the Austrian Rudi Hunger.

CAGIVA • Italy 1979–

Cagiva was formed in 1979 when brothers Claudio and Gianfranco Castiglioni bought the Aermacchi factory at Varese in Italy from Harley-Davidson. The first road bikes were simply rebadged versions of the Aermacchi two-strokes already in production and previously called Harley-Davidsons, but Cagiva signalled where its future lay by immediately entering Grand Prix racing, running a 500 square-four two-stroke, reputedly based on factory Suzuki RG500 crankcases. The marque's racers continued to resemble Japanese racers for some years and were unsuccessful, but by the mid-1980s Cagiva was getting serious with its first V-four 500.

This was contemporaneous with Cagiva's purchase of Ducati in 1985 from the state-owned company Finmeccanica, saving the name from oblivion. Cagiva had already been supplied with Ducati engines for some years, but the acquisition of the company allowed the Castiglionis to pursue their racing passion on two fronts. The cash input from Cagiva allowed Ducati to push ahead with its development programme and take up racing seriously, so that from the end of the 1980s Cagiva was effectively running Grand Prix and World Superbike teams. Success did come to the Italians though, with Ducati dominating World Superbikes, and in 1989 American Randy Mamola gave the Cagiva factory its first podium finish at the soaking Belgian GP and three years later four-times 500 world champion Eddie Lawson took Cagiva's first win, at a damp Hungarian GP.

By 1993 Cagiva's V593 was reckoned to be fully competitive with its Japanese rivals and John Kocinski won the marque's first dry-weather GP in the United States. The following year he led the world championship for a period, eventually finishing third overall, only for the Castiglioni brothers to announce their withdrawal from GP racing. This last - and best - Cagiva Grand Prix machine was the C594 which featured an 80 degree V-four reed-valve two-stroke producing around 180bhp at just under 13,000rpm.

The reason the racing had to stop was clear: it was financed almost entirely by the Ducati factory alone, as Cagiva was selling few motorcycles with its own name – in the important home market the name failed to gain credibility, the stark result of this being that in December 1995 for example, the year Cagiva withdrew from racing, it sold just seven of its 125cc Mito sports bikes in the home market. With Ducati only producing around 20,000 machines a year, the sums clearly didn't add up.

Even so, some success was had with the Elefant series, the big trail bike introduced in 1989. This was available with either the 750cc or 900cc V-twin engines from the Ducati SS series, and developed from Cagiva's successes in the Paris-Dakar rally. Although the bike was never a big seller, it built up a loyal following and proved one of the better, more wieldy machines of its type.

But compounding Cagiva's money problems was the attempt to develop a brand new four-cylinder superbike with which the Castiglionis planned to reintroduce the MV Agusta name, and at the end of 1996 Cagiva was forced to sell a 51 per cent share in Ducati to the American Texas Pacific group, simply to pay the bills.

124cc Cagiva Mito (two-stroke water-cooled single) 19

CAGIVA

124cc Cagiva Super City (water-cooled two-stroke single) 1997

124cc Cagiva motocross (water-cooled two-stroke) 1982

124.6cc Cagiva Roadster (air-cooled two-stroke single) 1998

The money from the sale allowed the MV project to continue, and at the 1997 Milan Show, the Massimo Tamburini-styled F4 was finally unveiled (see 'MV Agusta').

By the end of 1998 Cagiva's situation was looking healthier. Interest in the MV was enormous but the Elefant's replacement, the Gran Canyon, sells only in small numbers. Other Cagiva machines, such as the utility River 600, Canyon 600, Mito 50 and 125 and 125cc Planet are also destined for low volume production, while the recent rebadging of Taiwanese San Yang scooters as Cagivas is not a major money-spinner. What Cagiva desperately needs to secure its long-term future is a large volume, large capacity machine, to generate sufficient income to develop new models and to fully utilise the three factories at Varese which it owns. It is expected that the MV Agusta F4 engine will be adapted for other machines, some Cagiva-badged, others MV Agustas, with this in mind.

As a footnote, the Cagiva company changed its name to MV Agusta from July 1 1999, although this is not the end of the Cagiva name as it will still be used on a variety of machines coming from the Varese factory.

864cc Cagiva Gran Canyon (air-cooled ohc desmo V-twin Ducati) 1999

600cc Cagiva Canyon (air-cooled four-stroke single) 1998

493cc Calthorpe (ohc) 1926

496cc Calthorpe (ohv Matchless) 1939

198cc Cambra (sv) 1925

CALVERT • England 1899–1904

Motorcycle pioneer, who used Minerva engines as well as its own 2.25hp, 2.75hp and 3.25hp motors.

CAMBER • England 1920–1921

Built by a motorcycle dealer, these machines had 492cc sv Precision engines.

CAMBRA • Germany 1921–1926

The Berlin-built Cambra was (unlike most other Berlin-made motorcycles of that period) a four-stroke, of 180cc and 198cc and had its own sv engines.

CAMILLE-FOUCAUD • France 1952–1954

Producer of mini-scooters with 49cc, 70cc and 118cc engines.

CAMPION • England 1901–1926

Was a well-known bicycle factory at Nottingham, which used a variety of proprietary engines when it produced motorcycles. These had capacities from 147cc to 996cc. Engine suppliers were Minerva, MMC, Fafnir, Precision, Villiers, Blackburne and JAP. The big models with the V-twin JAP engines had Brough Superior-like petrol tanks. Campion also supplied frames to other firms and when Jock Porter's New Gerrard factory at Edinburgh could not cope with production, from 1924 to 1926 it had New Gerrards built at the Campion works.

CAN-AM • Canada 1973–1987

The Canadian Bombardier Snowmobile Group also owns the Austrian engine manufacturer Rotax, famous for its two-stroke twins (with disc valves, contra-rotating tandem crankshafts and water cooling), as well as its larger single-cylinder four-stroke engines, and as a development partner of Aprilia and BMW with the F650 and Pegaso 650cc singles. Can-Am was big in motocross and employed the famous ex-BSA team rider Jeff Smith for many years. Clean air legislation in the US market limited the scope of the two-strokes and, in 1987, manufacture of the Can-Am motorcycle was halted and efforts switched to snowmobiles and boats, produced

under the Bombardier name. Rotax engines, however, are still made, and the company is an important engine design consultant.

CANNONDALE • America 1998–

Cannondale was founded at the beginning of the 1980s to manufacture off-road bicycles, specialising in aluminum fabrications. At the end of the 1990s it turned its attention to motocross machines, introducing in 1999 the MX400, with aluminum frame and liquid-cooled four-stroke single-cylinder engine equipped with electric start, fuel injection, gear-driven dohc and reversed cylinder head.

CAPPONI • Italy 1924–1926

Two-stroke machines with own 173cc three-port engines. Limited production.

CAPRIOLO • Italy 1948–1963

Former aircraft factory which produced 73cc ohv machines with pressed steel frames and unit-design engines. Later models also included 123cc ohv versions with tubular frames. There were also NSU-engined two-strokes and some interesting face-cam ohc machines with capacities up to 123cc. Another interesting Trento-built Capriolo design was a 149cc flat twin with a transverse-mounted unit-design ohv engine and a pressed steel frame. Capriolo also built transport three-wheelers with 75cc and 150cc engines.

CAPRONI-VIZZOLA • Italy 1953–1959

Sturdily built machines with - mainly - engines supplied by NSU of Germany. The range included the 198cc Cavilux, as well as the 173cc and 248cc ohv singles. The last one was based on the NSU Max and was called Cavimax. This engine developed 17bhp at 6500rpm.

494cc Can-Am (Rotax ohc 4-valve single) 1982

400cc Cannondale MX400 (water-cooled two-stroke single) 1999

149cc Capriolo (ohv flat-twin) 1955

CARABELA • Mexico 1971–1979

Mainly built for the USA market, the Mexican Carabela showed typical Italian lines. The range included two-strokes of 102cc, 123cc, 173cc, 193cc and 245cc for motocross, trials, enduro and also use on normal roads. Earlier models used European engines, including Jawa and Villa.

CARBINE • Australia c1902–c1916

JAP and MAG-engined machines built by Williams Brothers of Sydney who later made Waratah machines. The name Carbine was adopted by the brothers who also made cycles and wheelchairs after the 1894 Melbourne Cup-winning racehorse Carbine.

CARDAN • France 1902–1908

Motorcycles with De Dion engines and shaft drive to the rear wheel.

CARFIELD • England 1919–1924

Equipped with spring frames, Carfield motorcycles had 247cc and 269cc Villiers two-stroke and 347cc Blackburne sv single-cylinder engines. Another model used the Coventry-Victor 688cc sv flat twin engine.

CARLEY • France 1950–1953

Mini-scooter with a flat 49cc two-stroke engine.

125cc Casal K260 (air-cooled two-stroke single) 1971

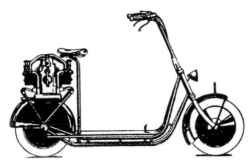

248cc CAS (sv flat twin) 1922

CARLTON • England 1913–1940

Bicycle factory which is now part of the Raleigh group. Owned in the 1930s by former tuning wizard and racing motorcyclist Don R. O'Donovan who was also motorcycle designer at Raleigh (Sturmey-Archer), Carlton produced 123cc two-strokes with Villiers engines and also supplied similar machines under a different name to a leading motorcycle dealer In London.

CARLTON • Scotland 1922

Orthodox lightweight machines with 269cc Villiers engines, built in limited numbers.

CARNIELLI • Italy 1951–circa 1965

Producer of the well-known 48cc Graziella folding mofa, Carnielli built during the years many different lightweights. These included 73cc two-strokes and also models with 98cc ohv NSU engines. There was also a co-operation with the German Victoria factory which supplied 48cc two-stroke and other engines.

CARPATI • Rumania 1960–

Leading moped producer in Rumania. Builds its own 65cc two-stroke engines.

CARPIO • France 1930–1935

Lightweight machines with 98cc and 124cc Aubier-Dunne and Stainless two-stroke engines.

CARREAU • France c1903

Produced motorcycles with 1.5hp engines.

CAS • Czechoslovakia 1921–1924

Designed by J. Reichziegal, the CAS scooter closely resembled the British ABC Skootamota, but used a flat twin 4-stroke engine of 130cc and then 150cc. CAS also made lightweight motorcycles, with 175cc and 225cc two stroke engines.

CASAL • Portugal 1964–

The first Casal machines had Zèndapp engines and also a Zündapp-like appearance. Afterwards it fitted its own two-stroke engines from 49cc to 248cc and also produced a water-cooled 49cc machine. Other versions included 74cc machines and various trials and motocross models. The 248cc trials model had a 27bhp motor. In the 1980s and 1990s Casal concentrated mainly on production of 50cc scooters and motorcycles, including some sports models.

CASALINI • Italy 1958–1963

Mini-scooter producer which switched to the manufacture of a wide range of 48cc mopeds.

CASOLI • Italy 1928–1933

Sporting 172cc machines with Villiers and own two-stroke engines. Limited production.

CASTADOT • Belgium 1900–1901

Only few of these machines - which had 1.5hp Zedel engines - were built.

CASTELL • England 1903

Assembler which fitted Minerva and Sarolea engines into its own frames.

CASWELL • England 1904–1905

Strengthened bicycle frames with 2.5hp, 2.75hp and 3.5hp Minerva engines.

CAYENNE • England 1912–1913

An obscure firm which might have been of continental origin, that entered a water-cooled ohv single in the 1913 Senior TT.

CAZALEX • France 1951–1955

Lightweight machines with two-stroke engines from 49cc to 124cc.

CAZANAVE • France 1955–1957

Producer of 49cc mopeds and lightweight machines.

CBR • Italy 1912–1914

Turin built machines. The range included two-strokes, a 225cc sv machine and also bigger models with 3hp, 5hp and 8hp engines.

CC • England 1921–1924

The initials 'CC' were those of Charles Chamberlain, a small producer in Bispham, Blackpool, Lancashire. CC machines were offered in capacities ranging from 147cc to 996cc, but it is not certain what went into production. Engines included a 269cc Villiers, and Blackburnes of 347 and 497cc.

CCM • Canada c1910–1914

Lightweights assembled using the Motosaccoche clip-on unit by the Canada Cycle & Motor Company, Toronto.

CCM • England 1971–

Maker of trials and motocross machines originally based on BSA engines, later extensively developed by founder Alan Clews. Many famous riders, such as Nick Jeffries, John Banks and Norman Barrow, rode CCMs. CCM was absorbed by Armstrong in 1980 and sold back to Clews in 1987, after which its success at producing enduro and motocross machines increased. In 1999 CCM unveiled its first road going single-cylinder machine, which because of interchangeable wheels could be converted between a trail bike and a supermoto.

CECCATO • Italy 1950–1963

Produced a wide range of two-strokes from 49cc to 173cc and also ohv and some ohc models from 73cc to 123cc. The 73cc ohc Super Sport produced 8bhp at 11,000rpm, the 98cc version 11bhp at 10,500rpm. The single ohc

600cc CCM Enduro supermoto (air-cooled ohc single Rotax) 1999

600cc CCM 604R (air-cooled ohc single Rotax) 1999

was driven by a train of gears; the top speed of these machines was 71.5 and 77.5mph respectively.

CEDOS • England 1919–1929

Well-made 211cc and 249cc two-strokes which were also delivered with open frames for use by ladies. From 1924 onwards, the range included also 348cc ohv models with Bradshaw and Blackburne engines, a 348cc sv Blackburne-engined version and a 990cc V-twin with an sv JAP engine and Brough Superior-like petrol tank.

CELTIC • Ireland c1910–1914

Irish assembled machines often sold to servicemen based at the Curragh, also opened London office.

CEMEC • France 1948–1955

Predecessor of Ratier and successor to CMR, CEMEC built mainly BMW-like 746cc transverse-mounted sv flat twins and a limited number of 746cc and 493cc ohv models on similar lines. All had plunger rear suspension and telescopic forks.

CENTAUR • Germany 1924–1925

Small assembler of lightweight machines with 1.5hp sv engines supplied by Gruhn of Berlin.

746cc CEMEC (sv flat twin) 1954

CENTAUR • England 1901–1915

Once a well-known make and also a technically interesting design. Among the models were 348cc V-twins and a 492cc sv single, which originally had the silencer inside the front down-tube. Later Centaur models used square cylinder cooling fins.

CENTER • Japan 1950–1962

Sporting 149cc ohv singles with own unit-design engines.

CENTURY • England 1902–1905

A long forgotten make which used Minerva and MMC engines.

CF • Italy 1928–1971

Designed by Catelli and Fiorani, these were potent 173cc and 248cc ohc singles, which won many Italian races. Fusi, closely connected with Belgian FN, bought the CF factory in 1937. After an interruption, a reorganized company built 49cc two-stroke machines from the late 1960s onwards.

CFC • France 1903–1906

Strengthened bicycle frames with 1.5hp engines.

C & G • England c1920s–early1930s

JAP-powered motorcycles built by Clifton and De Guerin, Bath.

CHAMPION • America 1911–1913

Made by Peerless at St. Louis, the air-cooled 1261cc in-line four Champion had a car-like frame built under Militaire licence and idler wheels on both sides. The ioe engine had ball gear-change and shaft drive to the rear wheel. Both wheels had wooden spokes. Production of these unconventional motorcycles was on a limited basis.

CHAMPION • Australia c1912–1924

Built in Tasmania by John King and Son, using JAP, MAG and Peugeot engines.

CHAMPION • Japan 1960–1967

These machines, made by Bridgestone Tire Co., had two-stroke engines from 49cc to 123cc.

CHANG JIANG • China 1985–

Produces the CJ750M1M, based on the 1957 BMW R71. The M1M is an update of the CJ750M1, the chief changes being the use of 12v electrics on the later bike, instead of 6v, and a small power increase (up from 21bhp at 4600rpm to 23bhp at 4500rpm).

CHARIOT • Czechoslovakia c1902–1906

Limited production of belt-driven pioneer machines.

CHARLETT • Germany 1921–1924

Lightweight machines with Charlett's own 195cc sv single-cylinder engines.

CHARLKRON • Germany 1925

Small producer of 348cc and 498cc single-cylinder machines with 3-valve ohc 'K' (Küchen) proprietary engines.

CHARLTON • England 1904–1908

These motorcycles were equipped with 402cc Buchet engines, which were originally made in France.

CHASE • England 1902–1906

Made by the Chase brothers, of London, then leading bicycle racers, Chase motorcycles had various engines made by Minerva, MMC and Precision.

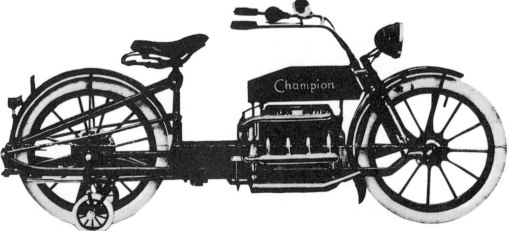

1306cc Champion (ioe Militaire-Patents four-cylinder) 1917

CHATER·LEA

545cc Chater Lea (own sv engine) 1926

348cc Chater Lea (ohc Camshaft model) 1926

CHATER LEA • England 1900–1937

Chater – soon Chater Lea – at first supplied components, such as frame lugs, forgings and castings and special gears, to the trade; it survived as a general engineering company for 50 years after it stopped making motorcycles. In later years, it made only a 550cc sv Blackburne-engined sidecar outfit, most of which were supplied to the AA for road patrol use. Manufacture ceased when Blackburne stopped making engines. Earlier, Chater Lea had used a very wide range of engines, including MAG, JAP and Villiers as well as Blackburne. It also made its own 350cc ohc engine in the 1920s and had some success with it, especially on the continent. This was actually a 'face cam' engine, not to be confused with the true ohc modified Blackburne 350cc engine. With that, in a Chater Lea frame, Doug Marchant exceeded 100mph – the first time for a 350cc machine – over a flying kilometre at Brooklands in 1924.

CHELL • England 1939

Lightweight machines with 123cc Villiers engines, made in limited numbers only.

CHIORDA • Italy 1954–1956

Produced 48cc ohv machines; afterwards mainly 49cc two-strokes with Franco Morini engines, including motocross versions.

CHRISTOPHE • France 1920s

Identical production to Automoto with two-strokes up to 248cc and sv models up to 498cc. The range also included 498cc double-port ohc models with unit-design engines.

CIE • Belgium 1900–1905

Pioneer in the motorcycle game with 3hp and 4hp machines designed by M. Coutourier and the famous Paul

Kelecom, who also built proprietary engines and became technical director at the FN works at Herstal.

CIMA • Italy 1924–1927

Assembler of sporting motorcycles with 247cc and 347cc sv and ohv Blackburne engines. Limited production.

CIMATTI • Italy 1949–1984

A cycle maker, which began making mopeds and lightweights soon after WW2 and steadily built up this business, refusing to move to larger machines. Engines included Franco Morini, Minarell, Demm, HWM and FBM. Despite Cimatti's apparent success (50,000 units in 1977), the company collapsed in 1984.

CITA • Belgium 1922–1925

Motorcycles with triangular frames and own 173cc, 198cc and 348cc ohv engines.

CITO • Germany 1905–1927

Old established bicycle factory. Produced first singles and V-twins with Fafnir engines and in the early 1920s a 346cc two-stroke with its own three-port engine. These machines were made at the branch factory of Cito-Cologne, at Suhl in Thuringia. Also at Suhl was the Krieger-Gnädig (KG)

motorcycle factory, which built 503cc and later 499cc singles of advanced design with shaft drive to the rear wheel. As the demand rose for these machines Cito took over the KG production, but in 1923 Cito became part of the Cologne-based Allright works. Allright was a motorcycle producer in its own right, but it continued with the manufacture of KG motorcycles until 1927 at the Suhl works, partly also at Cologne. Even when Allright ceased building motorcycles to concentrate on bicycles, forks, brake-hubs and other parts, the KG was not dead; production moved to the Paul Henkel bicycle factory at Mäbendorf near Suhl and continued until 1932.

CITYFIX • Germany 1949–1953

Produced mini-scooters and lightweight machines with 58cc Lutz and 98cc Sachs two-stroke engines.

CL • Germany 1951

Offered mini-scooters with 34cc engines. Production was very small.

CLAES • Germany 1904–1908

Made by a once well-known bicycle factory, Claes motorcycles with 3.5hp and 5hp Fafnir engines were also sold with the Pfeil badge on the tank.

346cc Cito (two-stroke) 1922

CLAEYS-FLANDRIA • Belgium 1954–1960

Limited production of Ilo-powered scooters.

CLARENDON • England 1901–1911

Coventry-based bicycle and car producer, whose motorcycles had not only its own 3hp engines, but also proprietary engines made by Scout, Birch, Hamilton, Whitley and Coronet. Clarendon machines were of sturdy design and had an excellent finish.

CLARK • America 1942–1947

Took over and continued manufacture of the Powell A-V-8 scooter.

CLAUDE DELAGE • France 1925

Small company which produced motorcycles and cars on a limited scale, but had no connection with the famous Delage car factory.

CLEMENT • France 1897–1905

Famous French motorcycle and car pioneer. Built singles and V-twins, in 1920 even a 998cc ohc racing V-twin. The last model built by the Louis Clement works - which still had the name Adolphe Clement on the door and which was at Levallo, Mézières - was a 63cc machine with an ohv unit-design engine.

CLEMENT-GARRARD • England 1902–1911

Clement-Garrard was connected with the French factory of Adolphe Clement. Its English importer was Charles Garrard who called the imported motorcycles Clement-Garrard. He was also connected with James Lansdowne Norton, who produced frames for him until Norton founded his own motorcycle factory and used these Clement-Gerrard 1.5hp and 2hp single and 3hp V-twins which had very large outside flywheels and very small crankcases.

CLEMENT-GLADIATOR • France 1901–1935

Produced large cars until it built motorcycles too. Became successful in the 1920s when some potent 248cc JAP-engined ohv machines left the old works on the Seine. Clement-Gladiator was also a pioneer of good rear suspension, which it used with triangular frames during the late 1920s and Andreino won many races on these machines. The range of models included machines from 98cc to 498cc with two-stroke sv and ohv engines.

CLESS & PLESSING • Austria 1903–1906

This Graz-built motorcycle had its own 2·75hp and 3·5hp single-cylinder and 5hp V-twin engines. In the Czech parts of the old Austro-Hungarian Empire, the Cless & Plessing was known as the Noricum.

CLEVELAND • America 1915–1929

Made by the once famous Cleveland car factory, the Cleveland motorcycle was of very sound design. The first machine was a 269cc two-stroke; in 1924 came a 347cc single with an ioe engine and soon afterwards a 746cc in-line four with air-cooling was built. The last Cleveland, built from 1928 onward, was an improved and modernised version of the 746cc four with a 996cc capacity.

CLEVELAND • England 1911–1914

Freddie Dixon, the famous rider, was closely connected with this Middlesbrough-based producer. The models included 2.75hp and 3.5hp singles with Precision engines.

CLUA • Spain 1952–1964

Connected with the Italian Alpino factory, Clua built two-strokes with 74cc, 98cc, 123cc and 173cc engines.

CLYDE • England 1898–1912

G. H. Wait of Leicester, designer and manufacturer of these superb machines, died in the 1950s. He was a pioneer who also built cars and three-wheelers. His machines had 2·75hp, 6·5hp and 8hp engines of JAP and also of his own manufacture. Some models already had water-cooled engines in 1903.

CLYNO • England 1911–1924

Another factory which built motorcycles and cars. Motorcycles had 5hp, 6hp and 8hp engines made partly by the Stevens brothers, who owned the AJS works at Wolverhampton, where the Clyno was built too. A reorganisation after WW1 led to new 269cc two-strokes and 925cc V-twin sv models. When in 1924 demand for Clyno cars increased, it was decided to drop motorcycle manufacture.

CM • Italy 1930–1957

Created by two famous riders and technicians Oreste Drusiani and Mario Cavedagna, the first CM was a 173cc ohc machine. Other models included 248cc, 348cc and 496cc ohc and also 496cc ohv singles. Headed now by Salvia, CM also built in the mid-1930s very fast 348cc ohc racing machines which were ridden by Guglielmo Sandri. After the war, all CM machines had 123cc, 158cc and 173cc single-cylinder and 248cc twin-cylinder two-stroke engines. In addition, there was the Francolino, a very sporting 173cc ohc machine built in the mid-1950s. This engine produced 9.5bhp at 6500rpm.

CM • Germany 1921–1923

The Munich-built CM had a 110cc Cockerell two-stroke engine and was in limited production only.

CMM • England 1919–1921

Small producer which fitted 292cc Union two-stroke engines into its own frames.

CMP • Italy 1953–1956

Fitted 48cc, 73cc, 98cc and 123cc Ceccato two-stroke engines and also 48cc Sachs two-strokes into modern frames of its own manufacture. Another model had the 123cc Ceccato ohv engine.

CMR • France 1945–1948

Produced after the war from existing and partly new parts BMW models R12 and R71 in France. These 745cc flat twins had 745cc and were, of course, transverse mounted.

COCKERELL • Germany 1919–1924

Designed by Fritz Cockerell, who also created the 5-cylinder Megola, these lightweight machines had his own flat single-cylinder two-stroke engines of 110cc, 145cc and 169.5cc capacity. Sporting versions had water-cooled power units. Cockerell also designed 38cc bicycle attachments and created many other engines in the late 1920s including a water-cooled four-cylinder motorcycle and diesel and two-stroke engines. In addition, he created four and six-cylinder two-stroke cars and other power units. Cockerell motorcycles were fast, economical and

269cc Cleveland (two-stroke) 1918

346cc Cleveland (ohv) 1925

746cc Cleveland (ioe four-in-line) 1926

reliable and in 1924 his riders on water-cooled 145cc racing machines - Karl Adam and Hans Letnar - won the Championship of Germany in the 150cc class.

CODRIDEX • France 1952–1956

Manufacturer of mopeds with 49cc and 65cc engines.

COFERSA • Spain 1953–1960

Assembler of two-stroke machines with engines from 98cc to 198cc.

COLEFORD • New Zealand 1913

3 ³/₄hp machine. Little is known of it.

COLIBRI • Austria 1952–1954

Scooters with 123cc two-stroke Auto-Union (DKW) engines. Limited production.

COLOMB • France 1950–1954

Small assembler of scooters and lightweight motorcycles.

996cc Cleveland (ioe four-in-line) 1929

COLONIAL • England 1911–1913

The Carter-designed single-cylinder machine had its own 450cc two-stroke engine.

COLUMBIA • America 1900–1905

Built at the Pope works, the Columbia had Pope-built single-cylinder and V-twin engines.

COLUMBIA • France 1922–1926

Sv singles of 197cc and 247cc capacity in simple and open frames.

745cc Cockerell (water-cooled two-stroke four-cylinder prototype) 1927

110cc Cockerell (two-stroke) 1922

COLUMBUS • Germany 1923–1924

Built good bicycle attachment engines and a 248cc ohv machine, which became the first Horex motorcycle when the Kleemann family bought the Columbus engine factory.

COM • Italy 1926–1928

One of the many small Italian producers of 123cc and 173cc machines.

COMERY • England 1919–1922

A factory owned by racing motorcyclist Archie Cook. Produced motorcycles with 269cc Villiers two-stroke engines.

COMET • America early 1940s

0.5hp scooters, made in Minneapolis.

COMET • England 1902–1907

Fitted Minerva engines of 2.75hp and 3.5hp into own frames made from BSA cycle parts.

COMET • Italy 1953–1957

Superb, but quite expensive 173cc ohv and 173cc as well as 246cc vertical twin ohc machines designed by Alfonso Drusiani and built in his own works.

COMMANDER • England 1952–1953

Made at the last pre-war Rudge factory at Hayes, the R. W. Dennis-designed Commander was an unorthodox design. It had a frame made from square tubes and a partly enclosed engine. This was a 98cc or 197cc Villiers two-stroke. The factory, belonging to the General Steel group, never went into quantity production.

CONDOR • England 1907–1914

Built proprietary engines and complete motorcycles. Unique was a single-cylinder model with 96mm bore and 122mm stroke. At 810cc this was probably the biggest single in commercial production.

CONDOR • Switzerland 1901–

Next to Motosacoche, Switzerland's leading motorcycle manufacturer. Fitted in early years Zedel, afterwards mainly MAG (Motosacoche) engines from 246cc to 746cc with ioe and some ohv engines. Small models had 147cc to 198cc Villiers motors. After 1945, a 346cc two-stroke twin was built but main production concentrated on 678cc flat twins with its own transverse-mounted sv engines and shaft drive to the rear wheel. Another Condor had its own 247cc ohv engine as well as shaft drive. Together with the twin, these machines were built mainly for the Swiss forces. There was also a 248cc machine which had an ohc engine, supplied by Ducati. Condor was a very active competitor in races and during the late 1920s and early 1930s when it used 248cc, 348cc and 498cc Marchant-designed ohc Motosacoche racing engines it was very successful. Among leading Condor riders were Georges Cordey, Ernst Hänny, Léon Divorne, Paul Wuillemin, Armin Bättig and Paul Dinkel.

CONDOR • Germany 1953–1954

Scooter-like motorcycles with 48cc two-stroke engines.

CONNAUGHT • England 1910–1927

Producer of excellent 293cc and 347cc two-stroke singles with belt or chain drive to the rear wheel. The range of models became larger when Connaught introduced 1925 models with 348cc sv and ohv Blackburne and ohv Bradshaw (oil-cooled) engines. Bert Perrigo, who

123cc Commander (two-stroke Villiers prototype) 1954

678cc Condor (sv flat twin) 1955

afterwards went to BSA, and Jack Sprosen were among leading Connaught riders. The Birmingham-based factory bought in 1924 the JES motorcycle production which was at Gloucester.

CONSUL • England 1916–1922

Small assembler, which produced Villiers-engined 269cc and 247cc models with orthodox frames.

CONTRAST-JAP • England c1912

Assembled motorcycles with JAP engines.

COOPER • America 1941–1942

Rebadged Powell A-V-8 scooters.

COOPER • America 1972–circa 1985

Made in Mexico by Islo at Salfillol for the American importer, Cooper machines were equipped with 246cc single-cylinder two-stroke engines, with different trials, enduro and motocross models.

CORAH • England 1905–1914

Superbly made 498cc single-cylinder sv machines and 746cc ohv V-twin JAP engined models. The small factory fitted upon request other proprietary engines as well.

CORGI • England 1946–1952

The tiny Corgi folding scooter was made by Brockhouse Engineering of Southport and was derived from the Excelsior Wellbike, designed to be dropped alongside airborne troops in wartime. The Corgi had a 98cc Excelsior Sprite engine whereas the Wellbike, confusingly, used a Villiers engine.

CORONA • England 1901–1904

Small producer of machines with 1.5hp Minerva, 2hp Clement and British 2.5hp proprietary engines.

CORONA • Germany 1902–1924

The first Corona motorcycles had single-cylinder and V-twin engines mounted between the saddle tube and the rear wheel. Zedel and Fafnir supplied the engines. Afterwards they had a more orthodox design. Motorcycle production stopped in 1907, but was taken up again in 1922, when Corona announced 346cc sv singles and 493cc flat twins. The later ones had BMW sv engines.

CORONA-JUNIOR • England 1919–1923

Concentrated manufacture on a 447cc single-cylinder sv machine which in 1919 was sold for £85 and in 1923 for £75.

CORRE • France 1901–1910

Better known as a car manufacturer which eventually was bought by La Licorne, Corre also built a range of motorcycles with Zurcher Peugeot and Zedel engines.

CORYDON • England 1904–1908

Produced 2.5hp single-cylinder and 3hp as well as 4.5hp V-twin machines of good quality.

COSMOS • Switzerland 1904–1907

Fitted 3hp and 4hp Zedel and Fafnir engines into strengthened bicycle frames.

COSSACK • Russia 1973–

Name for Russian-built motorcycles in some foreign countries. The Russian state-owned factories produce the 174cc Voskhod and 346cc Ish-Planeta single cylinder two-strokes, the 347cc Ish-Jupiter two-stroke twin, the BMW-like 650cc Ural flat twin with a transverse-mounted ohv engine and the Dniepr, which is a modernised version of the Ural, although both models produce only 32bhp. The Cossack name is now being phased out in preference to the original Neval badge. See under 'Neval'.

497cc Condor (ohv MAG) 1931

346cc Connaught (sv JAP) 1927

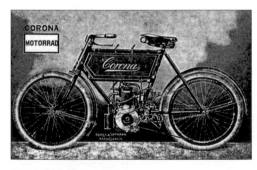

2¹/₂hp Corona (sv) 1904

COTTEREAU • France 1903–1909

One of the first car producers in France. Cottereau motorcycles had Minerva, Peugeot and also its own engines from 2hp to 6hp. From 1911 onward, Cottereau cars became known as CID cars.

346cc Cotton (ohv Blackburne) 1923

490cc Cotton (ohv JAP) 1938

650cc Cossack (D model) 1977

COTTON • England 1919–1980

F. W. Cotton designed and patented a frame with triangulated straight tubes and set up business in Gloucester to make motorcycles with Villiers two-strokes and ohv Blackburne engines. Stanley Woods first rode for Cotton in the 1922 Junior TT finishing fifth, but won easily the following year. Thereafter Cotton-Blackburnes became very popular and were raced successfully.

Cotton also used JAP Python and Villiers engines, but the company was run down by 1939. Post-war, it was bought by accountant Monty Denley and engineer Pat Onions. Completely fresh designs were made including Villiers-engined road, scramblers and trials machines. These, and Villiers 250cc Starmaker-engined road racers, were successful in the 1960s, a period when Derek Minter and Bill Ivy raced for Cotton. Later, a shortage of Villiers engines dictated the use of Italian Minarellis. Denley and Onions sold out and the new management concentrated on Austrian Rotax engines mainly for road racing, although some machines were made for the police. Production came to a halt in 1980.

COULSON • England 1919–1924

Built 347cc and 497cc sv singles and also 497cc ohv V-twins with JAP engines. The last Coulson-B had a 346cc ohv Bradshaw engine with oil cooling. Most models used a spring frame and Eric Longden gained many successes with F. Aslett Coulson-designed machines. Originally made at Kings Cross, London, the factory was afterwards bought by A. W. Wall and eventually H. R. Backhouse & Co. Ltd. of Birmingham.

COVENTRY-B&D • England 1923–1925

Barbary and Downes were ex-employees of the defunct Hobart motorcycle factory and founders of this make. They also built 170cc Wee-McGregor two-stroke machines. The Coventry-B&D was built with JAP engines of 346cc to 996cc and with the 346cc Barr & Stroud sleeve-valve engine. The production was on a limited scale.

COVENTRY-CHALLENGE • England
1903–1911

A bicycle dealer who fitted into strengthened frames engines made by Fafnir, Minerva and other makes. Designer-manufacturer was Edward O'Brien.

COVENTRY-EAGLE • England 1901–1939

Well-known assembler of superb machines. Owned by the Mayo family, Coventry-Eagle was originally a bicycle factory which built over the years motorcycles with engines from 98cc to 996cc. It used Villiers, JAP, Sturmey-Archer, Blackburne and Matchless engines. During the 1920s they had Brough-Superior-like petrol tanks and the Flying 8 was a popular model with the big 996cc V-twin sv JAP engine. Among the racing versions, the JAP-engined 248cc single, ridden by Mita Vychodil of Czechoslovakia and Martin Schneeweiss of Austria, won many events. At Brooklands a 996cc ohv JAP-engined V-twin broke records and when Bert Le Vack in 1922-1924 raced new ohc JAP engines, he used Coventry-Eagle frames too. An interesting frame was introduced in 1928. It was a pressed steel, channel-section frame, which over the years housed various Villiers engines. Mammut of Germany built this frame under licence. Another sensation was the Pullmann,

248cc Coventry-Eagle (ohv Blackburne) 1936

introduced in 1935 with a chassis-like pressed steel frame and rear suspension. The rear wheel was enclosed by deeply valanced mudguards. Engines for the Pullmann were the 247cc Villiers deflector-type, the 247cc Villiers flat-top and the 246cc ohv Blackburne. The last Coventry-Eagle motorcycles had tubular frames with 123cc Villiers engines and 247cc, 347cc and 497cc ohv single-cylinder power-units made by Matchless in London. Production ceased with the outbreak of WW2.

COVENTRY-MASCOT • England 1922–1924

Produced exclusively motorcycles with 348cc engines. Blackburne supplied sv versions, Bradshaw the oil cooled ohv motor and Barr & Stroud delivered its sleeve-valve power units to this small factory.

COVENTRY-MOTETTE • England 1899–1903

Improved Bollée design with a 2·5hp engine, designed by Turrell.

COVENTRY-STAR • England 1919–1921

Assembled machines with 269cc Liberty and Villiers engines.

COVENTRY-VICTOR • England 1919–1936

England's leading producer of opposed twin-cylinder engines of 499cc, 688cc and 749cc capacity and of complete motorcycles with these engines. From 1926 onwards there was also a three-wheeler in production; in 1929 Coventry-Victor also produced speedway machines with 499cc ohv flat twins. McKechnie, Bison, Jeecy-Vea, Socovel and others used C-V power units.

COVERT • New Zealand 1912

6hp machine - few details available.

CP-ROLEO • France 1924–1939

Interesting design, which used frames made from pressed steel and partly cast iron. These frames included the petrol and oil reservoir. Some models had normal tubular frames. Engines used were 247cc to 498cc sv and ohv JAP, Voisin, LMC and Chaise.

CR • Germany 1926–1930

Assembled machines with 172cc Villiers two-stroke engines.

CRESCENT • Sweden 1954–late 1970s

Like Monark and NV, Crescent was a member of the Swedish MCB group. It concentrated mainly on small proprietary engined two-stroke motorcycles, although in its main activity as out-board boat engine maker it had its own designs. One of these, a three cylinder 500cc water-cooled two-stroke, was often used in solo and sidecar racing by amateur constructors in the 1970s. Rudi Kurth indeed built such a solo for the Monark factory, but it was not successful.

CRESENT • USA 1901–c1904

The Western Wheel Works of Chicago was established in 1895, specialising in manufacturing electrical generators for household and commercial lighting equipment. It branched out to build a limited number of single-cylinder two-stroke machines.

497cc Coventry-Eagle (ohv Sturmey-Archer) 1926

172cc Coventry-Eagle (two-stroke Villers) 1931

497cc Coventry-Eagle (ohv Matchless) 1937

348cc Curwy (ohv) 1924

CREST • England 1923

Assembled machines with 346cc Barr & Stroud sleeve-valve and 347cc Villiers two-stroke engines.

CROCKER • American 1936–1941

Albert Crocker, with minimal facilities, built his 998cc ohv V-twins in a small Los Angeles workshop. Highly regarded by those who knew them, they rivalled and sometimes beat Harleys and Indians.

CROFT • England 1923–1926

Known also as Croft-Anzani, as most Croft machines housed 996cc four and eight-valve V-twin Anzani ohv engines, designed by the famous Hubert Hagens. A few Croft machines had the 1078cc Anzani engine and all had the Brough Superior-like petrol tank. The production was on a limited scale.

CROWNFIELD • England 1903–1904

These Jack Perkins-designed machines had open frames. Engines fitted were the 1.75hp and 2.25hp Kerry and Givaudan.

CRT • Italy 1925–1929

Designed and built at Treviso by Cavasini and Romin, the CRT was a sporting 248cc and 348cc machine with Blackburne ohv engine.

CRYPTO • England 1902–1908

Leading make during the period. Designed by W. G. James, most Crypto machines had 2.5hp and 3hp Peugeot and Coronet proprietary engines.

CSEPEL • Hungary 1932–1951

Once the leading Hungarian motorcycle factory, which was part of the great Manfred Weiss steel works at Budapest. The Laszlo Sagi-designed two-strokes had 98cc, 123cc and 146cc engines. During a reorganisation, the state-owned factory dropped the Csepel badge in 1952 and the new models got the Pannonia and Danuvia names on the petrol tank.

CUDELL • Germany 1898–1905

Pioneer which first built three-wheelers and afterwards 402cc and 510cc motorcycles with De Dion engines.

CURTISS • America 1903–1912

Glenn Curtiss, the famous pilot and aircraft engine producer, built single and V-twin motorcycles and also supplied his engines to other motorcycle producers, including Marvel. Riding a motorcycle with one of his air-cooled V-eight aircraft engines, he broke many records.

CURWY (CURSY) • Germany 1911–1931

Produced mainly 348cc and 498cc sv and ohv machines with own power units; a few 348cc ohc machines were also built. Curt Szymanski, the designer-manufacturer, changed in 1927 the name Curwy to Cursy, probably because the word 'curwe' means 'prostitute' in German.

CUSHMAN • America 1936–1965

A scooter marque that actually saw military service in WW2. Cushman of Lincoln, Nebraska, made many different scooters over almost 30 years. Cushman scooters were powered by its own four-stroke Husky engines of various capacities. Its scooters were also sold under the Allstate brand, and built under licence in Belgium. From 1961-1963 the company also sold Italian Vespa scooters under the Cushman name.

CUSTER • America 1938–1944

Primitive scooter with 2.5hp engine, built in Dayton, Ohio.

CYC-AUTO • England 1934–1956

Wellington Butt's early 'Autocycle' always had the 98cc engine ahead of the cycle pedal bracket, the crankshaft in line with the frame. He used own engine, then Villiers. Cyc-Auto was sold to Scott in 1937, which used its own 98cc engine unit, latterly with twin exhaust pipes. Final offering was a real motorcycle with shaft drive, but few, if any, were made or sold.

CYCLETTE • France c1920s

Autocycle-like machines with engines up to 100cc, made in Paris. The Cyclette won the 'velomoteurs' class in the 1924 Paris-Nice race.

CYCLON • Germany 1901–1905

Leading producer during the early years of motorcycle manufacture. Used De Dion, Werner and Zedel engines and concentrated eventually on the production of the three-wheeled Cyclonette.

CYCLONE • America 1913–1917

For many years the only commercially built 996cc V-twin with an ohc engine. Designed by Andrew Strand, the

996cc Cyclone (ohc V-twin) 1914

996cc Cyclone (ohc V-twin) 1913

Cyclone won many races but became outclassed when big factories including Harley-Davidson entered the market with 8-valve 996cc V-twins and entered racing with such machines. Only one other make - Koehler Escoffier in France - built big V-twin ohc machines before 1939.

CYCLOP • Germany 1922–1925

Assembled motorcycles with 127cc to 198cc two- and four-stroke engines made by Kurier, Bubi, Teco, Namapo and others.

CYKELAID • England 1919–1926

Attachment engines of 1.25hp and 1.50hp (133cc) for bicycles and also complete lightweight machines with these power units.

CYRUS • The Netherlands 1931–1971

Producer of bicycles and mopeds and motorcycles with 49cc to 148cc Villiers, Sachs, and llo two-stroke engines.

CZ • Czechoslovakia 1932–1997

See panel

CZ • Czechoslovakia 1932–1997

Started production with 73cc and 98cc lightweights and soon became a leading motorcycle factory in the country, originally belonging to the big Skoda works. CZ stands for Cveskà Zbrojovka, or Czech arms factory. Other pre-war models were good-looking 173cc and 248cc unit-design two-strokes with pressed steel frames. The factory also built 348cc two-strokes and even ohv prototypes, which never went into quantity production. A 496cc air-cooled vertical twin-cylinder, two-stroke machine suffered the same fate. After 1945, CZ fell under government control, becoming commercially and technically linked to Jawa, a co-operation which increased the years. Among the first post-war CZ machines were 123cc models, and other versions with tubular frames up to 348cc twins. The big Strakonice works had over the years many superb technicians and designers, including Vàclav Pavlic, Ignaz Uhl, J. F. Koch, Jaroslav Walter and Jaroslav Pudil; among successful riders in trials and races were Cyril Nemec, Cenek Kohlicek, Eman Marha, Josef Pastika, Milada Bayerovà, Jàn Bedrna, Dave Bickers, Friedrichs, De Coster, Jàn Lucàk, Frantisek Bartos, Vàclav Parus and others. Many among these were motocross specialists and while Jawa concentrated more on trials and road races it was up to CZ to succeed in motocross, with some excellent machines. After 1949 the Strakonice factory built superb 123cc, 248cc and 348cc road racing machines with ohc engines, of which most were designed by the late Jaroslav Walter. Redesigned water-cooled motocross models with 248cc and other engines came into production in 1978, proving fast and reasonably reliable. CZ's links with Jawa extended to the sharing of components as well as technology in the early 1980s, although it always remained independent, until dwindling sales of its increasingly anachronistic machines eventually led to its sale to the Italian Cagiva concern in 1992. Cagiva planned to use the factory to build and assemble some of its own lightweight motorcycles and scooters but this never really worked as it had hoped, and in July 1997, the CZ factory was finally closed, a victim of an almost complete lack of model development.

124cc CZ (two-stroke single) 1982

346cc CZ(two-stroke twin) 1982

173cc CZ (two-stroke) 1935

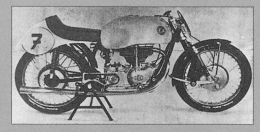

248cc CZ (dohc single works racer) 1957

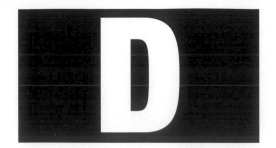

D

DAELIM • Korea 1978–

See DLM entry

DAK • Germany 1923–1925

Association of some German car manufacturers, which also sold 117cc and 147cc deflector-type two-strokes, assembled by Ilo of Pinneberg. When demand for Ilo proprietary engines increased, the factory stopped manufacture of complete machines.

DALESMAN • England 1969–1974

Financed mainly by US dollars, Dalesman built good competition machines with 98cc and 123cc Puch as well as 123cc Sachs engines.

DALTON • England 1920–1922

Some versions of Dalton motorcycles had disc wheels. The small factory fitted 347cc and 497cc sv Blackburne singles and 688 flat-twin cylinder Coventry-Victor engines into sturdy frames.

DANE • England 1919–1920

Limited production using 348cc two and four-stroke Precision engines and 990cc sv V-twin JAP engines.

DANUBIUS • German 1923–1924

Made by the big Ratibor machine factory Ganz & Co., the Danubius was a 198cc sv machine of conventional design.

DANUVIA • Hungary 1955–1963

Of Czepel design, the Danuvia was a mass-produced 123cc two-stroke machine.

DARDO • Italy 1924–1929

Well-made lightweights with horizontal 132cc and 174cc two-stroke engines.

DARLAN • Spain 1958-1960

Limited production of machines with own 94cc two-stroke engines.

DARLING • Switzerland 1924–1929

From 1928 produced new 498cc models with sv and ohv Sturmey-Archer single-cylinder engines.

DART • England 1923–1924

Built up-to-date 348cc single-cylinder ohc machines with 74mm bore and 81mm stroke. Designer was A. A. Sidney. Few machines were built.

DART • England 1901–1906

Designed by Frank Baker - not the Baker of Precision engine manufacture and of Baker motorcycles - the old Dart had 2·5hp engines made by Minerva and MMC.

DAVENTRY • Belgium 1951–1955

Assembled 123cc and 175cc two-strokes with Puch, Sachs, Ilo and other proprietary engines.

DAVISON • England 1902–1908

Good early motorcycles with English Simms and Belgian 2hp and 2.5hp Minerva engines.

DAW • England 1902–1905

Proprietary engine and carburetor manufacturer, Dalton & Wade also made a small number of motorcycles.

DAW • Germany 1924–1925

Unconventional fully enclosed motorcycle. Designed by Ernst Köhler, it had a single-cylinder 405cc two-stroke engine.

DAX • France 1932–1939

Excellently designed machines with two-stroke engines from 98cc to 174cc and four-stroke ohv unit-design engines from 123cc to 498cc.

DAYANG • China 1983–

Trade name for motorcycles produced by the Luoyang Northern EK Chor Motorcycle Co., Ltd. in Henan Province. Current production rate is around 500,000 machines annually from a staff of just under 3000. Most of the machines - lightweight motorcycles and scooters - are based on Japanese designs or produced under Japanese licencing agreements, but the company is investing heavily and rapidly expanding its technological capabilities, and will shortly be capable of generating its own designs.

DAY-LEEDS • England 1912–1914

Big machine factory which built three wheelers before

492cc Dax (ohv) 1932

998cc Della Ferrera (sv V-twin with sidecar) 1924

496cc Della Ferrera (ohv) 1927

entering motorcycle manufacture. The only model was a 496cc single with its own ioe engine. WW1 stopped manufacture.

DAYTON • America 1911–1917

Built by the Huffman Manufacturing Co. at Elkhart, Indiana, Dayton motorcycles had 7hp, later 9-10hp V-twin Spake engines.

DAYTON • England 1913–1920

The first product was a 162cc bicycle attachment engine; later Dayton designs had 269cc Villiers two-stroke engines.

DAYTON • England 1954–1960

Was among the first producers of modern scooters after WW2. They were respected scooters with 173cc, 198cc and 246cc Villiers engines.

DE-CA • Italy 1954–1957

Built interesting 48cc and 98cc ohv singles and also a 123cc vertical ohv twin in limited numbers and at a premium price. The smallest model had 39mm bore and 40mm stroke. It produced 2·4bhp at 6000rpm and had a 44mph top speed. The DE-CA range also included a 48cc ohv bicycle engine.

DE-DE • France 1923–1929

Limited production of a wide range of models. These included two-strokes from 98cc to 174cc and sv and ohv versions with JAP engines from 248cc to 498cc.

DE DION BOUTON • France 1926–1930

There was no real connection between the once famous engine and car factory of the same name and these motorcycles. These had 173cc and 247cc two-stroke, deflector-type engines; a bigger model a 348cc ohv engine.

DEFA • Germany 1921–1924

Built not only complete 198cc sv machines, but supplied other builders of motorcycle frames.

DEFY-ALL • England 1921–1922

Motorcycles with quite unusual spring frames. The engines fitted were the 269cc Villiers and the 348 sv single-cylinder made by Blackburne.

DEI • Italy 1932–1966

When Umberto Dei took over the Ancora motorcycle factory, he produced lightweights with 49cc, 60cc, 73cc and 98cc two-stroke engines, supplied partly by Sachs. Others had Mosquito power units.

DELAPLACE • France 1951–1953

Simple machine with 173cc and 247cc Ydral two-stroke engines of good design.

DELIN • Belgium 1899–1901

No details are available about this pioneer who, according to some sources, fitted 1.5hp and 2.5hp De Dion engines.

DELIUS • Germany 1949–1953

Large-wheeled Cityfix scooterette with engines from Lutz, KMS, Sachs and Ducati.

DE LUXE • America 1912–1915

Made by Excelsior, ie the Schwinn company of Chicago, De Luxe motorcycles had mainly V-twin proprietary engines made by F. W. Spake of Indianapolis.

DE LUXE • England 1920–1924

Everyone who bought a De Luxe with the 346cc Barr & Stroud sleeve-valve engine got a free sidecar frame. Earlier models had 269cc Villiers engines.

DELLA FERRERA • Italy 1909–1948

The Della Ferrera brothers built not very good-looking but interesting machines. Among them were the 498cc V-twin ohc racing machines of 1922, which had the overhead camshafts driven by chains. They won many hill-climbs and short-distance races despite the very high saddle position and exposed chains. Production versions included 498cc, 598cc, 746cc and 996cc sv V-twins as well as 498cc ohv and 637cc sv singles. The models had - even in the 1920s - a rear suspension. The last model built was a unit-design 499cc sv single.

DELOMA • Germany 1924

Lightweight built at Magdeburg (now DDR) with Julius Löwy's crude-oil 142cc two-stroke engine.

DELTA • Germany 1924

Very unorthodox fully enclosed motorcycle with a dual-seat and rear suspension by semi-elliptic leaf springs. The 499cc single-cylinder two-stroke engine with 75mm bore and 113mm stroke was a three-port deflector-type. Limited production.

246cc Delta Gnom (two-stroke) 1929

494cc Delta Gnom (ohv) 1929

248cc Delta Gnom (ohv JAP engine) 1935

174cc Demm (two-stroke) 1955

660cc Dennell (sv three-cylinder JAP) 1906

DELTA-GNOM • Austria 1925–1955

Was a well known make in Austria. The first machines had its own 246cc two-stroke engines, later versionsüü with one exception - sv and ohv JAP engines from 346cc to 996cc. The exception was the Hans Pitzek-designed 498cc ohv single, built from 1928 onwards. After 1945 the reorganized factory built only two-stroke machines with 98cc, 123cc and 173cc. The engines came from Rotax, Puch, Ilo and HMW. Many leading Austrian racing men, including Leopold Killmeyer, Karl Bohmann, Hans Walz, F. J. Meyer, Ladislaus Möslacher and Franz Behrendt rode Delta-Gnom machines in pre-war days.

DEMM • Italy 1953–1982

A factory famous in its day for lightweights of between 50cc and 175cc, both four- and two-stroke, Demm also sold engines to other makers from time to time as proprietary units and made small industrial vehicles. Was involved in racing and record breaking in the 1950s and early 1960s. In later years, concentrated on 50cc motorcycles and mopeds.

DENE • England 1903–1922

A motorcycle assembler. Dene machines had 2.5hp and 3.5hp Fafnir engines, 2.25hp to 8hp Precision engines, 3.75hp water-cooled Green-Precision engines, the 3.75hp Abingdon and also the 6–8hp JAP V-twin sv engine. Despite the wide range of models, Dene production was on a limited scale.

DENE • New Zealand 1912

4 1/2hp machine. No further details.

DENNELL • England 1903–1908

Designed by Herbert Dennell of Leeds, these machines had Minerva, NSU and JAP engines, but among the JAP-engined models was also the 660cc three-cylinder, which made headlines. The three single-cylinders were air-cooled and set in-line on a common crankcase. Rear drive was by belt. Dennell also fitted a few four-cylinder in-line Franklin & Isaacsson engines.

DERBI • Spain 1950–

Famous for its 50cc models, but also made machines of up to 350cc, all two-strokes. Won the 50cc and 125cc world championship, mainly with rider Angel Nieto in 1970-1-2. Today Derbi is Spain's largest and strongest surviving motorcycle maker, its range consisting of small two-stroke scooters and sports motorcycles.

DERNY • France 1949–1958

Quite unorthodox 123cc and 173cc two-stroke motorcycles in a range which also included 173cc scooters. Best known is the Taon of 1957, a small sports bike with integrated headlight and fuel tank styling, 124cc two-stroke AMC engine, leading link Earle's front forks, and a contemporary steel and chrome look.

DERONZIERE • France 1903–1914

Built 282cc singles with its own engines and other models with power units made by Zedel and Peugeot.

49cc Derbi Supermoto (two-stroke water-cooled single) 1999

348cc DFR (ohv) 1927

DESPATCH-RIDER • England 1915–1917

The name more or less states the purpose of these machines. They were powered by 210cc Peco and 269cc Villiers two-stroke engines.

DEVIL • Italy 1953–1957

Made at Bergamo, the Devil was a good motorcycle. Production included 48cc and 158cc two-strokes and 123cc and 173cc ohv singles with inclined cylinders on the beautiful Soncini-designed engines. The 173cc version had a five-speed gearbox in unit with the motor, and top speed was 81mph.

DFB • Germany 1922–1925

Producer of 159cc two-stroke bicycle engines and of complete machines with the same power units.

DFR • France 1921–1933

Ambitious factory. The first models had its own 346cc two-stroke engines, afterwards it also built sv and ohv versions. There was also a 248cc Bradshaw-engined single, probably a sleeved-down oil-cooled 346cc engine. The factory raced this machine with a supercharger and with Pierre in the saddle during 1925 - 1927. There were also MAG-engined 348cc and 498cc ohv singles and in 1932 DFR introduced a new model with a pressed steel frame and a 498cc vertical-twin ohv Dresch engine. It was later taken over by Dresch.

DGW • Germany 1927–1928

London's 1927 Olympia motorcycle exhibition first saw DKW machines with DGW on the petrol tank. The reason was a dispute with another German factory which already used the DKW trademark.

DIAG • Germany 1921–1928

Machine factory, which produced 83cc and 101cc bicycle attachment engines, afterwards also complete 173cc, 246cc and 346cc sv and ohv motorcycles. The frame design had the tubes above the crankcases; the engines virtually hung in the tubular frames. The Diag was never a widely known motorcycle.

DIAMANT • Germany 1903–1940

The first Diamant vehicles were three-wheelers and the first motorcycles made had Fafnir power units, afterwards its own single and V-twin engines. From 1907 or 1908 until 1926 there were no motorcycles made, but new models built from 1926 onward were designed by the famous Franz Gnädig and also had Gnädig-designed 346cc Kühne ohv engines, followed by 496cc sv and ohv versions. On special order, JAP engines could be fitted too. During the late 1920s, Diamant and the Elite car factory joined forces and while Elite faded out as a car manufacturer, part of the Diamant factory was taken over by Opel for producing 496cc Opel motorcycles with duralumin frames, a design by Ernst Neumann-Neander.

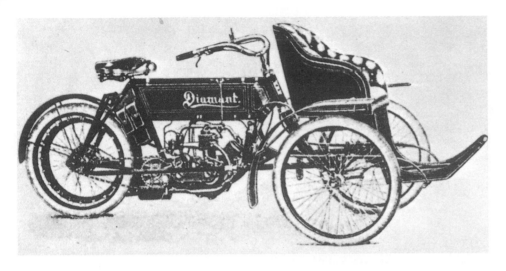

4hp Diamant (sx Forecar) 1905

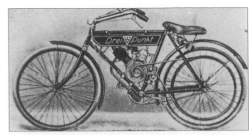

198cc Dieterle-Dessau (sv) 1923

When this production stopped in the early 1930s, a limited number of new 348cc and 498cc EO (Elite-Opel) machines - with Kèchen instead of the original Opel engines - were built before the factory closed forever as a motorcycle and car producer. The frames of the EO were nearly identical to the ones used in the late 1920s and early 1930s by Opel. From 1933 onward, production concentrated on 73cc and 98cc mopeds with Sachs two-stroke engines.

498cc Diamant (ohv Kühne) 1929

DIAMOND • England 1910–1938

Diamond motorcycles were made by the DF&M engineering company in Birmingham, and in the early days showed some remarkable enterprise. In the 1920 250cc class of the Junior TT, it entered an extremely advanced four-valve ohv-engined model, although reports of the time do not say how it performed. Much of Diamond's subsequent production used Villiers two-stroke engines and JAP, Blackburne and Bradshaw oil-cooled proprietary engines. Using JAP engines, Vic Brittain rode in the 250cc, 350cc and 500cc classes in the 1931 TT without any success. Thereafter, Diamond became just another maker of Villiers-engined utility machines, with production ending with the outbreak of war in 1939.

DI-BLASI • Italy 1992–

Manufactures small capacity runabouts, including fold-up 49cc scooter.

49cc Di-Blasi (air-cooled two-stroke single) 1997

346cc DKW RT350 (two-stroke two-cylinder) 1955

DIETERLE-DESSAU • Germany 1921–1925

Known also by the Dreipunkt trademark, Dieterle's factory built bicycles and lightweights. The last ones had 'exhaust-injected' 198cc and 248cc sv engines of patented design.

DIFRA • Germany 1923–1925

Assembler which fitted mainly 198cc sv Namapo engines into its own frames.

DIHL • Germany 1923–1924

Berlin-built 269cc single-cylinder two-stroke machines. Limited production.

DILECTAV • France 1920–1939

Producer of machines with engines from 98cc to 498cc. Engine suppliers were Villiers, Aubier-Dunne, Soyer, Chaise, JAP and others.

DJOUNN • Germany 1925

Designed by Alexander von Djounkowski, a former Russian pilot, the Djounn was built in Berlin. Its 499cc single-cylinder engine was full of new and undeveloped innovations which soon caused its commercial demise.

DKF • Germany 1923–1924

Assembler of lightweights with 148cc and 198cc sv engines.

DKR • England 1957–1966

Manufacturer of Villiers-engined scooters with 148cc, 173cc, 197cc and 247cc single-cylinder and 244cc vertical-twin power units.

DKW • Germany 1919–1981

See panel

DLM • South Korea 1972–

The Daelim Machinery Co. of Seoul is one of the leading producers of modern 124cc single-cylinder two-stroke machines in the country and produces 5,000 machines monthly. To put this in context, Suzuki has the same production level, while Honda builds 8,000 machines in a month. High taxes and petrol prices are keeping engines to small capacities.

DMF • The Netherlands 1940–1957

Owned by former racing driver Joop Verkerke, this assembler used proprietary engines made by Villiers, Ilo and Puch. They were of 123cc, 148cc and 173cc capacity. The last model made by DMF, which stood for Driebergsche Motorrijwielen Fabriek N.V., was an Ilo-engined 244cc two-stroke twin.

DMG • Germany 1921–1924

Limited production of 147cc sv single-cylinder bicycle engines and later of complete motorcycles with its own 198cc sv power units.

DMW • England 1945–1971

DMW made forks, hubs and other components for the trade, plus a range of road bikes, trials bikes and some interesting scooters, including the Villiers 250cc twin-engined Deemster, sold to several police forces. When Villiers stopped making motorcycle engines, DMW took over the stock, jigs and fixtures and continued to supply Villiers components. Under owner Harold Nock, who retired in 1971, DMW was an individualistic company. It made a 250cc Villiers Starmaker-engined road racing model; an interesting prototype had two Starmakers side by side.

DNB • Japan 1957–1961

Produced single-cylinder two-stroke machines of 123cc, 197cc and 247cc.

DNIEPR • Russia 1967–

Built as a sidecar machine, the BMW-based Dniepr, with its 647cc ohv engine and shaft-drive, is the simple home version of the newer Ural-3, which is basically the export model of Dniepr. Both are built at the Sverdlowsk machine works.

DOBRO-MOTORIST • Germany 1923–1925

Made by a branch of Mercur Aircraft of Berlin, this company built 145cc DKW two-stroke and 346cc sv and ohv JAP engines into triangular frames.

DKW • Germany 1919–1981

In the 1920s, DKW, founded in 1919 by Danish-born J. S. Rasmussen, was the world's largest motorcycle factory. It first produced a two-stroke 'clip on' engine, followed by various small two-strokes, designed by Hugo Ruppe. DKW supplied many other German makes with its two-stroke engines. It raced its Ruppe-designed water-cooled two-strokes, with patent 'Ladepump' inlet charging by a separate piston in the crankcase, in 175cc and later 250cc classes in the 1920s with considerable success. By the decade's end, DKW was producing road machines with single- and twin-cylinder deflector-piston engines of 150cc to 600cc.

In the 1930s, DKW became part of Auto Union (together with car makers Audi, Horch and Wanderer) and made two-stroke-engined light cars as well as motorcycles. As far as the latter were concerned, two radical decisions were made. One was to exploit the Schnurle 'flat-top piston' patents for road machines, which gave huge advantages in terms of power and reliability. The other decision was to race water-cooled 'split single' two-strokes - still with piston-pump inlet charging - designed by Swiss born Arnold Zoller, and developed through the 1930s by DKW's August Prussing.

These weirdly unorthodox (and very noisy) machines came to dominate the 250cc class and won many grand prix events, ridden notably by Walfred Winkler, Ewald Kluge, Siegried Wunsche and others. Kluge won the 1938 Lightweight TT at record speed. DKW was 1-2-3 in the 1938 250cc European Championship (the first year that a points scoring system was used) with riders Kluge, Petruschke and Gabentz. In 1939 Kluge was 250cc champion and Heiner Fleischman 350cc. The range of road machines covered all classes from 98cc to 500cc - the latter a superb air-cooled twin with electric starting.

Post war, DKW was split. The original factory at Zschopau, in the Russian zone, became IFA, then MZ.

DKW itself resumed production at Ingoldstat and later at Dusseldorf, West Germany. Mainstay of early production was an updated version of the famous RT125 introduced in 1939. The model sold well for DKW, but its real claim to fame was that it became the most copied motorcycle ever, with the BSA Bantam, Harley-Davidson Hummer, Soviet Moskva and Yamaha YA1 all being close copies or having strong DKW influences. DKW soon supplemented the RT125 with 200cc, 250cc and 350cc air-cooled twins. DKW also raced in the 125cc, 250cc and 350cc classes with normal piston-ported two-strokes (some had rotary inlet valves) with some success, but not as great as in pre-war days. The 350cc 'three' was especially technically interesting. Designed by Eric Wolf and radically developed by Helmut Görg, it was 'fast but fragile'.

Worrying business trends stopped the racing programme at the end of 1956. In 1957 DKW partly amalgamated with Victoria and Express to form the Zweirad Union, which, in turn, was taken over in 1966 by proprietary engine maker Fichtel and Sachs, which added Hercules to the Union. No longer an innovator or leader in two-stroke technology, DKW had become redundant, and the name was gradually subjugated to that of Hercules - although the DKW name was still retained for its earlier prestige in some markets. Apart from some very ordinary mopeds and lightweights, the DKW name was last seen on the Hercules Wankel W2000, which the company made great efforts to export to Britain and the USA. The W2000 had a Sachs snowmobile single-rotor air-cooled unit rated as 300cc, for which 32hp at 6500rpm was claimed. It had a 6-speed gearbox and chain drive. The W2000 never achieved acceptance, and it, and the DKW name, disappeared for good in the early 1980s. It was a sad end to a make that in its day had typified ingenuity and forward thinking in motorcycle design.

123cc DKW RT125 (two-stroke sing

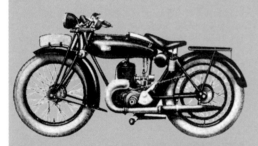

206cc DKW 206 (two-stroke single) 1925

174cc DKW (two-stroke water-cooled racer) 1926

122cc DKW Golem(two-stroke) 1921

124cc DKW RT125 (two-stroke single) 1972

148cc Dobro-Motorist (two-stroke DKW) 1925

492cc Dollar (ohv) 1931

746cc Donghai (transverse ohv flat-twin) 1982

DOGLIOLI & CIVARDI • Italy 1929–1935

Designed by Cesare Doglioli, these sporting machines had 170cc Norman ohv engines, later versions 173cc, 247cc, 347cc and 498cc JAP and four-valve ohv Python engines. Production was on a limited scale.

DOLF • Germany 1922–1925

Good, but very unorthodox 198cc two-stroke machines with unit-design engines of its own manufacture. The Dolf engines had no less than eight transfer and exhaust ports. In addition, they used a conic inlet rotary sleeve in the crankcase. The 62mm x 66mm bore/stroke engine developed 3hp.

DOLLAR • France 1925–1939

Once a leading French make, Dollar built many different models from 98cc to 748cc. Among them were two-strokes from 98cc to 246cc and 746cc models with four-cylinder unit-design air-cooled ohv engines. There were also Dollar machines with shaft drive and versions with power units made by Chaise.

DOMINISSIMI • Italy 1924–1928

Small producer of sporting 172cc and 248cc ohv single-cylinder machines.

DONGHAI • China 1978–

The first Chinese make to be exported, the very heavy 745cc vertical twin-cylinder ohv Donghai is, with its 33bhp at 5000 rpm, built to be used with a sidecar. With a top speed of not more than 58mph, it is a sturdy design on basically English lines with some Japanese technical influence. It is a cheap machine of limited performance.

DONISELLI • Italy 1951–1961

Once a producer of motorcycles with Ilo and Alpino engines from 63cc to 174cc, Doniselli later concentrated on different lightweights with engines of 49cc capacity.

DOPPER • The Netherlands 1904

Early ohv design of a 269cc single-cylinder machine, which had a long wheelbase and belt drive.

DORION • France 1932–1936

Lightweights with 98cc and 123cc Aubier-Dunne two-stroke engines.

DORMAN • Hungary 1920–1937

Assembled machines from 172cc to 499cc with Villiers, MAG and JAP proprietary engines. Limited production.

DOT • England 1903–1974

See panel

DOTTA • Italy 1924–1926

Small assembler which fitted 173cc Piazza two-stroke engines.

DOUE • France c1903

Long forgotten make. Fitted 1.5hp engines into bicycle frames.

DOT • England 1903–1974

Old established factory, founded by racing motorcyclist Harry Reed, who won the twin-cylinder class in the 1908 TT with a 680cc Peugeot-engined machine. He rode in 1924 in the sidecar TT and finished second on a Bradshaw-engined 348cc machine. DOT's heyday was during the 1920s, when it fitted not only Bradshaw engines, but mainly JAP motors from 246cc to 986cc V-twins. There were also Blackburne-engined 347cc versions and in the late 1920s and early 1930s machines with 173cc and 247cc Villiers two-stroke engines. The Manchester-based company gained further successes in TT races, when Syd Ollerhead was second in the 1924 Junior and Jack Cooke third in the Lightweight of the same year. Two third TT places were won in 1928, with Kenneth Twemlow in the Junior and his brother Eddy in the Lightweight. Kenneth was also second in the 1929 Lightweight. The engines were ohv racing singles, made by JAP. Some experimental racing DOTs had horizontal cylinders, but these failed to gain success. Motorcycle production stopped in 1932, but a reorganized company re-entered the market after 1948 and built a range of Villiers-engined two-strokes of 123cc to 246cc, of which many were motocross and trials machines.

Later, there were also Sachs and Minarelli-engined two-stroke models.

248cc DOT (two-stroke Villiers) 1957

346cc DOT (ohv JAP) 1926

D-RAD • Germany 1921–1933

Built at a state-owned former arms factory at Berlin-Spandau, the first machine was a 393cc flat twin, designed by Günther. Originally called the Star, it was renamed D-Rad and built until 1926. In the meantime chief designer Christiansen created the first true D-Rad, a heavy 496cc single-cylinder sv unit-design machine with a leaf-spring fork. The famous Martin Stolle, formerly with BMW and Victoria, joined the Spandau factory in 1927 and developed this design. In 1929 he created an ohv model (R10) with a new fork, coil springs and a separate gearbox, and in 1930 a similar machine, the R11, with an sv engine. The D-Rad motorcycles were always of sturdy design and often ridden with sidecars. Some regarded them as 'farmer's machines', but many big trials and long-distance events were won by these excellent machines, which also competed in races. Stolle was not only in charge of D-Rad design, but also of the very active competition department. Among leading riders in it were Curt Weichelt, Erich Tennigkeit, Franz Seelos, Max Polster, Hans Przybilski,

Franz Ischinger, Paul Bütow, Franz Heck and others. The last models built by D-Rad were 198cc and 246cc two-stroke singles with German Bark engines. Not many were made when NSU at Neckarsulm took over and stopped D-Rad motorcycle production.

DREADNOUGHT • England 1915–1925

Made by William Lloyds Cycle Ltd. at Birmingham, where it built Quadrant and LMC motorcycles too. The Dreadnought had an impressive name, but was only an assembled 269cc two-stroke machine with a Villiers engine.

DRESCH • France 1923–1939

Built many models over the years. These included 98cc to 246cc two-strokes and sv, ohv and ohc machines with Chaise, Aubier-Dunne, Stainless, Train, JAP, MAG and other proprietary engines up to 748cc. Among them were

models with shaft drive, pressed steel frames and 498cc and 748cc four-cylinder in-line versions. Also a 496cc vertical twin with pressed steel frame and shaft drive was built 1930–1932.

DREVON • France 1946–1953

Machines with engines from 98cc to 173cc.

DRYSDALE • Australia 1994–

Ian Drysdale has built several bikes from his Ausdale Engineering Company in Melbourne, including desert racers with two-wheel drive. At the end of 1998 he announced his 750cc V-eight, with cylinder heads from the Yamaha FZR400 and other home-built components. The V-eight is expensive at around £23,000, but Drysdale is developing slightly cheaper custom-styled V-eight of 1000cc capacity using Yamaha Fazer cylinder heads.

DOUGLAS • England 1907–1964

Famous for pioneering and for persisting with the flat twin engine, Bristol ironfounder Douglas took over J. F. Barter's Fairy (Fee) flat-twin motorcycle and developed it, in 350cc form with, from 1910, a two-speed gearbox with chain and belt transmission. Douglas was successful in long distance trials and in the TT. Harry Bashall won the 1912 Junior, which led directly to a War Office contract for despatch riders' machines for the British Army - thousands of which were used in WW1. Post-war, Les Bailey and Walter Moore designed an ohv model that sold well - the then future King George VI owned one! Douglas continued to perform successfully at Brooklands and Freddie Dixon won the 1923 sidecar TT and made the fastest lap in the 1924 Senior. Len Parker won the 1925 Sidecar TT. Sales of 350cc, 500cc and 600cc machines continued to be high through the 1920s. Freddie Dixon and Cyril Pullin designed the EW model with all-chain drive, three-speeds and a 350cc sv engine for 1925. Dixon also designed the 500cc and 600cc RA racing models, later developed into the 'Dirt track' Douglas, and into the super-sporting SW5 and SW6 road bikes.

In 1932, however, the Douglas family sold the company to a finance group and thereafter, the company appeared to lose its way, and was in and out of insolvency for the rest of the decade. However, it managed to produce a neat all-enclosed 150cc two-stroke and side-valve flat twins of 250cc - 750cc. In 1935 it was rechristened 'Aero Douglas', but production slowed down to a trickle of 600cc models, while, during WW2, it produced industrial trucks, aircraft parts and auxiliary engines.

The immediate post-war period saw a transverse-engined ohv 350cc with torsion bar suspension. In 1946 this became the T35 model, now with 'Radiadraulic' bottom link front forks. Despite some competition success, however, the T35 and its variants, the Plus 80 and Plus 90, never sold well, while the 350cc Dragonfly, with frame designed by Ernie Earles, did even worse. Between 1951 and 1964 Douglas undertook licensed manufacture of the Vespa scooter at its factory in Bristol. During that period it was bought by Westinghouse. Douglas (Sales and Service) continued to handle Italian-built Vespa scooters after it had ceased British production, until it was bought by the Heron Suzuki Group in the early 1980s.

350cc Douglas (sv flat twin) 1911

596cc Douglas Wessex (sv flat twin) 1934

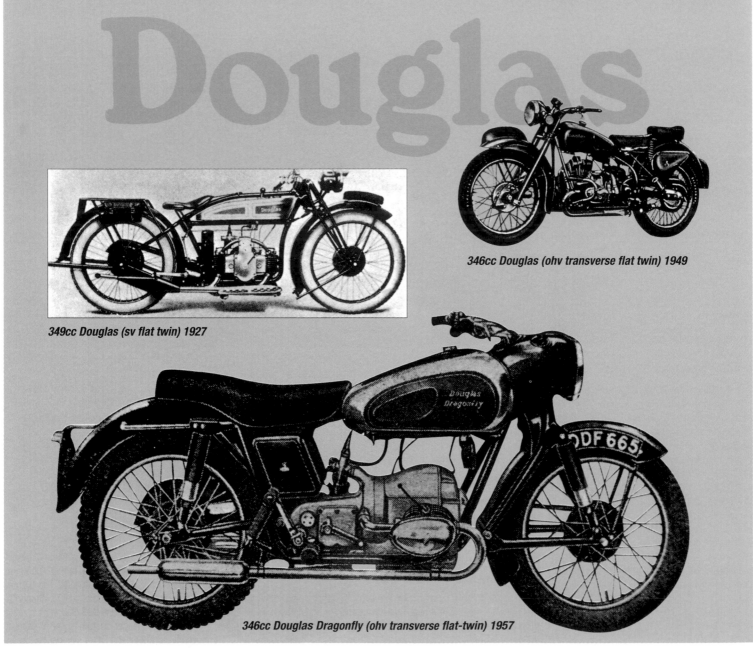

346cc Douglas (ohv transverse flat twin) 1949

349cc Douglas (sv flat twin) 1927

346cc Douglas Dragonfly (ohv transverse flat-twin) 1957

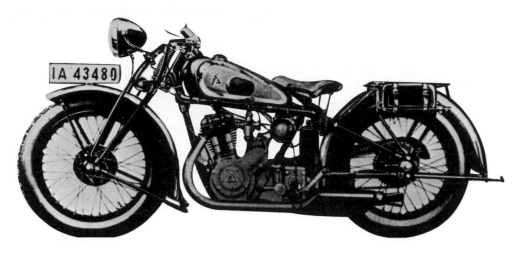

497cc D-Rad R11(sv Model) 1931

398cc D-Rad (sv flat twin) 1923

746cc DSH (sv V-twin JAP) 1929

173cc DS-Malterre (ohv AMC) 1955

248cc DS-Malterre (ohv AMC) 1954

498cc Dresch (sv two-cylinder, shaft drive) 1930

DS • Sweden 1924–1928

Made mainly for the Swedish armed forces, the DS had Swiss MAG ioe engines of 746cc.

DSH • Austria 1924–1932

The name came from the owners Döller, Seidl and Hauler. The first machines had 172cc and 246cc Villiers engines, later ones also 346cc, 490cc and 746cc sv and ohv JAP and MAG engines. The famous Rupert Karner, many times Austrian Champion, joined DSH in 1927 as a rider and with commercial interests. His death at the 1928 Hungarian TT when the fork on his 348cc machine broke during the race led to a hiatus for DSH until it was revived in 1929 by Franz Döller. He built new JAP-engined models with 246cc, 497cc and 746cc engines, among them a very sporting 246cc ohv double-port version. Among successful DSH riders were Anton Hunek, Josef Opawsky, Rudolf Runtsch and Friedrich Schwarz.

DS-MALTERRE • France 1920–1958

During the 1920s, production concentrated around a not very modern 496cc single-cylinder sv machine. After the war, DS - it stood for Deblades & Sigran - built Ydral-engined 123cc to 247cc two-stroke and 124cc to 248cc ohv versions with French-made AMC proprietary engines.

DSK • Japan 1954–1962

Built many two-strokes from 172cc upwards and also 497cc ohv machines with transverse-mounted flat-twin power units.

DUCATI • Italy 1946–

The Ducati company was formed in 1926 by Antonio Cavalieri Ducati and his three sons, Adriano, Bruno and Marcello, to manufacture radios and other electrical items - one of the first companies in Italy in this field. It grew rapidly, and by the time it moved to Borgo Paningale on the edge of Bologna nine years later, its present site, it had grown to a 2000 square metre factory with 100 employees.

The old factory was destroyed in the Second World War, but when it was rebuilt produced a wider range of goods from electric razors to movie cameras and refrigeration compressors, and seeing the demand for cheap personal mobility in the aftermath of the war, used its know-how to produce the Cucciolo in 1946, a four-stroke engine which strapped to a bicycle. The design and production machinery was bought from Aldo Farinelli, a lawyer and motoring enthusiast who had set up the SIATA factory in Turin to produce the engine, but found his factory did not have sufficient capacity. Despite - or because of - its very basic simplicity, the Cucciolo and its many variants went on to sell 100,000 units around the world.

Encouraged by this success, Ducati's designs became ever more ambitious - a racing version of the Cucciolo took only a year to arrive after the first road model!

By the early fifties Ducati was producing 'proper' motorcycles, such as the single cylinder 98, although the highly advanced Cruiser scooter, with hydraulic/direct drive switching, electric start and automatic gears, was a sales disaster as it was very expensive, slow and unreliable.

More importantly, on May 1, 1954, a young engineer called Fabio Taglioni joined the company, who went on to become one of the great motorcycle engineers.

Taglioni's brief was to design sports and racing machines, his first being the Marianna sohc Gran Sport 100 and 125 of 1955, which proved highly competitive, especially in long distance and endurance races which it dominated. Already the bike was sporting a distinctive helical drive to the overhead cam, something which Taglioni stuck with until the late 1970s. In 1956, in order to stay in front, Taglioni unveiled a dohc 125 Grand Prix bike, again with helical cam drive. The bike made sporadic appearances, until a new version made its debut at the Swedish Grand Prix late in the racing season. It won its inaugural race, but most significantly, also debuted the desmodromic valve gear which has been synonymous with Ducati ever since. Unlike later versions however, the first desmos featured three camshafts - two opening cams and one closing cam.

The design was a great success, finishing second and third in the 1958 Grand Prix, and larger versions followed, while road bikes such as the popular 175 Turismo, which

49cc Ducati Cucciolo (four-stroke single) 1946

*49cc Ducati Cucciolo Racing
(four-stroke single) 1947*

158cc Ducati (ohc) 1965

198cc Ducati (ohc) 1958

125cc Ducati Bialbero racer(four-stroke single) 1955

evolved into the 200cc Elite, mirrored this success. In 1960 financial restrictions curtailed the racing side of things, just as the development of twins was showing great promise (in the hands of Mike Hailwood among others), but a whole range of small capacity motorcycles, mopeds and scooters was produced throughout the sixties, such as the Diana 250 sports bike and Piuma moped of 1962, and Brio scooter a year later.

At this time, Ducati's American importer, Berliner, persuaded the Italians to build a machine for the US police market, the result being the prototype Apollo of 1963. This colossal 1257cc air-cooled, 90 degree V-four

produced 80bhp, which was just too much for the tires of the time and it proved dangerously unstable, even with power reduced to 65bhp.

More mainstream designs continued to do well, such as the 250 Mach 1 sports bike and Cadet 125, a basic, cheap runaround, but the next significant step happened in 1968, when a new generation of singles with larger crankcases (known as the 'wide case' singles) appeared, still with helical cam drives, and shortly with desmo valves for the first time on Ducati's road bikes. 250cc, 350cc and 450cc versions were produced, including the American styled Scrambler, an unlikely best seller for the

company. Production of the singles continued until 1975 in Italy, and for longer by Spanish Ducati importer and constructor Mototrans.

Taglioni meanwhile had spotted the trend towards larger bikes, and in 1971 the 90 degree V-twin GT750 appeared, the engine being an amalgam of two sohc singles on a common crankcase.

At the same time, a reasonably successful 500 twin Grand Prix bike was introduced, with the same V-twin configuration, but one of Ducati's most famous victories came in 1972 when British rider Paul Smart won at Imola the very first race of a new, desmo racing version of the

496cc Ducati (ohc two-cylinder) 1976

Mike Hailwood's 1978 TT winning Ducati 900SS

GT750, ahead of Bruno Spaggiari on a second Ducati and, amazingly, Giacomo Agostini on his MV Agusta.

Development of the desmo V-twins became intense, although the 750 Sport road bike of 1973 still did without them. That honour fell to the Super Sport 750 of 1974, a very expensive, limited edition machine (just 450 were made). Less successful was Ducati's foray into off-road two-stroke bikes with its Regolarita 125 in 1974, a route it soon abandoned.

Ducati's parallel twins of 1976 onwards proved to be another cul-de-sac (although the configuration appeared spasmodically in Ducati's history up to then). The styling

904cc Ducati 907ie (liquid-cooled ohc desmo) 1992

888cc Ducati 888 Strada (liquid-cooled dohc desmo) 1994

of the GTL350 and 500 was based on that of the previous year's 860GT V-twin, penned by car designer Giorgetto Giugiaro (who designed the first VW Golf), and did not look good, while the engines vibrated and the bikes were heavy. A few years later desmo versions with new styling did better, but were hardly a roaring success.

Meanwhile, the 860GT of 1975 received mixed reviews for its looks, but its reputation was ruined by poor electrics.

1977 proved significant for two reasons. Most public was the new 900SS, developed from the 750SS, famous for its excellent handling and good looks. The lean, aggressive SS also featured Ducati's trademark helical drive to the single overhead cam and desmo valve operation.

Behind the scenes, Taglioni began work on a new generation 500cc V-twin with belt-driven cams, the bike which was to become the Pantah and spawn a whole generation of two-valve desmo V-twins.

In 1978 came another famous Ducati victory when Mike Hailwood returned to the Isle of Man to win the Formula One TT after an eleven year absence from motorcycle racing. The bike was based on a 900SS, prepared by Steve Wynne of Sports Motorcycles with little help from the factory or its NCR racing team, although in 1980 the Italians still produced the Hailwood Replica road bike in the same Castrol racing colours.

The 860GT meanwhile had developed through the 900GTS to the Darmah (now with desmo valves) in 1978,

996cc Ducati 916SPS (liquid-cooled dohc desmo) 1998

the bike which started what was called 'Euro-styling' (the integration of fuel tank and seat unit). The real advances on this were the replacement of many unreliable Italian electrics with Japanese and German ones.

The Pantah arrived in 1979 to much acclaim, then was increased to 600cc in 1982 (this was the capacity originally planned, ironically, then reduced to 500cc for marketing reasons). The following year the last of the helical gear twins was produced, the S2 with Pantah-style fairing and 1000cc engine, but carburation was poor, the handling not good either and generally the bike epitomised the worst of results of a disinterested state ownership.

Luckily as it worked out, a partnership was formed with newly established Cagiva to supply engines.

In 1984 the situation had clearly become much worse, with one announcement stating Ducati was to cease bike production to concentrate on engine supply to Cagiva. But a protege of Taglioni, Massimo Bordi, took over as technical director, then in 1985 Cagiva's Claudio and Gianfranco Castiglioni negotiated an agreement to buy Ducati from Finmeccanica, the Italian state's holding company.

The Castiglionis decided Ducati must concentrate on racing, and the highly successful Pantah-based 750 F1 road bike was produced along with the Paris-Dakar-winning Cagiva Elefant. In a completely different vein, fairly successful were the Indiana 350cc, 650cc and 750cc custom-styled V-twins, and the influential 750 Paso, the first design for Ducati by Massimo Tamburini, brought to the Cagiva-Ducati Group from Bimota (which he founded) by the Castiglionis. This featured a 750 Pantah engine in box-section trellis frame hidden behind fully enclosed bodywork, which caused problems with heat build-up around the twin-choke Weber carburetor nestling in the engine's V causing fuel vaporisation, accelerating Ducati's fuel-injection development.

In 1987 a prototype of Ducati's 851cc liquid-cooled desmo with four valves per cylinder, developed by Massimo Bordi, was ridden to victory at Daytona by ageing racer Marco Lucchinelli. The bike, still with 750cc capacity, had already debuted unsuccessfully the previous year at the Bol d'Or, but in 1988 it achieved fifth, and went on to win for the first time with Frenchman Raymond Roche in 1990. Edi Orioli also won the Paris-Dakar that year on a Ducati-powered Cagiva.

The 851 Superbike Strada (Street) surprised many road testers with its speed, and once the fashionable but unsuitable 16 inch wheels were replaced with 17 inch items, its handling too. But it wasn't until 1990 when Japanese brakes and suspension were fitted that the true potential of the bikes for the road was revealed, and Ducati's reputation finally began to turn around solidly. Although called 851s, the racers and then homologation versions were taken out to 888cc. SP versions, (SP2, SP3, SP4 and SPS) were all effectively race bikes made road legal, but the 888 Strada was more usable and at last a real if expensive alternative to Japanese fours in terms of speed as well as handling.

904cc Ducati Hailwood Evoluzione prototype (air-cooled ohc desmo) 1999

The SS range meanwhile was relegated to the role of general sports bike, due to its older two-valve, air-cooled engines, though in 1992 was restyled once again, a chape it kept until the current look, drawn up by South African Pierre Terblanche for the 1998 model, when it also gained fuel injection.

The same engine was used in yet another highly influential Ducati, the M900 Monster, styled by Argentinian Miguel Galuzzi at Ducati's request in response to the growth in the retro bike market.

The same year the Supermono racer appeared, with an ingenious balance system using a second conrod to operate a bob weight positioned where the rear cylinder of a V-twin would be (the single even used V-twin crankcases). The engineering was the product of Claudio Domenicali and the styling Terblanche's, but there was more to the look than met the eye. Terblanche had been working with Tamburini at the San Marino-based Cagiva Research Center on the 888 replacement, and although the Supermono appeared first, it was influenced by Tamburini's pivotal 916, unveiled at the Milan Show at the end of that year. Although unmistakably Ducati with its trellis frame and desmo valves, the 916's low, wide pair of headlights, underseat exhaust and single-sided swingarm have been famously influential - the bike is regarded as one of the most beautiful ever made.

The success went beyond the looks with very strong sales and enormous success in World Superbikes, with the bike taking four of the five titles from 1994 to 1998, three with Briton Carl Fogarty and one in 1996 with Australian Troy Corser.

It was only at the end of 1998 that the 916 received a significant change, although the capacity increase to 996cc (made the previous year on the homologation special 916SPS) was still trivial by many manufacturers' standards.

Behind the scenes Ducati was fairing less well, largely due to the over-ambitious Cagiva simultaneously trying to run a 500cc Grand Prix team (with expensive, top class riders such as Randy Mamola, Eddie Lawson and John Kocinski) as well as the Ducati World Superbike effort, all on the back of Ducati's profits - Cagiva itself and its other marques were producing little of interest to the mass of motorcycle buyers. Suppliers were being paid later and later, until some refused to send more parts, resulting in faltering production and huge unmet demand for the 916, and eventually in September 1996 the American Texas Pacific Group acquired a majority holding in Ducati from Cagiva. Shortly after, the ST2 sports tourer was introduced, then the 916-powered ST4, but the new management, led by Federico Minoli, more importantly managed to turn the finances around and step up production to 28,000 motorcycles in 1998, double its 1996 levels.

In 1999 the company was successfully floated on the New York and Italian stock exchanges, and currently Ducati's future is looking very bright.

916cc Ducati ST4 (liquid-cooled dohc desmo) 1998

904cc Ducati M900 Monster (air-cooled ohc desmo) 1994

904cc Ducati ST2 (air-cooled ohc desmo) 1997

904cc Ducati 900SS (air-cooled ohc desmo) 1999

7hp Durkopp (sv V-twin) 1903

148cc Durkopp (two-stroke) 1952

246cc Dunelt (two-stroke) 1924

DUCATI • Italy 1946–

See panel

DUCATI (MOTOTRANS) • Spain 1959-1979

Produced for many years nearly identical models to the Bologna Ducati factory. Mototrans-Ducati of Barcelona is still closely connected with Italian Ducati, although it stopped building the machines under licence at the end of 1970s. When it did, it produced various 340cc ohc singles with touring and sporting specifications and also a 72cc trials two-stroke machine with 6bhp at 6100 rpm. The best known export model was the 24-Horas 346cc sporting single, although this was partly because of its reputation for unreliability. The last Spanish-built Ducati (Mototrans) models were Spanish-developed 246cc and 346cc ohc singles, called Forza and Vento.

DUCSON • Spain late 1950s-early 1960s

Small producer of 49cc two-stroke machines.

DÜMO • Germany 1924-1925

Sporting version of the 198cc Autinag, designed by Frankowski.

DUNEDIN • Scotland c1910-1912

JAP-powered motorcycles built by G. E. Rutherford, who started his Cycle Works in Edinburgh in 1898

DUNELT • England 1919-1956

Equipped with double-diameter pistons, the first Dunelt two-strokes had single-cylinder engines of 499cc. A similar version of 248cc was built from the 1920s onwards. From 1929 the factory also fitted 346cc, 498cc and 598cc sv and ohv engines made by Sturmey-Archer, as well as a 246cc version with the Sturmey-Archer face cam ohc engine. During the following years, the main range consisted of Villiers-engined machines up to 344cc and of sv and ohv models up to 498cc with engines made by Python (Rudge) and JAP. After a reorganization, the Birmingham factory moved in 1931 to Sheffield and

discontinued the manufacture of motorcycles in 1935. It re-entered the trade in 1955 with a 49cc moped with its own ohv engine, but had not much success. The greatest sporting success gained by Dunelt was winning the 1930 Maudes Trophy in the Isle of Man for the most meritorious performance of the year. Despite severe conditions, a 498cc Dunelt with an ohv engine covered 13,119 miles in 16 days at an average speed of 34.8mph.

DUNKLEY • England 1913-1915

Produced a variety of machines for a very few years with 199cc, 499cc, 746c and 988cc Precision engines, 342cc Peco two-strokes and also JAP-engined models from 293cc to 748cc.

DUNKLEY • England 1957–1959

Mopeds with own 61cc, 64cc and eventually 49cc ohv engines. These were of unit design, 'Whippet' was the trade name of these products.

DUNSTALL • England 1964–1982

Paul Dunstall became world famous for custom parts and for his Norton Dunstall Dominator twins, but was also a serious and successful race development engineer. In later years, Dunstall offered various customised bikes with big Japanese high performance engines, special frames etc, but these never had the huge success of his earlier products. In 1979 he collaborated with Heron Suzuki to produce in limited numbers a tuned version of the four-cylinder GS1000, badged the Dunstall Suzuki, which with its top speed of 153mph was hailed as the fastest production motorcycle of the time.

DURAND • France 1920–1923

Assembled motorcycles with Zurcher engines. Limited manufacture.

DURANDAL • France 1925–1932

Some models had pressed steel frames and most used JAP, Zurcher and Chaise proprietary engines from 246cc

to 490cc. There was also a successful works racing machine with a 348cc KTT Velocette ohc engine.

DÜRKOPP • Germany 1901–1959

Pioneer of the German motorcycle industry. In 1905, it already produced single and V-twin machines and an in-line four with air-cooled cylinders. Also a leading bicycle and car producer - now a leading manufacturer of needle bearings - Dürkopp stopped motorcycle production before WW1, built in the 1930s motorized bicycles and in 1949 resumed motorcycle manufacture with Sachs-engined 98cc and 123cc two-strokes. It also fitted Ilo engines of the same size and built after 1951 its own 147cc, 174cc and 198cc two-stroke engines designed by Goslau. A beautiful scooter, the 198cc Dürkopp Diana, came out in 1953 and was made until the famous factory stopped producing two-wheelers.

DUVAL • Belgium 1950–1955

Limited production of small 123cc two-stroke machines with engines supplied mainly by Royal Enfield.

DUX • England 1904–1906

Small assembler which used frames made by Rex at Coventry and engines supplied by Minerva, MMC, Sarolea and others. They were singles and V-twins.

DUZMO • England 1919–1923

A 496cc single-cylinder ohv machine designed by John Wallace and partly developed by the famous Bert le Vack, who was for a short period with Duzmo.

DWB • Germany 1924–1926

After Juhö closed down, Dorko Werke Bamberg took over manufacture of the 195cc sv machines and added in 1925 a 269cc two-stroke model to the range.

DYSON-MOTORETTE • England 1920–1922

Scooter-like lightweight with a 1·5hp engine on the left side and the petrol tank above the rear wheel.

EADIE • England 1898–1903

Pioneer make, which first built three-wheelers and then motorcycles with engines made by De Dion, Minerva, MMC and other factories. Eadie was also closely connected with the foundation of the Royal Enfield factory.

EAGLE • America 1910–1915

Well-made Spake-engined 4hp singles and 7hp and 9hp V-twins. According to the late Floyd Clymer, the Eagle was one of the best machines ever made in the USA.

EAGLE-TANDEM • England 1903–1905

Limited production of De Dion-engined machines, which were fitted with a chair-like seat.

EASY RIDER • China 1994–

Brand name given to Chinese-made mopeds and scooters on sale in Europe.

EBE • Sweden 1919–1930

After manufacturing 173cc bicycle engines, EBE produced motorcycles with own 172cc ohv and 598cc sv engines.

EBER • Germany 1924–1928

Motorcycles of typical English design with 347cc and 497cc sv and ohv Blackburne, then also 348cc and 498cc ohv Kühne and ohc Küchen engines.

EBO • England 1910–WW1

Assembler which fitted Precision engines and also single and V-twin JAP engines.

EBS • Germany 1924–1930

Berlin-based manufacturer which fitted engines of own manufacture of 198cc, 246cc, 348cc, 398cc, 496cc and a V-twin of 796cc. After 1928 a Villiers-engined 198cc two-stroke was added. The factory produced also three-wheeled transport vehicles with motorcycle engines.

EBU-STAR • Japan 1952–1955

Interesting 248cc twin-cylinder ohv machine with a vertical and a horizontal cylinder.

EBW • Germany 1923–1924

Assembled 139cc machine with engines made by Bekamo.

ECA • Germany 1923–1924

Simple 142cc two-stroke machines made in limited numbers.

ECEKA • Germany 1924–1925

Another small make which fitted 145cc and 173cc engines.

ECHO • Japan late 1950s–early 1960s

Producer of 123cc and 148cc two-stroke machines and the Pandra scooter.

ECKL • Germany 1923–1926

Hugo Eckl first produced bicycle attachment engines, afterwards also a 198cc single with its own ohv engine.

ECOMOBILE • Switzerland 1982–

Futuristic machines with bodywork fully enclosing the rider and exceptional aerodynamics as a result. Originally used BMW boxer engines, then four-cylinder K-Series motors. Machines feature very long wheelbases and outriggers to keep them upright when coming to a halt.

ECONOMIC • England 1921–1923

Unusual 165cc twin-cylinder two-stroke machines with friction drive of a design which came from the USA. The first models had the horizontally opposed twin fitted in orthodox fashion - in line. Afterwards it was transverse-mounted in a low duplex frame. Although its price was only £28.10s, it failed to make the grade.

ED • Germany 1923–1925

Equipped with low double-loop frames, the 139cc machines had flat single-cylinder Bekamo two-stroke pumping cylinder engines.

EDETA • Spain 1951–1960

Two-stroke machines with 147cc and 173cc engines.

EDMONTON • England 1903–c1910

Was a small assembler of motorcycles which fitted Minerva and Fafnir engines.

EDMUND • England 1907–1924

Made in Chester, the Edmund used Fafnir, MAG, JAP, Blackburne and Barr & Stroud proprietary engines. From about 1911, a 'spring frame' - actually an elaborate

49cc Easy Rider Holiday (two-stroke) 1998

198cc EBS (sv) 1924

246cc EBS (ohv) 1925

1047cc Egli (six-cylinder dohc Honda CBX) 1982

sub-frame pivoting on leaf springs and isolating the saddle and footrests - was featured, though it is doubtful if it justified its complication.

EDWORTHY • Australia 1896–1906

The Edworthy Motor & Cycle business of Granville, Sydney has been in business for over 100 years, but only built three motorcycles, using proprietary engines.

EENHORN • Holland 1905–1907

Based at Rotterdam, Eenhorn (Unicorn) built single-cylinder and V-twin sv machines on a limited scale. Produced from 3hp to 5.5hp.

149cc Eichler (two-stroke DKW) 1922

EGLI • Switzerland 1968–

Designed by Fritz W. Egli, the first machines had 996cc Vincent V-twin engines. The later Egli products included his frames with Japanese engines, including the 1047cc six-cylinder dohc Honda engine, and with 903cc to 1100cc four-cylinder dohc Kawasaki motors, including a modified turbo-engined Kawasaki version. Kawasaki and Honda also supplied big 500cc to 600cc single-cylinder ohc engines to Egli in the 1980s, although the machine which gained him the most publicity more recently was a turbo-charged Yamaha V-Max powered machine, with the 1200cc V-four engine.

EGA • Germany 1922–1926

Made by the Gaggenau iron works, the EGA machines had own 246cc and 346cc three-port, deflector-type two-stroke engines.

EICHELSDÖRFER • Germany 1929–1931

Builder of 198cc machines with ohv engines made by JAP.

EICHLER • Germany 1920–1925

Well-known assembler of lightweight motorcycles with 119cc, 145cc and 173cc DKW and 129cc to 149cc Bekamo two-stroke engines. Produced also DKW-designed 123cc Golem and 145cc Lomos scooters, then in Germany called Sesselräder. Ernst Eichler, founder of the factory, left in the mid-1920s and built machines with pressed-steel frames. After less than a year he returned to his old Berlin-based factory where he continued producing these red motorcycles.

EISENHAMMER • Germany 1923–1926

Two-stroke machines of heavy design with 206cc DKW and 225cc engines of own manufacture.

EISLER • Czechoslovakia 1920–1926

Agricultural machine factory which produced not only 148cc two-stroke bicycle attachment engines, but also complete lightweight motorcycles with these power units.

ELAND • The Netherlands 1955–1959

Small assembler, which fitted 123cc to 158cc two-stroke engines, mainly supplied by Sachs, into its own frames.

ELECT • Italy 1920–1923

Interesting design by Ladetto - later of Ladetto & Blatto fame - Ubertalli and Cavalchini. It was a horizontal twin with 492cc and three valves for each cylinder.

ELF • France 1977–1997

The first Elf race machines, financed by the eponymous French petroleum company, appeared in the late 1970s. Created by Renault and Peugeot race car designer Andre de Cortanze, and originally powered by Yamaha TZ750 race engines, they soon established a reputation for technical innovation or, as some people saw it, eccentricity.

De Cortanze favoured hub-center steering and other unconventional features, which were later incorporated in the marque's endurance racers, powered by factory Honda engines. In the mid 1980s the Elf project moved into GP racing with the Elf2, running Honda NS500 three-cylinder engines, with de Cortanze's deputy Dan Trema assuming the role of chief designer. The machines became gradually less radical as Elf management upped the pressure for results. The NSR500-powered Elf3 scored points in the 1986 500 world championship and won its first race at the non-championship Macau GP of the same year. The Elf4 and Elf5 of the following seasons were not so successful and wound up the company's racing involvement.

Elf returned to GP racing in 1996 with a V-four that had begun life as the Swissauto sidecar engine. Housed in a chassis built by the French ROC concern, the bike was an irregular points scorer over the next two seasons but never achieved its hoped-for success. The project was taken over in 1998 by the now Malaysian-owned MüZ factory.

ELFA • Germany 1926–1932

Built during the years a variety of models with 73cc, 98cc, 123cc, 198cc, 298cc, 346cc and 497cc proprietary engines made by DKW, Kühne, Küchen, Windhoff, Sachs, Bark and also JAP. Mofa production continued until 1940.

ELFE • Germany 1923–1925

Unorthodox frames with own 196cc three-port deflector-type engines built in small numbers.

ELF-KING • England 1907–1909

Equipped with hand-starters like cars, these machines had V-twin Minerva engines.

ELFSON • England 1923–1925

Well-designed machines with Elfson's own 294cc three-port two-stroke power units. Another model had 170cc Norman ohv engines.

ELI • England 1911–1912

Accessory factory which produced motorcycles with 3.5hp Precision engines.

ELIE HUIN • France early 1950s–early 1960s

The post-war Elie Huin machines had Ydral, AMC and other French proprietary engines from 123cc to 248cc.

196cc Elster (sv) 1925

ELIG • Spain 1956–1959

Small producer which used Hispano Villiers engines from 123cc to 198cc.

ELITE • Germany 1903–1940

Founded by Diamant, where motorcycles were built in 1903. Elite started car production in 1914 and the manufacture of a 1hp engine for bicycles in 1923. Elite and Diamant joined forces in 1927 and produced Diamant motorcycles until 1928-1929, when Opel took over the factory for the manufacture of its own 498cc motorcycles with duralumin frames. In 1932 these models were succeeded by similar machines called EO (Elit-Opel). These had 348cc and 498cc ohc engines made by Küchen, while the 'real' Opel motorcycles of that period had its own sv and ohv single-cylinder power units. Few EOs were actually built.

ELLEHAM • Denmark 1904–1909

One of the few Danish producers. The design included an open frame, a larger front wheel and a 2.75hp Peugeot engine.

ELMDON • England 1915–1921

Limited manufacture of 269cc two-strokes with Villiers engines.

ELRING • Germany 1924–1925

This was another name for the 196cc Elfe two-strokes.

ELSAVA • Germany 1907

Built by Volker & Prugel, Krenzmuhle, Germany. The company made its own engines with, unusually, the inlet valve fitted within the exhaust valve. Fuel supply was metered by an injector housed in the inlet tube. Although the design did work machines were built in limited numbers as mixture control was difficult and the buying public distrusted the idea.

ELSTAR • England 1968–1971

Produced mainly frames for competition machines, including motocross, grass track and speedway. Fitted Jawa, Bultaco and other mainly two-stroke engines. Production stopped when Ellis, the founder, was killed in a road accident.

ELSTER • Germany 1924–1926

A comparatively small factory which produced 197cc sv machines with engines of own design and manufacture.

ELSWICK • England 1903–1920

Well-known bicycle manufacturer which fitted 348cc and 498cc single-cylinder Precision proprietory engines.

ELVE • Belgium 1958–early 1960s

Moped producer which fitted 49cc Sachs engines.

EM • Austria 1928–1930

Produced one model only in limited numbers. It was a 497cc single-cylinder ohv machine with the MAG double-port engine.

EMA • Germany 1922–1926

Designed by Eduard Molitor, these low-built machines had 145cc DKW engines with a horizontal cylinder.

206cc EMA (two-stroke DKW) 1925

497cc EM (ohv MAG) 1929

340cc EMW (ohv shaft drive) 1953

EMB • America 1995–

Produces what is currently the world's only commercially available electric motorcycle, the Lectra VR24. Top speed is about 30mph, but it can be boosted to 45mph in short bursts at the expense of range, which can be around 60 miles.

EMBLEM • America 1909–1925

Big 996cc V-twin machines of sound design, which competed with success in sporting events.

EMC • England 1947–1988

The first machines had its own 348cc double-piston two-stroke engines. Afterwards the Ehrlich Motor Company fitted 123cc and 248cc Puch engines. A 123cc JAP-engined two-stroke exhibited at Earls Court in 1952 never went into quantity production. Joe Ehrlich built from 1960 to 1964 the 124cc de Havilland rotary disk two-stroke racing machines, which were ridden in races by such famous men as Mike Hailwood, Derek Minter, Phil Read, Rex Avery and Paddy Driver. Ehrlich returned to GP racing in 1987, running a Rotax-powered tandem-

twin 250. The bike was developed further over the next two seasons, Scot Donnie McLeod finishing the 1988 250 world championship a highly respectable 12th overall. Nevertheless, the project lacked the necessary finance to continue competition at world level. Although EMC stopped its involvement in motorcycling at this time, the company is still involved in other engineering projects.

EMH • Germany 1927–1929

Limited manufacture of 348cc and 498cc machines with open frames and Küchen ohc engines.

EMMAG • Hungary 1924–1927

Built unorthodox water-cooled 670cc two-stroke twins and also air-cooled 495cc two-stroke singles. Production was on a limited scale.

EMURO • Japan 1953–late 1950s

Produced two-stroke machines with own engines from 98cc to 248cc.

EMW • East Germany 1945–1956

Produced in the former Dixi-BMW car and motorcycle factory at Eisenach a 348cc single-cylinder ohv machine with shaft drive and pressed steel frame which was similar to a 1934 BMW model.

EMWE • Germany 1924–1925

Using a welded box frame, EMWE fitted a 293cc two-stroke engine of its own design.

ENAG • Germany 1924–1925

The Theo Steininger-designed two-stroke machines had 248cc and 348cc capacity, water-cooled barrels and air-cooled cylinder heads.

ENDRICK • England 1911–1915

Built different machines with Fafnir, Peugeot and JAP engines, until the Olton (Birmingham) factory concentrated on models with 346cc Peco two-stroke and 496cc Precision sv engines.

497cc EO (ohc Küchen prototype) 1930

499cc Enfield Bullet (ohv) 1999

ENDURANCE • England 1909–1924

Among the C. B. Harrison-designed models were those with 269cc Villiers engines and versions with its own 259cc and 297cc two-stroke three-port motors.

ENERGETTE • England 1907–1911

Designed by the famous J. L. Norton - founder of the Norton factory - the Energette had a British-built Moto-Rêve engine of 274cc. It was a V-twin with 50mm bore and 70mm stroke.

ENFIELD • India 1970–

Royal Enfield of Redditch sold its old tooling to Enfield India, who first made small two-strokes, then the 346cc ohv Bullet, and now the 493cc ohv model as well. The company changed its name to Royal Enfield in the mid-1990s, and production continues of the old British designed singles, albeit with various updates such as improved, 12 volt electrics. Further modifcations are planned, including electric starters.

ENGEE • Germany 1925

Single-cylinder ohv machines with Kühne proprietary power units. Apparently only a 348cc model was marketed.

EO • Germany 1930–1931

Mentioned already under Elite, the EO had an Opel-like frame made from duralumin and 348cc and 498cc ohc Küchen engines. Designer of the frame was Ernst Neumann-Neander.

EOLE • Belgium c1900

Built in the pioneer period, the Eole had Kelecom and Fafnir engines.

EPA • Germany 1924–1925

Small assembler, which fitted 293cc JAP sv engines into own frames.

ERCOLI-CAVALLONE • Italy 1922–1923

One of the few makes in the world which produced 496cc V-twin machines with two-stroke engines. Others were the British Stanger and WAG. None had much success and soon all disappeared from the market.

ERIE • America 1905–1911

The Hammondsport factory fitted Minerva, Spake and Curtiss engines and was commercially connected with the Glenn Curtiss factory.

ERIOL • France 1932–1939

Lightweight motorcycles with 98cc two-stroke engines.

ERKA • Germany 1924–1925

Simple 269cc two-stroke machines made by a small factory.

ERKÖ • Germany 1922–1924

Another small producer of lightweights with 145cc DKW motors.

ERMAG • Germany 1923–1930

Good machines designed by ex-Ziro designer Albert Roder. The first 246cc Ermag had a Dunelt-like double diameter piston and a rotary inlet valve for the single-cylinder two-stroke engine. From 1925 Ermag produced a fast 246cc ohv machine and sv singles with 497cc and 547cc capacity. Successful Ermag riders: Hans Hieronymus, Karl Perl, Paul Bittorf. Roder was with Victoria in the 1930s and before the war joined the NSU works at Neckarsulm.

ERNST EICHLER • Germany 1924–1925

Originally the founder of the Berlin-based Eichler motorcycle factory, Ernst Eichler left the works after differences and set up a new factory. There he created some interesting 142cc two-stroke and 172cc two and

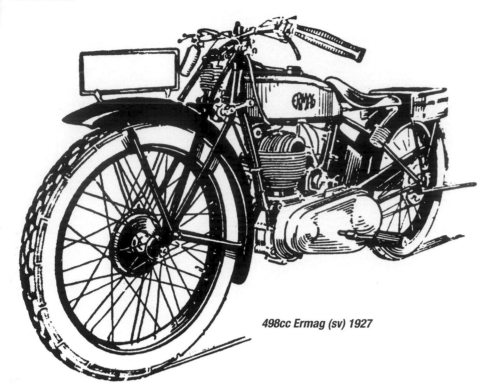

498cc Ermag (sv) 1927

246cc Ermag (ohv) 1927

four-stroke sv machines with frames made from pressed steel. After a comparatively short period he returned.

ERNST-MAG • Germany 1926–1930

The first machines had 348cc and 498cc ohc engines made by Kèchen, but from 1928 onwards the Silesian factory relied exclusively on Swiss MAG engines of 348, 498, 598, 746 and 996cc capacity. Among them were fast 348cc ohv double-port singles and 498cc and 598cc ohv V-twins. Factory riders even had some 498cc ohc V-twins. These included Landolph Rhode, Edgar Kittner and Orlindo Geissler.

ERR-ZETT • Austria 1938

Lightweights with 98cc Sachs and Ilo engines. As result of political circumstances at that period in Austria, only a few of these machines were built.

ESCHAG • Germany 1923–1925

Simple 298cc two-stroke machines with belt drive to the rear wheel.

ESCH-REKORD • Germany 1927–1930

Designed and built by racing motorcyclist Adolf Esch, these racing machines used 248cc, 348cc and 498cc engines made by Blackburne, MAG and JAP. Among the riders were Joseph Wenzel and Wilhelm Etzbach. The design resembled that of leading English machines.

ESCOL • Belgium 1925–1938

Built on English lines in limited numbers, Escol used Villiers engines from 147cc to 247cc. Larger models had 248cc to 596cc JAP and Python engines. The last Escol had its own 348cc two-stroke engine.

ESO • Czechoslovakia 1949–1962

Eventually absorbed by the Jawa factory, Eso was founded by ex-racing rider Jaroslav Simandl for the purpose of producing 498cc speedway ohv single-cylinder engines. Afterwards it built at the Divisov factory not only complete speedway machines but also models with modified 348cc and 498cc engines for road races and motocross events. It went on to produce track engines and ice-racing versions, and for Jawa very successful speedway engines with four-valve cylinder head.

ETA • England 1921

Interesting 870cc three-cylinder machine with a radial engine, unit-design and shaft drive. The Eta never went into quantity production.

ETOIL • France 1933–1939

Aubier-Dunne-engined two-strokes from 98cc to 198cc.

EUROPA • Germany 1931–1933

Made in Munich with 98cc and 146cc Villiers engines as well as with Berlin-built 147cc and 198cc Schliha two-strokes.

EVANS • America 1919–1924

One of the finest American lightweights ever built, the Evans had a 119cc two-stroke engine and also gained popularity in Germany. The Berlin-based Stock factory, then part of the Kuhn industrial empire, eventually took the Evans license and built these machines in improved form as the first models made by Stock.

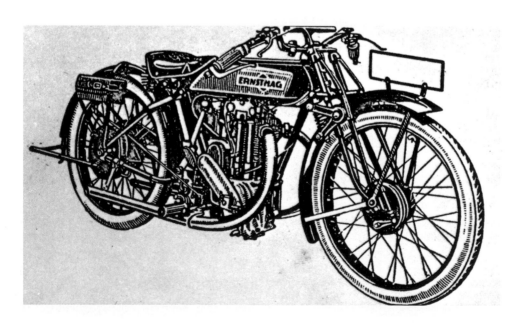

347cc Ernst-MAG (ohv MAG) 1927

198cc Europa (two-stroke Schliha) 1933

EVANS-PONDORF • Germany 1924–1925

Built also the 119cc Evans, but ran into license problems with Stock and tried to enter the market with a beautiful 496cc single of advanced design, which included foot-operated gearchange. Unfortunately lack of money prevented quantity production of this Pondorf design.

EVART-HALL • England 1903–1905

The first machines had single-cylinder engines fitted into strengthened bicycle frames and mounted near-horizontally above the pedalling gear. The 2.5hp engines had sight-feed lubrication, spray or surface carburetors and back-pedalling hub brakes. From 1904 onwards, Evart-Hall produced also the air-cooled in-line four-cylinder 385cc machine designed by Binks.

EVEREST • Germany 1925–1926

Offered by a Berlin-based company, the Everest was built by the G. A. Rempp factory at Münster. It was a heavy 496cc single with Everest's own ohv engine.

EVER ONWARD • Australia 1924

Prototype with 500cc Barr and Stroud sleeve-valve engine and Norton frame.

EVO • Germany 1923–1925

Designed by well-known motorcycle journalist Eduard Voigt, 146cc Evo machines had Ilo as well as its own two-stroke engines.

EVYCSA • Spain c1956

Well-designed 173cc machines with four-speed gearboxes made in limited numbers.

119cc Evans (two-stroke) 1922

EWABRA • Germany 1921–1924

Heavy 550cc single-cylinder sv machines, designed and built by Ewald Brackelsberg, a cousin of the late Bugatti driver Karl Brackelsberg.

EWB • Australia c1912–1915

Single-cylinder and V-twin JAP-powered machines built in Melbourne by E. W. Brown, JAP agent for Australia and New Zealand.

EXCELSIOR • England 1896–1964

See panel

EXCELSIOR • Germany 1923–1924

This company was evidently not considered a problem for the older German Excelsior factory at Brandenburg, for it apparently never fought the use of the Excelsior trademark. The short-lived Munich firm built only a simple 245cc two-stroke machine.

EXCELSIOR • Germany 1901–1939

This was originally a bicycle factory at Brandenburg. After using Minerva, Zedel and Fafnir engines, during the 1920s the factory used English 198cc, 298cc and 346cc sv and ohv JAP engines too. Its motorcycles, of typical English design, were not dissimilar to English Excelsiors, although there was no direct connection between Excelsior-Birmingham and Excelsior-Brandenburg. Never as famous as the English make, the German factory fitted in the 1930s 198cc two-stroke and 196cc to 496cc sv engines made

192cc Excelsior Germany (two-stroke Bark) 1936

EXCELSIOR • England 1896–1964

Baylis-Thomas of Coventry used De Dion, MMC and Minerva engines as early as 1900 and Harry Martin broke records at Canning Town cycle track on an Excelsior in 1903. A pause followed until 1910, when motorcycle production resumed under W. H. Carson, an advocate of 'big singles'. Pre-war, an 850cc sv single was offered. In 1920 there was a tie up with the Walker family of Tyseley, Birmingham, and Eric Walker took over the company's direction. In the 1920s, Villiers, JAP and Blackburne engines were used, and Excelsior-JAPs gained a reputation in racing. In 1933 a special Blackburne engine with four radial valves and twin carburetors was used, Syd Gleave winning the

Lightweight TT with it on its first appearance. Its subsequent record was disappointing.

In 1934 the Excelsior Manxman was produced, with a single ohc engine of 250cc and 350cc (and later 500cc); it was also sold in genuine racing form. For 1936, Excelsior made the 'Manxman' engines in its own factory, and, in 1937 and 1938, produced ohc four-valve racer engines (under Rudge patents) of 250cc and 350cc for works riders Tyrell Smith, Ginger Wood and occasionally Charlie Manders. Development was in the hands of Australian Alan Bruce. The four-valve engines were never sold to the public and for 1938 the factory reverted to two valves. Excelsior never won a TT with the Manxman (though it won several grands prix), but was second in 1937 and 1938. Dennis Parkinson won the Manx Grand

Prix in 1936, 1937 and 1938, on the last occasion with a rear sprung machine.

Excelsior built the wartime 'Welbike' with 98cc Villiers engine for airborne dropping for the army. Post-war, this with a 98cc Excelsior engine became the Brockhouse Corgi scooter. Excelsior now made its own 98cc, 125cc and twin 250cc engines - all two-strokes, and its Talisman twins, 250cc then 330cc became highly popular. Excelsior lightweights, with its own engines and later with Villiers units, sold well at home and in export, but with the death of the energetic Eric Walker, the company lost its driving force. Over a period of time production and sales fell away, until in the end only the 'Universal' model was being offered as a 'do it yourself' kit. The Walker brothers, Eric Walker's sons, eventually sold the factory to accessory maker and seat belt pioneer Britax.

490cc Excelsior GB (ohv JAP) 1930

248cc Excelsior GB (ohv 'Manxman') 1936

EXCELSIOR • America 1908–1931

This was the biggest factory producing Excelsior motorcycles. It was the Excelsior Supply & Mfg. Co at Chicago, part of the still-existing Schwinn bicycle empire. The range consisted of 269cc two-strokes built along the lines of the English Triumph Baby and of 499cc singles and 746cc to 996cc V-twins with its own ioe engines. Only a few 499cc and 996cc works racing models had ohc power units. There was a problem when the Chicago-based factory sold machines to England, so these were given the name American-X and in the mid-1920s all V-twins built by Schwinn were renamed Super-X. In addition, the factory produced since 1919 the famous Bill Henderson-designed in-line four machines, of which the last version was of 1301cc with ioe valves, separate cylinder barrels and a common cylinder head. Super-X and Henderson had next to Indian and Harley-Davidson the largest motorcycle production in the USA when Ignaz Schwinn decided in 1931 to stop manufacture of motorcycles.

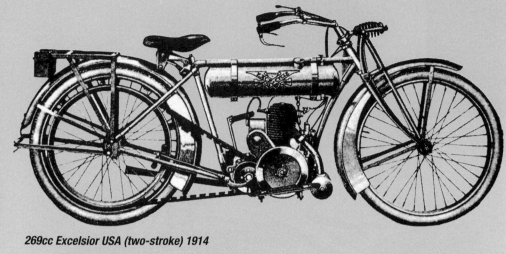

269cc Excelsior USA (two-stroke) 1914

992cc Excelsior USA (ioe V-twin) 1922

by Bark of Dresden, and while Walker built successful racing machines, Conrad & Patz - owners of the German factory - never showed any interest in sporting events.

EXCELSIOR-HENDERSON • America 1998–

Reformed to produce a modern custom-styled machine called the Super-X, after the original bike built by Excelsior in the 1920s. Production of the fuel-injected V-twin is due to begin in 1999.

EXPRESS • Germany 1903–late 1950s

Produced Fafnir-engined motorcycles in the early years of motorcycling. Resumed manufacture of mofas in the 1930s with 74cc and 98cc two-stroke engines and re-entered the market in 1949 with two-stroke motorcycles up to 248cc. An old bicycle factory, Express also supplied mofas and mopeds again. These now had 47cc engines. Experiments in the mid-1950s with the Küchen-designed 248cc twin-cylinder ohe engine proved not very successful. In 1957 Express became part of the then newly-founded Zweirad-Union at Nuremberg, together with Victoria and DKW, but the name Express was soon dropped.

EYSINK • The Netherlands 1899–1956

Leading Dutch motorcycle factory. Fitted first Minerva, Fafnir and other engines into own frames, built in 1905 vertical twins with Kindermann-designed Berkley engines and also entered car production. The most famous pre-1914 models were the 365cc and 425cc singles, used also by the Dutch forces during the war. There were also 366cc and 409cc singles and 774cc V-twins with own engines. During the early 1920s, a flat twin came into being. It was of 702cc and its engine was similar to the British Raleigh of that period. The first Villiers-engined two-strokes were built in 1926. Eysink built 147cc, 172cc and 198cc versions. The Dutch factory was also closely connected with foreign factories including New Hudson and Sunbeam in England and Dollar in France, which supplied certain parts to the Dutch. It also fitted the English Rudge-built 348cc and 498cc four-valve Python ohv engines and some JAP engines, including racing versions. In the mid-1930s bread-and-butter versions with Sachs and Ilo two-stroke engines up to 198cc came into production at the Amersfoort factory, then headed by Dick Eysink. After 1945 most Eysink machines had Villiers engines. During the late 1940s and early 1950s, very fast 172cc machines were developed.

247cc Express (two-stroke ILO 'Radex') 1952

123cc Eysink (two-stroke Villiers) 1939

492cc Fadag (ohv) 1926

246cc Fabula (two-stroke shaft drive) 1923

FABULA • Germany 1922–1924

Designed by ex-Dürkopp designer Nikolaus Henzel, the Fabula was of very advanced design. It had its own 246cc unit-design two-stroke deflector-type engine and shaft drive to the rear wheel. Many parts of it were made for Fabula by the superbly equipped Dürkopp factory at Bielefeld.

FADAG • Germany 1921–1925

Made by a car factory, Fadag's first product in the sphere of two-wheelers was a 118cc bicycle attachment engine. Motorcycles, built from 1923 onwards, had what Fadag appeared to claim were its own 497cc single cylinder sv and ohv engines although unconfirmed sources suggest they were supplied by Sarolea of Belgium to the Düsseldorf-based factory.

FAFNIR • Germany 1900–1914

Pioneer producer of proprietary engines and from 1903 onward of complete motorcycles, Fafnir supplied in the early years most German-made motorcycle power units. The Aachen-based factory had the Werner brothers licence for the manufacture of proprietary engines and produced many versions up to 8hp V-twins.

FAGAN • Ireland 1935–1937

Only one model, a Villiers-engined 123cc single, was made by the Irish factory.

FAGARD • Germany 1923–1925

Limited production of 145cc two-stroke machines with DKW engines, also known as FG.

FAGGI • Italy 1950–1953

Lightweight machines with Villiers engines from 123cc to 147cc. Good design, small production.

FAINI • Italy 1923–1927

Manufacturer of 108cc bicycle engines and of 198cc motorcycles with own sv engines.

FAIRFIELD • England 1914–1915

Only one model, a 269cc two-stroke, was built by this Warrington factory. The onset of WW1 prevented the output from increasing further.

FAKA • Germany 1952–1957

A scooter with 8 inch and later 10 inch wheels and Ilo engines of 147cc, 174cc and 197cc capacity.

FALCO • Italy 1950–1953

Built at Vercelli, the Falco was powered by German 98cc and 147cc Sachs engines.

FALKE • Germany 1923–1925

Assembled machines with 142cc Grade and 145cc DKW three-port, deflector-type two-stroke engines.

FALTER • Germany 1952–

Moped and mofa producer, whose products were also known as Stoewer Greif. The Bielefeld-based factory used mainly 49cc engines.

FAM • Italy 1951–1969

Founded by Giovanni Benelli - one of the five brothers of Benelli motorcycle fame of Pesaro - FAM produced 115cc singles and 195cc flat twins which used the B trademark. The egg-shaped engines were of contemporary design.

FAMA • Germany 1923–1925

Limited manufacture of 190cc ohv and 420cc sv single-cylinder machines with own engines.

FAMO • Germany 1923–1926

Triangular frames and 127cc two-stroke three-port engines formed the basis of all Famo models.

127cc Famo (two-stroke) 1925

FANTIC • Italy 1968–

Started out producing sporting 49cc and 124cc two-strokes with an eye on the American market, then focused more on Europe and the home market. Produced many types of models in the 1970s and 1980s, including choppers and sports mopeds as well as trials and motocross competition machines. The two-stroke trials machines of 79cc, 124cc, 157cc and 212cc were very successful in all levels of competition.

Currently produces a small range of scooters and lightweight sports motorcycles.

FAR • Austria 1924–1927

Assembled machines with 346cc and 490cc single-cylinder sv and ohv JAP engines. The name stood for Franz and Anton Rumpler.

123cc Fantic Caballero RC125 (two-stroke) 1976

79cc Fantic motocrosser (two-stroke) 1982

49cc Fantic GT Super (two-stroke air-cooled single) 1976

FARNELL • England c1901

Long forgotten make which had 2.75hp Minerva engines fitted into bicycle frames.

FAVOR • France 1919–1959

Was a well-known make in France. Built two-strokes from 98cc to 248cc and JAP-engined sv and ohv models with 346cc single-cylinder power units. After the war the Favor range included Aubier-Dunne-engined two-strokes and AMC-engined ohv singles up to 248cc.

FAVORIT • Germany 1933–1938

The first machines had 996cc V-twin JAP engines, afterwards the small manufacturer concentrated on 98cc and 123cc lightweights with Sachs engines. Favorit's main product was sidecars.

FB • Germany 1923–1925

The first machines were 269cc two-strokes, afterwards JAP and Blackburne-engined 348cc and 498cc sv and ohv models came into being. Designed by Friedrich Benz, these machines were also badged as the Meteor.

FB • England 1913–1922

Fowler and Bingham built proprietary two-stroke engines of 206cc, 269cc and 411cc and also complete motorcycles.

F.B. MONDIAL • Italy 1948–1979

Fratelli Boselli – the Boselli brothers – built industrial three-wheelers until 1944. Post war, Count Giuseppe Bosselli decided to advertise by racing in the new 125cc class and the 125cc dohc Mondial, designed by Alfonso Drusiani, swept all before it in 1948 and 1949. In 1949 Nello Pagani was world champion, in 1950, Bruno Ruffo and in 1951 Carlo Ubbiali. Cromie McCandless won the first 125cc TT for Mondial in 1951. 1950 saw the debut of Mondial's 125cc pushrod ohv road machines. Later production ranged from 50cc to 250cc two-strokes and four-strokes.

Mondial was always interested in racing and in 1957 Tarquinio Provini won the 125cc and Cecil Sandford the 250cc world titles. After 1960 Mondial raced two-strokes designed by Francesco Villa, although not very successfully. Thereafter, Mondial's fortunes declined, it became just another Italian company and late models even had Sachs engines.

FBM • Italy 1950–1955

Interesting designs with partly pressed steel frames and the horizontal single-cylinder engines mounted directly on the swinging arm of the rear suspension. The range included 48cc and 74cc two-strokes and ohv engines with 158cc and 198cc capacity.

FEARNOUGHT • New Zealand 1913

3½hp machine. Details are thin.

FECHTEL • Germany 1924–1926

Small assembler which fitted Hansa-built 198cc ohv engines into its own frames.

FEDERATION • England 1919–1937

The Co-op machine, built at Birmingham, was also known with the Federal trademark. Most models had the 269cc Villiers engine, later ones 147cc Villiers and 246cc ohv JAP engines. The price for the smaller model in 1936 was £25, for the bigger £44.

FEE • England 1905–1908

The Barter-designed sv flat twins had 198cc, 346cc and 676cc engines. Also known as the Fairy, the Fee was really the forerunner of the Douglas machines.

FEILBACH LIMITED • America 1912–1915

Like the Harley-Davidson, the Feilbach Limited was built at Milwaukee, Wisconsin, but unfortunately for a short period only. The range consisted of 548cc singles and

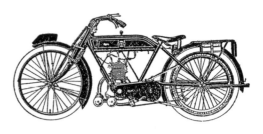

269cc Federal (two-stroke Villiers) 1921

990cc to 1130cc V-twins with its own ioe engines. Most models could be obtained with either chain or shaft drive.

FEMINIA • France 1933–1936

Assembled lightweights with 98cc and 123cc Aubier-Dunne and Stainless two-stroke engines.

FERBEDO • Germany 1954

Very simple but unsuccessful mini-scooter with 49cc Zündapp engines.

FERRARI • Italy 1951–1954

A big name, but a small factory, and no connection with Enzo Ferrari and his cars. Still, Ferrari motorcycles were of sound design and the range included two-stroke and ohv machines from 123cc to 248cc. The last model was a beautiful 173cc vertical-twin ohc machine.

FERRARIS • Italy 1903

Short-lived make which had 2hp Peugeot engines in bicycle frames.

FERT • Italy 1926–1929

Calamidas Fert machines had no connection with the then well-known Italian plug of the same name. The motorcycles

1196cc Feilbach (ioe V-twin) 1914

490cc FEW-Paramount (sv JAP) 1927

used 173cc ohv engines of Fert's own design and manufacture. Ridden by Passera and Aldi in races, they were not successful.

FEW-PARAMOUNT • England 1920–1927

Waller's long wheelbase design with two bucket seats and a fully enclosed engine did not win many customers. Offered with 498cc JAP and Blackburne as well as with 996cc V-twin JAP engines, only a few of these unorthodox machines were built.

FEX • Germany 1923–1924

Fitted DKW and Bekamo engines, after his own 170cc two-stroke proved to be a technical failure.

FG • Germany 1923–1925

Identical with Fagard.

FHG • Germany 1927–1929

Offered by the German AJS importer Pleus & Co., the FHG was probably a French Grimpeur 173cc two-stroke built to the Pleus specification.

FIAM • Italy 1923–1925

A 110cc bicycle attachment engine designed by Lelio Antonioli and built in limited numbers.

FIAMC • Germany 1951–1953

Producer of 123cc two-stroke motorcycles and of scooters with identical engines.

496cc Finzi (ohv transverse V-twin) 1924

FIDUCIA • Switzerland 1902–1905

Made by the Weber foundry at Zürich-Uster, these machines had own 450cc single-cylinder engines.

FIFI • Germany 1923–1924

Another name for the 145cc and 173cc Eichler motorcycles.

FIGINI • Italy 1899–1910

Luigi Figini together with Lazzati were pioneers in the motorcycle field. Figini produced its first machine in 1899 and entered commercial manufacture of motorcycles in 1902.

FIMER • Italy 1950–1951

Scooters using 125cc Villiers engines. Limited production.

298cc FKS (two-stroke flat twin) 1923

FLANDERS "4"

497cc Flanders (sv) 1913

FINZI • Italy 1923–1925

Built at the Maxima factory, the Finzi was a machine of advanced design with the 598cc ohv V-twin unit-design engine mounted transversely. It had a saddle sprung by leaf springs and a fully enclosed rear chain. Despite the modern conception, the Finzi was not a commercial success.

FIORELLI • Italy 1951–1968

Assembled machines with 123cc and 173cc Ilo engines and concentrated afterwards on the production of components for other factories and on bicycles and mopeds.

FIT • Italy 1950–1954

Another assembler, which fitted Ilo engines of 123cc and 147cc into own frames.

FIX • Germany 1922–1926

A branch of the Hansa-Lloyd car factory, Fix produced two-strokes with own 3hp engines.

FKS • Germany 1921–1926

Produced a range of machines with 149cc two-stroke engines. These were mounted originally above the front wheel, afterwards above the pedalling gear. Another model was a 298cc flat twin two-stroke, similar to the KC.

FLANDERS • America 1911–1914

Made by the Michigan car factory of the same name, the Flanders was a 499cc sv single with the exhaust valve on the rear side of the cylinder.

FLANDRIA • Belgium late 1950–1983

Well-known manufacturer of bicycles, mofas, mopeds and lightweight machines with 49cc two-stroke engines. In 1976 showed a very sporting motorcycle with a six-speed gearbox and 17 inch alloy wheels. All engines were made by the A. Claeys-Flandria N.V. at Zedelgem.

FLINK • Germany 1920–1922

Built by a company which is now part of BMW at Munich, the Flink was a 148cc two-stroke machine with a Kurier deflector-type proprietary engine. Not a very successful design.

980cc Flying Merkel (sv twin) 1913

FLM • England 1951–1953

Designed by former P&M Panther designer Frank Leach, the little lightweight had 123cc Villiers and JAP two-stroke engines and also 198cc Villiers power units.

FLOTTWEG • Germany 1921–1937

The first products were good 119cc bicycle attachment engines over the front wheel. They were followed by 183cc and 246cc ohv machines with its own engines. JAP-built 198cc and 346cc ohv engines powered Flottweg machines from 1928 to 1931. After an interruption, new models again with its own 198cc ohv engines came into being but did not sell well. The factory - not far from BMW at Munich - was eventually sold to that maker.

FLUX • Germany 1923–1924

Assembled motorcycles in limited numbers with 198cc two-stroke engines.

FLY • England c1901

Pioneer machines using engines made by Carlton, London.

FLYING MERKEL • America 1909–1915

The yellow Merkels were machines of contemporary and advanced design. The Middletown factory built 545cc

490cc Flying Merkel (sv single) 1917

119cc Flottweg (two-stroke) 1922

singles and 980cc ioe V-twins and in 1913 built models which had not only two-speed gearboxes, but spring frames and some even had electric starters.

FN • Belgium 1901–1957

Pioneer in the motorcycle field and for many years the leading make in Belgium. Became famous for using shaft drive from 1903 to 1923, for great successes in races and long distance events and after 1945 in motocross. Great designers, including Paul Kelecom, Van Hout, Dougal Marchant, George-William Patchett and others have been connected with this big factory of arms, motorcycles and cars. There were also famous racing men such as Kicken, Flintermann, Lovinfosse, Lempereur, Sbaiz, De Grady, Milhoux, Charlier, Demuiter, Noir, Van Gent, Renier, S. 'Ginger' Wood, Handley Mellors, Abarth and others, who - like Mingels, Leloup and R. Beaten in motocross - won many races. The first FN machines had 225cc and 286cc single-cylinder and 496cc and 748cc four-cylinder in-line engines. All models from 1924 onwards had chain-drive to the rear-wheel, as shaft drive production was then too expensive. Afterwards mainly

348cc and 498cc sv and ohv models were built. All had unit-design engines. There were also 596cc ohv versions, and in 1937 a BMW-like 992cc four-cylinder machine with a tranverse-mounted, air-cooled sv engine was made for the army. Already in 1931 there was a 198cc Villiers engined two-stroke in the FN range and when Marchant joined the Belgian factory in 1930, he created very fast 348cc and 498cc racing ohc singles. Van Hout developed these during the following years and designed in 1937 a super-charged 498cc vertical twin-cylinder ohc racing machine, which was ridden in 1938 by 'Ginger' Wood. The war prevented more successes by this fast machine. After the war, FN built a range of sv and ohv unit-design models of 249cc, 344cc, 444cc and 498cc and also two-strokes from 49cc to 248cc, mainly with its own Ilo engines. With mainly Belgian riders, it competed successfully with 498cc machines in motocross events, but withdrew in the mid-1950s. FN car production stopped before WW2.

283cc FN (sv shaft-drive) 1921

748cc FN (sv four-cylinder shaft-drive) 1921

493cc FN (sv four-cylinder shaft-drive) 1908

498cc FN Super-Sport (ohv) 1936

446cc FN (ohv) 1954

FRANCIS-BARNETT • England 1919–1964

The first models had 293cc and 346cc sv JAP engines. From 1924 onwards, the Coventry-based factory concentrated on bolted together triangular frames, in which Villiers engines from 147cc to 344cc and JAP sv engines of 174cc and 346cc were fitted. Among them also - from 1927 onwards - the vertical twin two-stroke of 344cc, made by Villiers. During the 1930s it built Villiers-engined machines from 148cc to 248cc with the exception of the Stag, which had a Blackburne-built 248cc ohv engine with entirely enclosed valve mechanism and crossed pushrods. Once more Villiers-engined two-strokes formed the backbone of the Francis-Barnett programme after the war; they were 98cc to 248cc. In the late 1950s AMC (Associated Motor Cycles Ltd.) took over the Coventry factory and built Piatti-designed 248cc two-stroke engines. It was not a successful venture and soon it reverted to Villiers power units. It also moved FB production to the James Works at Birmingham, another factory which belonged to AMC Ltd. Afterwards both makes ceased to exist.

346cc Francis-Barnett (sv JAP) 1927

246cc Francis-Barnett Cruiser (two-stroke Villiers) 1936

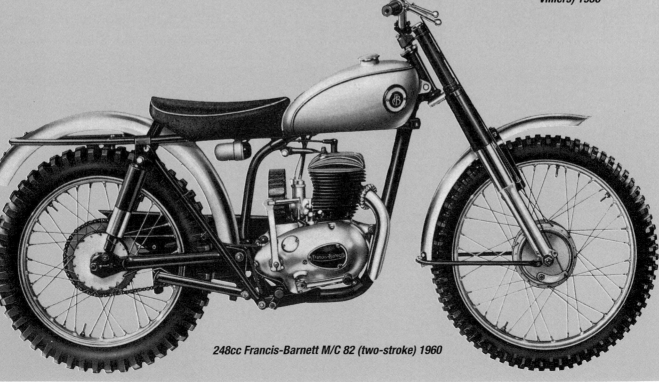

248cc Francis-Barnett M/C 82 (two-stroke) 1960

349cc Force (two-stroke) 1925

123cc Frera (two-stroke) 1958

346cc Freyler (ohc sleeve-valve) 1929

173cc FVL (ohv Moser) 1929

198cc Frischauf (two-stroke Villiers) 1932

FM • Italy 1925–1927

Very unorthodox frame, designed by the Molteni brothers. (Fratelli Molteni means Molteni Brothers in Italian.) The frame was made from cast aluminum alloy and allowed a low saddle position; it was also nice looking. Engines fitted were the 346cc MAG single and afterwards the 346cc ohv Bradshaw with oil cooling. In 1950, the brothers debuted a 125cc scooter, also extensively using cast aluminum, but it was only built for 3 years.

FMT • Italy 1922–1930

Small 124cc two-strokes built in limited numbers by Fratelli Mattarollo of Torino.

FN • Belgium 1901–1957

See panel

FOCESI • Italy 1952–1956

Well-designed 49cc two-stroke machines with the flat unit-design engine mounted directly on the swinging arm. The machines became known under the Gloria trade mark.

FOCHJ • Italy 1954–1957

Assembler which used German NSU two- and four-stroke engines from 49cc to 246cc. They included the famous Max single-cam engine.

FOLLIS • France 1903–1960

Fitted in pre-1939 days different proprietary engines made by JAP, Python and Blackburne; after 1945 machines from 124cc to 248cc with Ydral two-stroke and AMC ohv engines. The factory was at Lyon.

FONGRI • Italy 1919–1925

Designed by Eugenio Grignani, Fongri - the name came from Fontana and Fratelli Grignani - concentrated on machines with sv opposing twins having capacities of 579cc, 575cc and 499cc.

FORCE • Austria 1925–1926

Small producer of 346cc single-cylinder, two-stroke machines with its own three-port, deflector-type engines.

FORELLE • Germany 1955–1958

Bicycle factory, which built 49cc mopeds with Sachs and Ilo engines.

FORSTER • Switzerland 1921–1932

Producer of two-stroke machines with 140cc, 198cc and 246cc. Designer was Karl Kirschbaum.

FORTONIA • Germany 1924–1925

Motorcycles with 2.5hp and 3.8hp single-cylinder engines.

FORTUNA • Germany 1921–1928

Two-strokes with 247cc and 297cc three-port engines and big outside flywheels.

FORWARD • England 1909–1915

Produced by a leading bicycle, accessory and parts manufacturer, the Forward was really a comparatively backward motorcycle design with a strengthened bicycle frame and its own V-twin engines of 339cc and 479cc.

FOWLER & BINGHAM • England 1913–1922

The Birmingham-built lightweight was powered by F & B's own 269cc two-stroke single-cylinder engine. Also supplied proprietary engines and built the F. B. Wizard motorcycle.

FP • Hungary 1924–1925

Single-cylinder machines with own 346cc sv engines.

FRANCE • France 1931–1935

Two-stroke machines with own engines from 98cc to 245cc. The frames were of simple design.

FRANCIS-BARNETT • England 1919–1964

See panel

FRANCHI • Italy 1950–late 1950s

Assembler who fitted Sachs two-stroke engines of 98cc, 123cc, 147cc and 174cc and also called his machines Franchi-Sachs.

FRANKONIA • Germany 1923–1925

Another assembled machine. Used 145cc DKW engines with horizontal cylinders.

FRANZANI • Germany 1923–1932

Small factory. First used its own 283cc two-stroke engines, afterwards 198cc to 490cc JAP engines and the German 497cc Küchen ohc proprietary power unit.

FRAYS • England pre-WW1

One of three marques made at 66 Bishops Street, Birmingham. The other two were Kings Own and Priest.

FRECO • Germany 1923–1925

Fitted 145cc and 173cc DKW two-strokes, 197cc Runge sv engines and for racing purposes 173cc and 247cc ohv Blackburne engines. Production was on a limited scale.

496cc Fusi (ohv) 1939

FREITAL • Germany 1925–1926

For commercial reasons, the DKW factory at Zschopau used this name for a short period on 173cc machines.

FREJUS • Italy 1960–1968

Turin-built machines, including mofas, mopeds etc, from 48cc to 198cc.

FRERA • Italy 1906–1956

For many years a leading make. Built 320cc and 570cc singles and 795cc V-twins, afterwards also a big 1140cc sv V-twin. During the 1920s, Frera machines had a very Sunbeam-like black and gold appearance and were designed on English lines. A 269cc two-stroke was made for a short period, but 346cc and 496cc sv and ohv singles formed the main range in the period between the wars. Leading riders: Felice Macchi, Virginio Fieschi, Mario Acerboni, Edoardo Self, Mario Ventura, F. J. Meyer. Reorganization after 1945 resulted in 73cc and 124cc two-strokes and a 147cc ohv machine. The founder, Corrardo Frera, died before WW2.

FREYLER • Austria 1928–1929

This was a 'valveless' ohc machine of 348cc capacity. It used a rotary valve - driven by a vertical shaft - in the cylinder head. The interesting design by Adalbert Freyler was not fully developed when the Vienna-based factory closed.

FREYER & MILLER • America c1902

Had the engine behind the saddle and the petrol tank was mounted above the rear wheel. The Freyer & Miller was one of the first machines using a rotation magneto.

FRIMA • Germany 1923-1924

Made by Friedrich Marquardt of Friedburg, Frima used its own 2·5hp two-stroke engine.

FRIMO • Germany 1923–1925

Made by the Vis AG., producer of Vis-Simplex and Vis-Duplex machines, the Frimo was a conventional 246cc two-stroke machine with a three port engine.

FRISCHAUF • Germany 1928–1933

Assembled 198cc sv singles with JAP and Blackburne engines and 497cc ohc machines with the Küchen proprietary engine.

FRISONI • Italy 1951–1957

Produced 123cc Villiers-engined two-strokes and 160cc scooters in limited numbers.

FUBO • Germany 1923–1925

Two-strokes of 170cc and 269cc with its own engines, but also supplied 247cc and 347cc models with sv and ohv Blackburne engines.

FUCHS • Italy 1953–1957

Produced bicycle engines and 124cc to 159cc motorcycles with two-stroke and ohv engines.

FUJI • Japan early 1950s–early 1960s

Producer of the Gasuden scooter and of two-stroke machines from 49cc to 249cc. This factory was not the same as Fuji Heavy Industries Ltd.

FUJI HEAVY INDUSTRIES • Japan 1946–1960

Manufacturer of the well-respected Rabbit range of scooters, produced in various capacities from 90cc up to 270cc.

FULGOR • Italy 1922–1926

Lightweight two-strokes of 143cc, made by a small factory at Milan.

FURCH • Germany 1924–1925

Yet another small Berlin-built motorcycle which had an own-make 2.5hp sv motor. The production was on a limited scale.

FUSI • Italy 1932–1957

For many years Italian FN importer, Fusi bought the CF motorcycle factory in 1937 and produced first a 248cc ohc machine. It fitted 174cc, 246cc and 490cc JAP engines into its own frames, which also had many FN parts; according to some sources, FN even built the frames for Fusi machines. The JAP engines were made in Italy under licence. After 1945, Fusi built an improved 248cc machine with the old but developed CF ohc engine.

FVL • Italy 1926–1935

Designed by former racing motorcyclist Francesco Vincenzo Lanfranchi, the first FVL lightweight machines had 124cc and 174cc ohv Moser engines. Bonamore and Forlani, designers of the now defunct Fert factory, joined the Lanfranchi works in 1929 and created beautiful ohv machines with 174cc and in 1932 a 248cc. Another version had a 174cc ohc power unit.

GA • Italy 1925–1927

Assembler of sporting V-twin machines, Franco Azzara fitted 678cc ohv engines made by Blackburne in England.

GAB AUTO SCOOTER • England 1920–1921

Low powered scooter with seat rather than saddle, built in East Ham, London.

GABBIANO • Italy 1954–1956

One model, a 125cc two-stroke single.

GABY • England 1914–1915

Well-made 269cc machines with Metro three-port, deflector-type engines.

GADABOUT • England 1946–1951

Made by the Swallow sidecar factory, the Villiers-engined Gadabout was a 123cc scooter, which for various reasons could not beat the leading foreign scooters in England.

GAGGENAU • Germany 1925–1927

Sturdy two-stroke singles with 346cc and 396cc unit-design engines of own manufacture.

GAIA • Italy 1922–1932

The Turin-based factory always built machines of sound design. The first products were bicycles fitted with Rubinelli engines; the next were motorcycles with the then popular Swiss 123cc and 173cc ohv Moser engines. After 1927, most models had Ladetto & Blatto 173cc ohv units.

GALBAI • 1921–1925

Producer of 276cc, 301cc and 348cc two-stroke machines with own engines. Other models had 492cc V-twin MAG and oil-cooled 346cc single-cylinder Bradshaw ohv engines.

GALBUSERA • Italy 1934–1955

Sensationally exhibited an in-line mounted supercharged 498cc two-stroke V-eight prototype at the 1938 Milan show. There was also a V-four version of 248cc, built on identical lines. Plinio Galbusera's bread-and-butter models had 173cc, 246cc, 348cc and 498cc Rudge-built (Python) four-valve ohv engines, the smallest version supplied by Miller, which had exclusive rights to this engine. Technical head of Galbusera was Egyptian-born Adolf Marama, who rode Rudge-engined machines in all kinds of races. He was also responsible for the design of the speedway frames made by this Brescia factory, which after 1945 concentrated on lightweight machines with Sachs engines

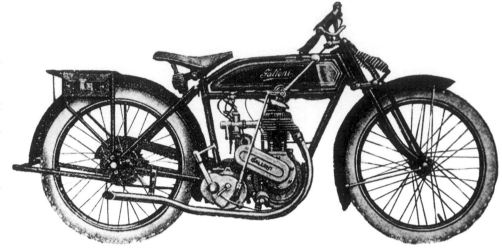

346cc Galloni Sport (sv) 1924

from 98cc to 173cc. The sensational two-strokes of the immediate pre-war period never went into production.

GALLONI • Italy 1920–1931

Was a leading make and also successful in many races with Alfredo Panella, Nino Bianchi and Augusto Rava. The early models had 494cc and 746cc V-twin sv engines; later ones 249cc, 349cc and 499cc sv and ohv single-cylinder engines of its own design and manufacture. From 1927 the red Galloni was overshadowed by the Bianchi, Frera and Moto Guzzi. The last Galloni was a 173cc ohv machine with a Blackburne engine.

GAMAGE • England c1905–1924

The motorcycles sold by the Gamage stores were made mainly in England by factories which included Wolfruna, Omega, Radco and others. The models included 269cc two-strokes and 293cc, 347cc and 497cc single-cylinder sv machines.

GANAREW • Wales c1903

Lightweight two-speeder built by the Ganarew Cycle Co. Ltd., Monmouth, and powered by French Clement engines.

GANNA • Italy 1923–late 1960s

Varese-built, the Ganna was a good machine with many different engines fitted during the years. Among the first were 347cc sv and ohv Blackburnes, afterwards 173cc, 248cc, 348cc and 498cc JAP engines, partly built under licence in Italy. There was in 1936 an interesting 499cc four-valve ohc model with a Ganna-designed and built engine. After the war and a reorganization of the company, most Gannas had two-stroke engines made by Puch, Sachs and Minarelli. They were from 48cc to 248cc. In addition, a 174cc ohv model was in the range too. Although

496cc Galbusera (two-stroke V-eight prototype) 1938

290cc Gamage (sv) 1903

Ganna was never a leading make in races, all models had a very sporting appearance and a superb finish.

GAOMO • Italy 1951–1954

Produced limited numbers of lightweight scooters of 62.5cc and 75cc.

GAR • Germany 1924–1926

The Rempp-designed 499cc ohv machines had Gar's own single-cylinder engines and were built in limited numbers only.

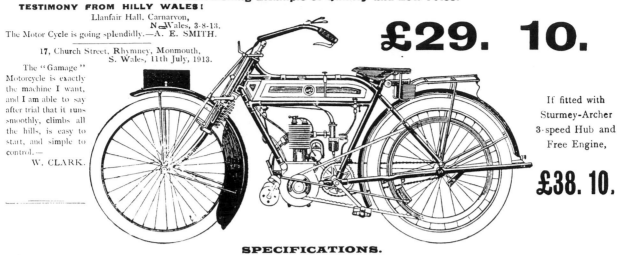

Page from Gamage's 1913 catalog

GARABELLO • Italy 1906–1929

Francesco Garabello was one of the pioneers of the Italian motorcycle industry. He produced 240cc and 480cc singles and from 1922 onward a big, water-cooled 984cc four-cylinder in-line model with shaft drive. Although a clever technician, he never achieved financial success. When Luigi Comini took over the Alba factory, he transferred it to Turin. Garabello's last (and unorthodox) design was a 173cc single with water-cooling and a rotary valve in the head. The drive to this valve as well as the rear wheel was by shaft. The radiator was mounted directly in front of the petrol tank, the carburettor in front of the vertically mounted cylinder. The design was unsuccessful.

GARANZINI • Italy 1921–1931

Made by a racing motorcyclist Oreste Garanzini - who imported the English Verus machines which were renamed Veros in Italy - the design was on typical English lines. Also from England came the 346cc sv JAP engines and on later models 147cc to 248cc Villiers and 248cc to 490cc sv and ohv power units made by JAP and Blackburne. Garanzini rode his machines in many races during the mid-1920s.

GARELLI • Italy 1918–

Alberto Garelli developed his 'split single' two-stroke between 1912 and 1918 and offered a 350cc version for sale in 1919. Successful in racing and record breaking, it sold freely until 1935, when the factory switched to aero engines. Post-war, production resumed with the Mosquito cycle attachment, made between 1947 and

1956. Between 1958 and 1961, Garelli merged with Agrati and thereafter specialised in mopeds and 50cc and 80cc lightweights. In the 1980s Garelli began building 125cc road bikes and contested the 125cc world championship with impressive success. The factory won six straight world titles from 1982 to 1987, running its super-fast, disc-valve, water-cooled two-stroke twins. Spanish legend Angel Nieto won a hat trick from 1982 to 1984, Italian Fausto Gresini took the title in 1985 and 1987, and compatriot Luca Cadalora secured the 1986 crown. Garelli lost its technical edge when the world championship switched to single-cylinder regulations in 1988 and withdrew from racing at the end of 1989.

The company continues to produce a range of lightweight motorcycles and scooters.

GARIN • France 1950–1953

Small producer of 49cc mopeds and 98cc two-stroke motorcycles.

GARLASCHELLI • Italy 1922–1927

Produced 65cc and 123cc two-strokes and from 1925 onwards also 173cc machines with two-stroke ohv engines.

GAS GAS • Spain 1982–

Gas Gas has produced the world's top-selling trials bike since 1995 when the Girona factory output 4000 machines. Formed by former competition riders Josep Pibernat and Narcis Casas, Gas Gas still leads the opposition as far as model choice is concerned with six different trials machines ranging from 50cc to 370cc.

996cc Garabello (sv water-cooled four-cylinder) 1926

346cc Garelli (two-stroke double-piston single racer) 1924

346cc Garanzini (sv JAP) 1926

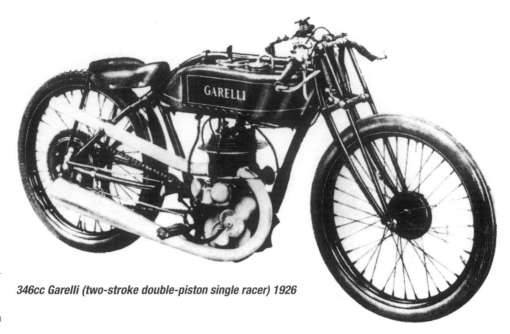

346cc Garelli (two-stroke double-piston single racer) 1926

Gas Gas won three World Trials Championship crowns with Jordi Tarres in 1993, 1994 and 1995 and also two World Enduro Championship titles with Paul Edmondson.

Gas Gas went into production with its first 125cc and 250cc motocross machines in 1997, but these have been less successful than the trials bikes. It is currently working on developing a four-stroke engine for motocross and enduro.

GATTI • Italy 1904–1906

Pioneer who fitted 1.75hp De Dion engines into strengthened bicycle frames.

GAZDA • Austria 1926–1927

Created by the inventor of the Gazda leaf-spring handlebars Anton Gazda, the 246cc two-stroke machines - built in small numbers only - were of unorthodox design. They had a pumping cylinder and three ports.

GAZELLE • The Netherlands 1903

Famous bicycle factory which fitted Sarolea engines into the first motorcycles made at the Dieren works. Resumed production of motorised two-wheelers in 1932 with Ilo-engined 60cc and 75cc machines. Motorcycles with Ilo and Villiers engines followed in the mid-1930s. They had 98cc, 123cc and 148cc. The range was similar after the war, until the Dutch factory concentrated on various models with 49cc engines, many of which had Minarelli engines.

GAZZI • Italy 1929–1932

A small factory which produced well-made 173cc ohv machines of modern design.

346cc Garelli (two-stroke double-piston single) 1935

GB • England 1905–1907

Motorcycles with different Minerva engines from 3.5hp to 5hp and a very long wheelbase.

GCS • Australia 1914–1917

Designed and built by George Charles Stilwell at Melbourne, GCS motorcycles were mainly V-twins with various sv engines made by JAP in England. Among them 490cc and 746cc models.

GD • Italy 1923–1938

Very fast 122cc two-strokes with a great racing history, ridden by such famous riders as Alfonso Drusiani, Frederico Castellani, Guglielmo Sandri, and Amilcare Rosetti. The GD stood for Ghirardi and Dall'-Oglio. From 1928, as well as these horizontal singles the factory built 248cc vertical twin two-strokes, 173cc ohc singles and 98cc two-stroke machines.

249cc Gas Gas MC Cross (two-stroke) 1998

148cc Geier (two-stroke Sachs) 1954

246cc Gazda (two-stroke prototype) 1926

148cc Geha (two-stroke) 1922

GECO-HERSTAL • France 1924–1928

Gérkinet's factory was closely connected with the Belgian Gillet works at Herstal, and also built part of the Gillet model range. In addition, it had its own 173cc to 346cc sv models.

GEELEY • China 1980–

Part of the China-Geeley Group of companies, state-owned Geeley is based in Taizhou in Zhejiang Province, and is one of the world's larger manufacturers, employing around 5000 staff. Currently produces a selection of lightweights it calls its LC models, in engine sizes 50cc, 100cc, 125cc and 150cc, both two- and four-strokes. The vast majority of machines are for the home market.

GEER • America 1905–1909

Early producer of single and V-twin machines. Fitted its engines into strengthened bicycle frames.

GEHA • Germany 1920–1924

Lightweight machines with Geha's own 1.5hp two-stroke engines.

GEIER • Germany 1934–early 1960s

Built mofas and motorcycles with 73cc, 98cc and after 1945 also 123cc, 147cc and 173cc Ilo and Sachs two-stroke engines.

GEKA • Germany 1924–1925

Fitted 173cc DKW engines into lightweights. Limited production.

GE-MA-HI • Germany 1924–1927

Built a wide range of machines with tubular and also with wide-tube petrol tank frames. The last ones were partly made from welded steel, not unlike the big Mars. Among the engines fitted were the 131cc Esbe, 149cc Bekamo, 149cc Grade and also the 147cc and 173cc DKW.

GEMINI • Taiwan 1970–

In the 1970s and 1980s produced older Suzuki-licenced designs, mostly trail bikes as well as a 49cc model with 8 inch wheels and more orthodox 78cc, 123cc and 173cc models, exporting many to the USA. Now concentrates more on scooters and lightweights.

GEMS • Italy 1921–1923

Light machines with 269cc two-stroke engines.

GENIAL-LUCIFER • France 1928–1956

Assembler of two-stroke machines with 98cc to 246cc Aubier Dunne, Train and Sabb engines.

GENTIL • France 1903–1904

With the horizontal single-cylinder engine in front of the pedalling gear, the Gentil had the look of a modern moped. Produced also V-twin machines and 98cc mopeds.

GEORGE ELIOT • England 1903–1904

A range of 2hp, 2·5hp and 3·5hp machines built by John North Birch of Nuneaton which were also sold as Birch motorcycles. Birch, designer of the Motor Wheel made and sold as Singer, was acquainted with the writer Mary Ann Evans who published under the pen name George Eliot, hence the name of his machines.

GEORGES RICHARD • France c1899

Assembled motorcycles with Minerva, Buchet, Zedel, Peugeot and other engines and later became part of the Unic car factory.

GEPPERT • Germany 1925–1926

Small factory which assembled two-stroke machines with 147cc Grade and DKW engines.

GERALD • France 1927–1932

Designed by Charles Gerald, these machines had 98cc and 173cc Aubier-Dunne two-stroke engines. Other models were powered by 248cc ohv JAP and 348cc and 498cc ohc Chaise power units.

GERARD • England 1913–1915

Of simple design, the 269cc Gerard had a Villiers engine and was built at Birmingham.

GERBI • Italy 1952–1953

Sachs-engined 98cc, 123cc and 173cc machines.

GERMAAN • The Netherlands 1935–1966

Another Dutch bicycle factory, which assembled good lightweight machines with 98cc Sachs and Ilo, as well as 123cc Ilo and 147cc Villiers engines. After the war, Germaan also used Hungarian 123cc Czepel engines and Ilo engines which included the 244cc vertical twin two-stroke. Germaan is now part of the Batavus group.

GERMANIA • Germany 1901–1908

These were actually Czechoslovakian Laurin & Klement motorcycles, built by the once famous Seidel & Naumann typewriter factory at Dresden under licence. The range

GERMANIA-MOTORRAD
mit 2 Cylindern, 3½ HP (System Laurin & Klement)

615cc Germania (sv V-twin) 1904

of models included 3.5hp and 4.5hp V-twins. Laurin & Klement was the forerunner of the present Skoda car factory.

GEROSA • Italy 1953–1985

Brescia-based factory which produced a variety of 49cc models and also 123cc two-strokes of sound design. Initially there were also 124cc and 174cc ohv machines in the range.

GERVO • Germany 1924–1925

Limited production of 198cc sv and 173cc DKW-engined two-stroke machines.

GH • Czechoslovakia 1924–1925

Gustav Heinz designed 172cc machines with Villiers power units. Heinz also produced Sirocco and Velamos motorcycles. Now nationalised, Velamos is one of the leading bicycle factories in the country.

GIACOMASSO • Italy 1926–1935

Superbly designed machines with 174cc Moser ohv engines, but from 1927 onward Felice Giacomasso designed his own power units with ohv and even ohc. New 489cc and 595cc ohv vertical twins appeared in 1933.

GIANCA • Italy 1946–1949

Producer of the 98cc Nibbio scooter before production was moved to San Cristoforo.

GIGANT • Austria 1936–1938

Designed by the former Delta-Gnom technician Johann Teichert, the light-green Gigant machines had 498cc and 598cc ohv and 746cc V-twin sv engines. All were of JAP manufacture. Also produced successful racing machines with 498cc ohv JAP and Husqvarna single-cylinder engines, which were ridden by the Austrian champion Martin Schneeweiss, Josef Lukes and others.

490cc Gigant (ohv JAP) 1936

GIGUET • France 1903

Equipped with strong frames, Giguet motorcycles had De Dion and Minerva engines.

GILERA • Italy 1909–

See panel

GILLET-HERSTAL • Belgium 1919–early 1960s

Together with FN and Sarolea, among the leading Belgian makes. Became famous for the rotary-valve 346cc two-stroke, which Robert Sexé rode around the world in the mid-1920s. Other models included 348cc and 498cc unit-design sv and ohv machines and a 996cc V-twin with the ioe engine, made by MAG in Switzerland. The factory also showed great interest in racing and had such riders as Kicken, Debay, Bentley, Milhoux, Jackl, Deimel, Uvira and others. Chief designer Van Oirbeck created in 1929 works machines with single-cylinder ohc engines and René Milhoux broke many records with them. Two-strokes from 98cc to 248cc were built after the war and there were also vertical-twins up to 720cc.

GIMA • France 1947–1956

The machines were beautiful lightweights with Ydral, AMC and other 123cc to 248cc engines.

GIMSON • Spain 1956–1964

Bicycle factory which built 49cc and 65cc mopeds.

GILERA • Italy 1909–

Giuseppe Gilera started his business in 1909 in Milan, but full-scale production only began when he moved to Arcore in 1920. Early models were sturdy sidevalves of 350cc, 500cc and 600cc. These sold well and competed in the ISDT, winning for Italy in 1930 and 1931. They also did well in races such as the Milan-Taranto. In 1935 Gilera bought the rights to the water-cooled, super-charged Rondine, which, under the direction of Gilera and Piero Taruffi, became the famous Gilera 'four'. With all-enclosing streamlining, Taruffi broke the world speed record at 170.15mph. The Gilera, ridden by Dorino Serafini won the 1939 European championship.

Post war, road bike manufacture began with the 500cc ohv Saturno, which was also developed as a 'production' racer to considerable effect. In 1947, Piero Remor (designer of the Rondine) designed a normally aspirated 500cc four for Gilera, which was to be extensively developed by Francesco Passoni. This machine took the 500cc world title in 1950 and 1952, ridden by Umberto Masetti and in 1953, 1954 and 1955 by Geoff Duke.

496cc Gilera (sv) 1921

250cc Gilera Nettuno (ohv) 1946

498cc Gilera (dohc aircooled four-cylinder racer) 1952

498cc Gilera (dohc four-cylinder racer) 1939

496cc Gilera Saturno (ohv single) 1939

498cc Gilera (dohc air-cooled four-cylinder racer) 1953

49cc Gilera trials (two-stroke) 1982

558cc Gilera RC600 (ohc) 1991

558cc Gilera Saturno (ohc) 1991

Duke also won the Senior TT in 1955, while Bob McIntyre did the 'double' - Junior and Senior TTs plus the first-ever 100mph lap in the Isle of Man in 1957. After this, Gilera withdrew from racing, only to be tempted back later in 1963, against its better judgement. Meanwhile, for the road, there were mainly rather depressingly uninspired ohv lightweights of 125cc, 175cc and a 300cc twin. The beautiful Saturno went out of production in 1959. Racing had all but bankrupted Gilera, while founder Giusepe Gilera had been deeply affected by the death of his energetic son Ferruccio in 1955 from a heart attack. In 1969, aged 80, Gilera sold his faltering company to Piaggio, maker of the Vespa scooter. Piaggio brought new energy to the production of lightweights from 50cc to 200cc, both two-strokes and four-strokes. Involvement in trials and motocross followed with no overwhelming success. However, the development work involved paid off in very sporting 125cc models for the road in the 1980s, which enjoyed considerable domestic sales. A half-hearted return to bigger bike manufacture was made in 1991 with the re-introduction of the Saturno name on a 500cc single-cylinder sports bike, aimed primarily at Japan, although a few filtered through onto some European markets. It was not a great sales success, and neither was the Nordwest of 1992, with a 558cc engine developed from the Saturno's, despite positive press reaction to its sharp handling and attractive supermoto styling.

At the same time, Gilera launched the CX125, a sporting single cylinder two-stroke with single sided rear swingarm and, radically, a single leg at the front, similar to an aircraft's undercarriage design. Again, sales were not good, and Piaggio bosses decided in light of a worldwide decline in motorcycle sales that there was no future in the production of bigger machines, and closed Gilera's Arcore factory in 1993. This was a shame for motorcycle sport as well as the road bikes and, of course, the factory workers themselves, as in 1992 Gilera had returned to world championship competition, with an impressive entry into 250 GPs. The reed-valve V-twin was never quite competitive over the next two seasons and its demise from racing only added to the management's determination to shut the factory down.

The name continues to be used on Piaggio scooters, such as the current 50cc, 125cc and 180cc Runner, as well as a 125cc custom machine called the Eaglet, but it is really no more than a badge.

There have been some hints from Piaggio bosses, however, that Gilera motorcycles might again be manufactured (an idea prompted by a resurgence of interest in larger motorcycles and the revival of famous Italian names such as MV Agusta and Benelli), possibly by the year 2001, although nothing definite has been confirmed. If so, it is possible they will be powered by Honda engines, as Piaggio has close links with the Japanese factory and some Honda-powered Gileras were being proposed in the late 1980s.

558cc Gilera Nordwest (ohc) 1991

124cc Gilera Cougar (ohc) 1998

180cc Gilera Runner SP (two-stroke) 1999

346cc Gillet-Herstal Tour du Monde (two-stroke) 1929

GIRARDENGO • Italy 1951–1954

Another Italian assembler who produced 123cc, 147cc and 173cc two-stroke engines.

GITAN • Italy 1951–1985

Old established producer of 49cc two-strokes, including motocross versions. In the early years of the company, motorcycles with up to 198cc two and four-stroke Minarelli engines were also built.

GITANE • France 1953–early 1960s

Well-known bicycle manufacturer, whose motorcycles had 49cc to 173cc and engines made by Ydral, VAP and Mistral.

GIULIETTA • Italy 1957–1980

Under this name and also that of Peripoli and, in England, AJW, Giulietta sold a wide range of mopeds and 50cc motorcycles using Sachs, Morini and Minarelli two-stroke engines. Popular and stylish in their day, but of no particular merit.

GIVAUDAN • England 1908–1914

An 'assembler' company that used various engines, including Precision and Blumfeld. A few used the Villiers four-stroke.

GKD • Italy 1978–

Younger manufacturer which concentrates on 99cc, 123cc and 242cc trials and motocross two-stroke singles.

GL • France 1919–1921

Mainly built from English components, this French design by Georges Lévy, had a 990cc V-twin JAP sv engine, Sturmey-Archer gearbox and Binks carburettor.

GLENDALE • England 1920–1921

Simple assembled machines with 269cc Villiers and 346cc Blackburne engines.

GLOBE • America 1948–1952

Aluminum chassis scooters powered by 2hp Continental Red Seal engines.

GLOBE • England 1901–1911

Produced different models with Minerva, MMC and Sarolea engines.

GLORIA • England 1924–1925

With frames built by Campion in Nottingham, the Gloria also had strong ties with France. In both countries it was sold with the 173cc Train two-stroke engine.

GLORIA • England 1931–1933

Made by Triumph at Coventry, this Gloria had a 98cc Villiers two-stroke engine.

GLORIA • Italy 1948–1955

Designed by Alfredo Focesi, the little Gloria had the 48cc two-stroke engine mounted directly on the rear swinging arm.

GLORIAL • France c1920s

George Dailliet of Douai made 2hp cycle attachments, 2½hp two-stroke lightweights with pumped oil lubrication and a 4½hp model.

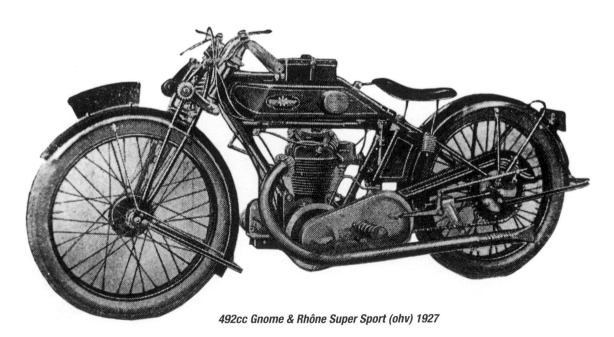

492cc Gnome & Rhône Super Sport (ohv) 1927

GNOME·RHONE

Type "JUNIOR"
250 cmc. — 3 CV
Soupapes latérales

Type "MAJOR"
350 cmc. — 4 CV
Soupapes latérales
4 vitesses

TYPE
"SUPER-MAJOR"
350 cmc. — 4 CV
Soupapes en tête
4 vitesses

Type D5
500 cmc . 1 cyl". - 5CV
Soupapes latérales
4 vitesses
Transmission par cardan

Type CV2
500 cmc . 2 cyl". - 5CV
4 vitesses
Transmission par cardan

Type X
750 cmc . 2 cyl". - 7CV
Soup. en tête - 4 vitesses
Transmission par cardan

UNE SEULE TECHNIQUE EN TOUTES CYLINDRÉES

Gnome & Rhône sales catalog

498cc Godden speedway racer (ohc) 1982

GNÄDIG • Germany 1925–1926

When KG at Suhl was sold to Allright, Franz Gnädig - one of the designers - left for Berlin and built his own 348cc ohv machines. Afterwards he took the design to Kühne at Dresden and it became the first engine built by this proprietary engine factory.

GNOM • Germany 1921–1923

Bicycle attachment engine of 63cc, built by the Columbus engine factory, which was eventually taken over by Horex of Bad Homburg.

GNOME & RHÔNE • France 1919–1959

Famous for its aircraft engines in WW1, Gnome & Rhône first built the English Bradshaw-designed 398cc machine, afterwards also a 498cc ABC with the flat-twin ohv engine transverse-mounted, under licence. Captain Bartlett headed the manufacture at the big Paris factory. Together with Naas he also won many races. From 1923 onwards, single-cylinder machines of own designs came into being. They consisted of 306cc sv, 344cc ohv and 498cc sv and ohv versions and again Naas, together with Georges Bernard, gained many successes. During the late 1920s, BMW-like sv and ohv flat twins, transverse-mounted in pressed steel frames, came into production. They were of 495cc and 745cc capacity. After 1945, Gnome & Rhône concentrated on small two-stroke machines, of which most were of 124cc and 174cc.

124cc Gori racer (two-stroke Sachs) 1974

GODDEN • England 1978–

Concentrates on the manufacture of grass-track racing machines with own ohv and sohc engines, including a 498cc sohc four-valve model with 64bhp.

GOEBEL • Germany 1951–1972

A producer of mofas and mopeds, Goebel used 49cc Sachs engines for his product.

GLORIA-REKORD • Germany 1924–1925

One of the many German companies which entered the market in the mid 1920s. Gloria-Rekord created its own 3hp single-cylinder two-stroke, but the engine proved unsuccessful

GN • Italy 1920–1925

Assembled mainly from English components, Giuseppe Navone's motorcycles had 346cc two-stroke single-cylinder engines. Navone was also closely connected with the Italian branch of the French Train engine works.

490cc Goetz (ohv JAP) 1933

GOETZ • Germany 1925–1935

Built in 10 years a total of 79 machines, most individually at the request of customers. They had 246cc Villiers, 346cc, 498cc and 676cc JAP, 498cc Küchen and even 796cc ohc vertical twin Columbus engines.

GOLEM • Germany 1921–1923

Called Sesselrad (chair-wheel), the DKW-built Golem was a scooter-like vehicle with a 122cc two-stroke engine which had a horizontal cylinder. The improved successor was the 144cc Lomos. When DKW dropped the production, Eichler at Berlin bought the production equipment and all rights to both designs.

GOGGO • Germany 1951–1956

Scooters built by Hans Glas Manufacturing, based in Dingolfing in Bavaria, with engines of 120cc, 150cc and 200cc. The Ilo-engined 200 produced 11hp and had a top speed of 65mph. A total of 46,500 scooters was built in this period, after which the factory turned to car production, including the 250cc Goggomobil. It was eventually taken over by BMW.

GOLD-RAD • Germany 1952–1980

Producer of mofas, mopeds etc. with 49cc Sachs and Ilo engines; now mainly importer of Italian Motograziela products, which also have 49cc power units.

GOLO • Austria 1923–1925

Limited manufacture of machines with 346cc and 490cc JAP and 347cc Bradshaw engines.

4¹/₂hp Göricke (sv V-twin) 1905

4¹/₂hp Göricke (sv V-twin Forecar) 1905

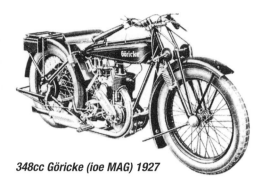

348cc Göricke (ioe MAG) 1927

49cc Göricke (two-stroke Sachs) 1956

132cc Grade (two-stroke) 1924

343cc Grigg (two-stroke Villiers) 1923

346cc Grindlay-Peerless (sleeve-valve Barr & Stroud) 1924

GONTHIER • Belgium 1907–1910

Early 748cc design with an air-cooled four-cylinder in-line engine of own manufacture, double-loop frame and chain drive.

GORI • Italy 1969–early 1980s

Gori produced sporting off-road and road-racing machines with highly-tuned Sachs 125cc engines. These enjoyed considerable success in Italy in the 1970s, with the result that the company was taken over by its ambitious rival, SWM, in 1979. SWM renamed the Gori 'Go-Motor' and continued production, but this ended shortly before SWM itself collapsed.

GÖRICKE • Germany 1903–

Once well-known for racing bicycles, Göricke was one of the pioneer motorcycle producers in Germany. Built in the early days single and V-twin machines and during the 1920s assembled models with 172cc to 247cc Villiers as well as 346cc and 496cc MAG engines. Touring versions had ioe and sporting machines ohv engines. There were also Blackburne-engined Göricke machines, but the motorcycle production was never very big. Designer was Alfred Ostertag. Still building mofas etc, Göricke also produced until the mid-1950s Sachs and Ilo-engined two-strokes from 98cc to 198cc.

GORRION • Spain 1952–1955

Sachs-engined mopeds and motorcycles. The range also included 124cc and 174cc machines.

GOUGH • England 1920–1923

Assembled machines with 293cc sv JAP and 548cc sv Blackburne engines.

GOUVERNEUR • Germany 1903–1907

Long forgotten make which used 3.5hp GN engines.

GR • Italy 1925–1926

After Count Mario Revelli won the 500cc class of the Grand Prix des Nations at Monza in 1925 on an Antonio Boudo-designed 490cc JAP-engined ohv single-cylinder machine, his brother Count Gino Revelli built these machines with the GR trade mark in limited numbers.

G & R • Holland c1935–1939

Autocycle-type machine with Fichtel and Sachs 1.25hp engine and hand-change gearbox built in The Hague by Goverse and Rotteveel.

GRADE • Germany 1903–1925

Designed by Hans Grade, a leading aircraft pioneer, all the products (airplanes, cars and motorcycles) had two-stroke engines. He also supplied engines to other producers. His 118cc and 132cc motorcycles were very successful and were really a creation of his designer-in-chief, Hans Plog. Leading Grade riders: Hans Przybilski and the Hartmann brothers.

GRANDEX-PRECISION (GRANDEX) • England 1917

As the factory first fitted Precision engines from 2.5hp to 6hp, the early machines used the Grandex-Precision trademark. The Precision was dropped when the factory also fitted 225cc, 293cc, 490cc, 597cc and 746cc JAP engines. Most of them were sv models.

490cc Grindlay-Peerless (ohv JAP) 1929

GREEVES • England 1952–1978

Unorthodox and sturdy machines with partly cast aluminum frames and own leading-link front forks, designed by Bert Greeves. Most used Villiers engine and gearbox units, but Greeves developed special cylinders and, later, complete engines. Brian Stonebridge pioneered Greeves' motocross career, but sales took off when Dave Bickers won the 1960 European Championship. The bikes, such as the 360cc and 380cc motocross models, were almost unbeatable in British scrambles and trials. Greeves also made a road racer, the 250cc Silverstone, which, ridden by Tom Phillips, won the ACU star in 1963, the 250cc Manx Grand Prix in 1964 (Gordon Keith) and in 1965 (Dennis Craine). There were road bikes, too – the 2T Villiers engined 'Essex Twin' being very well thought of. When Bert Greeves retired in 1973, the factory lost its lucrative American connection and declined.

248cc Greeves racer (two-stroke Villiers) 1963

197cc Greeves (two-stroke Villiers) 1963

247cc Greeves trials (two-stroke Villiers) 1963

GRAPHIC • England 1903–1906

Small producer which fitted De Dion, Minerva and MMC engines.

GRASETTI • Italy 1952–1965

Produced 123cc and 148cc machines with its own two-stroke power units.

GRATIEUX • France 1919–1921

Aircraft engine producer which tried building motorcycles with two-stroke radial engines.

GRAVES • England 1914–1915

This was a supermarket of that period which sold Speed King motorcycles with 293cc JAP sv engines and a simple specification. Producer was Omega at Wolverhampton on behalf of Graves.

GREEN • England 1919–1923

In pre-WW1 days closely connected with Green-Precision and Regal-Green. Charles Green was mainly an engine producer and a strong supporter of water-cooled power units. He produced mainly 3.33hp and 4hp singles. After the war he tried again to join the ranks of motorcycle manufacturers, but was not very successful. In his last years he offered to convert air-cooled Precision engines to water cooling.

GREEVES • England 1952–1978

See panel

GREYHOUND • England 1905–1907

Small assembler, which fitted proprietary engines made by Minerva, MMC and Fafnir.

49cc Gritzner (two-stroke Sachs) 1962

246cc Grizzly (two-stroke) 1929

GREYHOUND • America 1907–1914

Once a well-known make. The 4.5hp single-cylinder was developed and built at the Thor factory.

GRG • Italy 1926–1927

Technically interesting design with two coupled 174cc Della Ferrera single-cylinder ohv engines and rear suspension.

GRI • England 1921–1922

GR Inshaw's 350cc and 500cc engines used a combination of poppet valves and a rotary valve. As with so many rotary valves, this was not really satisfactory in practice.

GRIFFON • France 1902–late 1920s

Old established and once very successful make in competition. Built singles and V-twins, the last model being a nice 348cc single with sv and ohv engines. In the 1920's Peugeot took over Griffon.

GRIGG • England 1920–1925

A 1.75hp scooter was the first Grigg product. It was followed by a 161cc two-stroke and a 181cc ohv machine with Grigg's own engines. Other models had Villiers and Blackburne single and V-twin engines up to 680cc. The biggest model had the rare 990cc V-twin sv B&H engine.

GRINDLAY-PEERLESS • England 1923–1934

Originally a sidecar factory, the first motorcycle models had 490cc JAP single-cylinder and 996cc Barr & Stroud sleeve-valve V-twin engines. Machines with 346cc and 496cc single-cylinder Barr & Stroud motors followed. Many models had sv and ohv JAP engines from 248cc to 996cc and Brough Superior-like petrol tanks and there was a 490cc JAP-engined version with a Castle-type forks. Small models from 147cc to 247cc were powered by Villiers two-stroke engines and there were also Grindlay-Peerless machines with Rudge-built Python four-valve ohv engines from 248cc to 498cc. Bill Lacey, famous tuner and rider, broke many records on JAP engined machines while Karl Abarth of Austria and Jan Mocchari of Czechoslovakia gained many successes in road races and hill climbs with various grand prix machines. The Grindlay-Peerless factory was only a few hundred yards from the former Rudge works.

GRINDLEY SPORTING • England 1925–1926 and 1951

JAP-powered motorcycles built at Prees, Shropshire. The same firm later built Grindley 125cc racing machines.

GRINGO • America 1973–

Small make which concentrates on 248cc and 358cc single-cylinder two-stroke machines for motocross and flat tracks.

GRITZNER • Germany 1903–1962

A famous sewing-machine factory which during the early years built Fafnir-engined singles and V-twins. After WW2, motorcycle manufacture resumed and Sachs engines of 98cc, 147cc, and 174cc were fitted. The last Gritzner was a 49cc motorcycle of very sporting appearance and originally known as the Mars-built Monza. Gritzner-Kaiser AG is the factory name and the Kaiser part built three-wheelers in 1901.

GRIZZLY • Czechoslovakia 1925–1932

Designed by Josef Matyas, the Grizzly was a modern 246cc two-stroke machine with deflector-type three-port engine. The range included after 1929 348cc MAG-engined ioe and ohv models. Works rider Zdenek Hermann had a 348cc ohc MAG engine in his machine. Other riders: Trnka, Adamek, Korbel.

GROSE-SPUR • England 1934–1939

Lightweight machines with 123cc Villiers engines built by Carlton for the London-based dealer Grose.

GROTE • Germany 1924–1925

Very unorthodox 305cc two-stroke singles, which - by adding one or two more engines! - could be brought to 614cc or 921cc.

GRÖCO • Germany 1924–1925

Assembler which fitted 346cc Kühne ohv engines into simple frames.

GRUHN • Germany 1909–1932

Old-established Berlin-based manufacturer of sv machines and proprietary engines of 148cc, 196cc and 246cc. A new 198cc single-cylinder ohv machine came into production in 1928. It had shaft drive to the rear wheel and was of up-to-date design. The last Gruhn was a 123cc two-stroke. Richard Gruhn's machines never had any kind of sporting image.

148cc Guazzoni (two-stroke) 1966

198cc Gruhn (sv) 1922

348cc Grutzena (ohv Kühne) 1925

490cc Güldner (ohv) 1925

GRUHN • Germany 1920–1926

Another Berlin-based Gruhn, owned by Hugo Gruhn. He was Richard Gruhn's brother and concentrated mainly on the production of frames for others. His own machines housed the 198cc Alba single-cylinder sv engine.

GRUTZENA • Germany 1925–1926

Sturdy but not very modern 348cc singles with Kühne ohv engines. Production was on a limited scale.

GS • Germany 1920–1924

Lightweight machines with 129cc two-stroke engines. These could be bought also as bicycle attachments. This was the Gustav Schulze GS.

GS • Germany 1923–1925

This, the Georg Schroff - Berlin built - GS was a 145cc machine with Gruhn sv engines as well as many other Gruhn parts.

GSD • England 1921–1923

R. E. D. Grant's interesting design had a transverse-mounted 496cc flat-twin engine, four speeds and shaft drive to the rear wheel. A second model housed the 342cc White & Poppe single-cylinder two-stroke and also had shaft drive.

GUARALDI • Italy 1905–1916

The first machines had German Fafnir, later ones Belgian Sarolea engines with capacities up to 550cc.

GUAZZONI • Italy 1949–1977

After Aldo Guazzoni left Moto Morini, he created many interesting two-strokes and ohv models up to 248cc. Among them were some very fast 49cc versions. Later Guazzoni concentrated on 49cc mini-machines and 123cc models - two-strokes - for trials and motocross.

GUIA • Italy 1950–1954

Small assembler of 98cc, 123cc and 147cc two-stroke machines.

GUIGNARD • France 1933–1938

Jéan Guignard produced mainly 98cc and 123cc two-stroke machines.

GUILLER • France 1928–1956

Pre-war, manufactured lightweight mopeds and motorcycles using Madoz, Zurcher and Chaise motors. After 1945 became one of the leading French factories, producing light motorcycles from 49cc to 248cc with engines from AMC, Ydral, VAP, Aubier-Dunne and others, and also made the Italian SIM Moretti scooter under licence.

GUIZZARDI • Italy 1926–1932

Produced 124cc and 174cc ohv and also 174cc ohc singles with its own power units. They were modern machines of sound design.

GUIZZO • Italy 1955–1962

Built 48cc mopeds and a well-designed 149cc scooter in a period when others had dropped scooter manufacture.

GÜLDNER • Germany 1925

A short-lived but superb Norton-like 490cc ohv single-cylinder machine, built by a well-known agriculture machine factory. Dr. Güldner's design was so similar to Norton's that it was possible to use Norton spare parts after Güldner dropped motorcycle production. Top rider was Josef Klein, who later rode for DKW and Horex.

GUSTLOFF • Germany 1934–1940

Mopeds with 98cc Sachs engines, designed by Martin Stolle of D-Rad fame.

G & W • England 1902–1906

Long forgotten assembler which used Minerva, Peugeot and Fafnir proprietary engines.

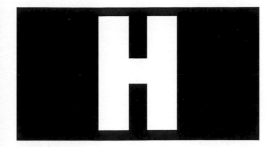

HACK • England 1920–1923

Mini-scooter with 103cc and 110cc Simplex two-stroke engines built in limited numbers.

HADEN • England 1920–1924

Built a single model only. It had a 347cc Precision two-stroke engine.

HAGEL • Germany 1925

Two-stroke machines with Hagel's own 247cc three-port engine.

HÄGGLUND • Sweden 1973–1978

Developed for the Swedish Army, this machine had a single-cylinder 345cc Rotax two-stroke engine with 76mm bore and stroke. It developed 24bhp at 5300rpm. The monocoque frame included the petrol tank; drive was by shaft, and the wheels were made from pressed steel. The weight was 135kg. Late in 1976, the army contract went to Husqvarna instead and Hägglund finally closed in 1978.

HAGG TANDEM • England 1920–1922

Enclosed motorcycles with two seats, powered by Union two-stroke and Barr and Stroud sleeve valve engines by St Albans firm. Also marketed as HT.

HAI • Austria 1938

Cast aluminum frame including the petrol tank. Own 110cc two-stroke engine. Hitler's production plans for the industry brought production of the Hai to an end.

HAJA • Germany 1924–1925

Simple 198cc sv machines with Hansa-built single-cylinder engines.

HAKO • Germany 1924–1925

Copies of HRD machines. Even the 348cc and 490cc ohv JAP engines used were identical.

HALESON • England c1912

Steam-powered machines built in limited numbers by Fred Hale, who built more prototypes than machines for sale.

HALUMO • Germany 1923–1926

Produced 147cc two-strokes, then 146cc and 198cc ohv machines with its own engines.

248cc Hansa (ohv) 1926

HAM • The Netherlands 1902–1906

Single-cylinder machines with 2hp (at 2000rpm) Altena engines.

HAMILTON • England 1901–1907

Built 2.25hp, 3.25hp and 4hp singles as well as 4.5hp V-twins and sold power units to other producers.

HAMPTON • England 1912–1914

Well-made 492cc sv machines with single-cylinder power units made by T. D. Cross.

HANFLAND • Germany 1920–1925

Built Hanfland and Kurier motorcycles with own 147cc two-stroke engines. Curt Hanfland also supplied these engines to Flink, a branch of the famous BMWfactory.

HANSA • Germany 1922–1926

Once a well-known factory at Bielefeld, Hansa produced two- and four-stroke singles of 148cc to 246cc. The last models had 198cc and 246cc ohv engines with horizontally-mounted valves and low triangular duplex frames.

HANSAN • England 1920–1922

Assembler which fitted 269cc Arden two-stroke and 346cc Blackburne sv engines.

HAPAMEE • Germany 1925-1926

Meinke-designed 198cc and 246cc two-strokes with own deflector-type motors.

HARDING-JAP • France 1912–1914

Built from English components, the Harding motorcycle had a 496cc V-twin JAP engine. H. J. Harding was an Englishman living in St. Cyr.

148cc Hanfland (two-stroke)

HAREWOOD • England 1920

Assembled machines with 269cc Villiers two-stroke and 346cc Precision sv engines.

HARRIS • England 1973–

Steve and Lester Harris began by building frames for racing bikes in their small workshop in Hertford, but soon bowed to demand from road riders for better frames and produced a series of tubular steel trellis frames under the Magnum name. These accepted the best contemporary engines, being the Kawasaki Z1/Z900/Z1000 in the first Magnum 1, then various Suzuki and Kawasaki motors in Magnums 2,3 and 4 (Suzuki GSX-R750/1100), although Harris would always adapt its frames to take other power units.

In 1992 Harris along with French frame builder ROC was selected by Yamaha to produce proprietory frames for 500cc grand prix machines to be powered by the Japanese V-four two-stroke engines, in a move designed to bring more privateers into the blue riband racing class by making cheaper but still competitive bikes available.

In 1997 Harris was chosen by Suzuki to manage its return to World Superbike racing by running the GSX-R750 racing bikes.

HARLETTE • France & Belgium 1925–1928

Puch split-single two-stroke made under licence and sold as Harlette in France, Belgium and Italy. However Gerkinet in France also made a 175cc model with an ohv Gillet Herstal engine. Painted to look like a miniature Harley-Davidson) and sold in France and Belgium.

HARLEY-DAVIDSON • America 1903–

Harley-Davidson was until quite recently America's only production motorcycle manufacturer, and certainly it can claim the distinction of being the oldest surviving motorcycle company in the world, having made and sold motorcycles since 1903.

Harley-Davidson has come a long way since then, when pattern maker Arthur Davidson and draughtsman William Harley came together to build their first motorcycles, with Davidson's brother, Walter, helping. When, in 1907, working from a small backyard shed, production reached 50, they decided to give up their regular jobs, and joined by another Davidson, brother William, they incorporated the company and moved into a larger factory. Progress from here was quite remarkable; by the time the USA entered WW1 in 1917, Harley-Davidson was making 17,000 motorcycles a year.

The 1907 model had a 475cc engine with an inlet valve opened by atmospheric pressure over the side exhaust valve, the engine being inclined forward in a sturdy loop frame, with characteristic bottom link front forks. The single-speed transmission was by flat belt, tensioned by a jockey pully. Surprisingly, almost alone in

the USA, Harley persisted with belt drive until as late as 1913. The bike had famously earned itself the name of 'Silent Grey Fellow' from as early as 1905, after Harley's practise of painting its bikes grey, fitting them with effective silencers and promoting the machines as close companions on the open road, a theme still used today.

The company's first 800cc 45 degree V-twin came in 1909. It had mechanically operated overhead inlet valves, a Schebler carburetor and a Bosch magneto. Engine capacity rose to 980cc in 1912. There was a clutch in 1911, a two-speed gear and chain drive for 1914 and a three-speed gear and kickstart a year later. In the war, Harley produced over 20,000 twins, most with sidecars for the US forces, of which about 7,000 went to France.

Post-war, a novel offering was a 600cc fore-and-aft flat twin, but it lasted for only four seasons, main production consisting of 1000cc and 1200 V twins. Cheap car prices forced a degree of conservatism on the company, which cut down on model changes, but in 1928 a significant development took place, with the introduction of the 750cc 'Forty five' with a straightforward side-valve layout. This D series twin was uprated until 1951, while its engine lasted for even longer, being used in the three-wheeled utility 'Servicar' from 1932 until 1975!

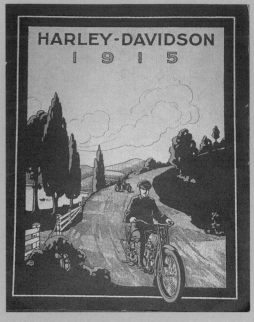

1915 poster for Harley-Davidson 61 Twin

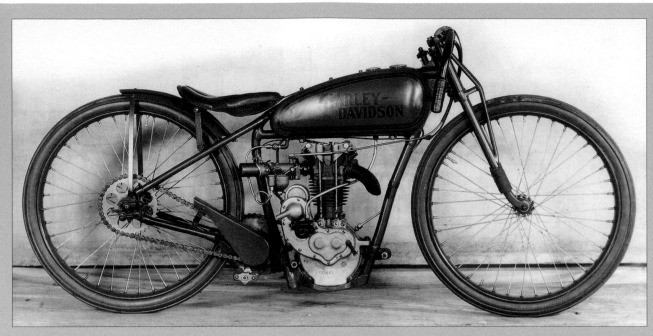

350cc Harley-Davidson 'Peashooter' (ohv) 1922

980cc Silent Grey Fellow (oh inlet valves, V-twin) 1912

There were also side-valve and ohv 350cc singles, perhaps owing something to the British AJS and intended more for export than for domestic sale. Harley's first ohv twin was the 1000cc 'Knucklehead' of 1936, supplemented in 1941 by a similar 1200cc version.

Post-WW2, Harley branched into lightweights with the 125cc Hummer, an even franker copy of the DKW RT125 than BSA's Bantam. This was uprated to 165cc before being dropped after 1952. Harley also briefly made a 165cc two-stroke scooter. Serious production, however, centred on the big twins, particularly on the 1948 'Panhead' ohv with light alloy heads and hydraulic tappets. This came in 1000cc and 1200cc capacities. In 1949, hydraulically-damped telescopic front forks were added and it was rechristened the Hydra Glide. In 1958,

with rear suspension, it became the Duo Glide and, in 1965, with 12 volt electric starting, the Electra Glide; it was then redesigned with 1200cc and 1340cc engines as the F series. In 1952 the unit-constructed sv K series was introduced, followed by the X series ohv in 1957, a model designation still in use. The original XL Sportster had a totally new 883cc engine and, for the first time, a unit construction gearbox. Continually developed since then, with a 1000cc option being introduced in 1972, this basic model has been subjected to a bewildering number of permutations.

Before WW1 Harley was content to let its customers' race results speak for themselves, but in 1916 it built special eight-valve ohv models, which were raced into the early 1920s by Harley's own team. Thereafter, racing

The first Harley-Davidson, 475cc single, 1903

61 cubic inch Harley-Davidson Knucklehead (ohv V-twin) 1936

HARLEY-
DAVIDSON

750cc Harley-Davidson Forty Five (sv V-twin) 1932

749cc Harley-Davidson Servicar (sv V-twin) 1934

1200cc Harley-Davidson Hydra Glide (ohv V-twin) 1953

models were sold, including the 350cc ohv 'Peashooter'. Originally intended for professional US dirt track and speedway racing, the 'Peashooter' had a significant influence on dirt track racing, first in Australia and then in Britain.

In the 1930s Class C amateur racing called for stock machines of 750cc, relieving Harley and its rivals of the task of fielding factory teams. But, inevitably, special machines were made and supplied to favoured dealers and riders - especially when Class C began to centre on the 200-mile race at Daytona beach. In the late 1930s honours in Class C were about equal between Indian and Harley, but in 1941 both concerns were shocked when the Daytona 200 was won by Canadian Billy Matthews on a 500cc ohc Norton. Another Norton came second in 1948, while Nortons won the race outright from 1949 and through to 1952. In 1953, however, Harley struck back with the remarkable KR750 side-valve, which became legendary before being replaced by the ohv XR750 in 1970.

Far from finding the KR750 a hard act to follow, the XR750 if anything shone even brighter, dominating American dirt track racing almost totally ever since. At first the bike was not a great success, but in 1972 the old iron-barrelled engine was replaced by an all aluminum unit and the titles started to gather. In the early 1970s Yamaha with the legendary Kenny Roberts took two titles on XS650-based machines, and a dozen years later Honda picked up four titles with its V-twin RS750, very loosely based on the CX500 road bike. These aberations aside, the XR750 has been in control, taking famous names such as Jay Springsteen and Scott Parker to a succession of championships.

883cc Harley-Davidson XL Sportster (ohv V-twin) 1957

883cc Harley-Davidson Sportster (ohv) 1958

901cc Harley-Davidson Sportster (ohv) 1965

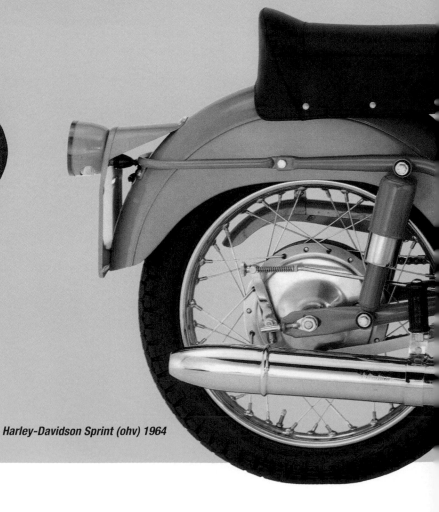

Harley-Davidson Sprint (ohv) 1964

1215cc Harley-Davidson Duo Glide (ohv V-twin) 1963

Between 1960 and 1978 Harley-Davidson at first partly and then fully-owned the Italian Aermacchi company, a link that provided it with a ready-made range of smaller machines for the domestic market. It also provided racing models, at first ohv four-strokes and, later, two-strokes. In 1974, 1975 and 1976 Walter Villa was 250cc road racing champion and in 1977 350cc champion on Harley-Davidson two-stroke twins. Aermacchi was sold to a new company, Cagiva, when US exhaust emission legislation made the continued sale of two-strokes impractical. The sale also relieved Harley of having to peddle an image with the small two-strokes which it was not really comfortable with.

In 1968 Harley-Davidson was bought by the large US conglomerate AMF American Machine and Foundry. Although the Davidson family was nominally involved, first Walter, then William G - chairman in 1971 - and John A Davidson left the board. The AMF period has been

1200cc Harley-Davidson FLH1200 Liberty Edition (ohv V-twin) 1976

347cc Harley-Davidson (ohv single) 1974

painted as a disaster for Harley, but, in fact, sales trebled, and the company also succesfully lobbied against the unfair pricing of Japanese imports - eventually the US government imposed tariffs on imported motorcyles of 700cc and over. By 1980, however, AMF was

disenchanted with the business, since it appeared difficult to make profits commensurate with the capital it had invested, so it responded favourably to offers of a buy-back by former and current members of the senior management, including William G. Davidson - but not

1200cc Harley-Davidson FXS Low Rider (ohv V-twin) 1977

*Grand National Champion Scott Parker at the Del Mar Mile
on his works XR750, 1995*

*1000cc Harley-Davidson XLCR Cafe Racer
(ohv V-twin) 1984*

brother John. The buy-back took place amicably for $75,000,000 in June 1981.

The first real fruit of the new dynamism and genuine understanding of the product which came with the buyout was the introduction of the new Evolution engine in 1984, a massive improvement in terms of reliability, power and smoothness compared with the old Shovelhead motor (thus named because of the shape of its rocker covers), yet entirely consistent with Harley values. In the next few years the Evo motor was phased in across the range, which the management concentrated on expanding at the same time as improving the build quality, which had become very shoddy in the AMF days. But the motor made its debut in a machine which was to show Harley exactly where much of its future lie, which ironically was in the past. The 1340cc Softail of 1984 used many older Harley styling cues, including a rear end which was sprung but disguised to look like the old hard-tail machines of the 1940s and earlier. This single feature has appeared on many Harley models since, as well as being copied by other manufacturers on their own custom machines, including all of the Japanese.

By the end of the 1980s Harley's range had expanded into double figures, traditional models such as the basic 883cc and 1200cc Sportsters appearing with various Lowriders (with non-unit engines) and Softails, including the still current Fat Boy, introduced in 1989, plus Glides including the luxurious Electra Glide Ultra Classic FLHTCU. All models except the Sportsters featured 1340cc engines.

More and more Harley was drawing on its rich heritage (and even introduced a model called the Heritage Softail Nostalgia in 1993!), with new models apeing machines from the 1970s, 1960s, and then with the Road King in 1994, the 1950s. Technical innovations were limited to the introduction of the Dyna chassis in 1993 on the FXDB Sturgis Dynaglide, which had two rubber engine mounts to isolate vibration and also instil some handling integrity, and then a basic fuel injection on the Electra Glide in 1995.

Harley has been less sure of itself in road racing, deciding it needed to compete, but as yet not having much success during the 1990s. It built the VR1000 in 1995 with a view to competing first in American Superbike racing, then World Superbikes, but the liquid-cooled, 60 degree V-twin engine with fuel injection, four valves per cylinder and dohc has rarely produced the necessary combination of power and reliability. Harley has toned down the project, but work on it is continuing.

The quality and reliability of the company's road bikes meanwhile increased steadily into the 1990s, and Harley's sales expanded considerably, especially in its export markets. Although the American market remained static throughout the 1990s, Harley retained around a 50 per cent share for much of the time, and recently is looking even stronger in its home territory despite increasingly convincing Japanese custom bikes and the

1340cc Harley-Davidson FXLR Low Rider Custom (ohv V-twin) 1987

1000cc Harley-Davidson XLCR Cafe Racer (ohv V-twin) 1977

1340cc Harley-Davidson FLT Tour Glide (ohv V-twin) 1980

1340cc Harley-Davidson FLSTN Heritage Softail (ohv V-twin) 1993

appearance of several new American manufacturers, including Excelsior-Henderson, Polaris and possibly Indian.

Harley-Davidson is continuing to invest heavily in its products though, in 1997 opening the Willie G Davidson Product Development Centre for its research, and in 1998 the company introduced a brand new engine, the Twin Cam 88. Visually similar to the old Evo motor (which is important in a Harley), the Twin Cam is a great improvement in terms of power, smoothness and torque, and should serve the company well into the next millenium.

For the year 2000, Harley has made sweeping changes to its range, finally taking on board criticisms from Europeans of poor brakes and suspension by uprating these, and more significantly, fitting twin balance shafts to the Twin Cam 88 engines used across the Softail range, to reduce vibration from the increasingly unacceptable levels of earlier models (the engines in Softails are rigidly attached, whereas other Harleys use two or three rubber mounts). The chassis are also extensively revised, the twin aims being cheaper production costs and improved ride and handling.

883cc Harley-Davidson Custom 53 (ohv V-twin) 1998

883cc Harley-Davidson Night Train (ohv V-twin) 1998

1340cc Harley-Davidson Road King Classic 95th Anniversary (ohv V-twin) 1997

1340cc Harley-Davidson FLHTCU Electra Glide Ultra Classic (ohv V-twin) 1997

HARLEY-DAVIDSON • America 1903–

See panel

HARPER • England 1954–1955

Scooter with 198cc Villiers two-stroke engine. The production was on a limited scale.

HARRAS • Germany 1922–1925

Fitted Ruppe's Bekamo two-stroke engines - built under licence - into own frames. They had 139cc and 145cc and a pumping cylinder, housed at the bottom of the crankcase.

HARWOOD • England 1920–1921

Design by Harold Harwood and built by the Harwood Motor Company, Bexleyheath. A heavyweight cycle motorised by a 133cc Harwood two-stroke engine with chain final drive.

HARSO • Germany 1925–1926

Small machines built by a small company, which fitted 174cc and 206cc DKW two-stroke proprietary engines into open frames.

HASCHO • Germany 1923–1926

Fitted first 143cc and 173cc DKW engines, superseded by English Villiers two-strokes.

HASCHOT • Germany 1929–1931

Limited production of machines with 172cc Villiers deflector-type engines.

HASTY • France 1930–1934

Lightweights with 98cc Aubier-Dunne two-stroke power units.

HAUSER • Germany 1981–

Took over the manufacture of the well-known Kramer trials, enduro and motocross machines. The range included 124cc, 248cc and 406cc versions with membrane and rotary-valve two-stroke engines.

HAUSMANN • Czechoslovakia c1950s

Scooter with twin air scoops to cool the engine fashioned in the vehicle's voluminous bodywork. Two headlights and a screen were included in the specification.

HAVERFORD • America 1909–1914

Small American factory. Built 4hp single-cylinder machines with automatic inlet valves.

493cc Helios (sv flat twin BMW) 1922

HAWEKA • Germany 1923–1926

Very English-looking motorcycles with 348cc, 490cc and 678cc sv and ohv JAP engines. Another model had the 497cc ioe MAG single-cylinder engine. Leading riders: Bremer and Schulz.

HAWKER • England 1920–1923

When ABC was liquidated, Tom Sopwith and Harry Hawker - Sopwith's test pilot - used the factory to make a small 300cc two-stroke motorcycle. Subsequently, Hawkers used 350cc and 550cc side-valve Blackburne engines. Hawker died in a flying accident in 1921 and production of Hawkers ended as Sopwith re-entered aircraft manufacture.

HAXEL-JAP • England 1911–1913

Assembler which fitted the 293cc JAP sv engine into a limited number of frames.

HAZEL • England 1906–1911

This was another assembler which fitted first V-twin Peugeot and from 1909 also 393cc JAP engines.

HAZLEWOOD • England 1905–1923

Once a big motorcycle factory, but never a well-known one at home. The Hazlewood production included V-twin sv machines of 499cc to 998cc and JAP-engined models from 245cc to 548cc and V-twins to 996cc in strong duplex frames. These were exported to the British

colonies: few reached the home market. A make which built exclusively road-going models.

HB • England 1919–1924

Simple well-made machines with 346cc and 498cc sv and ohv Blackburne engines.

HEC • England 1922–1923

The Hewin-built machine had 247cc Villiers two-stroke engines.

HEC • England 1938–1940

First seen at the 1938 British motorcycle show, the HEC was distinguished from most autocycles by its use of an 80cc engine made by the famous Levis factory at Stechford, Birmingham. When Levis was sold, supply of engines ceased and so did HEC production.

HECKER • Germany 1921–1956

Was a leading factory. Built 245cc two-stroke machines with its own engines, afterwards 346cc ohv models, with power units similar to the AJS of that period. They were followed by JAP-engined machines of 198cc to 548cc and a 746cc V-twin with the ioe MAG engine. The range also included from 1931 onwards Sachs-engined 73cc and 98cc two-strokes, some with frames made from square-section tubes. After 1945 Hecker machines housed Sachs and Ilo engines from 98cc to 248cc.

199cc Hecker (ohv JAP) 1931

247cc Hecker (two-stroke Ilo) 1954

346cc Haweka (sv) 1926

147cc Hella (two-stroke) 1922

490cc Hecker (sv JAP) 1928

HEIDEMANN • Germany 1949–1952

Well-known bicycle factory which built lightweights with 98cc and 123cc Sachs engines.

HEILO • Germany 1924–1925

Well-designed 348cc deflector-type, three-port, two-stroke single with own engine. Experimented also with supercharged two-strokes.

HEINKEL • Germany 1952–1962

Built 49cc mopeds and scooters with own 149cc ohv engines in a former aircraft factory. The range was extended by 123cc two-stroke and 174cc ohv scooters, which gained commercial success.

HELI • Germany 1923–1925

Water-cooled 246cc two-stroke, unit-design engine in tubular duplex frame, with belt drive and leaf-spring fork.

HELIOS • Germany 1921–1922

Although not designed by BMW, the machine was BMW built. Its engine was a 493cc BMW-made M2B15 proprietary sv flat twin. The Helios had many faults and so BMW decided to produce its own completely new motorcycles with transverse-mounted flat twin engines.

HELLA • Germany 1921–1924

Built at Munich, the Hella was a two-stroke with a horizontal cylinder. The range consisted of 147cc and 183cc models.

HELLER • Germany 1923–1926

The Heller used, like the Helios, the 493cc flat twin BMW M2B15 engine; from 1924 onwards also the similarly-built 746cc MJ (Mehne) sv flat twin power unit.

HELO • Germany 1923–1925

Fitted with 149cc Bekamo-type two-stroke, which had an additional piston in the crankcase. Production was on a small scale.

HELVETIA • Switzerland 1927–1930

Built by the Universal company, the little Helvetia had a 190cc PA two-stroke engine.

HELYETT • France 1926–1955

Produced motorcycles with 98cc to 996cc V-twins. Among them were transverse-mounted JAP-engined 746cc V-twins with shaft drive, which had the gearbox in unit with the engine. Also built some fast 996cc racing machines with 45bhp and 55bhp ohv JAP engines. After 1945 only two-strokes from 48cc to 123cc were made.

HENDERSON • America 1911–1931

See panel

HENDERSON • America 1911–1931

A famous four-cylinder design by William 'Bill' Henderson, whose father built Henderson cars. The motorcycles had air-cooled in-line unit-design engines of 1068cc and 1301cc and for a short period also 1168cc. The designer sold his creation to the Chicago-based Schwinn factory in 1917 and afterwards created the similar ACE. He was killed in 1922 in a road accident. Henderson motorcycles had three-speed gearboxes plus a reverse gear.

Another famous American designer, Arthur Lemon, continued after Henderson's death in developing the big four-cylinder until 1931, when Ignaz Schwinn decided to withdraw from the manufacture of motorcycles. According to experts who knew most American fours, which included the Militaire, the Champion, the Cleveland, the ACE, Indian-ACE and others, the big Henderson was the finest of them all. Red Wolverton, who rode Hendersons in the mid-1920s, won many races on them.

1301cc Henderson De Luxe (sv four-cylinder) 1925

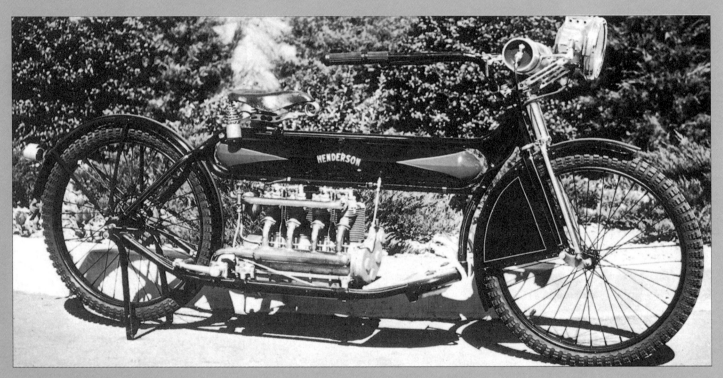

7hp Henderson (sv four-cylinder) 1913

HENKEL • Germany 1927–1932

Was the last in the line who built the once-famous 503cc and 497cc Krieger Gnädig (KG) motorcycles. This unit-design single with shaft drive was originally designed by the Kreiger brothers and Franz Gnädig. They handed production over to the Cito works, which eventually became part of the Allright factory. When in 1927 Allright decided to drop motorcycle production in favour of the manufacture of forks, hubs etc., it was Paul Henkel who built these machines. Rudi Albert had them redesigned and developed in the mid-1920s, but by 1932 they were outmoded. After 1929 Henkel made a 198cc sv single with a Blackburne engine.

HENLEY • England 1920–1929

Assembled machines with modern tubular frames. The first models had 269cc Villiers two-stroke and 497cc Blackburne sv engines. Other models with 248cc, 293cc and 346cc sv and ohv JAP and Blackburne engines followed. After a reorganization in 1927, the name became New Henley. Afterwards the make was bought by Arthur Greenwood and Jack Crump, and was transferred to Oldham from Birmingham. Among new models were 678cc and 748cc sv V-twins. Henley would fit MAG engines if required, mainly the 497cc double-port ohv model.

HERBI • Germany 1928–1932

Two models of sound design formed the Herbi production. One was a 198cc sv machine with Blackburne engine, the other a 498cc model with the ohc three-valve Küchen motor.

HER CHEE • Taiwan 1985–

Huge manufacturer of mopeds and scooters with its own 50cc and 100cc two-stroke engines, and more recently 125cc four-strokes. Sold under many brand names including: Adly, Italjet, Maico, Fantic and Siam.

HERCULES • Germany 1904–1992

Hercules, owned by engine maker Sachs, survived into the 1980s only as a producer of mopeds. From its early beginnings it used proprietary engines from many sources, and in the 1930s it achieved some good racing results with JAP-powered models. The company also made lightweights, down to as small as 75cc. Wartime bombing of Nuremburg put the Hercules factory out of action until 1950, when 98cc Sachs-engined and 125cc Ilo-engined models were both shown for the first time. Both sold well and were joined a year later by other lightweight models. By the mid-1950s, Hercules was exporting throughout Europe with models from 100cc to 250cc, the top of the range using a 250cc Ilo twin-cylinder engine. The company survived the problematical late 1950s that saw so many German motorcycle concerns flounder, becoming part of the Zweirad Union in 1966. Three years later, this was taken over by Fichtel and Sachs, which kept the famous name alive. The W2000 Wankel-engined model (promoted outside Germany as a DKW) followed in 1970. More profitable was a 125cc Sachs-engined model sold in large numbers to the German army. As part of its efforts to keep Hercules afloat, Sachs, for a while, sold a reasonably large range of enduro models of 125cc and 350cc in the USA. However, in 1980 economics dictated the range should be cut down solely to machines of 80cc, which used a water-cooled Sachs two-stroke. During the 1990s Hercules was only selling re-badged Peugeot scooters, but still remained in business.

198cc Hercules (two-stroke Ilo) 1951

49cc Hercules K50RX (two-stroke Sachs) 1971

294cc Hercules (Wankel rotary) 1975

198cc Hercules (sv JAP) 1930

197cc Hercules (ohv Moser) 1931

49cc Hercules K50RL (two-stroke Sachs) 1977

992cc Hesketh V1000 (dohc eight-valve V-twin) 1981

1488cc Hildebrand & Wolfmüller (two-cylinder, 2¹/₂hp at 240rpm) 1894

HERCULES • Germany 1904–1992

See panel

HERCULES • England 1902

Assembler which used engines made by MMC, Minerva and White & Poppe.

HERCULES-VICTOR • Australia c1920s

The English-built 588cc Coventry Victor sold under licence in Australia as Hercules-Victor.

HERDTLE-BRUNEAU • France 1902–1914

Produced a range of unorthodox motorcycles including a water-cooled 264cc (48mm bore x 73mm stroke) vertical twin. Other models had V-twin Bichrone two-stroke engines. Herdtle-Bruneau was also among the first motorcycle manufacturers using ohv engines.

HERKO • Germany 1922–1925

Built lightweight machines with 122cc and 158cc two-stroke engines and also 198cc sv engines. Engines as well as frames were also supplied to other makes.

HERKRA • Germany 1922–1923

Another small manufacturer of motorcycles with its own 141cc two-stroke engines.

HERMA • Germany 1921–1924

Bicycle attachment engines of 148cc which could be fitted on either front wheel or the rear. They were of Herma's own design.

HERMES • Germany 1922–1925

Designed by Berwald, the Cockerell-like machines used a 124cc horizontal single-cylinder two-stroke engine.

HERMES • Germany 1924–1925

JAP-engined 348cc, 490cc and 678cc motorcycles with sv engines and open frames. Production was on a limited scale.

HEROS • Germany 1921–1929

Built in the Saxony region, Heros machines had own 155cc, 185cc and 247cc engines with outside flywheels and used two- and three-speed gearboxes of own manufacture. The engines were two-strokes as well as four-strokes. The last ones had sv, in some cases also overhead-inlet and side-exhaust valves.

HEROS • Germany 1923–1924

Another Heros, made by a Berlin-based factory, which used 142cc DKW two-stroke engines.

HERTHA • Germany 1924–1925

Lightweights, made on the line of the Eichler. The Hertha had a 142cc DKW engine.

HESKETH • England 1981–

An attempt to market a British superbike, the impressive looking but highly flawed V1000, with a 992cc ohc 90 degree V-twin engine was based on a Weslake design. The company was started by Lord Alexander Hesketh from his Towcester estate, after he had established his motoring credentials as owner of a well-known Formula One car team, which at one stage included eventual world champion James Hunt. The V1000 appeared quite advanced, but serious gearbox problems, excessive fuel consumption and mechanical noise as well as poor reliability delayed its launch. Eventually only about 150 machines were delivered before financial problems hit the company, with the loss of substantial sums of money. It was liquidated in 1982, but was reformed by Lord Hesketh to produce the Vampire, a fully-faired tourer based on the V1000, and with a series of other improvements. But the reputation for

poor reliability was too strong, and again the company went bust with few being built.

Nevertheless, Heskeths are still being built to order on the Hesketh estate, by former employee Mick Broome.

HESS • Germany 1925

Made by a Darmstadt machine factory, the Hess was a 799cc air-cooled four-cylinder in-line motorcycle; the only such design ever made in Germany. Production was on a limited scale only.

HESSRAD • Germany 1923–1925

Single-cylinder sv machines with own 297cc and 347cc engines, built on a limited scale.

HEXE • Germany 1923–1925

Producer of bicycle attachment engines and of 142cc and 269cc two-stroke motorcycles. The last model was a 346cc sv single with belt drive.

HIEKEL • Germany 1925–1932

Only a single model was ever made by Hiekel. It was a sturdily built 348cc single-cylinder three-port two-stroke with a strong triangular frame, which provided a low saddle position.

HIGHLAND • Sweden 1997–

A company formed by a group of Swedish motorcycle enthusiasts. Its first bike, which started production in 1998, is a trail bike called the 950 V2 Outback, powered by a 950cc fuel injected 60-degree V-twin producing up to 100bhp. The motor was originally developed by Folen for another company which failed to reach production readiness, and was then further developed by Highland. Other machines are planned, including a supermoto-style machine and a 1200cc café racer.

950cc Highland 950 V2 Outback (dohc eight-valve, liquid-cooled 60 degree V-twin) 1999

HILAMAN • America 1906–late 1910s

Produced ioe single-cylinder and in 1912 also V-twin models with strong frames. Had a good reputation.

HILDEBRAND & WOLFMÜLLER • Germany 1894–1897

This was the first motorcycle built in the world on commercial lines. It was also the first two-wheeled machine called a Motorrad, or motorcycle. Heinrich Hildebrand and Alois Wolfmüller created it together with Hans Geisenhof, a clever mechanic. The Munich-based factory soon had five branch factories in Munich, but luck was not with them. After less than four years, the production of the Hildebrand & Wolfmüller had to be stopped forever. Although this factory ceased development and became uncompetitive, other factories - especially Werner in France - went on developing motorcycles. The number of machines made by Hildebrand & Wolfmüller is not known exactly. Some sources claim there were 2000 made; others say there were no more than 800 produced.

The Hildebrand & Wolfmüller had a low frame made from steel tubes and a horizontal four-stroke twin-cylinder engine, which developed 2·5hp at 240rpm. With a 90mm bore and 117mm stroke, it had a capacity of 1488cc. The connecting rods of both cylinders were connected directly to the rear wheel, which also acted as

the flywheel. Rubber bands assisted the rods in returning while the rear mudguard housed the radiator for water cooling the engine. Total loss lubrication, hot tube glow ignition and a surface carburetor were other features of this design.

Mr. Moritz Schulte bought such a machine in 1895 and took it to England, where it created great interest. A few years afterwards, Schulte became a director of Triumph at Coventry, but by then the original Hildebrand & Wolfmüller design was a thing of the past. Heinrich Hildebrand designed more engines in later years, but never regained the fame which he had with his original motorcycle.

HINDE • The Netherlands c1900–1938

Pioneer who used 2hp De Dion engines in his first motorcycles. After an interruption of many years, the reorganised factory built in the second half of the 1930s 98cc and 118cc two-stroke machines with Ilo engines.

HIRANO • Japan 1952–1961

Mini-scooter producer, which used 49cc and 78cc two-stroke engines. The motorcycle production included models with 123cc and 173cc two-stroke engines.

HIRONDELLE • France 1921–1926

Former arms factory which built motorcycles with 198cc sv and also other engines.

HIRSCH • Germany 1923–1924

Two-stroke machines with own 128cc and DKW 142cc engines. Small production. This was one of the many Berlin-based companies which built two-stroke motorcycles during the 1920s.

HIRTH • Germany 1923–1926

Racing two-strokes with water-cooled double-piston engines, designed for experimental purposes by the famous WW1 pilot and racing car driver Helmut Hirth. The experiments concerned the material 'Electron', used on these comparatively very powerful 144cc singles and 244cc vertical twins. Ridden by Hirth's famous brother Wolf Hirth, by Erwin Gehrung, Karl Fischer and others, these machines won many races. After they ceased racing, the Stuttgart Bosch factory used them for plug-testing purposes.

HIRUNDO • Italy 1950–1951

Limited production of 125cc and 150cc scooters.

HJ • England 1920–1921

Assembled machines which housed 269cc Liberty and Villiers engines.

HJH • Wales 1954–1956

Built in Neath in Wales, the Hulsman motorcycles were of orthodox design and housed 147cc, 197cc and 247cc Villiers two-stroke engines.

HKR • Germany 1925–1926

After a reorganization at Hako, these HRD-like machines became known as HKR, which stood for Hans Korn, Rothenburg. The range of these sporting machines included 348cc and 498cc models with sv and ohv engines made by JAP in London.

HM • Italy 1996–

HM is one of the newest motorcycle manufacturers in Italy, a business venture formed between the country's Honda and Montesa importer with backing from Honda Japan. HM produces a wide range of motocross, enduro and street-legal trail bikes from 50cc through to 500cc. Many look identical to Hondas, but a lot of the smaller 50-60cc schoolboy motocrossers and enduro bikes use different engines and bear HM's own logo on the crankcases.

HMK • Austria 1937–1938

Built in limited numbers, the HMK was a JAP-engined motorcycle built on typical English lines. Production included some sv, but mainly ohv models from 248cc to 594cc with single-cylinder engines.

HMW • Germany 1923–1928

Heavy single-cylinder 3hp machines with HMW's own sv engines.

HMW • Austria 1949–1964

The first product was the 49cc Fuchs bicycle engine. Afterwards a wide range of 49cc two-stroke mopeds and lightweight machines were built. The factory also supplied engines to other manufacturers.

HOBART • England 1901–1923

A big, Coventry-based factory which also supplied engines, frames and other parts to motorcycle assemblers. Built own machines with single-cylinder and V-twin engines, but also used own two-strokes as well as proprietary engines made by Morris, JAP, Villiers and Blackburne. 170cc Hobart two-strokes were popular. The last model built was a 246cc two-stroke with internal flywheel. McKenzie motorcycles also came from the Hobart works.

498cc Hochland (ohv flat twin) 1926

HOCHLAND • Germany 1926–1927

Limited in production numbers, the Hochland, designed by Emslander, was a well-made 496cc flat twin ohv machine.

HOCKLEY • England 1914–1916

As a result of WW1 only a limited number of Hockley machines, with 269cc two-stroke Liberty and Villiers engines, came into being.

HOCO • Germany 1924–1928

Interesting design with a wooden frame and on some models a fully enclosed engine. Nabob supplied 146cc and 246cc two-stroke engines; JAP sv engines of 293cc and 346cc capacity were also fitted.

HODAKA • Japan 1964–1977

When Yamaguchi, once a well-known motorcycle factory, closed down, the American Henry Koepke resumed work in this Negoya-based Japanese factory and called his new machines Hodaka. Main production went to the USA, although he also tried to gain sales in some European markets. Main production concentrated around motocross and enduro machines with 98cc, 123cc and 246cc two-stroke engines. The American importer of Hodaka was the Pacific Basin Trading Co. at Athena, Oregon.

HOENSON • The Netherlands 1953–1955

Bicycle factory, which built good-looking motorcycles with 147cc Sachs and 198cc Ilo single-cylinder two-stroke engines. The last model had the 244cc Ilo twin two-stroke motor.

HOFFMANN • Germany 1949–1954

Produced the Italian Vespa scooter under license for Germany, and in addition two-stroke motorcycles with Sachs and Ilo engines from 98cc to 247cc. Richard

490cc HMK (ohv JAP) 1938

2³/₄hp Hobart (sv) 1904

Küchen, one of the leading German motorcycle designers, created in the early 1950s beautiful BMW-like 246cc and 298cc machines with transverse-mounted horizontally-opposed twin-cylinder ohv unit design engines and shaft drive to the rear wheel. Called Gouverneur, these Hoffmann machines were of clean and up-to-date design with telescopic forks and plunger-type rear suspension. They were quite expensive to produce and the motorcycle market was not good at the time.

HOLDEN • England 1898–1903

Designed by Colonel H. Capel Holden, this machine had a water-cooled 3hp four-cylinder engine with direct drive to the small rear wheel. Some of these interesting machines are still in existence. Colonel Holden afterwards went to Australia.

246cc Hoffman (ohv flat twin) 1953

HOLLEY • America 1902–late 1910s

One of the first companies in the USA building motorcycles on a commercial basis. The machines had a rearward facing single-cylinder engine of about 2hp which was mounted in a strengthened bicycle frame.

HOLLOWAY • England c1902–1905

Limited number of machines built by Holloway, Shoreham-on-Sea, Sussex.

HOLLY • Australia c1909

Small number of 2³⁄₄hp machines assembled from proprietary parts in Brisbane.

HOLROYD • England 1922

Racing motorcyclist Jack Holroyd built a number of sporting machines with 246cc and 346cc ohv JAP engines, without much success.

HONDA • Japan 1948–

See panel

HONGDU • China 1957–

Started by producing copies of the Soviet M-72 for the Chinese army, then produced Czech Jawa machines for Chinese use. In the 1970s made a variety of machines, all based on eastern bloc designs, for the Chinese postal service.

Now produces lightweight motorcycles and scooters, most based on older Japanese designs, some with engines supplied directly from Japan.

HOOCK • Germany 1926–1928

Hoock & Co. of Cologne was the importer of English Villiers engines and built the 342cc single-cylinder three-port version into its own frames. Not many were made.

3hp Holden (first 4-cylinder machine built) 1897

HOREX • Germany 1923–

See panel

HORSY • France 1952–1953

Scooter with a 83cc two-stroke engine, made by a small factory.

HOSK • Japan 1953–early 1960s

Produced 123cc two-strokes, 248cc and 348cc ohv singles as well as 498cc vertical twins, which were not unlike the German Horex motorcycles.

HOSKISON • England 1919–1922

Assembler whose range consisted of three basic models, with 269cc Villiers, 292cc Union and 497cc sv Blackburne-engines. Small output and orthodox open frames. Like the Villiers, the Union was also a three-port two-stroke.

HOWARD • England 1905–1907

Interesting 2.5hp single, because the designer used fuel injection instead of a carburetor.

H&R (R&H) • England 1922–1925

A simple 147cc Villiers-engined two-stroke, hailing from Coventry. The H&R stood for Hailstone and Ravenhall, which occasionally became Ravenhall and Hailstone.

H&R • Germany 1921–1925

This H&R stood for Hartmann and Richter, the original name for Heros motorcycles which had its own 155cc, 185cc and 249cc sv engines.

HRD • England 1924–1950

See panel

HRD • Italy 1980–

Sporting machines with 49cc and 79cc two-strokes.

HT • England 1920–1922

Scooter-like design with two seats and with leaf rear suspension. Used first 292cc Union two-stroke, afterwards 346cc Barr & Stroud sleeve-valve engines. The engines were fully enclosed. The production was on a limited scale.

123cc Hodaka (two-stroke) 1974

HONDA • Japan 1948–

The 40-year-old Soichiro Honda already had one successful career behind him, having sold his piston ring manufacturing business just after WW2, which left him at a loose end in 1946. More as a hobby than anything else, he began converting surplus army two-stroke engines to power bicycles and the ready sale of these led him to design a motorcycle of his own. In 1948 the Honda Motor Co Ltd was incorporated; by 1950, production of the 98cc model D two-stroke was over 3,500. Honda's Model E was his first four-stroke. It had a pressed steel frame, telescopic front forks, and a 5.5hp, 150cc ohv engine. In 1953 Honda produced 32,000 of this model - very profitably. At the urging of financial partner Takeo Fujisawa (who steered the infant Honda Co through some difficult times), that profit was almost entirely ploughed back into the developing business.

In 1954 Honda and Fujisawa, who had decided that the company had to export or die, visited Europe. Grasping the advertising possibilities of racing they attended the 1954 TT in the Isle of Man and were overwhelmed by what they saw. In particular Honda was deeply impressed by the 125cc and 250cc NSU team, which won both its races (NSU was double world champion that year) and which displayed remarkable organisation and efficiency. 'I decided there and then that when Honda went racing that was how we too would do it, and that those were the sort of results that we, too, would obtain,' he later commented.

Starting in 1959 when Honda 125cc twins won the team prize in the TT, Honda was indeed obtaining `those sort of results' by 1961; between then and 1967, the company won every class in the TT - 18 victories in all - and had 16 world championships to its credit. Honda riders in those years included Tom Phillis, Tommy Robb, Mike Hailwood, Luigi Taveri, Ralph Bryans, and Jim Redman.

Other makers had won racing fame without parallel successful sales of road machines, but Honda combined the two. Its early 1960s road bikes were as strikingly different as its twin-, four-, five- and six-cylinder racers. The 125cc twin Benly and 250cc twin Dream had sturdy ohc engines that ran at very high rpm and produced remarkable power with very quiet exhausts. Pressed steel frames were used, while some models had electric starting.

Honda used clever advertising, and insisted on the competence of its sales outlets - a major reason for its success. Its 50cc Cub *f* and later 70cc and 90cc variants of this little 'step through' - achieved a market breakthrough rarely achieved before or since. Within a year of the Cub's introduction in 1959, nearly 170,000 had been sold. By the mid-1960s, Honda production of all models was 130,000 per month, and by the 1990s more than 23million had been built, making this the most successful vehicle in the world of any type.

The first hint of a challenge to British big bikes was the CB450 vertical twin of 1965, but neither it nor the later, larger CB500 were really successful, and British manufacturers gave a premature sigh of relief. But in 1969 the stunning CB750 Four appeared, a magnificently-styled machine with its transverse four-cylinder ohc engine, with four carburetors, a disk front brake and, of course, electric starting. The CB750 moved motorcycling into a new dimension. It was made in thousands, where British bikes were made only in hundreds, and it cut the heart out of the ailing British industry. Honda never looked back, even though Soichiro Honda and Takeo Fujisawa both retired at the end of 1973.

The next two decades saw a constant flow of innovation, always backed up by a range of down-to-earth reliable models for basic transportation. 1971 saw the delightful CB500 four and 1975 the CB400 Four. The

98cc Honda D-type (two-stroke) 1947

146cc Honda 3E-type (ohv single) 1953

246cc Honda Dream (ohc) 1960

same year, the then incredible 1000cc flat four, water-cooled, shaft-drive Gold Wing appeared. Ironically as it turned out, the Gold Wing was first intended to be a sports bike, but over successive years grew bodywork and then another two cylinders to become the GL1500, the ultimate in luxury touring machines.

While it generated something of a cult following in Europe, sales have always been small, although in the USA where it is now built the bike is an enormous success.

A more real-world machine was the CX500 of 1978, which grew into the CX650, CX650 Turbo and Gold Wing-style Silver Wing. Honda's versatility and imagination at the time was demonstrated by the introduction the same year of the six-cylinder CBX1000, with the transverse engine displaying six chromed exhaust pipes unhindered by frame downtubes.

This, and the Gold Wing, were made in Maryville, Ohio, in a new US factory, and by this time Honda had set up plants in Belgium, Taiwan, Thailand, Mexico and Brazil. These were followed by factories in Italy, Spain, Pakistan and China, with a major research and development center in Germany.

But the pace at which Honda was introducing new models, such as the double ohc CB900 sports bike, its CB750 derivative, CBX550, CB250RS single, CB250/400 T and then N Superdream models, was becoming too fast, even for Honda's massive research and development resources to keep up with, and the reliability of many machines suffered as a result. In particular, problems with camchains and camchain tensioners persisted for much of the early eighties, but Honda's reputation for good reliability was so deeply ingrained that amazingly it failed to be seriously dented.

The motivation for this breathless development pace was a declaration by Yamaha to become the world's number one manufacturer, a position Honda decided to defend fiercely.

Perhaps the worst example of rushed development was the V-four, shaft driven VF750 of 1982, intended by Honda to start a whole series of V-fours which would take over from the almost universal in-line layout. The bike suffered from camshaft, camchain and shaft drive problems, among many others, and ironically as a result, with Honda aiming to repair its reputation, led to the unveiling of the VFR750 in 1986. This is now considered a modern classic for its unsurpassed ability as an all-rounder, but more important at the time, it was soon known for its astonishing reliability. This in turn led to a racing classic, mentioned below, the RC30 of 1988.

Parallel to the frantic road bike development was a breathtakingly ambitious racing program, although it was far from successful. After a 10 year abeyance, Honda made a disastrous return to racing in 1979 with the infamous 32-valve, oval-piston four-stroke V-four NR500, a brave but perhaps Quixotic rage against the contemporary technological trend, as two-strokes had totally dominated GP racing since the early 1970s.

One of Honda's few outright failures, this exotic creation nevertheless garnered Honda plenty of cutting-edge four-stroke technology, which would later be incorporated into various road and race models, in particular the costly NR750 endurance racer and NR750 road bike. This was introduced in 1992 costing around six times a typical big capacity sports machine, and the majority ended up in collections rather than on the roads. To many, the bike appeared to be just a face-saving device to justify the whole oval-piston engine program, but aspects of its design inspired many bikes that followed, including possibly the Ducati 916 with its underseat exhaust, single-sided swingarm and narrow, twin headlights.

Unfortunately, Honda's hopes of further employing its oval-piston technology in racing circles were dashed when the FIM effectively banned oval pistons from

161cc Honda CB160 (ohc) 1965

competition, fearing this complex technology would dramatically escalate costs.

The NR (cruelly nicknamed the 'Never Ready' by the world's media) was replaced in 1982 by the two-stroke NS500 triple, which American Freddie Spencer rode to the following year's 500 World Championship. The NS was also different from the mainstream, since the opposition was made up entirely of four-cylinder machines. But by 1984 Honda was aware it too needed a more powerful 500 and unleashed its NSR500 V-four, with which Spencer took another crown in 1985 and which Australian Wayne Gardner used to win the 1987 title. Another Australian, Mick Doohan, had immense success on the NSR, winning more than 50 grands prix and five back-to-back titles from 1994-1998. He was still racing successfully on the NSR at the start of 1999, until a nasty leg injury took him out of the championship. During the period 1984-1998 the NSR won eight world championships and more than 100 grands prix.

Honda returned to 250 grands prix with a full-factory bike in 1985, its first attack on the 250 world title since Mike Hailwood won the 1967 series. Spencer rode the 'little brother' NSR250 to overall victory, becoming the only man in history to win simultaneous 500 and 250 titles. Over the next 12 seasons the factory won another six 250 world championships (Toni Mang 1987, Sito Pons 1988 and 1989, Luca Cadalora 1991 and 1992, Max Biaggi 1997).

Meanwhile, Honda first entered off-road competition seriously in the mid-70's and by the end of the decade, Englishman Graham Noyce had put it on the map here too with victory in the 1979 World 500cc Championship. Throughout the 1980s, the factory's CR500 two-stroke completely dominated the class, winning every 500cc world championship bar one from 1979 to 1994, when HRC - Honda's racing division - pulled its support and placed it in the more popular 250cc class.

49cc Honda C50 Cub (ohc) 1976

736cc Honda CB750-K6 (ohc four-cylinder) 1976

Honda, which has to date won 22 world motocross titles plus four world trials championships (1982-1984 and 1986) with Belgium's Eddy Lejeune, now focuses its development on the 125cc and 250cc classes, although the production 500cc two-stroke is still made in limited numbers.

With the 500cc motocross class moving more towards a four-stroke only series, Honda is currently working on a machine that is based around the long-established four-stroke enduro XR model.

Away from the two-stroke dominated grand prix and off-road arenas, the new range of V-four machines dominated the mid 1980s US Superbike scene in the hands of flamboyant Fred Merkel. In 1987, future 500

world champion Wayne Rainey took the crown on the VF's successor, the VFR750. In 1988 the remarkable RC30 V-four, a 'homologation special' for the new World Superbike championship, won the title for the first two years, ridden by Merkel.

The RC30 was phased out at the end of 1993 and replaced by the similar, but less successful RC45. Honda raced this new V-four 750 for four seasons before regaining the title in 1997 with another American, John Kocinski. For the 2000 season, however, Honda was planning to replace or supplement the RC45 with a V-twin machine based on its VTR1000 Firestorm road bike. In the WSB rule book V-twins enjoy a 250cc capacity advantage over four-cylinder bikes, and this benefit has

helped Ducati's V-twins dominate the series from the early 1990s.

Endurance racing has long been of great importance to Honda, for this most gruelling of motorsports emphasises a machine's reliability as well as its outright speed. The factory entered the FIM coupé d'endurance series for the first time in 1976, won every round with its 941cc four and continued to dominate the long-distance scene for the next five years.

Its V-four machines also won huge success in endurance and other international events - the legendary RVF750 (a Formula One-spec machine based around the VF750 and then VFR750 engines) taking the world title in 1984, 1985, 1986, 1989 and 1990. In 1994 the

999cc Honda GL1000 GoldWing (ohc liquid-cooled flat four) 1976

408cc Honda CB400F (ohc four-cylinder) 1976

124cc Honda CG125 (ohc single) 1976

198cc Honda CB200 (ohc twin) 1976

series switched from Formula One to Superbike regulations and the RC45 took the crown in 1995 and 1998. All but one of these titles were won with bikes and machines entered by Honda France, endurance racing being, above all, a French sport.

Honda, the last Japanese manufacturer to continue high-profile involvement in the infamous Isle of Man TT races, has dominated the Island's prestigious Formula One TT pretty much since it was introduced in 1977, winning all but two events up to 1998, initially with its in-line fours, then with its V-fours.

Meanwhile, something of a regrouping was taking place with the road bike models. New model development slowed so quality and reliability could be concentrated on, and Honda backed down from producing a flagship sports bike, apparently concerned such bikes might promote punitive legislation from concerned governments. So in 1987 its new 600cc and 1000cc fours were both designed as all-rounders, noted for their fully enclosing bodywork. The CBR1000F was moderately successful, but the CBR600F became yet another Honda classic, ironically noted as much for its leading-edge

748cc Honda CB750 F2 (dohc four-cylinder) 1982

493cc Honda CX500 (liquid-cooled ohc V-twin) 1982

Honda VF500F (dohc liquid-cooled V-four) 1985

sports ability as well as its highly capable touring and commuting abilities. The 600 was uprated several times, and has topped the 600 class consistently since then. The 1999 machine is entirely new again, but still follows the same philosophy and basic style.

The sports bike market remained strong, however, and mindful of missing out, at the end of the 1980s Honda began work on a new sports bike. The result, the CBR900RR of 1992, was an instant major success, redefining the parameters for the class with its ultra light dry weight of 408lb (185kg) matched to 122bhp power output, and pointed out a new direction for sports machines. This too was revised, and remained the definitive machine of its type until the Yamaha R1 of 1998.

Honda's mission to cover every class of machine has resulted in a wide variety of models. The most notable include the ST1100 Pan European of 1989, the 176mph CBR1100XX Blackbird of 1996 which took over from Kawasaki's ZZ-R1100 as the fastest production motorcycle until Suzuki's GSX1300R Hayabusa of 1999. With an eye on Ducati's success, Honda produced the VTR1000 Firestorm in 1997, a 1000cc V-twin in the all-rounder mould of the CBR600, but clearly, also mindfull of a World Superbike spin-off, which, as mentioned above, is likely to debut in 2000. Middleweight off-road machines were also a success, such as the V-twin XRV750 Africa Twin of 1989, single-cylinder NX650 Dominator of 1988 and XL600 Transalp of 1987, all three aimed more at the touring road rider than the true off-road enthusiast, and selling especially well in several continental European countries.

Throughout this period of often glamorous, expensive machines, sales of the Honda Cub continued, until in 1998 it quietly smashed the 21 million barrier, becoming the best selling motor vehicle of any kind in the world.

Just as important, Honda's reputation for high build quality and reliability as well as technological ability barely dipped in the 1980s and currently seems to be firmly established in the public's eye, justifiably so.

124cc Honda CB125T (ohc twin) 1988

447cc Honda CB450 (ohc six-valve twin) 1989

598cc Honda CBR600F (dohc liquid-cooled four-cylinder) 1987

998cc Honda CBR1000F (dohc liquid-cooled four-cylinder) 1987

1520cc Honda GL1500 GoldWing (ohc liquid-cooled flat six) 1998

647cc Honda Revere (ohc liquid-cooled V-twin) 1996

124cc Honda CG125 (ohv single) 1997

HONDA

1084cc Honda ST1100 Pan European (dohc liquid-cooled V-four) 1997

249cc Honda CR250R motocrosser (two-stroke liquid-cooled single) 1997

745cc Honda Shadow (ohc liquid-cooled V-twin) 1995

749cc Honda CB750 (dohc 16-valve four-cylinder) 1996

583cc Honda Transalp (ohc V-twin) 1987

742cc Honda XRV750 Africa Twin (ohc V-twin) 1997

996cc Honda VTR1000 Fire Storm (dohc liquid-cooled 90 degree V-twin) 1997

893cc Honda CBR900RR FireBlade (dohc 16-valve liquid-cooled four-cylinder) 1994

996cc Honda Varadero (dohc liquid-cooled V-twin) 1999

599cc Honda CBR600F (dohc 16-valve liquid four-cylinder) 1999

HONDA

Honda Shadow Custom (ohc liquid-cooled V-twin) 1998

...nda Hornet (dohc 16-valve liquid-cooled four-cylinder) 1998

124cc Honda Foresight (two-stroke single) 1998

1520cc Honda F6C Valkyrie (ohc liquid-cooled flat six) 1998

1137cc Honda CBR1100XX Blackbird (dohc 16-valve, liquid-cooled four-cylinder) 1997

HOREX • Germany 1923–

Built at Bad Homburg, the Horex was for many years a leading make in Germany. Fritz Kleemann, a well-known racing motorist, founded the factory together with his father, whose factory produced glassware under the Rex trade mark. From this name and from the first two letters of Homburg emerged the Horex trade mark. Closely connected with it was the Columbus proprietary engine factory; nearly all Horex motorcycles used these power units, although around 1930 some engines were made under Sturmey-Archer license. In addition, Columbus engines were used by other motorcycle factories including Victoria, AWD, Tornax etc. The first design was the Gnom, a 63cc bicycle attachment, which was fitted in front of the pedalling gear. The first Horex was a good-looking 246cc ohv single, which - ridden by Fritz Kleemann Junior and Phillip Karrer - won many sporting events. Bigger 498cc and 598cc sv and ohv singles and also 198cc, 298cc and 346cc ohv models followed. Hermann Reeb, then chief designer at Bad Homburg,

created in 1932 sensational 598cc and 796cc vertical twins with chain drive to the ohc. This was a technically very advanced design. Some of the bigger versions had their capacity increased to 980cc and competed successfully in the 1000cc sidecar racing class. Karl Braun used a supercharger on such an engine and won many races. Other models, especially 248cc and 498cc versions, ridden by Josef Klein, Franz Islinger and others were successful too and when Tom Bullus rode a 498cc Horex in the 1929 Grand Prix at the Nürburgring, he was leading the race until he had to retire. In the mid-1930s Horex also built 498cc four-valve ohv singles. After 1945, Horex was the first German motorcycle factory to get permission to build a motorcycle of more than 250cc. Some claimed it was because the Kleemanns had close connections with the Americans. At any rate the 349cc Horex Regina, an ohv single, was an excellent machine. There were also 248cc and 398cc versions of it, but none could outsell the 349cc version. It was, after many years, replaced by 248cc and 348cc

Resident singles and 398cc, 448cc and 498cc Imperator vertical twins. All these new models had modern ohv engines. In addition, Horex also produced 348cc and 498cc twin-cylinder double ohc machines for the works team, which included such famous riders as Kurt Mansfeld, Hugo Schmitz, Friedl Schön, Werner Gerber and Bill Petch. The last Horex racing machines were Apfelbeck-designed 348cc vertical dohc twins, ridden by Hans Bartl and Fritz Kläger. Kläger rode together with H. P. Müller, designer Roland Schnell, Georg Braun, Hermann Gablenz, Erwin Aldinger and Robert Zeller. Schnell also designed dohc 248cc, 348cc and 498cc singles which he built in conjunction with Horex. After the name Horex was sold during the late 1970s, new 49cc and 79cc two-strokes with German Sachs engines came into being. There is also the Horex Motorrad GmbH where the well-known designer Friedl Munch built for several years the luxurious 1326cc, 100bhp in-line four Horex 1400 Tl. The price of this hand-built motorcycle in 1982 was approximately £22,000.

792cc Horex Columbus (ohc twin) 1934

349cc Horex Regina Columbus (ohv) 1950

498cc Horex works racer (dohc twin) 1952

HUARI • China 1979–

Large state owned company located in Linyi City in Shandong Province, currently producing around 600,000 machines annually.Part of the Shandong Huari Group Corporation which also produces agricultural equipment, weapons and consumer goods. The Huari range consists of six basic machine types, all light motorcycles or scooters.

HUC • Germany 1924–1925

Designed by Max Hecker of Berlin, the HUC was fitted with 145cc and 172cc DKW two-stroke proprietary engines.

HUCKE-RINNE • Germany 1924–1926

Racing motorcyclist Max Hucke was building frames for 124cc, 174cc and 247cc Rinne engines, which had evaporation cooling.They were fast two-strokes and - ridden by Hucke, Rannacher, Lücke, Michael, Köhler etc. - won many races.

HÜFFER • Germany 1923–1925

An assembler of lightweights, Hüffer fitted engines of capacities from 150cc to 198cc, all bought in units made by DKW, Rapid, Baumi etc.

HULBERT-BRAMLEY • England 1903–1906

Successor to the Booth Motor Company. Produced three-wheelers, lightweights and the Binks-designed 385cc four-cylinder in-line machine.

HULLA • Germany 1925–1932

Fitted mainly DKW two-stroke engines of 173cc, 198cc, 206cc and 298cc into own frames. There was another model which housed the 293cc JAP sv engine. Hulla sales were concentrated in the northern parts of Germany.

HRD • England 1924–1950

Founded by famous racing motorcyclist Howard R. Davis, the company built Massey-designed machines of advanced design. They had 348cc and 490cc sv and mainly ohv JAP engines, a low saddle position and a very sporting appearance. H. R. Davis himself won the 1925 Senior TT and Freddy Dixon the 1927 Junior TT on these machines. In 1928 Bill Humphries of OK-Supreme fame bought HRD but soon sold it again to Phil Vincent, who continued production at Stevenage. In addition to JAP engines, he also used in the following years Villiers, Blackburne and four-valve ohv Python engines of 248cc to 498cc and fitted on all frames his unusual rear suspension. From 1934 onwards, his own high-camshaft 496cc ohv singles and from 1937 his 996cc high-camshaft V-twins were fitted into modern frames. (See also Vincent-HRD.) The original HRD design was copied by many other producers, including Hako.

498cc HRD racer (hc Vincent single) 1934

490cc HRD racer (ohv JAP) 1925

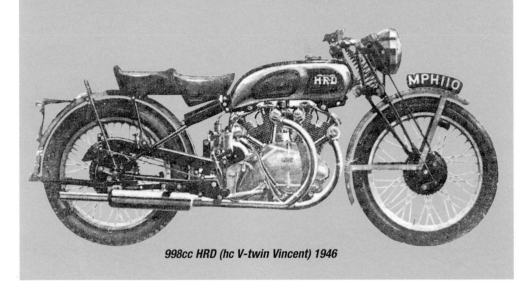
998cc HRD (hc V-twin Vincent) 1946

HULSMANN • The Netherlands 1939–1955

Bicycle factory which fitted for a long period 123cc Villiers engines. During the 1950s, Villiers engined 198cc and 225cc machines were added.`

HUMBER • England 1900–1930

Famous manufacturer of De Dion-engined three-wheelers and of cars, whose first motorcycles were built under Phelon & Moore license with a forward inclined single-cylinder engine. Models of own design had 496cc, 596cc and 746cc sv flat twin engines, of which the 596cc version was built until 1923. Afterwards Humber concentrated on 347cc singles with sv, ohv and ohc. A Humber ridden by P. J. Evans won the 1911 Junior TT.

HUMBLOT • France 1954–1956

Small scooters and cyclemotors using Lavalette and Franco Morini engines.

HUMMEL • Germany 1951–1954

Became known as producer of the Sitta scooter, which had 120cc, 123cc and 149cc Ilo engines. The motorcycles also had 49cc to 248cc Ilo two-stroke engines.

HUNWICK HALLAM • Australia 1998–

Innovative 996cc V-twin racer producing 176bhp called the X1R, with road version projected for production in late 1999. 1172cc V-twin unfaired V-twin called Rage also scheduled for production in 1999. Company is based in Sydney.

HURIKAN • Czechoslovakia 1947–1949

Designed by Jaroslav Vlk, the Hurikan was a luxurious 247cc ohc sports machine of advanced design. Only a few were made.

HURRICANE • Japan late 1950s–1961

Producer of the 90cc and 123cc Rabbit scooters and of motorcycles with two-stroke engines up to 248cc. The biggest model was a 348cc ohv single.

HURTU • France 1903–late 1950s

Once a well-known car factory which built lightweight motorcycles and after WW2 also 49cc attachment engines for bicycles.

HUSAR • Germany 1923–1925

Rear leaf spring suspension was common to all Husar machines. Engines were side-valve singles of 296cc capacity.

HUSQVARNA • Sweden 1903–

See panel

HUY • Germany 1923–1926

The first model made by this firm used the 198cc side-valve single engine built by Alba at Stettin. It won some popularity, although it had a very high riding position and somewhat uncomfortable front springing. Later, an additional model featured a 350cc 100 MAG engine, although in all probability this was made only in limited numbers.

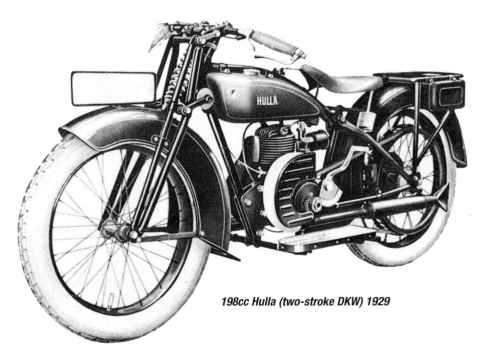
198cc Hulla (two-stroke DKW) 1929

HUSQVARNA • Sweden 1903–

As an industrial conglomerate, Husqvarna was not dependent upon the vagaries of the motorcycle trade for its prosperity, so production was spasmodic, rather than continuous, between 1903, when a proprietary engine was first fitted to a Husqvarna bicycle, and 1986 when the American dealer network and rights to the name were sold to the Italian Cagiva company. In the 1920s most models used JAP engines, although a 735cc ohv V-twin, specifically for sidecar use was designed for 1926, and 500cc versions were made for the ISDT in 1929. These engines were used very successfully for ice and later for road racing, although several excursions to the TT in the 1930s brought indifferent results. Husqvarna's best year was 1934, when Ernie Nott was third on a 350cc version in the Junior race and Stanley Woods made the fastest lap in the Senior before running out of fuel.

The factory then largely switched to making ultra-lightweight two-strokes, and continued along much the same lines after WW2, with 120cc and 150cc models. In the early 1950s, however, Husqvarna began to take trials and motocross seriously, offering special 175cc and 200cc machines that became extremely popular. By 1959, engine capacity was up to 250cc, and rider Rolf Tiblin contested and won the European 250cc Motocross Championship.

Another remarkable achievement followed in 1960 when Husqvarna built a 500cc machine from scratch and won the 500cc championship. However, sales had plunged, and for all its competition successes Husqvarna sold only 420 motorcycles in 1961. Manufacture of road-going motorcycles subsequently halted. Only 250cc competition and off-road models were now made, and a determined effort to sell them in the USA gradually succeeded. In 1962 Torsten Hallman won the World Motocross Championship and Rolf Tiblin the 500cc, although no 500cc machines were on offer to customers.

With some half-hearted excursions into road racing, Husqvarna thereafter concentrated on the off-road and competition market. A development in the 1970s was a 'clutchless' trials bike, followed by a genuinely fully automatic four-speed gearbox. Capacities grew to 360cc and 390cc, then to 430cc. But it is in enduros that the company earned its reputation, taking 13 world titles in 125cc-250cc and sidecar classes since the sport was given its international status in 1990.

Although a specialist in 125cc, 250cc and 500cc two-strokes, the factory pioneered the return of the four-stroke engine in motocross. Today, the TC610 is reckoned to be one of the best four-stroke motocrossers available.

498cc Husqvarna racer (ohv V-twin) 1934

124cc Husqvarna MC12.

354cc Husqvarna Automatic (two-stroke single) 1976

610cc Husqvarna TE6 enduro (four-stroke, liquid-cooled single) 1999

...vo-stroke) 1976

HYOSUNG • Korea 1980–

A firm that has strong technical ties with Suzuki, and produces some smaller Suzuki models for export. Main product lines are 50cc to 150cc custom style motorcycles and scooters, with both two- and four-stroke engines. Hyosung has been developing its own models since 1985, and is now successfully exporting them worldwide.

124cc Hyosung GA125F Cruise II (ohc single) 1999

124cc Hyosung GF125 (ohc single) 1999

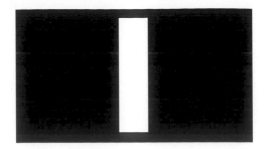

IBIS • Italy 1925–1928

Piazza-engined 173cc sports machines with ohv and an open frame built on English lines.

IDEAL • Germany 1924–1925

Two-strokes with 173cc deflector-type three-port engines of own manufacture.

IDEAL-JAWA • India 1961–

Closely connected with Jawa of Czechoslovakia, the Mysore factory started with the production of 248cc Jawa two-stroke singles, which were known also as 'Jawa-Jezdi'. Other models based on original Jawa designs followed.

IDRA • Italy 1923–1926

Designed by O. Idra, this 123cc ohv engine could be fitted into bicycles and was obtainable also as a complete lightweight with a strengthened bicycle frame.

IDROFLEX • Italy 1949–1954

Unusual 105cc two-stroke engine fitted to the rear swinging arm.

IFA • East Germany 1945–1960

Successor to the pre-war DKW motorcycles and made at the former DKW factory at Zschopau, the name IFA disappeared when it became superseded by the name MZ, which stands for Motorradwerke Zschopau. A nationalised factory, the production concentrated around two-stroke singles from 98cc to 298cc, built in large numbers. Most interesting was a twin-cylinder two-stroke of 346cc, which had the flat twin mounted transversely. It also had shaft final drive. The unique engine had 58mm bore, 65mm stroke and 15bhp at 5000rpm. Not a big output, but at that period everyone was glad to get a motorcycle at all. In addition, the 346cc IFA was comparatively cheap. When IFA disappeared and MZ took over, the only difference on the single-cylinder two-strokes up to 298cc was the badge on the petrol tank. IFA also built air-cooled 123cc and 248cc racing two-strokes. Among riders were such famous names as Petruschke,

342cc Ifa (two-stroke flat twin) 1955

98cc Imme R100 (two-stroke single) 1949

Brehm, Krumpholz, Fügner, Degner, etc. Racing manager was Walter Kaaden, also responsible for part of the development.

ILO • Germany 1923–1925

Famous manufacturer of two-stroke proprietary engines, which also built complete 117cc, 132cc, 147cc and 170cc motorcycles until the demand for engines forced the Pinneberg factory to give up manufacture of frames and other parts.

147cc Ilo (two-stroke) 1923

IMHOLZ • Switzerland 1924–1927

Built 123cc two-strokes, afterwards also 173cc versions with its own two-strokes and 173cc Moser ohv engines. Limited production.

IMME • Germany 1948–1951

Ingenious and very advanced 98cc two-stroke with a very compact egg-shaped single-cylinder two-stroke engine, often referred to as the 'German Hobby Horse'. The basic frame was a tubular steel spine with the engine slung beneath, with a single-sided fork at the front and single-sided rear swingarm, which allowed both wheels to be quickly detachable by undoing just three nuts. Rear suspension was a cantilever design, while the swingarm doubled as exhaust pipe. Before Imme closed down the factory at Immenstadt, Bavaria, Norbert Riedl, the creator of this design, produced a similar 148cc twin-cylinder model, which was made in only small numbers. But many of the Imme's features were later found on other manufacturers' models.

IMN • Italy 1950–1958

Concentrated first on 49cc to 248cc two-strokes, also built ohv machines and failed. It then created a sensational 198cc flat-twin ohv of unit design with shaft drive. This design was not fully developed when it was put on the market, and that was the end of the IMN Rocket.

IMPERIA • Germany 1923–1925

Assembler which fitted 346cc and 496cc JAP engines into open frames. No connection with the other German Imperia.

IMPERIA • Germany 1924–1935

Becker's Imperia factory at Cologne built 247cc and 347cc ohv Blackburne machines and versions with the single-cylinder ohv JAP, but most had Swiss MAG power units of 346cc, 496cc, 596cc, 746cc and 996cc. With the exception of the smallest, all were V-twins with ioe and

678cc Imperia (ohv V-twin JAP) 1929

346cc Imperia (ohv Bark) 1934

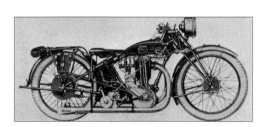

497cc Imperia (ohv MAG) 1928

ohv. Becker went broke in 1926 and the Schrödter family of Bad Godesberg bought Imperia. New models with 498cc single-cylinder double-port MAG ohv engines and 678cc V-twin ohv JAP engines came into being. During the 1930s there were also other models with MAG and Bark engines, but mainly 248cc, 348cc and 498cc four-valve ohv singles with Rudge-built Python proprietary power units. Racing versions ridden by Ernst Loof, A. F. Dom, Wilhelm Schminke, Sebastian Roth, Gerd in der Elst, Otto Kohfink etc. won many races and championships. Dom, born in the Dutch East Indies and formerly with Motosacoche and Standard, was a famous designer and rider. The same was the case with Ernst Loof, the top Imperia rider. In the mid-1930s import of foreign engines into Germany became nearly impossible. As a result, Imperia boss Rolf Schrödter

designed a range of new and very unconventional two-strokes. The first was a 348cc double-piston single with the pistons running in opposite directions and a single plug in the centre. There were two crankcases, one on each side of the cylinder. These were connected by a chain and on top was a supercharger. This air-cooled engine was not fully developed when Imperia ran out of money; the reason for this was too many unconventional features to produce with limited means. These included a 498cc transverse-mounted flat-twin two-stroke with Trilok gearbox and shaft drive as well as 746cc sports and racing cars.

IMPERIAL • England 1901–c1910

Fitted with 3.5hp Coronet engines, these machines had an early kind of disc brake.

IMPERIAL • America 1903–c1910

This was a 444cc single-cylinder machine, of which nothing else is known.

INDIAN • America 1901–

See panel

INDUS • Germany 1924–1927

Fitted with 346cc ohv Kühne engines, 346cc and 490cc ohv JAP engines and the 497cc ohc three-valve Küchen single-cylinder engine, Indus machines were built in limited numbers only. They had front and rear leaf-spring suspension.

INNOCENTI • Italy 1947–1971

Milanese manufacturer of the highly successful Lambretta scooters, as well as mopeds and three wheelers. See Lambretta.

INTRAMOTOR • Italy 1971–1989

Produced a variety of 49cc models with Minarelli two-stroke engines and also 122cc trials and motocross machines.

INVICTA • England 1902–1906

Assembled machines with Minerva and Kelecom engines.

INVICTA • England 1913–1923

Built at the Francis-Barnett factory at Coventry, the Arthur Barnett-designed machines had 269cc Villiers two-stroke engines, other models 499cc sv Abingdon and 346cc and 678cc sv JAP engines.

INVICTA • Italy 1951–1954

Two-strokes with engines from 74cc to 123cc of typical Italian design.

INVINCIBLE • New Zealand 1913

3 1/2hp machine. Sketchy details only.

INVINCIBLE-JAP • Australia 1922–1923

V-twin machines assembled with 700cc and 1000cc JAP engines and American Excelsior front forks, wheels and mudguards.

IRESA • Spain 1956–1959

Small assembler which fitted Spanish-built Villiers engines up to 198cc into own frames.

293cc Invicta (sv JAP) 1921

INDIAN • America 1901–

Although not the USA's first motorcycle concern, Indian was an early pioneer and, for many years, indisputably the country's leading make. Its story started when a successful bicycle manufacturer George M. Hendee commissioned an engine design from toolmaker Oscar Hedström, who was familiar with the De Dion. Hedström's engine, with automatic overhead inlet valve and a spray carburetor, was fitted into a cycle frame forming part of the seat pillar, and driving the rear wheel by chain. Three machines were extensively tested in 1901 and proved notably easy to start and control, due to the excellence of Hedström's carburetor. The next year, 143 Indians were sold and, from then on, progress was swift. The first 600cc V-twin appeared in 1907, it rapidly gained a spring front fork, twistgrip throttle control and an engine shaft shock absorber.

Indian won races and broke records. Its British agent, Billy Wells, entered George Lee Evans in the 1909 TT and Evans led for half the race to finish second. Always with an eye on export sales, Hendee entered four riders for the 1911 Senior TT on the Mountain circuit. In a thrilling race, Indian riders, helped by the new two-speed gearboxes, finished 1-2-3 and Indian's name was made in Europe. In 1912, over 20,000 machines were sold.

By 1914, Indian was offering a 7hp (1000cc) twin with spring frame, electric lights and even electric starting. Unfortunately, with this latter advance Indian had over-reached itself, as the innovation was a disaster. Even more unfortunately, the electric starting controversy had already led Oscar Hedström to leave the company, and indirectly to Hendee himself leaving in 1916. Hedstrom's replacements were Charles Gustafson and C. B. Franklin. Gustafson abandoned Hedström's inlet-over-exhaust-valve layout in favour of side-by-side valves with the 1000cc Powerplus of 1915. Franklin was to design the 600cc sv Scout for 1919. During WW1, Indian supplied 40,000 motorcycles to the US government. In the 1920s Indian consolidated its image with the Scout, the uprated Powerplus, the Chief, and the 1200cc Big Chief. There were also various smaller single-cylinder models, on rather European lines. Racing and record breaking were still important, as was the popular sport of hillclimbing.

Exports to Britain were devastated by tariffs imposed in 1924. Indeed, in the later 1920s, Indian profits were eroded overall by ever-cheaper cars that cost little more than a high-quality motorcycle. Nevertheless, Indian was able to acquire the moribund Ace company, maker of a famous four-cylinder motorcycle in 1927, together with the services of designer Arthur Lemon. Sold at first as the Indian Ace, later as the Indian four, the machine remained in production until 1942. Another new design in 1927 was the first 750cc Franklyn-designed Indian twin, which was to feature more importantly in Class C racing in the 1930s.

In 1930, Indian was taken over by E. P. Du Pont at a particularly difficult time. Production plunged: in 1933, for example, it was down to a miserable 1660 machines. Indeed, although Indian fought hard, the concern never really recovered from these grim depression years. Charles Franklyn died in 1932 and was replaced by Briggs Weaver. One of his early designs was the 750cc Sport Scout, which sold very well and became Indian's mainstay in Class C racing. Even so, Indian was, in the 1930s, running a poor second in sales to Harley-Davidson.

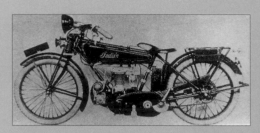

998cc Indian 'Electric Spec' (sv V-twin) 1914

1200cc Indian Big Chief 74 (sv V-twin) 1928

596cc Indian Scout (sv V-twin) 1926

1200cc Indian 4 (ohv in-line four cylinder) 1931

Post-war, Paul Du Pont sold Indian to industrialist Ralph B. Rogers, owner of Torque Engineering. While continuing to make the 1200cc Chief, Rogers instituted the Torque series of European-style singles and twins, designed by Briggs Weaver, that came on the market in 1947.

Unfortunately the Torque models were mechanically so unreliable that they earned themeselves an unenviable reputation. Money was injected into the company by British entrepreneur John Brockhouse, whose Brockhouse Engineering also provided a 250cc side-valve model, the Indian Brave. When Rogers resigned from Indian in 1949, Brockhouse assumed control, but continuing losses meant that in 1953 production in the USA of the 746cc Indian was terminated, the separate Indian Sales Corporation being subsequently sold. But the arm that sold the bikes, the Indian Sales Corporation, was still solvent and owned by Brockhouse who carried on using the network of Indian dealers to sell Royal Enfields and Velocettes with Indian badges.

This wasn't a success, so Brockhouse sold the Sales Corporation to AMC in England, owner of AJS, Matchless and others, which kept the dealer network together but eventually for English badged bikes only.

Then in 1963 a company called Berliner took over importing into America for AMC, and it never used the Indian name to which it still had some right. Meanwhile, Floyd Clymer, who'd originally tried to buy Indian rights from Brockhouse, now built his own Indians, buying engines from Europe and fitting them to frames he commissioned from Italjet in Italy. A few hundred were sold in the late 1960s in America with Indian badges.

In the early seventies Clymer died and his wife sold the now rather dubious Indian rights to a Californian entrepreneur who again imported European bikes rebadged as Indians. In the mid-1970s, he started manufacturing small bikes in Taiwan, all called Indians, but went bust, and the rights went to another Taiwanese company, which also went bust.

In the late 1970s an Indian spare parts business, which had been using the logo for years, claimed the rights, then sold them to the American Moped Association which sold them on to the Derbi Motor Corp, which then did nothing with the name, eventually selling half the rights to Philip Zanghi in 1991. He started selling Indian T-shirts before announcing a new Indian motorcycle and inviting investors to help him produce it, but was jailed for fraud.

Another entrepreneur, Wayne Baughman, decided the Indian name was now up for grabs, so he produced plans for bike production and requests for investors. This venture folded too.

A receiver named Richard Block was appointed in Colorado to sort it out, with the courts assigning all Indian rights to Block to dispose of as he saw fit to benefit the creditors. This arbitrarily overrode another court's decision in 1995 to allocate the Indian rights to Maurits Hayim-Langridge in return for paying off some creditors, but he lost an appeal for reversal.

This left two claimants - both of whom Block said must come up with credible schemes for producing Indian motorcycles - being Canadian Murray Smith whose T-shirt company had been making Indian-badged clothing for years, and Leonard Labriola, who had previously invested heavily in Baughman.

In the end Smith won, not only agreeing to pay $17 million to creditors, but also buying custom bike maker CMC to show he would build Indians, and in 1999 CMC produced a small batch of V-twin Indian-style machines while designs and plans for larger scale production are finalised.

Illustration from Indian Scout 37 brochure of 1926

218cc Indian (ohv) 1949

246cc Indian Brave (sv, Brockhouse-built) 1955

750cc Indian Scout 45 (sv V-twin) 1927

ITALJET • Italy 1966–

Evolved out of Leopoldo Tartarini's Italemmezetta, made from 1958 as a re-styled MZ for Italy. A wide variety of models was produced, from 50cc up to a Triumph 650cc Bonneville-engined road bike called the Grifon, although the concentration was on miniature motorcycles for children, and similar novelties. Attempts to move into more serious manufacture in the 1980s led to financial problems that Tartarini was lucky to overcome. In the early 1990s the firm dabbled with the import and rebadging of Taiwanese Her Chee 50cc scooters, before market growth inspired it to build its own scooter in the 1990s. The retro 50cc Velocifero became something of a fashion icon, while the Formula in 50cc and 125cc twin-cylinder guises became the first production scooter to be fitted with hub-centre steering. By 1999 the scooter range was using engines from Morini, Minarelli, and Piaggio, including the innovative space-framed Dragster model, with a maxi-scooter planned to be powered by 125cc and 250cc Yamaha four-stroke engines. In 2000, Italjet plans to enter 125cc Grand Prix racing with a motorcycle of its own design - the bike, called the Formula 125GP, was undergoing early development in 1999 in European and Italian national racing series. The company also announced plans to build a 900cc unfaired motorcycle powered by a Triumph three-cylinder engine. Like the original Bonneville-powered Italjet, it too will be called the Grifon.

49cc Italjet Velocifero (two-stroke Minarelli) 1997

124cc Italjet Dragster (two-stroke) 1998

746cc Itar (sv flat twin) 1929

IRIS • England 1902–1906

Quite unorthodox machines with 5hp V-twin water-cooled engines. There was also a hand starter and a friction clutch.

IRIS • Italy 1952–1953

Two-stroke machines with German 123cc Ilo engines. Limited production.

IRUNA • Spain 1953–late 1950s

Produced 123cc scooters with its own two-stroke engines.

ISH • Russia 1928–

The oldest Russian factory at Izevsk. Early models had 1200cc V-twin sv and 746cc ohv engines. They were followed by 198cc two-strokes and a Neander-like 498cc ohc machine. From 1938 onwards, the 348cc single-cylinder two-stroke Ish came into being and was built in large numbers. Early models had 18bhp, later ones 25bhp. Alongside this model is the 347cc Jupiter-3 with a twin-cylinder, two-stroke engine, designed on German lines. This engine produces 25bhp at 4600rpm. Another version is the single-cylinder Jupiter Planeta Sport, whose 348cc two-stroke engine has 76mm bore, 75mm stroke and

1090cc Iver-Johnson (sv V-twin) 1914

32bhp at 6500rpm. Top speed is 87·5mph. Ish machines are extremely outdated by western standards.

ISLO • Mexico 1960–1978

Used two-stroke engines built under Sachs licence from 48cc to 248cc. Also supplied Cooper-Islo machines to America.

ISO • Italy 1949–1964

Once a famous producer of luxury cars and also of scooters and motorcycles with its own double-piston two-stroke engines of up to 248cc. Fitted also 123cc and 173cc ohv engines, but a BMW-like 499cc machine with transverse-mounted ohv flat twin never went into quantity production.

ITALA • Italy 1933–1939

Giuseppe Navone's motorcycles were of sound design, but built in limited quantities. As he was importer of French Train proprietary engines, his first models used the 98cc Train two-stroke. Afterwards he used 173cc, 246cc and 346cc Chaise, as well as English 248cc, 348cc and 498cc Python four-valve ohv engines. The Super-Itala had an air-cooled 498cc Chaise four-cylinder engine.

ITALEMMEZETA • Italy 1958–1966

Designed by Leopoldo Tartarini, founder of Italjet, this

machine was really an MZ built on Italian lines with MZ two-stroke engines from 98cc to 248cc.

ITALJET • Italy 1966–

See panel

ITAR • Czechoslovakia 1921–1929

Produced the Zubaty-designed 750cc sv flat twin used by the Czechoslovakian army and also a civilian version. A 350cc single never went into quantity production. For 1928 it switched to 350cc and 500cc sv JAP engines.

ITOM • Italy 1948–1968

Maker of superb 50cc mopeds and lightweight motorcycles. The latter were the backbone of 50cc racing in Britain from 1958 to 1962, but the concern did not keep up with progress.

IVEL • England 1902–c1905

Used De Dion and MMC engines in strengthened bicycle frames.

IVER-JOHNSON • America 1907–1915

Superbly designed singles and V-twins with capacities up to 1090cc. Some models had rear suspension.

IVO LOLA RIBAR • Yugoslavia 1956–1965

Produced Italian 123cc Vespa scooters under licence.

IVY • England 1908–1932

Newman's first machines had Precision, water-cooled Green-Precision and JAP proprietary engines, plus own two-stroke engines of 225cc and 296cc. After 1919 there were also 246cc and 346cc versions with outside flywheels. After an interruption of some years, Ivy returned to motorcycle production with 248cc two-strokes and 293cc JAP-engined sv singles.

IXION • England 1901–1903

Bicycle producer which fitted De Dion, MMC and - according to unconfirmed sources - also French 1.5hp Bichrone two-stroke engines.

IXION • England c1900s–1923

Thke green machines used a variety of engines. Among them were the 670cc Abingdon V-twin, the 499cc and 597cc Precision sv singles and 349cc Precision and 293cc Peco two-strokes. When Ixion closed, New Hudson bought the trade mark.

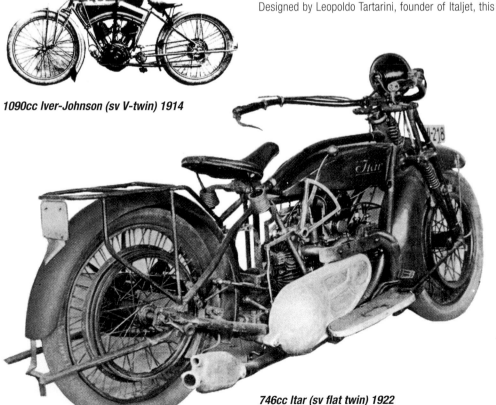

746cc Itar (sv flat twin) 1922

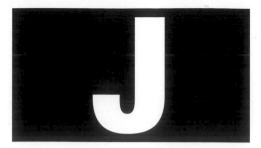

J

JAC • Czechoslovakia 1929–1932

Interesting 498cc single-cylinder sleeve-valve unit-design machine with shaft drive and a welded frame of triangular design, made from pressed steel. Designed by J. A. Cvach, the machine had a leaf-spring fork, a low saddle position and the triangular fuel tank between saddle and gearbox.

JAC • Japan c1928–c1930s

Side-valve 250cc motorcycles designed by Tetsuji Makita and built by the Nippon Car Company.

JACK & HEINZ • USA c1949–1951

Horizontal twin-cylinder two-stroke cycle attachment, also made complete pedal start machines. Jack & Heinz, Bedford, Ohio was a maker of aircraft electrical equipment.

JACKSON • England 1902–1908

Horsham, Sussex-based firm founded by George Jackson in 1890 which progressed from cycle hire in the 1890s to building cycles then motorcycles in moderate numbers, using Minerva and Fafnir engines. These were called Jackson Specials.

JACKSON-ROTRAX • England 1949–1966

Speedway machines with 499cc JAP single-cylinder ohv engines, designed and built by former rider Alec Jackson.

JACK SPORT • France 1927–1931

Assembler of motorcycles with 348cc and 498cc sv and ohv engines.

JAK • Germany 1922-1925

Lightweight machines, fitted with 119cc, 142cc and 173cc DKW and 129cc Bekamo engines, which had a charge-pump in the crankcase.

JALE • Germany 1923–1925

Produced air- and water-cooled 170cc two-strokes with deflector-type, three-port engines in limited numbers.

JAMATHI • The Netherlands 1973–1983

Limited manufacture of sporting 49cc two-strokes.

JAMES • England 1902–1964

See panel

JAP • England 1904–1908

Famous as manufacturer of proprietary engine of 123cc

498cc JAC (sleeve valve, shaft drive) 1930

to 1098cc, JAP also built complete motorcycles until 1908, when J. A. Prestwich of Tottenham (London) decided to concentrate on building power units only. After 1945 the engine factory was taken over by Villiers.

JAVON • Germany 1929–1932

Small assembler of JAP-engined motorcycles with 198cc and 498cc single-cylinder sv engines.

JAWA • Czechoslovakia 1929–

See panel

JD • England 1920–1926

Made by Bowden, the JD was a 116cc bicycle attachment engine. It was also supplied with a strengthened bicycle frame.

JE-BE • America late 1950s–late 1960s

German-built 98cc and 123cc two-stroke machines for the US market, with engines made by Fichtel & Sachs. The name stood for Joe Berliner, the importer.

JEAN THOMANN • France 1920–1930

Was part of the Alcyon Group and produced two-strokes of 98cc to 248cc. There was also a 499cc ohv single with a big outside flywheel.

JEECY-VEA • Belgium 1923–1927

Concentrated on producing motorcycles with opposing flat twin engines. These were 498cc ohv and 688cc sv Coventry-Victor power units as well as 746cc sv Watelet engines. The late King Albert of Belgium rode such a machine in the mid-1920s.

JEFFERSON • America 1911–1914

The superb Jefferson was a development of the Perry E. Mack-designed PEM machines. It had its own ohv engines of 499cc (singles) and 998cc (V-twins) a swinging arm fork and rear suspension.

JEHU • England 1901–c1910

Was in the pioneering years a well-known factory. The engines fitted were Minerva, MMC and also of the company's own design and manufacture. They produced 2·25hp, 2·5hp and 3hp.

JELINEK • Czechoslovakia 1904–1907

Produced motorcycles with engines made by Minerva, Orion and Fafnir. These produced from 2·5hp to 5hp.

JES • England 1910–1924

In pre-1914 days was already building 116cc and 189cc ohv machines. In the 1920s, models with 169cc and 247cc two-strokes came into production. There were also 246cc and 498cc sv and ohv singles with Blackburne engines when JES was taken over by Connaught.

JESMO • England 1911–1939

Machines assembled in Hull.

JESMOND • England 1899–1907

One of the pioneers in the motorcycle trade. Fitted De Dion, MMC and Sarolea engines into strengthened bicycle frames.

JFK • Czechoslovakia 1923–1926

Designed by J. F. Koch, this 348cc ohc single was of contemporary design. Koch was also the creator of BD, Praga, Koch and some CZ designs.

JAMES • England 1902–1964

Originally a cycle maker whose first motorcycle used a Minerva engine in a standard cycle frame. This was the work of Frank Kimberley, who was to be with James for the next 53 years, most of them as managing director. In 1908, the concern moved to a new factory at Greet, near Birmingham, where it remained until 1964, and expanded its production accordingly. The Safety James, a P. L. Renouf design with James' own 500cc engine, sold badly, but it was soon offering a lightweight two-stroke, a 500cc V-twin and a 600cc single. Post-WW1, a fire at Greet meant that full production did not start until 1922, but for the rest of the 1920s, James was prominent on the trials scene, with the 500cc V-twin as its prestige model. An ohv model was made in 1930, by which time James also had a range of Villiers two-strokes, based on Frank Baker's designs, which it had acquired. During the early 1930s, the fortunes of the four-strokes declined; by 1935 only two-strokes were being made, including, from 1939, an Autocycle. During WW2 James supplied the Military Lightweight, with Villiers 125cc 9D engine, to the British Army, phasing it in as a civilian model, the ML, after 1945.

In 1951, Kimberley sold James to AMC of Woolwich. In the early 1960s, James used the disastrous AMC Piatti-designed two-stroke engine, as did AMC's other lightweight maker Francis Barnett, which had been moved from Coventry to Greet. An unsuccessful James scooter was another nail in the coffin. AMC fortunes declined and, in 1966, the group - AJS, Matchless, Norton, James and Francis Barnett - was sold to Manganese Bronze Holdings. Norton alone was to be revived.

346cc James (sv) 1923

2³/₄hp James (sv) 1911

498cc James (ohv V-twin) 1929

248cc James Cotswold (two-stroke single)

198cc James Captain (two-stroke) 1957

JAWA • Czechoslovakia 1929–

In 1929 the arms manufacturer Frantisek Janecek of Prague decided to produce motorcycles. He obtained the licence for the German Wanderer design, eventually buying the production machinery for this model and thus entered the motorcycle market with a 498cc, single-cylinder unit-design ohv machine with shaft drive and a pressed steel frame. The leaf-sprung fork was also made from pressed steel. The whole design was expensive to produce and not fully developed when it was bought. There were many teething troubles with the lubrication system, the valve gear and the frame. The name Jawa was a combination of the first two letters of the names Janecek and Wanderer. This model, despite its faults, was quite successful in major trials, including the Scottish Six Days, with riders who included Jaroslav Kaiser, Antonin Vitvar, Franta Brand, Richard Dusil, Zdenek Houska, Robert Uvira and others.

George-William Patchett, the famous English designer, joined the Jawa factory in 1930 and soon created new racing machines with 498cc unit-design ohv engines and chain final drive. In later years they were fitted with separate gearboxes and were followed by 348cc, then 248cc and 173cc models, used exclusively by works riders such as Franta Juhan, Fritz Bardas, Leopold Killmayer, Vàclav Stanislav, Lada Nerad, Josef Pastika, Jiri Bayer, Hermann Gunzenhauser and others. Patchett himself was also a good rider, besides being designer-in-chief. The big 498cc production (ex-Wanderer) model was not a commercial success, but when in 1932

Jawa introduced an attractive 173cc two-stroke with Villiers deflector-type engine and a triangular frame also made from pressed steel, it was immediately a bestseller. These red and yellow machines became very popular; they were comparatively cheap as well as good-looking. Many riders who afterwards became famous started their careers on tuned versions of this little machine. Jawa afterwards built the Villiers engines under licence, while a 246cc two-stroke version of 1934 introduced the Schnürle patent flat-top two-stroke engine as then used by DKW in Germany, also under licence.

Patchett-designed 346cc sv and afterwards ohv models completed the Jawa range in the mid-1930s.

The last pre-war version was the Robot, designed by the famous Czech designer Josef Jozif. This was a 98cc two-stroke model. When the war broke out, Patchett returned to England and concentrated on the design of arms for Enfields and other firms, a job which brought him fame and financial rewards. Jawa at the Prague-Nusle and Tynec factories repaired motorcycles during the war for the German occupants, but Czech designers and other technicians secretly developed new machines for the immediate post-war period under the noses of the Germans. Among them was a highly sophisticated 248cc two-stroke single with unit design, automatic

98cc Jawa Robot (two-stroke) 1938

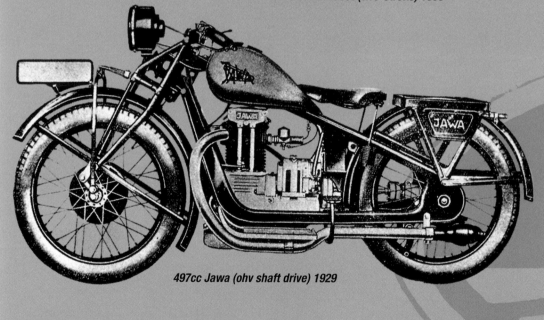

497cc Jawa (ohv shaft drive) 1929

246cc Jawa (two-stroke AU patent engine) 1936

498cc Jawa works racer (dohc twin-cylinder) 1955

174cc Jawa (two-stroke) 1966

343cc Jawa (two-stroke twin-cylinder) 1982

clutch, telescopic fork and plunger-type rear suspension. In 1947 Jawa took over the Ogar factory and added a new 346cc two-stroke twin in a frame identical to the 248cc machine to the range. Vàclav Sklenàr, another Czech designer, created in the same period new 348cc and 498cc supercharged and unsupercharged vertical-twin double ohc racing machines for the works riders. These included again Antonin Vitvar, Richard Dusil, Jan Novotny, Karel Rykr, Ladia Stainer and others. During the 1950s and 1960s, new racing twins came into being. Designers have been Josef Jozif, Jan Krivka and others. These new double ohc models were of 248cc, 348cc and 498cc capacities and in the mid-1950s there

was a 498cc production model with a single ohc vertical twin engine. With Frantisek Stastny and Gustav Havel in the saddle, the 348cc racing twins iwon many road races in the late 1950s and early 1960s. Afterwards Jawa - since 1945 a nationalised factory - built two-stroke machines - including 248cc and 348cc racing versions - only. It also produced very successful trials and motocross machines and, after taking over the Eso factory, very successful 498cc ohv singles for speedway, ice racing and so forth, which were exported worldwide. Even the most famous and successful speedway riders of the 1970s and early 1980s used Jawa machines, such as Barry Briggs and Ivan Mauger.

Jawa took over ESO in 1962 and thereafter produced Jawa-ESO speedway machines in large numbers, exporting them around the world.

In the early 1980s Jawa linked itself more closely to CZ technically, mostly by sharing suppliers, in order to reduce costs, although the two companies were never merged, nor did Jawa own CZ as many believe. Instead, production at Jawa continues of the same machines (whose designs are now so old-fashioned it is impossible to export them to many markets) albeit on a very small scale. The last model to be exported in any serious numbers was a basic two-stroke 350cc twin.

343cc Jawa Blue Style (two-stroke twin-cylinder) 1986

JH • England 1913–1915

Assembled machines with various JAP and 269cc Villiers engines. There was also a model with the 6hp V-twin MAG engine.

JIALING • China 1991–

Produces a selection of mopeds and scooters based on older Japanese designs.

JING GANG SHAN • China 1951–1955

China's first motorcycles were developed at the PLA Beijing No 6 Automotive Works in 1950, very closely based on

the Zündapp K500, and then sold under the Jing Gang Shan name. Around 5000 machines were made until the company was incorporated into the Beijing No.1 Automotive Accessory Factory, when production stopped.

JHC • Germany 1922–1924

Simple 183cc machines with JHC's own three-port, two-stroke engines.

JNU • England 1920–1922

The only model made had a 312cc two-stroke Dalm engine. The production was limited.

JNZ • New Zealand 1960–1975

The JNZ stands for Jawa New Zealand; the machine was built under Jawa licence.

JOERNS • America 1910–1915

Once a well-known motorcycle factory. Built singles and V-twins and fitted two-speed gearboxes. Also produced the 996cc Cyclone, probably the first V-twin ohc machine built in large numbers.

JOHNSON • England 1901–1902

Scunthorpe, Linconshire cycle shop and maker which built

124cc Jialing Trail (ohc single) 1998

six Minerva 1³/₄hp single-cylinder powered machines. One remained unsold and was fitted with a new-for-1902 JAP 293cc four-stroke unit.

JOHNSON • USA 1918–1920

Direct chain drive 175cc horizontally opposed two-stroke twin attachment for fitting to cycle built by the Johnson outboard motor firm of South Bend, Indiana. Also sold as a complete machine. Over 30,000 units were claimed to have been built.

JONGHI • France 1931–1956

Concentrated first on 348cc sv singles, designed by the Italian Giuseppe Remondini, who came to Jonghi from Negas & Ray. His first 348cc ohc machines were made in 1933 and were successful in races. Afterwards he also built 248cc and 173cc ohc versions. Famous Jonghi riders were Jeanin, Perrin, Renier (Senior) and the great Georges Monneret. The factory also built small two-strokes with

Aubier-Dunne engines. In the mid-1930s, Jonghi amalgamated with Prester. Most models built after 1945 had two-stroke engines of 98cc to 248cc. Jonghi machines also broke many long-distance records at the Montlhéry race track.

JOOS • Germany 1900–1907

Machine factory which built engines and later motorcycles, with horizontal twin-cylinder engines. Later models were orthodox singles and V-twins with Fafnir engines.

JOUCLARD • France 1903–1907

Was a machine equipped with 1.5hp and 2.25hp single-cylinder engines.

JOYBIKE • England 1959–1960

This was a cross between a lightweight and a scooter. It was powered by 70cc JAP and 49cc Trojan two-stroke engines.

JP • England 1913–1914

Lightweight, economically built machines with 300cc side-valve TDC engines, marketed as JP Impregnable Motor Cycle by motorcycle accessory dealer John Piggott Ltd, London. Machines were probably built by a contracted engineering company.

JSL • Germany 1923–1925

Lightweights with own 132cc and 180cc as well as 206cc DKW two-stroke three-port deflector-type engines.

JUCKES • England 1910–1926

Very underrated machines, made by a well-known engineering company at Wolverhampton. Produced well-made two-strokes of 269cc, 274cc and 399cc and a 348cc ohv single. All had its own engines and gearboxes; the last version of the four-stroke also had an additional tube on both sides, leading from the bottom of the steering head directly to the rear wheel hub.

116cc JD (two-stroke) 1923

998cc Jefferson (ohv V-twin) 1914

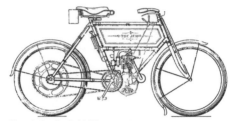

2hp Jehu (sv) 1903

123cc Jonghi (ohv) 1952

198cc Juhö (sv) 1923

JUERGENSEN • Denmark 1904–WW1

One of the first Danish motorcycle factories. Built English Humber machines under licence, which is interesting because these early Humber machines, with the cylinder inclined to the front and forming part of the front down-tube, were themselves made under Phelon & Moore licence.

JUERY • France 1931–1939

Paris-built 346cc and 498cc sv and ohv singles with Chaise as well as own engines.

JUHÖ • Germany 1922–1924

The name came from the manufacturer Julius Hölich. Designed by Leo Falk with own 148cc sv and 195cc two-stroke engines.

JULES • Czechoslovakia 1929–1934

These were 120cc two-stroke bicycle attachment engines and were also sold complete with the Leopold Skrivanek designed Praga bicycles. They had a single leaf spring below the saddle as suspension for the rear wheel. There was no connection between Praga motorcycles and the Jules.

JUNAK • Poland 1956–1964

Made at the former German town of Stettin, the Junak was the only four-stroke machine made after 1945 in Poland. Of sound design, it had its own 247cc and 347cc ohv single-cylinder engine.

JUNCKER • The Netherlands 1932–1935

Basically a bicycle factory, the Dutch firm built a range of two-strokes from 98cc to 198cc with Ilo and Villiers proprietary engines. They used triangular frames on some models, which were so similar to German Europa motorcycle frames that the impression was created that Juncker built them for the Munich company, although there was in fact no connection. After the war Juncker merged with Gazelle, another famous Dutch bicycle factory.

JUNCKER • France 1935–1937

Stainless and Aubier-Dunne two-stroke engines propelled these French-built 98cc, 123cc and 147cc lightweight machines.

JUNIOR • Italy 1924–1935

This Italian machine was made by Edoardo Mascagni, son of the opera composer Pietro Mascagni. Equipped with triangular duplex frames, the Junior housed its own 174cc and 346cc two-stroke engines, later models also 173cc to 499cc sv and ohv JAP and 248cc and 348cc ohv Blackburne engines. The end came when Edoardo Mascagni lost his life with Italian forces in Abyssinia.

JUNO • England 1904

Single-cylinder model offered by the Metropolitan Machinists Company which after a lull in production became the Juno Cycle Co. in 1911.

JUNO • England 1911–1923

Small assembler. When demand rose, it was the Birmingham-based Sun motorcycle factory which supplied the London-based Juno works with frames. Among the engines used were the 269cc Villiers, 597cc Precision and 770cc V-twin JAP. There was also a 147cc Villiers-engined model. If required, Juno was also prepared to supply motorcycles equipped with other proprietary engines.

JUPITER • Russia 1973–

Built in the same factory as the Ish, the Jupiter, created in 1981, uses an old-fashioned 346cc two-stroke two-cylinder engine producing 28bhp. There is an even older and cruder 346cc two-stroke single, which develops 32bhp and which looks like a combination of DKW, Jawa and MZ models.

JUPP • England 1921–1924

The Baker-designed Jupp was a cross between a scooter and a motorcycle. It had an open frame rear suspension and a 269cc Liberty two-stroke engine.

JURISCH • Germany 1926–1930

The designer/producer of this very unorthodox two-stroke was Carl Jurisch, a well-known technician and racing motorist. His own 248cc double-piston twin-cylinder racing machine was water-cooled and supercharged. Jurisch was a two-stroke specialist, who rode many such machines including Bekamo, Puch and DKW.

346cc Juckes (ohv) 1925

246cc Jurisch racer (two-stroke, water-cooled proto.) 1926

KADI • Germany 1924–1930

Small producer of good 198cc sv machines and of 498cc versions with the three-valve ohc Küchen proprietary single-cylinder engine.

KAHENA • Brazil 1989–1994

Produced only one model, a huge touring bike powered by a 1600cc, air-cooled four-cylinder boxer VW Beetle engine.

KANTO • Japan 1957–1960

Was one of the many Japanese factories which produced two-strokes, in this case a 124cc model only.

KAPTEIN • The Netherlands 1938–1951

Was closely connected with the French Motobecane factory and fitted 123cc sv and 173cc ohv Motobecane engines into his machines, which had many other parts from that source.

KARÜ • Germany 1922–1924

Designed by Dr. Karl Rühmer, who was also behind SMW motorcycles, these machines had opposing flat twin engines. One was the 398cc Bosch-Douglas, built by SMW under licence, the other the 492cc BMW flat twin.

KATAKURA • Japan late 1950s–late 1960s

Built a variety of two strokes, including mofas, mopeds etc., of 48cc to 248cc.

KATHO • Germany 1923–1925

Assembler of 198cc sv machines with engines supplied by Alba.

KAUBA • Austria 1953–1955

Scooters with 98cc and 124cc Rotax-Sachs engines, built in limited numbers.

KAWASAKI • Japan 1962–

See panel

KAWATA • Taiwan 1989–

Currently produces an electric scooter called the Swap.

KC • Germany 1921–1924

Designed by the motoring pioneer Fritz Kirchheim, the first KC product was a 105cc rotary-valve two-stroke bicycle engine with 1.2hp at 2100 rpm. Another product by KC which stood for Kirchheim & Co. was a two-stroke flat twin motorcycle of 257cc. Most parts including even the carburetor were made by KC.

KD • England 1903–1904

Marketed by Leo. Ripault & Co. of London the KD (Keller Dorian) featherweight motorcycle was powered by a 1 3/4hp single-cylinder engine with direct belt drive to the back wheel. Also sold as an attachment kit for fitting to sturdy bicycles.

398cc Karü (sv flat twin Bosch-Douglas) 1923

KEEN • America 1936–1944

Produced basic Power Cycle scooters powered by Lauson engines.

KELLER • Switzerland 1930–1932

Equipped with a triangular duplex frame of strong design, the 347cc Keller had its own sv single-cylinder unit-design engine of very clean lines. It could be taken very easily out of the frame and dismantled using very few tools. Even so, the Keller was not very successful.

KEMPTON • England 1921–1922

Lightweight machines and scooters with 124cc ohv engines supplied by ABC.

KENI • Germany 1921–1923

Yet another Berlin-based producer of two-stroke machines. The Kempff-designed machines had 145cc and 158cc deflector-type, three-port engines.

347cc Keller (sv) 1932

KAWASAKI • Japan 1962-

Shozo Kawasaki founded a shipyard in 1878 at Tsukiji, Tokyo, and the company, which later became Kawasaki Heavy Industries, went on to produce a wide range of products from railway rolling stock and engines to aircraft. After WW2 the aircraft division was no longer allowed to produce aircraft, so looked for other suitable engineering products. A subsidiary called Meihatsu (see Meihatsu entry) was formed to produce motorcycles, but these were generally old-fashioned and not developed much by the parent company, which at first saw this as a temporary measure to occupy its factories.

But although Kawasaki was an industrial giant, few people had heard of it and it decided to step up its motorcycle side to enhance the company image. The successful Meguro company was first affiliated then taken over in 1962 (see Meguro entry) and production of the Meguro range (with 50cc to 500cc machines, including a BSA A7 copy) continued while development went ahead.

The all-Kawasaki B8 125cc two-stroke was introduced in 1962, and soon there was a range from 50cc to 250cc, including the disc valve induction 250cc twin 'Samurai', which sold well in the USA. A range of lightweights followed in the 1960s, including several trail bikes (Japan's roads were still not good in more remote regions) such as the 120cc C2SS of 1967 and 175cc Bushwhacker of 1968, and British singles and twins were also copied, including the W1 of 1965 and its later sporting variants, the W1SS, W2SS and W2TT. This was a development of the Meguro K1, itself a copy of the 500cc BSA A7, but the W1 had the capacity enlarged to 624cc, among other changes. Much of the W1 was identical to the original BSA, but Kawasaki used one-piece connecting rods, a built-up crankshaft and roller bearings instead of the English bike's plain bearings. Incidentally, the W1 was to provide the marketing inspiration and some of the styling for the retro W650 of 1999.

Following an internal reorganization in 1969, the first of Kawasaki's three-cylinder air-cooled two-strokes, the 500cc H1, was produced. It became something of a cult motorcycle around the world due to its fearsome straight line performance, but built a reputation (not entirely justified) for dreadful handling, and the fuel consumption was very poor. But its popularity meant the three-cylinder format and the bike's basic styling was extended to 250cc, 350cc and 750cc versions, eventually all called the KH series. The 500cc H1R and 750cc H2R racer versions were extremely successful on the track, both as raced by the factory and as sold to private owners.

Due to impending strict air pollution laws in the USA, Kawasaki planned a new range of four-strokes, but was shocked when Honda unveiled a 750cc four at the 1969 Tokyo Show - that was exactly what it was about to launch itself! Kawasaki's chief designer, Ben Inamura, went back to the drawing board and came up with what has since been called the first real superbike, the 903cc Z1 of 1972, which had the Honda's four exhausts, dohc, electric start and disc brake, plus a then awesome amount of power and very handsome styling. The Z1 won itself a tremendous reputation, establishing Kawasaki as a major contender on the US motorcycle scene. The company still raced the three-cylinder two-strokes, however, and built successful single-cylinder motocross machines.

85cc Kawasaki (two-stroke) 1965

123cc Kawasaki racer (two-stroke) 1966

650cc Kawasaki (dohc four-cylinder) 1980

*748cc Kawasaki H2
(two-stroke three-cylinder) 1972*

650cc Kawasaki Z650 (dohc four-cylinder) 1980

1286cc Kawasaki Z1300 (dohc liquid-cooled transverse six-cylinder) 1979

Notable successes for the three-cylinder 'Green Meanies' (so called because of their vivid green livery) included Mick Grant's Isle of Man wins, in the 1975 Senior TT aboard a 500 triple and in the 1978 Classic TT on a 750, at an average speed of over 112mph. But the KR750 (as it became known) never won the big Daytona 200 race, despite repeated attempts by numerous factory riders. The bike was denied its greatest success in controversial circumstances: American Gary Nixon would have won the 1976 Formula 750 title on his KR750 if the FIM had not discounted the final race following a dispute.

Although Kawasaki has always been best known for its big-bore race bikes, the factory's first world title in fact came in the 125cc class, when British privateer Dave Simmons rode an ex-factory disc-valve twin to the 1969 125 crown.

Kawasaki had always raced what were basically standard road machines, but sprang a surprise in 1975 with an in-line 250cc two-stroke - in effect, two 125cc singles one behind the other. This was not a new idea, (in fact, copied from MZ) and Rotax also built engines on the same principle. The advantage of the layout is that the design of the transfer passages is unrestricted by the need to place the cylinders as close to one another as possible, as on a conventional twin. However, the in-line twin was a disappointment at first, since it suffered from severe vibration. Eventually, this was cured, and Mick Grant rode it in 1977 to good effect. In 1978, it was joined by a bored-out 350cc version which was immediately competitive. South African Kork Ballington rode the bikes to both the 250cc and 350cc world championships in 1978 and 1979 and then German Toni Mang took over the reins, winning the 1980 and 1981 250cc crowns and the 1981 and 1982 350cc titles.

Encouraged by its success in the smaller classes, Kawasaki built a 500cc square-four in 1980, also employing disc valve induction. Ballington was the obvious man to ride the innovative machine, but despite his skill, the bike never matched the success of its smaller brothers and was dropped at the end of the 1982 season, without ever having won a grand prix.

From this point onward Kawasaki switched its attentions to four-stroke racing, reflecting a move to road bikes powered by four-stroke engines. The Z1 inspired a whole dynasty of machines, from the Z900 to Z1000 and then Z1100, all with a reputation for exceptional engine strength and power, although often with less effective handling. But some smaller versions, especially the acclaimed Z650, matched fine engines to good handling chassis. Based on the Z bikes, but with liquid cooling, was the huge Z1300, a six-cylinder machine which really proved to be the end point of a line of development which simply seemed to offer more weight, more power and more of anything else that could be added.

249cc Kawasaki Scorpion 250 (twin-cylinder four-stroke) 1983

738cc Kawasaki Z750LTD (dohc transverse four-cylinder) 1980

738cc Kawasaki GPz750 Turbo (dohc turbocharged four-cylinder) 1984

738cc Kawasaki GPz750 (dohc transverse four-cylinder) 1982

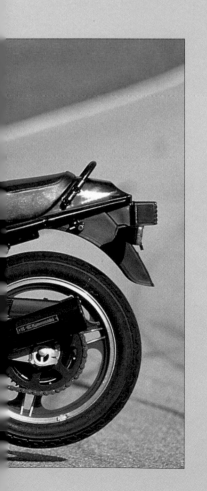

553cc Kawasaki GPz550 (dohc transverse four-cylinder) 1984

Kawasaki

123cc Kawasaki AR125 (two-stroke liquid-cooled single) 1981

592cc Kawasaki GPX600R ((dohc transverse four-cylinder) 1989

738cc Kawasaki GT750 (dohc transverse four-cylinder) 1988

More effective was the GPz range, topped by the GPz1100, which had better handling, but it was in 1984 that Kawasaki released the most influential sports bike of the 1980s, the 908cc GPZ900R, which not only produced a stunning 113bhp from its 16-valve, liquid-cooled engine and had a six-speed gearbox, it handled!

The bike was so right from the beginning, it outlasted several successors, which were the bigger, faster but less agile GPZ1000RX (capable of 160mph), then the even faster ZX-10, with production of the 900R only stopping after the ZZ-R1100 which followed the ZX-10 had been in production for nearly a decade (and had a major revamp). The 173mph ZZ-R1100 proved to be

another classic Kawasaki, holding the mantle of world's fastest motorcycle right up until 1998 when it finally gave way to the Honda Blackbird. Kawasaki will be hoping to regain the title from the Suzuki Hayabusa with a new ZX-12 planned for 2000.

Kawasaki's four-strokes meanwhile took longer to get going on the race track, but as far back as the late 1970s, Reg Pridmore had given an indication of what was to come, dominating three seasons of America's new Superbike class for road-based machines on his Z1000. As the series became established, Kawasaki entered factory-prepared Z1000s, which carried future

997cc Kawasaki GPZ1000RX (dohc transverse four-cylinder) 1986

997cc Kawasaki ZX-10 (dohc transverse four-cylinder) 1988

748cc Kawasaki ZXR750 H1 (dohc transverse four-cylinder) 1990

749cc Kawasaki ZXR750 J1 (dohc transverse four-cylinder) 1991

997cc Kawasaki GTR1000 (dohc transverse four-cylinder) 1986

124cc Kawasaki KMX125 (two-stroke liquid-cooled single) 1986

500 world champion Eddie Lawson to the 1980, 1981 and 1982 titles.

In 1981 and 1982 a French-entered factory team won the endurance world championship with Z1000-based machines, but an unlikely success in the 1983 US Superbike series with a slow but dependable GPz750 (ridden by another future 500 king, Wayne Rainey) was followed by a withdrawal from racing.

Globally, four-stroke racing had been downsized from 1000cc to 750cc, and at the time Kawasaki felt it didn't have machinery which was competitive enoughfor this new class.

The marque did little in roadracing until the 1990s, when its French-based long-distance team returned to endurance racing with the in-line four ZXR750, again painted in the lime-green livery that had made the 'Green Meanie' two-strokes so familiar in the 1970s.

Kawasaki had first made a name for itself in four-stroke racing with endurance machines in the 1970s (entered by Frenchmen Godier and Genoud) and it seemed only natural the factory should return to this now high-profile test of speed and endurance. At the same time Kawasaki began an official assault on the recently introduced World Superbike championship.

599cc Kawasaki ZZ-R600 (dohc transverse four-cylinder) 1990

553cc Kawasaki Zephyr 550 (dohc transverse four-cylinder) 1991

1052cc Kawasaki ZZ-R1100 (dohc transverse four-cylinder) 1991

Kawasaki

899cc Kawasaki ZX-9R Ninja (dohc four) 1994

In 1991 the ZXR won the world endurance crown with Frenchman Alex Vieira, a success repeated by Britons Carl Fogarty and Terry Rymer in 1992, by Frenchman Adrien Morillas in 1994 and Scot Brian Morrison in 1996.

Kawasaki had to wait a little longer for World Superbike success. Hard-riding Australian Rob Phillis took third overall in the 1991 and 1992 series, but it was left to Georgia, USA rider Scott Russell to win the factory's first WSB title in 1993, riding a factory ZXR entered and prepared by moustachioed American Bob Muzzy. Russell finished second in the 1994 championship battle, but the marque's WSB racer, now tagged ZX-7R, has been less competitive in recent years. Californian Doug Chandler overcame that to win a US Superbike double on his Muzzy-prepped bike in 1997 and 1997.

Success in off-road competition took much longer than on the tracks. Although best known now for its range of KX motocrossers and KDX enduro models, Kawasaki's first off-road success came from trials in the late 1960s and early 1970s.

Englishman Don Smith won the European Trials Championship riding a 250cc air-cooled Kawasaki which was later to become the forerunner of a commercially available KT250 production machine. Unfortunately, Kawasaki never did make a great success of trials and pulled its support, and its production machine from sale, to concentrate on the more popular motocross. Yet despite massive factory involvement and a wide range of KX two-stroke motocrossers ranging from children's KX60s to intimidating KX500s, a world number one plate eluded Kawasaki until as recently as 1995, when Belgian Stefan Everts clinched the World 250 Motocross Championship on a production-based two-stroke.

But throughout its history, Kawasaki has been unique among the Japanese factories in producing only

899cc Kawasaki ZX-9R Ninja (dohc liquid-cooled four-cylinder) 1998

enthusiast machines and leaving commuter and utility bikes out of its portfolio.

Kawasaki's range has included some fine motorcycles, such as the exceptional handling ZXR750, developed into the ZX-7R, the ZX-6R super sports 600, and the ZX-9R, although the first ZX-9R of 1994 was criticised in some quarters for poor handling. But no-one could deny the immense power of its engine, and it also marked 20 years of design by Ben Inamura, whose history now included this, the GPZ900R and the first Z1.

Like most manufacturers, Kawasaki's range has expanded into new areas, some being niches created by the Akashi company itself, such as retro bikes inspired by the Zephyr 750 and 550 of 1991. These had styling based on that of the old Z1, and appealed greatly to the older motorcyclists often returning to two wheels after a decade's break or more. Kawasaki has since drawn on other influences from the past, including the Drifter 800 and 1500 machines of 1999 which borrow styling cues from the Indian Chief of the late 1940s and the W650 which mimics 1960s British twins.

But whether it is with custom bikes, sports bikes or more basic machines, Kawasaki's fundamental philosophy is still driven by the original idea of promoting the company generally, and this has also given the company probably the strongest image and customer loyalty of any Japanese brand.

675cc Kawasaki W650 (ohc twin-cylinder) 1999

748cc Kawasaki ZX-7R Ninja (dohc liquid-cooled four-cylinder) 1996

1470cc Kawasaki VN1500 Classic Tourer (ohc V-twin liquid-cooled) 1998

498cc Kawasaki ER-5 (dohc liquid-cooled twin) 1997

347cc Keller (sv) 1932

KENZLER-WAVERLEY • America 1910–1914

Closely connected with Jefferson, Kenzler-Waverley also produced singles and V-twins with its own ohv engines.

KENILWORTH • England 1919–1924

Produced orthodox motorcycles with 293cc single-cylinder sv JAP engines. Another product was a scooter, supplied with various engines including the 143cc ohv Norman, 269cc Villiers and 293cc JAP. They had front and rear suspension and a hand starter. Despite the advanced design sales figures were poor.

KERRY • England 1902–early 1960s

Various sources claim that the first Kerry machines - equipped with Kelecom and FN engines - were made in Belgium for the London-based East London Rubber Co., which sold these machines in England. From 1910 onward Kerrys were made at the Abingdon factory with 499cc sv single-cylinder and 670cc V-twin sv engines. Production finished when WW1 broke out, but entirely different Kerry machines - 49cc mopeds - appeared in the late 1950s.

KERSTEIN • Holland c1932–1934

Tiny 98cc and 147cc two-stroke machines assembled in Rotterdam with Villiers engines and Albion gearbox.

KESTREL • England 1903

Assembled machines with 211cc Minerva and MMC engines.

KG • Germany 1919–1932

Very advanced single-cylinder design by the Krieger brothers and Franz Gnädig. The first models had a 503cc ioe engine, later ones 499cc ohv unit-design engines with shaft drive to the rear wheel. Early models had leaf-spring forks; from 1922 onwards, girder forks were used. At that time the KG was being built by the Cito works of Suhl in Thuringia, which in 1923 became part of the Allright factory at Cologne. When it stopped building motorcycles in 1927 Paul Henkel - formerly with Cito - bought the whole design including the production equipment and moved it to his

works at Mäbendorf near Suhl. So the original KG became the Cito-KG, the Allright-KG and eventually the Henkel-KG, but was after 1927 only a shadow of the major make of the early 1920s. Rudi Albert had it redesigned in 1924 and fitted with a horizontal shaft, but it could not compete with the latest BMW and other designs. Until the mid-1920s these machines gained many successes in sporting events. Leading riders were Max and Oskar Krieger, Hemming, Kniebecke, Faust, Ehrlenbruch, Greifzu, Roggebuck and others. When Allright took over, the Krieger brothers and Gnädig left the factory. The Kriegers afterwards built 'Original Krieger' motorcycles with Blackburne engines, and Gnädig created new 348cc ohv singles, bearing his name and eventually built by the Diamant works.

KH • Belgium c1923

Lightweight 150cc two-stroke with Albion two-speed gearbox and leaf spring suspension assembled by D. Hanlet, Herstal-Liege.

KIEFT • England 1955–1957

Produced small sports and racing cars and sold Hercules (Nuremberg-built) 147cc and 198cc scooters and 197cc two-stroke Sachs-engined motorcycles in England under the Kieft trade mark.

KILEAR • Czechoslovakia 1924–1926

Brno-based machine factory which built 247cc two-stroke machines with three-port, deflector-type engines.

KING • England 1901–1907

Pioneer which built three-wheelers and afterwards motorcycles. Both had De Dion Bouton engines, the motorcycles also Minerva, MMC, DAW, Antoine, Sarolea and other power units.

KING-JAP • Germany 1928–1931

Although built in Germany, most parts - including the 198cc, 346cc, 490cc and 545cc sv and ohv JAP engines - came from England.

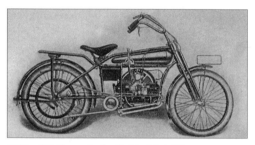

257cc KC (two-stroke flat twin) 1923

145cc Keni (two-stroke) 1923

498cc KG (ohv shaft drive) 1924

KINGSBURY • England 1919–1923

Aircraft engine factory, which after WW1 produced small cars, scooters similar to the Autoped and Krupp and also a 261cc motorcycle with its own engine.

KINGS OWN • England pre–WW1

One of three marques made at 66 Bishops Street, Birmingham. The other two were Frays and Priest.

246cc Klotz (two-stroke) 1925

3hp Komet (two-stroke) 1905

4.2hp KMB (sv) 1923

347cc Koehler-Escoffier (ohv) 1929

497cc Koehler-Escoffier (ohc) 1929

KINGSWAY • England 1921–1923

Motorcycles of simple design with 293cc sv JAP engines.

K&K • Germany 1924–1925

Two-stroke machines with own 170cc and 289cc three-port engines.

KLOTZ • Germany 1923–1926

Excellent 246cc two-stroke three-port deflector-type engines of its own manufacture in contemporary designed frames. Ridden by Gebhardt and others, Klotz machines gained many successes in trials and races. Connected with Klotz was Wilhelm Gutbrod, who after the demise of the Klotz make founded the Standard motorcycle factory.

KM • Germany 1924–1926

Produced 142cc and 159cc two-stroke machines with own three-port engines in limited numbers.

KMB • Germany 1923–1926

Built single-cylinder machines with 4.2hp two-valve and 6hp four-valve engines of own design and manufacture.

KMS • Germany 1922–1924

Interesting 196cc ohv singles with the valves in a sloping position. These engines were of own design and manufacture. A smaller model used the 142cc Grade two-stroke power unit.

KOBAS • Spain 1977–1986

The name given to the racing bikes produced by Antonio Cobas, famous for his pioneering engineering. Possibly best known for being the first to use the aluminum twin spar frame design, which he fitted with a 250cc Rotax two-stroke in 1983. The bike also incorporated rising rate rear suspension, previously only seen on motocross machines.

KÖBO • Germany 1923–1926

Köhler & Bovenkamp at Barmen-Hatzfeld was a well-known factory for chains. Motorcycles made by this company had own 276cc two-stroke engines and never gained the reputation of the chains made by Köbo.

KOCH • Czechoslovakia 1934–1935

When the Praga factory decided to give up manufacture of motorcycles, chief designer J. F. Koch founded his own factory. There he built very advanced 348cc unit-design ohc singles with four-speed gear boxes. Production was on a limited scale.

KOEHLER-ESCOFFIER • France 1912–1957

Designed by Roger Guignet, Koehler-Escoffier machines became famous during the 1920s with a 996cc V-twin which had - as the only machine of this capacity and configuration in the world - an ohc engine of its own design and manufacture. There was also a 498cc ohc single with a sloping cylinder. Other versions had 347cc and 497cc MAG and Chaise single-cylinder ohv engines. There was a great similarity with Monet-Goyon motorcycles, after the MG factory at Macon took over the Guignet works in 1929.

After 1945 Monet Goyon and Koehler-Escoffier motorcycles were near-identical. Most models had 98cc to 248cc Villiers two-stroke engines with J. A. Gregoire rear suspension. Among successful Koehler-Escoffier riders were the famous George Monneret and Jean Eddoura.

KOFA • Germany 1923–1925

Assembled machines with 283cc two-stroke engines.

KOHOUT • Czechoslovakia 1904–1906

Minerva and Fafnir-engined 2.5hp and 2.75hp single-cylinder machines.

KOLIBRI • Germany 1923–1930

A good 110cc two-stroke attachment engine supplied for existing bicycles and also with the firm's own bicycle.

KOMÁR • Poland late 1950s–late 1960s

Nationalised producer of various 48cc two-stroke mopeds.

KOMET • Germany 1902–1905

Originally a bicycle factory, Komet was among the first producers of two-stroke motorcycles in Germany. These engines were made under French Ixion licence and produced from 1hp to 4hp.

KONDOR • Germany 1924–1925

A two-model range which consisted of a 3hp version with an Ideal sv engine and a 3.5hp model, which had a Simplex single-cylinder two-stroke power unit.

KÖNIG • Germany 1972–1976

Built a four-cylinder opposed-piston two-stroke 500cc grand prix racer which debuted at the West German GP in 1972, where it finished an excellent third with Kim Newcombe aboard. The following year the König became the first motorcycle to beat Agostini's MV Agusta at top speed, and it led the world championship until the seventh round. Newcombe eventually finished

129cc Koster KS (two-stroke Bekamo) 1925

second in the championship, but not before winning the Yugoslav Grand Prix.

KOSMOS • Italy 1978–1986

Enduro and motocross machines with 123cc, 246cc, 310cc, 348cc and 480cc single-cylinder Sachs engines, built at Liscate near Milano.

KOSTER (KS) • Germany 1923–1925

Unorthodox lightweight with a frame made partly from pressed steel, partly from tubes. It was supplied with 123cc Bekamo or with 144cc Cockerell engines. The wheels were solid discs, the drives (chain and belt) fully enclosed while the petrol tank formed the top part of the frame.

KOVROVETZ • early 1960s

Was for a few years the leading 123cc and 174cc two-stroke single in Russia. Eventually superseded by the Voskhod.

KR • Germany 1924–1925

Successor to the Karü, the KR also used the old 492cc sv flat-twin BMW proprietary engines; another model was the big 998cc V-twin MAG with ioe valves and a duplex cradle frame.

KR • Germany 1930–1933

Although both KR machines were made in Munich, they had nothing in common. This one was an assembled machine with 198cc sv and ohv as well as 298cc sv engines made by JAP.

KRAMER • Germany 1977–1985

Manufacturer of trials, motocross and enduro models, with Rotax two-stroke engines of between 125cc and 280cc, which competed in the ISDT and later the ISD Enduro with distinction. Even so, falling sales meant an end to production in the mid-1980s.

KRAMER • Italy 1979–

Linked to, but independent of, the German Kramer factory, maker of similar Rotax-engined machines.

KRAMMER • Austria 1926–1929

Vienna-based Rudolf Krammer's first machines had 172cc Villiers two-stroke engines. His 496cc ohv models had the rare single-cylinder Anzani or the MAG engine; the 996cc V-twin versions housed 8-valve Anzani ohv engines. The production was on a limited scale.

KRASNY-OKTOBR • Russia 1930–1934

These were the first motorcycles made in large numbers in Russia. They were not unlike the German DKW machines of that period and had 296cc two-stroke engines.

KRAUSER • Germany 1979–

Best known now for its motorcycle luggage, Krauser also produced a series of BMW-based café racers during the 1980s, and had various racing sucesses in the same decade with 80cc Grand Prix bikes (winning one world championship) and sidecar racing chassis.

KREIDLER • Germany 1951–1982

See panel

KRIEGER (ORIGINAL KRIEGER) • Germany 1925–1926

After the Krieger brothers left the KG factory (taken over by Allright), they founded another motorcycle factory at Suhl in Thuringia, this time with the Original Krieger trademark. With frames very similar to the KG, this new machine had a 347cc sv Blackburne engine, but failed to gain much popularity. Interesting is the fact that the Kriegers also offered their old 499cc ohv single with its shaft drive until 1926, although the machine was made by then at the Allright-owned Cito factory at Suhl. They also produced frames for other companies and a Hamburg company supplied KG frames with various JAP engines.

KROBOTH • Germany 1951–1954

Produced scooters of sound design with 98cc, 147cc and 173cc Sachs two-stroke engines. Was already during the 1920s connected with motorcycles, when he not only raced on Roconova and Gillet-Herstal machines, but when the K&R (Kroboth & Richter) motorcycle was made. In the 1930s he was also behind the design of Favorit and Kroboth light cars.

KRS • Germany 1921–1926

Assembler, which fitted 148cc and 198cc ohv Paqué proprietary engines and also the 293cc Bosch-Douglas flat twin, made under licence by SMW.

KRUPP • Germany 1919–1921

The autoped-like scooters - called at that time Motorläufer in Germany - had 185cc and 198cc engines fitted outside the small front wheel. Producing scooters was not a good proposition then and even the financially strong Krupp group was not in the trade for long.

KSB • Germany 1924–1929

Small, but very active make. Fitted a variety of engines into own frames. These included the 142cc and 173cc DKW, 348cc ohv Kühne, 248cc Blackburne and eventually the 248cc and 490cc sv and ohv JAP single cylinder.

KTM • Austria 1953–

See panel

KUMFURT • England 1914–1916

With frames made under Waigh patents, these machines housed 269cc Villiers and 496cc Precision V-twin engines.

KURIER • Germany 1921–1924

Designed by Curt Hanfland, these 147cc two-stroke engines had square-finned barrels. Hanfland also supplied

KREIDLER • Germany 1951–1982

Concentrated on the production of 50cc machines, including mofas, mopeds etc. As a result of steady development, the motorcycles - equipped with flat two-stroke engines of 40mm bore, 39·7mm stroke and 6·25hp at 8500 rpm - were among the leaders in this class. Some Kreidler frames were made from pressed steel, others tubular steel. Top speed of the Florett was around 53mph. Designed by chief engineer Hilber, Kreidler machines included some very fast 49cc racing machines which have broken world records. Among leading riders were Anscheidt, Kunz (father and son), Rittenberger, Lazzarini, Dîrflinger and other successful men. In 1981 commercial difficulties led to a reorganization and new ownership of Kreidler, but to no avail. In 1982 the factory closed.

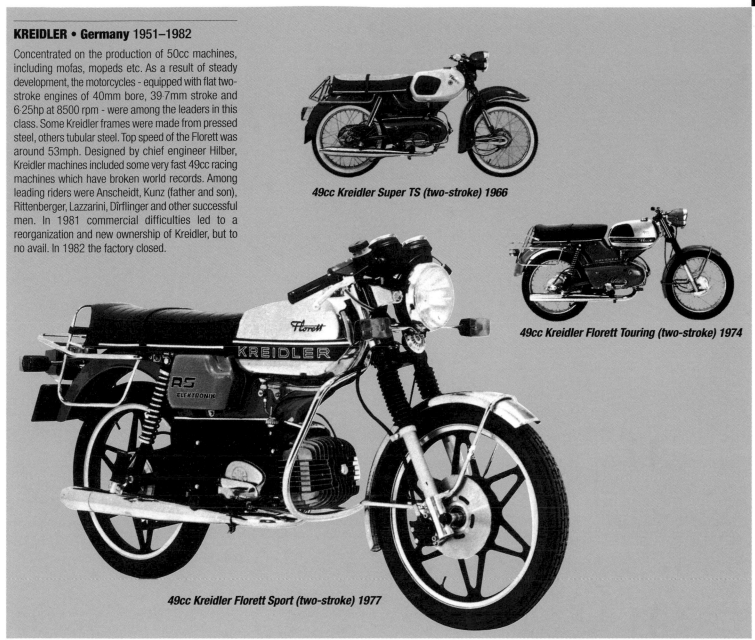

49cc Kreidler Super TS (two-stroke) 1966

49cc Kreidler Florett Touring (two-stroke) 1974

49cc Kreidler Florett Sport (two-stroke) 1977

such engines to other manufacturers, including the Bavarian Flink.

KUROGANE • Japan 1937

1300cc V-twin. Little else known.

KURRAS • Germany 1925–1927

The Kurras sport machines had triangular frames with water-cooled 173cc Bekamo two-stroke engines, which had an additional pumping piston at the bottom of the crankcase. Not many were made.

KV • Germany 1924–1927

Simple ohv machines with own 197cc and 246cc single-cylinder engines.

KYMCO • Taiwan 1963–

The name is an abbreviation of Kwang Yang Motor Company, which manufactures a range of scooters and small motorcycles using its own two- and four-stroke engines, up to 150cc. Started out producing Hondas under licence, but grew fast and now has its own research facilities.

KYNOCH • England 1912–1913

Now an unknown make, but Kynoch was once a famous arms factory at Birmingham. Produced mainly 488cc single-cylinder and 770cc V-twin sv machines with own engines of first class design and quality. Kynoch's Perry Barr factory later housed the Amal carburetor works.

KYRLE • England c1903

Made by G. W. Butcher, Ross-on-Wye who also made and repaired cycles and motors.

KZ • Germany 1924–1925

Assembler, which fitted 198cc sv Alba engines and 348cc ohv engines made by Kühne at Dresden. They were designed by Franz Gnädig, formerly of KG (Krieger-Gnädig) fame.

497cc Krammer (ohv Anzani) 1928

346cc KZ (ohv Kühne) 1925

KTM • Austria 1953–

A make that seemed to spring from nowhere, and, for no particular reason at first, became extremely popular very quickly. Excellent styling was probably the reason, which helped KTM build up a following among younger riders of 50cc machines. Its bikes used 125cc and 150cc Rotax and also Puch and Sachs engines. In the 1960s KTM began serious efforts in trials and motocross, progressing in the 1970s to making its own two-stroke engine and gearbox units, although a number of Rotax engines still featured. In the 1980s KTM became ever more deeply involved in world motocross competition with its typical single-cylinder water-cooled two-stroke machines. Success on the tracks, however, did not bring the rewards that might have been expected - or hoped for. By the end of 1991, KTM's financial situation was such that the company was expected to collapse. A management buy-out rescued the situation, and now the company's future is looking much better, especially since the introduction of the Duke series of supermoto road bikes, in addition to substantial off-road successes (including a massive Paris-Dakar Rallye presence) and work in hand on a big V-twin engine for road and off road use.

49cc KTM Comet (two-stroke Sachs) 1971

49cc KTM Comet GP50RS
(two-stroke) 1977

390cc KTM GS390 (two-stroke) 1982

246cc KTM 250GS (two-stroke) 1

600cc KTM Dukc 2 (ohc liquid-cooled single) 1999

British rider John Deacon on his KTM Rallye in the 1998 Paris-Dakar Rally

L-300 • Russia 1932–

Produced DKW-like 294cc and 346cc two-strokes and - in 1940 - also a 348cc single-cylinder machine. The two-strokes were built in large numbers for the Russian forces.

LABOR • France 1908–1960

One of the many motorcycle factories belonging to the Alcyon group of companies. Labor produced 98cc to 248cc two-strokes and mainly ohv models from 174cc to 498cc.

LAC • England c1896–1906

The London Auto Co. was established in 1896 but didn't begin assembling complete motorcycles until later. LAC claimed to build complete machines around any standard engine.

LACOMBE • France 1948–1949

Basic scooter produced in limited numbers, fitted with 49cc Roussey engine.

LADETTO (LADETTO & BLATTO) • Italy 1923-1932

Like other Italian factories, Ladetto's first machines were 123cc and 173cc two-strokes. After Emilio and Giovanni Ladetto were joined by Angelo Blatto they built potent 173cc sv and ohv models and a 247cc sv machine with own engines. Alfredo Panella won his class in the 1928 Grand Prix of Europe at the Meyrin Circuit in Switzerland, where the 173cc Ladetto & Blatto was extremely fast. Blatto left the Turin-based factory in 1930.

LADIES PACER • England 1914

Built in Guernsey, this open-framed machine housed a 110cc two-stroke engine, made by JES at Gloucester.

LADY • Belgium 1925–1938

Designed by Lambert van Ouwerkerk, these well-made machines had 172cc to 498cc proprietary engines made by Villiers, MAG, Blackburne, JAP and Python (Rudge) and - on some models - as early as 1932 a good rear suspension.

LAFOUR & NOUGIER • France 1927–1936

A variety of engines made by Aubier-Dunne, Chaise, Stainless, Train, Villiers and JAP powered these machines, from 98cc to 498cc capacity.

LAG • Austria 1921–1929

The first products were 118cc and 148cc two-stroke bicycle engines. Afterwards a few JAP engines of 346cc and 490cc were fitted into LAG frames. A 246cc two-stroke came into production in 1925, but from 1927 until the demise of motorcycle manufacture, only a single model with a 346cc two-stroke engine was made by the Liesing factory, sited near Vienna. LAG also fitted these engines to Draisines. A 348cc model with an ohc engine, designed by LAG designer Ludwig Stein, never came into quantity production. The two-strokes had 70mm bore, 90mm stroke, Tiger forks, Sturmey-Archer 3-speed gearboxes and - in the last models - modern saddle tanks.

LA GALBAI • Italy 1921–1925

Equipped with own 276cc, 301cc and 347cc single-cylinder and 492cc V-twin two-stroke engines of own design and manufacture, these machines were not well-known internationally.

LAGONDA • England 1902–1905

The Lagonda factory owner was an American, Wilbur Gunn, who came to England to build motor vehicles. His first products were three wheelers, followed by cars and motorcycles. Most had De Dion, MMC or Minerva engines.

L'ALBA • Italy 1924–1926

Slightly modified German 198cc Alba sv machines, assembled at Milan by Valeri.

L'ALBATROS • France c1904–1906

Cycle manufacturer with offices in Paris which offered single- and twin-cylinder motorcycles as well as making cars.

LA LORRAINE • France 1922–1925

Lightweight machines with own two-stroke engines from 98cc to 248cc.

LAMAUDIÈRE • France 1901–1907

Used big engines and there was even a single-cylinder engine with a capacity of 942cc.

LAMBRETTA • Italy (India) 1946–1998

The Innocenti-built Lambretta was one of the first and most sucessful scooters on the international market. Lambretta scooters began life with 123cc engines, bigger than the great competitor Vespa, and featured an exposed engine and open design. Full bodywork didn't appear until the LC125 (Luxury C) of 1951. In the same year R. Ferri took the 125cc fully enclosed streamliner Lambretta, powered by a supercharged Lambretta LC motor, to a speed of 121mph, which secured the 125cc and 175cc motorcycle flying speed records for many years after. A

497cc Lady (sv Blackburne) 1930

496cc La Mondiale (ohc Chaise) 1928

special racing motorcycle bearing the name Lambretta and designed by the famous Salmaggi was a 248cc transverse-mounted dohc V-twin. Pagani rode it in a few races during the early 1950s. Production of Lambretta scooters was licensed to companies in Spain, France, Germany, India and Argentina.

In 1958 Lambretta introduced the LI series scooter, with a horizontal cylinder layout and enclosed drive chain. In various forms, this two-stroke engine of 125cc to 198cc went on to be the mainstay of the popular models until the brand's demise at the hands of car giant British Leyland, which took over the manufacturer Innocenti in 1971.

The Indian government stepped in to buy all the Lambretta tooling in the early 1970s and set up several manufacturing companies in India. The last survivor, Scooters India Limited, ceased Lambretta production in 1998.

LA MONDIALE • Belgium 1924–1933

These machines had nothing in common with the Italian-built Mondial. Blavier's La Mondiale, built at Brussels, was one of the first machines using a pressed steel frame and fork. The two-stroke engines were of 308cc (75mm x 68mm bore/stroke) and 349cc (75mm x 79mm bore/ stroke); bigger versions used 346cc and 498cc Chaise ohc engines. There was also a 347cc Villiers-engined model and there were JAP-engined 346cc (70mm x 90mm bore/stroke) and 490cc (85.7mm x 85mm bore/stroke) sv and ohv singles. Thanks to triangular frames, La Mondiale machines had a very low saddle position. Among the works riders were Fondu and Schuoppe, who rode 248cc ohv racing machines with JAP engines.

4hp Laurin & Klement Type CCD (sv V-twin) 1904

496cc Lanco (ohv) 1924

LAMPO • Italy 1925–1927

Well-designed lightweight machines with 123cc, 173cc, 198cc and 247cc two-stroke and 173cc ohv engines. The last came from Piazza.

LANCER • England c1904

Minerva, MMC and its own engines powered these 2hp, 2·75hp and 3·5hp machines.

LANCER • Japan 1957–early 1960s

Produced two-stroke machines up to 248cc and built a Lilac-like 248cc V-twin, which was transverse-mounted in the frame and had shaft drive to the rear wheel.

LANCO • Austria 1922–1926

The best-known model built by Lanco was the Josef Wild-designed 496cc machine with its own ohv single-cylinder engine. There was also an sv version and earlier models had 492cc, 746cc and 986cc ioe MAG engines.

LANDI • Italy 1923–1926

Built 122cc and 172cc machines with own two-stroke three-port deflector-type engines.

LANYING • China 1985–

Name used in Europe for Changjiang machines (see Changjiang).

LA PANTHERRE • France 1928–1932

Chiefly assembled orthodox machines with 346cc and 490cc sv and ohv JAP engines.

LA PETITE MOTO • France c1923–1924

Four-stroke lightweight offered either as a single speeder or with gears by Messers Beaufrere, Paris.

LAPIZE • France 1930–1937

Another small but active factory. Fitted different engines, including Aubier-Dunne, LMP, JAP and others into machines from 98cc to 498cc.

3hp Laurin & Klement Type B (sv) 1903

198cc Lambretta GP200 (two-stroke single) 1998

LATSCHA • France 1948–1953

Assembler, which fitted 98cc and 123cc Aubier-Dunne two-stroke engines into own frames.

LAURIN & KLEMENT • Austria (Czechoslovakia) 1899–1908

One of the leading motorcycle factories in the early years, Laurin & Klement produced singles, V-twins and even four-cylinder in-line machines. Some models were water-cooled. The first models had the engine above the front wheel; thereafter a wide variety of engine placements were designed. Famous were the single-cylinder BZ with 2·5hp, L model with 2·75-3hp and BZP model with 2·5hp. The CC model was a V-twin with 3hp and front suspension, the CCD a stronger version with 3·5hp to 4hp and the CCRW was a water-cooled 4·5hp to 5hp machine. The first in-line four was built in 1905. Motorcycle production stopped in 1908 when Laurin & Klement concentrated on car production. The L&K motorcycles - then an Austrian make

- were built in Germany with the Germania trade mark under license. In the mid-1920s, Laurin & Klement was bought by the Skoda works. While producing motorcycles, the factory won many major races with riders including Vondrich, Podsednicek, Toman, Count Kolowrat, Merfeit etc.

L'AVENIR • Belgium 1959–

Producer of 49cc mofas, mopeds etc. with HMW and Sachs engines.

LAVERDA • Italy 1949–

See panel

LAZZATI • Italy 1899–1904

The Milan factory was among the first in Italy producing motorcycles. The De Dion engines were mounted into strengthened bicycle frames.

L&C • London c1904

Small assembler, which fitted De Dion, Minerva and Antoine engines.

LDR • Germany 1922–1925

Designed by Josef Herz, the 548cc sv single was a primitive design, although it had a low saddle position. The engine had an outside flywheel and neither chain was sufficiently enclosed. Early machines had belt drive to the rear wheel.

LEADER • England c1903

Built in Bristol by Eli Clarke.

LEA FRANCIS • England 1911–1926

George Bernard Shaw was a Lea Francis customer. He rode a MAG-engined 592cc ioe V-twin. Other models had 496cc versions of the same make of engine. Until 1920, the Coventry-based car and motorcycle factory also fitted V-twin sv JAP engines - including 746cc power units - into its own frames.

592cc Lea Francis (ioe V-twin MAG) 1923

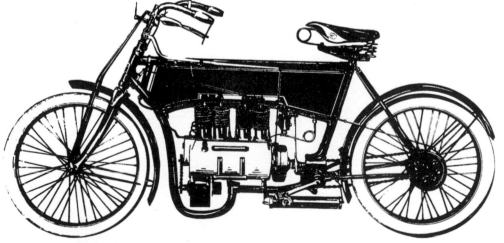

5hp Laurin & Klement Type CCCC II (sv) 1905

4hp Laurin & Klement Type CCD (sv V-twin) 1904

LAVERDA • Italy 1949–

Francesco Laverda made his first 75cc ohv motorcycle entirely on his own and solely for his personal use. Local enthusiasm pushed him into making replicas for sale, and by 1951, 500 had been produced. Entries in the Milan-Taranto road race of 1953 culminated in Laverdas taking the first 14 places in their class! Next came a 100cc model and 50cc and 60cc scooters.

Laverda started in a totally new direction in 1961 with a 200cc ohc twin, but the company's fortunes were really transformed by a brand new 650cc ohc twin, designed by Francesco Laverda's son, Massimo, and launched in 1967. Uprated to 750cc for 1969, these 750GT and GTL twins sold well, and helped found a reputation for the company as a producer of high performance machines. In 1971 the 750 SF1 was introduced, with lighter crank, bigger 36mm carburetors and bigger valves. Its drum brake was superseded by a single disk on the SF2 and twin discs on the SF3, which also had a rear disk and electronic ignition plus cast aluminum wheels.

The SFC of 1974 was an exotic machine designed to homologate Laverda's race endurance bikes - only 500 were built. This had many magnesium components, a tuned engine and lighter frame.

New twins were developed from the SF series, in 1978 appearing as the 497cc Alpina, with its homologation race variant, the fast but fragile Montjuich, arriving the following year.

But it was Laverda's triples which were the most glamorous machines. In 1973 the dohc, 981cc 3C was introduced, which formed the basis of the Jota in 1976, a model created by UK importer Slater Bros which was effectively a tuned 3C. This became one of the classic bikes of the 1970s, due to its 143mph top speed and aggressive good looks. More triples appeared, including

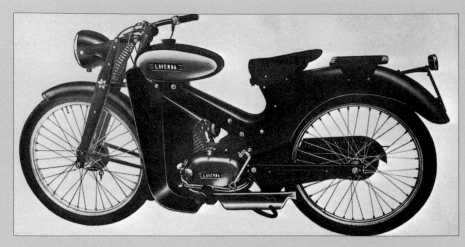

75cc Laverda (ohv) 1951

124cc Laverda Trail (ohc single) 1969

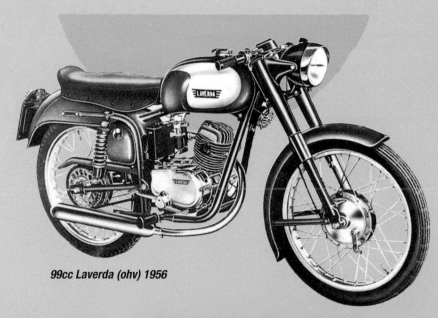

99cc Laverda (ohv) 1956

744cc Laverda 750S (ohc twin) 1969

980cc Laverda (ohc) 1972

1200cc Laverda Mirage (dohc three-cylinder) 1978

981cc Laverda RGS1000 (dohc three-cylinder) 1981

981cc Laverda Jota (dohc triple) 1982

497cc Laverda (dohc twin) 1977

124cc Laverda 125 Lesmo (two-stroke single) 1983

the half-faired RGS1000 of 1983, and the sportier SFC1000 the following year. The bigger engined 1200cc Mirage, which ran from 1978 to 1983 was the touring version of the triple.

Laverda also experimented in 1978 with a very costly V-six for endurance racing, but this proved too fragile - it retired early in its only race, the Bol d'Or.

But Laverda's high prices kept sales low, and the company went into receivership in 1987. A rescue operation in 1989 - without the original Laverda family - only kept the company on the brink of bankruptcy, although a new 650cc twin did undergo some development. Then in 1994 a financial package put together by local entrepreneur Francesco Tognon allowed new investment and a move from the Breganze factory to one of Tognon's then-empty textile factories in nearby Zane, and production of the 650 twin was started. From this were produced many variants in the next five years, including uprated engines which were taken out to 750cc.

Laverda's longer term plans also include a liquid-cooled triple of 900cc, with which the company is hoping to enter World Superbike racing early in the new Millennium.

124cc Laverda 125LB Uno (two-stroke single)

Laverda 600 Atlas (ohc single) 1985

124cc Laverda CU125 Ride (two-stroke single) 1985

748cc Laverda Ghost Strike (dohc twin) 1998

748cc Laverda 750S (dohc twin) 1998

748cc Laverda Formula 750 (dohc twin) 1998

Tradizione e innovazione nella Moto

LEVIS • England 1911–1939

Levis made the first practical lightweight two-stroke motorcycle and led the world in two-stroke development into the 1920s. For many years, it was one of England's leading manufacturers of two-stroke machines. Racing successes included winning the 250cc class of the 1920 Junior TT and the first Lightweight TT, the French and Belgian grands prix -all in 1922. Top Levis riders included Geoff Davidson, R.O. Clark and Phil Pike, among others. Lightweights of first 211cc and then 250cc were very popular in the early 1920s, and sold all over the world. For 1927 Levis designer and development engineer Bob Newey, the brother-in-law of the Butterfield brothers, who owned the company, devised a simple 350cc ohv four-stroke engine that was originally offered in the same frame as the contemporary model O 250cc two-stroke. Although two-strokes continued to be produced, the ohv machines gained in popularity and were made in 250cc, 350cc, 500cc and latterly 600cc versions.

Although never a high volume producer, Levis was highly regarded. However, in 1939, the Butterfield brothers sold the factory to an air compressor manufacturer, the marque coming to an end as a result.

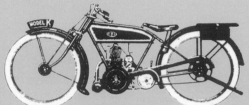

246cc Levis K (two-stroke) 1926

246cc Levis O (two-stroke) 1927

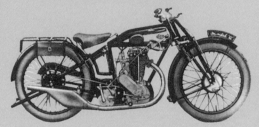

346cc Levis A (ohv) 1928

496cc Levis D-Special (ohv) 1938

Successful Levis rider Percy Hunt on his 346cc machine

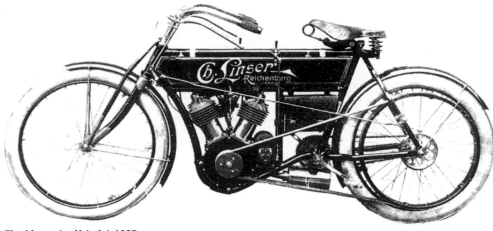

5hp Linser (sv V-twin) 1905

3¹/₂hp Linser (sv) 1905

LEBELT • Germany 1924–1925

Small producer of machines with own 3·8hp two-stroke and 4.6hp sv engines.

LECCE • Italy 1930–1932

Built 173cc ohv machines with modified Swiss-made Moser engines. Otello Albanese, the Lecce boss, modified the cylinder heads to V-valves.

LEFOL • France 1953–1955

Folding Scoot-Air scooter designed to be dropped by parachute, powered by a 98cc Comet engine.

LE FRANCAISE-DIAMANT • France 1912–1959

Another Alcyon-owned motorcycle producer, which built machines from 98cc to 498cc. After the war, only two-strokes up to 248cc were made.

LEGNANO • Italy 1954–

Concentrated on mopeds, mofas and other lightweights with 49cc engines, made mainly by Sachs and Minarelli.

LE GRIMPEUR • France c1900–1932

Produced a variety of machines from 98cc two-strokes to big V-twins with engines made by MAG, JAP, Aubier-Dunne, Stainless, Chaise etc. Another French factory, Dresch bought Le Grimpeur in the late 1920s.

LEIFA • Germany 1924–1925

Lightweights with 148cc sv engines, built by a former shipyard.

LELIOR • France 1922–1924

Built an Evans-like 246cc two-stroke machine and also a 174cc two-stroke flat twin.

LEM • Italy 1974–1983

Produced a range of lightweights and children's motorcycles, using 50cc Morini and Minarelli engines.

LENNOX • Australia c1916–1918

Approximately 12 single- and twin-cylinder machines were made by Robert King, an undertaker of Lennox Street, Richmond, Victoria.

LENOBLE • Belgium 1952

Produced a limited number of Kon-Tiki and Phenix scooters.

LEONARD • England 1903–1906

Small assembler of motorcycles with Minerva, MMC and Fafnir engines.

LEONARDO FRERA • Italy 1930–1934

When Frera founder Corrado Frera retired in 1929 and Emilio Fossio took over the famous factory, young Leonardo Frera became technical director. Two years later he left and founded his own motorcycle works at Tradate. There he built 173cc to 346cc sv and ohv machines with JAP single-cylinder engines.

LEOPARD • Germany 1921–1926

Produced 248cc and 346cc two-strokes with its own engines, and later 248cc and 348cc ohv models.

LEPROTTO • Italy 1951–1954

Well-made two- and four-stroke ohv models of 123cc, 158cc and 198cc capacity.

LETHBRIDGE • England 1922–1923

Small assembler of machines with 247cc and 269cc Villiers two-stroke three-port engines.

LETO • Germany 1926–1928

Interesting design with a frame made of pressed steel, which was welded together and included the petrol tank. Lehmann, the designer, fitted 173cc and 198cc Rinne two-stroke engines into his unusual frames.

LE VACK • England 1923

Famous designer-rider Herbert Le Vack—who was also with JAP, Duzmo, New Hudson, Indian and Motosacoche—built for a short period his own 346cc ohv single-cylinder machines, using JAP engines.

LE VELOMOTOR • France c1922–1923

Two-stroke pedal start autocycle-type machine with own engine built by M. R. Chevillard, Montrogue.

LEVIS • England 1911–1939

See panel

490cc Lloyd (ohv JAP) 1925

LEWIS • Australia 1911–1913

Small factory at Adelaide which used English 546cc single-cylinder water-cooled Precision engines in own simple and open frames.

LFG • Germany 1921–1925

The first product of this former airship manufacturer was a separate small wheel with a 163.5cc sv engine, which could be attached to any bicycle. More unorthodox was a 305cc single-cylinder two-stroke motorcycle, which had an airship-like body.

LGC • England 1926–1932

Made at Birmingham by the Leonard Gundle Motor Co., a manufacturer of delivery three-wheelers, this machine had a very sporting appearance, but was never built in large quantities. Engines fitted were the 247cc Villiers, 293cc sv JAP and both 346cc sv and ohv JAP single-cylinder versions.

LIAUDOIS • France 1923–1927

Assembled machines with Train two-stroke engines from 98cc to 173cc.

LIBERATOR • France 1902–late 1920s

Old producer which fitted mainly Antoine, Saro lea and JAP proprietary engines.

LIBERIA • France 1920–1965

Bicycle factory which produced motorcycles mainly with Aubier-Dunne two-stroke engines from 98cc to 248cc.

LILAC • Japan 1952–1961

Was a leading make and built many expensive and luxurious models. Among them were shaft-driven 246cc flat and transverse-mounted ohv V-twins, 173cc ohv

singles with shaft drive, etc. Lilac also produced 49cc mopeds, mofas, etc.

246cc Lilac (ohv transverse V-twin) 1960

LILIPUT • Germany 1923–1926

In a modest way assembled motorcycles with proprietary engines made by Namapo, DKW, Baumi, Gruhn and others.

LILLIPUT • Italy 1899–c1906

Produced machines with 269cc, 293cc and 499cc engines. Made by Minerva, Villiers and TDC.

LILY • England 1906–1914

Another assembler of motorcycles with 269cc, 293cc and 499cc engines, made by Minerva, Villiers and TDC (Cross).

LINCOLN-ELK • England 1902–1924

Was a well-known make. Designed by James Kirby, pre-WW1 models had his own 402cc and 499cc single-cylinder sv engines. After the war, production concentrated around 349cc and 596cc sv singles and 770cc sv V-twins.

LINER • Japan 1961

Like Lilac, Liner also built quite expensive motorcycles. Among them were 148cc ohv singles and a 246cc vertical twin, which had - like the Sunbeam S7 and S8 models -

one cylinder behind the other. It had an ohc unit-design engine and also shaft drive to the rear wheel.

LINSER • Austria (Czechoslovakia) 1904–1910

Linser motorcycles were also known under the Zeus trade mark. The range consisted of 492cc singles and 618cc V-twins with Linser's own sv power units.

LINSNER • Germany 1922–1924

Assembled flat twin machines with 293cc Bosch-Douglas and 492cc BMW sv proprietary engines.

LINTO • Italy 1965–1968

Designed by the famous Lino Tonti, these 498cc dohc road racing vertical twins were built in very limited numbers. The riders included Alberto Pagani, Jack Findlay, John Dodds and Marszowsky.

LINX • Italy 1929–1941

Made by a small factory, Linx motorcycles were of contemporary design. The engines were 173cc to 598cc sv and ohv singles, made by Blackburne, Piazza, and JAP, and the four-valve Rudge-built Python.

LION-RAPIDE • Belgium 1936–1953

Assembled machines with 98cc to 247cc Villiers and Ilo two-stroke engines and there were also models with the 347cc FN engine.

LITO • Sweden 1959–1965

Produced 498cc ohv motocross machines with modified single-cylinder BSA and Husqvarna engines. One of its own engines, designed by Folke Mannerstedt, had 87mm bore, 83.5mm stroke, 496cc and semi-desmodromic overhead valves The clutch and the declutching mechanism was built into the graduated flywheel.

98cc Lohner Sissy (two-stroke Ilo) 1957

LITTLE GIANT • England 1913–1915

Assembled machines with 225cc two-stroke and 199cc sv single-cylinder Precision engines.

LLOYD • England 1903–1923

Heavy machines, built mainly for use in the former British colonies. The range included 499cc and 497cc singles and 842cc V-twins, all with its own sv engines.

LLOYD • Germany 1922–1926

Produced only a single model, a 144cc two-stroke.

LLOYD • Germany 1923–1926

The first product was an Ottmar Cramer designed 137cc bicycle engine. Bigger machines included 293cc, 346cc and 490cc JAP-engined sv and ohv models of typical English design and with many parts made in England.

LLOYD • The Netherlands 1930–1931

Was closely connected with the German DKW and Hulla factories, which supplied the 198cc two-stroke engine and (Hulla) most of the parts for the frames. The frame was made from pressed steel.

LML • India 1984–

Indian producer of Piaggio Vespa scooters under license in 100cc, 125cc and 150cc forms.

LMP • France 1921–1931

Was really an engine factory which also built JAP engines under license in France. The range of LMP motorcycles included 173cc and 248cc two-strokes and sv and ohv single-cylinder models from 247cc to 497cc. Marc and CP Roleo fitted LMP engines.

LMS • Germany 1923

Another builder of airships which tried to produce unorthodox motorcycles with airship-like bodies. Only a very few machines were built and all of these had 142cc DKW engines before production ceased.

LOCAL • Australia c1909

Small number of 3½hp motorcycles assembled by Brisbane firm from proprietary parts.

LOCOMOTIEF • The Netherlands 1957–early 1960s

Mopeds with 49cc Pluvier and Sachs engines. Successful but little known.

LOHNER • Austria 1950–1958

Produced first class car bodies etc. and also Porsche-designed electric motor vehicles. The scooters had 98cc and 123cc Rotax-Sachs and 198cc Ilo engines.

LOMOS • Germany 1922–1924

Early scooter with a pressed steel frame, made by DKW and afterwards by Eichler of Berlin. A 142cc DKW two-stroke engine was used.

LONDON • England c1903

Forgotten producer, whose machines housed De Dion, Minerva and MMC engines.

LORD • Germany 1929–1931

Despite the English name, a German machine with a 198cc JAP sv engine.

LORENZ • Germany 1921–1922

Another early scooter with a 211cc two-stroke engine which soon disappeared from the market.

LORENZ • Germany 1921–1925

Also kown as the Rapid bicycle attachment engine, the interesting Lorenz was a 126cc two-stroke flat twin. It was also supplied as a complete machine with a strengthened bicycle frame.

LORIOT • France 1927–1930

Bredier & Charon, a French gearbox factory, supplied units which could be attached to existing JAP proprietary engines to provide shaft drive to the rear wheel.

LOT • Poland 1937

Unit-design machine with a 346cc single-cylinder two-stroke engine and shaft drive, built in limited numbers.

LOUIS CLEMENT • France 1920–1932

Limited production of 598cc and 996cc V-twins with Louis Clement's own ohc engines. From 1928 onwards, manufacture concentrated around 98cc two-stroke machines and production of the V-twins ceased.

LOUIS JANIOR • France 1921–1924

Heavy machines with 499cc flat twin sv engines.

LOWTHER • America late 1940s

Lightweight scooters, also sold by Indian under its own name.

LTN • France c1923

A 3hp motorcycle with Nouguier three-speed gearbox and sprung frame built by Lafont and Nouguier, Nimes.

LUBE • Spain 1949–1965

For many years closely connected with NSU of Germany, Louis Bojarano, the head of this Spanish factory, built NSU-engined two- and four-strokes from 49cc to 246cc into his own frames. Only after NSU gave up motorcycle production did Lube build its own two-strokes.

LUCAS • Germany 1923–1924

The first models had the 129cc Bekamo two-stroke engine with pumping cylinder; later ones its own 148cc ohv engines.

LUCER • France 1953–1956

Most models had 173cc AMC ohv engines, others the Aubier-Dunne two-strokes from 98cc to 173cc.

LUCIFER • France 1928–1956

Used a variety of the proprietary engines. These included the 98cc to 246cc two-stroke Train, 248cc to 496cc ohv MAG and Chaise and also the 498cc unit-design ohc Chaise.

LUDOLPH • Germany 1924–1926

Fitted own two-strokes of 247cc and 299cc into simple frames.

LUGTON • England 1912–1914

Limited production of 498cc machines with Precision and JAP engines.

LUMEN • France c1920

Scooters of 143cc, said to be capable of 15mph.

LUPUS • Germany 1923–1926

The Stuttgart-based factory concentrated production on a single model with its own 148cc two-stroke engine.

LUTÈCE • France 1921–1926

Heavy and luxurious 997cc and 1016cc vertical twins with strong duplex frames, built much on American lines. They had shaft drive to the rear wheel. The last model was a 98cc two-stroke with belt drive.

LUTRAU • Germany 1924–1933

A producer of car accessories, whose two-stroke singles had 198cc, 246cc and 346cc engines of own design and manufacture. There was also a 497cc sv single-cylinder model. Designer: Ludwig Traunspurger.

LUTZ • Germany 1949–1954

Produced 48cc and 49cc two-strokes, mainly scooters and mopeds. The last Lutz scooter had a 173cc two-stroke engine.

LUWE • Germany 1924–1928

Designed by Ludwig Weber, the first models had 148cc and 198cc Paqué ohv engines. There was also a version with the 198cc ohc engine made by Paqué. Other models used the 348cc ohv Kühne engine and 348cc to 746cc singles and V-twins made by JAP, MAG and Blackburne.

LWD • Germany 1923–1926

A small factory, which produced 197cc and 247cc sv engines and fitted them into simple tubular frames.

LYLE • England 1912–1913

Small number of machines assembled in Portsmouth using Precision engines.

126cc Lorenz (two-stroke flat twin bicycle engine) 1923

MABECO • Germany 1923–1927

This design was a perfect copy of the American Indian Scout. Built by Max Bernhardt & Co. at Berlin, the engines were really made by Siemens & Halske. They were 596cc and 749cc sv V-twins and in 1925 a 749cc ohv version which in racing trim had four exhaust pipes, was added. Originally green in colour, Mabecos became eventually red like the Indians of that period. This led to difficulties, as the Springfield company went to court. Mabeco was liquidated, but after a change of name from Max Bernhardt & Co. to Mabeco-Werke GmbH, it re-entered motorcycle production, still with the big Siemens & Halske Group as the main shareholder. A few 996cc ohv racing machines and 346cc double-piston single-cylinder two-strokes built under Garelli licence were made too. Mabeco gained many racing successes with such riders as Hermann Rossner, Erich Tennigkeit and others.

MABON • England c1905

Strengthened bicycle frames with MMC, Fafnir and own engines. Limited production.

MABRET • Germany 1927–1928

Small assembler, whose machines had 346cc sv and ohv Kühne engines; a few also the 496cc Kühne sv single.

MACKLUM • England 1920–1922

Scooter-like machines with 292cc Union two-stroke engines. Production was on a limited scale.

MACO • Germany 1921–1926

Produced a variety of DKW-engined two-strokes and also 198cc sv machines with own engines.

MACQUET • France 1951–1954

Two-strokes with 123cc and 174cc, built into modern frames.

MADC • Switzerland 1901–1905

This was the original name for the 215cc Motosacoche bicycle-attachment engines, built by the Dufaux brothers.

MAER • Italy 1978–

One of the many new German producers of 123cc and 246cc motocross, trials and enduro two-strokes.

MAFA • Germany 1923–1927

Bicycle factory which used 119cc to 246cc DKW two-stroke engines as well as the 348cc ohv and 496cc sv single-cylinder Kühne power units.

749cc Mabeco Luxus (sv V-twin) 1927

MAFALDA • Italy 1923–1928

Sporting two-stroke machines with own 123cc and 173cc three-port, deflector-type engines.

MAFFEIS • Italy 1903–1935

Like the Maserati brothers in the racing car field, the Maffeis brothers built and raced their own product. The first Maffeis machines had Belgian 2.25hp Sarolea engines. Maffeis chief Bernardo Maffeis later designed 348cc single-cylinder and also V-twin models, but concentrated during the 1920s on producing machines with 248cc, 348cc and 496cc sv and ohv Blackburne engines.

MAGATY • France 1931–1937

Small assembler of 98cc two-stroke machines with Train and Stainless engines.

MAGDA • France 1933–1936

Small production of 98cc and 123cc two-stroke machines.

MAGNAT-DEBON • France 1906–late 1950s

Was among the leading French makes. Built different V-twins partly with Moto-Rêve engines in pre-1914 days. After WW1 new two-strokes and single-cylinder sv and ohv models to 498cc capacity were built.

The company became part of Terrot in Dijon during the 1930s and had more or less identical models to the Terrot, among them, after 1945, mopeds, scooters and ohv singles up to 499cc with its own single-cylinder power units. Top rider in pre-war days was Paul Boetsch, who joined Terrot together with others when Magnat-Debon was taken over.

749cc Mabeco Sport (ohv V-twin) 1927

4¹/₂hp Magnet (sv V-twin) 1906

MAGNAT-MOSER • France 1906–1914

A Magnat-Debon branch factory which also had a works at Grenoble, that fitted Swiss Moser engines of up to 746cc capacity.

MAGNEET • The Netherlands 1950s to early 1960s

Moped and mofa producer. Used mainly 48cc Sachs two-stroke engines.

MAGNET • Germany 1901–1924

Leading motorcycle producer in pre-1914 days, which also built own ioe and sv engines. Most famous was the 4.5hp V-twin model.

MAICO • Germany 1935–1987

The first pre-WW2 Maicos used 120cc and 145cc Ilo two-stroke engines, but when motorcycle production resumed after the war in 1948, Maico's own 125cc two-stroke took their place. In 1951, the company launched the sensational enclosed Maico Mobil, with a 175cc fan-cooled engine. This was not a scooter, but had many of a scooter's advantages. With more conventional 175cc machinery, Maico took part in the ISDT and similar events successfully, also becoming increasingly involved in motocross. For 1954, there was the 350cc or 400cc two-stroke twin Taifun, with beautifully detailed pressed frame-cum-bodywork, and for 1955 the new Maicoletta scooter.

Through the years Maico's involvement with off-road sport increased, and many machines were sold in the USA. There was also some involvement with road racing in the 125cc class and the Maico 125cc R5 model was popular and successful with private owners. The German army used 250cc Maicos, based on the company's motocross experience, in the 1970s. In the 1980s, however, financial problems dictated a policy of making only off-road models, or lightweights with off-road styling, with water-cooling, monoshock suspension etc.

In 1987, Maico collapsed, with most of its employees being dismissed. However, a buyer was at hand, the concern moving to Bavaria as a result. Restarting production took time, and the company stills produces some off-road styled machines.

174cc Maico 175SS (two-stroke) 1960

123cc Maico MD125 racer (two-stroke) 1969

386cc Maico MC400 motocrosser (two-stroke) 1977

490cc Maico motocross (two-stroke) 1982

MAGNI • Italy 1928–1930

The most interesting model which appeared under this name was a 348cc ohc twin-cylinder machine with the two cylinders facing forward. Another model had a vertical 498cc single-cylinder. Both models were put into limited production by the designer Luigi Magni.

MAGNI • Italy 1977–

Company formed by former MV Agusta race team manager Arturo Magni, originally to produce chain drive conversions and frame kits for MVs, then his own Honda CB900F-powered machine, followed by a BMW boxer-powered bike. Magni then went on to produce bikes powered by Moto Guzzi V-twins, including the 1100cc Sfida.

MAICO • Germany 1935–1987

See panel

MAINO • Italy 1902–1956

A small factory which built motorcycles in limited numbers and with interruption. In early years it fitted Swiss 2.25hp Souverain engines; after a long period of abstaining from building motorcycles, Giovanni Maino produced after 1945 lightweights with 38cc Mosquito and Sachs and NSU engines from 98cc to 147cc.

MAJESTIC • Belgium 1928–1931

Made from English components, this machine was fitted with 346cc and 490cc single-cylinder sv and ohv JAP engines, Burman gearboxes, Amal carburettors and other proprietary parts.

MAJESTIC • England 1904

Small production run of single-cylinder JAP-engined machines.

MAJESTIC • England 1933

An attempt by Ernie Humphries of OK Supreme to move up-market in the early 1930s. The very nicely styled and made 250cc, 350cc and 500cc Majestic had engines made by the Stevens brothers under the name AJAX, after they had been forced to sell their AJS company to the London Matchless firm.

MAJESTIC • France 1927–1934

Another assembled machine, using Train, Chaise and JAP engines up to 498cc. A sensational 498cc four-in-line model with an air-cooled Train engine and a car-like bonnet over the power unit, with duplex steering, a car-like frame and rear suspension, never went into quantity production.

MAJOR • Italy 1947–1948

Yet another motorcycle with a fully enclosed engine and

992cc Magni Sfida 1000 high cam 8-valve V-twin Moto Guzzi) 1993

with shaft-drive to the rear wheel. Designed by Salvatore Majorca, this machine had a 347cc engine of his own design.

MAKO • Switzerland 1953

Lambretta lookalike scooter powered by a 125cc Ilo engine.

MALAGUTI • Italy 1958–

Malaguti has grown substantially only in recent years, although it has been producing first scooters then children's motorcycles for many years, originally using Mosquito, then Sachs, Franco Morini and Minarelli engines. In the mid-1990s the Minarelli-powered F10 and F12 Phantom scooters proved massively successful, precipitating the company's rapid expansion and the building of two new factories near Bologna. The upmarket, stylish Firefox F15 and retro-styled Yesterday added to the success, and recently Malaguti has introduced 100cc machines and has plans for 125cc and 250cc maxi-scooters, powered by Yamaha/Minarelli engines.

MALANCA • Italy 1957–

Produces like Malaguti a wide range of 49cc mopeds etc. and also 124cc and 149cc two-stroke machines with twin-cylinder engines. Malanca's 123cc water-cooled two-stroke racer built in the mid-1970s was a very successful vertical twin.

MALVERN STAR • Australia 1938–1952

Autocycles using Villiers 98cc single-speed engines assembled in Malvern, Australia with parts supplied by English maker Norman.

MAMMUT • Germany 1925–1933

The first models had 198cc Baumi, afterwards 197cc and 246cc own two-stroke engines. From 1928 onwards, Mammut used 198cc Villiers and 198cc to 497cc Black-burne engines. Mammut also built Coventry-Eagle frames under licence. They were made from pressed and rivetted steel.

MAMMUT • Germany 1953–1956

Had nothing in common with the other Mammut. Production concentrated on 49cc mopeds and lightweights of 123cc, 147cc, 173cc and 198cc two-stroke machines with Sachs and Ilo proprietary engines. Identical to these

124cc Malanca Sport (two-stroke) 1976

Bielefeld-built machines were also Meister and Phänomen motorcycles, also Doppler products.

MAMOF • Germany 1922–1924

Assembled machines with 145cc DKW and Grade two-stroke engines. Also small production of machines with own 155cc sv motors.

MANET • Czechoslovakia 1948–1967

This factory in Slovakia is part of the nationalised Czechoslovakian motorcycle industry. The only motorcycle built under this name was an 89cc double-piston two-stroke single, designed by Vincenz Sklenaf; afterwards the factory produced scooters with 123cc engines and is still working closely together with Jawa and CZ.

MANON • France 1903–c1906

Strengthened bicycle frames with its own 1.5hp engines.

MANTOVANI • Italy 1902–1910

Produced 1.5hp, 2.75hp and 4hp machines, of which some had water-cooled engines of own manufacture.

MANURHIN • France 1955–1962

After DKW (Auto Union) stopped manufacture of the Hobby scooter in 1955, Manurhin took over production and supplied it with a 75cc two-stroke engine.

MANUFRANCE • France 1951–1955

Lightweight machines and scooters with 124cc and 174cc engines.

49cc Malaguti Yesterday (two-stroke) 1999

MAORI • New Zealand 1914

A batch of 350cc Maori motorcycles was made in England for sale in New Zealand but were lost in a shipwreck off Cape Town. Only a prototype imported earlier to New Zealand by George Johns of Bannister & Johns, which was raced with success in grass track events by Johns. A small number of Maoris were registered in England.

70cc Malaguti Firefox RR (two-stroke) 1999

749cc March Superbike racer early mock-up. The bike's development was taken over by Norton in 1998

198cc Mammut (sv JAP) 1931

346cc Mammut (sv JAP) 1925

MARANELLO-MOTO • Italy 1977–

Sachs, Simonini and other two-stroke engines of 49cc, 123cc and 247cc are used by this small company for powering a variety of trial, motocross and other competition machinery.

MARATHON • America 1910

A two-stroke twin with shaft drive. It has been impossible to find out if this design was marketed.

MARC • France 1926–1951

Well-known make which built machines of typical English design. The range included models with 247cc Staub-JAP and 347cc and 490cc sv and ohv engines made by JAP and LMP.

MARCH • England 1996–1997

A revival of the famous March racing car name, funded by American money to produce an exotic 750cc four-cylinder race bike to compete in World Superbike racing, as well as a single cylinder sports bike and large capacity custom cruiser. With development well under way, the designs, with engines by British engineer Al Melling, were transferred to the revived Norton company, where development is continuing.

MARCK • Belgium 1904–1908

Produced single-cylinder machines with own 499cc ioe engines.

MARIANI • Italy 1930–1934

Interesting 496cc single-cylinder sv machines, supplied with two valves for the use of petrol and with three valves for running on naphta. They never became a world-sensation.

MARS (MA) • Germany 1903–1957

Swiss Zedel and German Fafnir engines powered Mars motorcycles built in Nuremberg before WW1. Fame came in 1920 when Franzenberg designed the famous white Mars with a box frame made from welded and rivetted pressed steel. The engine was exclusively made by the Maybach car and aircraft engine factory for Mars. It was a 956cc sv flat twin. The first models had a two-speed gearbox with two chains to the rear wheel; from 1927 onwards, a three-speed gearbox was used. There was a hand starter below the low saddle; the gearchange was inside the petrol tank and so was the tool kit. Early models had a swinging arm on the front, later ones a

Druid-like Tiger fork. Half of the rear wheel was enclosed and leg shields were standard. For a couple of years, this Mars—which was delivered in white, afterwards also in green, violet and dark red—was a good seller. During the hyper-inflation period in Germany the factory ran into difficulties, and production stopped between late 1924 and 1926, when Johann and Karl Müller, two leading technicians of the Mars works, started up again with improved models. As they could not use the Mars trademark, the machines were known for a while as 'MA'. In 1929 they added new models with MAG, later also with Sturmey-Archer, JAP and Villiers engines from 198cc to 596cc. During the 1930s, manufacture concentrated on bicycles and mopeds with 75cc and 98cc Sachs engines.

There was a 60cc two-stroke lightweight with 57mm bore x 68mm stroke. Typical for all Mars and MA products was the excellent workmanship and finish. This was still true after 1945, when Rudi Albert—formerly designer with Allright and Phänomen—created the unorthodox Mars Stella, with a low frame, small-diameter wheels and rubber suspension for the fork and the saddle. Sachs supplied the 147cc, 174cc and 198cc two-stroke engines. Albert also designed the last Mars model, the sporty Monza with a Sachs 49cc engine. When the factory closed down, Gritzner took over manufacture of this lightweight. Chief designer Albert left and joined the Fichtel & Sachs proprietary engine factory.

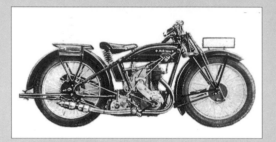

497cc Mars Germany (ioe MAG) 1929

956cc Mars Germany (sv flat twin Maybach) 1923

147cc Mars Stella Germany (two-stroke Sachs) 1952

MARINI • Italy 1924–1928

Not to be confused with Morini, Emilio Marini's machines were only built in limited numbers. They used 124cc two-stroke engines, although it is not clear whether these were Marini's own or proprietary units.

MARLOE • England 1920–1922

Small assembler, who fitted 346cc Precision and 348cc and 498cc sv Blackburne engines into open frames, making the bikes easier and more graceful for ladies with long skirts to ride.

MARLOW • England 1920–1922

There was no connection with the Warwick-built Marlow, as many believe. The Marlow premises were in Birmingham, where the main production concentrated on 269cc Villiers-engined machines. Models with 346cc and 490cc JAP engines were built to order.

MARMON • America 1948

Two-stroke twin cycle attachment built by a Californian company owned by Zeppo Marx (of the Marx brothers). Complete machines were assembled too.

MARS (MA) • Germany 1903–1957

See panel

MARMONNIER • France 1947–1951

Produced mainly 124cc and 174cc machines with Aubier-Dunne engines.

MARS • England 1905–1908

Small factory which—like the German Mars—also fitted Fafnir engines into strengthened bicycle frames. It is not

498cc Marusho Magnum (ohv flat twin) 1965

known if there was a connection with the German factory. The London-based firm also used the 211cc Minerva engine, which was not used by Mars in Germany.

MARS • England 1923–1926

A variety of engines powered these well-made machines, built in Coventry. Among them were the 247cc Villiers two-stroke, 293cc and 346cc JAP sv models, the 348cc sleeve-valve Barr & Stroud and the 348cc oil-cooled Bradshaw. Production was on a small scale, but workmanship was excellent. Mars already used modern saddle tanks in late 1923.

MARSH • America 1901–late 1910s

Pioneer of the American motorcycle industry. Produced singles and V-twins with its own engines. After it bought the Metz motorcycle factory, Marsh's machines became known as MM, which stood for Marsh-Metz.

346cc Martinsyde (ohc) 1923

676cc Martinsyde (ioe V-twin) 1923

MARSHALL • England 1905

Limited assembly of 2hp Minerva-engined machines by Henry Marshall, Cycle & Motor Works, Clay Cross which went on to build the Lily from 1906-1914.

MARSEEL • England 1920–1921

Designed by racing-driver D. M. K. Marendaz, the Marseel was a 232cc scooter which failed to make the grade.

MARTIN • England 1911–1922

Assembled standard-looking machines with 198cc Precision and 293cc, 347cc and 490cc sv JAP engines. There was also a V-twin with the 64.5mm x 76mm bore/stroke 498cc JAP engine.

MARTIN • Japan 1956–1961

Assembled two-stroke singles with 124cc, 198cc and 246cc engines.

MARTINA • Italy 1924–1927

Small producer of 173cc two-stroke machines.

MARTIN-JAP • England 1929–1957

Specialist in the manufacture of JAP-engined 348cc and 498cc speedway machines. Was known all over the world and supplied such machines to many famous riders.

MARTINSHAW • England 1923–1924

Fitted the 346cc Bradshaw 'oilboiler' (oil-cooled) engine into its own frames. Production of this ohv single was limited.

MARTINSYDE • England 1919–1925

A former aircraft factory which built 346cc singles and 498cc to 676cc V-twins with its own eoi (exhaust over

inlet) engines. Of good design and quality, the biggest version had 70mm bore and 88mm stroke, drip lubrication, an AJS three-speed gearbox and Amac carburettor. When this factory closed down, BAT in London bought the remains and the name.

MARUSHO • Japan 1964–c1969

Was a very BMW-like 498cc transverse-mounted ohv flat-twin with unit-design engine, four-speed gearbox and shaft drive to the rear wheel. The Marusho was built in the former Lilac factory and destined mainly for the USA market.

MARVEL • America 1910–1913

Closely connected with Glenn Curtiss, Marvel used Curtiss single-cylinder and V-twin engines.

MARVEL-JAP • England 1909–1912

Fitted JAP proprietary engines into standard frames, especially the 4.5hp V-twins. Limited production.

MAS • Italy 1920–1956

Founded by Alberico Seilig, one of Italy's leading designers of motorcycles, the first machines were strengthened bicycles with its own 123cc ohv engines. The first motorcycles made by MAS had 148cc and 173cc ohv engines with big outside flywheels and pedalling gears. 173cc sv and 244cc ohv singles followed. During the 1930s the range included 248cc and 348cc sv machines and a 568cc sv single. There were also 348cc and 498cc ohv models, which—like the sv versions—had inclined cylinders. Although main production concentrated for a long time on 173cc ohv models in different shapes, Seilig had already designed in 1929 a modern 492cc vertical-twin with an sv engine, and later, very good rear suspension for nearly the whole range. He left the MAS factory in 1938 and founded the Altea. After the war he was in Argentina for many years, but eventually returned to Italy, where he

496cc MAS Italy (ohv) 1938

died. MAS during the war supplied 498cc ohv singles to the Italian forces and also produced the 173cc Lupatta two-stroke, followed by a 340cc sv and a new version of the 598cc ohv model. The 122cc Stella Alpina, with cooling by forced air, was interesting but not a success. That was soon after the war, and in 1950 a new 492cc vertical-twin with a single ohc engine also failed to make the grade. Better was the 173cc Zenith of 1951, a very modern ohv single with telescopic forks and swinging arm rear suspension. Another model had a 173cc ohc engine and was exhibited in 1954 at the Milan show. Other models included a range of 124cc two-strokes and a Sachs-engined 49cc mini-scooter.

159cc Maserati (ohv) 1953

248cc Maserati (ohv) 1955

MAS • Germany 1923–1924

Built 183cc two-strokes in small numbers.

MASCOTTE • France 1923–1924

Lightweight machines with own 174cc sv engines.

MASERATI • Italy 1953–1961

Famous factory which entered motorcycle production with contemporary 123cc two-strokes and 158cc ohv models. There were also 248cc ohv and 173cc ohc singles, a 158cc two-stroke and eventually a 248cc vertical twin with an ohc engine, built in small numbers only. Although of excellent design and finish. Maserati motorcycles never became as famous as the cars.

MASON & BROWN • England 1903–c1908

Assembled machines with De Dion, Antoine and mainly the 2hp Minerva engine.

MASSEY (MASSEY-ARRAN) • England 1920–1931

Designed by E. J. Massey, these machines had a hectic life, as the company moved nearly every year. It built good, light motorcycles with 172cc to 490cc engines made by Villiers, Jap, Blackburne and Bradshaw. Massey also designed the first HRD motorcycles.

MAT • Czechoslovakia 1929–1930

Similar to the Ariel Square Four, the 498cc Votroubek-designed MAT had a square four-cylinder engine, but Votroubek used an sv design with shaft drive to the rear wheel. The factory, owned by Bugatti racing driver Milos Bondy, built only few of these machines.

MATADOR • Germany 1925–1926

Limited production of lightweights with its own 269cc two-stroke engines.

MATADOR • England 1922–1927

Concentrated on 348cc machines with Blackburne sv and ohv engines and with the oil-cooled Bradshaw ohv engine. Bert Houlding, the designer, also built Toreador motorcycles. Successful riders: B. Houlding, A. Tinkler.

MATCHLESS • England 1901–1969 (revived 1987)

See panel

MATRA • Hungary 1938–1947

Designed by former racing motorcyclist Laszlo Urbach, these machines had 98cc and 198cc Sachs and Ardie two-stroke engines.

MAURER • Germany 1922–1926

Produced 1.5hp bicycle attachments with rotary disc-valve two-stroke engines. Maurer motorcycles had water-cooled vertical 247cc and horizontal water-cooled 494cc twin-cylinder two-stroke motors. With its opposing cylinders in line with the duplex frame, this model was probably the only water-cooled two-stroke flat-twin built as a production model. Production was not large-scale. Interesting was the big outside flywheel and the position of the forward-facing carburettor, which was connected with the rearward-facing cylinder via a long inlet pipe and had a shorter pipe to the forward-facing cylinder. It is unlikely that this unusual system worked satisfactorily. Also odd was the position of the radiator. The single-cylinder Maurer had it below the saddle, where four-strokes usually have the oil tank. The flat twin had the radiator directly below the full length of the petrol tank.

MAUSER • Germany 1923–1927 (1932)

Extremely unorthodox two-wheeler with a car-like body and outrigger wheels on both sides. The chassis comprised two pressed steel channel members, while steering was by a huge D-shaped handlebar. The water-cooled single-cylinder 510cc sv engine produced 10bhp at

496cc Maxima (sv flat twin) 1922

490cc Mawi (sv JAP) 1930

3400rpm. It was mounted in front of the rear wheel and had the cylinder mounted horizontally. Chains drove the gearbox and rear wheel. At 638lb it was a heavy vehicle, and business for the producer, the Mauser arms factory, was not brisk. The Mauser did not look very safe. When Mauser in 1927 abandoned manufacture of this 'Einspurauto' (single-track car), another company at Oberndorf/Neckar—Gustav Winkler—continued production until 1932. During the second half of the 1920s, the French firm Monotrace built the Mauser under licence.

MAV • Italy 1977–

Another Italian assembler of motocross and trials machines with 49cc, 123cc and 244cc two-stroke singles, made by Minarelli, Hiro and Sachs.

MAVISA • Spain 1957–c1960

Luxurious lightweight with a horizontal 248cc two-stroke, twin-cylinder engine of unit design and with shaft drive to the rear wheel.

350cc Majestic 1930

MATCHLESS • England 1901–1969 (revived 1987)

Harry Collier senior and his sons Harry and Charlie Collier were famous pioneers, who started the Matchless company in London in 1901 using De Dion and MMC engines from a very early date. They were early customers, too, for JAP engines, which they raced successfully. Competing in the scandalous International Cup Race in Austria in 1906 so disgusted them that they urged the Auto Cycle Club to stage a `fair' race in the Isle of Man. As a result the TT was born. The Collier brothers either won or came second in six TT races between 1907 and 1911 and set many records at Brooklands and elsewhere.

By this time, Matchless was mainly using JAP and MAG engines, but it began to make its own after WW1. In the 1920s, Harry and Charlie Collier were joined by Bert Collier, their younger brother, though their father died in 1926. Two years later, in 1928, Matchless became a public company. The designs of the period were unexciting by and large, and not enhanced by the strange shade of khaki green chosen for most models. Matchless briefly flirted with Brough Superior-type petrol tanks, before settling on somewhat slab-sided saddle tanks, enamelled white with black lining.

Two designs of more interest were the Silver Arrow of 1929 and Silver Hawk of 1930. Both had very narrow-angle V engines—a side-valve twin of 400cc for the Arrow and, for the Hawk, a 600cc four with overhead camshaft. Despite their advanced specifications, including spring frames, neither was a sales success.

Even so, Matchless was a well run and profitable company, as became evident in 1931, when AJS at Wolverhampton hit financial trouble. Matchless outbid BSA to acquire the company. At first, Matchless made the AJS as a separate range, but, as parts were used up, the two makes were rationalised and, by the end of the 1930s, were virtually identical, the exception being the 350cc and 500cc ohc race models. These were sold only as AJS.

Associated Motorcycles – AMC, frequently termed the Matchless/AJS set-up – also built and raced an impressive supercharged ohc V-four 500cc AJS, originally seen at the 1935 Show as a sports model! After a disappointing 1936 season, it disappeared, only to return in 1938, now water-cooled with a spring frame. It was ferociously fast but almost unrideable, and won no races before the war. However, ridden by Jock West, it did win the 1946 Albi Grand Prix, before the FICM banned supercharging. Following WW2, AMC launched the 500cc twin `Porcupine' and the 350cc single-cylinder 7R, both with AJS on the tank.

During the war, Matchless supplied many thousands of G3 and then G3L (Lightweight) 350cc machines to the armed forces. Fitted with AMC's version of BMW's hydraulically damped telescopic (`Teledraulic') front forks, the G3L was the favorite of many wartime desptach riders. Post war, similar 350cc and 500cc singles soon were also fitted with oil-damped swinging arm rear suspension at the insistence of Jock West, the company's new sales manager. There was also a 500cc vertical twin, followed by 550cc, 600cc and 650cc variants, all of which shared a central main bearing.

In the 1950s, Matchless acquired the Norton, Francis Barnett and James companies and the Matchless name appeared for the first time in many years on a

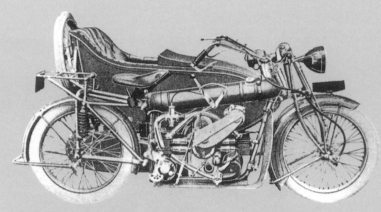

986cc Matchless (sv flat twin) 1916

976cc Matchless (sv V-twin JAP) 1923

347cc Matchless Comfort (sv) 1925

398cc Matchless Silver Arrow (sv V-twin) 1930

498cc Matchless G9 (ohv vertical twin) 1960

646cc Matchless G12 CSR (ohv twin) 1961

248cc Matchless G2 (ohv single) 1960

347cc Matchless G3 (ohv single) 1960

496cc Matchless G6 (ohc single) 1960

346cc Matchless (ohv) 1947

racing model. This was the G45, a 500cc twin, which was followed by the 500cc G50, in effect a stretched 7R.

With the passing of the Collier brothers, however, the quality of AMC's management declined sharply and rapidly and the decision to manufacture an AMC two-stroke engine for use in the James and Francis Barnett range proved disastrous.

The design of 'Lightweight' 250cc and 350cc models, and a frantic mix of AMC and Norton parts to create special bikes for the US market did little to arrest the company's slide. As early as 1961, there had been a shareholders' revolt, but, as so frequently happens, this led to nothing. Jock West resigned in disgust. Matchless management quarrelled with its American distributor, the able and energetic Joe Berliner, and became involved with the moribund Indian Sales Corporation, which by that time had nothing to do with manufacturing. By 1969 AMC—Matchless—was effectively bankrupt and was sold to Dennis Poore's Manganese Bronze Holdings group. Norton was revived and AJS put on hold. Matchless simply disappeared.

However, in 1987, the name was revived. Les Harris, British bike spare parts manufacturer and maker (under licence) of the post-Triumph 'Bonneville' bought the Matchless name from Manganese Bronze and launched a new machine with an ohc 494cc Austrian Rotax engine. The frame was British-built, and largely equipped with Italian hubs, brakes, front forks and rear suspension. At best this G80 model would only have scored a small number of niche sales, but the styling was too angular to really appeal to old bike fans, while the handling and performance fell well short of contemporary standards. Production continued for a few years then stopped.

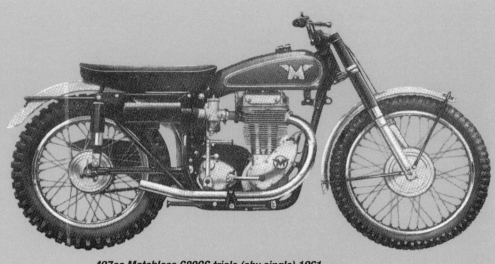

497cc Matchless G80CS trials (ohv single) 1961

494cc Matchless G80 (ohc Rotax) 1987

MAWI • Germany 1923–1930

Assembled machines with 142cc and 173cc DKW two-stroke and 198cc to 546cc sv and ohv single-cylinder four-stroke JAP engines.

MAX • Germany 1923–1925

Produced 180cc two-stroke and 446cc sv machines with its own power units.

MAX • France 1927–1930

French and English proprietary engines from 98cc to 496cc were fitted into motorcycles made by this small company.

MAXIM • England 1919–1921

One of the many assemblers. Fitted 318cc Dalm single-cylinder two-stroke engines.

MAXIMA • Italy 1920–1925

Well-designed 690cc and 747cc horizontal twins with opposing cylinders. The sv engines were of its own design and manufacture.

MAY BROS • England 1903–1906

Motorcycles with Minerva, MMC, Sarolea and other engines made to order.

MAZUE • France 1911–1914

This company built at Lyon 346cc and 496cc single-cylinder machines with ohv engines of its own manufacture.

MAZZUCHELLI • Italy 1925–1928

A long name, a small factory and a German 198cc Alba single-cylinder sv engine in a simple frame.

MB • Czechoslovakia 1927–1928

Built, like the Mat, in the Avia factory of racing car driver Milos Bondy, the Slechta-designed 498cc single-cylinder MB machine was quite unusual because it had a rotary valve in the cylinder head which steered the incoming and outgoing fuel mixtures and gases respectively. The design was never fully developed and became superseded by the Mat.

MB • America 1916–1920

Contemporary-designed machines with 746cc parallel-twin engines and shaft drive to the rear wheel. The design was never fully developed.

MBK • France 1987–

Yamaha bought the French Motobecane factory in 1987 as a local production facility for mopeds and scooters up to 125cc. Machines produced there are badged either Yamaha or MBK (a nickname for Motobecane), depending on the destination market.

MBM • Italy 1973–

Concentrates on 49cc mopeds and similar small transport.

MBR • Italy 1923–1926

This firm was a small producer of 124cc two-stroke machines.

MC • Czechoslovakia 1923–1927

Concentrated on the manufacture of a 996cc V-twin sv machine for use with a sidecar. The design by Vladimir Guth was based on English lines.

MCB • Sweden 1902–

Famous factory which now includes former motorcycle producers as Hermes, Monark (Esse), Nordstjernan, NV-Bohlin, Apollo and others. The main range of models includes two-strokes from 48cc to 123cc with mainly Sachs and Franco-Morini engines.

MCC • England 1903–c1910

Fitted De Dion, Minerva and other engines. Produced also its own engines using Minerva patents.

MEGOLA • Germany 1921–1925

This was probably the most unorthodox motorcycle ever made on a commercial basis. Designed by Fritz Cockerell, the 640cc Megola had an air-cooled five-cylinder radial engine with the side-valves built directly into the front wheel. It had no clutch or gearbox, but a lot of power at the low end. Starting was by pushing or by 'kicking with the heel into the spokes of the front wheel' while the machine was on the stand. The petrol tank was in the normal position, but petrol first had to be pumped into a smaller tank, mounted on the right side of the leaf-sprung fork. Below it, outside the front axle, was the carburetor, on the opposite side the magneto. Some models also had rear suspension by means of half-elliptic springs. Changing ratios was by using bigger front wheels. Racing models had top speeds of around 85mph, production versions of 68mph to 70mph. Thanks to the low centre of gravity, Megolas had first class road-holding qualities. The company won many races and trials with a works team which consisted of Toni Bauhofer, Sepp Stelzer and Albin Tommasi. The name Megola came from the first two letters of the three men who founded this Munich-based factory: Meixner, Cockerell and Landgraf. Interesting, because Cockerell in this case wrote his name with G instead of the usual C as with his second motorcycle enterprise, the Cockerell lightweight motorcycles.

The design of the spokes of the front wheel enabled the dismantling of the cylinders without taking a spoke out of the wheel. There was also a specially designed tube in the tires which could be changed without dismantling the wheel, ie it was an open tube, which could be 'pushed' together. The five small cylinders had 52mm bore and 60mm stroke; the frame consisted of a welded and rivetted box. Touring models had mostly bucket-seats; sports versions had saddles. Today, the Megola—of which nearly 2000 were made—is one of the most valued collector's machines.

640cc Megola Sport (sv air-cooled radial five-cylinder) 1922

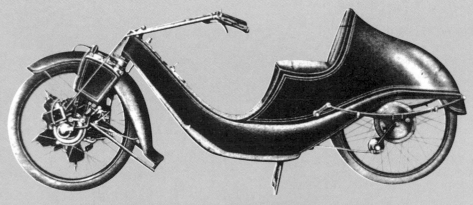

640cc Megola (sv air-cooled radial five-cylinder) 1921

614cc Menos (sv flat twin water-cooled) 1923

McEVOY • England 1926–1929

Michael McEvoy, the founder of this Derby-based factory, was earlier with Rolls-Royce; Cecil Allerhead Birkin, who financed the enterprise, was a brother of famous racing-car driver Tim Birkin; and George Patchett, the leading technician, came from George Brough's Brough Superior works at Nottingham. McEvoy soon offered machines from the Villiers-engined 172cc two-stroke and 248cc, 348cc and 498cc sv and ohv singles with Blackburne and JAP engines, to 998cc JAP and Anzani-engined sv and ohv V-twins, including 8-valve versions and racing engines. George Patchett—who eventually became FN and Jawa designer—also rode in 1926–1927 a supercharged 996cc McEvoy with the big JAP racing engine. McEvoy and Cecil Birkin also competed in sporting events and when Birkin was killed in a TT practice accident in 1927, the factory got into difficulties. Before McEvoy closed down, he built prototypes of a 346cc three-valve ohc single and of an air-cooled ohc 498cc in-line four. He was an expert on supercharging, and later represented German Zoller superchargers in England and also built some supercharged cars.

McKECHNIE • England 1922

Luxurious twin-cylinder with a 688cc Coventry-Victor flat twin engine. The McKechnie had rear suspension and a very strong duplex frame. The production was on a limited scale.

McKENZIE • England 1921–1925

Lightweight machine with 169cc two-stroke engine, which was also supplied in open frames for ladies. McKenzie machines were made for this London-based company by the Hobart works at Coventry.

MDS • Italy 1955–1960

Produced modern lightweights with own unit-design, single-cylinder ohv engines of 65cc, 70cc, 75cc and 80cc. There was also a miniscooter with a 65cc engine. Some versions of the motorcycle had separate gearboxes.

MEAD • England 1911–1916

According to some sources, Premier in Coventry was the producer of machines for the Liverpool-based Mead Cycle Co. The range included Precision-engined 198cc, 492cc and 592cc models, 293cc JAP-engined singles and 746cc and 980cc versions with V-twin Premier engines.

MEAD • England 1922–1924

Assembler which used 1.75hp, 2.75hp and 3.75hp Precision, Wall and Villiers engines.

MEGOLA • Germany 1921–1925

See panel

MEGURO • Japan 1932–1962

Two young men, Takaji Suzuki and Nobuji Murato, founded the Murato Iron Works, which in 1922 made a copy of a Harley-Davidson hoping to impress a Japanese defence procurement department. But the single prototype was rejected, so the foundry instead decided to specialise in motorcycle components instead of whole machines, choosing transmissions and founding in 1928 Meguro Seisakusho to supply them to the motorcycle industry.

In 1932 a deal was done with Harley-Davidson to produce an old design of V-twin which became the Rikuo, but most importantly Meguro learned a great deal about heat treating steel and modern production techniques.

In 1937 Meguro produced the twin port Z97, a 500cc single which was a copy of the 1935 Velocette MSS. Production of the Rikuo increased during the war, but afterwards Meguro had to wait until 1948 before restarting production, with 250cc and 350cc ohv singles being added to the two-bike range, then a basic 125. In the mid-1950s a newer 500cc single and then a twin, the Senior, were introduced, and the range sold well enough for Meguro to become one of Japan's major manufacturers. In 1960 Meguro became affiliated with Kawasaki, which was looking to begin motorcycle production to improve the company image, and in 1962 the company name changed to Kawasaki Meguro. The following year it was completely merged with Kawasaki and the name no longer used.

MEIHATSU • Japan 1953–1961

Meihatsu Industries was formed by Kawasaki to sell its motorcycles, the first of which was a 125cc two-stroke, with an engine based, like so many others around the world, on the DKW RT125 (which inspired the BSA Bantam). Other machines were similar utility motorcycles, including one produced in 1961 which was later sold as the B8 with the Kawasaki badge, the first machine to wear it.

498cc Meguro (ohv twin cylinder) 1959

346cc Meray (ohv JAP) 1929

MEISTER • Germany 1949–early 1960s

The Alfred Ostertag-designed machines were of standard design and good finish. Production included 49cc Zündapp-engined mopeds and motorcycles with 98cc, 123cc, 147cc, 173cc and 198cc Sachs as well as Ilo two-stroke power units.

MELDI • Italy 1927–1937

Concentrated on the production of racing machines with 248cc, 348cc and 498cc ohv JAP and Python (Rudge product) engines.

MEMINI • Italy 1946–1947

Concentrated on a limited manufacture of 173cc two-strokes with own engines.

MENON • Italy 1930–1932

Touring machines with inclined 174cc and 198cc single-cylinder sv engines.

MENOS • Germany 1922–1923

This was nothing else but a slightly redesigned and renamed Aristos. Identical was the water-cooled 614cc flat-twin sv engine, the rivetted and welded box frame made from pressed steel and the position of the radiators on both sides of the rear wheel. Only differences were a new fork design and a Zebra-like enamelling of the whole machine.

MERAY • Hungary 1921–1944

Was once the leading Hungarian make over the years produced machines from 172cc to 996cc with Villiers, Moto-Rêve, Puch, Blackburne, and JAP engines. After 1936 also had its own 346cc and 496cc single-cylinder engines. Ferencz Meray, Laszlo Erdêly, Bertalan Szoter, Josef Weber etc. won many races on these machines.

MERCIER • France 1950–1962

Built 49cc machines, mainly mofas, with Lafalette engines. Also mini-scooters and afterwards motorcycles with 98cc to 173cc Villiers and Ydral engines.

MERCO • Germany 1922–1924

Very simple design of 148cc two-stroke machine with deflector-type three-port engines of its own manufacture.

MERCURY • England 1956–1958

Offered a wide range of 49cc and 98cc motorcycles and mini-scooters, but production was limited. Among the models were the Dolphin, Hermes and Whippet scooters.

MERKEL • America 1902–1922

For many years a leading make, Merkel built well-designed singles and V-twins up to 986cc. Some models already had rear suspension before WW1. The end came when Indian bought the Milwaukee factory.

MERLI • Italy 1929–1931

Small production of 173cc two-stroke machines with French Train engines.

MERLIN • Spain 1982–1989

A competition machine designed by Ignacio Bulto, formerly of Bultaco fame. Merlins used Italian 248cc Cagiva two-stroke engines.

MERLONGHI • Italy 1927–1930

Small producer of small 132cc two-stroke two-speed machines.

MESSERSCHMITT • Germany 1955–1961

The famous wartime aircraft company produced the Vespa scooter under licence after the previous German producer, Hoffman, ceased production.

MESSNER • Austria 1928–1933

Racing motorcyclist who produced 248cc racing machines with ohv JAP and his own ohc engines.

METEOR • Czechoslovakia 1909–1926

The first products were 211cc bicycle attachment engines.

The motorcycles had 147cc and 169cc two-stroke deflector-type three-port engines.

METEOR • Germany 1925–1926

Simple machines with 185cc sv engines. Limited production.

METEOR • Germany 1923–1926

Lightweights with 172cc two-stroke engines which came probably from Thumann in France.

METEORA • Italy 1955–1966

Produced 49cc NSU-engined and 123cc FBM-engined two-strokes and also a 148cc ohv model. Later models had 49cc Franco-Morini engines and included motocross versions.

METISSE • England 1962–mid 1980s

Famous motocross riders Don and Derek Rickman built their own machines using Triumph engines, which became very popular and successful. They diversified into road racing and pioneered disc brakes. They also made road machinery with both British and Japanese engines, and even sold such machines to the police. They abandoned motorcycles in the 1980s.

METRO • England 1912–1919

Well-made machines with own 269cc two-stroke engines. See also next entry.

METRO-TYLER • England 1919–1923

The Metro became the Metro-Tyler when the London-based Tyler Apparatus Co., Ltd. bought the remains of the Birmingham-based Metro Manufacturing and Engineering Co. The price in 1921 for the 269cc two-speed model was £80, for the three-speed version £85.

MEYBEIN • Germany 1922–1926.

Fitted 119cc and 142cc DKW two-stroke engines into its own very low and very simple frames. Some versions had a horizontal cylinder.

650cc MF (flat twin Citroen) 1981

MEYBRA • Germany 1923–1925

Another simple machine with its own 168cc two-stroke engine.

MEZO • Austria 1923–1926

Designed by Medinger, who was a racing motorcyclist and also importer of English engines into Austria, the Mezo range included 172cc and 247cc two-strokes with Villiers engines and 293cc, 346cc and 490cc sv and ohv singles with JAP engines. Production was on a limited scale, partly because of Medinger's injuries, sustained in 1924 in the Austrian Tourist Trophy race.

MF • France 1981–1982

The MF used a modified Citroen 'Visa' flat twin car engine of 650cc in a nicely styled chassis in what was at the time a modern design with cast aluminium wheels and so on. Very few were made, however.

MF • Germany 1922–1925

The Nuremberg-built, Max Fischer-designed machine first had 492cc flat twin sv engines made by BMW, afterwards 347cc and 497cc sv engines made by Blackburne in England.

MFB • Germany 1923–1924

The frames were made of wood. Engines fitted were the German 198cc Nabob and the English 293cc sv JAP. When this Hamburg factory went bust, Hoco in Minden took over.

MFB • Germany 1925–1926

Small assembler of 206cc two-stroke machines with DKW engines.

MFB • Italy 1957–1964

Bologna-built 48cc, 74cc and 124cc two-strokes and 174cc ohv singles.

MFZ • Germany 1921–1928

Always produced workhorse models and never machines with any sporting pretensions. Nearly all models had MFZ's own ohv engines with 198cc, 247cc and 347cc capacities. The biggest version in 1926 had chain drive and three instead of two speeds.

346cc MFZ (ohv) 1927

MGC • France 1927–1929

Interesting design with an aluminium frame which included the petrol tank. Most engines fitted were JAP or Chaise of ohv 248cc, 348cc and 498cc specifications.

MGF • Italy 1921–1925

Designed by a well-known racing motorcyclist, the MGF—Motocicli Garanzini Francesco—machines had Blackburne ohv engines from 248cc to 498cc and also its own 142cc two-stroke engines.

MGF • Germany 1923–1931

Produced quite a large number of 122cc, 140cc, 173cc and 198cc two-stroke three-port and also Bekamo-licenced pumping-cylinder two-stroke machines.

MG-TAURUS • Italy 1933–late 1950s

Vittorio Guerzoni first used 173cc two-stroke Train engines, then his own 248cc ohv and 496cc ohv and ohc models. There were also Sachs-engined mofas and after 1945 two-strokes and ohv models from 75cc to 198cc.

MICHAELSON • America 1910–1915

Used 492cc single-cylinder and 992cc V-twin engines. They had overhead inlet and side exhaust valves, duplex frames, leaf-sprung forks and chain drive to the rear wheel, when most other factories used belt drive.

MICHAUX-PERREAUX • France 1868-1871

This steam-powered machine was created by Louis Guillaume Perreaux by fitting a small commercial steam engine to a Michaux bicycle, with relatively simple modifications. It went into commercial production at the rate of several hundred a year until around 1871, and is thought to be the world's first poduction motorcycle.

MIDGET BICAR • England 1908–1912, USA 1908–1909

Made by J. F. Brown of Reading, England, the Midget Bicar featured a pressed and rivetted sheet steel frame, and a variable pulley gear. Late models had 500cc and 600cc Precision engines. The design was licensed to the American Walton Motor Company, which used its own V-twin engines to power it.

Michaux-Perreaux Steam Velocipede, probably the world's first commercially produced motorcycle

MIDGET MOTORS • America 1960–1962

Mini-motorcycles with optional disc brake.

MIELE • Germany 1953–1962

Big and still famous factory which before WW2 built bicycles with 73cc and 98cc Sachs two-stroke engines. After the war, the same make of proprietary engine powered machines from 48cc to 147cc. Miele products were known for their high quality.

MIG • China 1993–1996

The MIG badge was applied to several Chinese makes of motorcycle brought to the UK and some other export markets.

MIGNON • Italy 1923–1932

After producing 123cc bicycle attachment engines, Vittorio Guerzoni designed the modern Mignon with a vertical 246cc twin-cylinder sv engine and a crankcase made of Elektron. That was in 1925 and in 1932 his next design

appeared. This was a 498cc single with ohv and chain-driven ohc. Other models were 173cc versions with ioe and also ohv.

MILANI • Italy 1970–1984

Produced a wide range of Minarelli-engined 49cc models and also 124cc models for trials and motocross. Most of the production went to the USA.

MILITAIRE (MILITOR) • America 1911–1917

Heavy four-cylinder in-line car-type air-cooled 1306cc ohv unit-design engine fitted into unusual frame with shaft drive. The frame consisted of a one piece stamping while the front suspension embodied coil springs in the front fork tubes. There was also a rear suspension which included quarter-elliptic cantilever springs mounted on a patented axle suspension. The gearbox had three speeds and a reverse gear; lubrication was full force feed by gear pump. The whole design was unorthodox and very expensive in production. In the seven years of limited production, these machines were made by eight companies in

Cleveland, Buffalo, New Jersey, Springfield and Bridgeport. The total output was probably less than 100 units. A single-cylinder version, built in the early years, never reached even this figure. This single had 480cc capacity, a steering wheel instead of handlebars, a bucket seat instead of a saddle and, like the four, wheels with wooden spokes.

MILLER-BALSAMO • Italy 1921–1959

Was a leading make in Italy, first with 123cc two-strokes, afterwards with very fast 174cc ohv machines, which had Swiss Moser and afterwards also Miller-built English Rudge (Python) four-valve single-cylinder engines. In addition, there were also Miller models with 248cc, 348cc and 498cc four-valve Pythons. Carlo Fumagalli, Aldo Pigorini, Silvio Vailati, Gino Zanchetta and others won many races and on 174cc Python-engined racing machines broke world records. The range of models included after 1934 98cc Sachs-engined two-strokes and a 246cc ohv model with its own single-cylinder engine. A completely enclosed version, built just before the war, had a 198cc two-stroke engine. After 1945, production concentrated around two-

98cc Miele (two-stroke) 1952

strokes from 123cc to 246cc and the 246cc ohv model, but Ernest Balsamo's machines never regained the popularity they had in the late 1920s and early 1930s. The big 499cc ohv singles, built after the war, were basically pre-war models slightly modernised. They were soon dropped, while a new 169cc ohc single made its appearance in the 1950s. The last model was a 49cc two-stroke.

MILLFORD • England 1904

A range of single-cylinder motorcycles and forecars marketed and sometimes assembled by Mills and Fulford, the Coventry sidecar maker. The 2¹/₄hp and 3¹/₄hp machines were built for Mills and Fulford by the Whitley Motor Co. and Hamilton Motor Co. of Coventry.

MILLIONMOBILE • England c1902

Motorised bicycle with a 1.5hp engine.

MIMOA • Germany 1924

Used a 142cc Albertus two-stroke engine, designed by Julius Löwy. This power unit could be run also on crude oil, but lacked power and reliability.

MINERVA • Belgium 1901–1914, 1953–1954

A famous name in the motoring world, Minerva not only built complete motorcycles with its own engines from 2hp to 8hp, but supplied these engines to other producers, as well as licences for manufacture in other countries. The Minerva name was also used by Van Hauwaert, who had bought the name, on a small range of two-stroke scooters in 1953 and 1954.

MINETTI • Italy 1923–1927

One of the many small Italian producers of 124cc two-strokes with three-port engines.

MINEUR • Belgium 1923–1928

Liege was once the centre of the motorcycle industry in Belgium. Paul Mineur produced there his 348cc and 496cc sv and ohv singles with a variety of proprietary engines. These included JAP, Bradshaw, MAG and Liége-built Sarolea motors.

MINISCOOT • France 1960–1962

This was a folding miniscooter with a 74cc two-stroke engine.

MINNEAPOLIS • America c1900–1915

Well-designed singles and V-twins with two-speed gearboxes in unit. The Minneapolis-based factory used telescopic forks and produced also three-wheelers.

MINSK • Russia 1953–early 1960s

Produced inside the Russian motorcycle industry two-strokes up to 246cc vertical-twins, but was also closely connected with other Russian works via the CKEB, the common design centre.

MIRANDA • Germany 1951–1954

Originally known as Schweppe scooter, the design was renamed Miranda when the Dortmund-based Pirol works took over its manufacture. It was offered with 173cc Sachs and 198cc Küchen two-stroke engines.

246cc Miami (sv) 1916

13hp Michaelson (ioe V-twin) 1913

246cc Mignon (two-stroke twin) 1926

4hp Militaire (single) 1912

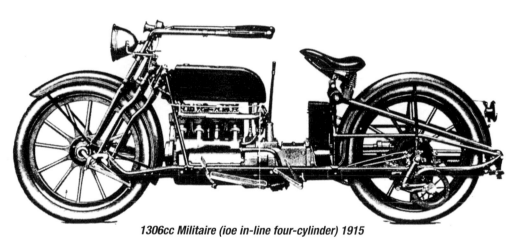

1306cc Militaire (ioe in-line four-cylinder) 1915

173cc Miller (ohv Moser) 1926

MISTRAL • France 1902–early 1960s

Produced lightweights with 1.75hp engines and after WW2 modern lightweights from 49cc to 247cc until it specialised in various 49cc models and also supplied the power units to other mofa and moped manufacturers.

MITCHELL • America 1901–c1906

Was a famous car factory which also built 345cc single-cylinder motorcycles with rearward-facing cylinders.

MITSUBISHI • Japan 1948–1964

This huge industrial concern had considerable success with its Pigeon scooters, powered by engines from a 115cc two-stroke to a 210cc four-stroke.

MIVAL • Italy 1950–1966

Produced 123cc two-strokes and in 1954 took over the licence for the German Messerschmitt cabin-scooter. It fitted a 172cc two-stroke engine into this three-wheeled vehicle and used a four-speed gearbox with it. New motorcycles included 123cc, 174cc and 199cc ohv versions. There was also a racy-looking 174cc single-cylinder dohc machine and a similar motocross version with a sohc engine. The production included 49cc bicycle attachment engines and also 248cc ohc motocross models, of which some had five- and even six-speed gearboxes. Mival also built trials versions.

MIYATA • Japan 1909–1964

Old factory which produced Asahi motorcycles after WW2. Among the models were 249cc sv and ohv singles, 344cc ohv singles and 496cc vertical twins with ohv engines. Other models included 123cc two-strokes. Based on English lines, Asahis were never imported into Europe.

MJ • Germany 1925

Produced experimental 249cc two-stroke machines which never went into quantity production. Concentrated on the manufacture of air- and water-cooled flat twin engines of 596cc and 746cc, supplied to motorcycle producers such as Heller. Mehne, another machine factory, took over MJ when it ran into financial difficulties.

MJS • Germany 1923–1925

Motorcycles of simple design with its own 245cc three-port deflector-type two-stroke engines.

MM • America 1906–WW1

The MM had, like other early American motorcycles, single-cylinder rearward facing sv engines, supplied by Thomas. Afterwards it used single-cylinder and V-twin power units made by Marsh, Royal, Holley and Pope.

MM • Italy 1923–1964

This MM was founded by Angelo Mattei, Mario Mazzetti, Alfonso Morini (who became founder of the Morini works) and Giuseppe Massi. Afterwards Massi and Mattei left and Antonio Salvia joined the MM factory, where they built superb 123cc and later 173cc two-strokes with a forward-facing horizontal cylinder. In 1927 Alfonso Morini and Amedeo Tigli, riding 123cc two-strokes which had the gearbox in unit with the engine, broke world records and reached speeds of over 66 mph. A 173cc ohv machine and 348cc sv and ohv singles as well as 248cc ohv and 496cc sv models followed. New racing singles with 173cc and 348cc chain-driven ohc engines came into production in 1932 and 1936 respectively. Both proved to be very successful. Luigi Bonazzi broke the world record for the flying kilometre with the 348cc version and reached 116.6 mph, while Guglielmo Sandri won many races with this machine. He also ran it under the CM trademark. Michaele Mangione became Champion of Italy in 1938 on an improved version of this 348cc single with the chain-drive sohc engine; Salvia was responsible for the design. All MM machines were superbly made and had an excellent finish; this was the case with a new 248cc ohc single built in 1947, and with 346cc and 492cc sv singles made in the same period. MM afterwards dropped the big model and concentrated on 247cc and 347cc ohc singles. Unfortunately it never built racing machines after the war, only 247cc motocrossers. The last MM design was a 173cc ohc single, although it also built 123cc two-strokes of excellent design. A 247cc production racer was the 1956–built Sport SS, with an sohc unit-design engine.

122cc MM racer (two-stroke) 1927

M&M • England 1914

Assembled machine with open frame and 269cc Villiers two-stroke engine.

MMM • Germany 1925–1927

Small producer of 148cc two-stroke machines.

MODENAS • Malaysia 1975–

A manufacturer of scooters, Modenas is owned by the DRB-HICOM group of companies that also owns the Malaysian car manufacturer, Proton, and holds a controlling share in Lotus cars.

The company's 110cc four-stroke step-thrus were originally sold on the home market only, but Modenas has recently expanded into overseas markets.

246cc MM (ohv) 1936

In 1997 the marque came to prominence internationally when it bought into a 500 grand prix project headed by racing legend Kenny Roberts. The team's V-three two-stroke Modenas KR3 was a TWR design, built mainly in Britain using Formula One car know-how. Kenny Roberts Junior raced the bike to 16th and 13th in the 1997 and 1998 500 world championships.

MOCHET • France 1950–1955

Lightweights with 149cc Ydral two-stroke engines.

MOFA • Germany 1920–1925

Produced 70cc and 148cc bicycle attachment engines and also complete lightweight machines.

248cc MM Super Sports (ohv) 1956

498cc Modenas Grand Prix racer (two-stroke liquid-cooled three cylinder) 1997

MOHAWK • England 1903–1925

The first models had 2.5hp and 3hp engines. After an interruption of some years, the bicycle factory re-entered the motorcycle market in the 1920s. The wide range of assembled machines included models with 269cc Villiers, 293cc JAP and 492cc Abingdon engines. Other models used a 154cc two-stroke flat twin Economic power unit and a 346cc sv JAP engine.

MOLARONI • Italy 1921–1927

Made by the Molaroni brothers at Pesaro, early models were 296cc two-stroke singles of its own design and manufacture. Others housed a 596cc flat twin two-stroke with automatic lubrication. Designed by Alfredo Sgrignani, a new range of models included the improved 296cc model with 70mm bore and 78mm stroke, a 344cc version with 75mm bore and 78mm stroke and a 348cc ohv single

with 74mm bore and 81mm stroke which had a Blackburne engine.

MOLTENI • Italy 1925–1927, 1950–1953

Very ambitious design of a frame and fork, chaincases etc. made from aluminum alloy. The good-looking Molteni, fitted with 348cc oil-cooled Bradshaw and 492cc MAG single-cylinder engines, was not a commercial success. In 1950 the Molteni brothers had a second attempt at producing a cast aluminum machine, this time a 125cc scooter. Despite its beautiful construction it only lasted for three years in production.

MONA • Australia c1915

Limited production of a belt-driven flat twin cylinder machine built in Alexandria, NSW and marketed by Quirk's

Lighting and Engineering Co., Melbourne.

MONACO-BAUDO • Italy 1926–1928

After Augusto Monaco produced an experimental 246cc vertical twin engine at the Della Ferrera factory, he built a 496cc single-cylinder sv model with a unit-design engine and a big outside flywheel. Co-designer was Antonio Baudo, whose earlier V-twin engines were of 474cc, 686cc and 996cc capacity. Other models housed 346cc and 490cc single-cylinder JAP and Blackburne sv and ohv engines.

MONARCH • America 1912–1915

Another USA factory which produced 496cc singles and 990cc V-twins with its own ioe engines and spring frames.

10hp Monarch (ioe V-twin) 1913

244cc Monark (two-stroke twin Ilo) 1952

MONARCH • England 1919–1921

Made by Excelsior of Birmingham, the Monarch was a cheaper version. It had 296cc Villiers and 293cc JAP sv engines.

MONARCH • Japan 1955–1962

Produced Norton-like 346cc and 496cc ohv single-cylinder machines.

MONARK • Sweden 1920–late 1970s

Monark began by making a 175cc two-stroke motorised bicycle under the name of Essc, but changed this when it started making four-strokes, from 250cc to 600cc. In the 1930s, it began to use Ilo two-strokes, and, during the war, 500cc Husqvarna four-strokes. Post war, production was of lightweights, again with proprietary engines. BSA originally made the `Bantam' engine for Monark, with others coming from Ilo, CZ and Adler. In the late 1950s and early 1960s, Monark built 500cc ohv motocross machines and rider Sten Lundin, supported by Ove Lundell, won the world championship in 1959 and 1961. However, production increasingly centred on 50cc off-road machines with Sachs and Franco Morini engines, headed by the 175cc Enduro model. Monark, like several other Swedish motorcycle manufacturers, was owned by the MCB group which in the late 1970s decided to concentrate on enterprises other than motorcycle racing.

498cc Monark works motocrosser (ohv single) 1959

MONET GOYON • France 1917–1957

Was for many years a leading make successful in races. The first product was a wheel with a small engine, which could be attached to any bicycle. It was of 114cc with ioe valves. Motorcycles made by the Macon works used for many years 147cc, 172cc, 247cc and 342cc Villiers two-stroke and 347cc and 497cc ioe and ohv single-cylinder MAG power units. With Sourdot, Hommaire, Goussorgues and Debaisieux many races were won, partly with Brooklands-Villiers 172cc two-stroke engines, partly with ohv and ohc MAG 347cc and 497cc singles. The ohc versions were works engines; Monet Goyon as one of the biggest MAG engine customers was the only French factory to get

them from the Swiss engine works. The only engine built by Monet Goyon around the early 1930s was a 344cc sv single of unit design and with a slightly inclined cylinder. After the war, new 98cc, 124cc, 198cc and 232cc two-strokes and 345cc sv and ohv singles came into production. There was also—from 1953 onwards—the Starlet, a nice 98cc two-stroke scooter. Many of these machines had J. A. Grégoire rear suspension. The same was the case with similar Koehler Escoffier models, which were also built by Monet Goyon. Both makes used Villiers engines made under licence. They were also fitted to the Lemardelé-designed fully enclosed motorcycles and scooters.

MONFORT • Spain late 1950s

Assembled machines with 124cc and 198cc two-stroke engines in limited numbers.

MON-GRIMPIER • France 1913–1921

A single-cylinder 211cc two-stroke. No further information is available.

MONOPOLE • England 1911–1924

One of the best assembled machines. Fitted 247cc and 269cc Villiers engines, 293cc and 680cc sv JAP motors and also the 499cc Abingdon single-cylinder sv engine.

MONOTRACE • France 1926–1928

Licence-built German Mauser one-track car. Had a water-cooled 520cc engine, a car-like open body and on each side an outrigger wheel.

MONTEROSA • Italy 1953–1958

Producer of 49cc mopeds. Small factory and limited output.

MONTESA • Spain 1945–

See panel

MONTGOMERY • England 1902–1939

Before WW1 William Montgomery built motorcycles with

MONTESA • Spain 1945–

Pedro Permanyar and Xavier Bulto built up Spain's first post-war motorcycle factory with 100cc and 125cc two-stroke machines of Bulto's design. They did well in racing, and in 1956 Marcello Cama finished second in the 125cc TT. Bulto left the company in 1958, to be replaced by Leo Mila, who designed the 175cc two-stroke Impala. Its excellent sales led to another model, the 250cc Sport. Both models did well in long distance races, such as the Barcelona 24 hours.

From the early 1960s too, sales were good in the USA, especially of trials bikes, while in Europe, Montesa did well in one-day trials. By the late 1970s, it offered a full range of two-strokes from 50cc to 350cc. With the general decline of the Spanish industry, however, Montesa was taken over by Honda. Following this, a development budget was granted to the research and development department in 1995 that led to the first of the modern-day Cota trials bikes with which the factory re-took the World Trials Championship in 1996 with France's Marc Colomer. Montesa also produces a selection of lightweight Hondas at the factory.

349cc Montesa 360H7 Enduro (two-stroke) 1982

247cc Montesa Cappra (two-stroke single) 1974

247cc Montesa Cota (two-stroke single)

World Trials Champion Marc Colomer, 1996

249cc Montesa Cota 315R (liquid-cooled two-stroke single) 1996

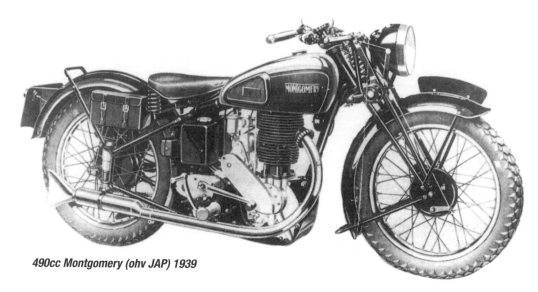

490cc Montgomery (ohv JAP) 1939

996cc Montgomery (ohv V-twin Anzani) 1939

498cc Monet-Goyon (ohv MAG) 1931

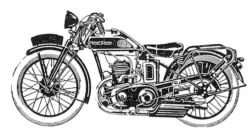

342cc Monet-Goyon (two-stroke Villiers) 1930

346cc Monet-Goyon (sv) 1931

proprietary engines at Bury St. Edmunds. Afterwards he moved to Coventry, where his products included not only a model with a 688cc flat twin sv engine but also sidecars. After the war his son Jack Montgomery resumed motorcycle production and built a wide range of machines from 147cc Villiers-engined two-strokes to 996cc V-twins with ohv Anzani and JAP engines. There were also models with 348cc Bradshaw engines, but from the mid-1930s onwards, only 246cc, 346cc and 496cc ohv JAP engines were fitted. The sporting Greyhound models with JAP special engines were famous; successful also were some JAP-engined racing models. Riders included Sid Jackson, Erich Hiller, Otto Kohfink and Mita Vychodil. Montgomery built the first Brough Superior frames in 1920/1922 and afterwards produced the P&P motorcycle frames. In 1925 a fire destroyed the Montgomery works; P&P also had to interrupt production.

MONTLHERY • Austria 1926–1928

Limited production of 346cc sv and ohv machines with JAP engines.

MONVISO • Italy 1951–1956

Sachs-engined 98cc, 123cc, 147cc and 173cc two-strokes of typical Italian design.

MOONBEAM • England 1920–1921

Utility machines with 296cc Villiers two-stroke.

MORIDELLI (MBA) • Italy 1969–1982

Racing enthusiast Giancario Morbidelli sponsored 50cc and then 125cc racing two-strokes, designed by Franco Rhingini. This was followed by a water-cooled 125cc twin with disc valve induction, which ridden by Gilberto Parlotti, was sensationally successful in 1970 and 1971. Following Parlotti's death in the 1972 TT, Morbidelli partially withdrew from racing for the next two years; however, with riders Pileri and Bianchi, it later dominated the 125cc class, winning the world title for three years in a row from 1975. The same year, it produced a 250cc twin in a Bimota frame, with which Mario Lega won the 250cc world championship in 1977.

In 1978, Morbidelli 125cc and 250cc racers, built at the nearby Benelli Armi factory, were offered for sale for the first time and quickly became enormously successful in the hands of private owners. Designer Jorg Moller, the brains behind the earlier Van Veen Kreidlers, was associated with these later machines. Giancarlo Morbidelli himself withdrew after overspending on unsuccessful 350cc and 500cc four-cylinder machinery, but by now the marque was well established as MBA (Morbidelli Benelli Armi).

Morbidelli's interest in motorcycles then appeared to wane, until in 1994 he unveiled a prototype exotic road bike with an 850cc V-eight engine and bodywork by famous Italian automotive stylist Pininfarina, all funded by Giancarlo Morbidelli's huge woodworking machinery company. However, the general reaction to the V-eight was that it was ugly, and a restyled version was shown a year later. Even this did not generate the enthusiasm Morbidelli had been hoping for, and for the moment the plan to produce the bike in limited numbers is on hold, although the prototype is occasionally displayed at woodworking and furniture exhibitions.

MORETTI • Italy 1933–1952

Known as a producer of small sports cars, Giovanni Moretti began producing machines with Ladetto, DKW and JAP engines, mainly lightweights up to 248cc. After 1945 the range included 123cc and 248cc ohc machines and also a 246cc vertical twin with shaft drive.

MORINI • Italy 1946–1987

See panel

MORRIS • England 1902–1905

Founder of this factory was William Morris, who later became Lord Nuffield of what is now the Leyland car group. His motorcycles had 2.75hp single-cylinder engines made by De Dion and MMC.

MORRIS • England 1913–1922

Had no connection with the above factory. Produced a single model, a 247cc two-stroke with its own three-port, deflector-type engine.

MORRIS-WARNE • England 1922

A 248cc two-stroke single, which was offered with a vertical as well as a horizontal cylinder. They were built in limited numbers.

MORS (SPEED) • France 1951–1956

Cars bearing this name were among the finest products in the pioneer period. In the 1950s a branch of the

748cc Morbidelli prototype (dohc V-eight) 1996

original Mors factory produced scooters with 60cc, 115cc and 124cc two-stroke engines, unusually, some of which were liquid-cooled.

MORSE-BEAUREGARD • America 1912–1917

Very advanced 492cc vertical-twin unit-design machines, which had the cylinders mounted in line with the frame. Drive to the rear wheel was by shaft.

MORTON-ADAM • England 1923–1924

Produced 292cc three-port, deflector-type two-strokes in small numbers and also Harry Sidney-designed 248cc and 348cc ohc models with chain-driven camshafts.

MOSER • Switzerland 1905–1935

Was—like Motosacoche—not only producing complete motorcycles from 123cc to 598cc, but also a leading supplier of proprietary engines to factories like Miller-

Balsamo, FVL, Lecco, Dollar and others. Most were ohv singles and the 123cc and 173cc versions gained great popularity, especially in Italy. Both models also won many big races and during the 1920s in a grand prix in Switzerland, Lehman and Brehm riding 123cc ohv Moser machines gained first and second place with the great Italian rider Omobono Tenni on a GD in third position. Another quite popular Moser model was the 198cc ohv version fitted also by Hercules of Germany in the early 1930s. These engines had 60mm bore and 70mm stroke, the 173cc version 60mm bore and 61mm stroke. The biggest Moser engine, the 598cc single, had 85mm bore and 106mm stroke, double-port and a JAP-like appearance.

MOSER • Austria 1953–

This make, which produced 98cc and 123cc two-stroke machines with Rotax engines has been defunct for many years. It was the make from which the present KTM motorcycles were developed.

123cc Moser (ohv) 1927

496cc Moser (ohv) 1932

MORINI • Italy 1946–1987

Alfonso Morini, Mario Mazzetti's one-time partner in the pre-war MM company, began motorcycle manufacture on his own account with yet another copy of the RT125 DKW. Production racers soon followed, with works two-strokes being raced by Nello Pagani.

To try to match the all-conquering Mondials, Morini turned to four-strokes in 1950. A 175cc ohv road model appeared in 1952 and in 1955, the ohc 175cc Rebelo was introduced, much used in production racing. The 1958 dohc 250cc was so successful that the great Tarquinio Provini joined the works team for the 1960 season. Over the next four seasons, Provini was to challenge the world, and almost, but not quite, succeeded in winning the 1963 world title.

In 1973 Morini broke away from run-of-the-mill production of 125cc and 150cc models with the very unusual 350cc 3½ V-twin. This introduced a concept that lasted for 20 years, continuously developed and uprated by designer Franco Lambertini. Air-cooled, and using flat cylinder heads with combustion chambers in the pistons (Heron configuration), the V-twin engine was subsequently made in 250cc and 500cc configurations, while 125cc and 250cc singles were also part of the range.

In the mid-1980s, Morini followed the common trend and styled many of its machines in off-road and custom guises. Worries about future development costs were in the air, as it was evident that a new generation of water-cooled engines would soon be necessary. However, in 1987, Morini, together with several other companies, was absorbed by the growing Cagiva company.

344cc Morini 3½ (ohv air-cooled V-twin) 1974

174cc Morini Rebello racer (dohc) 1957

MOTOBECANE • France 1923–

For many years, Motobecane was France's largest motorcycle manufacturer; not the least of the company's claims to fame is to have made the Mobylette moped from 1949 onwards. Motobecane took over engine builder Polymechanique in 1928 and Motoconfort in 1930 and applied the Motoconfort name to some models – notably a superb 500cc in-line four-cylinder side valve (later 750cc ohc), with unit gearbox and shaft drive, sold in the early 1930s as both Motobecane and Motoconfort. Such flights of fancy were rare, though Motobecane prided itself on some nice British-styled ohv singles. Best seller in the 1930s, apart from the inevitable Velomoteur type of machine, was the 100cc ohv model Z (later in 125cc and 175cc versions) that lasted until as late as 1963. Post war, too, there was a neat and technically interesting 350cc vertical twin but, as ever, the real profits were in moped manufacture, although during the 1950s the company produced several different scooters. Again, in 1972, Motobecane produced a range of modern Japanese-styled two-strokes, but these were too expensive, and the Mobylette range continued to be the company's salvation. Alessandro de Tomaso briefly owned Motobecane in the late 1970s, before the company was nationalised, then sold to Yamaha in 1984 to become a European manufacturing base for the Japanese. Since then the factory has flourished, producing a wide range of mopeds and scooters, sold both as Yamahas and MBKs throughout Europe.

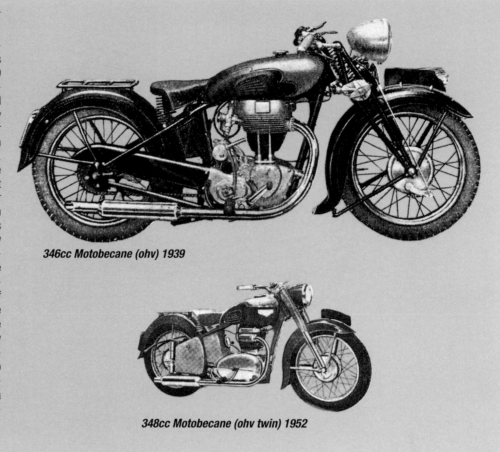

346cc Motobecane (ohv) 1939

348cc Motobecane (ohv twin) 1952

MOSKVA • Russia 1940–early 1960s

Produced heavy V-twins during the war, called M-72, for the Russian forces. Peace-time production consisted of 123cc and 173cc DKW-like two-strokes, which were superseded by the 174cc Voskhod. Other models connected with this factory were the shaft-driven M-31 with a 346cc ohv engine and the BMW-like M-61, a 592cc ohv flat-twin, transverse-mounted, which eventually became the 649cc Dneipr M-10, with 34bhp at 5200rpm.

MOTAG • Germany 1923–1924

Advanced design by Josef Schneeweiss. The Motag had a cast aluminum frame and was offered with three variants of vertical twin-cylinder ohv engines and also—as required—with air- or water-cooling. The engines were of 514cc, 642cc and 804cc. The production must have been very small as only very few of these machines reached the market.

MOTA-WIESEL • Germany 1948–1952

The original name was Motra-Wiesel. It was a cross between moped and scooter with small wheels and 74cc and 98cc two-stroke engines.

MOTEURCYCLE • France 1921–1924

Unusual 206cc two-stroke machine with friction drive to the rear wheel.

MOTOBECANE • France 1923–

See panel

MOTOBI • Italy 1951–1976

Designed by Giovanni Benelli, who had left his brothers in the Pesaro factory but later returned—now with the Motobi—to the old Benelli home, the first Motobi machines had 98cc, 114cc and 123cc flat single-cylinder egg-shaped two-stroke engines and also 198cc twin-cylinder versions. Afterwards he also built ohv models of similar design with capacities up to 248cc. That was in 1956, when the B on the petrol tanks was superseded by the Motobi name. Bestsellers were the 173cc Catria single with ohv, and 198cc and 248cc Spring Lasting two-stroke twins. A scooter with a 74cc two-stroke engine failed to succeed. After the return of Motobi to Benelli, some models stayed in production and there were others sold with both names, according to the demand. There were still 123cc and 245cc ohv singles being sold as Benellis in 1976 catalogues. The only model in the increasingly rare Motobi range was the 231cc ohc four-cylinder version, built to order with a 26bhp engine. The last model offered was the 250cc Cafe Racer twin—really a Benelli—after which the Motobi name disappeared.

MOTOBIC • Spain 1949/1965

Began with 50cc mopeds, then made a motorcycle with 125cc Hispano Villiers engine.

652cc Motag (ohv water-cooled twin) 1923

123cc Motobi (two-stroke) 1955

MOTOBIMM • Italy 1969–1971

Was a small factory which built 49cc motocross and trials machines with FB-Minarelli two-stroke engines.

MOTOBLOC • France 1948–late 1950s

Made at Vichy, the Motobloc products included 44cc mopeds, 65cc Sulky scooters and motorcycles from 124cc to 248cc with Villiers and Aubier-Dunn two-strokes and French AMC 123cc and 248cc ohv engines.

MOTO-BORGO • Italy 1906–1926

Designed by Carlo and Alberto Borgo—and also successfully raced by them—the early single-cylinder models had 493cc, 693cc and even 827cc engines. During WW1 V-twins of 990cc and afterwards 746cc came into being. Most of these machines had overhead inlet and side exhaust valves and there was during that period a cooperation with the English Rudge-Whitworth works at Coventry too; hence a certain similarity between Borgo and

496cc Moto-Borgo (ohv V-twin) 1926

Rudge machines. New 477cc V-twins with unit-design ohv engines came into production in 1921. Improved versions for sporting purposes had four-valve heads. The last Moto-Borgo, built from 1925 onwards, was a neat design with a two-speed gearbox built into the engine unit; it was one of the few 492cc ohv V-twins ever made on a commercial basis. The Borgos gave up motorcycle production soon afterwards and subsequently concentrated their efforts on the manufacture of pistons.

MOTOCLETTE • Switzerland 1903–1915

Small producer which fitted Zedel and later Moser single-cylinder proprietary engines.

MOTO GELIS • Argentina 1963–

Two-stroke machines up to 246cc with engines and other parts imported from Italy.

MOTO GUZZI • Italy 1921–

See panel

MOTOM • Italy 1947–early 1960s

Produced a variety of lightweight-machines with pressed steel frames. Most engines used were ohv units; the first a 48cc bicycle engine with pedalling gear. The next design was the 147cc Delfino, which eventually got a 163cc ohv engine. In this form it produced 8bhp at 6000rpm. Very popular was a 98cc ohv model with a horizontal fully-enclosed engine. There were also versions of 92cc and 98cc, models with tubular frames and also—in 1964—a 48cc version with a Peugeot two-stroke engine. There were many versions with automatic gearboxes, motocross

models and some machines with foreign engines, including the 49cc Zündapp two-stroke, which had a four-speed gearbox.

MOTO MARTIN • France 1975-

Specialist chassis company formed by Georges Martin, built dramatically styled, steel trellis-framed rolling chassis for a variety of Japanese multi-cylinder engines, especially the Kawasaki Z900/1000, Suzuki GSX750/1100 and Honda's six-cylinder CBX. Still involved in the production of specialist accessories.

MOTO MONTE • France 1932–WW2

Small manufacturer of 98cc two-stroke machines.

MOTOPEDALE • France 1933–1939

Two-strokes with 98cc and 123cc Aubier-Dunne engines. Other models included 248cc, 348cc and 498cc JAP and Python single cylinder engines. Limited production.

48cc Motom (ohv) 1958

MOTO GUZZI • Italy 1921–

Engineer Carlo Guzzi and wealthy enthusiast Giorgio Parodi created the first horizontally engined Moto Guzzi at Mandello del Lario in 1921 and continued to work together amicably for 30 odd more years. The Moto Guzzi theme of a horizontal engine with outside flywheel and unit gearbox in a low-built frame similarly lasted until the late 1960s with one or two variations.

The first Guzzis were 500cc; as early as 1923, now with overhead camshaft valve operation, they were already famous in racing. In 1926 Carlo Guzzi designed a similar 250cc machine; in that year's TT, Pietro Gherzi made fastest lap in the Lightweight TT and finished second—only to be disqualified over a technicality. Its natural disappointment did not stop Guzzi returning to the Isle of Man, a course of action that culminated in Stanley Wood's magnificent double win in Lightweight and Senior races in 1935. The Senior win was on the wide angle even-firing `Bicylindrica' 120°V twin, a 1933 Carlo Guzzi design, while both wins were the first ever by machines with spring frames, of a type designed by Carlo Guzzi in 1928. The victories were the first of a total of nine TT triumphs before Moto Guzzi withdrew from racing after 1957.

Successful production of motorcycles and light trucks continued in the 1930s and a prestige model, the 500cc transverse three-cylinder, was an interesting, if little known offering, in 1932 and 1933. The horizontal single-cylinder models were much more popular and, in the 1930s Guzzi was one of the few to successfully super-charge a single. It was with such a machine that Stanley Woods made fastest lap in the 1939 Lightweight TT.

Post war, the 500cc Bicylindrica was redesigned by Ing. Antonio Miccuchi, who also designed from scratch a superb 250cc twin that was foolishy discarded when Miccuchi took over the design of the road models. He

499cc Moto Guzzi (ioe) 1921

499cc Moto Guzzi racer (ohc) 1926

498cc Moto Guzzi racer (ohv V-twin) 1935

500cc Moto Guzzi C4V racer (ohc single) 1924

had already laid the foundations of Moto Guzzi's post-war prosperity with the 1946 design of the 65cc two-stroke Moto Leggera that sold in tens of thousands. Other post-war designs included the Galletto – a cross between a motorcycle and a scooter, and the Zigolo, an all-enclosed 100cc (later 110cc) two-stroke with a rotary inlet valve. Another post-war design – Carlo Guzzi's own – was the 175cc (later 235cc) Lodola of 1956, with a sloping, rather than horizontal, cylinder. The Lodola was very successful in the ISDT and similar events, as well as selling well in standard form. The traditional horizontal singles continued as the 250cc Airone and the 500cc Astora and Falcone.

Post-war racing took off in 1949 with, for the first time, an integrated factory racing department with Ing. Giulio Carcano in charge and British rider Fergus Anderson as development rider and team leader. After a promising start with 250cc singles and yet another redesign of the 500cc twin, with Bruno Ruffo winning the 250cc world championship Moto Guzzi had a poor year in 1950 and with drew to recoup. In 1951 Moto Guzzi rider Tommy Wood won the Lightweight TT and Bruno Ruffo again won the 250cc Championship. In 1952 Guzzi was 1–2–3 in the Lightweight TT and Enrico Lorenzetti was world champion.

499cc Moto Guzzi racer (dohc three-cylinder supercharged) 1940

246cc Moto Guzzi Albatros (ohc) 1947

499cc Moto Guzzi racer (dohc four-cylinder) 1953

98cc Moto Guzzi Zigolo (two-stroke) 1958

498cc Moto Guzzi works racer (dohc V-eight) 1955

844cc Moto Guzzi 850 T3 California (ohv V-twin) 1981

844cc Moto Guzzi California II (ohv V-twin) 1982

844cc Moto Guzzi Le Mans III (ohv V-twin) 1981

This, however, was Moto Guzzi's last year of 250cc supremacy, for in 1953 and 1954 it was overwhelmed by the German NSU twins. Now Carcano developed single-cylinder 350cc machines that had a remarkable run of success over the next four seasons, with two Junior TT wins and four consecutive world titles. Not so good was the record of an in-line 500cc water-cooled four-cylinder racer with shaft drive, one that had been commissioned elsewhere by Giorgio Parodi. Though bristling with novelties, it was not an easy machine to ride, and was abandoned after a couple of half-hearted seasons, perhaps prematurely.

Its immediate replacement was another single-cylinder model, but this was a relatively unsuccessful stop gap. For 1955, Carcano designed one of the most extraordinary racing motorcycles of all time, the 500cc V-eight. Of incredible complexity, its technical brilliance seems to have blinded many commentators to the fact that, even with two full seasons of development behind it, it was really a failure. It was also hideously expensive, and no doubt contributed considerably to the financial troubles that forced Moto Guzzi to withdraw from racing at the end of 1957 and disband the racing department.

For a time, Moto Guzzi was in grave danger of collapse, and indeed was briefly in receivership in 1966, due to changing social attitudes to motorcycles and

124cc Moto Guzzi 125TT (two-stroke) 1985

949cc Moto Guzzi Le Mans 1000 (ohv V-twin) 1984

346cc Moto Guzzi 350NTX (ohv V-twin) 1987

744cc Moto Guzzi Targa (ohv V-twin) 1990

346cc Moto Guzzi V35 III (ohv V-twin)

the Fiat 500 car, which brought cheap four-wheeled transport to the masses.

But the situation was retrieved by one machine, the V7. Work on it had started in 1964 as a military machine, but a civilian version was shown at Milan in 1965 and was a big hit. This 700cc V-twin with its in-line crank was eventually developed into the machines Moto Guzzi is still producing at the end of the 1990s, but initially it was produced in just two guises, civilian and softer tuned military versions.

In 1968 the V7 became the 757cc V7 Special (Ambassador in the USA), but it was at the Milan Show of 1971 that Guzzi unveiled perhaps its finest sporting machine, the V7 Sport. The first version, called the Telaio Rosso (red frame) was a limited edition special to homologate racing versions, and featured a lightweight chrome-molybdenum frame and hand-built internals. Some 200 were made, but even the later production versions performed extremely well, with a top speed of more than 125mph (faster even than the Honda CB750 and Kawasaki H2).

In 1973 industrialist Alessandro De Tomaso bought Moto Guzzi, and development of the twins slowed as he preferred four-cylinder machines. In 1974 the lower specification 750S replaced the V7 Sport, while the touring 850GT became the 850T. In 1975 the 750 S3 was produced, which carried a disappointing number of the touring 850 T3's components.

The 844cc engine also proved significant for Moto Guzzi, as the US variant, the Eldorado, was also offered as the California, which in much uprated form is still in

1064cc Moto Guzzi Quota (ohv V-twin) 1998

949cc Moto Guzzi 1000S (ohv V-twin) 1990

949cc Moto Guzzi California III Classic (ohv V-twin) 1991

744cc Moto Guzzi Strada (ohv V-twin) 1993

744cc Moto Guzzi Nevada (ohv V-twin) 1993

992cc Moto Guzzi Daytona 1000ie (high cam V-twin) 1993

1064cc Moto Guzzi 1100 Sport (ohv V-twin) 1993

1064cc Moto Guzzi V11 Sport (ohv V-twin) 1999

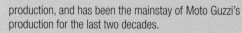

production, and has been the mainstay of Moto Guzzi's production for the last two decades.

Interesting technologically but a commercial failure was the V1000 Convert, with car-type automatic transmission, inspired by De Tomaso's automotive bias.

In 1978 Guzzi took on BMW's sports tourers with the SP1000 Spada, which continued in production until 1983, although its performance was generally poor. In 1984 the SPII appeared, with a 949cc square-finned engine shared with the California II and running gear from the T5.

But in 1975 Moto Guzzi unveiled the machine most remembered today, the Le Mans. Essentially an uprated V7 with an 844cc engine, the styling was highly attractive and the performance exceptional. In 1978 the Le Mans II superseded the original, but lost some of its appeal because of the bulkier fairing replacing the small nose cone. The Le Mans series continued to the Le Mans V, which was finally replaced by the eight-valve Daytona, designed by Dr John Wittner, an American Moto Guzzi racing enthusiast (and former dentist) who ended up working for the factory.

Smaller V-twins were also being produced, starting with the V50 and V35 in 1977, with sporting Imola and Monza versions following shortly. The designs were clever in some respects, but build quality and performance were poor.

Various versions and capacities were produced, including the 750cc V75, 650cc V65 Lario, enduro-styled V65 TT and the later V65 NTX, and custom variants including the V65 Florida.

The 750 Targa of 1989 underlined how far behind Moto Guzzi was falling though, as it was the slowest sports 750 of the early 1990s.

The John Wittner-developed Daytona RS of 1991 restored some faith in Guzzi's products, although sales remained low into the 1990s, when the range also included the 949cc Quota trail bike of 1992, the Strada 1000 roadster, and uprated California 1100 of 1993. In 1997 this became the fuel injected California EV, which ran alongside the two-valve per cylinder 1100 Sport of 1994, a bike which proved more popular than the Daytona as it offered similar performance for less money.

In 1996 Guzzi offered the strangely styled Centauro, then in 1998 the Quota grew into the Quota ES, with a 1064cc engine and major styling revisions. Production of the new V11 Sport - first unveiled at Milan in 1997, started in 1999, while in 1998 the company displayed a technically advanced 75 degree V-twin engine intended for supersports use and as a World Superbike contender. For the moment, the California and its two variants, the Special and Jackal, are still Guzzi's best selling machines.

However, the company's future is currently uncertain as a proposed move from the original, cramped Mandello site to a new factory at Monza was cancelled after causing considerable unrest among the workforce. Managing director Oscar Cecchinato was sacked and Guzzi will now be uprating its old, Mandello factory instead.

MOTOSACOCHE (MAG) • Switzerland
1899–1957

Founders Armand and Henry Dufaux gained fame with 241cc and 290cc bicycle attachments. Afterwards they built a seven-cylinder radial engine, but production models had 247cc to 996cc ioe and partly ohv single-cylinder and V-twin engines. From 1930 onward new sv versions superseded the ioe engines. In addition to motorcycles, the Swiss factory also supplied proprietary power units to motorcycle factories in many countries. There were also branch factories in Lyon and Milan; other firms including Royal Enfield in England and Triumph in Germany built Motosacoche engines under licence. Among factories which fitted these superb engines in England were Brough Superior, Matchless, Ariel, Rex Acme, New Henley, Lea Francis, Morgan and New Hudson. Motosacoche proprietary engines were also known as MAG. Other factories included the German Standard, OD, Triumph (Orial), Imperia, Spiegler, MA, Bayern, Neander, Luwe, Hecker, Bücker; the Austrian DSH, Werner-MAG, EM; the French Monet Goyon; the Hungarian Meray, the Swiss Condor and Allegro. Very prominent were the 347cc and 498cc ohv singles, also 497cc and 597cc ioe and ohv V-twins.

Dougal Marchant and Bert Le Vack were among leading Motosacoche designers and it was Marchant who produced between 1927 and 1929 extremely fast 248cc, 348cc and 498cc ohc single-cylinder works racing engines. Only a few favoured MAG engine customers, including Standard, Triumph, Monet-Goyon etc., received such engines for their works riders. Wal Handley won in 1928 the 350cc and 500cc class in the Grand Prix of Europe on them. For its own works riders Motosacoche also had in the years up to 1927 a few 498cc and 748cc V-twins with ohc engines, but these were suitable only for the many hillclimbs of that period. Among leading Motosacoche works riders were Francesco Franconi, Luigi and Bruno Martinelli, Paul Oilter, Artur Bizzozero, Ernst Haenny, Jean Gex, Augsburger, Rossi and among foreign works riders besides Handley, Luigi Arcangeli, Carlo Barsanti, Charly Dodson, Artur Simcock, Ignaco Faura, Hans Soenius and Anton Uroic. There were also other riders such as Otto Ley, Toni Fleischmann (both Triumph); Artur Dom, Karl Gall, Paul Rüttchen, Rudi Ecker and Hermann Lang (all Standard); Jean Goussorgues and Pierre Debasieux (all Monet Goyon) etc. who won races on MAG-engined machines.

Privateers got from 1931 onwards a 498cc ohv racer, the D50, with a special engine which had both pushrods in a central tube and looked like an ohc design. These engines were catalogued not only in Motosacoche's own motorcycles, but also at Standard, OD, Triumph and other factories. Among riders of such `private' racers were Count von Alvensleben, Fritz Köhler, Franz Hecker and others. Production engines of the 1930s included besides 347cc and 497cc sv singles and 497cc ohv singles also a superb 846cc sv V-twin touring model, the last Le Vack design before he was killed when testing a model. A few new 498cc ohc singles were built in the mid-1930s for the works team, but no new designs appeared from that time until after the war, when Dougal Marchant created a very unorthodox 235cc single-cylinder sv model, which never went into quantity production. The only post-war versions built were a 248cc ohv single with unit-design engine and shaft-drive and a 246cc vertical twin with the Richard Küchen-designed Opti ohc motor.

498cc Motosacoche (ioe V-twin) 1924

598cc Motosacoche (ioe V-twin) 1926

496cc Motosacoche (sv) 1933

498cc Motosacoche (sv) 1921

246cc Motosacoche (ohc twin Opti) 1955

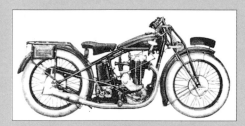

496cc Motosacoche (ohv) 1929

498cc Motosacoche (ohv) 1931

746cc Motosacoche (ioe V-twin) 1931

MOTOPIANA • Italy 1923–1931

Initially fitted 147cc to 247cc Villiers-engines and also 246cc to 490cc JAP sv and ohv motors into its own very sporty frames. Late in 1927, Gualtiero Piana produced his first 248cc sv engine, and afterwards an ohv version.

MOTO ROMA • England 1999-

Range of scooters built by the Taiwanese Her Chee company to the specifications of Bicester-based E. P. Barrus, a marine and agricultural business, in response to the rapidly growing UK scooter market. The range comprises GoGo, Roadrunner and Grand Prix models with two-stroke engines of 50cc and 100cc, and a 125cc four-stroke. The brand name is only used in the UK.

MOTO REVE • Switzerland (England) 1903–1925

Once a leading motorcycle and proprietary engine manufacturer. Built 298cc, 403cc and 497cc V-twins and in 1909 a vertical twin. It had a branch factory in England which produced Alp motorcycles. Its last model, in 1925, had a modern 346cc ohv engine.

MOTORMEYER • The Netherlands 1949–1951

Built a limited number of 346cc two-stroke, double-piston, single-cylinder machines.

MOTOSACOCHE (MAG) • Switzerland 1899–1957

See panel

MOTO-SCOOT • America 1936–1949

Basic Lauson-powered scooters which sold reasonably well up to WW2.

MOTOTRANS • Spain 1957–1982

Under the Franco regime, the import of foreign motorcycles into Spain was prohibited, so Mototrans manufactured Italian Ducati designs. In time, the company branched out with its own machines, mainly off-road and trial bikes with proprietary two-stroke engines of 50cc. Mototrans was taken over and closed by Semsa Yamaha in 1982.

MOUNTAINEER • England 1902–1926

Early machines had Minerva, Fafnir and MMC engines. After the war, only one model, a 269cc two-stroke with a three-port engine, was built in small numbers. It had an Albion two-speed gearbox and belt drive.

MOVESA • Spain 1952–early 1960s

Closely connected with Peugeot of France, the Movesa had a 173cc Peugeot two-stroke engine.

MOVEO • England c1907

Assembled machines with 3.5hp single-cylinder and 5hp V-twin JAP engines.

MOWAG • Switzerland 1958

Produced the Volksroller scooter in limited numbers, using a 50cc two-stroke engine.

MOWE • Germany 1903–1908

Produced by the same factory which in later years built Walter motorcycles, the Mowe was equipped with 3.25hp and 3.50hp single-cylinder and 5hp V-twin Fafnir engines.

MOY • Poland 1937–1940

Small factory which produced lightweights with own 172cc two-stroke engines.

M&P • France late 1920s to late 1930s

Producer of lightweight-machines with 98cc and 123cc Aubier-Dunne engines.

MP • Italy 1933–1935

Built by Mario Penazio at Turin, the MP had a modern pressed steel frame and English Sturmey-Archer proprietary engines, ie ohv singles with 347cc and 497cc.

MPH • England 1920–1924

Like the Mountaineer a very simple machine. The 269cc Wall two-stroke engine was fitted. The gearbox was a two-speed Roc.

MR • France 1923–1926

Equipped with various Train engines, the Italian MR was made by the Officine Mecchaniche Romeo Raimondi at Turin. Most versions had 174cc two-stroke engines; earlier ones 98cc.

MR • France 1926

This MR also concentrated on lightweights. 98cc and 123cc Aubier-Dunne, Ydral and Sachs engines played a major part. Special versions made by the factory competed successfully in long distance events.

1197cc Münch 4 (ohc four-cylinder NSU) 1971

MT • Italy 1949–1953

Teresio Muratore designed modern 248cc vertical ohc twins, but was unable to produce larger numbers of these interesting touring and sports machines.

MT • Austria 1925–1937

The Austrian MT was designed by Count Matthias Thun on typical English lines with mainly English parts. Among them were 147cc to 344cc Villiers engines as well as 346cc, 490cc and 746cc JAP sv and ohv engines. The last ones were V-twins. Special models, mainly racing machines, had also 248cc ohv Blackburne and 497cc ohv MAG motors. Thun, who also imported Villiers engines into Austria, used the 344cc Villiers vertical-twin and the water-cooled 247cc single-cylinder engine. Among leading MT riders were Count Phillip Boos-Waldeck, Josef Opawsky, Friedrich Schwarz, Robert Wolf, F. J. Meyer and Lorenz Hubbauer.

MUCO • Germany 1921–1924

Bicycle attachment engines of 118cc, which had to be fitted outside of the rear wheels.

MUFI (IMPERATOR) • Germany 1925–1926

Built one model only. This was a simple 348cc two-stroke machine with a three-port, deflector-type engine.

MULLER • Italy 1950–late 1970s

Made by a German expatriate, these machines used both two and four-stroke NSU engines. With NSU's withdrawal from manufacturing, Muller switched to Sachs, Franco Morini and latterly Hiro engines for their trail models.

MULLER • Austria 1923–1926

A simple design of two-stroke, the Austrian Muller was a 183cc machine with a strengthened bicycle frame and a unit-design engine, which had a two-speed gearbox and a big outside flywheel.

MUNCH • Germany 1966–

For many years, Friedl Münch worked in the racing department at Horex. After Horex closed in 1959, he was involved in a number of racing projects, plus a collaboration with American Floyd Clymer in an abortive effort to revive manufacture of the Indian motorcycle. Another involvement was with Helmut Fath and the four-cylinder URS engine. However, he is best-known for his design and construction of the 'Mammoth' four-cylinder motorcycle, using a modified NSU Prinz car engine, a 1000cc air-cooled ohc four cylinder that gave 55hp at 5800rpm, the engine being set transversely and driving a special four-speed gearbox by chain. Subsequent 1300cc engines gave considerably more power.

The Mammoth was no one-off special, but a series-produced machine, though, being hand made and very expensive, it was not produced in large numbers. Over the years several different backers came and went, but despite financial ups and downs the enterprise continued. Though at the time of writing it is not entirely clear whether Münch is currently building Mammoths to order (he is now well into his 60s) the project has never been publicly abandoned.

MUSTANG • America 1946–1964

Destined mainly for town-riding, the primitively built Mustang had a 314cc sv single-cylinder engine.

MV AGUSTA • Italy 1945–1978

See panel

MVB • Italy 1953–1956

Produced 49cc mopeds and motorcycles with 123cc and 147cc two-strokes in limited numbers.

MW • Germany 1923–1926

The MW, designed by Paul Paffrath, was an unorthodox design with a frame partly constructed from aluminum and partly pressed steel, welded and rivetted. The first version had a 249cc ohv single-cylinder engine and three-speed gearbox; the second model a 144cc two-stroke vertical-twin of its own design and manufacture. Both machines had rear suspension. After WW2, Paffrath—whose original home was in East Germany—lived in West Germany and from 1949 to 1953 produced a bicycle attachment engine, called Eilenriede.

MYMSA • Spain 1953–1962

Produced a wide range of small two-strokes of 75cc, 99cc, 123cc and 175cc in limited numbers.

MZ • (East) Germany 1953–

See panel

MV AGUSTA • Italy 1945–1977, 1999-

Meccanica Verghera Agusta holds the considerable distinction of having won more world titles in road racing than almost all other makes put together. Between 1952 and 1974, the company captured no fewer than 37 titles in every class from 125cc to 500cc–all this from a company whose main business was not motorcycles at all, but the design and manufacture of helicopters.

The first MV dates from 1945. Conceived by aircraft manufacturer Count Domenico Agusta to take advantage of the post-war shortage of transport, it was a 100cc two-stroke with two-speed gearbox. A 125cc, four-speed racing version, with three gears and telescopic forks, appeared in 1948.

The two-stroke MV was no match for the dohc FB Mondial, however, so Count Agusta poached Arturo Magini and Ing. Pietro Remor from Gilera and set them to work. Remor designed a 125cc dohc single and a 500cc four and Magni had them running within six months, the new machines first appearing at the 1950 Belgian Grand Prix. It was not until 1952, however, that they really started to make a mark, with Cecil Sandford winning the 125cc TT and Les Graham's excellent second in the Senior on the four. Sandford went on to win that year's 125cc championship, but the MV four continued to be overshadowed by the Gilera until Gilera withdrew from racing at the end of 1957. Thereafter, with the removal of direct competition from the racing scene, winning the Senior world title became almost taken for granted.

In contrast to the long record of track success, MV's road-going machinery was almost all thoroughly uninspired. It lacked any hint of the style of the racing bikes, and the factory seemed for a long time to be more interested in scooters than in designing and making road-

147cc MV Agusta (two-stroke) 1957

743cc MV Agusta 750S (dohc four cylinder) 1975

349cc MV Agusta 350GT EL (ohv twin) 1975

743cc MV Agusta 750GT (dohc four-cylinder) 1975

going motorcycles. Attempts to export to England even when the MV name was at the height of its fame were almost entirely fruitless, while so few of the later four-cylinder road bikes were produced that they might as well have been made to special order.

Racing success continued, however. In 1953, a 350cc four appeared alongside the 500cc model, but that same year Les Graham was tragically killed in the Senior TT, so little development work was done on it. It was not until 1956 that the fours really lived up to their promise, with John Surtees riding for MV. Remor had left MV by then, development thereafter being in the hands of Arturo Magni. Over the years, the MV fours (and three-cylinder models) were to be ridden by some of the world's finest – including Mike Hailwood, Giacomo Agostini and Phil Read. On 125cc and 250cc, there were such legends as Carlo Ubbialli, Tarquinio Provini and Luigi Taveri. When the Japanese began their thrust forward in the 125cc and 250cc classes, MV withdrew to concentrate on the larger ones, Ubbiali's 125cc and 250cc titles in 1960 were the last for MV.

When Count Agusta died in 1971, it was universally expected that MV's racing involvement would cease, especially as the Japanese were now threatening to compete in the larger classes, while lack of racing success by three- and four-cylinder racing models added to the pessimism that started to pervade the works. However, Corrido Agusta took up the challenge, and Arturo Magni and designer Ruggero Mazza kept MV ahead, but only for a few short years. Corrido lacked Domenico's passionate enthusiasm, and anyway the company simply could not match the natural superiority of two-strokes in grand prix racing - in 1976 an MV was the last four-stroke to win a grand prix race.

The road bike side of the business had never been particularly successful since the utility machines of the early days, despite the exotic nature of the later machines and their desirability, simply because they were so expensive to produce, and initially did not take advantage of the racing bikes' successes. The first road-going four-cylinder MV for example was not a sports bike but an unattractively styled 600cc tourer, although in 1970 MV relented and produced the 750 Sport, with dohc, four cylinders and shaft drive. In 1975 MV produced the 750S America, with a full fairing and new, highly attractive styling, for which there was great demand despite the very high price, but again it did not make a profit for the company.

Other factors were also involved in the demise of MV Agusta motorcycles. In 1973 the Italian government bought a 51 per cent in the company, as it regarded it primarily as a defence contractor because of the very successful production of helicopters, and as such the motorcycle arm was considered unimportant. Finally, MV forged a plan to produce two helicopters, the A109 and A129 Mangusta, to take it to the forefront of world helicopter design. The very high cost of development meant all of the company's funds had to be concentrated on this project, and the motorcycles suffered as a result.

499cc MV Agusta works grand prix racer (dohc four) 1956

Production ceased in 1977, although bikes continued to be sold from stocks until around 1981, and that appeared to be the end of motorcycling's most glamorous name.

But in 1992 the rights to the MV Agusta title were bought by Cagiva, who by this stage also owned Ducati among other names. Work started on a four-cylinder machine which Cagiva insisted would be badged Cagiva and not MV Agusta, although few believed this.

Initial engine work was carried out in conjunction with Ferrari, but this proved too costly, and Cagiva began suffering financial problems which slowed development. But the sale of Ducati in 1997 generated much needed funds, and the MV project restarted at full pace, the bike being designed by Massimo Tamburini who had previously been responsible for the Ducati 916. The new MV Agusta 750 F4 was finally unveiled at the Milan show in 1997, and went into production in 1999 in two versions, the expensive Serie Oro (gold series) with carbon fiber bodywork and magnesium castings, and the less expensive F4S, with conventional aluminum and injection-moulded plastic components.

In early tests the 172mph machine has been acclaimed for its handling and performance, and is also regarded as one of the most beautiful motorcycles ever made, so is seen as a fitting legacy to MV's glorious past. It only remains to be seen how the racing version will do in World Superbike racing.

As a footnote, Cagiva announced that it is changing its name to MV Agusta from July 1999, although the Cagiva badge will be retained, effectively reviving in full this famous Italian manufacturer.

749cc MV Agusta F4 (dohc fuel-injected, liquid-cooled transverse four-cylinder) 1999

MZ (MÜZ) • (East) Germany 1953–

MZ (Motorad Zschopau) was the successor of IFA, in turn the successor to the pre-war DKW from 1946, working from the old DKW factory at Zschopau. Taking the pre-war DKW RT125 as a basis, Walter Kaaden developed 125cc single and 250cc twin racers, with disk valve induction, which, by the late 1950s, first matched and then exceeded the specific power outputs of the best four-strokes of the day. A major blow at the end of 1961 was the defection of top rider Ernst Deger to Suzuki, to whom he revealed most of MZ's technology and, although MZ continued to race, it now put more emphasis on models for the ISDT and similar events.

Road machines of 125cc and 250cc based on this experience were offered for sale and exported to a number of countries at very competitive prices. However, when faced with the ramshackle East German economy,

even Walter Kaaden's dedication and hard work on the development side was not enough to keep MZ ahead. Although its domestic customers had no choice, other European customers did, and MZ gradually lost sales to the Japanese industry. Long before the re-unification of Germany, MZ was in financial difficulties, and, when state aid was withdrawn, the company came near to collapse.

At the end of 1991 the company shed many jobs and announced plans for a drastic reorganization, but it wasn't until 1994 that it made a credible comeback. Production of the old two-strokes was now to be continued under license in Turkey: the models now available were the ETZ251 and ETZ300, developments of the ETZ250 which first appeared in 1984 as an updated version of the older TS250, still with its distinctive stack of large, horizontal engine cooling fins.

In this year the company name changed to MüZ (Motorad über Zschopau), and it displayed the attractive

Skorpion, styled by British consultancy Seymour Powell and powered by a Yamaha XTZ660 single-cylinder four-stroke engine. When the bike was eventually produced around 18 months later, build quality was still not up to Japanese standards and a fairly high price prevented great sales success, but it did well enough for MüZ to produce more single-cylinder machines, such as the Baghira.

More excitingly, in 1998 the company returned to grand prix racing, taking over the French Elf racing project and signalling the possibility of a brighter future for a company which has spent many years on the brink of collapse.

This followed the takeover of MüZ by a Malaysian auto company, with a much-needed injection of funds, although the subsequent collapse of the far eastern economies has meant once again money is tighter than it might have been.

123cc MZ 125/G (two-stroke single) 1966

248cc MZ works racer (two-stroke twin) 1959

248cc MZ works racer (two-stroke twin) 1972

248cc MZ 250/1 G (two-stroke single) 1967

243cc MZ ETZ251 (two-stroke single) 1982

*660cc MüZ Skorpion Traveler
(ohv single Yamaha) 1999*

*660cc MüZ Skorpion Tour
(ohv single Yamaha) 1999*

660cc MüZ Skorpion Sport (ohv single Yamaha) 1999

660cc MüZ Baghira (ohv single Yamaha) 1999

660cc MüZ Mastiff (ohv single Yamaha) 1999

N

NAMAPO • Germany 1921–1924

Designed by Bernhard Nagl, the Namapo was built in the northern part of Germany—at Stettin which belongs now to Poland—and was nearly unknown in the south. It was made with own 147cc and 197cc sv single-cylinder engines. The smaller version was sold also as a bicycle attachment engine.

NARCISSE • France 1950–1953

Assembler of two-stroke machines with 48cc and 98cc Aubier-Dunne and some Sachs engines.

NARCLA • Spain 1955–1967

Small assembler which concentrated on 123cc two-strokes.

NASSETTI • Italy 1951–1957

Manufacturer of accessories, whose lightweight motorcycles—which included the 49cc Pellegrino with a horizontal cylinder and friction drive—had two-stroke engines and modern frames with telescopic forks. Ettore Nassetti, the designer-manufacturer, used tubular and pressed steel frames for his motorcycles.

NASSOVIA • Germany 1925

Small producer, whose motorcycles had the rare 2.75hp Anzani engine.

NAZZARO • Italy 1926–1928

Made by Eugenio Nazzaro of Turin, brother of the famous racing-car driver Felice Nazzaro (Fiat), the machine had a 173cc ohv engine and was built in limited numbers only.

NEAL-DALM • England 1920-1921

Made in Sparkbrook, Birmingham by cycle shop owner S. G. Neal using 318cc engines built by J.C. Dalman & Son, Birmingham.

NEALL • England 1910–1914

Fitted with 2.5hp and 3hp Precision proprietary engines, the Neall was an assembled machine.

NEANDER • Germany 1924–1929

Designed by the famous Ernst Neumann-Neander, who was known for his unorthodox creations, the Neander had a frame made from duralumin covered with cadmium, so that enamelling of the frame was not necessary. The frame included the gasoline tank. A fork with small leaf springs and a bucket seat were other features of the Neander, which was also built under licence by the famous Opel car

factory. While Opel fitted its own 498cc engines, all Neander machines had proprietary power units of 122cc to 996cc. These were Villiers two-strokes, Küchen single-cylinder ohc engines of 347cc and 497cc, MAG engines with ioe valves of 497cc, 746cc and 996cc, JAP sv and ohv engines from 490cc to 996cc and if required other power units could also be fitted. Racing successes were gained by 172cc models with Villiers Brooklands engines ridden by Gohr and Goretzki.

NECCHI • Italy 1951–1953

Assembled motorcycles with 98cc and 123cc Villiers two-stroke engines.

NECO • Czechoslovakia 1923–1927

Limited production of 346cc and 490cc sv and ohv machines with JAP engines.

NEGAS & RAY • Italy 1925–1928

Milan motorcycle importer which ventured into motorcycle production with 348cc unit-design sv singles which had big outside flywheels. Giuseppe Remondini, the designer, also built an ohv version in 1927 and in the 1930s joined the French Jonghi factory.

NEGRINI • Italy 1954–1984

Concentrated on the quantity production of 48cc and 49cc two-stroke machines, with three and four-speeds, as well as motocrossers. Earlier models had 110cc and 123cc two-stroke engines.

NEMALETTE • Germany 1924–1925

Unorthodox design with two rear wheels, a car-like body and a 173cc DKW two-stroke engine. It is not known if this machine was produced in any large quantities.

NERA • Germany 1949–1950

Designed by W. Neuscheler, the Nera was among the first post-war scooters in the country. Engines used were the 120cc Ilo and the 149cc Sachs.

NER-A-CAR • America (England) 1921–1926

Designed by J. Neracher, the American-built machine had a low, channel-steel car-like frame. The engine used was a 283cc two-stroke with friction drive to the rear wheel. Built under licence in England, developed versions of this unorthodox machine had 347cc Blackburne sv and ohv engines. Some models built in 1925 and 1926 also had bucket seats and deeply valanced mudguards. The Ner-a-car was a comfortable machine with excellent road-holding. The machines built in England had chain drive and also an improved fork design.

172cc Neander (two-stroke Villiers) 1925

996cc Neander (ioe V-twin MAG) 1929

348cc Ner-a-Car (sv Blackburne) 1924

285cc Ner-a-Car (two-stroke Simplex) 1923

NERVOR • France 1947–1958

Closely connected with Radior, Nervor produced well-finished machines with engines from 48cc to 248cc. Among them were its own power units, but also proprietary engines made by NSU and the French AMC. Nervor's top model was a 248cc vertical two-stroke twin with air cooling.

NESTOR • England 1913–1914

Produced Villiers-engined 269cc two-strokes and Precision-engined 296cc and 347cc sv machines, in limited numbers.

348cc Ner-a-Car De Luxe (sv Blackburne) 1924

496cc Nestoria (sv Sturmey-Archer) 1930

346cc Nestoria (two-stroke) 1925

NESTORIA • Germany 1923–1931

Produced 289cc and 346cc two-strokes with its own engines; took over the Astoria factory in 1925 and then built Küchen-engined 348cc and 498cc three-valve, single-cylinder ohc machines. Other versions had 496cc and 596cc MAG engines with ioe valves and eventually 198cc ohv Sturmey-Archer and 497cc sv Sturmey-Archer single-cylinder engines.

NETTUNIA • Italy 1950–1953

Equipped with Busi-designed 123cc and 158cc two-stroke engines, all Nettunia machines had four-speed gearboxes and were of sound design.

NEVA • France 1926–1927

Made by a small factory, these machines had 347cc ohv Anzani single-cylinder engines.

NEVAL • Russia 1973–

The factory was originally state owned until the shortly after the break up of the Soviet Union, when it has been attempting to become independent. It still produces the 174cc Voshkod and 346cc Ish-Planeta single-cylinder two-strokes, the 347cc Ish-Jupiter two-stroke twin and several versions of a 650cc boxer twin, based on an old BMW design, called the Ural and Dnepr. These include the Dnepr Classic and Dnepr Phoenix, with upswept exhaust pipes.

NEVE-ILO • Germany 1924–1926

Was among the first factories which fitted the then new 132cc and 170cc Ilo two-stroke proprietary engines into its own frames. Ilo became eventually one of the leading producers of two-stroke proprietary engines in the world.

NEW COMET • England 1905–1932

Built motorcycles with interruptions. Haden, the designer-manufacturer, used Villiers, Peco, JAP and Precision engines for his frames and there was also a Climax-engined 293cc two-stroke version. A major break in production occurred from 1924 to 1931, when the last New Comet machines were built. They were equipped with 198cc Villiers engines.

NEW COULSON • England 1922–1924

Originally the Coulson-B, the New Coulson had long leaf springs on either side of the rear wheel and a double leaf-sprung front fork. Otherwise it was a conventional motorcycle with 269cc two-stroke and 346cc and 498cc sv and ohv engines made by Bradshaw and Blackburne. Eric Longden won many races on Blackburne-engined machines. Some racing models had also JAP engines, including a V-twin ohv version of 496cc.

NEW ERA • America c1908–1913

Open-framed unorthodox design with a 546cc sv engine below the bucket seat and the gasoline tank above the rear wheel.

NEW ERA • England 1920–1922

Used mainly the 311cc Dalm two-stroke engine, but also other power units made by Precision and JAP.

NEW GERRARD • England 1922–1940

To be exact, this machine was really a Scottish product, made by famous racing motorcyclist Jock Porter. For a period when demand was bigger than production at Edinburgh, Campion in Nottingham produced frames on behalf of the Scottish factory. For years Porter fitted Blackburne engines from 173cc to 498cc into good and comparatively light frames, but concentrated from the late 1920s onward on 348cc models with ohv engines. When Blackburne stopped supplying such engines, Porter switched to JAP. He won TT and grand prix races on his machines. Other successful riders were the Austrians Georg Gartner, Karl Gall, Willi Melichar and Franz Putzker. Scottish patriots could get Scottish proprietary engines fitted; around 1922–1923 346cc sleeve-valve Barr & Stroud engines were available.

NEW HENLEY • England 1920–1929

This make is already mentioned under Henley, as there was not much difference between the Henley and the New

346cc New Hudson (ohv) 1927

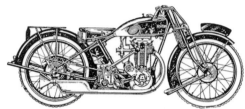

496cc New Hudson (ohv) 1929

496cc New Hudson (ohv) 1930

348cc New Gerrard (ohv JAP) 1928

348cc New Henley (ohv JAP) 1929

246cc New Imperial (ohv) 1926

246cc New Imperial (ohv JAP) 1927

248cc New Imperial (ohv Grand Prix) 1938

Henley. The Clarke brothers, original owners of the Birmingham-based factory, had to sell it when their father, who put up the money, withdrew his support.

NEW HOTSPUR • England c1914

JAP-powered machines built by Stutter and Abrey, Tottenham, London.

NEW HUDSON • England 1909–1957

Was a well-known motorcycle factory, which had in Fred Hutton and Bert Le Vack two leading designers and riders. Other famous racing men with this make were Jimmy Guthrie and Tom Bullus. Most models built were sv and ohv singles with own 346cc, 496cc and 598cc engines, although a 211cc two-stroke was also made around WW1. This nice little machine had 62mm x 70mm bore and stroke, a two-speed gearbox, and according to the model, belt or chain drive. Le Vack broke many records at Brooklands in the late 1920s; soon afterwards further development led to models with sheet metal panels over engines and gearboxes. Vic Mole, a motorcycle sales expert, was the man behind this idea, which was not too successful. Motorcycle production was stopped in 1933 and the name revived by BSA after 1945, when it produced mopeds with 98cc Villiers engines, in contrast to the big V-twins also made by New Hudson in pre-WW1 days. There were also MAG-engined three-wheelers built between the wars; via Bert Le Vack, the English factory had good connections with the Swiss make.

NEW IMPERIAL • England 1910–1939

Norman T. Downs, who presided over New Imperial from 1899 to his death in 1936, made his first JAP-engined motorcycle in 1910. After WW1 it concentrated on JAP-engined lightweights, scoring its first TT win in the 1921 Lightweight race and its last (of six) in 1936 – the last time a British bike won the race. From 1926, New Imperial made its own engine, designed by the 20-year-old Matt Wright, who remained development engineer and in charge of racing until 1937. Very well made and sporting, the marque sold well in the 1920s. In the 1930s 150cc, 250cc, 350cc and 500cc unit construction models were developed, offered later with optional spring frames. In 1934 Wright built a 500cc twin that Ginger Wood rode at Brooklands to put 102.27 miles into an hour –

the first `hour' at over 100mph by a 500cc `multi'. A supercharged version was also built. Unlike the 250cc racers, the V-twin was a notoriously difficult machine to race, so much so that Stanley Woods declined to ride it after one trial!

New Imperial was very successful until Norman Downs' death late in 1936. Bob Foster's TT win that year brought business which the factory could not cope with, and it resorted to sub-contracting with disastrous results. The resulting claims for rectification work bankrupted the concern, which was sold to Triumph's Jack Sangster in 1939 and moved to Coventry. It was Sangster's intention to revive New Imperial after the war, but German bombing destroyed the factory.

NEW KNIGHT • England 1923–1931

Small assembler of motorcycles with 147cc to 344cc Villiers two-stroke and 293cc JAP sv engines.

NEW MAP • France 1920-late 1950s

Built during the years a wide range of assembled machines with engines from 98cc to 998cc and engines made by Zurcher, JAP, Chaise, Blackburne, MAG, Ydral, AMC, Aubier Dunne, Sachs and Opti. New Map built also Mistral-engined 48cc mopeds and even small minicars with 123cc two-stroke engines. That was in the early 1950s, when motorcycle production concentrated around Ydral and AMC-engined models from 98cc to 248cc with two-stroke and ohv power units. Scooters and fully enclosed motorcycles were other products of this very versatile French factory.

NEW MOTORCYCLE • France 1925–1930

The Georges Roy-designed New Motorcycle had 246cc two-stroke and also 346cc ohv and ohc engines made by Chaise and MAG. Other power units made by these factories were also fitted.

NEWMOUNT • England 1929–1933

These machines—put together at Coventry—were really German Zündapp products with tubular frames. Engines fitted were 198cc, 248cc and 298cc Zündapp three-port deflector-type two-strokes and 348cc and 498cc Python four-valve ohv single-cylinders.

246cc New Imperial (ohv) 1938

496cc New Imperial (ohv) 1936

NEW PARAGON • England 1919–1923

Produced a range of single-cylinder two-stroke machines with 235cc, 347cc and 478cc engines of own manufacture and with half-elliptic leaf-springs.

NEW RAPID • The Netherlands 1933–1936

Made by the Amsterdam factory of P. J. Meyer, New Rapid supplied Villiers-engined two-strokes of 98cc, 148cc, 196cc, 248cc and 346cc and four-strokes with ohv engines. These included 248cc, 348cc and 498cc four-valve Python engines and also 346cc and 498cc two-valve JAP ohv versions.

NEW RYDER • England 1913–1922

Assembled machines with single-cylinder and V-twin Precision engines in early years, but concentrated after 1918 on Villiers-engined 269cc models.

NEW SCALE • England 1909–1925

Harry Scale first built his Scale motorcycles in very small numbers, but when he reorganized his production in 1919, he called them New Scale. They were assembled machines with 348cc Precision two-stroke and 499cc Blackburne sv engines. They had two-speed gears and chain-cum-belt drive. Later the range of models was expanded by the addition of 346cc versions with Bradshaw ohv engines and mainly with sv and ohv Blackburne engines of similar size. An interesting model which was built by order had the 347cc ohc Dart engine, designed by Sidney. When

New Scale came into difficulties, the factory was taken over by Dot.

NEWTON • England 1921–1922

Villiers-engined 269cc two-strokes of cheap design.

NICHOLAS • England pre-WW1

This small and now forgotten producer of motorcycles built machines equipped with 1.5hp engines which were probably made by MMC.

NICKSON • England 1920–1924

Assembled a variety of models with proprietary engines. These included the 247cc and 269cc Villiers two-strokes, the oil-cooled 348cc ohv Bradshaw and Blackburne's 346cc, and 499cc to 546cc sv singles.

NIESNER • Austria 1905–1911

Designed by Josef Niesner, the Vienna-built 3hp, 3.5hp and 5hp Minerva- and Fafnir-engined motorcycles were among the first made in the old Austro-Hungarian Empire. They were of sound and strong design. Niesner was afterwards Austrian importer for Norton, Royal Enfield and other makes.

NIMBUS • Denmark 1920–1957

Denmark's largest motorcycle factory ever, Fisker & Nielsen Ltd. at Copenhagen, concentrated all those years on only one model. This was a 746cc air-cooled in-line four with ioe and later ohv unit-design engines. With frames made from pressed steel, even the early models had rear suspension, which used open coil springs and a tank consisting of a wide diameter tube. The trailing arm front suspension was superseded by telescopic forks and a triangular tank superseded the earlier one. Common to all Nimbus models was shaft drive. Exports were very limited.

NINON • France 1931–1935

Small producer of ohv 499cc JAP-engined machine.

NIS • Germany 1925–1926

Another small factory which fitted 269cc two-stroke and 293cc JAP sv engines into orthodox frames of own manufacture.

NISSAN • Japan 1951–1956

Now a major car producer, Nissan once produced a range of 60cc machines with its own ohv single-cylinder engines.

746cc Nimbus (ioe four-cylinder) 1924

746cc Nimbus (ohc four-cylinder) 1935

NKF • Germany 1924–1925

Lightweight motorcycles with 132cc Bekamolicence engines, which used a pumping piston in the crankcase.

NLG • England 1905–1912

This maker achieved fame when an NLG racing machine with a large, 2913cc ohv V-twin JAP engine ridden by Cook, reached 90mph in 1909. Production versions housed 499cc single and 770cc V-twin JAP engines.

NMC • Japan early 1950s-early 1960s

Small 123cc and 173cc two-stroke machines, built by a small factory.

NOBLE • England 1901–c1906

The Noble was one of the first makes using the new central Werner position of engine location. The 2.25hp to 4.5hp engines came from De Dion, Minerva, MMC and Coronet as well as its own units.

NON BETTER • Holland 1932–3

Lightweight motorcycles with 98cc Villiers engines built by P. J. Meijer, Amsterdam. The marque was renamed the New Rapid in 1933.

NORBRECK • England 1921–1924

D. H. Valentine's Norbreck machines housed 269cc Villiers and Arden (70mm bore and stroke) two-stroke

NORTON · England 1902–

James Lansdowne Norton made his first Norton motorcycle in 1902, using a French Clement engine in his own frame. This was soon supplemented by a Peugeot-engined V-twin model, on an example of which Rem Fowler won the twin-cylinder race in the first TT of 1907. In the same year, Norton designed the first engine of his own manufacture. He himself competed in the TT in 1909, 1910 and 1911, on the last occasion using the first of his 'Long stroke' engines of 79mm x 100mm, 490cc, dimensions that were to become a Norton tradition.

Illness meant that in 1911 Norton lost control of his own company, which passed to the Vandervell family, although Norton remained as joint managing director with R. T. Shelley. Although Norton did not win a TT again until 1924 (one was second in the 1920 Senior), the exploits at Brooklands of record breaker 'Wizard' O'Donovan secured a ready market for 490cc sv Brooklands Road Special models in the days just before and just after WW1. Post war, Norton took on an even more sporting image, and in 1922 raced an ohv model. 1924 saw Alex Bennett win the Senior TT and George Tucker the sidecar race, while O'Donovan, Rex Judd and, later, Bert Denly continued to break records at Brooklands.

Through these years, Norton offered 500cc sv (16H) 633cc sv (Big four) and 500cc ohv (Model 18) variants. Although James Norton himself, a victim of heart trouble, died in April 1925, the greatest days of his company were still to come. Norton won the Maudes trophy for various achievements five times during the 1920s. It also won the 1926 and 1927 Senior TTs, the latter with the first ohc Norton, which became the CS1 model. This engine however, was, relatively unsuccessful, and was redesigned in both 500cc and 350cc form by Arthur Carroll for 1931. Standing over Carroll's shoulder was Irishman Joe Craig, a Norton rider of the 1920s who, between 1926 and 1955, masterminded Norton's racing success. During the 1930s the ohc Nortons won no less than 14

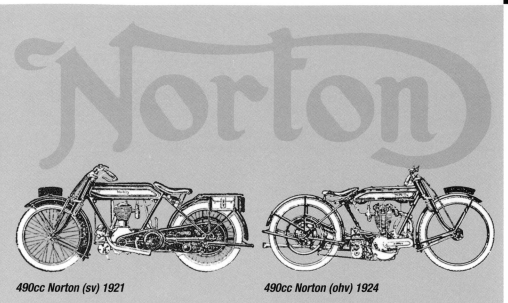

490cc Norton (sv) 1921   *490cc Norton (ohv) 1924*

490cc Norton (ohv) 192

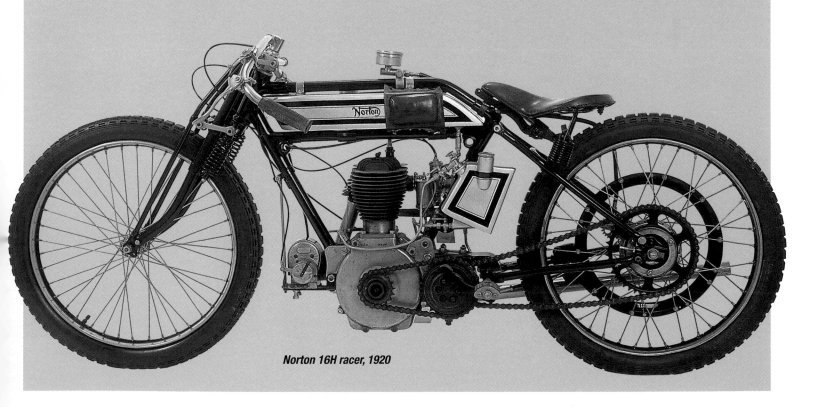

Norton 16H racer, 1920

TTs. At the top of the range, the CSI and 350cc CSJ were superseded by `International' models, which `prepared to Manx specification' were offered for sale as genuine racing machines.

In the years between the two world wars, there is no doubt that the Norton racing success of such star riders as Alex Bennet, Stanley Woods, Tim Hunt, Harold Daniel, Freddie Frith and many more, effectively sold the more mundane road machinery. Successes after 1945 continued the process, as newer stars like Artie Bell and, above all, Geoff Duke continued to win, aided and abetted by the extraordinarily successful McCandless-designed Featherbed frame of 1950 and engine development by Joe Craig and Leo Kuzmicki. However, the single-cylinder Norton could not stave off the challenge of the Gilera Four for ever. Even so, after Gilera withdrew from racing, Norton scored one last TT `double', with Mike Hailwood winning the 1961 Senior race and Phil Read the Junior, and Nortons continued to win the Manx Grand Prix for some years to come.

Norton's 500cc vertical twin, the Dominator, was designed by Bert Hopwood in 1947, but not marketed until after he had left the company, in 1949. During the 1950s Norton design by and large stagnated, although the Featherbed frame became common to all models, including the venerable 16H sv which finally expired in 1954. Hopwood returned to Norton to design the 250cc Jubilee twin of 1958 and the 350cc Navigator in 1960. By that time Norton was owned by AMC (Matchless and AJS) having been sold in anticipation of death duties by the Vandervell family in 1952. The company eventually moved from Birmingham to the AMC factory in Plumstead in 1962. In 1966, AMC collapsed and was sold to Denis Poore's Manganese Bronze Holdings which concentrated its

490cc Norton CS1 (ohc) 1927

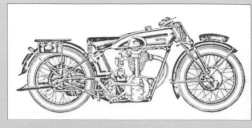

490cc Norton CS1(ohc) 1930

490cc Norton Model 18 (ohv) 1927

490cc Norton (sv) 1931

490cc Norton International (ohc)1933

490cc Norton trials (ohv) 1935

496cc Norton Internatioal (ohc) 1935

Military version of the Norton 16H, 1942

efforts on the Atlas engine, as the 750cc version was known, the original Dominator twin having been increased in capacity over the years from 500cc to 600cc, 650cc, 750cc, and finally (and amazingly in retrospect) 850cc in the last Commando.

A totally new frame was conceived that isolated engine vibration from the main frame – the 'Isolastic' system – and the Norton Commando was revealed at the 1967 Motorcycle Show. The Commando launched a remarkable revival of Norton's fortunes, and in uprated form, stayed in production for ten years. Its engine also formed the basis of Norton's successful re-entry into racing in the production class, and also in the newly instituted Formula 750cc class. Rider-designer Peter Williams was responsible for much of the riding and almost all of the design work involved. After an encouraging second place in the 1970 production TT with a Commando, Dennis Poore gave the go-ahead for an F750 TT and an enthusiastic Poore obtained sponsorship for a full racing team from Imperial Tobacco, which financed the F750 John Player Nortons in 1972, 1973 and 1974. In a program that had its ups and downs over the three seasons, the highest spot was the win in the 1973 F750 TT at over 105mph by Williams with team mate Mick Grant second. The machines in question employed superb streamlining and stainless steel monocoque frames designed by Williams.

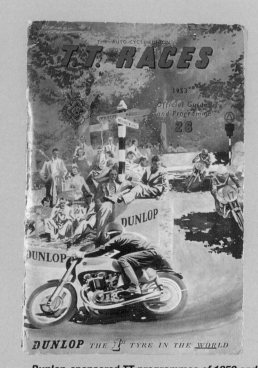

Dunlop-sponsored TT programmes of 1952 and 1953 (right and left)

498cc Manx Norton (ohc) 1947

348cc Manx Norton (ohc) 1938

498cc Manx Norton (dohc) 1962

497cc Norton (ohv twin) 1949

However, 1974 was not so fortunate, with Williams suffering an accident half way through the season. Sponsorship ended – just as a new twin-cylinder engine, the `Challenge', designed by Keith Duckworth of Cosworth Engineering, became available. Planned not only as a 100bhp racing engine, but as the basis of a whole new generation of Norton road bikes, it incorporated four-valve cylinder heads, water-cooling, balancer shafts and a unitary five-speed gearbox. Alas, it was to come to nothing – a Challenge racer was ridden just once by Dave Croxford at the end of 1975 when it was eliminated by a first lap crash. Nor was the road bike ever built. Denis Poore's Norton-Villiers company had, in 1973, been

asked to take over the ailing Triumph-BSA company, and NVT – Norton-Villiers-Triumph – had been formed. But almost immediately, the new company was in trouble with its work force at the Triumph factory at Meriden, which Poore estimated was costing NVT £20,000 a week in disputes and disrupted production, not only at Meriden but as BSA as well. In 1976 the position became impossible and, although government aid was promised, it was not forthcoming in the event. In effect, production ceased, though quite a few Commandos and Interpol police bikes were assembled in 1977 and early 1978.

However, it was not the end. Poore retained the Norton name, and set up a new division at Andover. Part of this

Norton 650SS (ohv twin) 1966

828cc Norton Commando Roadster (ohv twin) 1974

was given the name Norton Motors (1978) Ltd and its brief was to continue the pursuit of a motorcycle powered by a Wankel rotary engine design that Poore had inherited from BSA in 1973. Quite a bit of work had already been done on the running gear, and in 1979 25 machines were made with air-cooled rotary engines for evaluation and testing. In 1981–82, an improved machine was developed, famous ex-Norton and Triumph development engineeer Doug Hele joined the company and in 1983 about 170 `Interpol II' rotary-engined machines were sold to the police, armed forces and the RAC. Overheating and other problems dictated a water-cooled engine and development began again.

In 1987, the company was sold as part of a package to financier Phillippe le Roux and renamed Norton plc. Apparently fascinated by the Norton name, and impressed by the work in hand, Le Roux demanded a production model. As a token for the future, 100 air-cooled `Classic' models were made and sold. At the same time, the engine was being developed for light aircraft and a racing project had been set up which was to produce some encouraging results.

The water-cooled version of the rotary was first sold to the public as the Commander touring bike in 1988, developed alongside a competition version with which Norton returned to racing during 1987. The Spondon-framed 588cc rotary twin engine was developed by a bunch of factory enthusiasts, including project leader Brian Crighton. The rotary motor was then deemed eligible for Formula One racing and Norton was back in national competition the following year, Trevor Nation winning the bike's first high-profile race at the Mallory Park round of the British F1 championship.

It was back in force for a full campaign in 1989, with Nation and new signing Steve Spray running in JPS colours, contesting both the British and World F1 series. Spray won the British Formula One title in fine style, although the factory's world-level outings were less successful. Over the next two seasons the bikes were still a prominent feature of the British championships even though they failed to regain the crown. In 1991 the rotary was deemed eligible for 500 GP racing and Ron Haslam scored a 12th-place finish in a one-off ride at the British GP.

The following year it was Steve Hislop's turn to revive the glory days, the Scot winning the Senior TT to score Norton's first Isle of Man success in 19 years, at an average speed of 121.28mph. Against the odds the rotary went on to win the 1994 British Superbike championship in the hands of another Scot, Ian Simpson. Then tagged the RF1, Crighton claimed 150bhp from the water-cooled rotary motor. This was the last year of the rotary racer.

A road replica called the F1 had appeared in 1990, but despite good handling and performance, the power delivery was very difficult to live with and the bike did not sell in large numbers.

828cc Norton Commando Interpol (ohv twin) 1974

828cc Norton Commando 'John Player' (ohv twin) 1975

In 1991 le Roux left Norton siting problems with American and German subsidiaries, but increasing suspicions about le Roux's motivations led to his conviction several years later of financial irregularities involving the sale of Norton shares.

Ownership of the company meanwhile had passed on to the Canadian Aquilini Group, with rights to the name in Germany passing on to the German Norton importer, Joachim Seifert. At the time this appeared to have no significance, but with the Aquilini Group showing no apparent interest in producing further Norton motorcycles, Seifert, very much a Norton enthusiast, took it upon himself to create a new Norton to celebrate 100 years of the company's existence (albeit very troubled in more recent years), and at the NEC Motorcycle Show in Birmingham in 1997 displayed his C652SM, with a frame designed and built by English frame specialist Tigcraft and powered by a single-cylinder BMW F650 engine. Seifert began production of 101 machines, numbered from 1898 to 1998 for each year of Norton's history, but was not allowed to sell them in the UK, due to objections from the Aquilini Group.

Meanwhile, and possibly spurred on by Seifert's actions, Norton in the UK, with funding from Aquilini, took over development of the March superbike project and its other projected machines, all being designed by engineering consultant Al Melling. First of these machines intended for production is a fabulous 1500cc V-eight with a projected top speed of more than 200mph, called the Nemesis, although there is some scepticism as to when it will eventually be produced, as during 1999 it has already been subjected to considerable delays and wranglings. Other new projected Nortons include a 750cc, four-cylinder sports bike, a version of which it is hoped will compete in World Superbike racing, plus a large capacity V-twin cruiser primarily for the American market.

At the moment, these bikes appear to be some way from production.

588cc Norton F1 (twin rotor Wankel) 1990

588cc Norton Commander (twin rotor Wankel) 1988

652cc Norton C652SM (ohc single Rotax) 1999

1500cc Norton Nemesis prototype (dohc V-eight) 1998

NSU • Germany 1901–1965

A pioneer firm which began by fitting Swiss Zedel engines to ordinary bicycles before making its own engines from 1903. NSU developed a simple free-engine clutch and a two-speed epicyclic gear that fitted into the engine pulley of the belt drive. It was a strong exporter, even penetrating the US market at an early date, but, although it competed in the TT before WW1, it met with no great success. In the 1920s, NSU pioneered mass production; in the 1930s, it concentrated on smaller machines, though there were larger prestige models. Walter Moore, from Norton, was the designer at that time. He is best remembered for his Norton look alike ohc racer, although he actually developed a wide range of models, including the 98cc Quick two-stroke, in production from 1936 to 1953. The English rider Tommy Bullus joined NSU at about the same time and won many racing successes for it in the early 1930s.

Both men returned to England in 1939. Post war, designer Albert Roder introduced pressed steel frames and patent leading link forks. In 1949 NSU signed an agreement to make and sell the Lambretta scooter in Germany, which became a steady and lucrative source of income.

For 1953, NSU announced a new ohc 250cc four-stroke, with some striking features that included drive to the camshaft by eccentrics and straps (the system used by the Dart motorcycle 30 years earlier, and also by W. O. Bentley for some of his car engines). The Max, Special Max and Super Max were in production until 1963, and set new standards of excellence in the 250cc class. So did NSU's racing motorcycles of 1953 and 1954, the 125cc single-cylinder Rennfox and 250cc Rennmax twin. Derived from an earlier and relatively unsuccessful 500cc four, these machines won the 125cc and 250cc titles in 1953 and 1954 and, ridden by Werner Haas, Rupert Hollaus, H P Muller and Irishman Reg Armstrong, dominated their classes.

NSU was also in the forefront of record breaking. In 1951 Willi Herz had broken the world speed record on a streamlined 500cc supercharged twin that dated back to before the war, at a top speed of over 180mph. In April 1954 Gustav Baum broke world records in the 50cc and 100cc classes on (or rather in) a streamlined, cigar-shaped, feet-first projectile that became known as the `Flying Hammock'. Later he was to achieve over 134mph, using a 125cc engine.

NSU also sold a `production racer', the 250cc Sportmax that earned an enviable reputation in private hands between 1954 and about 1962. Although engine and frame closely resembled those of the 250cc road-going Max, they were in fact very special, and commanded a high price. Riders such as John Surtees, Mike Hailwood, Dan Shorey and many more were customers. H. P. Muller won the 1955 Riders' Championship in the 250cc road racing class using a Sportmax.

However, NSU had no hesitation in abandoning racing at the end of 1954. It had proved its point and that was enough. It was anticipating the expiry of its Lambretta license, and needed to develop its own scooter model, the NSU Prima. Announced in January 1956 it was another success. So, too, was the 50cc NSU Quickly, the original `moped' first sold in 1953 and of which NSU made well over a million. Later 50cc models were the sporting miniature motorcycles, the Quickly Cavallino and Quick 50.

By the late 1950s, however, NSU was finding the going harder than it should have been. As with most of the German industry, motorcycle sales were suffering, as growing affluence made light cars available to a wider public. NSU itself had begun to make four wheelers, after a long lapse, with the Prinz air-cooled car, and felt reasonably confident of being able to successfully `change horses'. It might well have done so, but for its unfortunate obsession with the Wankel rotary engine. Motorcycle production was deliberately run down as the company devoted more and more time and money to the Wankel. By 1969 the company had gone, ruined by warranty claims on the disastrous NSU Ro80 car. It was taken over by VW-Audi and the name was abandoned.

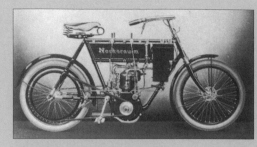

4hp NSU (sv water-cooled) 1905)

6hp NSU racer (ohv V-twin) 1909

326cc NSU (sv spring-frame) 1914

1hp NSU (sv Zedel) 1903

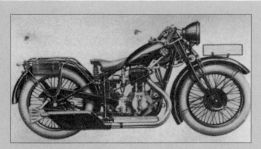

592cc NSU (sv) 1935

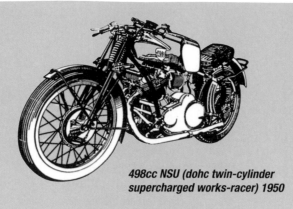

498cc NSU (dohc twin-cylinder supercharged works-racer) 1950

494cc NSU Sport (ohv) 1935

124cc NSU Fox (two-stroke) 1951

248cc NSU Supermax (ohc) 1957

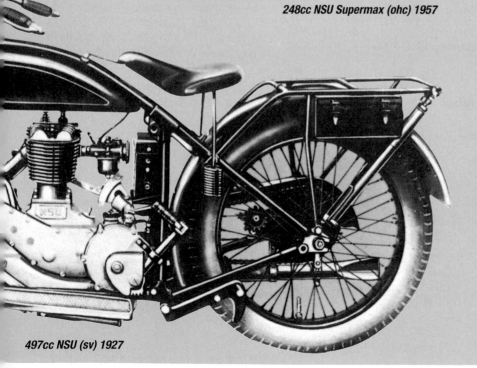

497cc NSU (sv) 1927

174cc NSU Maxi (ohc) 1957

engines. Models with 346cc and 496cc sv Blackburne engines built on request.

NORDSTERN • Germany 1922–1924

Produced 2.5hp two-strokes with own deflector-type engines. SFW took over this design when the original producer went bankrupt.

NORICUM • Austria (Czechoslovakia) 1903–1906

Built by Cless & Plessing at Graz in Austria (then the Austro-Hungarian Empire) the 2.75hp and 3`5hp singles and 5hp V-twins supplied to the Czechoslovakian part of the Empire were renamed Noricum.

NORMAN • England 1937–1961

Entered the market with 98cc Autocycles, took over the design and production equipment for the 98cc Rudge Autocycle and also built motorcycles with 98cc to 247cc Villiers two-stroke engines. In some countries they were renamed Rambler. In the late 1950s it bought the remains of the German Achilles factory. In the early 1960s the Norman brothers sold out to the big Raleigh group of companies, and manufacture of Norman motorcycles came to an end.

NORTHUMBRIAN • England 1920

3 ¹/₂hp machine. No further details.

NORTON • England 1902–

See panel

NORVED • Germany 1924–1925

Limited assembly of 348cc and 498cc machines with ohv and sv Kühne proprietary engines. Blackburne single-cylinder engines could be fitted to order.

NOVA • Hungary 1925–1928

Produced sporting machines with engines from 248cc to 498cc. The single-cylinder engines came from the JAP and Blackburne factories. Also most other parts such as Amal carburetors, Best & Lloyd oil pumps, Sturmey-Archer gearboxes, Druid forks etc. came from England. Among successful Nova competition riders were both Stefan and Nikolaus von Horthy, the sons of Hungary's Reichsverweser (head of state), Stephan Kiss and Karoly von Hild.

NOVICUM • Czechoslovakia 1904-8

A range of 1 ¹/₂hp - 4hp models with Fafnir, Minerva or Peugeot engines fitted, built by Mechanika Dilna, Praha-Smichov at Ladislav Svestka.

NOVY • Belgium early 1930s to early 1960s

Produced two-strokes from 48cc to 244cc with mainly Ilo engines. Among the models also was a vertical twin.

NS • Japan 1909

Rigid single-speed, single-cylinder machines built in limited numbers by Narazo Shamazu who built Aero machines in the 1920s.

NSH • Germany 1923–1928

Not to be confused with NSU, the NSH was an assembled machine with 173cc, 346cc Villiers and 490cc JAP engines. The Villiers-engined versions included the vertical 344cc twin of 1927–1928.

NSU • Germany 1901–1965

See panel

NUT • England 1912–1933

Although founded only in 1912, NUT was already in 1913 a TT winner, when Hugh Mason won on a V-twin the Junior

246cc Norman trials (two-stroke Villiers) 1962

344cc NSH (two-stroke twin Villiers) 1927

TT in the Isle of Man. The name was always closely connected with V-twins, with machines of 498cc, 678cc, 698cc and 746cc capacity. Engines came from JAP as well as from its own production. There were four-port 498cc and 698cc ohv models, and there were also 172cc Villiers-engined two-strokes and 248cc and 348cc ohv singles with JAP power units.

NUX • Germany 1924–1925

Small producer of 170cc machines with own three-port deflector-type two-stroke engines.

NV • Sweden 1926–

Now part of the big MCB-Monark group of companies, NV became known for fast 246cc ohv single-cylinder unit-design engines in excellent frames. There were afterwards two-strokes up to 123cc in production which had proprietary engines made by DKW, Royal Enfield, Sachs and others.

N-ZETA • New Zealand 1957–1962

Little known local licensed production of the 171cc Czechoslovakian Czeta scooter.

698cc NUT (sv V-twin) 1923

498cc NUT (ohv V-twin four-port) 1927

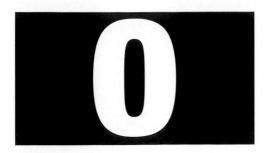

OASA • Italy 1930–1932

Designed and produced by the Aliprandi brothers, the Oasa had Ladetto's 173cc ohv engines and also 246cc and 346cc JAP single-cylinder ohv engines.

OB • Austria 1904–1907

Made at Vienna by Messrs. Opel & Beyschlag who imported Opel cars into the Austro-Hungarian Empire, the OB motorcycles had its own 2hp single-cylinder and 3.5hp V-twin power units and shaft drive.

OBERLE • Germany 1927–1929

Villiers-engined 147cc and 172cc two-stroke machines, designed by the racing motorcyclist Eugen Oberle.

OCMA (DEVIL) • Italy 1953–1957

These are the 123cc to 244cc two- and four-stroke machines which have already been mentioned under Devil.

OCRA • Germany 1923–1925

Ottomar Cramer, who built Lloyd motorcycles, was also designer and manufacturer of the 137cc Ocra bicycle attachment engines and of 293cc and 346cc sv and ohv motorcycles.

OD • Germany 1927–1935

The blue-grey machines produced by the Willy Ostner factory at Dresden were of good and sturdy design. Most models had 347cc, 497cc, 597cc and 996cc ioe and ohv MAG engines; only some special racing versions

996cc OD (ioe V-twin MAG) 1930

498cc OD (ioe MAG) 1931

including the 996cc 55hp V-twin ohv sidecar racer ridden by works rider Arno Zaspel had JAP power units. The big production 996cc MAG-engined version was the only German machine of the late 1920s and early 1930s with a reverse gear. Among the machines made were also 497cc racing models with the MAG ohv racing D50 engine and from 1931 onwards a MAG-engined 846cc V-twin with the Le Vack-designed sv engine. There were also 198cc and 246cc models with Bark two-stroke engines and frames made from cast aluminum. After the mid-1930s OD concentrated on three-wheelers, which were also made after 1945, when Ostner lived in West Germany. OD racing men besides Zaspel included Franz Heck, Ernst Bocktenk and Willi Zwolle.

498cc OD production racer (ohv MAG) 1932

ODA • Germany 1925–1926

Simple and cheaply built 293cc motorcycles with the JAP sv engine.

OEC • England 1901–1954

See panel

498cc OD Sport (ohv MAG) 1934

OFRAN • Germany 1923–1925

Concentrated on the production of a single model with its own 425cc two-stroke three-port engine.

OGAR • Czechoslovakia 1934–1950

Closely connected to a big accessory firm, Ogar was building superb 246cc two-stroke machines of very sporting appearance. Concentrating on this one model, it developed it from year to year. It also built a few water-cooled versions for the works riders, who competed successfully in races and trials. There were also a few Ogar-built 498cc speedway machines with ohv JAP and also its own ohv power units. The black and green machines designed by Frantisek Bartuska were very popular among younger riders, and some leading racing men including Jan Lucak, Frantisek Fiala, Lada Steiner, Vasek Liska, Jiri Plichta and Anton Mikl rode them too. The speedway machines were ridden by Lucak and Hugo Rosak; afterwards by Simek, Spinka and Nemecek. After 1945 and nationalisation, Ogar designer Vincenz Sklenar

346cc Ogar (two-stroke twin) 1948

OEC • England 1901–1954

The name came from Osborn Engineering Company. Frederick Osborn built his first machines with Minerva and MMC engines. After an interruption of some years, his son John Osborn resumed manufacture in 1920, after the Blackburne factory decided to concentrate on producing proprietary engines only. That was the birth of the OEC-Blackburne, which later became just OEC. Fred Wood was also connected with the factory; he was a clever technician and invented among other things the duplex steering on OEC machines. There were 348cc and 547cc singles and 998cc V-twins with sv engines in the range of models in 1922–1923, among them a big 998cc sidecar version with a steering wheel instead of handlebars, which was also available with a 1096cc V-twin Blackburne engine. Very sporting was a 348cc ohv single. OEC also built many frames for record-breaking V-twins, among them the frame for Claude Temple's 996cc Hubert Hagens-designed British-Anzani ohc power unit. This was a double-loop frame with Harley-Davidson-type bottom-link forks. Another OEC design was the duplex steering frame, used in 1930 by Joe Wright with a supercharged 85hp 996cc V-twin ohv JAP engine, when he reached a speed of 137.3mph. This machine was fitted with a Powerplus supercharger. Another interesting frame was built in 1928, when the factory was on the verge of building the unorthodox Tinkler design in quantities. The Tinkler, first seen in the 1927 TT practice, had a fully enclosed 497cc flat single-cylinder engine with water-cooling. The OEC production range included after 1925 347cc and 497cc Atlanta single-cylinder ohc engines with the camshafts driven by two pairs of bevel gears and a vertical shaft. Other models had Villiers two-stroke engines from 147cc to 342cc and JAP as well as Blackburne engines from 173cc to 998cc, including 678cc, 746cc and 998cc V-twins with sv and ohv engines. Villiers-engined machines and 498cc special Speedway versions which had been made from 1929 onwards again came into production after 1945. Among the models built in the second half of the 1930s were 248cc and 498cc, afterwards also 347cc singles and 998cc V-twins with JAP and Matchless ohv engines. Only the big version had a sv engine. The range included also the unorthodox Atlanta-Duo model with a 498cc ohv JAP and 746cc V-twin sv JAP engine. A 498cc ohv JAP engine was fitted to post-war speedway models. Road-going OEC machines had besides Villiers engines the Brookhouse-built Indian 246cc sv unit-design single-cylinder engine.

346cc OEC racer (ohv Blackburne) 1924

496cc OEC with Duplex steering (ohv Matchless) 1937

347cc OEC (ohv Matchless) 1938

`986cc OEC Taxi (sv V-twin Blackburne) 1923

OK (OK-SUPREME) • England 1899–1939

Early OK motorcycles had De Dion, Minerva, Precision and Green engines. After WW1, the range used the company's own 292cc (70mm x 76mm bore/stroke) two-stroke and Blackburne 247cc and 347cc sv and ohv engines. There were also 348cc machines with the oil-cooled Bradshaw engine and also JAP-engined versions of 246cc to 496cc. The 248cc racing models were famous; the young Walter Handley rode Blackburne-engined racers in 1922. From the mid-1920s onwards, JAP engines powered the 248cc racing models. Ridden by Frank Longmann, Alec Bennett, C. T. Ashby, Joe Sarkis, Rudolf Runtsch, Vic Anstice and others, they won many races. New Jones-designed 248cc long-stroke engines replaced the proprietary racing engines in the early 1930s, and 348cc ohc engines were added to the range of machines, which still relied on JAP engines of up to 498cc. There was also a special grass-track version with a 348cc JAP ohv engine, still available in limited numbers after the war until the death of John Humphries, the son of one of the founders of OK, the late Ernest Humphries. Among the last OK-Supreme models were ohv JAP-engined high-camshaft versions with 248cc, 348cc and 498cc single-cylinder engines.

293cc OK (sv JAP) 1926

346cc OK (ohv oil-cooled Bradshaw) 1926

248cc OK-Supreme (ohv JAP) 1928

348cc OK-Supreme racer (ohc) 1936

248cc OK-Supreme (ohc) 1936

created a new and modern 348cc ohc single with unit-design engine, telescopic forks and plunger-type rear suspension. It never went into quantity production. The new Ogar was really a 346cc twin-cylinder two-stroke, designed on the lines of the 246cc Jawa by Jawa designers. It had for some time the Ogar badge, but became eventually the forerunner of all the twins made by the big Czechoslovakian factory.

OGE • Germany 1921–1924

This was a 118cc two-stroke bicycle engine, designed by Oskar Giebel.

OGSTON • England 1911–1913

Name used during a short period for Wilkinson-TMC motorcycles.

OHB • Germany 1927–1928

Designed by Otto Hoffmann, this was an English-looking 490cc single with the JAP sv engine. Small scale production.

OK (OK-SUPREME) • England 1899–1939

See panel

OLD • France 1959

Produced a 50cc automatic scooter called the Miniscoot.

OLIVA • Italy 1920–1925

The Oliva brothers first built 120cc bicycle engines, then a 173cc two-stroke motorcycle with the French Train engine.

OLIVERIO • Italy 1929–1932

Assembled motorcycles with 346cc and 496cc Sturmey-Archer ohv engines.

OLIVOS • England 1920–1921

Blackburne-engined 496cc sv singles in spring frames of the company's own design and limited manufacture.

OLLEARO • Italy 1923–1952

With the exception of early 131cc two-strokes, Olleario became known as a producer of heavy motorcycles with unit-design 173cc to 499cc single-cylinder ohv engines and with shaft drive to the rear wheel. The 173cc models had two-stroke engines as well as ohv versions. They were probably the first shaft-driven, four-speed, unit-design 173cc models built commercially. After 1945, a 45cc bicy-

cle engine with 1.25hp at 4500rpm was made, followed by slightly modernised pre-war 173cc, 246cc, 346cc and 496cc singles. Neftali Olleario, the founder of the factory, never showed interest in racing; his machines were designed solely as touring motorcycles.

OLMO • Italy 1951–1961

Produced lightweights, including mopeds, with 38cc Mosquito and 48cc two-strokes of various makes.

OLYMPIC • England 1903–1923

MMC engines with 2.75hp powered the first Olympic motorcycles. After a long interruption, new 1919 models had 269cc Verus and afterwards 261cc Orbit two-stroke engines. Frank H Parkyn's factory supplied frames to other companies, also fitted Villiers, JAP and Blackburne engines and produced under the New Courier trademark cheap versions of Olympic machines.

OLYMPIQUE • France 1922–1958

For many years Zurcher proprietary engines (two- and four-stroke) and also JAP engines powered these Courbevoie-built machines. Most models were of 98cc, 173cc and 346cc. After 1945 the range consisted of two-strokes of 98cc to 173cc and also of a Zurcher-engined

170cc Omega Junior (two-stroke) 1923

348cc Ollearo (ohv shaft drive) 1935

346cc Omega (ohv JAP) 1926

230cc model. There were also AMC-engined 123cc, 173cc and 248cc ohv and partly ohc singles and a 123cc scooter with a two-stroke engine. Like Thomann, Armor, La Francaise and other companies, Olympique was part of the Aleyon group.

OLYMPUS-KING • Japan 1956–1960

Built on English lines, most models had 123cc two-stroke and 346cc ohv single-cylinder engines.

OM • Germany 1923–1925

These machines had 173cc ohv, 346cc and 490cc JAP sv and ohv engines. The total production was small.

OMA • Italy 1952–1955

Built 173cc unit-design ohv and ohc singles with three-speed gearboxes.

OMB • Italy 1933–1934

Modern Angelo Blatto-designed 174cc ohv single-cylinder machines. Blatto was also connected with the machines produced by the Ladetto & Blatto concern.

OMC • Italy 1933–1935

This Giovanni Ladetto-designed 174cc machine was built by the Officine Meccaniche Calabresi. The engine was an ohv single.

OMC • England 1930

An offshoot of Vale Onslow's S.O.S. firm. Very small production of 175cc Villiers trials machines.

OMEA • Italy 1950–1953

Interesting machine with a cast alloy frame designed by Carlo Bottari. There was a leading link fork and swinging arm rear suspension. The engine was a 124cc two-stroke with 5.4hp at 5400rpm.

OMEGA • England 1909

Designed by A. J. Dorsett of Diamond fame, the Omega had a horizontal 1.5hp engine.

OMEGA • England 1919–1927

When Premier in Coventry closed down, factory manager W.J. Green founded the Omega works. The first models had 269cc Villiers and 499cc Blackburne engines. Other models included Omega's own 170cc and 348cc two-stroke engines as well as JAP, Blackburne, Bradshaw and Barr & Stroud engines up to 678cc.

OMEGA • Japan 1960s

These were Kawasaki machines renamed for the American market.

OMER • Italy 1968–

Sporting lightweights with 49cc FB-Minarelli two-stroke engines.

OMN • Italy 1924–1925

Villiers-engined 147cc and 172cc two-strokes, built in limited numbers.

OMNIA • Germany 1931–1933

Cheap two-strokes with 98cc and 147cc Villiers and 198cc Bark engines, built by the Imperia motorcycle works at Bad Godesberg.

OMT • Italy 1949–1953

Identical machines—248cc ohc vertical twins—to the MT.

ONAWAY • England 1904–1908

Unconventional design with low triangular frames, bucket seats and Kelecom 5hp V-twins or the Berkley vertical-twin power unit.

OPRA • Italy 1927–1929

Designed by two famous designers, Pietro Remor and Carlo Gianini, the OPRA was an air-cooled 490cc four-cylinder in-line ohc racing machine with the power unit mounted transversely. In later years it formed the basic

OPEL • Germany 1901–1930

There were different periods when the big Opel car factory at Rüsselsheim, now owned by General Motors, built motorcycles too. The earliest models produced 1.75hp-2hp and bigger versions had 2.25hp-2.75hp single-cylinder engines in open as well as closed tubular frames. Production seems to have stopped around 1907 and was resumed soon after WW1. Leading link forks were used in 1906-1907. The next motorcycle engine, designed in 1914 but built after 1918, was a four-stroke sv bicycle attachment engine of about 123cc, which was fitted on the left side of the rear wheel. Opel, then a leading bicycle manufacturer, also supplied complete machines with strengthened frames and tanks which looked like fire extinguishers. There were also complete motorcycles with 148cc ioe engines and two-speed gearboxes from 1922 to 1925. From 1926-1927

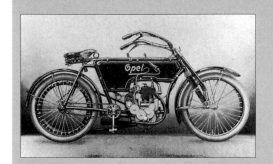

2 ³/₄ hp Opel (sv) 1905

140cc Opel (sv rear engine) 1921

204cc Opel track racer (ohv water-cooled) 1922

there was a 498cc single with an 84mm bore and 90mm stroke sv engine. 1928 saw the production of designer Ernst Neumann's Opel frames made from pressed steel, identical to the original Neander products. Opel built them under license at the former Elite-Diamant car factory, after it stopped building Diamant motorcycles and Elite cars. The new models, known as Motoclub, had 499cc sv and ohv engines producing 16hp and 22hp respectively. These models were the last motorcycles made by this famous car factory. There were two interesting non-production Opel machines, ridden from 1922 to 1924 by Fritz von Opel and Philipp Karrer. One was a water-cooled track-racing machine with a 204cc ohv engine, rearward facing exhaust port and a big outside flywheel. And a 1928 Motoclub with a 499cc ohv engine was tested—also by Fritz von Opel—with six rockets, three on each side of the rear wheel. The experiment was soon dropped.

148cc Opel (sv) 1924

498cc Opel Motoclub (ohv) 1928

498cc Opel Motoclub (ohv) 1928

design for the famous Rondine 4, which in 1937 became the first water-cooled and supercharged 498cc Gilera Four and the forerunner of the later air-cooled Gilera and MV Agusta four-cylinder works racing models.

OR • Italy 1928–1931

Produced bicycle engines and 173cc motorcycles which were equipped with its own sv and ohv engines.

ORBIT • England 1913–1924

The versatile Dorsett also designed Orbit motorcycles, first with 346cc sv engines, and after 1919 with 261cc two-strokes. Although there was only a small output from the works, models with various Barr & Stroud, Bradshaw and Blackburne engines were added.

OREOL • France 1903–WWI

Pioneer motorcycle producer, whose rider Cissac broke many records on a 333cc single-cylinder model. Oreol also built V-twins with Zedel, Moto-Reve and other engines.

ORI • Germany 1923–1925

Lightweight machines with 145cc two-stroke engines.

ORIAL • France 1919–1926

Was closely connected with the French MAG branch factory at Lyon and fitted MAG 346cc and 496cc ioe and ohv single-cylinder and V-twin engines into its own frames.

ORIAL • Germany 1929–1931

This name came into being when the marriage between Triumph (TEC) in Coventry and Triumph (TWN) in Nuremberg was dissolved. The Germans had until then used mainly Coventry-made engines and parts. Now they fitted Swiss MAG engines and renamed the machines Orial for export into certain countries. Afterwards they changed to TWN, which stood for Triumph Werke Nèrnberg.

ORIENT • America 1900–c1906

Excellent design by Harry Metz, who fitted 2.25hp and 2.5hp engines into strong modified bicycle frames.

ORIGAN • France 1933–early 1950s

Lightweights with two-stroke engines (mainly Aubier-Dunne) from 98cc to 174cc.

ORIGINAL-KRIEGER • Germany 1925–1926

After the original KG design was sold to Cito and via

347cc Orial France (ioe MAG) 1924

348cc Orial Germany (ohv MAG) 1929

2¹/₂hp Orient (sv Aster) 1901

Clto to Allright, the Krieger brothers left and founded a new company, producing first their 498cc models. After Allright intervention, they had to stop and used 346cc Blackburne sv engines in the slightly modified KG frames.

ORION • Czechoslovakia 1902–1933

Vilém Michl, the designer-manufacturer, built in the early years superb singles and V-twins with his own engines. He was assisted in the works by his sons, especially Zdenek Michl who created many interesting designs after WW1. There was a good 346cc two-stroke single as well as a 594cc double-piston two-stroke single. From 1927 onwards Orion made 496cc and 598cc sv singles and also a 496cc ohv machine. With Z. Michl, Vaclav Liska, Jarda Melzer etc. Orion machines gained many successes in sporting events.

ORIONE • Italy 1923–1928

Guido Carpi produced very fast 123cc and 173cc two-strokes with three-port deflector-type engines. Nello Pagani, Raffaele Alberti and Martino Soffientini were among the successful racing riders.

347cc Orion (two-stroke) 1923

4hp Orion Model W (sv V-twin) 1908

ORIONETTE • Germany 1921–1925

Built a range of good 129cc, 137cc, 148cc and 346cc two-stroke machines with mainly unit-design engines and two- or three-speed gearboxes. The design department, headed by Engelbert Zaschka, also produced some interesting unorthodox designs. Among them was a `combined' two and four-stroke with a valve in the crankcase. Only few of these `overhead two-strokes' were actually made.

ORIX • Italy 1949–1954

Designed by Amedeo Prina, Orix built Ilo-engined 173cc two-strokes as well as a variety of 123cc and 173cc two-stroke scooters.

ORLESTONE • England c1902–1905

Single-cylinder motorcycles with automatic ioe and trembler coil ignition. Built by J. Caffyn & Son, East Ham, Kent. The company was also a Baker, confectioner, cycle agent and the manufacturer of Orlestone bicycles and motorcycles.

ORLICE • Czechoslovakia 1906–1908

Limited production of belt-drive motorcycles.

ORMONDE • England 1900–c1906

Once a well-known make. Fitted 2.25hp and 2.75hp Kelecom as well as 3.5hp Antoine engines.

ORTLOFF • Germany 1924–1926

Lightweights with 185cc and 198cc Gruhn sv engines.

ORTONA • England 1904–1906

A 3.5hp single-cylinder machine was the only model built by this factory.

ORUK • Germany 1922–1924

Interesting design. Oruk means without belt and chain (ohne Riemen und Kette). The engine was—not unlike the Opel of that period—a 189cc sv single, mounted outside the rear wheel with a direct shaft drive. It was not a great commercial success and Oruk was taken over by the Schüttoff works.

OSA • Poland 1958–

Made by WFM (Warszawska Fabrica Motocyklowa), a leading motorcycle factory, the OSA was a scooter with 123cc to 173cc two-stroke engines and a nice appearance.

OSA-LIBERTY • France 1926–1932

Assembled good motorcycles with JAP license-built 346cc and 490cc sv and ohv engines. Manufacturer of the power units was the French Staub factory. Small 173cc and 246cc two-stroke engines were the company's own design and manufacture.

497cc Orion (ohv) 1929

OSCAR • England 1953–1955

The only product of this short-lived English make was a scooter with 122cc and 197cc Villiers two-stroke engines.

OSCAR • Italy 1965–1982

Franco-Morini-engined 49cc and 84cc lightweights of sporting appearance.

OSCHA • Germany 1924–1925

Water-cooled 496cc flat twins. The sv engine was designed by Otto Schaaf. Only a small number was built.

OSMOND • England 1911–1924

A company belonging to James in Birmingham. Built machines with 485cc Precision single-cylinder engines, and after 1918 small 102cc and 110cc machines resembling mopeds with Simplex two-stroke motors.

OSSA • Spain 1951–1980s

Maker of excellent two-strokes designed by Eduardo Giro, usually of 250cc, but also the 500cc twin 'Yankee'. Sales of trail bikes in America and trials models in Britain were good in the 1960s. At home, Ossa was strong in road racing and competed in grands prix with an advanced aluminum monocoque-framed 250cc disc valve single. Santiago Herrero was third in the 1969 TT and world championship, but was killed in the 1970 TT. Sales fell in the USA in the 1970s and in 1984 the factory passed into the hands of a 'workers' co-operative' with inevitable results.

230cc Ossa Sport (two-stroke) 1966

250cc Ossa Explorer (two-stroke) 1976

244cc Ossa Sixdays (two-stroke) 1973

246cc Ossa Enduro America (two-stroke) 1973

189cc Oruk (ohv rear-engine) 1923

The last model had a 239cc two-stroke engine of Osmond's design and manufacture.

OSSA • Spain 1951–1980s

See panel

OTTO • Germany 1921–1937

These were really Flottweg machines with the Otto trademark. The Otto works produced Flottweg machines; the Otto name was used mainly in the late 1920s, when the factory built machines with 293cc and 198cc sv JAP engines.

OTTOLENGHI • Italy 1928–1932

Concentrated on the production of well-made sporting 174cc ohv machines with a variety of engines, including Piazza, Ladetto & Blatto and JAP. The JAP-powered versions had 246cc and 346cc ohv engines.

OVER • Japan 1988–

Specialist producer mostly of highly respected racing machines, founded by Kensei Sato. Frequently the frames are of a trellis design, built using oval-section aluminum.

OVERDALE • England 1921–1922

The word England is not exact in this case, because the Overdale was offered by a Glasgow company, but the factory was in the Midlands, where the simple frame was fitted with a 269cc Villiers engine.

OVERSEAS • England 1909–1915

Built motorcycles exclusively for British colonies, with strong, heavy frames. Engines were sv V-twins of 842cc.

346cc Orionette (two-stroke) 1925

246cc Orionette prototype (two-stroke with ohv) 1925

P

PA • Belgium 1921–1929

For many years a leading make in Belgian races, the Praillet-designed machines were of typical English design. Equipped with 174cc, 247cc and 347cc sv and ohv Blackburne engines, they were occasionally ridden by Blackburne's British works riders, which included Paddy Johnston and Ernie Remington. From 1925 onwards, PA built its own 245cc two-stroke and 345cc ohv engines and also fitted after 1927 348cc and 490cc JAP and MAG sv and ohv engines.

PACER • England 1914

This short-lived motorcycle was built on Guernsey in the Channel Islands. The engine used was a 116cc single, made by JES.

PAFFRATH • Germany 1923–1926

Very interesting and unusual machines, designed by Paul Paffrath. For a description see MW. In 1949 Paffrath designed and built the Eilenriede bicycle attachment power units.

PAGLIANTI • Italy 1958–1966

Built 49cc mopeds and 75cc miniscooters with two-stroke engines.

PAKEHA • New Zealand 1915

2 3/4hp machine. No further details.

PALLION • England 1905–1914

Assembled machines with various engines made by Minerva, Fafnir, JAP and Villiers.

PALOMA • France early 1950s to late 1960s

A fully enclosed three-speed scooter with a 70cc engine was among the first products. Other models included 74cc and 123cc scooters, lightweights and also 49cc and 58cc mopeds etc. with Lavalette and René Gillet two-strokes.

246cc Pannonia (two-stroke twin) 1974

PAMAG • Germany 1952–1953

When Anker stopped production of motorcycles, Pamag took over and built 123cc, 174cc and 197cc two-strokes with Sachs and Ilo engines.

PAN • Germany 1924–1925

Equipped with an unusual leaf-sprung fork, these motorcycles were driven by 346cc ohv Kühne engines.

PANDA • Italy 1980–

Assembler of trials machines with German Sachs engines of 79cc capacity.

PANDRA • Japan early 1950s to early 1960s

Ceased production in the early 1960s.

PANNI • Hungary 1959–1962

Miniscooters with 48cc two-stroke power-units built by the state-owned Czepel works.

PANNONIA • Hungary 1951–1970s

Also made by the Czepel works, the Pannonia motorcycles had some similarity to Jawa products. The 247cc two-stroke was built with one and two cylinders and was also exported to European countries.

PANTHER (P&M) • England 1900–1967

See panel

PANTHER • Germany 1933–mid-1970s

Built in pre-war days mofas with 73cc and 98cc Sachs and Ilo two-strokes, after the war a wide range of 32cc and 48cc mopeds as well as motorcycles from 98cc to 174cc with Sachs engines. When Panther offered motorcycles in England during the 1950s, they had to be renamed Leopard, as there was already a Panther motorcycle factory in the UK.

PAQUE • Germany 1921–1925

The first product was a 140cc bicycle engine. Motorcycles had 147cc and 197cc ohv engines, which were also built as proprietary engines for Busse, Zürtz, Ammon and other factories. The last Paqué models had its own 497cc sv single-cylinder engines and there were also a few 198cc ohc engines built.

PARAGON • England 1919–1923

Produced a single model, a 348cc three-port deflector-type, only. The engine had 76mm bore and 79mm stroke and an Albion two-speed gear box.

PARAMOUNT-DUO • England 1926–1927

Unusual design without top tube, with two bucket seats, a fully enclosed engine and rear wheel half enclosed by panels. This design was offered with 490cc and 990cc sv JAP or Blackburne engine, but neither model succeeded in gaining many customers.

PARILLA • Italy 1946–1967

Giovanni Parilla's first design, a 248cc single-cylinder ohc machine, created quite a sensation, and the 1947 racing version an even greater one. It was a beautiful design, but unfortunately never as fast as Moto Guzzi's production racer, the Albatross. Luigi Ciai and others rode the Parilla, but the best racing model was in Germany, where it was developed by Roland Schnell and its rider Hermann Gablenz. Schnell also built a 348cc version and developed improved frames for both models. The normal model had 17hp at 7250rpm, racing versions around 30hp. These had two overhead camshafts and elektron crankcases. The first production model was a 247cc two-stroke of unit design, followed by 98cc and 123cc two-stroke versions. There was also a fully enclosed 123cc two-stroke scooter with a three-speed gearbox. The following models had 248cc and 348cc vertical-twin ohv engines. Two very fast 123cc models had a two-stroke engine and a dohc engine with telescopic forks and swinging arm rear suspension. The last one, a racing machine, developed 13.5hp at 10,000rpm. Less hot machines were 148cc and 158cc two-strokes; a range of 173cc dohc sports machines with engines which were also supplied to the German Victoria works; an improved 347cc vertical twin and a 98cc version; and the Slughi, with an enclosure which was nearly complete but also sporting. Engines fitted were a 98cc two-stroke with 50mm bore and 50mm stroke and a similar ohv version of 97.7cc with 52mm bore and 46mm stroke. Other Parillas included the Oscar scooter with a 158cc flat twin two-stroke engine and a range of 48cc mopeds and sporting motorcycles up to 247cc. These included the 99cc Olympia, a Slughi design with an open engine which was either a 99cc ohv or a 123cc two-stroke unit. A special version called Impala was made exclusively for the US.

98cc Parilla Slughi (ohv) 1958

PANTHER (P&M) • England 1900–1967

Yorkshiremen Joah Phelon and Harry Rainer patented the use of the cylinder and crankcase of an engine as a stressed member of a motorcycle frame in 1900, and licensed the idea to Humber of Coventry which used it extensively for its motorcycles and forecars. In 1903, Rainer died in a road accident and Phelon took Richard Moore, who had designed a two-speed gear using two primary chains and clutches, into partnership. The company now became P&M, making motorcycles with Moore's gear and chain drive and its own 500cc sv engine at Cleckheaton. The machine was developed year by year and, in 1914, was adopted by the Royal Flying Corps (later the RAF) as its standard despatch riders' machine.

Post war, production resumed, with minor improvements and a 555cc engine for some models. For 1924 there was a proper four-speed gearbox, and the P&M Panther, with a new ohv 500cc engine designed by Granville Bradshaw. This very sporting machine proved a good seller and Tommy Bullus finished fourth on a virtually standard model in the 1925 Senior TT. Unfortunately, another Bradshaw design, the 1926 250cc transverse V-twin Panthette was disastrously inept and came close to ruining the company on the very eve of the depression of the early 1930s.

Production continued with small Villiers-engined two strokes and with 500cc and 600cc Slopers. Frank Leach designed conventional framed 250cc and 350cc ohv models in 1932. The 250cc, in a special deal with London retailer Pride & Clarke, was sold as the Red Panther for less than £30! After 1945, the 600cc Sloper, now known as the Model 100, gained Dowty air spring telescopic forks, which were also fitted to the 250cc and 350cc ohv Frank Leach designs. These were available additionally in trials trim as the Stroud. Villiers-engined 200cc and 250cc singles were introduced; later the Villiers 250cc and 325cc twins were used. The 600cc was supplemented by the 650cc Model 120. An involvement with the importing of Terrot mopeds and scooters caused financial difficulties, as did an unsuccessful scooter, the Panther Princess, at a time when, in any case, the British market was declining. The last 650cc Slopers — still with engines as a stressed frame member — were made in 1967.

Royal Automobile Club patrolman on a P&M, 1920s

246cc Panther P&M Panthette (ohv V-twin) 1928

645cc Panther ohv with Viceroy sidecar 1964

499cc Panther P&M TT(ohv) 1925

173cc Patria (two-stroke Ilo) 1950

344cc Per (two-stroke) 1925

PARK • New Zealand 1911

3 1/2hp machine. No further details.

PARVUS • Italy 1921–1926

Was among the first Italian producers of bicycle engines. In this case they were 104cc two-strokes. Motorcycles, made from 1923, had 123cc two-stroke engines.

PASCO • Australia 1919–1922

Built partly on American lines, these motorcycles had English 548cc single-cylinder and 746cc V-twin sv engines made by JAP.

PASCO-JAP • Australia 1919–1922

Produced V-twins with 496cc and 990cc JAP and MAG engines and English components.

PASQUET • France 1932–WWII

Aubier-Dunne 98cc and 123cc engines in motorcycles made in limited quantities.

PASSONI • Italy 1902–1904

Pioneer of the motorcycle trade. Used own 2hp engines in strengthened bicycle frames.

PATRIA • Germany 1925–1950

The first models had 248cc and 348cc Roconova single-cylinder ohc engines, designed by Johannes Rölssig, but from 1927 to 1949 only mopeds were made. 98cc and 123cc Sachs and 98cc Imme engines powered post-war Patria motorcycles, which were of good design. Hans A. May, the owner of the Patria works, died suddenly in 1950 and the factory closed down.

PATRIARCA • Italy 1925–1933

Well-designed 124cc, 174cc and eventually 248cc singles, designed by Gustav Patriarca, who was one of Italy's better designers. Most models had ohv heads and the two- or three-speed gearboxes in unit with the engine.

PAUVERT • France 1933–WWII

Assembler of two-stroke machines with 98cc to 198cc. Limited production.

PAWA • Germany 1922–1923

Very unorthodox motorcycle designed by Kurt Passow. It had an unusually long wheelbase, a complete fairing from steering head to the center of the rear wheel, partly enclosed front wheel, a bucket seat but a completely open chain to the rear wheel. The 226cc two-stroke engine had a 60mm bore and 80mm stroke; a valve regulated the incoming mixture, but neither the engine nor the frame parts were properly developed. The whole machine was more a designer's dream than a good commercial proposition and production ceased in 1923.

PAWI • Germany 1922–1924

Made by a small car factory at Berlin, Pawi motorcycles were built in small numbers only. They were powered by the well-known 493cc sv flat-twin proprietary BMW engine with 68mm bore and stroke.

PAX • England 1920–1922

Orthodox motorcycles with 348cc and 499cc Blackburne single-cylinder sv engines. The bigger model had a three-speed Sturmey-Archer gearbox and a Senspray carburetor. The cost was £120.

PDC • England 1903–1906

Made by the old Imperial Company, these machines had Coronet 2hp, 2.75hp and 3.5hp proprietary engines.

PE • Germany 1923–1924

Lightweights with own 132cc three-port, deflector-type, two-stroke engines.

PEARSON • England 1903–1904

Equipped with 3hp Aster engines, the Pearson is now a forgotten make.

PEARSON & COX • England 1912

The only steam-driven motorcycle ever offered to the British public. Though not many were sold, the Pearson & Cox definitely reached production. One, with a sectioned engine, is in the Science Museum, London.

PEBOK • England 1903–1909

Was among leading English motorcycle producers. The 2.25hp, 2.75hp and 3.5hp engines were of its own design and manufacture.

PECO • England 1913–1915

Supplied 349cc proprietary two-stroke engines and also complete motorcycles, when Calthorpe bought the Peco works at Birmingham.

PEERLESS • America 1913–1916

Strong 4hp, 5hp and 8hp motorcycles with own ioe single-cylinder and V-twin engines, double-loop frames, telescopic forks and shaft drive. The factory was also connected with the four-cylinder Champion machines, made at the St. Louis works. The Peerless was built at Boston.

PEERLESS • Australia c1912

Fafnir single-cylinder sv motorcycles built by A. G. Healing, who also built the De Luxe.

PEUGEOT • France 1899–

Lion Peugeot, famous pioneer of both cars and motor-cycles, was an offshoot of the giant Peugeot Frères conglomerate. As well as its own motorcycles, it sold V-twin proprietary engines to several firms, notably Vindec, DOT, and Norton. Rem Fowler's win for Norton in the 1907 twin-cylinder TT was with a Peugeot engine. Peugeot itself raced – curiously, its machines were still using atmospheric inlet valves as late as 1912 – and was an early user of the distinctive Truffault swinging arm front forks. In 1913, it revealed 500cc vertical twin racing motorcycles with dohc, designed by the famous Ernest Henry, who had pioneered the double overhead camshaft

engine in the Peugeot grand prix car of 1912. Although the cycle parts appear primitive in today's eyes, the engines – with unit construction gearbox – were of a sophistication not to be seen elsewhere for years to come. Both before and after the war, these twins won many races and broke records on the continent. In 1923 they were redesigned by Tony Antoniescu with sohc valve gear, neat four-speed gearboxes and more modern cycle parts. Again, they were very successful, although when ridden in the 1924 Senior TT by Pean, Richard and Gillard, they made no impression. The post-WW1 range of road bikes had 300cc, 350cc and 750cc V-twin engines; in 1921, a single-cylinder 270cc two-stroke was added.

Pierre Péan on his works Peugeot (ohc single) 1924

Champoneau on a racing Peugeot (V-twin) 1904

173cc Peugeot (two-stroke) 1927

49cc Peugeot Vivacity (two-stroke single) 1999

During the late 1920s, Peugeot made various other two-strokes, and a sporting ohv single of 350cc. However the trend in France was towards ultra lightweight 'Velomoteurs' of 100cc, which could be ridden by anybody without a license or payment of tax. Peugeot, naturally enough, followed this mood, which came to dominate the French industry in the 1930s and, in the course of time, abandoned all its previous sporting pretentions. After WW2, it was still France's largest manufacturer, with 50cc mopeds, 100cc and 125cc two-strokes, and 250cc and 350cc two-stroke twins. It also made several different models of scooters. In common with most French firms, production declined in the 1970s, despite a brief undercover tie-up with Piaggio-owned Gilera in Italy, but during the 1980s the company was caught up in the European scooter revival and expanded rapidly, sales being helped in many markets by the familiarity and trustworthiness of the Peugeot name gained via the car division.

Peugeot's Speedfight (available in 50cc and 100cc capacities) is one of Europe's best selling two-wheelers, and other models such as the Trekker and latest executive scooter, the Elyseo are also big sellers.

49cc Peugeot Trekker (two-stroke single) 1998

125cc Peugeot Elyseo (two-stroke single) 1999

49cc Peugeot SV (two-stroke single) 1985

344cc Per (two-stroke) 1925

PEERLESS • England 1902–c1908

These machines were identical with Bradburys built at Oldham. They had 2hp and 2.5hp engines, built like the frames under Birch patents.

PEERLESS • England 1913–1914

Small assembler which fitted 292cc and 499cc Veloce (later Velocette) engines. The producer—International Mfg. Co. Ltd.—might have been a branch of Veloce Ltd.

PEGASO • Italy 1956–1964

Lightweight with 48cc ohv engine, built in large numbers. Producer was SIM (Societa Italiana Motori), a company with many ex-Motom employees.

PEM • America 1910–1915

This motorcycle manufacturer was well known in the United States in the period before WW1. It produced a single-cylinder 4hp motorcycle with its own ohv engine.

PENNINGTON • England 1897

Regarded in some circles as a pioneer, the American `inventor' E. J. Pennington was really a businessman who made promises to keep shareholders happy. His design had two horizontal and totally uncooled cylinders arranged behind the rear wheel spindle and driving the wheel, which had a flywheel built into it, directly via cranks. At the invitation of Harry John Lawson, Pennington came to England in 1896 and built two of his machines at the Coventry-based Humber Company, which was controlled by Lawson and his associates. Pennington reportedly took £100,000 for his design, which proved to be a complete failure. Only the two machines were built when Pennington bought a return ticket to America, instead of keeping his promise to motorise England.

PER • Germany 1924–1926

Kurt Passow, who created the unlucky Pawa, also built the 308cc Per. Compared with the Pawa, the Per was a much improved design. He again put the power unit behind a steel cover and used additional steel plates for covering most other parts. Again a bucket seat was used and everything done to make riding comfortable. The original 308cc engine was superseded by a more powerful 342cc unit of 12hp, but it was no use. The whole design was not really developed as it should have been. According to the designer, the two-stroke engine could run on anything, including crude oil, benzol, spirit etc. The smaller model had a two-speed gearbox and belt drive; the bigger version two- or three-speed gearboxes and—if required—chain drive to the rear wheel.

49cc Peugeot Speedake (two-stroke single) 1995

PERFECT • England c1913–4

Small production of 3 ¹/₂hp machines by the Perfect Cycle Company.

PERFECTA • Switzerland 1946–1950

Fitted French AMC ohv engines of 123cc, 148cc and 173cc into modern frames.

PERIPOLI • Italy 1957–1980

Producer of the Giulietta who also has a big output of 47cc and 49cc mofas, mopeds and similar light-weight models. Engines used included the German Zündapp.

PERLEX • Germany 1924–1926

One of the many small producers of the mid-1920s. Fitted 197cc sv Gruhn engines into simple frames.

PERKS & BIRCH • England 1899–1901

This was a 222cc sv single-cylinder engine, built into a driving wheel as a complete unit. These wheels were fitted to two- and three-wheeled vehicles. The design was eventually taken over by the Singer factory.

PERMO • Germany 1952–1954

Mopeds with 32cc Victoria two-stroke engines.

PERNOD • France c1900

Very much like the Birch design, the 1hp Pernod engine was fitted to a separate wheel which could be bought and attached as a 'pusher' to existing bicycles.

PERPEDES • Austria 1922–1926

Another bicycle attachment engine. In this case the 110cc two-stroke had to be fitted above the rear wheel directly to the bicycle. Drive was by belt.

PERSCH • Austria 1922–1925

Built 110cc bicycle engines at a factory near the Puch works at Graz. Frames for Persch engines (strengthened bicycles with special attachments) were built by Krammer of Vienna.

PERUGINA • Italy 1953–1962

Menicucci built very nice 158cc and 173cc two-stroke and ohv machines and after 1956 248cc versions. He was also the man behind BMP motorcycles. The range also included 123cc versions and a fast 173cc ohc single.

PERUN • Czechoslovakia 1904–1924

Built 3.5hp single-cylinder and 4.5hp V-twin motorcycles probably with Fafnir engines. After 1918 manufacture concentrated on 1.4hp bicycle engines.

PETA • Czechoslovakia 1921–1924

Lightweight motorcycles and scooters with 170cc two-stroke engines, built in small numbers.

PETERS • Germany 1924

Lightweights equipped with 143cc DKW two-stroke engines. These machines were only built in small numbers.

PETERS • England 1921–1925

One of the few motorcycles made in the Isle of Man, from an address in Ramsey. The Mk I had Peters' own 350cc two-stroke engine as a stressed frame member, with a strong steel fuel tank and a large diameter saddle tube as the other components. There was cantilever rear springing and belt drive with a variable engine pulley. The belt tension was maintained by rear wheel movement controlled by foot pedals! The Mk II Peters dispensed with the stressed member frame, though the general appearance remained the same. The machine used Blackburne four-stroke and Villiers two-stroke engines, a three-speed Jardine gearbox and all-chain drive. Sales were never large.

PEUGEOT • France 1899–

See panel

PG • Italy 1927–1931

Produced 123cc and 173cc ohv machines, gave up the smaller versions in 1929 and concentrated on different models of the bigger PG, designed by Giuseppe Parena.

PGO • Taiwan 1956–

Founded initially to build up Vespa scooters from Italian components, but has since gone on to produce a range of its own two-stroke and four-stroke automatic scooters of 50cc to 125cc, with assistance and license agreements from Yamaha.

The company also flagged an intention to move into the production of larger machines with the presentation in 1991 of the V2 prototype, a 1596cc liquid-cooled V-twin with aluminum ladder-style frame. But to date, nothing further has materialised.

PHANOMEN • Germany 1903–1940

Produced in early years Fafnir-engined singles and V-

246cc Phantom (sv) 1923

2¹/₂ hp Phoenix (sv) 1903

twins, afterwards three-wheelers called Phänomobil, and cars. Motorcycle manufacture was resumed in 1930 with motorised bicycles which had 74cc Sachs engines and afterwards with 98cc and 123cc Sachs-engined lightweights, designed by Rudi Albert. These Ahoj models used rubber suspension both for the forks and for the saddle.

PHANOMEN • Germany 1950–1956

Identical model range to the Meister and Mammut. Engines fitted were from 98cc to 197cc, made by Sachs and Ilo.

PHANTOM • Germany 1921–1928

A manufacturer of touring motorcycles, Phantom built its own 148cc, 198cc and 246cc sv engines and also fitted from 1926 onward JAP sv engines of 173cc to 490cc.

PHILLIPS • England 1954–1964

Built mofas and mopeds with 48cc two-stroke engines. Part of the big Raleigh group of companies.

PHOENIX • England 1900–1908

A factory founded by former racing cyclist and motorcyclist, J. V. Hooydonk. Excellent design with 211cc and 345cc Minerva engines. Built also engines of the company's own design.

490cc Pimph (sv JAP) 1926

948cc Pirate (ioe V-twin) 1911

PHOENIX • England 1955–1964

The Eric Barrett-designed scooters had Villiers-engines from 147cc to 323cc. Barrett also built a range of mainly JAP-engined ohv racing machines of 248cc to 498cc, which he rode in many races, including the TT.

PHOENIX • Germany 1933–1939

Made by RMW of Neheim-Ruhr, the Phoenix range was identical to RMW's models. It included Bark-engined 198cc and 246cc two-strokes and sv, ohv and ohc models of 346cc to 498cc with Sturmey-Archer, Moser, Bark, Küchen and MAG engines. The company tried to return to motorcycle manufacture with its own 246cc two-strokes after 1945, but few were made.

PIAGGIO • Italy 1946–

See panel

PIANA • Italy 1923–1931

The first machines designed by Gualtiero Piana had 147cc Villiers engines, afterwards models with 247cc Villiers and 346cc and 490cc JAP sv and ohv engines followed. 248cc JAP-engined models were superseded from 1927 onward by Piana's own 248cc ohv motors in complete and very sporting machines.

PIATTI • Belgium 1955–1958

Designed by an Italian, the 123cc scooter was built in England and sold by a Belgian company. Piatti designed afterwards 248cc two-stroke engines for Associated

Motorcycles Ltd. in London. But it failed to find many customers for this product.

PIAZZA • Italy 1924–1934

Small 124cc two-stroke bicycle engines were Antonio Piazza's first creations. Complete 174cc sv and ohv motorcycles followed and a 496cc ohv JAP-engined machine was added during the 1930s. While they were made in limited numbers only, 173cc Piazza ohv engines were popular and were also used by other Italian motorcycle producers.

PICK • England 1908–

Rare V-twin machines which comprised many 'bought in' and home produced parts. Made by the Pick Motor Company (1898-1925), Stamford, Lincs, which built and repaired vehicles until Jack Pick got fed up and opened a greengrocery business.

PIERCE (ARROW) • America 1909–1913

Interesting design, in which a wide diameter tube formed the tank. There were single-cylinder and 4hp four-cylinder models with air-cooling and the cylinders in line. This model was offered for $400 and had, like the single-cylinder version, shaft drive to the rear wheel. Pierce-Arrow was also a manufacturer of expensive motor cars.

PIERME • France 1922–1923

Two-stroke lightweight assembled in Paris using a Madoz engine.

PIERTON • France 1922–1925

Assembler, whose motorcycles had Aubier Dunne, Train, Villiers, Blackburne and JAP engines of 98cc to 498cc.

PILOT • England 1903–1915

Well-known factory. Produced 318cc two-strokes and also fitted Precision and JAP engines from 174cc to 598cc.

PIMPH • Germany 1924–1926

Assembled motorcycles with 490cc sv and ohv JAP engines and V-twin MAG power units as well.

PIOLA • Italy 1919–1921

The 620cc sv flat twin machines were only made in small numbers.

PIRATE • America 1911–1915

Ambitious factory which built ioe singles and V-

twins of 3hp, 6hp and 8hp. Most models had pedalling gears.

PIROL • Germany 1950–1952

Small-scale scooter manufacturer using 143cc and 198cc Ilo engines.

PIROTTA • Italy 1949–1955

Built 49cc bicycle engines designed by Gianfranco Viviani, afterwards also two-stroke and ohv motorcycles up to 158cc.

PITTY • East Germany 1955–late 1960s

Scooter with 147cc MZ two-stroke engines, built in large numbers.

PLANET • England 1919–1920

Fitted 269cc Villiers engines and 293cc to 546cc Union and Blackburne engines into open frames.

PLASSON • France 1921–1924

Lightweight machines of primitive design. Plasson fitted two-stroke and also 197cc sv engines of its own manufacture.

PMC • England 1908–1915

The name stood for Premier Motorcycle Company, but was not the Coventry based Premier. PMC of Birmingham was somehow connected with Wall (Roc) and Rex and produced motorcycles and three-wheelers under names like Warwick, Rex-JAP etc. with JAP engines of 393cc to 996cc.

PMZ • Russia 1931–WW2

One of the oldest motorcycle factories in Russia. The company originally produced bicycle engines, and subsequently progressed to 746cc and 996cc motorcycles with BMW-like flat twin sv engines, and V-twin engines reminiscent of the Harley-Davidson design. These were used by the Russian Army.

PO • Italy 1921–1923

Built a variety of 346cc single-cylinder two-strokes, designed by Pagni.

POINARD • France 1951–1956

Built motorcycles and scooters with 123cc to 248cc Aubier-Dunne, Ydral and four-stroke AMC ohv engines.

PIAGGIO • Italy 1946–

Piaggio was established in 1881 by Enrico Piaggio to produce naval fittings, and under his son Rinaldo it expanded into railway rolling stock production, then aeronautical design.

At the end of WW2 the company was headed by Rinaldo's two sons, Armando and Enrico, who identified the urgent need for cheap transport in Italy and set aeronautical engineer Corradino D'Ascanio to the task of designing a functional two-wheeler. In 1946 his design, the Vespa scooter was unveiled, and it went on to change the face of motorcycling and sell hundreds of thousands around the world. The Vespa was and continues to be produced in many countries under license, as well as at the original Pontedera factory in Italy. Licencees include Douglas (England), ACMA (France), MotoVespa (Spain), Hoffman and Messerschmidt (Germany), Baja and LML (India), and recently manufacturing facilities have been set up in China. A new, modern automatic version was introduced in 1997, but the original two-stroke in 125cc and 200cc guises with its trademark hand gearchange and spare wheel under a side panel (all missing on the current ET2 and ET4 Vespas) continues to be built alongside.

Most other modern automatic scooters from the company are marketed under the Piaggio name, the current range including the Typhoon, Sfera, Liberty and Hexagon among others. Engines used are mostly Piaggio's own two-stroke designs, with capacities from 50cc to 180cc, although the Hexagon 250GT uses a Honda-sourced single-cylinder four-stroke. In turn, Piaggio also sells its own engines to other manufacturers.

Piaggio's most sporting scooters use the Gilera badge, owned by Piaggio since it bought the ailing motorcycle company in 1969, but the Gilera factory at Arcore was closed in 1993, and any intention to produce Gilera motorcycles appeared to be finished with it (although one or two hints have come from Piaggio at the end of the 1990s that Gilera motorcycles might yet reappear).

Piaggio is currently one of the world's largest producers of powered two-wheelers, ahead even of Kawasaki in numbers.

124cc Piaggio Liberty (two-stroke single) 1998

249cc Piaggio Hexagon GT250 (ohc single cylinder Honda) 1998

124cc Piaggio Skipper (two-stroke single) 1998

1500cc Polaris Victory V92SC (ohc V-twin) 1998

POINTER • Japan 1946–1962

Two-strokes from 123cc to 247cc with own engines. Was a big factory.

POLARIS • America 1998–

The long-established and highly respected major manufacturer of various powered products, most notably snowmobiles, moved into motorcycle manufacture with a Harley-Davidson-style V-twin cruiser called the Victory. Currently the well-received Victory is sold only in America, but exports are expected in the next few years.

POLENGHI • Italy 1950–1955

Mopeds, mofas and similar 48cc vehicles.

POLET • Italy 1923–1924

Made 481cc singles with own ioe engines.

PONNY • Germany 1924–1926

Lightweights with mainly 142cc and 172cc DKW two-stroke engines.

PONY • Germany 1924–1926

Not to be confused with the Ponny company which was in operation for the same period of time. Pony used 185cc sv engines.

PONY • Spain 1952–1954

Assembled machines with Hispano-Villiers 123cc two-stroke engines.

PONY-MONARK • Japan 1951–early 1960s

Produced 147cc ohv and 123cc to 247cc two-stroke motorcycles.

POPE • USA 1911–1918

Made by a branch of a famous car factory, Pope motorcycles used 500cc single and 1000cc V-twins. These were excellent sporting machines, some with plunger rear springing.

POPET • Japan 1957–early 1960s

Miniscooter with 47cc two-stroke engines.

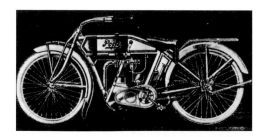

499cc Pope (ohv) 1913

998cc Pope (ohv V-twin) 1914

348cc Praga (dohc shaft-drive) 1932

2¹/₄hp Powerful (sv Buchet) 1903

POPMANLEE • Japan late 1950s–late1960s

Motorcycles with 124cc to 174cc and scooters with 49cc and 79cc two-stroke engines.

PORTLAND • England 1910–1911

This was the make of a big dealer in London, Maudes Motor Mart. Engines fitted were 498cc JAP and Peugeot.

POSDAM • Italy 1926–1929

The Alberto Da Milano-designed machines had 123cc, 147cc and 173cc ioe single-cylinder engines and with the exception of the 173cc machine, belt drive to the rear wheel. The biggest model had chain drive.

POSTLER • Germany 1920–1924

Designed by Walter Postler, who was a well-known racing-car driver, the first products were scooters with own 252cc ioe engines. After 1923 he also built a 246cc ohv machine with his own single-cylinder engine.

POTTHOFF • Germany 1924–1926

Built in limited quantities 185cc ohv machines with English Norman proprietary engines.

POUNCY • England 1930–1938

Built a range of Villiers-engined two-strokes, which included 147cc, 247cc and 346cc single-cylinder versions. The quarter-litre machine was also supplied with flat-top piston engines. From 1935 onwards, OEC rear suspension was available on all Pouncy models.

POUSTKA • Czechoslovakia 1924–1934

Made from English components, the Poustka had 147cc, 247cc and 346cc Villiers two-stroke engines. Like the Pouncy, it was a hand-made machine built in limited quantities.

POWELL • America 1939–1951

Los Angeles-based manufacturer of scooters and mini-motorcycles with four-stroke engines of up to 392cc.

POWELL • England 1921–1926

The first Powell with its 547cc Blackburne sv engine was a design which did not attract many customers. The factory also built 168cc, 198cc and 245cc two-strokes with its own engines.

POWERFUL • England 1903–c1906

French 2.25hp Buchet and English MMC engines powered these machines.

P&P • England 1922–1930

P&P stood for Packmann & Poppe of Coventry. Ealing Poppe, whose father owned the White & Poppe engine factory, designed these well-made sporting motorcycles. He made the first serious attempt to reduce engine noise and at the same time to keep the machine and the rider clean by introducing the superbly silenced and fully enclosed Silent Three, with a Barr & Stroud sleeve-valve power unit. Other models had JAP engines from 248cc to 996cc, which were made by the Montgomery works for

P&P. When a fire destroyed Montgomery's in 1925 P&P machines were not available for some time.

PRAGA • Czechoslovakia 1929–1935

Well-known car factory which merged with the Breitfeld-Danek machine works and also took over the J. F. Koch-designed 499cc BD motorcycle. This single-cylinder ohc machine had 84mm bore and 90mm stroke. A 346cc ohc Praga was built in 1932 with 70mm bore and 90mm stroke. This time the forks and frame were made from pressed steel and the unit-design engine had shaft drive to the rear wheel.

PRECISION • England 1912–1919

Frank Baker worked for many years in the US motorcycle industry before returning to England to set up the very successful Precision proprietary engine manufacturing company. Like JAP before and Blackburne after him, Baker discovered that making his own motorcycle upset the customers who were buying his engines, so Precision motorcycles, mainly of 500cc, were sold exclusively in Australia, a country without a large domestic motorcycle manufacturing industry.

PRECISION • England 1902–1906

No connection with F. E. Baker's Precision works. Produced motorcycles with mainly 211cc Minerva engines.

PREMIER • England 1908–1920

Once a great name in the British motorcycle industry, Premier in Coventry built big V-twins with outside flywheels, afterwards mainly singles with 348cc, 445cc and 490cc engines of Premier's own manufacture. After a reorganization in November 1914, the name was changed to Coventry-Premier. The last design was a 322cc two-stroke vertical twin arranged lengthwise in the frame. It never went into quantity production, and there were no Premier motorcycles built in England after 1915. The factory,

348cc Premier (sv) 1913 (German)

498cc Premier (sv) 1930 (Czechoslovakia)

498cc Premier Longstroke (ohv) 1930 (Czechoslovakia)

founded by Messrs. Hillmann, Herbert and Cooper, was really controlled by the Rotherham family, which in 1910 founded a branch in Germany. It was headed by Basil Jones, who raced Premiers in the TT races and who eventually became a brother-in-law of Geoffrey Rotherham, who controlled in the 1920s and early 1930s yet another Premier factory. Coventry-Premier produced three-wheeled and even four-wheeled light cars when it was absorbed in the early 1920s by Singer.

PREMIER • Germany 1910–1913

This was the Nuremberg-based branch of Premier in Coventry. Real owner was the machine factory J. C. Braun, but Basil Jones controlled production which consisted of a 346cc single-cylinder sv machine, and also bicycles and prams. A bad economic situation forced a transfer of the factory over the border into the Austro-Hungarian Empire, to Eger which in 1918 became part of Czechoslovakia.

PREMIER • Czechoslovakia 1913–1933

This was the most active period for Premier, although real motorcycle production did not start until 1923. Earlier it produced only the 346cc sv single and the manufacture of a few experimental light cars, as in England. Production at Eger commenced with a 269cc two-stroke, based on the English Triumph Baby. It had a round tank at first and was built for nearly ten years. Other models included JAP-engined 348cc and 498cc sv and ohv singles. From 1927 onwards, Premier's own engines of the same size were fitted, a 746cc V-twin sv engine added. New in 1929 was a 498cc long stroke ohv sloping engine. The factory, at that time the leading motorcycle producer in the country, was headed by Geoffrey Rotherham. Chief designer

was Hans Baumann, but the long stroke engine was created by Otto Lausmann. The factory had a racing department, where it used JAP engines, until the long stroke came into service. The JAP racing motors were of 348cc, 490cc, 746cc and 998cc; the leading riders Alois Kraus, Václav Lischka, Karl Tauber, Mila Stipek, Ernst Haubner etc.

PREMO • England 1908–1915

One of the names under which Premier (PMC) of Birmingham traded its motorcycles.

PREMOLI • Italy 1935–WW2

Racing motorcyclist Guido Premoli built 498cc motorcycles of sporting appearance with four-valve Python (Rudge) and OMB engines. In addition, he created 174cc singles with his own ohc engines which he raced himself.

PRESTER (JONGHI) • France 1926–late 1950s

Produced a wide range of models from 98cc to 496cc with Aubier-Dunne and Chaise engines. A merger with Jonghi in 1936 led to new models which included the famous Remondini-designed 174cc, 248cc and 348cc dohc racing machines. After the war, production concentrated on models of 98cc to 248cc and included beautiful 123cc ohv machines, 248cc two-strokes and also a nice 123cc scooter.

PRESTO • Germany 1901–1940

Was a well-known car factory, but little known as a producer of motorcycles. In the early years it used Zedel, Minerva and Fafnir engines; after WW1 the 197cc Alba sv engine was fitted, but production of Presto motorcycles was never large. During the 1930s Presto produced mopeds with 74cc and 98cc Sachs two-stroke engines.

PRIDE & CLARKE • England 1938–1940

A lightweight offered by a famous London-based motorcycle dealer. It had a 63cc two-stroke engine.

PUCH • Austria 1899–1991

Johann Puch's factory at Graz, Austria, started by making bicycles in 1899 and rapidly expanded over the next decade, producing cars, lorries and even railway locomotives by 1914. The sturdy, conventional four-strokes, singles and V-twins of between 300cc and 800cc were therefore only a minor part of Puch's output. During WW1 Puch concentrated on armament manufacture, but after it, eventually decided to concentrate on bicycles and motorcycles. For the latter, a design by Giovanni Marcellino of a 175cc 'split single' two-stroke engine was chosen and, although the design was to be altered and updated continuously, this engine configuration remained in use for the next 50 odd years. It powered the original Puch 'Harlette', a spindly affair described by the British magazine 'The Motor Cycle' as a 'motorised bicycle', but it did have a two-speed gear and clutch, in the rear hub. Almost from the start, Puch raced in the 175cc and later in the 250cc class, using an auxiliary charging pump and, on later models, water-cooling. The 250cc Puch's finest hour was the 1931 German Grand Prix, when Elvetio Toricelli won the 250cc class beating the works New Imperial, Rudge and Excelsior teams, and convincing

DKW that the 'blown' split single was its future salvation in racing. Unfortunately, Puch was badly hit by the depression of the early 1930s and withdrew from racing.

Split single two-strokes were Puch's strong point in the 1930s, although a flat four-cylinder four-stroke model was introduced in 1936. Manufacture of this was dropped after WW2, although the split singles continued to be made in various capacities. In the 1960s however, new, more orthodox, two-stroke engines appeared in the 50cc to 125cc capacities, while production diversified into small scooters, off-road machines and mopeds. Puch had long since had a reputation in ISDT-type events, and the new models were just as successful—and in motocross as well, with new 250cc designs.

In the late 1970s Puch began to use two-stroke and four-stroke Rotax engines for competition models, but more and more the 50cc class beckoned with ready sales of small motorcycles and mopeds. The Puch Maxi moped was a world best seller in the early 1980s. However, Puch was no more proof against the decline of the motorcycle market than the other European motorcycle manufacturers, and sales fell away badly in the late 1980s. In 1991 Puch was taken over by the Italian company Piaggio and now only makes mopeds.

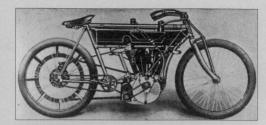

9hp Puch works racer (sv V-twin) 1907

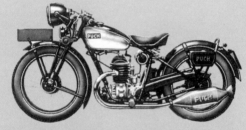

496cc Puch (two-stroke twin-cylinder, double piston) 1932

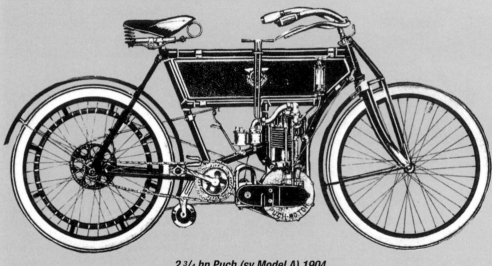

2 3/4 hp Puch (sv Model A) 1904

246cc Puch (two-stroke double piston) 1932

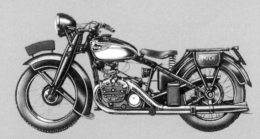

792cc Puch (sv transverse flat four) 1936

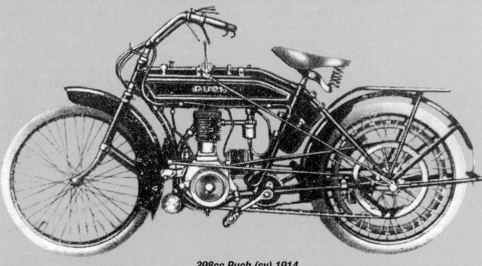

398cc Puch (sv) 1914

348cc Puch GS trials (two-stroke double piston) 1938

246cc Puch SGS (two-stroke double-piston) 1966

49cc Puch M50 Racing (two-stroke single) 1974

49cc Puch Monza GP (two-stroke) 1982

498cc Puch enduro (ohc single Rotax) 1982

976cc PV (sv V-twin JAP) 1923

PRIEST • England pre-WW1

One of three marques made at 66 Bishops Street, Birmingham. The other two were Frays and Kings Own.

PRIM • England 1906–1907

Money's Prim machines had a wide diameter petrol tank which formed the top part of the frame. The engine was a Belgian 5hp V-twin, made by Sarolea of Liège.

PRINA • Italy 1949–1954

Offered under the Orix trade mark, Prina's motorcycles and scooters had 123cc, 147cc and 173cc two-stroke engines made by Ilo of Germany.

PRINCEPS • England 1903–1907

Once a well-known producer of singles and V-twins with the factory's own engines.

PRINETTI & STUCCHI • Italy 1898–1911

Famous pioneer who built bicycles, three- and four-wheeled vehicles and afterwards motorcycles with engines designed by Carlo Leidi. Ettore Bugatti, whose Bugatti cars are still regarded as masterpieces, spent his first years in the trade with Prinetti & Stucchi. The first motorcycles had 2hp engines, but there were also bigger models built.

PRIOR • Germany 1904

A German make yet unknown in Germany. The motorcycles were Hercules products renamed Prior for sale in Britain, where there was already a Hercules factory owned by a British company.

PRIORY • England 1919–1926

Assembler of two-stroke motorcycles with 269cc Arden, 292cc Union and 147cc to 247cc Villiers engines.

PROGRESS • Germany 1901–1914

One of the leading makes in the early years of motorcycle production in Germany. Fitted Zedel and Fafnir proprietary singles and V-twins. Afterwards models with its own 532cc single-cylinder and 698cc V-twin engines came onto the market.

PROGRESS • England 1902–1908

The English Progress was a well-known motorcycle. Minerva, MMC, Antoine and other engines were fitted into strong frames.

PROGRESS • Germany 1951–1957

Another Progress, but this was a Sachs-engined 98cc, 147cc, 173cc and 198cc scooter. It was also built under license in Britain using 148cc and 197cc Villiers engines.

PROMOT • Poland late 1960s–early 1970s

Trials and motocross machines with 123cc Puch two-stroke engines.

PROPUL • France 1923–1926

Limited assembly of motorcycles with 246cc, 346cc and 498cc single-cylinder sv and ohv engines made by JAP, MAG and Blackburne. Built also a 98cc two-stroke.

P & S • England 1921

Made by Norfolk Engineering Works, Worthing.

PSW • Germany 1924–1929

Produced interesting 247cc two-strokes with inlet and exhaust ports in front of the cylinder, built a range of JAP and Blackburne-engined racing machines from 248cc to 490cc with single cylinder ohv engines, and even mini-cars with 98cc engines for children.

PUCH • Austria 1899-1991–

See panel

3¹/₂hp Progress (sv) 1905 (Germany)

PUMA • Argentine 1954–early 1960s

Mopeds and lightweights with 98cc two-stroke engines.

P&S • England 1919–1921

Identical with Pearson models, but the last versions built had the name changed to P&S (Pearson & Sopwith). They were made by Excelsior of Birmingham, owned by the Walker family.

PUMPHREY • England 1905–1908

Limited production of 2 ³/₄hp and 3 ¹/₂hp White & Poppe single-cylinder machines built by Pumphrey & Co. of Streatham, London.

PV • England 1910–1925

This London-based make fitted a variety of proprietary engines into sturdy spring-frames of its own design. JAP supplied mainly sv engines from 293cc to 996cc, Villiers two-strokes from 247cc to 347cc, while Barr & Stroud supplied 346cc sleeve-valve and Bradshaw 348cc oil-cooled ohv engines.

PZI • Poland 1936–1937

Small producer of motorcycles with own 598cc single-cylinder and 1196cc V-twin engines. Most were supplied to the Polish army.

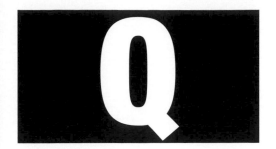

QINGQI • China 1956–

China's oldest and largest existing motorcycle manufacturer based in Jinan city, Shandong province, and despite being almost unheard of in most western countries, also one of the biggest in the world, with annual production of 1.663 million units in 1998. The majority of machines are lightweight motorcycles and scooters, mostly now based on older Japanese designs, although in the past Soviet and Czech designs were either copied or produced under license. In the past supplied only the military and state enterprises, now also supplies the domestic market where its Mulan single-cylinder motorcycle is the country's best-selling two-wheeler, although the Qingqi name is also used on many machines. Also exports to more than 50 countries, mostly in Asia.

QUADRANT • England 1901–1929

Superbly made W. L. Lloyd-designed motorcycles. The first models had 211cc Minerva engines, but from 1903 onwards, the Birmingham works also produced engines of its own design. They included 374cc two-strokes: 498cc, 554cc, 654cc and even 780cc singles and 1130cc V-twins with sv engines as well as a 498cc ohv version. There was also a 654cc version with ioe valves, while other models had splash lubrication. Tom Silver, one of the great English pioneers, rode these machines successfully in sporting events for many years.

QUAGLIOTTI • Italy 1902–1907

Producer of 2hp and 3hp single-cylinder and of 5hp V-twin machines. Carlo Quagliotti was regarded as one of the leading designer-manufacturer pioneers in the country.

QUASAR • England 1976–1994

The creation of innovative English engineer Malcolm Newell, the Quasar utilised a feet-forward riding position and streamlined bodywork complete with a roof. A number were sold to enthusiasts. The high tech exterior hid a low-powered, four-cylinder Reliant car engine, but the machine's low drag characteristics still helped it achieve more than 100mph.

Newell also experimented with other power units, including a six-cylinder Kawasaki-powered Phasar, until his death in 1995.

QUIRKS • Australia 1913–1915

Built 496cc sv flat twins on a small scale. The frames were of double-loop variety.

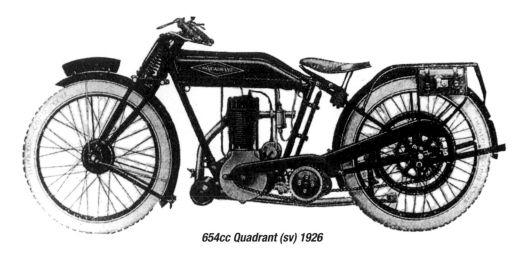

654cc Quadrant (sv) 1926

2hp Quadrant with spring forks 1905

1000cc Quasar (ohv 4-cylinder Reliant) 1976

RABBIT • Japan 1946–1968

A very popular scooter with own make 90cc, 123cc and 199cc two-stroke engines.

RABENEICK • Germany 1933–1958

Produced in pre-war days mopeds with 74cc Sachs engines, after 1945 38cc and 48cc mofas and mopeds and a range of motorcycles with 98cc, 123cc, 147cc, 173cc, 244cc and 247cc Ilo and Sachs engines. The machines were of excellent design and good finish. The works was bought by Fichtel & Sachs and went on to recondition car clutches.

248cc Rabeneick prototype (ohv shaft-drive) 1955

RACER • France 1953–1956

Small factory which produced bicycle engines and lightweight motorcycles with own 49cc and 74cc two-stroke engines.

RADCO • England 1913–1932

Excellent 211cc and 247cc two-strokes with outside flywheels, afterwards 247cc ohv models with Radco's own engines and Villiers-engined 145cc and 198cc two-strokes. JAP-engined versions had 293cc and 490cc sv and 248cc and 490cc ohv motors. All had one cylinder, but the 490cc ohv machine was built in three versions: Touring, Sport and Super-Sport.

RADEX • Germany 1951–late 1950s

This name was used for some post-war machines built by the Express motorcycle factory. See also Express.

RADIOLA • France 1933–1939

These were bicycle attachments with a capacity of 98cc.

RADIOR • France 1904–1960

Old established factory. Fitted Peugeot and Antoine engines and during the 1920s its own 98cc to 247cc two-strokes

269cc Radco (two-stroke) 1915

490cc Radco (ohv JAP) 1928

246cc Radco (two-stroke) 1923

as well as JAP and Chaise engines from 247cc to 498cc. Most Chaise-engined models were of unit design, some had ohv, others ohc. After 1945, most engines were supplied by the associated Nervor works, by AMC and NSU. The German factory also supplied 48cc and 98cc two-strokes for mopeds, lightweights etc. while Radior production included ohv models up to 248cc and also some interesting two-stroke vertical twins of the same capacity.

RADIUM • Australia c1912–c1915

Limited assembly of JAP and Precision-engined machines by the Alex Osborne Cycle Works, Burnie, Tasmania.

RALEIGH • England 1899–1970s

Raleigh was a famous bicycle maker which also produced proprietary Sturmey-Archer gearboxes and later, engines. Its first motorcycles, unashamed copies of the Werner Motocyclette, gave way in 1902 to a more orthodox model, notable for using Bowden cable controls. Production of this ceased in 1905 and Raleigh did not return to the motorcycle scene until 1919, when a new 650cc flat twin appeared, followed by a wide range of singles and twins designed by William Comery. These worthy (but rather dull) machines did very well in trials in the 1920s under publicity chief Hugh Gibson, a particular star being the brilliant lady rider Marjorie Cottle. In later years, Raleigh strove for a more sporting image,

hiring 'Wizard' O'Donovan (of Brooklands and Norton fame) to design TT racers, which, although promising, never really justified their considerable cost. In the depressed early 1930s Raleigh decided that bicycles were more profitable, and motorcycle production ended in 1933.

Raleigh re-entered the market again 25 years later with a Sturmey-Archer-engined moped, but soon found it cheaper to import a range of machines with automatic transmission—the Mobylette, built in France by Motobëcane. A small-wheeled version was the Raleigh Wisp. The Raleigh Roma was a 75cc (Bianchi) scooter.

In the late 1970s, Raleigh again decided that bicycles were a better it by now owned many other famous names and it gave up on the moped market.

3hp Raleigh No. 2 aircooled 1905   *3¹/₂hp Raleigh watercooled 'Raleighette' 1905*

173cc Raleigh (sv) 1924

490cc Radior (ohv JAP) 1929

RADMILL • England 1912–1914

Assembled motorcycles with 269cc Villiers and 346cc Precision two-stroke engines. If required other Precision engines could also be supplied.

RADVAN • Czechoslovakia 1909–1926

See also Meteor. After 1924 Radvan supplied under his own name 145cc and 174cc DKW-engined two-strokes.

RAGLAN • England 1909–1913

Built motorcycles with 292cc, 347cc and 496cc Precision sv engines, water-cooled 490cc Green-Precision singles and also with its own power units.

RALEIGH • England 1899–1970s

See panel

RAMBLER • America 1903–WW1

Made 4hp singles and 6hp V-twins.

175cc Radior (ohv single AMC) 1952

RAMBLER • England 1937–1961

This was the trademark for some Norman models—especially the Villiers-engined 197cc two-stroke—in some export markets.

RANZANI • Italy 1923–1931

Interesting make because the Ranzani used not only 175cc sv engines from the German Heros factory, but also 170cc ohv engines from Norman in England, a proprietary engine factory which was not connected with Norman motorcycles. The last Ranzani motorcycles had its own unit-design ohv 173cc engines.

RAPID • NETHERLANDS 1923

Belt-driven lightweights built by Renner Rijwiefabriek, Rotterdam.

RAS • Italy 1932–1936

Made by Fusi, for many years Belgian FN importer to Italy, the RAS had mainly JAP ohv engines of 173cc to 490cc, and some frame parts made by the FN works. A nice 248cc ohc single of its own design and manufacture was built in 1935. It was the last RAS model; after 1936, all machines used the Fusi badge.

RASSER • France 1922–1923

Unusual design with rivetted pressed steel frame and 98cc two-stroke engine.

RATIER • France 1955–1962

Produced in the late 1920s small cars and was successor to the CMR and CEMEC works, which after 1945 built BMW-like motorcycles with parts which were partly made in France by BMW for the German army during the war, and partly after the war in French factories. The first models were 746cc sv flat twins. Ratier built mainly 494cc and 597cc ohv models of pure French design and manufacture.

496cc Ratier (ohv transverse flat twin) 1958

RATINGIA • Germany 1923–1925

Lightweights with 170cc and 195cc sv engines.

990cc Reading-Standard (sv V-twin) 1917

990cc Reading-Standard works racer (ohc V-twin) 1921

RAVAT • France 1898–late 1950s

Produced a range of models up to 498cc including two-strokes of 98cc and 173cc. Also built the Italian Simonetta scooter under license.

RAY • England 1919–1920

Limited production of motorcycles with own 331cc two-stroke engines.

RAY • England 1922–1925

W. H. Raven designed the beautiful 193cc sv monobloc Ray, which weighed only 130lb with a saddle height of 24in. Another model with a Cohen-designed 172cc Villiers-Jardine engine was added in 1924, after the factory moved from Nottingham to Leicester.

RAYMO • France c1928

Assembled motorcycles with proprietary engines including Blackburne.

RAYNAL • England 1914–1953

Early models used the 269cc Villiers two-stroke engine; during the mid-1930s and after 1945 the machines had 98cc Villiers engines.

READING-STANDARD • America 1903–1922

A leading make of the period and together with Indian,

Harley-Davidson, Super-X, Henderson, ACE and Cleveland a very popular one. The production included 499cc singles and V-twins of 990cc and 1170cc. Most had sv engines, some racing versions ohv and even ohc power units, but the ohc engines were used by works riders only and were not for sale.

READY • England 1920–1922

Assembled machines of simple design. Engines used were JAP 293cc and 346cc sv units. Built later the 147cc Villiers-engined Rebro.

READY • Belgium 1924–1939

Originally known as Ready-Courtrai, the Ready motorcycles were of typical English design. Most engines came from England: Villiers, JAP, Blackburne and Python. The exception was the Swiss MAG. Models built were of 173cc to 498cc.

REAL • Germany 1981–

Producer of various light machines including a 79cc enduro model called 'Nevada'.

REBRO • England 1922–1928

Of simple design, the Rebro, priced at £37, had a 147cc Villiers engine. After Rebro closed, Ready took over production of this model, but only very few such machines appeared.

RECORD • Germany 1922–1924

Equipped machines of simple design with its own 147cc two-stroke engines.

REDDIS • Spain 1957–1960

Small producer of 124cc two-stroke machines with Hispano-Villiers engines.

REDRUP • England 1919–1922

Created by a former aircraft engine designer Charles Redrup, these machines had a 304cc radial three-cylinder sv engine of simple and practical appearance. Although also offered by two other makes—Beaumont and British Radial—the production of the engine was limited. Redrup also built a six-cylinder prototype by putting two such engines together. It was a smooth machine, but not a viable commercial proposition.

RED STAR • Belgium 1902

Built at Antwerp and fitted with a 211cc Minerva engine.

REFORM • Austria 1903–1905

Monarch in Birmingham, better known as the Excelsior works, supplied 2.25hp sv engines for the Vienna-based Austrian manufacturer.

REGAL • England 1909–1915

Excellent machines of sound design. The range included 349cc two-strokes with Peco engines, 346cc and 492cc sv and ohv singles with air-cooled Precision and water-cooled Green-Precision engines, while a 602cc twin was also made by Precision.

REGENT • England 1920–1921

Small manufacturer which fitted 688cc Coventry-Victor flat twin sv engines into heavy frames of its own design and manufacture.

REGENT • Russia 1965–

Producer of lightweight machines based, like the BSA Bantam and many others, on the RT125W DKW design of 1939.

REGINA • England 1903–1915

Early models had Minerva, MMC and Fafnir engines. Production stopped in 1907, but was resumed just before WW1, when the factory fitted its own 292cc two-stroke engines into orthodox frames. This machine was made at Ilford in Essex; at the same time identical machines were offered from an address in Derby.

REGINA • France 1905–WWI

Early French machines with Zurcher, Buchet and Peugeot proprietary engines.

REGNIS • Australia 1919–1923

Built by the Singer importer at Melbourne, the Regnis housed a 746cc ioe V-twin engine of Swiss MAG (Motosacoche) manufacture.

REH • Germany 1948–1953

The Richard Engelbrecht-designed Reh was made in small numbers and was of good design and quality. The engines fitted were of Ilo manufacture and were of 173cc, 198cc, 244cc and 248cc.

REITER • Italy 1927–1929

Despite the German name, the Reiter was a sporting Italian machine, made mainly from English components. Timone and Fresia built these at Turin. The engines used were the 247cc sv and ohv Blackburne and the oil-cooled 348cc ohv Bradshaw, the so-called 'oilboiler'.

123cc Regent Roadster 125 (two-stroke single) 1996

RELIANCE • America 1912–1915

One of the smaller US works, Reliance built 4.5hp single cylinder machines with ioe engines.

REMUS • England 1920–1922

Concentrated on the assembly of 211cc two-strokes engines built by Radco of Birmingham.

REN • Australia c1914

Single-speed two-stroke machines built by Warren Bros, Walkerville, South Australia. Also made a light delivery vehicle based on the Ren motorcycle.

RENÉ-GILLET • France 1898–1957

Excellent heavy machines used by the French armed forces and the police. Most of these were 748cc and 996cc V-twins with sv engines, which were run with sidecars attached. Another popular model was the 346cc single-cylinder sv model. Improved versions of the big V-twins were built after the war, while main production switched to two-strokes of 48cc, 123cc and 246cc. All engines were of its own design and manufacture. Never regarded as a very sporting make, René-Gillet machines were known as 'unbreakable' touring machines.

RENNER-ORIGINAL • Germany 1924–1932

Designed by Carl Ostner, brother of the manufacturer of OD motorcycles, Renner-Original concentrated on 346cc single-cylinder and 678cc V-twin machines with sv JAP engines. On request, it also supplied other JAP power units and German Kahne and Kachen engines.

RENNSTEIG • Germany 1925–1930

Arms factory which took over the production of Original-Krieger machines and fitted 198cc to 497cc Blackburne engines into typical KG (Krieger-Gnüdig) double-loop frames.

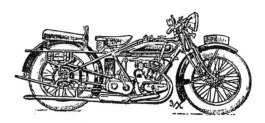

346cc René-Gillet (sv) 1928

248cc René-Gillet (two-stroke) 1952

346cc Renner-Original (sv JAP) 1927

REX (REX ACME) • England 1900–1933

Under two energetic brothers, Harold and Billy Williamson, Rex of Coventry became one of the leading motorcycle manufacturers in England. From the start, it made its own single-cylinder and V-twin engines with characteristic square finning and was among the first to fit spring front forks, with a telescopic action. Rex was prominent in all sorts of competition and its lady rider Muriel Hind won considerable publicity for it in long distance trials and speed hill climbs. In 1908 Rex entered into an agreement with Premier in Birmingham to build proprietary engined models under the name Rex-JAP.

Later in 1911 the Williamson brothers left the company after a board room argument, and George Hemingway took over, continuing to expand the Rex company until WW1. During the war Rex was engaged in defence work and made only a batch of 50 V-twins for Russia and a few sidecar outfits for the Daily Mail's distribution fleet. Post war, Rex at first offered advanced singles and twins with its own engines, but few of these were made and following its takeover of the smaller Acme company, it now began to use JAP and Blackburne engines. After the 1922 Lightweight TT rider Walter Handley (who had made the fastest lap before crashing) quarrelled violently with Ernie Humphries, his boss at OK Motor Cycles. He was signed up on the spot by Hemingway, starting a partnership that was to make motorcycle racing history. Between 1923 and 1927, Handley won three TTs and made five fastest TT laps for Rex Acme, as well as scoring grand prix victories and innumerable other wins and places. His career, although brief, raised him to a level comparable to, later, Stanley Woods, Geoff Duke and Mike Hailwood, simply the best in the world in their time.

In the 1920s, Rex Acme offered a wide range of machines, with Villiers two-strokes, JAP, Blackburne and MAG singles and twins. It also produced some oddities, such as an Aza two-stroke 175cc model and another 175cc ohv machine with what it claimed was its own engine, but which, in fact, was an AKD. It sold TT replica models and genuine racing machines that were very successful and earned Rex Acme a sporting reputation second to none.

However, the survival rate of 'vintage' Rex Acmes is low, and overall sales were probably not high enough. The company showed signs of faltering when Handley left in 1929, and it collapsed in the depression of 1930. It was bought by the Mills Fulford sidecar manufacturing concern, but a re-launch of the Rex Acme name in 1932 was not a success, and it and Mills Fulford disappeared forever in 1933.

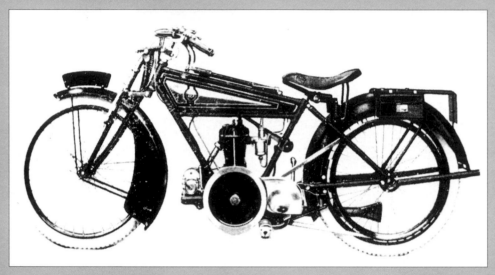

346cc Rex (sv Blackburne) 1922

3¹/₂hp Rex (sv) 1905

346cc Rex-Acme (ohv MAG) 1928

REPUBLIC • Czechoslovakia 1899–1908

Made by the Laurin & Klement factory (now Skoda) in the old Austro-Hungarian Empire, these machines were identical to Laurin & Klement products.

REVERE • England 1915–1922

Small two-strokes with 269cc Villiers engines with frames, built by Sparkbrook for White-house & Co., the Revere manufacturer.

REVOLUTION • England 1904–1906

This was a conventional 2.75hp single with power units made by NRCC.

REX (REX ACME) • England 1900–1933

See panel

REX • Germany 1923–1925

Produced 283cc two-stroke machines in a small factory near Nuremberg.

REX • Germany 1948–1964

Built bicycle attachment engines with 31cc, 34cc and 40cc, afterwards a large number of mofas, mopeds and lightweights with 48cc two-stroke power units.

REX • Sweden 1908–

The first machines had Swiss Motosacoche engines. In 1908 Rex built its own 2.5hp V-twin engines. Later there were Villiers and JAP-engined models from 147cc to 746cc. After WW1 Sachs, Ilo, Husqvarna and other two-stroke engines from 48cc to 248cc were fitted.

REX JAP • England 1908–1915

Made by the Premier company for Rex to use JAP engines in Rex running gear. The Williamson brothers (see Rex) wanted to expand Rex engine production facilities, but other directors did not. This confrontation led to boardroom conflict and eventually the Williamsons resigned.

49cc Rieju RS1 Evolution (two-stroke) 1998

269cc Reynolds-Runabout (TS Liberty-engine) 1921

903cc Rickman (ohc four-cylinder Kawasaki engine) 1977

REYNOLDS-RUNABOUT • England 1919–1922

Fully enclosed scooter-like machines with small wheels and a very low center of gravity. Engines used were the 269cc Liberty two-stroke and the 346cc sv JAP.

REYNOLDS-SPECIAL • England 1930–1933

Made by Albert Reynolds, who founded in 1938 the AER motorcycle works and who for many years was closely connected with Scott. The Reynolds-Specials were modified and improved 498cc and 598cc two-stroke, twin-cylinder water-cooled Scotts.

R&F • Germany 1924–1926

Another German 348cc ohv machine, but in this case the engine was R&F's own design and manufacture.

RHONSON • France 1952–1958

Built the 49cc Rhonsonette mopeds and other small machines and also 123cc two-stroke motorcycles.

RHONY-X • France 1924–1932

Built over the years a wide range of models. These included 185cc and 246cc two-strokes, in the late 1920s and 1930s also 98cc versions as well as JAP and Chaise-engined sv and ohv models up to 498cc. Some of the Chaise engines were ohc unit-design models.

RIBI • Germany 1923–1925

A Berlin-based manufacturer of 196cc and 248cc ohv single-cylinder machines with its own engines.

RICHARD • France 1901–1904

Car and motorcycle manufacturer, whose motorcycles had engines made by Peugeot and other proprietary engine manufacturers.

RICKMAN • England 1959–

Produced a variety of chassis kits, including racers for Triumph twins and in 1971 a rolling chassis for the Royal Enfield 350/500cc single, called the Interceptor. This was followed during the 1970s by successful kits for Japanese multi-cylinder engines, most notably the Kawasaki Z900/1000, Suzuki GS750/1000 and Honda CB900.

By the early 1980s demand for aftermarket chassis kits waned as the handling of the manufacturers' own machines improved, and Rickman turned to the production of motorcycle accessories.

RIEDEL • Germany 1951

Norbert Riedel designed the Riedel horizontally opposed twin cylinder two-stroke starter engine for Junkers Jumo engines used in Messerschmitts, then worked in the DKW plant at Zschopau after WW2. He went on to design and build the Imme. Before he closed his own factory he made 25 horizontally opposed 150cc two-stroke twin machines marketed as the Riedel .

RIEJU • Spain 1952–

Maker of two-stroke and four-stroke motorcycles and scooters of between 125cc and 175cc. Latterly has specialized in 50cc and 75cc lightweights, including 50cc sports motorcycles.

RIGAT • Italy 1912–1914

Produced motorcycles with 487cc single-cylinder Fafnir engines.

RIKUO • Japan 1932–1962

Not a manufacturer as many believe, but a copy of an early Harley-Davidson V-twin produced under license from the US factory, and built by Meguro. See Meguro entry.

RILEY • England 1901–c1908

The Riley brothers were pioneer makers of two- and three-wheeled vehicles, using De Dion engines and then their own, before turning to cars. Percy Riley was the first designer to use mechanically operated inlet valves and patented `overlap' valve timing.

RINNE • Germany 1924–1932

Concentrated on 124cc, 174cc and 248cc two-stroke engines. Complete machines were made in limited numbers with a horizontal cylinder. Racing versions were ridden by Max Hucke, Lücke and Rannacher and it was Hucke who built Rinne frames.

RIP • England 1905–1908

Peugeot, Stevens and White & Poppe engines drove these early machines, which had spring frames.

RITSURIN • Japan c1936

500cc ohv. Little else known.

RIVIERRE • France c1903

Had a Megola-like engine, ie a 1.75hp radial engine built into the rear wheel, but designer Gaston Rivierre offered also stronger engines up to 20hp, built on similar lines. They were really two-strokes with the opposite cylinder working as a kind of scavenging pump for the intake of the mixture.

RIWINA • Germany 1924–1925

Assembler who built his machines at Bielefeld, then a center of the German bicycle industry. The engine was a 142cc two-stroke, made by DKW. Other power units were also fitted.

RIXE • Germany 1934–1985

Pre war, Rixe made Sachs-engined motorised bicycles, and, post war, continued with Sachs two-strokes from 50cc up to 250cc. In the 1970s, production was almost entirely of 50cc models, but Rixe's last offering was a water-cooled 80cc sports model with five gears.

RIZZATO • Italy 1972–

Small factory that used 125cc Minarelli engines in sports machines, mostly trials models. During the 1990s Rizzato produced mopeds and scooters under the Atala brand name, mostly using Franco Morini two-stroke engines.

R&K • Czechoslovakia 1924–1926

Equipped lightweight motorcycles with 147cc and 172cc Villiers two-stroke engines. Kroboth later designed and built cars and – in Germany after the war – scooters.

RM • France c1923

All-enclosed two-stroke machine with monocoque construction built in Paris.

RMW • Germany 1925–1955

The first machines built had its own 132cc and 148cc two-stroke engines. Later ones also had 198cc versions with 62mm bore and 66mm stroke. Four-stroke models used a variety of proprietary engines up to 498cc. Among them were Sturmey-Archer, MAG, JAP, Küchen, Moser and Bark products. RMW took over the Phoenix motorcycle works, used for some time screwed-together frames and had after 1945 a comparatively small production.

ROA • Spain 1952–early 1960s

Built motorcycles and three-wheeled transport vehicles with Hispano-Villiers engines with capacities up to 325cc.

ROAMER • Australia 1936-1952

English-made Norman motorcycles sold under license in Australia.

ROBAKO • Germany 1924–1926

One of the many Berlin-based motorcycle assemblers of the 1920s. Fitted 129cc Bekamo and 132cc MGF two-stroke engines.

ROC • England 1904–1915

Designed by one of the great pioneers, A. W. Wall. The works, based at Guildford and afterwards at Birmingham, was financed by the famous author Conan-Doyle. Roc motorcycles had unusually long wheelbases with Precision and Roc engines of 2hp, 2.5hp and 3hp; most of them were V-twins. The versatile A. W. Wall designed during the years many different and often unorthodox vehicles and other products. They included different kinds of gearboxes, three-wheelers with motorcycle engines and car-like bodies, bicycle attachment engines etc.

ROC • France 1985-

Small but highly respected racing chassis builder which came to prominence in 1992 when it was selected by Yamaha, along with English company Harris, to build Yamaha-designed chassis for the Japanese four-cylinder two-stroke grand prix engine, a move designed to make competitive privateer grand prix racing bikes available at a reasonable price. The company is run by Serge Rosset.

ROCHESTER • France 1923–1929

Concentrated on lightweight machines with engines up to 174cc.

ROCHET • France 1902–c1908

Was among the first producers of motorcycles with two-speed gears. The single-cylinder 1.75hp ioe engine was of its own manufacture.

ROCKET • Italy 1953–1958

For its period an ultra-modern flat-twin ohv machine of 198cc only. The opposing cylinders were transverse-mounted and in unit with the engine. Drive to the rear wheel was by shaft. Made by IMN of Naples, the Rocket was an expensive, probably over ambitious design.

ROCK-OLA • America 1938–1940

Lightweight Johnson-powered scooter built by the famous juke-box manufacturer.

ROCKSON • England 1920–1923

Assembler which used 269cc Villiers two-strokes and 346cc Blackburne sv engines.

ROCO • Germany 1922–1925

Beautiful lightweight machines of 110cc, afterwards also 147cc two-stroke engines. Unconfirmed sources claim the engines were supplied by Cockerell. Among the owners of the Roco works were the famous designer and racing motorist Johannes Rössig and the Rosner brothers, also well-known racing men. The Roco had a triangular double-loop frame and a very low saddle position.

ROCONOVA • Germany 1924–1926

Designed by Johannes Rössig, who raced Douglas and Victoria machines, the Roconovas were the first 248cc and 348cc ohc singles built commercially in Germany. Racing versions of the quarter-litre machine won many races. Among the riders were Rössig, Thevis, Zadek, Count Bismarck, Perl, Nakonzer, Elsner, Pohle and others.

Roconova also supplied engines to other factories including TX and Patria.

248cc Roconova (ohc) 1925

ROÈS • France 1932–1934

Lightweight machines with 98cc and 123cc two-stroke engines.

ROESSLER & JAUERNIGG • Czechoslovakia 1902–1907

Another make born in the old Austro-Hungarian Empire, in a town called Aussig. The Fehers-designed singles and V-twins were of excellent quality. Some models had rear suspension. The engines were of 2hp, 2.75hp and 4hp.

ROHR • Germany 1952–1958

Scooters made by an agricultural-machine factory with 197cc Ilo engines.

ROLAND • Germany 1904–1907

Roland, Allright, Tiger, Vindec-Special etc. were all trademarks used by the Küln-Lindenthaler Motorenwerke AG at Cologne. Like the others, early Roland machines had Kelecom, FN and other engines built under license. These engines were singles of 2.25hp and 2.75hp and V-twins of 5hp. Roland motorcycles were also made available equipped with Truffault swinging-arm forks.

ROLAND • Germany 1923–1924

Small producer of two-strokes with 132cc Bekamo and 145cc DKW engines.

2³/₄hp Roland (sv Truffault fork) 1905

ROLEO • France 1924–1939

See CP Roleo

ROLFE • England 1911–1914

Ambitious factory which built good motorcycles with 498cc single-cylinder and 746cc V-twin sv JAP engines.

ROLL • France c1920s

Maker of lightweights including 250cc and 175cc models fitted with Train engines and Albion gearboxes. A 250cc Roll won its class in the 1924 Paris-Nice race. The machines were produced by Delaune-Berger, Paris.

ROMEO • Italy 1969–1975

A make of the younger Italian generation. Romeo concentrated on 49cc two-stroke machines with Minarelli engines.

ROMP • England 1913–1914

Short-lived 499cc sv single with Precision engine.

ROMPER • England 1920

Direct belt-drive single-speed 2 ³/₄hp Union-engined two-strokes.

RONDINE • Italy 1923–1928

Prinelli's two-stroke Rondine lightweights with 98cc Train engines had no connection with Rondine racing Fours.

RONDINE • Italy 1934–1935

Designed by Carlo Gianini and Piero Remor, the Rondine was a supercharged, water-cooled 499cc four-cylinder racing machine. Its production by the Compagnia Nazionale Aeronautica at Rome was financed by Count Bonmartini. He also entered a team in races. His top riders: Piero Taruffi and Amilcare Rosetti. The design was bought by Gilera in 1936 and raced until after the war under that name.

RONDINE • Italy 1951–1954

These Rondines, designed by Martino Siccomario, had 124cc and 147cc Sachs two-stroke engines.

RONDINE • Italy 1968–early 1970s

Yet another Rondine, designed by former MV-Agusta racing-team member Alfredo Copeta. His motocross and racing version had 48cc two-stroke engines.

ROND-SACHS • The Netherlands 1971–1975

Concentrated on the production of 49cc and 123cc motocross machines with Sachs two-stroke engines. The bigger produced 22bhp at 9300rpm.

ROSENGART • France 1922–1923

Rosengart was connected with a lightweight motorcycle with a 98cc Train two-stroke engine, which did not sell well. A little later, the company was better known for building the Austin Seven under license, as did Dixi-BMW in Germany.

ROSSELLI • Italy 1899–1910

Probably the most famous pioneer of the Italian motorcycle industry, Emanuel di Rosselli produced first his 1hp Lilliput, a bicycle with the engine in front of the pedalling gear. His next models included a 1.75hp ladies motorcycle and a 258cc, 2.5hp machine. Rosselli also produced cars.

ROSSI • Italy 1950–1955

The Parma-built machines had 123cc Sachs engines and proved the excellent design with successes in trials.

ROSSI • Italy 1929

With its frame made from aluminum alloy the 348cc 90 degree V-twin was a technically interesting but commercially not very successful design. Paolo Rossi, the designer, had insufficient resources to market this motorcycle on a bigger scale.

ROTARY • Japan early 1950s-1961

Modern two-strokes of 124cc, built by one of Japan's bigger factories.

ROTER TEUFEL • Germany 1923–1925

Berlin had many producers of two-strokes, but only a few factories which built four-stroke motorcycles. This was one of them. The machines had 170cc sv engines.

ROTTER • Germany 1924–1925

Before WW1 the Rotter factory had been used to build the Weltrad. For a time in the mid 1920s it fitted DKW engines into simple frames.

ROULETTE • England 1918–1919

Assembled machines with 269cc Villiers two-stroke, three-port, deflector-type engines.

ROUSSEY • France 1948–1956

Concentrated on lightweights, including 48cc bicycle

engines as well as motorcycles and scooters with 123cc and 174cc power units.

ROVA-KENT • Australia 1913–1914

Unit-design 496cc single-cylinder machine with its own four-valve ohv engine.

ROVER • England 1902–1925

Equipped with orthodox diamond frames, Rover motorcycles were known for their sound design and excellent workmanship. In pre-1914 days Rover had an excellent 496cc sv single, which was also built after 1918. The engine had 85mm bore and 88mm stroke. There were also JAP-engined models, including 676cc V-twins. The last Rover models built had 248cc and 348cc ohv single-cylinder engines of its own design and manufacture.

ROVENA • Spain 1960s

Rovena was made by Sanglas, being so named because of Sanglas's involvement with single-cylinder four-strokes. The first Rovenas used 250cc and 325cc two-stroke twin engines from Hispano Villiers, and later there were 50cc and 100cc Zundapp-engined models and a 250cc sports model (Hispano Villiers), credited with a 90mph top speed. Sanglas's success with police contracts led to it winding-up the manufacture of Rovenas in 1968.

496cc Rover (sv) 1921

ROVETTA • Italy 1900–1906

Once a well-known factory, Rovetta produced as easrly as 1904 water-cooled machines with its own 2.5hp engines.

ROVIN • France 1920–1934

Roaul de Rovin was a very versatile man. He built motorcycles from 98cc to 499cc with two-stroke engines and also JAP and MAG sv and ohv engines. He built three-wheelers and very fast small sports and racing cars with JAP racing engines, which he successfully drove in races. He raced also Delage GP cars, bought in 1929 the San-Sou-Pap motorcycle factory and built after 1945 very neat small cars.

ROYAL ENFIELD • England 1901–1970

Bicycle maker Royal Enfield experimented with De Dion engines and, in 1901, produced a motorcycle with a Minerva engine over the front wheel and driving the rear wheel by a crossed belt. However, no motorcycles were made between 1904 and 1911. Then, Royal Enfield offered a single-speed model with a 425cc MAG V-twin engine, revising it the same year to include the RE two-speed gear, which worked by selecting either one of two different ratios of primary chain drive. In 1912, there was a much larger 770cc JAP engined V-twin, also with two-speed gear and with a patented 'cush drive' in the rear hub. In 1913, an improved MAG engine, again of 425cc, with overhead inlet valves was fitted to the smaller model and, in 1914, a 225cc two-stroke was introduced. After WW1, the small twin was phased out and, until 1924, only the two-stroke and an 8hp JAP V-twin sidecar model were offered.

In 1924 engine designer E. O. (Ted) Pardoe joined Royal Enfield and a year later so did development engineer Tony Wilson-Jones. Both men saw long service, Pardoe staying with Royal Enfield until the mid-1950s and Wilson-Jones virtually until the end. So did Major Frank Smith who was first joint managing director from 1914 to 1933 and then sole managing director until his death in 1963. This continuity at the the top explains the steady evolution of Royal Enfield designs over long periods.

With Pardoe's arrival, Royal Enfield began to develop its own engines, which, by the late 1920s, powered the whole range. Although its designs were generally conservative, Royal Enfield was not afraid to experiment. In the 1930s it tried four-valve and three-valve cylinder heads, while the 150cc two-stroke 'Cycar' of 1932 featured a pressed steel frame that doubled as the enclosing bodywork. It also offered a 150cc ohv ultra-lightweight to take advantage of 1933 tax concessions. The main-

stay of the range, however, were the sporting ohv Bullets of 250cc, 350cc and 500cc.

Royal Enfield also produced a luxurious 1140cc side-valve V-twin model, in theory for export only until 1938, but in fact available to special order. Export also provided the company with yet another model. Just before WW2, Royal Enfield had made a 125cc copy of a DKW two-stroke, specifically for export to Holland. During the war this was supplied to the British Army as the 'Flying Flea', and it remained in the post-war range, uprated later to 150cc, until the early 1950s.

Post war, Royal Enfield was quick to specify telescopic forks, and in 1949 swinging arm rear suspension. There were new 250cc and 350cc Bullets, and in 1949, a brand new 500cc vertical twin. Later, in 1953, this was to be joined by the 700cc Meteor twin (later developed into the Constellation. In the same decade, Johnny Brittain re-established the Royal Enfield name on the trials scene, winning many major events and proving the value of rear suspension. A major innovation was the 1957 unit construction 250cc Crusader that was to become hugely popular later as the sporting Continental GT. Royal Enfield also investigated streamlining and offered fully aerodynamic Airflow fairings.

When Frank Smith died in 1963, the company was sold to the E. & H. P. Smith engineering group. An unfortunate excursion into racing with a 250cc two-stroke was a failure, but happier memories are of the 250cc Villiers-engined Turbo Twin made from 1964. A rapid decline in British sales after 1965 led to the drastic pruning of the range, the last new model being the 736cc Interceptor twin with production of the once popular 250cc models ceasing in 1967. Thereafter, only the Interceptor twin was made, almost entirely for export to the USA. The original Redditch factory was sold, the twins being made by new owner NVT at Bradford-on-Avon. An involvement with Floyd Clymer's Indian company and with the Rickman brothers was no more than a sideshow.

348cc Royal Enfield Bullet (ohv single) 1959

692cc Royal Enfield Super Meteor (ohv twin) 1959

223cc Royal Enfield (two-stroke) 1923

346cc Royal Enfield 352 (ohv) 1926

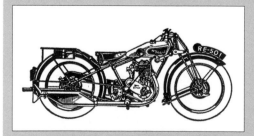

496cc Royal Enfield 501 (sv) 1929

496cc Royal Enfield GL31 (ohv) 1931

692cc Royal Enfield Airflow Meteor (ohv twin) 1960

ROVLANTE • France 1929–1935

Built 98cc and 124cc two-stroke machines.

ROYAL • America 1901–c1908

Typical American design with the 445cc cylinder sloping rearward and the petrol tank above the rear wheel of a strengthened bicycle frame.

ROYAL • Switzerland 1900–1908

Was one of the first motorcycle producers in the country. The 1.5hp and 2hp engines were of Zedel manufacture.

ROYAL • Italy 1923–1928

Built by the Santogastino brothers at Milan, the little machine had Royal's own 132cc two-stroke engine. In addition, it built a limited number of JAP-engined 346cc and 490cc sv and ohv machines.

ROYAL-AJAX • England 1901–c1908

Single-cylinder machines with 2.5hp—probably MMC—engines.

ROYAL-EAGLE • England 1901–1939

This name on the tank of Coventry-Eagle machines was available until 1910.

ROYAL ENFIELD • India 1996

Enfield India has been producing English Royal Enfield designs since 1956, but it was only in 1996 that it changed its name to Royal Enfield, long after the original Redditch factory had closed. See Enfield India entry.

ROYAL ENFIELD • England 1901–1970

See panel

ROYAL-MOTO • France 1923–1933

Built a wide range of lightweight machines with 98cc, 174cc and 244cc Massardin two-strokes and also four-strokes with 246cc to 498cc sv and ohv engines.

ROYAL NORD • Belgium 1950–early 1960s

Produced 48cc mofas, mopeds etc. and also motorcycles up to 248cc with Villiers, Maico, Sachs and other engines.

ROYAL-RUBY • England 1909–1933

Excellent machines which even before WW1 already had fully enclosed rear drive chains. Most models had the company's own sv engines, including 349cc and 375cc single-cylinder versions. The JAP-engined 976cc V-twin had leaf springs on both sides. Double-loop frames and saddle tanks were introduced in 1927, when the factory fitted 172cc to 346cc Villiers engines and 248cc and 348cc JAP ohv engines. The factory also built three-wheelers with motorcycle engines.

ROYAL RYDAL • England 1902-1904

Pedal start Minerva-engined 2hp motorcycles built by Coventry-based cycle manufacturer.

ROYAL SCOT • Scotland 1922–1924

The badge was probably the only genuine connection with the Glasgow Royal Scot works. The frame was built at the Glasgow Victoria motorcycle works for Royal Scot and the 348cc sleeve-valve engine was made in the nearby Barr & Stroud factory; most other parts and accessories were bought in England from specialised factories.

ROYAL SOVEREIGN • England c1902

Unorthodox machines with 211cc Minerva engines.

2¹/₂hp Royal Sovereign (sv) 1903

ROYAL STANDARD • Switzerland 1928–1932

Pauchand's design was a vertical 398cc twin-cylinder unit-design machine, with a Zurcher engine built exclusively for this make. The design was ahead of its time.

398cc Royal Standard (ohc twin) 1932

RUDGE • England 1911–1940

Though famous for its bicycles, Rudge resisted making motorcycles until its single-cylinder 500cc ioe engine and direct belt drive model of 1911. That year, Rudge rider Victor Surridge broke records at Brooklands, including 'the hour' at over 65mph. The company entered the 1911 TT in force, but, after Surridge was killed in practice, the team withdrew. It returned in 1913, when Ray Abbot finished second, while in 1914, Cyril Pullin won the only two-day Senior TT ever staged. By then, Rudge had proven its expanding-pulley belt-drive Multi gear and was making a 750cc multi-gear single for sidecar use.

Post war, the 500cc Multi was very popular, until belt drive began to lose favor. A 1000cc V-twin was generally unsatisfactory, but served to introduce chain drive and Rudge's own four-speed gearbox. For 1924, there were new four-valve ohv 350cc and 500cc singles with four speeds and chain drive. Such was the demand that only the 500cc model could be made. A tentative return to the Senior TT in 1926 revealed cycle part shortcomings, especially with the rim brakes, and for 1927 there was another design.

A vigorous racing program ensued, strongly supported by managing director J. V. Pugh with George Hack as designer and development engineer. This produced excellent results. In 1928 and 1929 rider Graham Walker won the Ulster Grand Prix, gaining Rudge a reputation that lasted until the end. Along with Walker, Ernie Nott and Tyrell Smith also won many other races in those years, 1930 being Rudge's greatest year, when Walter Handley won the Senior TT and with Walker second. In addition, with brand new Junior machines featuring four radially arranged valves, Rudge took the top three places in this class.

Thereafter things went wrong. Rudge was hit far harder than most of its competitors by the depression of the early 1930s—not helped by some catastrophic business decisions by J. V. Pugh. A 1–2–4 finish in the 1931 Lightweight TT was not enough. Rudge did its best to retrieve the situation, offering 250cc, 350cc and 500cc engines to other makers as 'Pythons', which sold well, but by 1933 it was in receivership and J. V. Pugh had left the company.

Production continued, however; Rudges even finished 1–2–3 in the 1934 Lightweight TT. In 1936 the company was sold to the electrical and electronics company EMI, and although sales were small, development of road bikes continued. A two-valve 250cc proved briefly popular. In 1938 EMI moved the factory from Coventy to Hayes in Middlesex and in 1939 a Villiers-engined autocycle joined the range. However, with the outbreak of war, although a 250cc machine was scheduled for acceptance by the British Army, production ceased after only 200 had been made. The Hayes factory was now devoted to making vitally needed radar equipment. The Autocycle was sold to Norman cycles, and the Rudge name acquired by Raleigh.

Post war, Rudge spares were privately manufactured from original jigs and patterns, and an attempt was made to revive the marque, using AMC cycle parts. There was even a 1000cc V-twin prototype. But effectively Rudge had disappeared for ever.

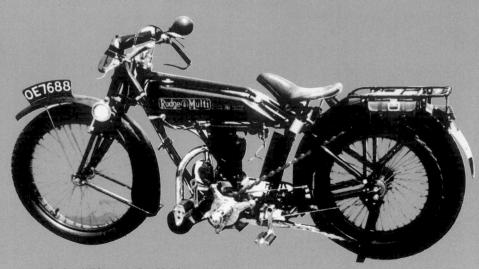

499cc Rudge-Whitworth (ioe Multi-gear) 1914

499cc Rudge-Whitworth Standard (ohv four-valve) 1926

499cc Rudge-Whitworth Sport (ohv four-valve) 1926

Rudge

499cc Rudge-Whitworth Ulster (ohv) 1929

499cc Rudge-Whitworth Special (ohv four-valve) 1931

499cc Rudge-Whitworth Ulster (ohv four-valve) 1935

499cc Rudge-Whitworth Ulster (ohv four-valve) 1938

499cc Rudge-Whitworth Ulster (ohv) 1929

ROYAL SUPER • Italy 1923–1928

Identical with the 132cc Royal two-stroke models.

ROYAL WELLINGTON • England c1901

Strengthened bicycle frames with 211cc Minerva engines.

R&P • England 1902–c1906

Was among the first commercially-built motorcycles in England. Most machines had 346cc single-cylinder engines with its own engine fitted in what is now the standard center position, developed by the Werner brothers in France.

RS • Germany 1924–1925

Unusual two-stroke, whose 380cc vertical-twin unit-design engine had a crankpin rotary valve. The design was probably not fully developed when it was sold to another firm, and never appeared on the market.

RS • Germany 1925–1928

This was the successor to the above RS, but with an orthodox engine, the old 493cc BMW flat-twin. Still a mystery, because BMW stopped producing that engine in 1922. Such engines were probably still in stock with some dealers.

RSI SULKY • France 1951-1955

Small producer of 65cc, 98cc and 125cc scooters.

RUBINELLI • Italy 1921–1927

Built 122cc and 172cc two-strokes and also supplied these engines to other small motorcycle assemblers.

RUCHE • France 1952–1954

A short-lived producer of 123cc and 173cc two-stroke machines.

RUD • Germany 1927–1930

Assembled motorcycles in small numbers with Kühne, MAG and JAP engines from 348cc to 748cc.

RUDGE • England 1911–1940

See panel

RUEDER • Germany late 1910s to early 1920s

Assembler which used 348cc Kühne ohv engines in orthodox frames.

RULLIER • France 1953

Limited production of scooters powered by 70cc Lavalette engines.

RULLIERS • Czechoslovakia 1924–1929

Two-stroke motorcycles with 147cc, 172cc and 346cc Villiers engines.

RUMI • Italy 1949–

Designed by Dr. Rumi at Bergamo, these were excellent 124cc twin-cylinder two-stroke machines with forward-facing horizontal cylinders and sporting appearance. The cylinders each had 42mm bore and 45mm stroke. The production sport model had a top speed of 80 mph,

racing versions were even faster. Rumi also built scooters and introduced a range of very unorthodox V-twin ohc machines of 98cc, 124cc and 174cc, which never went into quantity production. There was in the mid-1950s also a Salmaggi-designed 248cc twin-cylinder dohc racing machine, which was never fully developed and never ran in a big race. Rumi's heyday was around 1952 with the small Bees.

The Rumi family remained involved in racing with two Rumi cousins setting up race teams, one of which ran Honda's World Superbike team for several years. A limited run of single-cylinder sports bikes called the RMS650 was built, using a Honda Dominator engine in a twin spar, aluminum frame with high quality suspension components.

RUNGE • Germany 1923–1926

A small company which built 197cc sv machines on a limited scale.

RUPP • Germany 1928–1932

Produced two models. One was a 198cc ohv machine with its own engine, the other with a 498cc ohc single-cylinder three-valve Küchen power plant.

RUSH • Belgium 1922–1934

Became well known when the manufacturer-rider Van Geert won the 250cc class at the 1924 Monza GP. His machine had a 248cc Blackburne ohv engine. He also built 348cc single-cylinder ohv models. He built his own engines after 1927, when the range included 397cc, 497cc and 597cc sv and ohv models.

RUSPA • Italy 1926–1929

Built 124cc two-strokes and 174cc two-stroke and ohv machines. A 347cc single with chain-driven ohc was built in very small numbers only.

RUSSELL • England 1913

Limited production of 172cc and 492cc ohv machines.

RUT • Germany 1923–1924

Two-strokes of simple design with 124cc and an outside flywheel.

RUTER • Spain 1957–1960

Assembled machines with 95cc and 124cc two-stroke engines, supplied to the factory by Hispano-Villiers.

RUWISCH • Germany 1948–1949

Mini-scooter with 38cc Victoria bicycle engines.

RWC • Austria 1949–late 1950s

Lightweight motorcycles made by a bicycle factory. The engine was a 98cc Rotax-Sachs.

RW SCOUT • England 1920–1922

Made by R. Wheaterell of London, was an assembled machine with 269cc Villiers and 318cc Dalm two-stroke engines, but Blackburne 346cc sv and ohv engines could also be fitted.

123cc Rumi (two-stroke flat twin) 1952

173cc Rumi (ohv v-twin) 1960

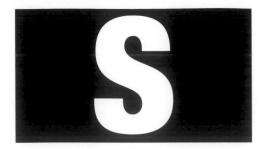

SACI • Brazil 1959–late 1960s

Scooter made with 174cc two-stroke engines.

SADEM • France 1951–1954

Lightweight machines with engines up to 98cc.

SADRIAN • Spain 1956–1963

Producer of three-wheelers, which also built Hispano-Villiers-engined 123cc to 198cc two-stroke motorcycles.

SAGITTA • Czechoslovakia 1928–1930

Limited assembly of machines with 247cc Villiers engines.

SALIRA • Belgium 1955–early 1960s

Assembler which used 98cc to 197cc Villiers engines, among others.

SALSBURY • America 1935–1949

Innovative scooter manufacturer which used Evinrude, Johnson and Lauson engines. Credited with development of the first 'variomatic' stepless variable ratio transmission, as used almost universally on modern scooters.

SALTLEY • England 1919–1924

An assembler whose machines had 269cc Villiers, 347cc Vulcanus and 497cc sv Blackburne engines.

SALVE • Italy 1925–1926

The only model had a 496cc unit-design sv engine.

SANCHOC • France 1922–1924

Built two-strokes of 98cc to 246cc and sv machines up to 346cc.

SAN CHRISTOPHORO • Italy 1951–1954

One of the small Italian producers of 124cc two-stroke machines. The Simonetta had 54mm bore/stroke and produced 6bhp at 4800rpm.

SANGLAS • Spain 1942–1982

Exclusively a maker of single-cylinder four-strokes, widely used by the Spanish police and army. Sanglas began with a 350cc model of extremely advanced design with telescopic forks, unit engine and four-speed gearbox. A 500cc model for police use appeared in 1956. Later 500cc and 400cc models had electric starting. Sanglas was taken over by Yamaha in 1978, and a model fitted with the XS400 twin engine was launched. By 1982, however, even the name Sanglas had disappeared.

SANKO-KOGYO • Japan 1954

Produced the Jet scooter with a choice of 172cc or 250cc engines.

SAN-SOU-PAP • France 1923–1936

The name stands for 'without any valves', but this was correct only until the factory built Train-engined 98cc to 248cc two-strokes and commenced manufacture of 248cc to 498cc sv and ohv singles with JAP and MAG power-units. San-Sou-Pap became part of the Rovin works in 1929.

SANTAMARIA • Italy 1951–1963

Mofas, mopeds, etc. with 49cc, 69cc, 98cccc, 123 and 147cc Zündapp, Sachs and Ilo engines.

SAN YANG • Taiwan 1962–

Assembled and built partly under license various Honda models in Taiwan. Since 1995 has marketed its scooters and motorcycles in some foreign markets under the name SYM.

SANYO • Japan 1958–1962

Sporting machines, singles with Sanyo's own 248cc ohv engines.

SAR • Italy 1920–1925

Based on the design of the Elect, the 498cc SAR was a sv then ohv flat twin machine. Another model had the oil-cooled 346cc Bradshaw ohv engine, which had 68mm bore and 96mm stroke with automatic lubrication.

SAR • Germany 1923–1930

The Raetsch-designed SAR engines were three-port two-strokes of 122cc, 147cc and 198cc.

348cc SAR (ohv Bradshaw) 1924

SARACEN • England 1967–1973

Concentrated on the manufacture of Sachs-engined 123cc, 188cc and trials machines, and on 244cc Mickmar-engined motocross machines.

SARCO (SARCO-RELIANCE) • England 1920–1923

Concentrated on a 261cc two-stroke single with 68mm bore x 72mm stroke and a Burman two-speed gearbox.

SARENKA • Poland 1961–

A 123cc two-stroke, built by the well-known Polish WSK factory.

SARKANA-SWAIGSNE • Latvia 1958–

Supplies 49cc mofas, mopeds and similar means of transport.

SAROLEA • Belgium 1898–1957

Was among the first producers of motorcycles and of proprietary single-cylinder and V-twin engines. Became famous during the 1920s with with English-looking 346cc and 496cc sv and ohv singles. It built in the 1930s 124cc, 147cc and 174cc two-strokes and 596cc ohv models. The works rider 'Grizzly' Gilbert de Ridder rode after 1935 348cc and 498cc machines with its own ohc racing engines. Other well known Sarolea riders were Gregoire, Claessens, Tom, Vidal, Stobart, Poncin of Luxembourg, Stépan of Czechoslovakia, Dirtl, Gayer, Runtsch, Benesch and Trella of Austria, Arcangeli and Colombo of Italy and others. After the war, there was a production co-operative created with other Belgian factories, and Sarolea's production concentrated on two-strokes of 49cc to 248cc. During the 1950s the Sarolea brand name was also used to re-badge Italian Moto Rumi scooters for the Belgian market.

496cc Sarolea (ohv) 1927

496cc Sarolea (ohv racing model) 1930

347cc Sarolea (ohv sport model) 1931

596cc Sarolea (ohv) 1932

SARTORIUS • Germany 1924–1926

Limited production of 195cc sv and 348cc Kühne ohv engined singles.

SATAN • Czechoslovakia 1929

This was a machine with Satan's own sloping 548cc sv engine. Small production.

SATURN • Germany 1921–1927

Made by the Steudel car and boat engine works, Saturn motorcycles had 246cc two-stroke, 348cc ohv and 497cc V-twin sv engines. There was also a 149cc bicycle sv engine and a prototype of a shaft-driven version of the 497cc V-twin, built at a Steudel branch factory at Leipzig.

SATURN • England 1925–1926

Produced a small number of 346cc singles with own two-stroke engines.

SAUND • India 1970–

Originally a 98cc two-stroke DKW (Zweirad Union) design, the Saund—built with many parts made in India—is still influenced by the German design. The 98cc engine produces 9.7bhp at 6800rpm.

SBD • German 1923–1924

Munich-built motorcycles with the 293cc Bosch-Douglas flat twin sv engine.

SCARAB • Italy 1967–1985

Scarabs, in effect, were Ancilotti motorcycles under a different name. Like Ancilotti, they were fitted with various makes of small capacity two-stroke German and Italian engines. The range was mostly 50cc and 125cc and styled in off-road fashion. The marque did not survive Ancilotti's demise.

SCARABEO • Italy 1968–1980

A division of Aprilla, concentrating on smaller motorcycles and mopeds with mostly 50cc and 125cc Sachs or Hiro two-stroke engines. Off-road styling as trials and motocross machinery. Now used only as a name on Aprilia scooters.

SCHEIBERT • Austria 1911–1913

Motorcycles with strengthened frames and a 197cc sv engine mounted above the front wheel.

SCHICKEL • America 1912–1915

Interesting design with a cast aluminum alloy frame which incorporated the petrol tank. Its engine was a 648cc two-stroke single.

SHIFTY • Italy 1979–

Big assembled machines with 903cc and 1049cc four-cylinder ohc and dohc engines, supplied partially by Abarth.

SCHLIHA • Germany 1924–1933

Was one of the many unorthodox two-stroke designs built during the 1920s and early 1930s in Berlin. Designed by Heinrich Schlèpmann, Schliha motorcycles were ohv singles of 129cc to 596cc.

198cc Schliha (two-stroke with ohv) 1930

SCHLIMME • Germany 1924–1925

Assembled machines with 142cc and 173cc DKW two-stroke engines.

SCHMIDT • Germany 1921–1924

Produced bicycle engines and 196cc lightweight motorcycles. The sv engines were of Schmidt's own design and manufacture.

SCHNEIDER • Germany 1924–1926

Another assembler, which fitted 142cc, 173cc and 206cc DKW engines.

SCHNELL-HOREX • Germany 1952–1954

Designed by racing motorcyclist Roland Schnell, who built these racing machines with 248cc, 348cc and 498cc single-cylinder gear-driven ohc engines in conjunction with the Horex works, the Schnell-Horex was made in limited numbers only but proved especially formidable in the 350cc size. Among the riders besides Schnell were Hermann Gablenz, H. P. Müller, Robert Zeller, Georg Braun, Erwin Aldinger, Fritz Klüger and others.

SCHROFF-RECORD • Germany 1923–1925

Simple 148cc three-port two-strokes with sloping engines.

SCHUNK • Germany 1924–1926

Little 198cc ohv machines with own unit-design engines and belt drive.

SCHÜRHOFF • Germany 1949–1953

Producer of mofas, mopeds etc. with 49cc Sachs, Ilo and Zündapp engines and of lightweights with bolt-together triangular frames and 123cc to 173cc Ilo two-stroke engines.

124cc Schürhoff (two-stroke Ilo) 1953

SCHÜTT • Germany 1933–1934

Equipped with frames made from duralumin, the Paul Schütt-designed 196cc two-strokes had a transverse-mounted engine of his design.

SCHÜTTOFF • Germany 1924–1933

Made by a machine factory, Schüttoff motorcycles had 246cc sv, afterwards 346cc sv and ohv as well as 496cc sv and ohv single-cylinder engines. From 1930 onwards, it also fitted 198cc and 298cc DKW two-stroke power units. In 1932 Schüttoff became part of the DKW works. The 348cc ohv models were very successful from 1925 to 1929. With a works team consisting of the riders Ihle, Lohse, A. Müller, E. Hirth etc. it won many races, while

SCOTT • England 1909–late 1960s

Few designs have inspired such devotion from admirers as the Scott. Yorkshire engineer Alfred Scott developed a twin-cylinder two-stroke engine small and powerful enough to use in a motorcycle, and built six prototypes in 1908. Production began the next year. Early Scotts had air-cooled cylinders and water-cooled heads, but the water-cooling was soon extended to the cylinders. There was a triangulated frame with straight tubes, telescopic front forks, a two-speed gearbox which selected one or other of two different ratio primary chain drives, and a kickstarter – the world's first. Chain final drive was used from the beginning. Petrol was carried in an oval drum beneath the saddle. Scotts did well in trials and racing, including four fastest laps in the Senior TT between 1911 and 1914 and wins in 1912 and 1913.

Alfred Scott left the company late in 1918 to devote his time to an unorthodox three-wheeler, the Scott Sociable, and the designer throughout the 1920s was Harry Shackleton. The Scott gained more powerful engines of 498cc and 596cc, a more orthodox fuel tank and a three-speed gearbox. But sales, hitherto respectable, plunged disastrously in the depressed early 1930s. Most machines built after that were made from components held in stock, the company becoming involved in more general engineering. However, in the mid 1930s, new designer Bill Cull became involved in developing a three-cylinder in—line two-stroke, first of 750cc then of 1000cc, of which six were made.

Post war, production resumed with what was virtually a pre-war model, but with new brakes and Dowty air-sprung telescopic forks. In 1950, the company was sold to Matt Holder, who moved it from Shipley to Birmingham. He modernised the Scott's appearance with a new spring frame, a shapely petrol tank and a dual seat, but the 1930s-style engine and three-speed gearbox were retained. However, though a small, steady demand existed, production came to an end when Birmingham city development forced Holder to move his engineering business in the late 1960s. He also developed a 350cc air-cooled two-stroke twin, which was raced but never went into production.

498cc Scott (two-stroke water-cooled twin) 1925

595cc Scott Flying Squirrel (two-stroke water-cooled twin) 1926

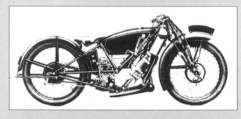

498cc Scott TT (two-stroke water-cooled twin) 1929

498cc Scott TT prototype (two-stroke water-cooled twin) 1930

996cc Scott (two-stroke water-cooled three-cylinder) 1935

486cc Scott (two-stroke water-cooled twin) 1914

596cc Scott (two-stroke water-cooled twin) 1948

347cc Schüttoff Sport (ohv) 1927

Josef Mittenzwei gained success in trials with a 498cc sidecar outfit.

SCHWALBE • Germany 1922–1924

Lightweight motorcycles with 124cc and 198cc flat twin engines. The smaller version was also available as a bicycle attachment engine. Producers of these machines, the Spiegler brothers, afterwards built Spiegler motorcycles at their Aalen factory.

SCHWALBE • Switzerland 1901–1905

The Rugg-designed Schwalbe had a strengthened bicycle frame and a 2.75hp Zedel engine.

SCHWEPPE • Germany 1949–1950

A scooter with swinging arms at both ends and 143cc to 184cc Ilo engines, which eventually became the Pirol scooter.

SCK • Germany 1924–1925

Assembler which fitted 348cc and 498cc sv and ohv JAP and MAG engines into own frames. Production was on a small scale.

SCOOTAVIA • France 1951–1956

Luxurious scooters with 173cc ohv AMC single-cylinder engines.

SCOOTERMOBILE • England 1954–1957

Unsuccessful English scooter built by Harper of Exeter.

SCOOTMULE • France 1962

Odd mini-bike powered by a 50cc Mosquito engine.

SCORPION • England mid 1960s

Motorcycles with pressed steel frames and 197cc and 246cc Villiers two-stroke engines.

SCOTO • France 1949–early 1950s

Miniscooter with 39cc Mosquito engine.

SCOTT • England 1909–late 1960s

See panel

SCOTT-CYC-AUTO • England 1934–1950

Early and typical English moped with Scott-built 98cc two-stroke engine.

SCOUT • England 1912–1913

Produced motorcycles with 498cc Precision single-cylinder sv engines.

SCYLLA • France 1931–1937

Lightweight machines with 98cc and 123cc Aubier-Dunne two-stroke engines.

SEAL • England 1914–1921

Very unorthodox motorcycle with a 996cc V-twin JAP sv engine, without handlebar and without saddle. It had a steering wheel in the attached sidecar.

SEARS • America 1912–1916

Made for Sears, Roebuck & Co. at Chicago, these machines had 9hp to 10hp V twin engines produced by Spake. See also Allstate.

SEEGARD • Germany 1924–1925

Built singles with its own sv 146cc and 197cc engines.

SEELEY • England 1966–1992

Colin Seeley took over production of the AJS 7R and Matchless G50 racing engines from AMC and built successful racing motorcycles with his own frames and fittings. Production ceased when they became uncompetitive, but later was resumed by Mick Rutter for

Classic racing. Rutter's products were marketed as replicas, though very close in specification to the originals. Seeley also produced very many other frames for all types of racing motorcycles during the early 1970s, so many in fact that he is credited with almost single-handedly 'saving' British motorcycle racing in this period.

SEGALE • Italy 1977–

Luigi Segale has been producing specialist frames for a variety of engines for many years, ranging from the first Kawasaki Z900/1000 fours to the Honda Fireblade.

SEILING • Italy 1938–1939

After MAS motorcycle manufacturer Alberico Seilig left that make, he produced 247cc and 347cc sv singles with his own unit-design engines and rear suspension.

346cc Seiling (sv) 1938

SEITH • Germany 1949–1950

Mini-vehicles for children with 38cc Victoria two-stroke engines.

SENIOR • Italy 1913–1914

Sporting machines with 296cc and 330cc single-cylinder and 499cc V-twin engines supplied by Moser of Switzerland.

SERTUM • Italy 1931–1951

Precision instruments were the first products made by Fausto Alberti's Milan factory. The first motorcycle was

49cc Siamoto S-Cross (two-stroke single) 1998

a 174cc sv machine, which was followed by a 120cc two-stroke. Other models were 174cc ioe and ohv and 246cc sv and ohv versions. A 498cc unit-design sv vertical-twin with a four-speed gearbox was built in the mid 1930s. There were also 248cc ohv machines and the 174cc models were replaced by 198cc machines. 120cc, 248cc and 498cc models were also built after the war, when the 498cc vertical twin was dropped and a 498cc sv single took its place. Until 1950, when a new 125cc two-stroke single appeared on the market, all Sertum machines were of strong and heavy design. It competed in many trials with such riders as Grieco, Fornasari, Ventura and several others, but never in bigger races. In 1949-1950 the factory moved to new, modern and much bigger buildings, but two years later Sertum—despite a first class reputation for quality and finish—had to close down.

496cc Sertum (sv twin) 1938

SERVETTA • Spain 1973–1989

Originally a producer of 50cc lightweights, it went on to make and export Lambretta scooters under license.

SERVICE • England c1900–1912

A sales organisation which sold under its own name motorcycles built by Connaught and Wartnaby & Draper.

SERVOS • Germany circa 1953

Lightweight scooter with 40cc Victoria engine driving the front wheel.

SESSA • Italy 1950–1956

Small assembler of motorcycles with 147cc Ilo engines.

SETTER • Spain 1954–1956

Lightweight machines with its own 60cc engines.

SEWUT • Germany 1924–1926

DWK-engined 142cc, 173cc and 206cc two-strokes, built in limited numbers.

SFM • Poland 1956–1964

While most motorcycles built in eastern countries are two-strokes, the machine built by SFM at Szeczin was a contemporary ohv design with 248cc and 348cc single-cylinder engines. It was called Junak.

S-FORTIS • Czechoslovakia 1929–1931

Produced a single model only, a 598cc ohv single with an engine supplied by Sarolea. Few were made.

SFW • Germany 1924–1926

After Nordstern went bankrupt, SFW took over the manufacture of its 2.5hp two-stroke machine.

S&G • Germany 1926–1932

A Nuremberg machine factory which produced 346cc ohv single-cylinder engines for the Hecker factory. These had much in common with similar AJS motors of that period. When S&G (Scharrer & Gross) built complete motorcycles, the range consisted of 346cc, 496cc and 596cc sv and 496cc ohv single-cylinder models. The factory also built three-wheeled delivery vehicles with motorcycle engines. The last motorcycles made had 172cc and 198cc two-stroke engines.

SGS • England 1927–1931

The name stood for Syd Gleave Special, after the well-known racing motorcyclist who won the 1933 Lightweight TT on a four-valve 248cc ohv Excelsior Mechanical Marvel. His motorcycles had Villiers engines from 147cc and JAP ohv motors from 248cc to 490cc.

496cc S&G (sv) 1930

SH • Germany 1925–1928

Identical to RS motorcycles.

SHACKLOCK • England 1915

Limited production of friction-drive transverse V-twin machines made by S. & C. Shacklock, Wolverhampton.

SHANKS • Arbroath 1923-1925

Lightweights built by the lawn mower manufacturer Shanks & Sons, using 269cc Villiers two-stroke or 346cc Barr & Stroud sleeve valve engines.

SHARRATT • England 1920–1930

Assembler of good machines with JAP engines from 293cc up to 996cc V-twins. After 1924 reduced production levels. Also fitted Villiers and MAG engines, but the last Sharratt motorcycles had 346cc sv and ohv JAP engines.

SHAW • America 1909–1923

Produced two single-cylinder 2.5hp and 3.5hp models, which had clutchless sv engines of its own manufacture.

SHAW • England 1904–1922

Early machines had Kelecom and Minerva engines. After a long interruption, this company supplied American 115cc

498cc Sieg (ohv V-twin MAG engine) 1928

bicycle attachment engines made by Shaw Mfg. Co. at Galesburg, Kansas.

SHEFFIELD-HENDERSON • England 1919–1923

A sidecar factory which produced 348cc ohv and 498cc sv machines with single-cylinder Blackburne engines.

346cc Sheffield-Henderson racer (ohv Blackburne) 1922

SHIN MEIWA • Japan early 1950s to early 1960s

Scooter-like machines with pressed steel frames and flat 89cc, 123cc and 153cc two-stroke engines.

SHL • Poland 1935–

Probably the oldest Polish motorcycle factory. Produced in the 1930s Villiers-engined 123cc machines and after 1945 a range of 123cc, 147cc and 174cc two-stroke machines.

SHOWA • Japan early 1950s to 1960

Manufacturer of 49cc mopeds and of motorcycles from 123cc to 247cc with its own two-stroke engines. In addition there was also a 173cc ohv machine. Now a highly respected manufacturer of motorcycle suspension, used by many modern manufacturers.

SIAMOTO • Italy 1995-

Originally a scooter importer, the company began manufacture in 1995, first with the knobbly-tyred S-Cross, powered by a 50cc Franco Morini engine. The retro-styled Capri of 1999 uses either a 125cc or 180cc two-stroke engine, produced by Siamoto.

SIAMT • Italy 1907–1914

Designed by Luigi Semeria, the Siamt was an excellent machine and very successful in races. The range included 260cc, 262cc and 344cc singles and 494cc, 688cc and 731cc V-twins.

SIAT • Italy 1924–1926

Once a popular bicycle engine with 75cc capacity. The Turin-built Siat was a lightweight with two-stroke and ohv engines from 98cc to 198cc.

SIC • France 1921–1925

Assembler which fitted 98cc to 346cc proprietary engines made by Aubier-Dunne, Zurcher and Train.

SICRAF • France 1947–1953

Paul Vallée not only produced motorcycles, mofas, scooters, three-wheelers etc. with 49cc to 246cc Ydral and AMC engines, but was also the owner of some F1 racing cars.

SIEG • Germany 1922–1930

Designed by H. Jüngst, the Sieg was supplied with a wide range of engines from 110cc to 598cc. These engines were made by DKW, Cockerell, Ilo, Bober, Alba, Hansa, Villiers, JAP, MAG and especially Blackburne.

SIEGFRIED • Germany 1925

Lightweights with 142cc DKW engines.

SIGNORELLI • Italy 1928–1930

One of the many Italian producers of 173cc two-strokes in the late 1920s.

SILK • England 1974–early 1980s

George Silk fitted a modified vintage Scott engine and Velocette four-speed gearbox into a special frame. There was a commercial demand for replicas, but difficulty in obtaining engines led to the design and manufacture of a special 700cc unit of Silk's own. About 150 such machines were made.

SILVA • England 1919–1920

One of the first scooters built in England. The ohv engine was 117cc.

SILVER PIDGEON • Japan early 1950s to 1965

Made by the Mitsubishi group, the Silver Pidgeon was a mass-produced scooter with 87cc two-stroke and 192cc ohv engines.

SILVER PRINCE • England 1919–1924

Was one of the many small motorcycle assemblers of the early 1920s. Engines used were the 148cc, 248cc and 269cc Villiers and the 346cc Blackburne.

SILVER STAR • Japan 1953–1958

Lightweights with own 123cc and 147cc ohv engines.

SIM • Italy 1953–1955

Produced unconventional Moretti scooters with 123cc and 147cc Puch engines. Also 147cc two-stroke machines with shaft drive to the rear wheel.

SIMARD • France 1951–1954

Lambretta-like scooters with 174cc Ydral engines.

SIMONCELLI • Italy 1927–1935

Concentrated on the production of 174cc machines, first with Train two-stroke and then with sv and ohv JAP engines. In 1934 the Simoncelli company had already introduced a good rear suspension.

SIMONETTA • Italy 1951–1954

This was a 124cc two-stroke machine, built at the San Christoforo works.

SIMONINI • Italy 1970–1983

Enzo Simonini produced excellent off-road machines with Sachs engines before selling out to Fornetti Impianti of Maranello in 1975. A superb 125cc roadster appeared in 1979 with full fairing, cast wheels, Brembo disc brakes and a 90mph top speed. Unfortunately, Fornetti Impianti in turn sold the company and its fortunes declined sharply under the new management, ending in failure.

SIMPLEX • The Netherlands 1902–1968

Was for many years the leading motorcycle factory. Fitted Minerva, Fafnir and MAG engines from 2hp to 6hp; from the mid-1920s also 346cc ohv Blackburne, 498cc sv Blackburne and 348cc ohv Bradshaw engines with oil-cooling into strong frames. Other engines fitted were the 98cc and 148cc Villiers and the 98cc Sachs; during the late 1930s also the 60cc Sachs and the 124cc Villiers. In the years after the war, there was a close connection with Juncker and Gazelle. Leading-link forks and duplex frames were used in 1911, 9hp V-twins with ioe Motosacoche engines were built in 1921, triangular frames were used in the mid-1920s and a 246cc single built in 1935 which had a water-cooled Villiers two-stroke power unit.

SIMPLEX • England 1919–1922

Producer of 105cc 1hp two-stroke bicycle attachment engines.

SIMPLEX • Italy 1921–1950

Luigi Pellini built beautiful little 124cc auxiliary engines and from 1927 onwards 149cc ohv machines with its own unit-design engines, followed by 174cc models. Improved `Ala d'Oro' (Gold Wing) versions with engines which had

173cc Simplex (ohv) 1929 (Italy)

fully enclosed valves and other modern design features were built in 1930. The range included also a 210cc and from 1934 a 496cc ohv with four-speed gearboxes. After 1945 models of 148cc to 248cc based on pre-war designs were built in limited numbers.

SIMPLEX SERVI-CYCLE • America 1935-1960

Basic 125cc single-cylinder single-speed two-stroke machine with belt drive designed by Joseph P. Treen and built by the Simplex Manufacturing Co., New Orleans. 198cc Clinton Industrial four-stroke sv engine also used later. Built in quantity and was used by the military as a runabout 'on camp.' Became a great favorite of paper boys and girls.

198cc Simplex (two-stroke Clinton Industrial engine) 1966 (USA)

SIMSON • East Germany 1950–

Originally called AWO, this one-time car factory made 250cc ohv models with shaft drive until 1960, changing the name to Simson along the way. Thereafter, it concentrated on smaller 50cc x 75cc two-stroke roadsters and mopeds. Was particularly successful in the ISDT and similar events. As with MZ, with whom it has commercial ties, Simson made strenuous efforts to export, but ran into difficulties with German re-unification.

49cc Simson Enduro (two-stroke) 1982

SINGER • England 1900–1915

The first products were three-wheelers, followed by Perks & Birch-licenced motorwheels, which with its 208cc engines were fitted into bicycles. In later years a wide range of Singer motorcycles of sturdy conventional design appeared on the market. These included water-cooled sin-

gles and 346cc two-strokes, but the best sellers were sv models of 299cc, 499cc and 535cc. These had some monobloc engines and a variety of gearboxes. Everything was of Singer's own design and manufacture. Singer bought Premier of Coventry in the early 1920s, but was by then a car manufacturer only.

SIPHAX • France 1951–1956

Small factory which produced 98cc two-strokes with a horizontal cylinder. The engines were of AMC manufacture.

SIROCCO • Czechoslovakia 1925–1928

Designed by Gustav Heinz, the Sirocco was built on English lines and also had English Villiers engines of 147cc to 346cc.

SIRRAH • England 1922–1925

The Sirrah, designed by Harris, was available with a wide range of engines. These included the 211cc Wisemann and 292cc Union two-strokes and 248cc, 348cc and 490cc sv and ohv Blackburne and JAP engines. Wisemann at Birmingham—manufacturer of the Sirrah—produced also the Verus motorcycles. The Sirrah (Harris in reverse) was a cheaper version of the Verus. There was also a 996cc Sirrah model with the V-twin sv JAP engine.

SIS • Portugal 1950–

Bicycle producer J. Simones Costa became the Portuguese importer of Sachs two-stroke engines and founded his own motorcycle factory. His machines are fitted with 49cc and 98cc Sachs power units.

SISSY • Austria 1957–1960

Unorthodox miniscooter with 98cc and 123cc Rotax two-stroke engines. Produced by the old-established Lohner works.

SITTA • Germany 1950–1955

Scooters with 119cc and 123cc Ilo engines, 49cc mopeds and also Ilo-engined motorcycles from 123cc to 247cc.

173cc Sitta (two-stroke Ilo) 1953

SJK • Japan 1956–early 1960s

Built a variety of mopeds and motorcycles from 49cc to 249cc with its own two-stroke engines, but like several other manufacturers failed during the slump in the Japanese motorcycle industry.

SKF • Russia 1961–1965

Russian Jawa-like 348cc double-ohc racing twins, destined for official works riders only.

SKO • Czechoslovakia 1924–1926

Designed by Frantisek Skopec, the SKO had a 498cc single-cylinder two-stroke deflector-type three-port engine.

SKOOTAMOTA

See ABC Skootamota

SL • England 1924–1925

Produced in limited numbers a 345cc single-cylinder machine with two inlet valves and one exhaust valve.

SLADE-JAP • England 1920–1923

A machine with a 346cc sv JAP engine. Small production.

SLANEY • England 1921–1922

Only one model was made by H. H. Timbrell's factory. It had a 688cc flat twin Coventry-Victor sv engine.

SLAVIA • Czechoslovakia 1899–1908

The Slavia was built in the Austro-Hungarian Empire by the Czech Laurin & Klement factory. The name Slavia was also used by the Laurin & Klement machines built under license in Germany.

SLINGER • England 1900–1901

Extremely unorthodox motorcycle with three wheels in line. The two small front wheels, one of which was directly driven by chain from the water-cooled 3.5hp single-cylinder De Dion Bouton engine, had a common frame; the rear part was more or less an orthodox bicycle frame.

SM • Poland 1935

Had a 346cc single-cylinder ohv unit-design engine with shaft drive to the rear wheel. Was built in small numbers only.

SMART • Austria 1925–1932

Assembled motorcycles with sv and ohv JAP engines of 346cc, 498cc and 596cc.

SMART • France 1922–1927

Lightweight motorcycles with 198cc sv engines of own manufacture.

346cc Smart (sv JAP) 1928

SMC • America c1912–1915

An 80cc two-stroke lightweight built by the SM Company of New York.

SMITH • England c1900–1905

Built by Smith & Son, Camberley using Fafnir and other period proprietary engines installed in frames of its own design and manufacture.

SMS • England 1913–1914

Unorthodox 211cc two-stroke with a patented inlet port arrangement.

SMW • Germany 1923–1933

Built two types of motorcycles with flat twin engines. One had the 293cc Bosch Douglas, built under license, the other the 493cc BMW, as found in the Victoria and other makes. New models appeared in 1928, when chief designer Karl Rühmer designed 198cc two-strokes with Villiers engines and 198cc as well as 498cc singles with sv and ohv Blackburne and Sturmey-Archer engines.

S&N • Germany 1901–1908

Big machine factory which also built Erika typewriters. The motorcycles were called Germania, and for a short period Slavia. They were made under Laurin & Klement license, and were partly directly imported from the then famous L&K factory at Jungbunzlau.

SNOB • Germany 1921–1925

Was the leading four-stroke lightweight machine in Germany during the early 1920s. Production versions had 154cc ioe single-cylinder engines, while works racing models had ohv engines. Designed by Karl Düpfner.

SOCVEL • France 1951–1952

Limited production of lightweight Stefa scooter using 98cc Sachs and 125cc AMC engines.

SOCOVEL • Belgium 1947–1955

The first 123cc Socovel was a quite orthodox two-stroke lightweight. Less orthodox were the following Villiers-engined 123cc and 197cc machines with completely enclosed engines and pressed steel frames. They had a triangular shape, plunger-type rear suspension and teleforks. The next model was a 98cc Autocycle, followed by entirely new 246cc two-strokes with Jawa engines and Jawa-like frames. There was also a 346cc Jawa-engined twin. Other versions had Ilo, Sachs and also Coventry-Victor 296cc flat twin engines; the last ones with opposing cylinders and transverse-mounted.

SODORBLOM • Sweden c1902–1903

Belt-drive single-speed 'clip on' mounted on sturdy bicycles with direct belt drive to the back wheel. Built by lorry maker Sodorblom, Giuteri-Akteiebolag of Eskilstuna.

SOK • Sweden 1925–1928

Concentrated on a 346cc ohv machine with mainly JAP engines.

SOKOL • Poland 1936–1939

The Sokol was a 598cc sloper, not unlike earlier BSA models, with own sv engine. Production of this motorcycle was destined for the army.

SOLO • Germany 1949–188

Produced a variety of mofas and mopeds with its own 49cc two-stroke engines including water-cooled versions and an electric moped.

49cc Solo 40 (two-stroke single) 1982

498cc Spiegler (sv) 1928

244cc Sparta (two-stroke twin Ilo) 1954

SOMMAIRE • France c1906–1910

Single cylinder and V-twin motorcycles.

SOORAJ • India c1960–

Maker of a range of functional utility machines including a 325cc diesel model assembled with an Italian-made engine.

SOS • England 1927–1939

Villiers engines always played an important part in the production of these machines. A few 490cc JAP-engined machines were made in earlier years but most models had 147cc to 347cc Villiers two-strokes. Among the models was a 172cc road-racer and a 172cc speedway machine. Earlier versions had three-port, deflector piston-type motors, later ones the flat-top piston Villiers. There were also water-cooled 249cc versions and models with the 346cc Villiers Longstroke.

SOUPLEX • Belgium 1947–1953

Produced 123cc two-strokes with Villiers engines and afterwards 296cc sv twin-cylinder machines with transverse-mounted horizontal Coventry-Victor engines.

SOUTHEY • England 1905–1925

This was a small company which built its own motorcycles as well as frames for other motorcycle assemblers. The company's own machines had 246cc, 249cc and 346cc engines. The first ones were made by Villiers and the last one was a side valve Blackburne.

SOYER • France 1920–1935

The first models had 247cc engines, and a ladies' version had a frame without a top tube. Afterwards 98cc and 174cc two-strokes and sv as well as ohv models from 248cc to 498cc with Chaise, Sturmey-Archer and JAP engines were made. The two-stroke engines were of its own manufacture. A Soyer with C. J. Williams in the saddle won the 1930 French Grand Prix. The engine used was a 498cc Sturmey-Archer ohv single.

SPA-JAP • England 1921–1923

Small assembler, whose machines had 246cc and 293cc sv JAP engines.

SPAKE • America 1911–1914

Produced strong and heavy 550cc single-cylinder and 980cc V-twin models with own ioe engines. The engines were also sold to other manufacturers.

SPARK • England 1921–1923

Made by Sparkbrook, the Spark was a utility model with the 269cc Villiers engine.

SPARK • England 1903–1904

This much older Spark had a 2hp engine and a patented surface carburetor.

SPARKBROOK • England 1912–1925

A well-known manufacturer which fitted in the early years 746cc and 980cc V-twin JAP engines and after WW1 a 269cc two-stroke Villiers. There were also 247cc and 346cc models with the two-strokes from Wolverhampton as well as 346cc singles with the JAP sv engine, the sleeve-valve Barr & Stroud and the oil-cooled Bradshaw.

SPARTA • The Netherlands 1931–1972

Bicycle factory, which produced 49cc machines with attachment engines, and afterwards models with 98cc Sachs and Villiers engines. There were also 74cc Sachs-engined and eventually 198cc Villiers-engined motorcycles. During the late 1930s, 120cc and 123cc two-strokes with Ilo and Sachs engines were added. Improved versions with 123cc to 198cc Villiers engines came after 1945; a 246cc two-stroke with a Victoria double-port engine was added in 1951. The Dutch factory also built a machine with the 244cc Ilo vertical two-stroke twin, but concentrated since the early 1960s on 49cc mopeds.

SPARTAN • England 1920–1922

Small production of 349cc single-cylinder two-stroke motorcycles with Broler three-port deflector-type engines.

SPARTON • Wales 1976–1980s

A co-operation between Spondon Engineering and Barton Engineering to build racing two-strokes designed by Barry Hart. Success with a simple air-cooled three-cylinder 500cc model led Sparton to over-reach itself with the Phoenix, a vastly more complicated square four.

SPAVIERO • Italy 1955

A 100cc ohv twin model, the Sparrow, offered for only one season by the Chiorda factory. Very few were made.

SPECIAL-MONNERET • France 1952–1958

Georges Monneret, famous French racing motorcyclist, produced in Paris his own lightweight motorcycles of sporting appearance. The engines were 49cc VAP and Sachs.

SPEED • France 1951–1956

This was a scooter with 60cc, 115cc and 124cc engines, manufactured by a branch of the former Mors car works.

SPEED-KING-JAP • England 1913–1914

These motorcycles were made to a low price for a chain store. They were equipped with 293cc JAP sv engines.

SPEEDWELL • New Zealand 1914

5/6hp machine. Few details.

SPENCER • Australia c1909

All-Australian motorcycle with engines built by Spencer itself.

SPHINX • Belgium 1923–1926

Made from mainly English components, the Sphinx had 346cc and 490cc sv and ohv engines made by JAP in London.

SPIEGLER • Germany 1923–1932

This make was the successor to the Schwalbe machines, also built by the Spiegler works at Aalen. The unusual frames, made from pressed steel and tubes with the tank forming the backbone of the frame, housed 346cc, 498cc and 598cc single-cylinder sv and ohv engines, made by JAP, MAG and at the works. A 198cc JAP-engined ohv single was introduced in 1929.

498cc Spiegler (ohv) 1929

SPIESS • Germany 1903–1905

Assembler who bought his 2hp to 2.75hp engines from the Minerva, Zedel and Fafnir factories.

SPINDLER • Germany 1922–1925

Bekamo-engined 149cc two-strokes, built in limited numbers.

SPIRIC • England 1901–1904

Cycle making brothers Eddie and Walter Crips from Kent built a limited number of motorcycles fitting proprietary engines to heavy weight Spiric Cycle frames.

SPIRIDITIS • Latvia early 1950s–circa 1985

These machines, built by the Sarkana-Swaigsne motorcycle works, had 123cc and 246cc two-stroke engines. According to unconfirmed information, the Riga factory was producing 49cc machines, mainly mopeds, during the 1980s, but no longer appears to be in production.

SPONDON • England, 1969–

Specialist chassis builder founded by Bob Stevenson and Stuart Tiller. Originally produced frames for racing bikes, especially Yamaha two-strokes, then went on to make frames for road bikes, which used a wide variety of engines. Also designed and built the frames

for Norton's rotary engined racing bikes in the early 1990s.

SPRING • Belgium 1910–1940

The first model was a four-cylinder with a frame which was sprung both front and back. New models which appeared after 1920 had transverse-mounted V-twin engines with 496cc, 746cc and 996cc. The last one was equipped with a reverse gear.

SPRINGFIELD • The Netherlands 1921

A range of Villiers and JAP-powered machine which were built in Birmingham, England by Wolf to be imported and sold in the Netherlands as Springfields by the Siebol Brothers of Amsterdam.

SPRITE • England 1965–1971

Frank Hipkin made trials and motocross machines, latterly with his own copies of Husqvarna two-stroke engines. An over-ambitious American venture ended the company.

SQUALO • Australia 1997-

Ducati-powered sports bike with Squalo's own frame.

SSD • Japan 1930s

Built by the Shishido Bros in 350cc and 500cc sv form.

STABIL • Belgium 1931–1933

Limited production of 98cc and 123cc machines with Villiers engines.

STADION • Czechoslovakia 1958–1966

Moped factory, which used 49cc engines supplied by Jawa.

STAFFETT • Norway 1953–early 1960s

Another moped producer fitting 49cc engines.

STAFFORD MOBILE PUP • England 1920-1921

Single-speed scooter with engine mounted by the front wheel. Early product of the Alvis car company.

STAG • England 1912–1914

The factory was at Sherwood Forest, Nottingham. Used Precision engines from 4.5hp to 6hp.

STAHL • America 1910–1914

Built at Philadelphia, the Stahl motorcycles had 4.5hp single-cylinder and 7hp V-twin engines.

STANDARD • Germany 1922–1924

One of the many workshops which built motorcycles in the early 1920s. These had simple frames with basic 132cc and 148cc three-port two-stroke engines.

STANDARD • Germany/Switzerland 1925–early 1950s

This was a very successful make. Wilhelm Gutbrod, who founded the factory, had been with the Klotz works until 1925. The first models had 248cc and 348cc ohv JAP engines, but he soon switched to Swiss MAG proprietary engines of 347cc to 998cc with ioe and partly ohv engines. Works racing models in 1929 had 347cc and 497cc Marchant-designed MAG ohc engines. A few 998cc racing V-twins with ohv JAP racing engines were also built. 1930 saw the introduction of 198cc and 248cc ohv singles with its own engines, and in 1931 came the 498cc production racer with the then-new ohv MAG racing engine. Brough licenced forks were used from 1929 onwards on many

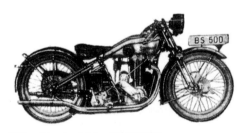

347cc Standard racer (ohv JAP) 1929

497cc Standard (ohv MAG) 1931

198cc Standard (ohv JAP-licenced) 1932

846cc Standard (sv V-twin MAG) 1935

models, including the Rex models of the mid-1930s with Standard's own 348cc engine. Standard built Josef Ganz-designed small cars and mainly 198cc and 248cc two-strokes during the late 1930s. In the 1920s Wilhelm Gutbrod had bought the Swiss Zehnder factory and continued manufacture of these good lightweight machines; he also owned another Swiss factory where he built bigger machines, among them a beautiful 846cc V-twin with the MAG sv engine. There were Swiss versions of the popular 497cc MAG-engined ohv singles. There were attempts after 1945 to re-enter motorcycle production with modern two-strokes up to 248cc and there were also prototypes of various ohv models; unfortunately, few Standard machines were built in the early post-war period. Wilhelm Gutbrod died soon after the war and his sons concentrated on the production of Gutbrod cars and on agricultural machinery. Now it produces lawn mowers among other things. Connected with Standard motorcycles were such famous racing men as A. F. Dom (who was also an excellent designer), Karl Gall, Paul Rüttchen, Hermann Lang, Franz Ecker, Konrad Dürr. With first class design, quality workmanship and excellent finish, Standard motorcycles were among the best built between the wars.

STANGER • England 1921–1923

Interesting design, as the 538cc Stanger had a 70mm bore x 70mm stroke V-twin two-stroke engine and was probably the very first half-litre motorcycle with such an engine configuration. It also had a spring frame and was offered for £95 in 1923. The engine with its big outside flywheel had a tendency to overheat, and the plugs to become fouled with oil.

STANLEY • England c1902

Made by a well-known bicycle factory, Stanley motorcycles had 2.5hp power units and friction drive to the rear wheel. The production was taken over by Singer.

STAR • England 1898–1914

Big factory with wide interests. Produced first three-wheelers and then motorcycles with De Dion engines. There was also a co-operation with Griffon of France. The last motorcycles built by Star were JAP-engined 625cc singles and

770cc V-twins. Star was also a well-known manufacturer of cars.

STAR • Germany 1895–c1900

According to unconfirmed information, Star built motorcycles under Werner license with the 1.5hp engines above the front wheel. This may have been around 1898 or possibly 1895, but this is doubtful.

STAR • Germany 1920–1922

Flat twins designed by H. F. Günther which eventually became the first D-Rad motorcycles. The 393cc engines with opposing cylinders were of the company's own design and manufacture. The first D-Rad versions were identical to the Star machines.

STAR • England 1919–1921

This was a small assembly plant for motorcycles with 269cc Villiers engines.

STAR-GEM • Belgium 1930–1933

Built small machines of 98cc and 123cc with its own and also Sachs two-stroke engines.

STEFFEY • America c1902–1910

Supplied 1.25hp and 3hp single-cylinder machines with air-cooled and water-cooled engines of its own manufacturer.

STEIDINGER • Germany 1925–1927

Lightweight machines with triangular frames. The two-stroke engines were of 199cc.

STELLA • Belgium 1921–1936

The Stella range included frames made from tubes as well as pressed steel. Engines were 98cc two-strokes and 346cc and 490cc sv and ohv singles made in France by Staub under JAP license.

STELLA • New Zealand c1900

A one-off machine built by Ray Every while working at the Temuka Cycle Works, near Christchurch. It used a single-cylinder Minerva engine clipped to a heavy cycle-type frame. The Stella was the first motorcycle in New Zealand and won the first motor race held in Christchurch.

STELLAR • England 1912–1914

Interesting design of a vertical-twin two-stroke machine with its own water-cooled 784cc engine and shaft drive to the rear wheel.

STEPHENSON-PEACH • England c1905

W. J. Stephenson-Peach, engineering schoolmaster of Repton School, Derby, built a very limited number of machines using his own single-cylinder engine. While a schoolmaster at Malvern College, Worcestershire, Stephenson-Peach helped HFS Morgan build his prototype Morgan three-wheeler.

STERLING • France 1952–1954

Scooter with a fully enclosed 123cc Ydral two-stroke engine.

STERNA • Germany 1922–1924

This water-cooled 614cc sv flat twin with opposing cylinders was nearly identical to Aristos and Menos motorcycles.

614cc Sterna (sv water-cooled flat twin) 1922

STERVA • France 1953–1956

Another French scooter of the early 1950s. Engines used were the 98cc and 123cc Sabb.

STERZI • Italy 1948–early 1960s

Well-designed lightweight machines from the 47cc ohv Pony to 174cc ohv models. Among them were 123cc and 158cc two-stroke versions in a variety of models.

STEVENS • England 1934–1937

The Stevens brothers, founders of AJS, who lost that factory in 1931 to the Colliers brothers in London, re-entered the motorcycle market with 248cc, 348cc and 498cc single-cylinder ohv models.
They also supplied AJW with 498cc proprietary engines. Stevens motorcycles were of typical English design and were supplied for use in trials with upswept exhaust pipes.

STICHERLING • Germany 1923–1926

DKW-engined 145cc, 173cc and 206cc two-strokes, built by a small factory.

748cc Stuart (TS water-cooled twin, shaft drive) 1912

496cc Stevens Sport (ohv) 1937

STIMULA • France 1902–WWI

Built motorcycles with Minerva, Buchet, Peugeot and also 346cc and 492cc sv and ohv engines of its own.

STOCK • Germany 1924–1933

The first Stock, a 119cc two-stroke, was made under Evans license. Entirely new Heuss-designed 173cc, 198cc, 246cc and 298cc models appeared in 1929. Of advanced design with own unit-design three-port two-stroke engines, shaft drive to the rear wheel and double-loop frames.

119cc Stock (two-stroke Evans licenced) 1925

246cc Stock (two-stroke shaft-drive) 1931

STOEWER • Germany 1904–1905

Was a well-known car factory which built three-wheelers first and then for a short period Fafnir-engined 2.75hp motorcycles.

STOLCO • Germany 1922–1924

Lightweight machines with Grade-built 144cc two-stroke motors.

STRAND • Australia c1913–1915

Assembled in limited numbers using proprietary parts and 269cc Villiers two-stroke engines.

STROLCH • Germany 1950–1958

Gassmann-designed scooters with 98cc, 147cc, 173cc and 198cc Sachs engines. After a short period the company was renamed Progress.

STRUCO • Germany 1922–1925

Built 147cc two-strokes and also 198cc models with its own sv engines.

STUART • England 1911–1912

This factory also built Stellar motorcycles. The Stuart was a single-cylinder 298cc two-stroke.

STUCCHI • Italy 1901–1927

Ettore Bugatti, Carlo Leidi and Adalberto Garelli were among famous technicians who were working for this once-famous firm, which built three-wheelers, motorcycles and four-wheeled vehicles. See also Prinetti & Stucchi.

STURM • Germany 1923–1925

These were assembled motorcycles equipped with 147cc Alba engines.

STYLSON • France 1919–WWII

Assembled motorcycles with JAP and Staub (JAP license) engines up to 996cc. Some Staub engines were modified to unit-design with shaft drive to the rear wheel. Other versions had the V-engine transverse-mounted. The company competed officially in races and Pierre Amort won many sidecar events with a 996cc JAP-engined racing machine.

STYRIA • Austria 1905–1908

The machines produced by this early Austrian factory had 2hp single-cylinder and 5hp V-twin Fafnir proprietary engines.

SUCCESS • The Netherlands c1906–c1912

Built by Dutch cycle maker with Zwdle and Fafnir engines.

SUDBRACK • Germany 1949–1951

Bicycle factory with 98cc and 123cc motorcycles. The machines were equipped with two-stroke engines of Ilo manufacture.

SUDBROOK • England 1919–1920

This short-lived company assembled machines which were equipped with 269cc two-stroke Villiers engines.

SUECIA • Sweden 1928–1940

Built 248cc, 348cc and 490cc machines with JAP engines. There were also Suecia two-stroke models up to 248cc, made by Sparta of The Netherlands.

SULKY • France 1954–1957

Built by Motobloc, the Sulky miniscooter had AMC two-stroke engines of 98cc, 117cc and 124cc.

SUMITA • Japan 1951–1955

Producer of 123cc and 148cc motorcycles with its own ohv engines.

SUN • England 1911–1961

Belonging to the Parkes family and then the Raleigh group, Sun produced bicycles and accessories before it entered motorcycle production with 346cc singles, which had Villiers ioe engines.

After 1918 the range included 269cc and eventually 247cc models with Vitesse rotary-valve two-stroke engines as well as Villiers-engined models from 147cc to 247cc. Others had 346cc Blackburne and 246cc to 746cc sv and ohv JAP engines.

There was no motorcycle manufacture during the second half of the 1930s. After 1945 production was resumed; now all models had Villiers two-stroke engines, including a scooter called Sunwasp. Engines used were of 98cc to 225cc.

SUNBEAM • England 1912–1957

See panel

SUNBEAM • England 1912–1957

Sunbeam motorcycles were first made by the famous bicycle maker John Marston of Wolverhampton. After WW1 the company was sold to Nobel Industries (later ICI), which allowed Sunbeam considerable autonomy. In 1936 ICI sold the name and precious little else to the Collier brothers' London-based AMC. Finally the name was purchased by BSA.

From 1912 to 1936, Sunbeam designs were by the highly respected J.E. Greenwood. Marston (and ICI) Sunbeams were famous for their superb black enamel finish, their sporting performance and, on many models, their all-enclosed chain drive. Although before 1914 Sunbeam made a 350cc single-cylinder model and later several proprietary-engined V-twins, its early reputation was founded on its 500cc sv singles, one of which, ridden by H.R. Davies, was second in the 1914 Senior TT. T. C. de la Hay won on a Sunbeam in 1920, and Alec Bennett in 1923. Thereafter, Sunbeam raced ohv models (an ohc version in 1925 was not successful) and Charlie Dodson won the 1928 and 1929 Senior TTs. Racing ended with the depression of the early 1930s, when Sunbeam sales declined badly.

When AMC took over and moved production to London, Sunbeam produced new 250cc, 350cc and 500cc models with Collier-designed high camshaft ohv engines, seen at the 1938 Show. These scarcely had a chance to prove themselves, being killed off by the outbreak of war in 1939. During the war, the name was sold to BSA. The post-war Sunbeam S7 was designed by Ehrling Poppe, once partner in P & P Motorcycles, who leaned heavily on the 1939 BMW for many of its features and styling. The twin-cylinder 500cc all-aluminum ohc engine was rubber mounted in line with the frame, with a unit four-speed gearbox, shaft drive and worm and gear final transmission. With its four-inch 'balloon' tyres there was nothing sporting about the S7, but it was a refined and pleasant touring machine. Unfortunately it sold better abroad than at home, and even the S8, a sports model with lighter-looking front forks, tyres and brakes, did not sell in the quantities which BSA had hoped for. Reluctantly, BSA ended Sunbeam production in 1957 and thereafter used the name on bicycles, as well as producing a BSA-Sunbeam scooter, but this had absolutely nothing in common with the once great name it bore.

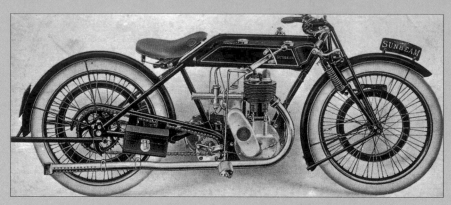

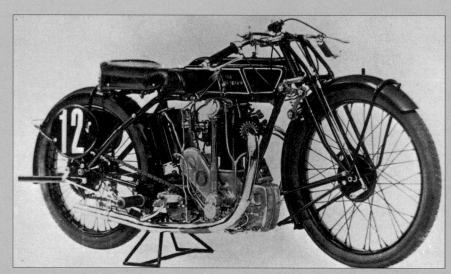

492cc Sunbeam Longstroke (sv) 1924

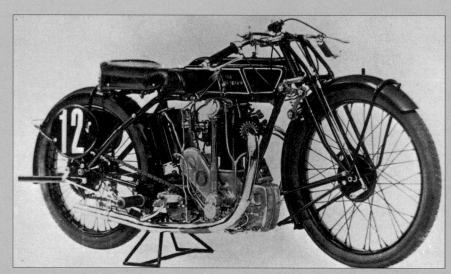

497cc Sunbeam works racer (ohc) 1925

493cc Sunbeam TT90 (ohv) 1927

493cc Sunbeam TT90 (ohv) 1929

497cc Sunbeam Sports (hc) 1939

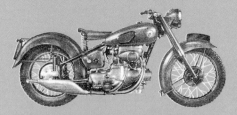

497cc Sunbeam S8 (ohc twin) 1950

SUZUKI • Japan 1952–

Suzuki was a long established and successful maker of textile machinery, which, in 1952, took advantage of the demand in Japan for cheap transport and produced a simple 36cc two-stroke engine called the Power Free, designed to clip onto a bicycle. The following year a 60cc version called the Diamond Free was introduced. Three years later – after, in common with so many other concerns, a close study of a DKW RT125 two-stroke – Suzuki produced its first real motorcycle. This was the 125cc two-stroke Colleda, also available with a 90cc engine, which was raced somewhat half-heartedly at Asama Plains in 1955 and then not again until 1959. The following year, Suzuki unexpectedly entered the TT with 125cc twin-cylinder two-strokes, and in 1961 it raced 125cc and 250cc twins. Performance in both classes was dire, but Suzuki had an ace up its sleeve.

In 1961, the East German MZ company was enjoying an extraordinarily successful season in the 125cc class. But in a truly cloak and dagger operation worthy of any thriller, Suzuki persuaded rider-technician Ernst Degner and his family to defect to the West, and more specifically to Suzuki to hand over MZ's secrets. With Degner's assistance, Suzuki won the newly-instituted 50cc world championship in 1962 and the 50cc and 125cc titles the next year. It won the 50cc title again in 1964, 1966 and 1967 and the 125cc title again in 1965 before withdrawing from grand prix racing. However success in the 250cc class continued to elude it at this time, despite investing heavily in an advanced square four racer, campaigned in 1964 and 1965.

125cc Suzuki S30 (two-stroke twin) 1966

247cc Suzuki T20 (two-stroke twin) 1967

49cc Suzuki Sport 50 M12 (two-stroke single) 1966

49cc Suzuki M15 (two-stroke single) 1966

Suzuki's 1960s success extended to motocross (then called scrambling) and the company has done extremely well in this field since. It is currently the most successful manufacturer in terms of world championship motocross titles.

Joel Robert won the 250cc title in 1970, and since 1971, when Belgian Roger De Coster claimed the 500cc title, it has won the amazing total of 26 world titles in the 125cc, 250cc and 500cc classes. Suzuki led the way in changing the focus of motocross in recent years. It was the first Japanese manufacturer to pull out of production of the 500cc two-stroke in the early 1980s to concentrate on developing the more accessible RM125 and 250 machines, a move which signalled the decline of the 500s as the most prestigious category in favour of the 250s.

A new venture in the mid 1980s, fuelled by demand from a new sport in America, was quad racing. A variety of 250cc and 500cc liquid-cooled two-strokes was produced and later a 200cc four-stroke, but production was cut in the early 1990s. Now, with the resurgence of interest in the sport, Suzuki, like other manufacturers, is considering a comeback.

Suzuki was also a hot contender in world trials throughout the 1980s. A UK operation called Beamish Suzuki was formed which manufactured machines under license from Suzuki. The RL250 Beamish Suzuki used many parts from an earlier Japanese-built and unpopular machine, fitted to a Whitelock frame with revised wheels, tyres and gearing, and the bike recorded much British Championship success, although a world title eluded it.

118cc Suzuki 120 B100P (two-stroke) 1967

247cc Suzuki GT250 (two-stroke twin) 1975

492cc Suzuki T500 (two-stroke twin) 1973

49cc Suzuki A50 (two-stroke single) 1975

Meanwhile, the company sold 50cc, 125cc and 250cc two-strokes for the road, which became ever more sophisticated from crude beginnings. A landmark was the T20 Super Six (for the six-speed gearbox) two-stroke twin of 1965. The air-cooled 500cc twin T500 Cobra (known in the USA as the Titan) followed in 1967, and in 1971 the very impressive 749cc three-cylinder water-cooled GT750 was launched. Its transverse engine produced 70bhvp, an enormous power output for the time which gace the bike a breathtaking performance, although as with most early Japanese superbikes, this was barely matched by the GT750's brakes and handling. Suzuki followed this up with smaller air-cooled triples – the 380cc, GT380 and 550cc GT550.

The export market to the USA was very important to Suzuki, and, claiming to be the world's largest maker of two-stroke motorcycles, it was extremely conscious of the growing threat from American anti-pollution laws. It now made a major error in staking a great deal on Wankel engine technology, which had become fashionable at the time. In 1970 it had taken out a Wankel development license from NSU, and in 1974 revealed what it hoped would be the motorcycle of the future – the (nominally 500cc) rotary-engined RE5.

The RE5 was not an entirely bad motorcycle, but it was not a good one and for all its novelty, it did not sell. The engine looked messy, bulky and was too high in the frame. The bike was heavy, it guzzled petrol and performance was far from impressive, while its one-off technology made it extremely expensive to service and maintain. The machine lasted for only two disappointing seasons before Suzuki hastily rushed into production a close copy of Kawasaki's Z1000, reduced to 750cc as the Suzuki GS750. This was followed by the GS1000, and both machines were very well received for both their engine performance and handling. Both sold well and Suzuki settled into a new generation of four-stroke fours and twins, which in turn were developed into the 16-valve GSX range in 1980. Both the GSX750, with dumpy, squared-off styling, and similar looking 1100cc version were worthy bikes, but it was the European Target-designed GSX1100S Katana which grabbed the public's attention with its space age looks in 1982. This was also available with a 1000cc engine to homologate an American racing version. The Katana generated plenty of headlines but relatively few sales, although since that time has become something of a cult machine.

As with the GS range, the GSX machines were also available as twins, and these further established Suzuki's reputation for producing fast, reliable and reasonably well handling four-stroke machines.

Suzuki kept producing road-going two-stroke sports bikes, the RG250 Gamma race replica succeeding the GT250 in 1984, being most notable for its exceptionally good-handling aluminum chassis. In 1989 this was replaced by the highly successful RGV250 which remained on sale for another seven years until being

749cc Suzuki GT750 (two-stroke liquid-cooled three cylinder) 1974

replaced by the RGV250-SP, a completely new machine sadly only available on the Japanese market in restricted form.

Although it had abandoned grand prix racing, the company raced the T500 two-stroke twin at Daytona from 1968 on. In that year Ron Grant was fifth on his TR500 and in 1969 he was second. In Europe, Jack Findley had successes on a TR500, including victories in the 1971 Ulster Grand Prix and the 1978 Senior TT with a later water-cooled version.

The TR750, a racing version of the road-going GT750, was very impressive, but despite a claimed 115hp, failed to score at Daytona, destroying chains and rear tyres faster than they could be replaced. Suzuki re-entered grand prix racing in 1974 with its square-four, disc-valve RG500 ridden by Briton Barry Sheene and Findlay. Two years later Sheene won the factory's first 500 title aboard the RG and retained the crown in 1977. The same year Sheene rode an over-bored 650cc version to the British Superbike championship. At this time the RG became the most popular machine in 500 racing only three of the top 30 riders in the 1977 championship used different machinery. Factory versions recorded two more world championship successes (with Marco Lucchinelli in 1981 and Franco Uncini in 1982), but subsequently the bike became uncompetitive and the factory withdrew from 500 racing at the end of 1983, although several semi-factory efforts bravely continued for the next few seasons.

747cc Suzuki GS750 (dohc transverse four) 1977

997cc Suzuki GS1000S (dohc transverse four) 1980

747cc Suzuki GS 1000 1978

1075cc Suzuki GSX1100S Katana (dohc transverse four) 1982

Suzuki was back again in 1987 with a reed-valve induction V-four, the configuration now preferred by all major 500 protagonists, although the RGV500 was not an immediate success. The factory's real weapon was rider Kevin Schwantz, who gave the bike its first GP win the following year and stayed with the factory until his retirement in 1995. However, the ebullient Texan was a spectacular but inconsistent rider and although he won many GPs on the RGV (25 in all), he didn't take the championship until 1993.

An uncharacteristic period of poor results at this highest level finally looks to have come to an end in 1999 with American Kenny Roberts Junior achieving several grand prix wins on the company's latest RGV500.

Suzuki also re-joined the 250 class in 1991 with a reed-valve V-twin, the RGV250, but this was an altogether less successful venture, failing to produce a single victory in five seasons of grand prix competition.

The factory first became involved in four-stroke racing in the late 1970s, following the launch of the GS750 and GS1000 road models. American Wes Cooley scored the GS1000's first major success when he took the US Superbike title in 1979, riding a high-handlebar machine prepared by legendary Japanese tuner Pops Yoshimura, who would continue to play a major role in the success of Suzuki four-strokes for many years.

247cc Suzuki RG250 (two-stroke twin) 1983

498cc Suzuki RG500 Gamma (two-stroke four-cylinder) 1985

1127cc Suzuki GSX1100E (dohc transverse four) 1986

572cc Suzuki GSX550E (dohc transverse four) 1986

SUZUKI

In 1983 Frenchman Herve Moineau and Richard Hubin took the marque's first world endurance title on its factory GS1000. Riding a GSX-R750, Moineau regained the title in 1987 (riding with Bruno Le Bihan) and won it again the following season (with Thierry Crine).

The GSX-R initially fast but fragile as a racer became a hugely popular mount in endurance, Formula One and Superbike events. Yet while Jamie James rode a Yoshimura-fettled GSX-R to the 1989 US Superbike crown, the bike has rarely been on the pace in World Superbike racing. During the championship's first 11 seasons the GSX-R won just three WSB races (Gary Goodfellow in 1988, Doug Polen in 1989 and Keiichi Kitagawa in 1998).

But the road version of the GSX-R has become something of a modern classic. It was introduced in 1985, and developed constantly over the years, gaining power and some weight but never really losing its reputation as one of the wilder race replica machines. It was only in 1992 that its trademark oil-cooled engine was replaced by a conventional water-cooled one, and twin cradle aluminum frame was substituted for a conventional twin spar one in 1996.

The GSX-R1100 was introduced a year later than the 750, but its development was less smooth, the 1989 K model for example having notoriously poor handling. The model was dropped at the end of 1995.

749cc Suzuki GSX-R750 (dohc transverse four) 1985

749cc Suzuki GSX-R750W (dohc transverse four) 1992

1052cc Suzuki GSX-R1100 (dohc transverse four)1986

749cc Suzuki GSX-R750 (dohc transverse four) 1985

Suzuki's range in the 1980s also included some single-cylinder trail and commuter machines, but gradually the company expanded into a wider range of niches, becoming more serious about custom bikes towards the 1990s with the VS750 Harley-style V-twin of 1986, then the similar VS1400 and the single-cylinder LS650 Savage in 1987.

A particular success was the GSF600 Bandit (one of many Suzukis using a version of the oil-cooled GSX-R engines) which took over from Yamaha's Diversion as the most popular budget middleweight for several years after its introduction at the end of 1995.

Like Honda, Suzuki was slow to move into the fashion scooter market, growing rapidly in Europe in the 1990s and dominated by the Italians and Peugeot, eventually introducing the AY50 Katana in 1997. At the other end of the scale, in 1999 Suzuki took on the challenge of producing the fastest production road bike, and won, with the GSX1300R Hayabusa, a 1300cc machine with controversial aerodynamic styling, producing 173bhp and capable of more than 190mph. This followed Suzuki's first big capacity sports V-twins, first the TL1000S in 1997, then the race replica TL1000R the following year. The R was designed to spawn a World Superbike racer in the wake of Ducati's success with the format, and included several innovations such as its rotary rear damper unit. But an initial year's racing in the USA made little progress, and the WSB project was abandoned. The appeal of the V-twin was recognised though, and the smaller capacity V-twin SV650 was successfully launched with a budget price tag in 1999.

249cc Suzuki RGV250 Gamma (two-stroke twin) 1991

349cc Suzuki DR350S (ohc single) 1990

SUZUKI

487cc Suzuki GS500E (dohc twin) 1993

599cc Suzuki GSF600S Bandit (dohc transverse four) 1995

1462cc Suzuki VL1500LC Intruder (ohc V-twin) 1998

748cc Suzuki GSX750W (dohc transverse four) 1998

749cc Suzuki GSX750F (dohc transverse four)

996cc Suzuki TL1000S (dohc eight valve V-twin, liquid-cooled, fuel injection) 1997

249cc Suzuki RM250 motocross (two-stroke single) 1994

49cc Suzuki Street Magic (two-stroke single) 1998

249cc Suzuki TU250 (ohc single) 1998

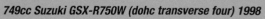

749cc Suzuki GSX-R750W (dohc transverse four) 1998

996cc Suzuki TL1000R (dohc eight valve V-twin, liquid-cooled, fuel injection) 1998

1300cc Suzuki GSX1300R Hayabusa (dohc 16-valve transverse four, liquid-cooled, fuel injection) 1999

650cc Suzuki SV650S (dohc V-twin) 1999

746cc Super-X (ioe V-twin) 1927

SUPER-X • America 1924–1930

Made by the Schwinn company of Chicago, the 746cc and 996cc Super-X machines were really successors to the American X. All models had V twin ioe engines and were of excellent design.

SUZUKI • Japan 1952–

See panel

SUZY • France 1932–1933

Made by a small factory, the Suzy had a fully enclosed 498cc ohc Chaise unit-design engine.

SWALLOW • England 1946–1951

The Swallow Gadabout scooter was designed by Frank Rainbow and had 125cc and 197cc Villiers engines. Swallow, who also made sidecars, was an early offshoot of SS (later Jaguar).

SWALLOW • Japan 1955–circa 1960

Manufacturer of the Pop scooter, with 125cc, 165cc and 175cc engines.

SWASTIKA • Australia 1913–1916

There was, during the 1920s a Swastika bicycle factory in Germany, but this at Adelaide built motorcycles with no German connections. Using English components this machine had a sv engine of 746cc.

SWIFT • England 1898–1915

Famous pioneer which built De Dion-engined three-wheelers and motorcycles with shaft drive for Starley. The Coventry-based factory also built cars. The Swift motorcycles had White & Poppe as well as its own 492cc and 768cc

746cc Super-X (ioe V-twin) 1930

V-twin engines. Commercially and technically Swift was closely connected with the Ariel works at Birmingham, then headed by Charles Sangster.

SWM • Italy 1971–1985

SWM was extremely successful in the 1970s, making 125cc Sachs and 250cc Rotax engines for off-road motorcycles. It over-reached itself by acquiring the Gori company, however, and foundered in the face of the market downturn of the early 1980s.

SYM • Taiwan 1995

Export brand name used on San Yang scooters. See San Yang.

SYMPLEX • England 1913–1922

Simple machines with 311cc Dalm two-stroke engines. Designer was J. J. Allen.

SYPHAX • France early 1950s

Built nice lightweights with flat 98cc single-cylinder AMC two-stroke engines and bigger two-stroke models with vertical Aubier-Dunne engine of 123cc and 174cc. Other versions housed ohv AMC engines of 123cc and 174cc.

TAC • England 1910-

A four-cylinder machine invented by Mr Tacchi Sn. Designed a radial-engined three-cylinder bike in the 1930s.

TANDON • England 1948–1957

A range of simple Villiers-engined lightweights of 125cc, 200cc and 225cc, later, Villiers 250cc and 325cc twins were used.

TAPELLA-FUCHS • Italy c1957

Concentrated on mopeds and used 49cc Fuchs two-stroke engines exclusively.

TAS • Germany 1924–1931

A bicycle factory which was closely connected with the French Gnome & Rhône works. The result was the use of 173cc and 248cc two-stroke and of 346cc and 498cc four-stroke sv and ohv engines made by the G&R works in TAS frames. When it broke that connection the German factory used Swiss MAG 347cc and 497cc ioe and ohv single-cylinder engines.

TAURA • Italy 1927–1930

Giulio Doglioli's motorcycles relied on English JAP and Blackburne engines. The range included first 173cc sv versions only, but in the next years models up to 490cc were built. Most of them had the 490cc ohv double-port JAP engine. A three-wheeler for invalids was also built.

TAURUS • Italy 1933–1966

The first models were 173cc two-strokes and a 173cc ohv version. Contemporary 346cc and 496cc ohc singles with unit-design four-speed gearboxes were built in 1934. New pre-war models were also 246cc and 498cc ohv singles, which had rear suspension, but the top design was without doubt the 1938 498cc dohc single. Unfortunately Taurus could not afford competing officially in races, but it was a superb design which needed only more development to become a first-class racing machine. The production version produced 34bhp at 6000rpm and had a top speed of 108mph. A 248cc single-ohc model built after 1945 produced 14bhp at 7000rpm. After the war, production included 49cc engines, 158cc two-stroke machines and a beautiful 199cc ohv unit-design machine, while the older 248cc ohc single was superseded by a quite tame 248cc ohv version. New also was a 173cc ohv model.

TAUTZ • Germany 1921–1923

One of the first German scooters built. It had a 118cc DKW two-stroke engine.

119cc Tautz (two-stroke) 1922

TAVERNIER • France 1921–1923

Assembler which built a range of machines with Zurcher, JAP and Blackburne engines.

TECNOMOTO • Italy 1968–1977

Maker of small motocross and enduro models which switched to the manufacture of children's motorcycles. Tecnomoto was sold to a British company in 1977, but did not survive.

TECO • Germany 1920–1926

Built mainly 198cc machines with sv, ioe and ohv engines of Alba manufacture although the crankcase bore the name Teco. The last model had a 346cc Kühne ohv engine.

TEDDY • France 1922–1924

Lightweight machines with 203cc sv engines.

TEE-BEE • England 1908–1911

Assembled machines with its own and also 293cc JAP sv engines.

TEHUELCHE • Argentina 1958–1962

75cc ohv machine of Italian design, built with many parts imported from Italy.

TEMPERINO • Italy 1906–1925

Limited motorcycle production by Maurizio and Jim Temperino, Turin, which was better known as a cyclecar manufacturer. Also marketed machines as the Mead Flyer.

TEMPLE • England 1924–1928

The Temple was part of the OEC range of models. Claude Temple was a well-known rider and breaker of records as well as a technician. He broke many records on 996cc V-twins, which had Hubert Hagens-designed ohc Anzani engines. This 1923 machine developed 58hp. Production versions had 496cc four-valve ohv Vulpine and 347cc and 497cc ohc Atlanta engines. From 1927 onwards the OEC also had duplex steering.

TEMPO • Germany 1924–1927

Built 197cc single-cylinder two-strokes and also 297cc sv machines in limited numbers, noted for their very strong frames.

TEMPO • Norway 1949–

Built a range of lightweights with 49cc and 123cc two-stroke engines. Among the engines used were the Villiers, Ilo, CZ and Sachs.

TERRA • Germany 1922–1924

Simple two-strokes of own design and manufacture. They were of 127cc, 143cc and 172cc.

TERROT • France 1901–early 1960s

This was for many years the factory with the largest motorcycle production in France. Terrot in Dijon was also a well-known make in races during the 1920s. It built motorcycles on English lines, including 98cc, 174cc and 246cc two-strokes and sv and ohv models from 246cc to 746cc. The last ones were V-twins. Used Blackburne, JAP and mainly its own engines, of which in pre-war days the 246cc ohv singles were extremely popular. There was also in the late 1920s a Blackburne-engined 174cc ohv racing model. A 498cc works racing model, built in 1937, had a transverse-mounted ohv V-twin engine. After 1945, Terrot built a range of modern ohv singles up to 498cc and also two-strokes, including scooters of advanced design. Famous Terrot riders in the period between the wars: Rolland, Perrotin, Coulon, Fraichard, Durant, Boetsch, Simo, Riha, J. and H. Tichy, Zukal, Raab and others.

TERROT • Czechoslovakia 1933–1935

A branch factory of Terrot-Dijon built a 346cc sv model in Czechoslovakia.

238cc Terrot Sport (two-strokc) 1923

348cc Terrot (ohv) 1930

498cc Terrot (ohv) 1952

TESTI • Italy 1951–1983

Testi built a vast range of proprietary-engined lightweight motorcycles and mopeds, using Sachs, Franco Massimi, Demm and Minarelli engines. At different times, Testis were sold in Germany as Horex, and elsewhere as Gitanes, although there was no direct connection between these companies. Like so many other small and quite vigorous companies, Testi did not have the resources to survive the depression of the early 1980s.

TETGE • Germany 1923–1926

Produced on a limited scale 148cc and 172cc sv singles and also machines with MAG 597cc V-twins.

TGM • Italy 1974–

Maker of trials and motocross models, with Hella, Danth and Villa two-stroke engines. Sammy Miller acted as a design consultant. Though not owned by Cagiva, TGM has had a 'working relationship' with it in recent years.

6hp Thor (ioe V-twin) 1915

THIEM • America 1903–1914

Built like other American factories of that period 550cc ioe single-cylinder and 890cc as well as 996cc V-twin machines of advanced design. Some had two-speed gearboxes.

THOMANN • France 1912–1939

Built two-strokes from 98cc to 248cc and was another factory which belonged to the Alcyon group from the mid-1920s onward.

THOMAS • England 1904

Assembler which built a limited number of motorcycles with various engines including Minerva and Sarolea engines.

THOMAS • America 1907–1908

Made in a branch of the Thomas car works, the motorcycles had 3hp single-cylinder engines with a sloping cylinder and belt drive to the rear wheel. The price: $175.

THOMASSIN • Belgium 1902

Built by J. Thomassin, Blegny with Herman of Herstal, Belgium engine.

THOR • America 1903–1916

Produced proprietary engines for various factories, including Indian at Springfield. The Aurora Automatic Machinery Co. later built complete V-twin motorcycles with 6hp and 9hp ioe engines, which had an excellent reputation among riders.

THOROUGH • England 1903

Another small assembler of motorcycles. These had MMC and Coronet engines.

THREE-SPIRES • England 1931–1932

Made by Coventry Bicycles Ltd, these little 147cc two-stroke machines were offered for £18.18s.

THUMANN • Germany 1925–1926

Although a comparatively small factory, Thumann built its own 246cc and 346cc sv engines.

THUNDER • Italy 1952–1954

Very up-to-date but expensive design of a 127cc vertical twin unit-design ohv machine with telescopic forks, swinging arm rear suspension, the dynamo incorporated in the crankcase, four-speed gearbox etc. The price was 285,000 lire, which was approximately 100,000 lire higher than normal 124cc two-strokes.

TICKLE • England 1967–1973

Producer of 348cc and 499cc Manx Norton single-cylinder dohc racing machines, after the Norton works decided to drop the manufacture of this model. Tickle also produced spares and parts when the originals were no longer available.

TIGER • America 1915–1916

Attempted to produce a lightweight machine in the USA. The Fredricksen-designed Tiger had a 241cc two-stroke engine.

TIKA • Germany 1921–1924

Assembled machines with 145cc and 197cc Herko sv engines.

TILBROOK • Australia 1950–1953

Designed by Rex Tilbrook, these Villiers-engined 123cc and 198cc two-strokes were of advanced design, but the company failed to stay in business. A 123cc racing model was successful in Australian road events.

TILSTON • England 1919

Short-lived producer, whose machines had 225cc Precision two-stroke engines.

TITAN • America 1993–

Hand builds in small numbers high performance custom-styled machines with Harley-Davidson-style engines made from aftermarket components. The retail prices are around double those of contemporary Harleys.

TITAN • Austria 1927–1933

The first product of this factory was the 144cc two-stroke, two-cylinder Austro-Motorette; the second design by Karl Schüber was the 346cc two-stroke Titan. This was probably the first commercially built two-stroke engine with the incoming mixture controlled by membranes.

The air-cooled engine had 75mm bore and 77mm stroke and produced 10hp. Another model had first the 490cc sv JAP and later a Blackburne sv engine.

TITAN • San Marino 1975–

Motocross machines with 49cc two-stroke engines built in the smallest European republic by a small factory.

TIZ-AM • Russia 1931–1940

Heavy 596cc single-cylinder sv machines built at the Taganrog factory.

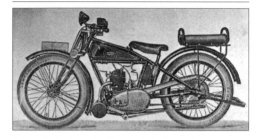

346cc Titan Touring (two-stroke) 1928

TM • Italy 1977–

Produces exclusive hand-made machines for motocross and enduro. The Pesaro factory's two-strokes are fitted with hand-made swingarms, titanium hand-welded exhaust systems, Öhlins front forks and rear shock and an abundance of carbon fibre. The factory has expanded rapidly in the past five years and upped its range to include seven motocross, four enduro and two children's 50cc models. It has yet to win a world championship, but it is tipped to do so in the near future.

TOHATSU • Japan 1935–1966

Was one of the leading Japanese motorcycle factories. Built two-strokes from 48cc to 248cc with rotary valves, including very fast 124cc two-cylinder racing versions.

TOMASELLI • Italy 1931–1939

Assembled sporting motorcycles with 173cc to 490cc sv and ohv JAP engines. The production was small.

TOMMASI • Italy 1926–1927

Produced 123cc and 246cc two-stroke machines with engines supplied by Della Ferrera. The bigger model had two 123cc power units coupled.

TOMOS • Yugoslavia 1956–

Leading motorcycle factory in Yugoslavia, which concentrated for many years on a variety of 49cc lightweights.

There were also racing machines. Bigger machines were added more recently, among them modern 87cc and 174cc single-cylinder versions with 18bhp at 7000rpm and sports models with 22bhp at 8200 rpm. There is now also a branch factory at Epe in The Netherlands.

TOREADOR • England 1924–1926

Closely connected with Granville Bradshaw, designer of the oil-cooled Bradshaw engines, Bert Houlding's factory produced not only 348cc ohv models, but also the rare 348cc Bradshaw ohc version, of which only very few were built. The Toreador range included models with 346cc and 490cc JAP and 496cc MAG ohv engines.

TORNAX • Germany 1925–1955, 1982–84

Superbly built motorcycles with a variety of proprietary engines. These included JAP sv and ohv engines from 346cc to 996cc, Columbus vertical twin-cylinder 598cc and 798cc ohc engines and also 496cc and 596cc single-cylinder ohv versions made by the same factory. After 1945, Tornax production concentrated on two-stroke machines up to 248cc with mainly Ilo engines. A few 247cc models with the Küchen-designed Opti vertical twin-cylinder ohc engine were built as well. Tornax produced in the mid-1930s a well-regarded sports car with the DKW two-stroke engine and built also many racing machines; the last one was a 124cc ohc single in 1952 which had a Küchen-designed engine.

The Tornax name was revived 1982 by a company in Frankfurt who used it on a range of small Franco Morini engined lightweights, but the revival was short lived.

346cc Toreador (ohv oil-cooled Bradshaw) 1926

TORPADO • Italy 1950–

Lightweight machines with 38cc Mosquito and 48cc and 74cc Minarelli two-stroke engines.

TORPEDO • America 1905–1908

A range of road-going and race machines built with 2 1/4hp, 3hp and 5hp Thor and 4hp Antoine engines.

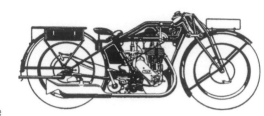

548cc Tornax (sv JAP) 1927

596cc Tornax Superior (ohv Columbus) 1934

80cc Tornax RX80 (two-stroke Franco Morini) 1982

TORPEDO • Czechoslovakia 1903–1912

When Czechoslovakia was still part of the Austro-Hungarian Empire, the Torpedo was one of the best machines. Designed by Frantisek Trojan, it was built entirely at the Kolin factory. Not only the ioe engines but even the carburettors were made there. Single-cylinder Torpedo engines produced 3.5hp and 4hp, V-twin versions 6hp and 8hp.

TORPEDO • England 1910–1920

Another Torpedo bicycle factory which built strong frames with 294cc, 346cc and 499cc single-cylinder and V-twin Precision engines.

TORPEDO • Germany 1901–1907

Assembled motorcycles with single-cylinder and V-twin Zedel and Fafnir engines.

TORPEDO • Germany 1928–1956

Well-known bicycle factory which concentrated on 198cc machines with Blackburne sv engines and later with mainly Sachs and Ilo two-strokes.

124cc TM125 Cross (two-stroke single, liquid-cooled) 1999

TORROT • Spain 1960–

Originally an offshoot of the French Terrot company, one of the few surviving small Spanish factories which makes motorcycles, mopeds and trail bikes with 50cc Sachs engines.

TOURISTE • France 1927

Basic lightweight.

TOWNEND • England 1901–1904

Pioneer who fitted 2hp and 2.5hp engines into heavy bicycle frames.

TOYOMOTOR • Japan 1957–early 1960s

Built 246cc two-stroke twins, which had much in common with German Adler motorcycles.

TRAFALGAR • England 1902–1905

Pioneer motorcycle producer which used MMC and Minerva engines and was also involved in the manufacture of wicker sidecars.

TRAFFORD • England 1919–1922

Assembled on a small scale motorcycles with 269cc Villiers engines. These were not particularly successful, and no other machines were produced,

TRAGATSCH • Czechoslovakia 1946–1949

This racing shop, owned by the original author of this book, Erwin Tragatsch, built track-racing machines with 348cc and 498cc JAP ohv engines. Long-track versions had a rear suspension which could be regulated to give various degrees of movement. Top rider: Hugo Rosak.

TRAIN • France 1913–1939

Was for many years a supplier of engines to other factories, many of which found their way to Italy, where the 173cc two-stroke versions became especially popular. Complete Train machines had two-stroke engines of 98cc to 346cc and sv and ohv engines from 246cc to 995cc. Among them were 746cc and 995cc V-twins. Also a 124cc racing two-stroke was built and most versions were available with water-cooling. The twin-carburetor racing engine produced 6hp at 5000 rpm and had a top speed of 63mph. 1930 saw the introduction of a 496cc in-line four ohc engine which had shaft drive and—like most Train models of that period—a unit design.

TRANS-AMA • Italy 1979–

Concentrates on motocross and trials machines with two-stroke engines of 49.6cc, 80cc, 124.8cc, 244cc and 321.5cc capacity.

TREBLOC • England 1922–1925

Lightweight machines with cwn 63cc engines.

346cc Train (ohv) 1931

TREDAGH • Eire 1902

Single-cylinder pioneer machine which transmitted power to the drive belt pulley by gear wheels.

TREMO • Germany 1925–1928

Singles with its own 308cc sv and ohv unit-design engines. Production on a limited scale.

TRENT • England 1902–c1906

Produced strengthened bicycles with 207cc power units.

TRESPEDI • Italy 1926–1930

Built good 173cc and 246cc two-stroke machines with its own engines, which were of the three-port deflector-type.

TRIANON • Germany 1922–1926

Bicycle producer which built only one motorcycle model, with its own 232cc two-stroke engine.

TRIUMPH • England 1902–

German immigrants Siegried Bettmann and Maurice Schulte started building bicycles in Coventry in 1887, in 1902 they fitted a Minerva engine into one and a new make of motorcycle was born. Improved Minerva, Fafnir and JAP engined models followed, but in 1905 Charles Hathaway was engaged to design a new 300cc side-valve engine to be manufactured by Triumph itself. Hathaway also designed front forks with a peculiar fore-and-aft movement, which were used by Triumph for many years. Production rose to 500 machines in 1906; in 1907 the engine capacity was raised to 450cc and then to 475cc. Triumph at this time built up a reputation for exceptional reliability, and it was at this time that the well-known phrase 'the trusty Triumph' came into usage.

Some have even credited Triumph, rather optimistically, with ensuring the continued production of motorcycles generally by proving they could be viable road-going transport.

Success followed quickly. Jack Marshall was second in the first TT in 1907 and won the second in 1908. These results, plus the addition of a `free engine' clutch in the rear hub, led to sales of 3000 Triumphs in 1909. For 1910, engine capacity was raised further to a full 500cc. In 1913, the Baby Triumph, a 225cc two-stroke, was introduced, while late in 1914 came the 550cc sv model H, with three-speed Sturmey-Archer gearbox, chain and belt drive. Over 30,000 of these were supplied to the British Army between 1914 and 1918. In 1920 the model H became the SD (Spring Drive), with all-chain transmission, while 1921 saw a new ohv model, the four-valve Ricardo. This was conceived as a racing machine, but was more successful as a sports model for the road.

Maurice Schulte left in 1922 to be succeeded by Colonel Claude Holbrook, who steered the company into car manufacture – not, as it turned out, the wisest of moves. The little two-stroke was enlarged to 250cc and given a kickstarter and clutch, but was killed off in 1925 to make room for production of the sensationally successful Model P, which at less than £43 was the cheapest-ever 500cc motorcycle in the world. Production of the P was soon up to 1000 per week.

The demands of the car program and depressed trading conditions after 1930 meant stagnation in the motorcycle side of the business. Even the arrival of designer Val Page in 1932 – he was responsible for the 650cc

499cc Triumph Ricardo (ohv four-valve) 1923

Triumph Ricardo racer (dohc) 1925

496cc Triumph Horsmann TT (ohv) 1927

148cc Triumph (ohv) 1935

6/1 vertical twin of 1933 and new 250cc, 350cc and 500cc ohv singles – could not arrest Triumph's decline. In 1936, entrepreneur Jack Sangster bought the Triumph motorcycle division for an almost nominal price and installed Edward Turner as general manager. Turner, recognized generally as an all round genius, first redesigned and restyled the range of ohv singles as the Tiger 70, 80 and 90, which were soon best sellers. He then produced the 500cc Triumph Speed Twin (and the later Tiger 100), which broke new ground and inspired nearly 50 years of development of a basic theme.

Triumph's most famous vertical twin, and the one which survived the longest, was the T120 Bonneville. This was introduced in 1959 as a sportier version of the Tiger 110, featuring splayed inlet ports and twin Amal carburetors. The Bonneville was uprated steadily over the years, losing its early heavy looks while the handling improved considerably too. A unit construction engine and gearbox was fitted in 1963, new oil-in-frame chassis in 1971 and in 1973 the capacity was taken out to 744cc (and the bike called the T140 Bonneville).

Meanwhile, sales success in the important American market started up more slowly. It was Turner's convic-

tion that the Speed Twin would sell in the USA but he had to wait until the end of WW2 to vindicate his belief. In 1949, US sales escalated with the 650cc Thunderbird, while, for those looking for smaller models, there were 350cc and 500cc twins, plus the single-cylinder 150cc Terrier, which developed into the long-running 200cc Tiger Cub.

In 1951 Sangster sold Triumph to BSA, but both companies retained their automony until Turner's retirement in 1964. Unfortunately, both BSA and Triumph were thereafter managed by men from outside the industry who, by and large, showed a lamentable ignorance of its peculiar problems, and investment in new design anfd machinery was minimal. Even the 750cc in-line three-cylinder model which became the Triumph Trident and BSA Rocket 3, was effectively no more than one and a half twins, meaning it was very old fashioned against the new Honda CB750. It performed very well nevertheless, but build quality was poor and it lacked the glamour of the Honda, and could not save against the increasingly sharp Japanese competition. Despite all the difficulties, Triumph commissioned, in a typically roundabout and almost underhand way, American stylist Craig Vetter to add an

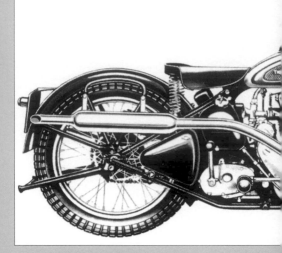

246cc Triumph Tiger 70 (ohv) 1938

499cc Triumph Mk 10 racer (ohc) 1935

trans-Atlantic flavour to the Trident. He came up with the X-75 Hurricane which gained many fans for its swoopy styling blending tank and seat unit, and the stack of three silencers on the bike's right hand side. But this was only produced in limited numbers, despite the bike's apparent potential. This was just one of many problems though. A series of appalling blunders led BSA into bankruptcy in 1973. A rescue operation of Triumph by Dennis Poore's Norton Villiers group was mounted with government aid, but the plan did not work, and resulted in a sit-in at the Meridan Triumph factory and the formation of a workers' cooperative.

This ill-conceived and ill-managed venture absorbed millions of pounds of tax-payers' money, only to founder finally in 1983.

All interests in Triumph were purchased by successful builder and entrepreneur John Bloor, who licensed production of the 750cc T140 Bonneville to Racing Spares' Les Harris. After considerable preparation, production began in 1985 at Newton Abbot, Devon, but, despite a motorcycle that was vastly improved in detail and quality control, the firm was allowed to continue only until March 1988, to make way for Bloor's new machines.

650cc Triumph 6/1 (ohv twin) 1935

Triumph Tiger 100 (ohv twin) 1939

497cc Triumph Grand Prix (ohv twin) 1947

At a purpose-built factory in Hinckley, he invested millions in the design, tooling, testing and manufacture of a new generation of Triumph motorcycles. These were revealed at the Cologne Show at the end of 1990 under the names Daytona, Trophy and Trident, names borrowed from Triumph's history, but both the new factory and the technology were otherwise thoroughly modern.

The new models were powered by 750cc and 900cc triples, plus 1000cc and 1200cc fours, although the engine range was of a modular design, sharing the majority of components to allow more economical production. The bikes also shared many other components, including the frames and most other chassis parts plus fuel tanks and some other bodywork. The technology, although reasonably modern, was still conservative compared with the latest sports bikes from Japan, but it allowed Triumph to re-establish itself as a serious mass producer of modern motorcycles with acceptable reliability and build quality.

As sales grew, so Triumph produced machines with an increasing number of unique parts and features, the 885cc Tiger trail bike of late 1992 for example being the first Hinckley Triumph to feature its own individual fuel tank (the first plastic one allowed in the UK, after a change in the law brought about by pressure from Triumph). The less successful modular engines were quickly dropped, notably the 1000cc Daytona unsuccessfully marketed as a sports bike, and work began on all-new engines. The first of these powered the Daytona T595 of 1997, an entirely new supersports machine designed to take on Honda's definitive Fireblade directly, a job it did reasonably convincingly, despite a well-publicised factory recall to replace troublesome early versions of its unique tubular aluminum trellis frame.

Triumph 3T (ohv twin) 1947

200cc Triumph Tiger Cub (ohv single) 1957

Other Triumphs followed the 1990s trend for retro machines, having the advantage of being able to draw more authentically from Triumph's own history, starting with the three-cylinder Thunderbird.

Other notable Hinckley Triumphs have included the streetfighter-styled Speed Triple T509, launched with the T595 Daytona and sharing many chassis components, and in 1999 the sports tourer Sprint ST, acclaimed as possibly the best machine in a highly competitive class (which includes Honda's definitive VFR750/800).

Triumph's technological capability has escalated rapidly, and with its growth has given it the confidence to take on the Japanese in other fiercely fought-out classes - a four-cylinder 600cc sports bike is slated for appearance at the end of 1999.

The company has grown from a production rate of about 5000 machines annually in 1993 to 15,000 in 1999, close to the capacity of the current factory. A second factory next to the current one is due to come on line in 2002, and it will approximately double this.

Triumph's initial foray into the American market was not a success in 1995, and exports to the important German market were also slow initially, both due to marketing reasons rather than any particular deficiencies in the bikes. Triumph is now overcoming both, and the company exports to more than 30 countries worldwide.

Its revival has been sustained and the prospects are looking particularly bright.

740cc Triumph Trident T150 (ohv three-cylinder) 1969

646cc Triumph T120 Bonneville (ohv twin) 1968

740cc Triumph X75 Hurricane (ohv three-cylinder) 1971

740cc Triumph T160 Trident (ohv three-cylinder) 1975

746cc Triumph T140V Bonneville (ohv twin) 1976

740cc Triumph Trident racer 'Slippery Sam' 1970

998cc Triumph Daytona 1000 (dohc liquid-cooled four-cylinder) 1994

885cc Triumph Sprint (dohc triple liquid-cooled) 1994

885cc Triumph Tiger (dohc three-cylinder liquid-cooled fuel injection) 1999

885cc Triumph Tiger (dohc triple liquid-cooled) 1994

995cc Triumph Sprint ST (dohc triple liquid-cooled fuel injection) 1999

885cc Triumph Thunderbird Sport (dohc triple liquid-cooled) 1998

995cc Triumph T595 Daytona (dohc triple liquid-cooled fuel injection) 1997

199cc TMZ 5.952 (two-stroke single) 1997

TRIBUNE • America 1903–WW1

As far as we know these machines had Aster and later Thor engines.

TRIPLE-H • England 1921–1923

The name came from the three founders of this make: Hobbis, Hobbis and Horrell. The machine was a simple 246cc two-stroke with a John Morris engine.

TRIPLETTE • England 1923–1925

Made at a low price, the Triplette was a simple machine with a 147cc Villiers motor.

TRIPOL • Czechoslovakia 1925–1926

Bicycle factory which built 246cc two-stroke Villiers-engined machines in limited numbers.

TRITON • c1960–

Not a marque in its own right, but certainly deserving of inclusion here as this was a highly popular home-built café racer creation using Triumph's parallel twin engines in the excellent handling Norton Featherbed frame. Many thousands were built, the majority by enthusiasts at home. The machine came to epitomise the 1960s motorcycling era.

TRIUMPH • America 1912

There was a small branch Triumph factory at Detroit, where machines with parts from the 548cc sv single were built. After WW2, Triumph had headquarters at Baltimore and Pasadena.

TRIUMPH • England 1902–

See panel

TROBIKE • England 1960–1963

British mini-bike built by Trojan of Croydon using American Clinton engines.

TROLL • East Germany 1964–1990

Boxy 143cc two-stroke scooter.

TROPFEN • Germany 1923–1924

An airship firm which built very unorthodox 248cc and 308cc two-stroke motorcycles. Everything—engine, frame, wheels and all—was enclosed in an airship-shaped shell. The whole thing was so unusual that hardly anybody bought it.

TRUMP (TRUMP-JAP) • England 1906–1923

Two leading racing men, F. A. McNab and Colonel Stewart, were among the owners of this ambitious factory, which built a couple of very fast racing machines. Together with Mrs. Stewart—who eventually became the famous Gwenda Hawkes of racing car fame—they broke many records. Trump motorcycles were not only built with 248cc to 996cc JAP engines, but also with 269cc Peco two-strokes and the big 996cc V-twin ohv engine made by British Anzani.

TRUSTY • Germany 1926–1930

Moderate production of lightweights at its Reichenberg premises with 147cc–172cc Villiers two-stroke engines.

TSUBASA • Japan 1950s

Built a range of 246cc machines with its own ohv engines.

TUK • Germany 1921–1922

Narrow-angle 397cc sv V-twins with comparatively short and high single-loop frames, built by a small company.

TULAMASHZAVOD (TMZ) • Russia 1957–

The company began in 1879 as an iron foundry in Tula, south of Moscow, and subsequently produced many goods. In 1957 it produced its first two-wheeler (by which time the company name had become Tulamashzavod), the T-200 which was a copy of the Goggo Isaria scooter using TMZ's own 197cc two-stroke engine. Various models were developed from this, and in 1985 the company started a range of all-terrain and sport motorcycles, including Franco Morini powered mini-motorcycles with balloon-type tyres designed for export.

TURKHEIMER • Italy 1902–1905

The designer, a leading Milan-based motorcycle importer who imported the first Hildebrand & Wolfmüller motorcycles into Italy in 1896, fitted 1.25hp engines into his own machines.

TWM • Italy 1979–

This producer concentrates on competition machines, especially trials and motocross versions with 123cc, 173cc and 244cc engines.

TX • Germany 1924–1926

One of the most unorthodox machines ever built, the TX had a tube of wide diameter which acted as a tank and replaced the steering head too. The tank cap was in front of the steering and the front forks, which used a leaf spring, were made from pressed steel. The 132cc and 174cc two-stroke Bekamo-licensed engines had forced induction by using a second piston as a pump in the bottom of the crankcase. A few 248cc ohc racing machines with Roconova engines were also built. Designer was Kurt Pohle.

TYLER • England 1913–1923

Built lightweight motorcycles with 198cc Precision, 269cc Villiers and also with own 269cc two-stroke engines.

TYPHOON • Sweden 1949–1951

Designed by the famous Folke Mannerstedt, this machine was a 198cc two-stroke of advanced design.

TYPHOON • The Netherlands 1955–early 1960s

Well-known manufacturer of mofas, mopeds etc. with 49cc two-stroke engines.

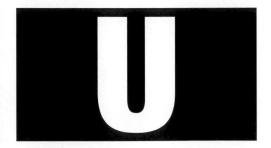

U

UDE • Germany 1924–1925

A small producer of a 249cc two-stroke machine with a deflector-type three-port engine.

ULTIMA • France 1908–1958

Built a range of machines with Zurcher, Aubier-Dunne, JAP and other engines. Among them were 248cc and 348cc single-cylinder and 498cc V-twin sv machines. After WW2, the factory concentrated on two-strokes up to 198cc, among which was a very successful 124cc model with a horizontal cylinder. Ultima built new 498cc twin-cylinder dohc racing machines with horizontally-mounted cylinders in 1951, but the promising design was never fully developed.

UNIBUS • England 1920–1922

The Boultbee-designed Unibus was one of the best scooters made immediately after WW1. It had a 269cc two-stroke engine and 16 inch x 2·5 inch tyres. With the exception of the handlebar, everything was fully enclosed. The pressed steel chassis was made on car lines and leaf suspension was used.

UNION • Sweden 1943–1952

Sporting single-cylinder machines with 348cc and 498cc JAP ohv engines.

UNIVERSAL • Switzerland 1928–1964

Famous factory which produced Helvetia motorcycles with 170cc PA engines before it built Universal machines. These had a variety of proprietary engines including JAP, Python, Anzani, Ilo and others with capacities up to 998cc. Among them were racing versions with big V-twin JAP ohv engines of 55bhp and Python-engined 248cc racing machines. Universal's own 676cc and 990cc sv V-twin engines were made for the Swiss Army. The outstanding model after the war was a 578cc flat-twin with the ohv engine transverse-mounted and with shaft drive to the rear wheel. The engine was of Universal's own design and manufacture. The same was true of a 248cc ohv single, which came on the market in 1956. Like the bigger twin, it too had a unit-design engine and shaft drive. A license was sold to the German Rabeneick factory, but this factory never went into quantity production. Famous riders such as Kirsch, Franconi, Alfter, Bianchi, and H. Taveri raced the machines between the wars.

UNIVERSELLE (UNIVERSAL) • Germany 1925–1929

Designed by Erich Landgrebe and made by a cigarette machine factory, the little ioe four-stroke machines originally had 183cc unit-design engines with big outside fly-wheels. Improved versions with 197cc and 247cc followed. Universelle built also delivery three-wheelers.

URAL • Russia 1979–

This is the export version of the 650cc Dnepr transverse-mounted ohv flat-twin sidecar machine. Basically a BMW-like design, the M66 Ural develops 32bhp at 4500rpm.

URANIA • Germany 1934–1939

Assembled 98cc and 123cc two-stroke machines with Sachs and Ilo engines.

UT • Germany 1922–1959

Built on English lines, UT motorcycles were assembled machines with Bekamo, Blackburne, JAP, Küchen and Bark engines in pre-war days, while Sachs and Ilo engines played the most important part after 1945. The first 247cc two-strokes built in the mid-1920s had flat single-cylinder engines and triangular frames; the biggest models had 598cc single-cylinder JAP and Blackburne ohv engines. The two-strokes which were built after the war had 122cc, 173cc, 197cc and 244cc engines. The last one was a vertical twin with an Ilo engine. Some 246cc twins with the Küchen-designed Opti ohc engine were also built. The factory had a successful racing department in the 1920s with Frenzen, Kohfink, Blind and other good riders.

UTILIA • France 1929–1936

Was a well-known producer of two-strokes from 98cc to 498cc and of sv and ohv machines with JAP, LMP and Chaise engines. The two-stroke engines came from the Sachs, Duten and Train factories; some were also built by Utilia.

678cc Universal (ohv transverse flat twin, shaft drive) 1955

244cc Universal (two-stroke twin Ilo) 1952

996cc Universal (ohv V-twin JAP) 1937

VAGA • Italy 1925–1935

Produced 124cc two-strokes, afterwards 174cc machines with JAP and Blackburne sv and ohv as well as CF ohc engines. The last models, 348cc ohv versions, had Sturmey-Archer engines.

VAL • England 1913–1914

Sidecar producer which built JAP-engined 488cc sv machines in limited quantities.

VALENTI • Italy 1979–

A company making motocross and enduro models, with 125cc and 250cc proprietary two-stroke engines.

VALIANT • America late 1960s

Produced Simplex lightweight machines with modified 124cc Clinton lawn-mower engines.

VALMOBILE • France 1954

Small folding scooter by Martin Moulet and licensed for production in England, the USA and Japan.

VAN VEEN • Germany 1978–1981

The Dutch Van Veen OCR1000, built in a German factory, was a 498cc 100bhp Wankel-engined, water/oil-cooled luxury motorcycle, built with the French-licenced motor in limited numbers. Van Veen also built the successful 49cc Kreidler-Van Veen racing machines.

VAP • France early 1950s to early 1960s

VAP was a mass-producer of 49cc mopeds, mofas etc. and was closely connected with Alcyon, Rhonson, Lucer and other factories.

VAREL • Germany 1952–1953

Mopeds and mini-scooters with own 43cc engines and scooters with 99cc Mota two-stroke engines.

VASCO • England 1921–1923

Only a single model was made by this small factory. It had 261cc Orbit engines; when Orbit went out of business, Vasco switched over to 349cc Broler engines. Both were single-cylinder two-strokes.

VASSENA • Italy 1926–1929

Designed by Pietro Vassena, these machines had 124cc two-stroke engines with a horizontal cylinder.

VELOCETTE • England 1904–1968

Two brothers, Percy and Eugene Goodman made several earlier forays into motorcycle design and construction before Velocette was established, with Percy Goodman's neat and advanced 206cc two-stroke of 1913. Sales were brisk, and even better post war with 220cc, followed by 250cc, models. Velocette two-strokes did well in trials, speed hill climbs and even the TT. However, the firm's fortunes were really established by Percy Goodman's 350cc ohc model K of 1925. A poor showing in that year's TT led to a redesigned engine and a win by Alex Bennett in 1926. It was the first of six victories, and guaranteed a volume of orders that forced a move into larger premises. Harold Willis joined the company in 1927 as rider and development engineer, contributing the positive stop foot change and experimenting with rear springing and supercharging. Before his untimely death in 1939, he designed the remarkable blown 'Roarer' twin.

Riders of KTT production racers won five Manx Grands Prix between 1929 and 1938 and in 1930 filled the first six places! The 1939 KTT was given swinging arm rear suspension, as used on the factory bikes since 1936. Stanley Woods won the 1938 and 1939 Junior TTs and was second in the 1937 and 1938 Senior races.

Road-going KTS and KSS ohc models sold well in the 1930s, and there was a 250cc two-stroke in the range until 1939. Popular, too, were the pushrod high camshaft series, the 250cc MOV and 350cc MAC of 1933 and the 500cc MSS of 1935.

Post-war, Velocette won the 1949 and 1950 350cc world championships, made a few VIII KTTs and sold the KSS until 1947. Its main gamble, however, was on the remarkable LE model, with its water-cooled transverse horizontally-opposed twin-cylinder 150cc (later 192cc) side-valve engine, shaft drive and wonderfully clean pressed steel chassis-cum-bodywork. Unfortunately, it never sold in large enough numbers, although it was popular with the police, being superbly reliable and so silent as to be ideal for patrol duties. Variants were the fibre glass-bodied Vogue and the 200cc ohv air-cooled Valiant, a sporting model with a conventional tubular frame, but these too were badly received. These disappointments stimulated development of the pushrod models, which, much modernised, became the 350cc Viper and 500cc Venom, also sold as Clubman production racing versions.

In 1961 a Venom Clubman, with an Avon fairing and megaphone exhaust but otherwise standard, averaged 100.05mph at the Montlhery track in France for 24 hours. The attempt was sponsored by the French Velocette importer and involved four French and four British riders. Viper and Venom Clubman racers did very well in production racing in the 1950s and 1960s, selling to the sort of rider who for a couple of generations had bought the KTS model for the road. The ultimate development was the Thruxton Velocette Venom of 1964, equally at home on road or race-track, and of stunning appearance and performance. But several bad decisions, including the manufacture of a truly awful scooter with a flat twin two-stroke engine and shaft drive, weakened the fragile company and the relatively small sales of the Thruxton could not stave off the inevitable liquidation in 1968.

Velocette advertising poster

249cc Velocette (two-stroke) 1924

349cc Velocette MAC (ohc) 1935

*For learner
and expert*

348cc Velocette KTT racer (ohc single) 1929

348cc Velocette KTS (ohc single) 1936

348cc Velocette Mk 8 KTT racer (ohc) 1950

149cc Velocette LE (sv water-cooled transverse flat-twin) 1948

VESPA • Italy 1946–

Designed by aircraft engineer Corradino d'Ascanio to be built from a pressed steel monocoque, the Vespa has survived for more than 50 years. The Vespa design has been produced in 13 countries around the world in both licensed and unlicensed forms, with many variants from 50cc to 198cc, famous for using a three- or four-speed twistgrip gearchange.

In 1996 producer of the Vespa, Piaggio, celebrated the Vespa's 50th birthday with the release of two new monocoque Vespas. The 125cc ET4 was the first variomatic transmission four-stroke Vespa, while the 50cc two-stroke ET2 is Piaggio's first production machine with a form of fuel injection.

Interesting Vespa achievements: 1951 Vespa 125cc record breaker hits 114mph on the flying kilometre. Factory-built high performance Vespas win nine gold medals at the Italian International Six Days road trial in 1951. Two PX Vespas complete the Paris-Dakar rally route in 1980. Vespas ridden on many round-the-world tours including one by Australian Geoff Dean, and during the 1990s Italian Giorgio Bettinelli.

The original two-stroke, hand gearchange Vespa continues to be produced in 1999 alongside the modern ET models in 125cc and 200cc form.

(See also the Piaggio entry)

198cc Vespa PX200 (two-stroke single) 1999

VATERLAND • Germany 1933–1939

A bicycle factory which built lightweight machines with 98cc and 120cc Sachs engines and closed just before the outbreak of war.

VECCHIETTI • Italy 1954–1957

Moped producer which used 49cc two-stroke engines made by Victoria in Germany.

VELAMOS • Czechoslovakia 1927–1930

Like the Sirocco, the Velamos was made by Gustav Heinz. While the Sirocco had Villiers engines, the Velamos had its own two-stroke engines with 246cc, 346cc and 496cc. All were singles with three ports and deflector-type pistons. In races they were ridden by Kliwar, Zwesper and Heinz. Velamos still exists as a nationalised bicycle factory.

VELOCETTE • England 1904–1968

See panel

VELOSTYLE • France 1949

Scooterette powered by 49cc VAP engine and built by Mochet. Not successful.

VELOX • Czechoslovakia 1923–1926

Designed by racing motorcyclist Hynek Vohanka, Velox lightweights had 147cc Villiers and afterwards 123cc and 174cc Bekamo two-stroke engines.

VELOSOLEX • France 1945–

A 50cc moped with friction drive to the front wheel. Extremely large production numbers.

VENUS • England 1920–1922

Only a single model with the 318cc Dalm engine was produced.

VENUS • Germany 1952–1955

Scooter with 98cc, 147cc and 174cc Sachs engines, made by a small factory.

VERGA • Italy 1951–1954

Small two-strokes with 73cc and frames with swinging arm rear suspension.

VERLOR • France 1930–1938

Aubier-Dunne and Stainless-engined 98cc and 124cc two-stroke machines.

VICTORIA • Germany 1899–1966

Founded in 1886 by Max Frankenburger and Max Ottenstein as a bicycle factory, Victoria built its first motorcycles 13 years later and fitted Zedel and Fafnir engines into its own frames. After WW1, production concentrated on 493cc machines with two horizontally opposed cylinders in the popular sv proprietary engine built by BMW. When the Munich factory decided to produce complete motorcycles, Victoria of Nuremberg engaged the former BMW designer Martin Stolle, who designed new ohv engines which were built for Victoria at the Sedlbauer factory at Munich. After a while Victoria bought the engine factory and continued building ohv 498cc and afterwards 598cc ohv flat-twins. Successor to Stolle after 1924 was Gustav Steinlein, who designed in 1925 the first supercharged racing machines with 498cc flat twin engines in Germany, which in 1926 broke the German speed record with nearly 104mph. New single-cylinder models were introduced in 1928. The engines were of Sturmey-Archer manufacture and were of 198cc to 499cc; a 348cc ohv version was built by Horex (Columbus) under Sturmey-Archer license for Victoria. Racing versions of this and 499cc machines as well as 598cc flat twins were officially raced by the works, which had excellent riders in Kurt Füglein, Othmar Mühlbacher, Josef Möritz, Adolf Brudes, Hans Escoffier, Albert Richter, Josef Alt, H. P. Müller, Karl Bodmer, Eugen Grohmann, Georg Dotterweich and others. Among models built during the 1930s were two-strokes from 98cc to 198cc and new Stolle-designed 497cc vertical ioe and ohv twins with triangular pressed steel frames and completely enclosed unit-design engines. Richard Küchen and Albert Roder were Victoria designers in the 1930s. After 1945 production concentrated first on two-strokes from 38cc - a bicycle attachment - to 248cc. The first new four stroke came into production in 1953. Also designed by Küchen, it had a transverse-mounted 348cc ohv V-twin unit-design engine with shaft drive to the rear wheel, telescopic forks and plunger-type rear suspension. New also were scooters, 38cc and 48cc mopeds, and the 198cc Swing, a very modern motorcycle with the engine and rear wheel on a swinging arm. Designed by Norbert Riedel, it was costly to produce. The last new model had a 173cc ohv engine, made by Parilla in Italy. Victoria supplied to the Italians in exchange small 49cc two-stroke moped motors. Soon afterwards the Zweirad-Union was founded and Victoria became part of it. While motorcycle manufacture stopped immediately, production of mopeds etc. under the Victoria name continued for some time.

4½hp Victoria (ioe Fafnir) 1904

493cc Victoria (sv flat twin BMW) 1920

496cc Victoria (ohv flat twin) 1923

496cc Victoria KR9 (ohv twin-cylinder) 1937

346cc Victoria (ohv transverse V-twin, shaft-drive) 1955

VINCENT (VINCENT-HRD) • England
1928–1956

In 1928 Philip Vincent bought the manufacturing rights of HRD, the make founded in 1924 by Howard R. Davies, the well-known racing motorcyclist. Vincent continued using 346cc, 498cc and 598cc sv and ohv JAP engines, but equipped the new models with a rear suspension of his own design. Entirely new 497cc high-camshaft ohv engines of his own design and manufacture came into production in 1935 and machines with this engine were priced from £79.10s. to £98 for the TT Replica racing model. Late in 1936 appeared the first 998cc Vincent with its V-twin high-camshaft engine, rear-wheel springing and twin brakes in each wheel. The cylinders were set at 47 degrees and were nearly identical to those used on the 497cc Meteor single. After the war, Vincent concentrated on improved versions of this big twin such as the Black Knight, the Black Prince and the very fast Black Lightning, a racing version of the 84mm bore x 90mm stroke 100bhp engine, which broke many speed records in the hands of George Brown, Roland Free, René Milhoux and others. Free reached 156.71mph with his special machine, running on alcohol fuel. In 1950 Vincent also brought back 499cc singles, effectively the twins without the rear cylinder. A racing version, the Grey Flash, was built but did not win many road races. John Surtees rode them successfully. The 998cc twins won many races, including the Clubmans TT and among the riders were Phil Heath, Dennis Lashmar, Cliff Horn, Jock Daniels, Joe Davis and others. The last works riders competed in 1937 races. Phil Vincent's big twins had gained a world-wide reputation and there were times when demand was much bigger than supply. But they were expensive to produce and when motorcycle sales went down in the late 1950s the situation became very difficult. Despite the manufacture of the Firefly bicycle engine and co-operation with NSU of Germany, Vincent closed in 1956.

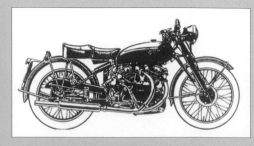

996cc Vincent Rapide (ohv V-twin) 1954

996cc Vincent Black Knight (ohv V-twin) 1955

996cc Vincent Black Lightning (ohv V-twin) 1956

998cc Vincent Series C Rapide (ohv V-twin) 1949

2³⁄₄hp Vindec-Special (sv FN) 1903

VERNET • Switzerland c1908–1912

V-twin Moto-Rêve-engined lightweight built in Grenoble by A. Vernet.

VEROS • Italy 1922–1924

Blackburne-engined 346cc sv and ohv machines built by Verus in England were renamed Veros when exported to racing motorcyclist Oreste Garanzini, who represented this make in Italy. One of the design differences was the fully enclosed rear chain on the Veros sv models.

346cc Veros (sv Blackburne engine) 1925

VERUS • England 1919–1925

Made by Wisemann in Birmingham, Verus's motorcycles had its own 211cc and 269cc two-stroke engines and also 246cc to 996cc four-strokes made by Blackburne and JAP. Wisemann built also Sirrah and Weaver motorcycles.

VESPA • Italy 1946–

See panel

VESUV • Germany 1924–1926

A small make. Had an open frame and its own 246cc two-stroke engine.

VIATKA • Russia 1958–

Leading scooter in the USSR. The engine is a 148cc two-stroke.

VIBERTI • Italy 1955–late 1960s

Built Victoria-engined 47cc mofas, mopeds and similar machines. Motorcycles made by this factory had 123cc ohv engines.

VICTA • England 1912–1913

Built 499cc single-cylinder motorcycles with Precision proprietary engines.

VICTOR • Austalia 1903

Minerva-powered belt-driven motorcycle built in limited numbers at Feeling, South Australia.

VICTORIA • Scotland 1902–1926

The Victoria motorcycle for many years was Scotland's leading make, being built at Glasgow (Dennistoun) and never in England. The whole design and most of the components were typically English though. Villiers, JAP, Blackburne and Coventry-Victor engines of 127cc to 688cc were mounted in Scottish frames, which were of excellent quality. There was no connection between this factory and the German-built motorcycles of the same name.

VICTORIA • Germany 1899–1966

See panel

VINCENT (VINCENT-HRD) • England 1928–1956

See panel

VINCO • England 1903–1905

Small firm which built motorcycles with 211cc Minerva engines.

VINDEC • England 1902–1929

These machines were made by Brown Bros. Ltd., a well-known supplier of parts and accessories. The range included 172cc and 224cc two-strokes and 490cc JAP-engined sv machines; the last model built had the 293cc JAP sv engine.

VINDEC-SPECIAL (VS) • England 1903–1914

A machine built for the English market by Allright of Cologne in Germany and identical to Allright models of the time. The South British Trading Co. in London was the importer.

Most versions had V-twin engines, made by FN, Minerva, Fafnir etc. There were Truffault-designed swinging arm front forks from 1905 onwards. After 1909 the machines were renamed VS to avoid confusion with the Brown brothers' Vindec motorcycles.

VIPER • England 1919–1922

Limited production of machines with 293cc sv JAP engines in open frames.

VIRATELLE • France 1907–1924

Built many models with proprietary engines, some of them unusual. The last one was a 686cc V-twin sv machine with a very long wheelbase.

VIS • Germany 1923–1925

Very interesting design. There was the comparatively orthodox 249cc two-stroke Vis-Simplex single with a forward inclined engine, but there was also the Vis-Duplex with a 496cc opposed twin-cylinder two-stroke engine, built in line with the duplex cradle frame. This engine suffered from overheating of the rear cylinder and was built in limited numbers only.

VITTORIA • Italy 1931–1972

Carnielli's machines had 98cc Sachs, 173cc and 248cc JAP, 346cc and 496cc Küchen and 499cc four-valve Python ohv engines. Most models built since the war - including delivery three-wheelers - had two-stroke engines up to 98cc.

VJATKA • Russia 1958–1975

Once the USSR's leading scooter, a 148cc two-stroke which was an unashamed, unlicensed copy of the Vespa.

VOLLBLUT • Germany 1925–1927

Assembler of sporting motorcycles with 248cc and 348cc ohv Blackburne engines.

VOLUGRAFO • Italy 1940–1945

Produced the first Italian production scooter of the modern type, called the Aermoto. It was built in Turin using 98cc Sachs engines. Military versions had a pair of front tyres.

VOMO • Germany 1922–1931

Moped-like machines with 1hp and 1.75hp two-stroke engines.

VORAN • Germany 1921–1924

Yet another small motorcycle, a typical lightweight with a 143cc two-stroke deflector-type three-port motor.

VOSKHOD • Russia late 1940s–

These are mass-produced Russian 174cc two-strokes. Now with 10·5bhp at 5500rpm, they are developments of old DKW and Jawa designs, and crude and basic compared with modern machines.

174cc Voskhod (two-stroke) 1981

1000cc Voxan Roadster (dohc V-twin) 1999

VOXAN • France 1999–

Formed in 1995 by Jacques Gardette to produce entirely French superbikes. In 1997 the first attractive and originally styled prototypes were displayed at the Paris motorcycle show, and by 1999 were available for sale in France. The first two models are the Café Racer and Roadster, each with 1000cc, liquid-cooled, 72 degree V-twin engines producing 120bhp and 108bhp respectively (but restricted to 100bhp for the French market). Exports are planned in the next few years.

VULCAAN • The Netherlands 1911–1927

Was closely connected with Zedel, the proprietary engine factory. Built 264cc and 299cc sv singles and also a range of sv V-twins, of which some were Vulcaan's own power units, probably built with some Zedel parts.

VULCAN • Czechoslovakia 1904–1924

See also Perun motorcycles, built by Zdarsky. The successor Ruzicka concentrated on the manufacture of spare parts after WW1.

VULCAN • England 1922–1924

Like other English firms, this one concentrated on 248cc two-strokes and on 293cc sv machines with JAP engines.

1000cc Voxan Café Racer (dohc V-twin) 1999

WACKWITZ • Germany 1920–1922

These 108cc engines were bicycle attachments or complete with strengthened bicycle frames.

WADDINGTON • England 1902–1906

Single-cylinder motorcycles with a variety of engines which included Minerva and MMC.

WADDON-EHRLICH • England 1981–1983

Built Rotax-engined racing two-strokes, on one of which Irishman Con Law won the 1982 250cc TT at over 105mph. However, Dr Erhlich left later that year to make his own 250cc and 350cc Rotax-engined EMC racing machines.

248cc Waddon-Ehrlich (two-stroke Rotax) 1981

WAG • England 1924–1925

One of the very few makes which produced 496cc V-twin machines with two-stroke engines. The production was limited.

WAGNER • Czechoslovakia 1930–1935

Offered motorcycles from 98cc to 499cc with two-stroke as well as sv, ohv and ohc engines.

WAGNER • America 1901–1914

One of the pioneers of the American motorcycle industry. This firm built 1·5hp, 2hp and 2·5hp machines equipped with its own and Thor engines.

WAKEFIELD • England c1902

One of the factories fitting Minerva and MMC engines above the pedalling gear of bicycles.

WALBA • Germany 1949–1952

Ilo-engined scooters from 98cc to 173cc, designed by W. Baibaschewski.

346cc Wallis (ohv Blackburne) 1926

WALLIS • England 1925–1926

Technically interesting 348cc and 498cc machines with hub-centre steering, similar to the Ner-a-car. The engines used were mainly JAP ohv units. Wallis, a superb technician, was also the designer of Comerford-Wallis speedway frames.

WALMET • Germany 1924–1926

Limited production of 246cc two-strokes with its own engines and 346cc models with Kühne ohv power units.

WALTER • Germany 1903–1942

Assembler whose first machines had Fafnir engines. From the 1920s to the mid-1930s Villiers two-strokes of 172cc to 347cc were fitted into excellent frames of modern design. After 1935 production concentrated on mopeds with 98cc Sachs and Ilo engines.

WALTER • Czechoslovakia 1923–1926

The factory, still headed by Josef Walter, designed in 1917 a 746cc flat twin machine. It never went into production when Josef Zubatý, the designer, left. The Itar factory took over manufacture after the war in 1922, when Walter director Plocek had a new 746cc on the drawing board.

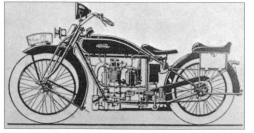

746cc Walter (ohv V-twin) 1923 (Czechoslovakia)

This was a transverse-mounted ohv V-twin machine and was built - like the Itar - mainly for the Czech army. The factory, now also building cars and aircraft engines, also produced a few enlarged 998cc racing machines, which proved very fast. Demand for cars and aircraft engines increased, and that was the end of the motorcycle manufacture at the Jinonice Walter factory. Successful Walter riders: Vasek Liska, Bohumil Turek, Stanislav Chaloupka, Jaroslav Knapp.

WALTER • Czechoslovakia 1900–1949

Josef Walter built first-class single-cylinder and V-twin motorcycles with his own engines, afterwards also three-wheelers with modified motorcycle power units. In 1922 he left the Walter works and founded a new Walter factory for the manufacture of gears, sprockets etc. There he designed - in conjunction with his sons Jaroslav and Jan

4½hp Walter B (sv V-twin) 1906 (Czechoslovakia)

- new 496cc sv singles in 1926. In 1938 Jaroslav Walter created superb 248cc ohv racing engines and soon afterwards an even better ohc version, which after the war gained many racing successes on road and track. In 1947 a new 348cc ohc racing single was added which - together with the 248cc ohc engine - was taken over in 1949 by the big CZ factory, when Jaroslav Walter joined the Strakonice works. Successful Walter riders: Vaclav Hovorka, Jan Lucak, Vojta Divis, Jan Horak, Vaclav Stanislav, Eman Hajek, Jarda Kost, Peter Kopal, Lada Steiner and others.

WANDERER • Germany 1902–1929

Was a well-known manufacturer of high-class motorcycles. Built 327cc and 387cc singles and 408cc and 616cc V-twins with its own sv engines. Many of them were used by the Germans during WW1. After the war, Wanderer built

4½hp Wanderer (sv V-twin) 1923

a nice 184cc ohv single with a horizontal cylinder and a range of 708cc and 749cc ohv V-twins with unit-design engines, some with eight valves. A new 498cc ohv single with unit-design engine, shaft drive and pressed steel frame, designed by Alexander Novikoff, was built in 1927. In 1929 this design, complete with all drawings and production equipment, was sold to Jawa at Prague, then a new company. That was practically the end of Wanderer motorcycle production, although it signed an agreement with NSU and produced during the 1930s motorised bicycles. Wanderer was a successful make in races during the 1920s. The top riders were Schuster, Urban, Kohlrausch, Ebert.

WARATAH • Australia 1930s–1950s

Popular Villiers-powered lightweights assembled by the Williams Brothers of Sydney who had earlier built Carbine motorcycles.

WARD • England 1915–1916

Two strokes with 298cc engines. The war prevented production on a bigger scale.

WARDILL • England 1924–1926

Unorthodox two-stroke machines with a patented 346cc engine, which was not fully developed when it was put on the market.

WARRIOR • England 1921–1923

Concentrated on one model with the 247cc Villiers engine.

WASP • England 1968–

Long established as chassis and complete motorcycle builder specifically for off-road competition. Wasp has mostly used modified bought-in engines but also produced its own one litre, twin-cylinder engine for sidecar motocross use in 1983.

WASSELL • England 1970–1975

Built excellent 123cc trials and motocross machines with German Sachs two-stroke engines; the untimely death of W. E. Wassell led to the demise of motorcycle production by this well-known accessories factory.

WATNEY • England 1922–1923

Assembler which fitted 269cc Villiers, 293cc sv JAP and 346cc sv Blackburne engines.

WATT • Latvia 1917

Direct belt-driven single-cylinder machines powered by Swiss-made Motosacoche engines.

WAVERLEY • America 1911–1913

Perry Mack of the Waverley Mfg. Co., Jefferson, Wisconsin, built 4hp machines which were later sold under the PEM and Jefferson IV labels.

WAVERLEY • England 1921–1923

Assembler whose Harry Cox-designed motorcycles had 269cc Peco two-strokes and 346cc and 496cc Blackburne sv engines.

WD • England 1911–1913

Modern 496cc single-cylinder machines with own ioe power units.

WEARWELL • England 1901–c1906

One of the first factories producing motorcycles in England. The company also built Wolfruna and Wolf machines as well as frames for other factories and assemblers. The first engines used for Wearwell machines produced 2·5hp and 3·25hp and were a product of the Stevens brothers.

WEATHERELL • England 1922–1923

Concentrated on sporting Blackburne engined 349cc ohv machines, but also supplied 248cc versions and a machine with an ohv 676cc V-twin Blackburne engine.

WEAVER • England 1922–1925

The original model had a 142cc ohv single-cylinder engine, other versions used 147cc Villiers and AZA two-stroke engines.

WEBER-MAG • Germany 1926–1927

Assembled motorcycles with MAG engines of 346cc, 498cc and 746cc. All had ioe engines.

WEBER & REICHMANN • Czechoslovakia 1923–1926

Produced 142cc and 172cc machines with pressed steel frames under DKW license. The engines were supplied directly by DKW.

WECOOB • Germany 1925–1930

Built a variety of motorcycles with 142cc Rinne two-stroke engines, 172cc to 347cc Villiers motors and also 348cc to 996cc JAP power units. Despite the large number of models, production was small.

WEE McGREGOR • England 1922–1925

Made at Coventry Bicycles Ltd. by former Hobart employees, this was a 170cc two-stroke machine, with the engine capacity later increased to 202cc.

WEGRO • Germany 1922–1923

Very unorthodox - and not very good - Passow-designed 452cc vertical two-stroke twin with a very long wheelbase and disk wheels.

WEISS • Germany 1925–1928

Munich-built 198cc unit-design ohv machines with belt-drive to the rear wheel and two-speed gearboxes.

346cc Wels (ohv Kühne) 1925

WELA • Germany 1925–1927

Assembled 348cc single with the Gnädig-designed Kühne ohv engine.

WELLER • England 1902–1905

Pioneer factory, which also produced cars. The motorcycles used its own 1·75hp and 2·25hp singles.

WELS • Germany 1925–1926

These machines had a BMW-like frame with 348cc Kühne ohv and 490cc JAP ohv engines fitted.

WELT-RAD • Germany 1901–1907

A bicycle factory and motorcycle pioneer which fitted its own 3·5hp single-cylinder and 6hp V-twin engines.

WERBI • Germany c1925

Lightweight machines, weighing only 85kg.

WERNER • France 1897–1908

The Werner brothers, Russians living in Paris, were innovative motorcycling pioneers. Their 1897 Motocyclette, with its engine over the front wheel, was the first popular motorcycle to be produced. In 1901, they moved the engine ahead of the pedalling gear, such a machine won the Paris-Vienna race of 1901. In 1904 there was a side-by-side vertical twin. The company was still thriving when first one and then the other brother died and, without their enterprise, the company soon followed.

217cc Werner (sv) 1901

WERNER-MAG • Austria 1928–1930

Designed by Konstantin Leschan, Werner-MAG motorcycles used 498cc double-port single-cylinder ohv engines. 746cc and 996cc capacity had MAG ioe V-twins.

WERNO • Germany 1921–1924

The Werner Noel-designed ohv singles had its own 154cc and 197cc engines.

WESPE • Austria 1937–1938

Designed by Thos. G. Harbourn, who for many years imported English Triumph motorcycles into Austria, the 123cc Wespe had an unlucky life. Just when it started, Hitler entered Austria, and production came to an end.

WESTFALIA • Germany 1901–1906

Used Zedel, De Dion and Fafnir 1.75hp and 2.5hp engines.

WESTFIELD • England c1903

Assembler which fitted 2.75hp MMC power-units.

WESTOVIAN • England 1914–1916

Had a big model range with TDC, Villiers, Precision and JAP engines from 197cc to 498cc.

WFM • Poland 1947–

Well-known make which concentrated on the production of well-designed 123cc, 147cc and 173cc two-strokes.

W&G • England 1927–1928

A transverse-mounted 490cc two-stroke twin with the cylinders facing slightly forward, not unlike the big DKW twin of that period. But while the DKW was a success, the W&G soon disappeared.

WHEATCROFT • England 1924

Was the successor to the New Era and had 318cc Dalm two-stroke and 546cc Blackburne sv engines.

WHIPPET • England 1903–c1906

This factory had many patents for engines and motorcycles and produced 1.75hp, 2.25hp, 2.5hp and 3hp machines. Early models used Aster and FN engines.

WHIPPET • England 1920–1921

Scooter of advanced design with 180cc ohv engines and 16-inch wheels.

WHIPPET • England 1957–1959

Unusual lightweight which really was a combination scooter and moped. It had ohv engines of 49cc, 61cc and 64cc.

WHIRLWIND • England 1901–1903

Made by the Dorman Engineering Co., the factory which in 1925-1927 built Granville Bradshaw's 348cc 'oilboilers', ie oil-cooled ohv proprietary engines. Among earlier products was a 1.5hp bicycle engine and complete motorcycles with 2hp and 2.5hp.

WHITE & POPPE • England 1902–1922

Built V-twin motorcycles and in 1906 a 489cc vertical twin which was available with air- and water-cooling. The factory produced also proprietary engines for motorcycles and cars, which included at that time the 493cc Ariel engines and after 1918 a 347cc two-stroke.

996cc Werner-MAG (ioe V-twin MAG) 1928

2¾hp Whitley (ioe) 1903

173cc Wimmer (ohv water-cooled) 1925

247cc Wimmer (ohv) 1931

346cc Wimmer (ohv Model GS) 1936

WHITING • Australia c1915

V-four motorcycle.

WHITLEY • England 1902–c1906

Another manufacturer of proprietary engines, whose own motorcycles had 2.75hp and 3.5hp single-cylinder engines.

WHITWOOD • England 1934–1936

Offered with 248cc, 348cc and 490cc ohv JAP engines, the OEC-built Whitwood-Monocar was a motorcycle with a car-like body, not unlike the Mauser Einspurauto of ten years earlier. It was an unusual vehicle which did not find many customers.

WHIZZER • America 1947–1954

Moped-like means of transport, of quite unusual appearance. The engine was a 199cc sv unit.

WIGA • Germany 1928–1932

Made by a small factory, the Wiga was of good design and while production stopped in the early 1930s, there was a prototype of a new JAP-engined model with rear suspension made in 1938.

The range included Küchen and JAP-engined models of 198cc, 93cc, 348cc and 498cc. The ohc Küchen engines had three valves.

WIGAN-BARLOW • England 1921

Small production of motorcycles with 293cc sv JAP and 346cc Barr & Stroud sleeve-valve engines.

WIKRO • Germany 1924–1926

The first machines had 346cc Precision engines while newer versions were powered by 347cc and 497cc Blackburne sv engines.

WILBEE • England 1902–c1906

Advanced design with 2hp Minerva engines and good frames made from BSA parts.

WILHELMINA • The Netherlands 1903–1915

A motorcycle importer which built a range of machines in earlier years, but had the biggest output just before WW1 with a 2.5hp single-cylinder Precision-engined model that proved to be particularly popular.

WILIER • Italy 1962–c1970

Concentrated on 49cc mopeds and lightweight machines, but strong competition forced it out of business.

WILKIN • England 1919–1923

Was using 499cc sv Blackburne engines in spring frames, but had a small output only. A 346cc model with an identical frame was also built.

WILKINSON-ANTOINE • England 1903–1906

Built in England 2.25hp and 2.75hp machines with Belgian Antoine single-cylinder power-units.

844cc Wilkinson-TMC (ioe air-cooled four-cylinder) 1911

WILKINSON • England 1909–1916

The Wilkinson Sword Company made the luxurious 680cc air-cooled in-line four-cylinder TAC (Touring Autocycle), with separate gearbox and shaft drive, until 1911 and thereafter the 850cc (and later 1000cc) water-cooled TMC (Touring Motorcycle). Early in 1914, Wilkinson sold its motorcycling interests to the Ogston Motor Co, which continued to make an improved TMC until 1916. The engine was later used in a light car, the Ogston Deemster.

WILLIAMS • America 1912–1920

Unusual design with a rotating single-cylinder engine built into the rear wheel.

WILLIAMSON • England 1912–1920

Excellent air- and water-cooled 996cc flat twins with opposing cylinders. The engines were made by Douglas exclusively for Williamson. Machines built after 1919 had 770cc V-twin sv JAP engines.

WILLOW • England 1920

Another early scooter which was not a success. The engine used was the 269cc Villiers two-stroke.

WIMMER • Germany 1921–1939

Over the years built 134cc bicycle engines, then 137cc and 172cc single-cylinder ohv unit-design motorcycles with water-cooling. The last ones proved very successful in races with such riders as Kolm, Kolmsperger, Gmelch and others. From 1928 onwards air-cooled 198cc and 247cc models, afterwards 299cc and 497cc versions

were also made. During the 1930s there was also a 346cc ohv trials version and a 198cc two-stroke, both with Bark engines. No Wimmer motorcycles were made after the war.

WIN • England 1908–1914

Built a two-model range with 499cc and 599cc Precision single-cylinder sv engines.

WINCO • England 1920–1922

Assembled motorcycles with 261cc Orbit two-stroke engines.

WINDHOFF • Germany 1924–1933

Built radiators before entering motorcycle production with superb water-cooled 122cc and 173cc two-strokes. These had Bekamo-type horizontal-cylinder engines with a second scavenging piston at the bottom of the crankcase. They were very successful in races. A sensational Windhoff appeared on the market in 1927: an oil-cooled 746cc four-cylinder unit-design ohc engine as the centre of the whole machine. There was no real frame; everything was bolted onto the power unit. Shaft drive was another feature. A 996cc model built on similar lines was in prototype stage, but never built in quantities. Instead, a BMW-like 996cc Windhoff was built. It had a twin-cylinder sv engine transverse-mounted, shaft drive and was, like the smaller four, without a real frame. The last Windhoffs were the most conventional, using

173cc Windhoff (two-stroke water-cooled Bekamo licensed) 1926

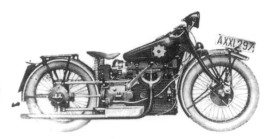

746cc Windhoff (ohc oil-cooled four-cylinder) 1928

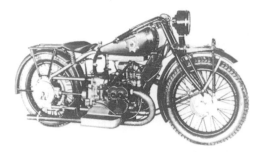

996cc Windhoff (sv transverse flat-twin, shaft-drive) 1929

198cc and 298cc Villiers-licensed two-stroke engines. The Berlin-based factory also supplied these power units to other motorcycle manufacturers. Successful Windhoff riders: Erich Tennigkeit, Walter Ebstein, Karl Wittig, Richard Scholz.

WITTALL • England 1919–1923

Assembled machines with 269cc Villiers engines.

248cc Wittler (two-stroke) 1925

WITTEKIND • Germany 1952–1954

Moped producer which fitted 40cc Komet engines.

WITTLER • Germany 1924–1953

Produced during the 1920s a 249cc two-stroke machine with its own engine. After 1949 production of 49cc mopeds with Sachs and Zündapp engines was resumed and there was also a 124cc lightweight with the Sachs engine.

WIZARD • Wales 1920–1922

Used a Wall-designed 269cc Liberty two-stroke.

WK • Germany 1920–1922

This was a 249cc sv engine built into a wheel which could be attached to any bicycle.

WKB • Austria 1923–1924

A 183cc two-stroke, three-port bicycle attachment engine designed by Hermann Medinger.

WMB • Germany 1924–1926

Lightweight machines with WMB's own 1·8hp sv engines. Small production.

WOLF • England 1901–1939

Besides Wolf motorcycles, the company also built the Wear-well and Wolfruna at the Wolverhampton works. In

247cc Wolf (two-stroke Villiers) 1936

the early years Moto-Rêve engines were used; all Wolf machines had proprietary power units, among them Blackburne and JAP engines up to 678cc. From 1928, Villiers two-strokes up to 248cc were used including deflector-less flat-top versions of 123cc and 248cc.

WOTAN • Germany 1923–1925

Like many others of that period, the Wotan was a simple 170cc two-stroke with a three-port engine.

WOOLER • England 1911–1955

John Wooler was a designer with many brilliant ideas and all his creations were very unconventional. His first 344cc two-stroke had a horizontal single cylinder and a double-ended piston, using the bottom part for pre-compression inside the crankcase. The machine had both wheels sprung by plunger suspension and was of advanced design throughout. Similar frames were used for 346cc and 496cc twins with horizontally opposed cylinders and overhead valves on the sides of the cylinder heads. A 611cc single, the only vertical engine known to be made by John Wooler, was built in 1926 as a prototype, but never in quantities. After WW2 he built a variety of 498cc four-cylinder machines with opposing cylinders transversely mounted, shaft drive, spring frames etc. These beautiful ohv machines were built in very small numbers; the last one was priced at £292.4s.1d.

WSE • Germany 1924–1925

Small producer of 249cc sv machines, which also supplied the engines to other assemblers.

WSK • Poland 1946–1978

Once a leading factory. Produced contemporary 123cc and 173cc sporting two-strokes and a 240cc version.

WSM • Germany 1919–1923

Built 496cc Stolle-designed ohv flat twins for Victoria until that company bought the whole WSM (Sedlbauer) factory

at Munich. Earlier machines had 493cc BMW-made flat twin sv engines, but the manufacture of complete Sedlbauer motorcycles was never on a large scale.

WUCO • Germany 1925

Lightweights with own 174cc sv engines. JAP-engined 248cc, 348cc and 490cc models were also made.

WURRING • Germany 1921–1959

Known for its excellent frames, Wurring motorcycles had a variety of proprietary engines. Among them were DKW, Villiers, Küchen, Kühne, Columbus, Bark, Sachs, Ilo and other makes with capacities from 142cc to 596cc. The last ones were 244cc Ilo vertical two-stroke twins. See also AWD.

WUYANG-HONDA • China 1992–

Joint manufacturing venture established between Honda Japan and the Chinese government-owned Guangzhou Motor Group to produce utility motorcycles in Guangzhou. Typically Chinese huge output of around 400,000 units annually, comprising the WY125 series of machines, including the WY125-A, WY125-B, WY125-C (with electric starter), WY125J (police version), as well as the WH125LZ scooter and SCR100 scooter, all essentially Honda based designs. Honda's stake rose from 35 per cent to 50 per cent at the end of 1994. Employs around 3500 staff for production levels of around 400,000 machines, up from 50,000 in the first year.

WÜRTTEMBERGIA • Germany 1925–1933

Made by a big agricultural machine factory, these machines all had 198cc to 596cc sv and ohv engines made by Blackburne. Good design and workmanship.

W&WA • Austria 1925–1927

The Josef Wild-designed machines had 498cc single-cylinder MAG ioe engines while 746cc and 996cc V-twins - also MAGs - could be supplied to order.

499cc Wooler (semi-ohv flat-twin) 1924

XING FU • China 1992–

Name used by the Shanghai Ek-Chor Motorcycle Co. Ltd for its XF250A two-stroke twin, based on an old east European design.

XL • England 1921–1923

Strong machines with double loop frames and 490cc JAP and 538cc Blackburne single-cylinder sv engines.

XL-ALL • England 1902–c1906

Built 2hp and 4hp V-twins with its own engines which, according to the producer, could run on one cylinder if for any reason the other one failed. Early models were lightweights and had the cylinders set at 90 degrees. The frames were of the loop bicycle type and had a long wheelbase.

X-TRA • England 1920–1922

This was really a three-wheeler with a 346cc single-cylinder Villiers engine. It had two front wheels and a body which was similar to early 1920s sidecars.

YALE • America 1902–1915

Was a well-known machine in the USA; especially the big 950cc V-twin with two-speed gearbox and chain drive to the rear wheel. The price in 1915: $260.

YAMAGUCHI • Japan 1941–1964

Once a leading factory, Yamaguchi concentrated on a variety of 49cc models including mofas, mopeds etc. and also built 123cc two-strokes with vertical twin-cylinder engines. The range included trials machines. When the factory closed, Hodaka took over the works.

YAMAHA • Japan 1955–

See panel

YAMARTAGO • Japan c1929

Single-cylinder machine with 350cc and 500cc JAP or JAP-copied engines. Many examples were fitted with a back axle, twin rear wheels and small pick-up body. Yamartago imported other components from England for its machines, including Amac Carburetors, ML magnetos and Sturmey-Archer gearboxes.

YEZDI • India 1960-

The company which trades as Ideal Jawa (India) has built since 1960 250cc-350cc licensed Jawa designs.

YI FA • China 1992–

Beijing-based company which produces an ungainly looking air-cooled two-stroke single called the YF250, of Chinese design.

YOUNG • England 1919–1923

Made by the producer of Mohawk motorcycles, the Young was a 269cc bicycle engine which could be mounted above the rear wheel. A new 130cc two-stroke version was introduced in 1923, but production of it went to the Waltham Engineering Co. Ltd.

YVEL • France 1921–1924

Light 174cc and 233cc machines with own sv engines.

490cc York (sv JAP) 1929

YAMAHA • Japan 1955–

The Yamaha Fukin Works was established in 1887 by Torakusu Yamaha to produce organs, and although it closed after only three years, Yamaha went on to establish the Nippon Gakki Company in 1897, this time to mass produce and export organs. Nippon Gakki had turned to production of various military items during WW2, and after the war found it had surplus machine tool capacity beyond its ability to produce piano frames, so looked around for another suitable marketable product. At first aircraft propellers were produced, but in 1953 the company president, Genichi Kawakami, decided to look for something more lucrative, and a decision was made to produce motorcycles.

After Yamaha representatives visited various Japanese and European manufacturers, the first Yamaha design was produced, the YA-1 being a close copy, like so many other machines, of the DKW RT125.

Production started in 1955 in Nippon Gakki's Hamana factory, the name Yamaha being chosen after the company's original founder. Even this early on, Yamaha decided that it would help sales to go racing, and entered the Fuji Tozan and Asama Kazan races, the two largest in Japan in the 1950s, and won them both.

In 1957 the YA-1 was joined by the YD-1, a 250cc two-stroke copied from the Adler MB250, which was also raced, and also sold well.

In 1959 Yamaha introduced the tubular framed YDS1, a 250cc twin with five speed gearbox that was to be the basis for its development of 250cc and 350cc two-strokes for the next 20 odd years. But for a while in the early 1960s the company's future was looking precarious, as its scooters and mopeds (the 175cc SC-1 and 50cc MF-1) proved problematical - stock prices collapsed and dividend payments weren't paid, almost bringing the company down. A new sales director was appointed, Hisao Koike, who set up new sales structures and reformed the engineering team, which in turn developed the Yamaha Autolube separate lubrication system for two-strokes which transformed reliability and customer usability. This was a major factor in putting the company back on track.

Two racing divisions, one for development of machines for private customers and the other for the factory to develop its own grand prix machines, which went on to win the 250cc world title in 1964 and 1965. The customer TD series was comparatively ineffectual until the TD1C of 1967, which was enormously successful. Thereafter, especially with the water-cooled TR and TZ models, Yamaha achieved a total domination of the 250cc and 350cc classes. The grand prix models, which were successfully raced between 1960 and 1968, were the most effective two-strokes ever seen until that time, and raced on level terms in the 250cc class with Honda, and in the 125cc with Honda and Suzuki.

The bare statistics - five TT wins and seven second places, and five world championships and seven second places - scarcely conveys the influence exerted by Yamaha on motorcycle racing in the 1960s. More than any other manufacturer, it was responsible for the development of the modern racing two-stroke still being used today. Similarly, it undoubtedly led the world in the 1960s and 1970s in the quality and performance of two-stroke road machines of between 50cc and 350cc. Consequently, it was with some reluctance that it acknowledged in the early 1970s that US anti-pollution laws forced the development of four-stroke engines.

123cc Yamaha YA 1 (two-stroke single) 1955

Yamaha YL-1 brochure of 1967

123cc Yamaha YA-6 (two-stroke single) 1967

In fact, having taken the decision, Yamaha applied its efforts just as vigorously to development of the four-stroke as it had previously to the two-stroke. Starting with the 650cc XS-1 four-stroke twin in 1970, it rapidly developed a full range of four-strokes, which included single-cylinder engines, twins, threes and, of course, fours, many of which had shaft-drive transmission.

Gradually, the range of road-going two-strokes was reduced in number, but racing success continued. Some gauge of Yamaha's status in 1970s two-stroke competition can be judged from its history in the big Daytona 200 Mile race, which Yamaha made its own, winning 13 back-to-back 200 milers from 1972 (Don Emde) to 1983 (Kenny Roberts). In World Championship circles, Yamaha won its first 500 title (with Italian legend Giacomo Agostini) in 1975 and has won a further ten 500 crowns to date. The factory has won no less than 13 titles in the 250 category, Briton Phil Read taking the first in 1964, aboard an air-cooled, disk-valve twin. In the 125 class, Yamaha won four world championships, between 1967 (Bill Ivy) and 1974 (Kent Andersson).

In the late 1970s Yamaha also ruled the short-lived Formula 750 world series. Originally intended as a 'production bike' championship, Yamaha made the class its own when it created the TZ750, a homologation special. This water-cooled, four-cylinder two-stroke missile became the definitive big-bike racer of the era, winning all three F750 world titles (with Canadian Steve Baker in 1977, Venezuelan Johnny Cecotto in 1978 and Frenchman Patrick Pons in 1979).

Yamaha's prominence in two-stroke racing has been consistent to this day, and has been joined by an impressive four-stroke effort. Although its water-cooled in-line twin TZ250 and 350 machines, which dominated GP grids in the 1970s and early 1980s, are no longer the automatic choice for most riders, the factory features strongly in today's major two-stroke world championships: the 250 and 500 classes.

Yamaha's modern era of success began with Kenny Roberts, who won three back-to-back 500 crowns from 1978 to 1980 aboard the marque's in-line fours. Later, Yamaha moved to square-four and then V-four configurations, the latter YZR machines taking American Eddie Lawson to the 1984, 1986 and 1988 championships, and compatriot Wayne Rainey to the 1990, 1991 and 1992 crowns. Since then Yamaha has failed to regain the title, but YZR500 is still a GP winner.

The factory's 250 racers have enjoyed less world championship success since the end of the TZ era. In the late 1980s Yamaha switch its factory 250s to a V-configuration, half a 500 V-four. The YZR250 won the 1987 title in the hands of mercurial Venezuelan Carlos Lavado, and American John Kocinski took the 1990 crown on a later version of the same bike. Three years later Japanese Tetsuya Harada regained the 250 championship, aboard his factory V-twin (which Yamaha then tagged a TZ).

Yamaha's four-stroke racing commenced in the mid-1980s. In 1986 Eddie Lawson scored the factory's first major four-stroke success when he won the Daytona 200 on the new FZ750 Superbike. Developments of this machine became potent tools in Formula One and endurance, though Yamaha has never taken long-distance racing as seriously as Honda, Kawasaki and Suzuki. In 1987 Rainey and Australian Kevin Magee won the marque's first victory in the prestigious Suzuka Eight Hours race in Japan, riding a YZF750.

73cc Yamaha Eighty Sports YGS-1 (two-stroke single)

*73cc Yamaha Eighty YG-1
(two-stroke single) 1967*

49cc Yamaha V50 (two-stroke single) 1972

YAMAHA
SPORTS 350 model R-3

Yamaha 350 R-3 brochure from 1970

Yamaha has yet to win a World Superbike crown, although the factory has stepped up its commitment to the street-based series in recent years. Australian Mick Doohan won its first WSB race at Sugo, Japan, in 1988, riding an FZR750. Yamaha's latest WSB machine, the R7, was launched in 1999 and borrows heavily from its 500 GP cousin's chassis technology.

At the time of publication Yamaha also held the lap record around the notorious Isle of Man TT circuit.

In off-road competition Yamaha also impressed, although it achieved less success the road racers. In 1973, Sweden's Hakan Andersson put Yamaha on the World Motocross Championship map with victory in the 250cc class. Five years later, fellow countryman Hakan Carlqvist clinched the 1978 500cc Motocross series in what was its first and last 500cc title.

In 1982, American Danny La Porte scored the next major success for Yamaha's YZ250 - the second of five 250cc titles and two 125cc crowns for the factory.

Although Yamaha's success hasn't been as great as some manufacturers, it was nevertheless the world leader in terms of technical advancement for motocross bikes: in 1987, it launched the revolutionary YZM into the then-booming 500cc class in a bid to topple Honda's stranglehold. The bike, ridden by Kurt Ljungqvist, Leif Persson and Jacky Martens was the forerunner of today's modern-day motocrosser and featured a liquid-cooled 499cc motor laced into a twin-spar frame, with upside-down forks and disk brakes.

The machine won several GP races, but was never further developed as a production 500cc bike as Yamaha turned its attention to the more hotly-contested 125cc and 250cc classes, but using much of the technical findings from the bigger bike to conceive a new breed of smaller-capacity motocrossers.

Yamaha's latest motocross development is the YZ400 four-stroke, a more environmentally friendly machine that, since its launch in 1997, has been in huge demand in the American and European markets. The bike has already proved itself in the USA and is a major contender for honors in the 1999 world 500cc Motocross Championship.

In the trials world, Yamaha was very forward thinking early on. The TY175 was the top-selling trials bike in the UK in the mid-to-late 1970s and won major acclaim from both youth riders and adults. This was eventually superseded by the TY250, which, like Suzuki's RL became more competitive when bastardised by a British company - this time John E. Shirt - who turned the basic Yamaha components into a British Championship-winning and world-class machine in the early 1980s.

The Yamaha factory fired back in the mid-1980s with the new-style TY250 monoshock: still air-cooled, but its best trials machine to date. It ran on in production for 10 years, virtually unchanged, until replaced by the TYZ water-cooled model that brought the factory bang up-to-date in terms of technical features alongside its competitors.

Yamaha hired several top trials riders, but failed to win a World Trials championship and, due to comparatively small sales, production of the TYZ ended in 1998.

Meanwhile, the company's road bike program continued its policy of expanding into every market niche. The XS-1 became the improved XS-2, with much needed frame improvements carried out in conjunction with British racer Percy Tait, and went on to become the

347cc Yamaha 350 R5-F (two-stroke twin) 1972

YAMAHA

743cc Yamaha TX750 (ohc twin-cylinder) 1972

*195cc Yamaha 200 CS3E
(two-stroke twin) 1972*

XS650, which was produced up to 1981. This was joined in 1977 by the dohc shaft driven triple XS750, expanded to 826cc for the XS850 (1981-1984), while the XT500 single trail bike of 1978 became a huge success. The road styled version, the SR500 of 1979 was not a great seller in many countries, but continues in production even today.

But during the 1970s and early 1980s, it was still Yamaha's two-strokes which kept the company to the fore in road sports bikes, the YA series of two-stroke twins developing into the classic RD250 and 350 air-cooled twins, then the RD400 of 1976, which all set the performance standards of their time. But it was the 1980 RD350LC (and the 250cc version) with its liquid-cooling and attractive styling that's best remembered, the bike becoming the first to feature variable exhaust port timing in 1985 as the RD350 YPVS (Yamaha Power Valve System). Production stopped in Japan in 1985 but continued at Yamaha's Brazilian factory into the 1990s.

171cc Yamaha 175 CT1-C (two-stroke single) 1979

246cc Yamaha 250 DT2 (two-stroke single) 1972

499cc Yamaha XT500C (ohc single) 1976

Less successful was the eagerly anticipated 1984 four-cylinder RD500LC, potentially a grand prix bike for the road but which proved a little too gentle-natured to match the 350LC's raw appeal.

It was during the 1980s that Yamaha's ambition overreached itself. The company announced its intention to relegate Honda to second position in the world, and initiated an intense program of new bike development which ultimately almost led to its downfall. A peace treaty was signed at the 'neutral' Kawasaki factory in 1982, but not before severely underdeveloped machines such as the complex and quirky XZ550 V-twin came onto the market. Yamaha flirted briefly with the then-fashionable turbocharging in this period with the poor handling XJ650 Turbo.

But in 1984 Yamaha returned to form, transferring its sporting ability to its four-strokes with the FZ750 749cc dohc four, the first road bike to feature five valves per cylinder and using Yamaha's 'Genesis' frame technology (forward inclined engine in twin spar frame).

This spawned the homologation special OW-01 of 1989, which eclipsed even the Honda RC30, but it was the company's FZR1000 of 1987 which really underlined the company's strength. As the FZR1000R EXUP of 1988, with a variable volume exhaust system, this redefined expectations of a sports bike with its excellent handling and power. Other notable machines of the time were the FJ1100 of 1984, originally a sports bike but soon marketed as tourer (due to the superior ability of the Kawasaki GPZ900R), becoming the FJ1200 in 1986, various middleweight fours such as the XJ550, 600, 650 and 750, the XV535 of 1988, still available and one of the best selling custom bikes ever, the FZR600 middleweight sports bike of 1989, and the V-four 1200cc V-Max, a unique street rod-style machine styled in the USA and notable for its aggressive styling and staggering straight line speed. This is still in production and selling well, and has become something of a cult machine.

Yamaha lost the sports bike lead to Honda in 1992 when the FireBlade was introduced, and learned after

49cc Yamaha FS1DX (two-stroke single) 1979

195cc Yamaha RD200 (two-stroke) 1979

YAMAHA

the moderately successful Thunderace of 1996 that sports bike riders weren't so keen on a compromise between speed and comfort. So in 1998 it introduced the YZF1000R-1, producing a huge 148bhp from its dohc four cylinder, 20-valve motor yet weighing just 177kg, with race track handling yet easy road manners. This is currently the definitive big sports bike.

With most markets focusing on 600cc sports bikes rather than 750s, Yamaha followed the R1 up with the R6, and equally uncompromised machine capable of revving beyond 15,000rpm, and producing a claimed 118bhp, while reserving the exotic, limited production R7 for the 750cc class to homologate its World Superbike racers.

Yamaha's range is now comprehensive, with a wide selection of custom bikes (by far the most successful Japanese ones), sports and sports touring machines (although a gap followed the cessation of FJ1200 production in 1996), trail bikes and budget machines, from scooters up to the four-cylinder XJ900. Especially

653cc Yamaha XJ650 Turbo (dohc four-cylinder turbocharged) 1984

550cc Yamaha XZ550 (dohc V-twin) 1984

996cc Yamaha TR1 (ohc V-twin) 1984

347cc Yamaha RD350LC (two-stroke twin liquid-cooled) 1983

notable is the XJ600 Diversion, which when it was introduced in 1992 reinvented the budget middleweight class. The lead was taken over by the Suzuki GSF600 Bandit in 1995, but Yamaha claimed it back convincingly in 1998 with the excellent FZS600 Fazer. Yamaha appears to be more willing to try new ideas than the other Japanese companies, which has often led to great success, but one machine that failed dismally despite impressive technical credentials was the GTS1000 of 1993. Despite its innovative hub-center steering, unusual frame, fuel injection and ABS brakes, it was heavy, blandly styled and very expensive. Originally Yamaha had attempted to build a hub-center steered supersports machine, but could never match the performance of more conventional telescopic fork-equipped bikes, so the GTS was something of a compromise, and it showed. Even so, if anything radically new is to come from Japan in the future, the chances are it will wear the famous triple tuning fork Yamaha badge.

1198cc Yamaha VMX1200 V-Max (dohc V-four liquid-cooled) 1984

1097cc Yamaha FJ1100 (dohc transverse four) 1984

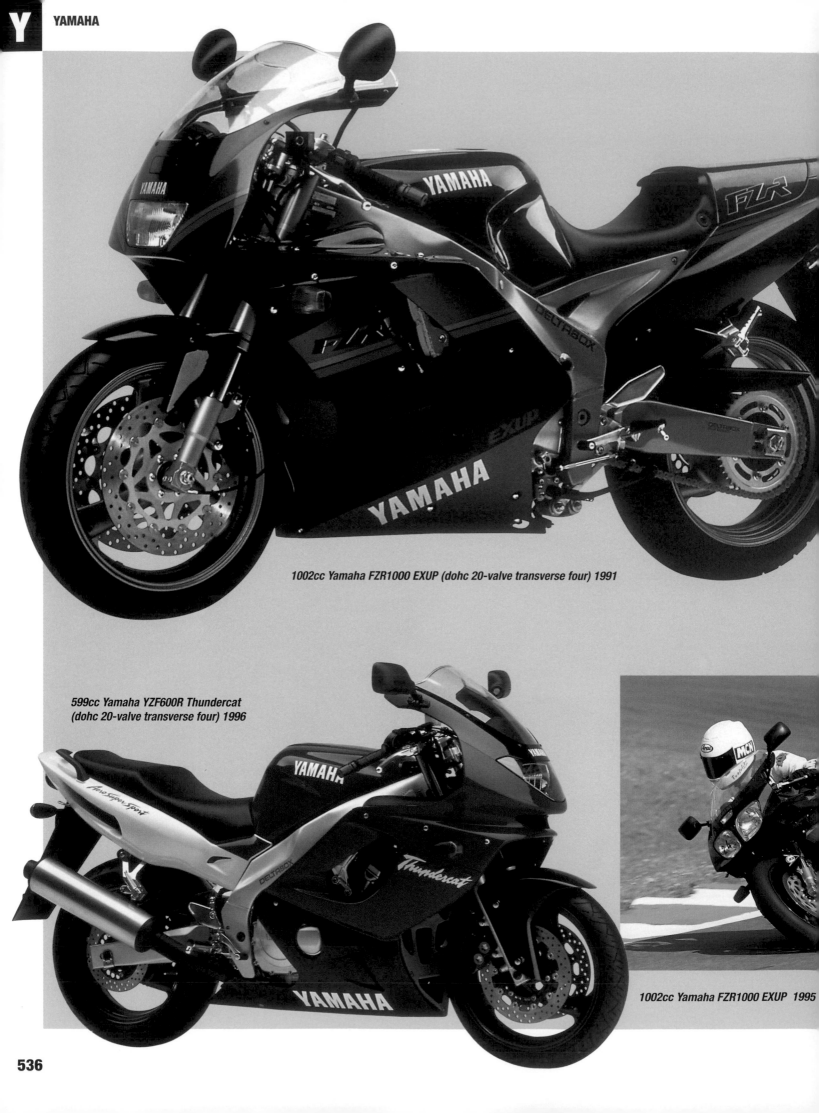

1002cc Yamaha FZR1000 EXUP (dohc 20-valve transverse four) 1991

599cc Yamaha YZF600R Thundercat
(dohc 20-valve transverse four) 1996

1002cc Yamaha FZR1000 EXUP 1995

249cc Yamaha TZ250 racer (two-stroke twin liquid-cooled) 1995

749cc Yamaha YZF750R (dohc 20-valve transverse four) 1994

1002cc Yamaha GTS1000 (dohc 20-valve transverse four) 1993

400cc Yamaha WR400F enduro (dohc single) 1998

892cc Yamaha XJ900S (dohc transverse four) 1995

599cc Yamaha FZS600 Fazer (dohc transverse four) 1998

599cc Yamaha YZF-R6 (dohc transverse four) 1999

749cc Yamaha YZF-R7 (dohc transverse four) 1999

998cc Yamaha YZF-R1(dohc 20-valve transverse four) 1999

1294cc Yamaha Venture Tour (ohc V-four) 1999

1063cc Yamaha Drag Star 1100 (ohc V-twin) 1998

Z

ZANELLA • Argentina 1958–late 1960s

Built on Italian lines, the Zanella was a sporting two-stroke design which used partly Italian components. The machines were of 49cc, 98cc and 123cc.

123cc Zanella (two-stroke) 1963

ZEDEL • France 1902–1915

While the Swiss parent company Zürcher & Lüthi concentrated on the manufacture of proprietary engines, the French branch supplied complete machines with 2hp, 2·25hp, 2·5hp, 2·75hp, and 3·5hp single-cylinder and V-twin engines.

ZEGEMO • Germany 1924–1925

When some partners of the Zetge factory left, they founded the Zegemo works. Designed by Hans Knipp, the Zegemo was a 248cc two-stroke with the rare Baumi engine.

ZEHNDER • Switzerland 1923–1939

The 110 Zehnder, called Zehnderli, was a very popular lightweight. It had a two-stroke engine with a horizontal cylinder, not unlike the German Cockerell. Zehnder's racing versions had 123cc engines with water-cooling. There were 148cc models and from 1929 onwards a 248cc two-stroke single with a vertical cylinder, which was also built as a sports model. In the early 1930s the factory was bought by Wilhelm Gutbrod, owner of the German Standard motorcycle works, who continued the production of Zehnder machines in Switzerland. Otto Zehnder won many races in the 125cc and 250cc class. The quarter-liter racing models also had water-cooled engines. Leading riders were Graf, Wiedmer, and Liechti. After 1945 there were to be new Zehnder motorcycles; a design was ready for production when the designer, Robert Zehnder, died suddenly. Price for the complete 110cc 2.2hp Zehnder in 1929: Fr. 885, in 1937: Fr. 700.

ZEHNER • Germany 1924–1926

The Zehner was a 197cc sv machine, designed by Otto Dehne. Made by a small manufacturer, comparatively few machines reached the market.

ZENITH • England 1904–1950

Freddie Barnes established Zenith at Weybridge to build a strange machine with hub-center steering and a Fafnir engine, known as Tooley's patent Bicar. This metamorphosed into the Zenette, which had a sprung sub-frame, and from 1908, Barnes' patent Gradua infinitely variable gear. This used an engine pulley with flanges that moved in and out under the control of a hand wheel, the belt tension being maintained by a linked mechanism that moved the rear wheel back and forwards in the frame. Applied to 500cc, 750cc and 1000cc JAP-engined motor cycles of otherwise conventional construction, the system was enormously successful and gained Zenith a great reputation.

Post-WW1, Zenith continued with the Gradua gear, until belt drive became discredited. Granville Bradshaw was briefly associated with Zenith after Sopwith's ABC company collapsed, introducing his flat twin 500cc oil-cooled engine in a 1922 Zenith model. However, later Zeniths were entirely orthodox machines, mainly using single-cylinder and V-twin JAP engines and later small Villiers four-strokes. Zenith gained quite a reputation in the late 1920s for racing and record breaking successes with 1000cc JAP engines, but in late 1930 Barnes lost control and the company was sold to London dealer Writers. Limited production continued in the 1930s and even after WW2, but the great days were over. Using old stocks of JAP engines, Zenith lasted until 1950.

496cc Zenith (ohv oil-cooled Bradshaw flat twin) 1922

348cc Zenith (ohv JAP) 1929

1096cc Zenith (sv V-twin JAP) 1936

110cc Zehnder (TS horizontal single) 1926

ZENIT • Italy 1954–1956

Assembled machines with French 123cc and 174cc AMC ohv engines.

ZENITH • England 1904–1950

See panel

ZEPHYR • England 1922–1923

Made bicycle engines which were also available as complete lightweight machines. The two-stroke engine had 131cc and was of the deflector-type three-port variety.

ZETA • Italy 1948–1954

Very ordinary and primitive scooter-like vehicles with 48cc and 60cc proprietary engines, built by Ducati and other producers of similar small power units. The Zeta had very small wheels.

ZETGE • Germany 1922–1925

Built well-designed two-strokes with 142cc and 173cc DKW engines as well as with 147cc to 173cc engines of Zetge (Gehlich) design and manufacture.

ZEUGNER • Germany 1903–1906

Pioneer assembler which fitted Fafnir, Zedel, Minerva, FN, Peugeot and other proprietary engines.

ZEUS • Czechoslovakia 1902–1912

The Christian Linser-designed Zeus machines, made when Czechoslovakia was still part of the Austro-Hungarian Empire, were among the leading singles and V-twins built. The range included 3hp and 3·5hp singles and 4hp and 4·5hp V-twins. Zeus machines were also sold under the Linser name.

ZEUS • Germany 1925–1927

Equipped with double-loop frames, German Zeus

motorcycles had 348cc and 498cc Küchen three-valve ohc engines.

ZIEJAN • Germany 1924–1926

Built 211cc and 246cc two-strokes, while a 449cc single-cylinder two-stroke never went into production. Instead the factory assembled motorcycles with 348cc and 498cc sv and ohv JAP engines.

ZIRO • Germany 1919–1924

Designed by Albert Roder, who eventually became chief designer at the NSU works, the 148cc and 346cc Ziro were excellent two-strokes with a rotary valve in the crankcase. After Ziro closed down, Roder was with Ermag, Zündapp and Victoria before he eventually joined the firm of NSU.

ZOPPOLI • Italy 1947–1951

Mini-motorcycles built using 48cc and 60cc Ducati Cucciolo engines.

ZÜNDAPP • Germany 1921–1985

See panel opposite

ZÜRTZ-REKORD • Germany 1922–1926

Interesting design with a wide top tube, which also served as the fuel tank. The Zürtz brothers used a variety of engines including 142cc and 173cc DKW two-strokes, the rare 198cc ohv Paqué and also the ohv 249cc Columbus, as used by the first Horex. A small number had 346cc and 490cc sv and ohv JAP engines.

ZWEIRAD-UNION • Germany 1958–1974

Originally a combination of the DKW, Express and Victoria works with the HQ at the Nuremberg Victoria factory. Hercules was added in 1966 and eventually taken over by the big Fichtel & Sachs group of companies.

ZWERG • Germany 1924–1925

Lightweights with own 147cc and 187cc two-stroke deflector-type engines.

ZWI • Israel 1952–1955

The only motorcycle factory in Israel. Founded by former Hungarian racing rider Stefan Ausländer, it built exclusively 123cc two-stroke machines with JAP and Villiers engines.

ZZR • Poland 1960–

Concentrates on the manufacture of 49cc two-stroke machines, which are being sold under the Komar name.

ZÜNDAPP • Germany 1921–1985

Zündapp, which became part of a giant engineering conglomerate, was at one time one of Europe's largest motorcycle manufacturers. Its involvement began in 1921 with a remarkably frank copy of the successful British 211cc Levis two-stroke, and continued in this vein until 1926, Levis models being copied in every detail without the least acknowledgement! Thereafter Zündapp began to produce two-strokes of its own design. In response to the depression of the early 1930s, the company called in Richard Küchen, who designed a range of transverse horizontally opposed engines, gearboxes that used chains and sprockets, shaft drive and characteristic pressed steel frames. There were side-valve twins of 400cc and 500cc and a four-cylinder of 600cc, which were immediately successful.

Later development centred on the 597cc KS600 flat twin, while, from 1939 to 1945, the company's efforts were devoted to the production of the 750cc KS750 sidecar outfit with sidecar wheel drive and reverse gears. Post-war motorcycle production resumed in 1947, with a 200cc two-stroke. The KS600 was re-introduced, to be replaced in 1951 by the KS601 with a new ohv design. This was highly successful in the ISDT and similar events through the 1950s. Zündapp also introduced a clip-on engine for bicycles, the 50cc Combimot, later to become a moped – the Combinette.

There were other larger two-strokes and, in 1953, the 150cc and later 200cc Bella scooter was introduced. It was to be one of Zündapp's most successful products, lasting until 1964 in various forms. However, although exports were still good in the 1950s, the German market was shrinking.

In the 1960s Zündapps of 50cc, 75cc and 100cc put up some remarkable performances in the ISDT and other important events, and production consisted mainly of such smaller two-strokes. A 50cc Zundapp with streamlining broke some world records at Monza in 1965, including the hour at over 101mph! Zündapp now moved increasingly towards 50cc sports machines and mopeds, and entered the 1950s with only two capacities, 175cc and 50cc. Sales plunged disastrously, so a water-cooled 80cc sports model was introduced in 1981. Zündapp raced in the 80cc class, and won the world championship in 1983, 1984 and 1985, but such success did not save the company, which went into liquidation on the eve of the 1985 Cologne Show. In 1986, it was sold in its entirety to China.

78cc Zündapp K80 (two-stroke) 1982

211cc Zündapp Z22 (two-stroke) 1921

797cc Zündapp (sv transverse flat four) 1936

249cc Zündapp K249(two-stroke) 1927

746cc Zündapp KS750 army model (ohv transverse flat twin) 1941

298cc Zündapp Z300 (two-stroke) 1929

123cc Zündapp KS 125 Sport (two-stroke) 1971

598cc Zündapp KS601(ohv transverse flat twin) 1950

THE LEADING MODELS FROM THE GOLDEN AGE TO THE PRESENT

THE 1920s

MARQUE	COUNTRY	CYL	BORE	STROKE	CC	HP	2/4-STROKE	ENGINE
AJS	GB	1	74	81	349	2 3/4	sv	own
		2 V	74	93	799	4–7	sv	
Albertus	D	1	60	75	212	3	2	Löwy
Alecto	GB	1	76	76	344	3 1/2	2	own
Allon	GB	1	70	76	292	2 1/2	2	own
Ardie	D	1	72	75	305	3	2	own
Ariel	GB	1	60	88	249	2 1/2	sv	Blackburne
		1	92	100	662	4 1/2	sv	own
		2 V	73	95	796	6–7	ioe	MAG
		2 V	82	94	994	8	ioe	MAG
BAT	GB	1	70	90	347	2 3/4	sv	JAP
		2 V	70	88	676	5	sv	JAP
		2 V	85.5	85	986	8	sv	JAP
Beardmore	GB	1	70	90	347	2 3/4	sv	Precision
		1	81	96	494	3 1/2	sv	Precision
		1	89	96	598	4 1/2	sv	Precision
Bekamo	D	1	50	66	129	2 1/2	2	own
BMW	D	1	68	68	249	2 1/2	ohv	own
		2	68	68	493	6.5	sv	own
		2	68	68	493	16	ohv	own
Bianchi	I	2 V	70	78	600	—	sv	own
Bradbury	GB	1	74.5	80	349	2 3/4	sv	own
		1	89	89	554	4	sv	own
		2 V	74.5	86	749	6	sv	own
Brough	GB	2 F	70	64.5	496	3 1/2	ohv	own
		2 F	70	90	692	5–6	sv	own
Brough-Superior	GB	2 V	72	91	742	6	ioe	MAG
		2 V	85.5	86	976	8	sv	JAP
		2 V	90	77.5	984	8	ohv	JAP
B.S.A.	GB	1	72	85.5	349	2 3/4	sv	own
		1	80	98	493	3 1/2	sv	own
		1	85	98	557	4 1/4	sv	own
		2 V	76	85	770	6	sv	own
		2 V	80	98	985	8	sv	own
Burney	GB	1	81	96	495	3 1/2	sv	own
Calthorpe	GB	1	67	69	247	2 1/2	2	Peco
Campion	GB	1	70	76	293	2 3/4	sv	JAP
		1	71	88	347	2 3/4	sv	JAP
		2 V	85.5	85	976	8	sv	JAP
Cedos	GB	1	62	70	211	2 1/4	2	own
		1	67	70	247	2 3/4	2	own
Chater Lea	GB	1	70	70	269	2 1/2	2	own
		1	71	88	349	2 3/4	sv	Blackburne
		1	85	96	545	4 1/4	sv	own
		2 V	85.5	85	976	8	sv	own
Clement	F	2 V	54	75	345	3	sv	own
		2 V	64	77	496	3 1/2	sv	own
Cleveland	USA	1	70	70	269	3 1/2	2	own
Clyno	GB	1	70	70	269	2 1/2	2	own
		2 V	76	102	925	8	sv	own
Connaught	GB	1	73	70	293	2 1/2	2	own
		1	76	77	348	2 3/4	2	own
Cotton	GB	1	70	70	269	2 1/2	2	Villiers
		1	60	88	248	2 1/2	sv	Blackburne
		1	71	88	348	2 3/4	sv	Blackburne
		1	71	88	348	2 3/4	ohv	Blackburne
Coventry-Eagle	GB	1	55	60	147	1 3/4	2	Villiers
		1	71	88	348	2 3/4	sv	Blackburne
		2 V	85	85	998	8	sv	JAP
Coventry-Mascot	GB	1	70	90.6	349	2 3/4	sleeve	Barr & Stroud
Coventry-Victor	GB	2 F	75	78	688	6	sv	own
D-Rad	D	1	82	94	496	10	sv	own
Diamond	GB	1	55	62	147	1 3/4	2	Villiers
		1	70	90.6	349	2 3/4	sleeve	Barr & Stroud
Dolf	D	1	62	66	199	3	2	own
Dot	GB	1	60	70	198	2 1/4	2	own
		1	70	70	269	2 3/4	2	Villiers
		1	70	76	293	2 3/4	sv	JAP
		2 V	85	85	986	8	sv	JAP
Douglas	GB	2 F	60.8	60	348	2 3/4	sv	own
		2 F	68	68	496	3 1/2	sv	own
		2 F	74.5	68	595	4	sv	own
		2 F	83	68	733	6	ohv	own
Dunelt	GB	1	85	88	499	3 1/2	2	own
Duzmo	GB	1	89	79	497	3 1/2	ohv	own
Economic	GB	2 F	52.5	38.5	163	1 3/4	2	own
Excelsior	GB	1	55	62	147	1 3/4	2	Villiers
		1	67	70	247	2 1/2	2	Villiers
		1	71	88	348	2 3/4	sv	Blackburne
		2 V	76	85	770	6	sv	JAP
		2 V	85.5	85	976	8	sv	JAP
FN	B	1	65	86	285	2 3/4	sv	own
		1	74	80.5	348	2 3/4	sv	own
		4	52	88	749	8	sv	own
Francis-Barnett	GB	1	70	76	293	2 3/4	sv	JAP
		1	70	90	346	2 3/4	sv	JAP
Garelli	I	1	50	89	348	2 3/4	2	own 2-Piston
Gnome & Rhone	F	1	85	88	499	3 1/2	sv	own
Hanfland	D	1	55	65	149	3	2	own
Harley-Davidson	USA	2 F	69	76	584	5	sv	own
		2 V	84	88.9	989	9	ioe	own
		2 V	87	101	1208	12	ioe	own
HEC	GB	1	67	70	247	2 1/4	2	Villiers
Henderson	USA	4	68.3	88.9	303	11 1/2	sv	own
Henley	GB	1	68	96	348	2 3/4	ohv	Bradshaw
Hobart	GB	1	60	88	248	2 1/4	sv	Blackburne
		1	71	88	348	2 3/4	sv	Blackburne
Humber	GB	1	75	79	348	2 3/4	sv	own
		2 F	75	68	600	4 1/2	sv	own
Indian	USA	2 V	70	78	596	4	sv	own
		2 V	79	100	998	7–8	sv	own
		2 V	82	112	1204	10	sv	own
Invicta	GB	1	70	90	346	2 3/4	sv	JAP
Ivy	GB	1	75	79	348	2 3/4	2	own
James	GB	1	73	83.5	349	2 3/4	sv	own

THE 1920s

MARQUE	COUNTRY	CYL	BORE	STROKE	CC	HP	2/4-STROKE	ENGINE
James	GB	2 V	64	77	499	3 1/2	sv	own
		2 V	73	89.5	749	7	sv	own
JES	GB	1	60	60	169	1 1/2	2	own
JNU	GB	1	73	76	318	2 3/4	2	Dalm
KG	D	1	80	99	497	4	ohv	own
Lea Francis	GB	2 V	64	77	497	3 1/2	ioe	MAG
		2 V	64	92	592	5	ioe	MAG
Levis	GB	1	62	70	211	2.1	2	own
Lutece	F	2	75	113	997	7	sv	own
Mabeco	D	2 V	70	78	600	11	sv	Simens & Halske
Mars	D	2 F	80	95	956	7.3	sv	Maybach
Martinsyde	GB	1	70	90	437	2 3/4	eoi	own
		2 V	70	88	678	6	eoi	own
Massey	GB	1	71	88	348	2 3/4	sv	Blackburne
Matchless	GB	1	71	88	348	2 3/4	sv	Blackburne
		2 V	85	85	980	8	sv	JAP
		2 V	82	94	993	8	ioe	MAG
McKenzie	GB	1	60	60	170	1 1/4	2	own
Metro-Tyler	GB	1	70	70	269	2 1/2	2	own
Megola	D	5	52	60	640	6.5–14	sv	own Radial
MFZ	D	1	64	77	249	3	2	own
Mohawk	GB	1	70	70	269	2 1/2	2	Villiers
Moto-Râve	CH	1	61	85	248	2 1/2	ohv	own
Motosacoche	CH	2 V	54	75	345	3	ioe	MAG
		2 V	64	77	496	4	ioe	MAG
		2 V	72	91	750	6	ioe	MAG
New Comet	GB	1	70	76	293	2 1/2	2	Climax
New Gerrard	GB	1	70	90.5	384	2 3/4	Sleeve	Barr & Stroud
New Hudson	GB	1	62	70	211	1 3/4	2	own
		1	70	90	346	2 3/4	sv	own
		1	79.5	100	498	3 1/2	sv	own
		1	87	100	596	4	sv	own
New Imperial	GB	1	70	76	293	2′	sv	JAP
		1	70	90	348	2 3/4	sv	JAP
		2 V	85.5	85	976	8	sv	JAP
Nimbus	DK	4	60	66	746	7	ioe	own
Norton	GB	1	79	100	490	3 1/2	sv	own
		1	79	100	490	3 1/2	ohv	own
		1	82	120	633	4	sv	own
NSU	D	1	58	72	190	1 1/2	ioe	own
		1	73	78	326	2 1/2	ioe	own
		1	85	88	499	3 1/2	ioe	own
		2 V	58	75	396	3	ioe	own
		2 V	63	80	499	3 1/2	ioe	own
		2 V	72.5	90	749	6–14	ioe	own
		2 V	75	94	931	6 1/2	ioe	own
		2 V	80	99	998	8–17	ioe	own
NUT	GB	2 V	64.5	76	499	3 1/2	sv	own
		2 V	64.5	76	499	3 1/2	ohv	own
		2 V	70	88	676	4 1/2	sv	own
OEC	GB	1	71	88	348	2 3/4	sv	Blackburne
		1	85	96.8	549	4	sv	Blackburne
		2 V	85	88	998	8	sv	Blackburne
OK	GB	1	70	70	269	2 1/2	2	Villiers
		1	60	88	248	2 1/2		Blackburne
Olympic	GB	1	68	72	261	2 1/2	2	Orbit
Omega	GB	1	60	60	170	1 1/2	2	own
		1	71	88	348	2 3/4	2	own
Paragon	GB	1	76	79	349	2 3/4	2	own
Peugeot	F	1	52	52	110	1	2	own
Puch	A	1	36 x 2	60	123	1	2	own
P & M (Panther)	GB	1	84.1	100	555	5	sv	own
P & P	GB	1	70	90.5	349	2 3/4	Sleeve	Barr & Stroud
Quadrant	GB	1	79	100	490	3 1/2	sv	own
		1	87	110	654	4 1/2	ioe	own
Radco	GB	1	67	70	247	2 1/2	2	own
Raleigh	GB	1	71	88	348	2 3/4	sv	own
		2 F	77	75	698	5–6	sv	own
Ray	GB	1	60	70	198	1 1/2	sv	own
Reading-Standard	USA	2 V	85.7	101.6	1170	10	sv	own
Ready	GB	1	70	76	293	2 3/4		JAP
Rex-Acme	GB	1	70	90.5	349	2 3/4	Sleeve	Barr & Stroud
		1	85	95	550	4	sv	JAP
		I	60	88				
Rover	GB	1	63	80	249	2 1/2	ohv	own
		2 V	70	88	678	5	sv	JAP
Royal Enfield	GB	1	64	70	225	2.5	sv	own
		2 V	85.5	85	976	8	sv	JAP
Rudge	GB	1	85	88	499	3 1/2	ioe	own
		2 V	85	88	998	7–9	ioe	own
R & H	GB	1	55	62	147	1 1/4	2	Villiers
Sarolea	B	1	85	97	553	4	sv	own
Scott	GB	2	70	63.5	487	3.5	2	own
		2	73	63.5	532	3 3/4	2	own
Sparkbrook	GB	1	67	70	247	2 1/2	2	Villiers
Sun	GB	1	70	70	269	2 1/2	2	Vitesse
		1	71	88	348	2 3/4	sv	Blackburne
Sunbeam	GB	1	70	90	347	2 3/4	sv	own
		1	77	105.5	492	3 1/2	sv	own
		1	85	88	499	3 1/2	sv	own
	GB	1	85	105.5	599	4 1/2	sv	own
		2 V	85.5	85	976	6–8	sv	JAP
Stanger	GB	2 V	70	70	538	4	2	own
Triumph	D	1	70	72	277	2 1/2	2	own
Triumph	GB	1	67.2	70	249	2 1/4	2	own
		1	80.9	97	499	3 1/2	ohv	own
		1	85	97	550	4	sv	own
Trump	GB	1	70	90	348	2 3/4	sv	JAP
		2 V	76	85	748	6	sv	JAP
Velocette	GB	1	62	73	220	1 3/4	2	own
		1	63	80	247	2 1/2	2	own
Victoria	GB	1	79	70	347	2 3/4	2	Villiers
Victoria	D	2 F	70.5	64	499	6.5	ohv	own
Vindec	GB	1	70	76	293	2 1/2	sv	JAP
		2 V	85.5	85	976	8	sv	JAP
Vis-Duplex	D	2 F	63	80	498	3 1/2	2	own
Wanderer	D	1	65	76	251	2	sv	own
		2 V	65	76	502	4	sv	own
		2 V	70	80	615	4	sv	own
		2 V	71	94	749	6	ohv	own
Weaver	GB	1	56	61	149	1 1/4	ohv	own
Wee McGregor	GB	1	60	60	170	1 1/4	2	own
Wolf	GB	1	71	88	348	2 3/4	sv	Blackburne
Wooler	GB	2 F	60	60.5	345	2 3/4	ioe	own
Zenith	GB	1	70	76	293	2 3/4	sv	JAP
		1	70	90	348	2 3/4	sv	JAP
		2 F	68	68	496	3 1/2	ohv	Bradshaw
		2 V	70	88	678	5	sv	JAP
		2 V	85.5	85	976	8	sv	JAP
Zündapp	D	1	62	70	211	2 1/4	2	own

THE 1930s

MARQUE	MODEL	COUNTRY	CYL	BORE	STROKE	CC	2/4-STROKE	ENGINE
AJS	S 4	GB	1	74	93	399	sv	own

THE 1930s

MARQUE	MODEL	COUNTRY	CYL	BORE	STROKE	CC	2/4-STROKE	ENGINE
AJS	S 5	GB	1	74	81	349	sv	own
	S 6		1	74	81	349	ohv	own
	S 8		1	84	90	498	ohv	own
	S 2		2 V	84	90	996	sv	own
AJW	B. Fox	GB	1	57.1	67	172	2	Villiers
	Flying Fox		1	70	90.5	348	ohv	Python
	Flying Foy		1	85	88	499	ohv	Python
	680		2 V	70	88	675	ohv	JAP
	8/55		2 V	80	90	996	ohv	JAP
AKD	70 Merkur	GB	1	60	61	172	ohv	own
	40 Polar		1	76	77	348	sv	own
Allegro	Supersp.	CH	1	57	67	172	2	Villiers
	Grand Sport		1	79	101	498	ohv	Sturmey-Archer
Ardie	Jubilee	D	1	85.7	85	490	sv	JAP
	Silberpfeil		1	85.7	85	490	ohv	JAP
	750		2 V	70	97	743	sv	JAP
Ariel	L 1 F	GB	1	65	75	248	ohv	own
	V F		1	81.8	95	497	ohv	own
	S B		1	86.4	95	557	sv	own
	4 F		4 Sq	51	61	497	ohc	own
Austria		A	1	70	90	346	2	Villiers
Bianchi		I	1	59.5	62.5	174	ohv	own
BMW	R 2	D	1	63	64	198	ohv	own
	R 52		2 F	63	78	486	sv	own
	R 57		2 F	68	68	494	ohv	own
	R 62		2 F	78	78	745	sv	own
	R 63		2 F	83	68	735	ohv	own
Brough-Superior	500	GB	2 V	62.5	80	492	ohv	JAP
	680		2 V	70	88	676	ohv	JAP
	SS 80		2 V	85	85.7	998	sv	JAP
	SS 100		2 V	80	99	998	ohv	JAP
BSA	B 1	GB	1	63	80	249	sv	own
	B 3		1	63	80	249	ohv	own
	L 5		1	72	85.5	349	sv	own
	L 6		1	72	85.5	349	ohv	own
	S 7		1	80	98	493	sv	own
	S 9		1	80	98	493	ohv	own
	E 11		2 V	76	85	770	sv	own
	G 12		2 V	80	98	986	sv	own
Condor	312	CH	1	72	85	348	ioe	MAG
	322		1	82	94	498	ioe	MAG
	GP 572		1	82	94	498	ohv	MAG
Calthorpe	Ivory	GB	1	74	81	348	ohv	own
Coventry-Eagle	G 22	GB	1	67	67	196	2	Villiers
	G 45		1	70	90	348	sv	Sturmey-Archer
	G 44		1	71	88	348	ohv	Sturmey-Archer
	G 54		1	79	101	496	ohv	Sturmey-Archer
	G 55		1	85.7	85	490	ohv	JAP
	F 130		2 V	85.5	85	996	sv	JAP
Diamond		GB	1	67	70	247	2	Villiers
Delta-Gnom		A	1	71	88	348	ohv	Sturmey-Archer
			1	82	94	496	ohv	own
			2 V	85.5	85	996	sv	JAP
DKW	VR	D	1	63	64	198	2	own
	300		1	74	68	296	2	own
	500		2	68	68	494	2	own
Dollar		F	1	66	70	239	ohv	Chaise
			1	75	79	349	ohv	Chaise
			1	89	79	492	ohv	Chaise
Douglas	B	GB	2 F	60.8	60	347	sv	own
	D		2 F	68	82	595	sv	own
	G		2 F	68	82	595	ohv	own
D-Rad	R9	D	1	82	94	496	sv	own
	R10		1	82	94	496	ohv	own
Dresch	E	F	1	76	77	348	sv	own
	C		2	64	77	495	sv	own
Dunelt	J2	GB	1	65.5	88	298	sv	Sturmey-Archer
	J4		1	71	88	348	ohv	Sturmey-Archer
	J5		1	79	101	496	ohv	Sturmey-Archer
	J7		1	86.8	101	598	sv	Sturmey-Archer
Elfa	T200	D	1	63	64	198	2	Windhoff
	LS300	D	1	68	64	294	2	Kähne
	LS350		1	70	90	346	ohv	Kåchen
	LS500		1	79	100	492	sv	Kåchen
Elite (E.O.)	Sport	D	1	86	86	496	ohv	Kåchen
Excelsior	A 4	GB	1	61	67	196	2	Villiers
	A 9		1	62.5	90	248	ohv	JAP
	A 12		1	85.7	85	490	ohv	JAP
FN		B	1	74	80.5	348	sv	own
			1	85	87	495	sv	own
			1	85	87	495	ohv	own
Francis-Barnett	Hawk	GB	1	61	67	196	2	Villiers
	18 Falcon		1	61	67	196	2	Villiers-DP
Frera	Sport	I	1	53	79	174	sv	own
	Sport		1	63	79	247	sv	own
	Sport		1	71	88	347	sv	own
	Spinta		1	84.5	88	497	ohv	own
Garelli	314	I	1	50	82	348	2	own 2 Piston
	315		1	50	89	349	2	own 2 Piston
Gilera	Sixdays	I	1	84	90	498	sv	own
Gillet Herstal	Welttur	B	1	79.5	70	348	2	own
	SS		1	70	90	348	ohv	own
	T		1	84	90	498	sv	own
	Rekord		1	84	90	498	ohv	own
Gnome Rhone	Touring	F	1	69	82	306	sv	own
	CM 1 GS		1	73	82	344	ohv	own
	GS 500		1	85	88	497	sv	own
	V2		2 F	68	68	495	sv	own
Harley-Davidson	C	USA	2 V	70.6	101.6	493	sv	own
	D		2 V	69.8	96.8	743	sv	own
	V		2 V	86.9	101.6	1208	sv	own
Henderson	De Luxe	USA	4	58.8	89	1301	ioe	own
Horex	S 200	D	1	57	78	198	ohv	Columbus
	T 500		1	80	99	496	sv	Columbus
	S 500		1	79	101	496	ohv	Columbus-S.A.
	T 600		1	80	118	596	sv	Columbus
Hulla	Bremen	D	1	60	68	196	2	DKW
Husqvarna		S	1	64.5	76	248	sv	own
			1	62.5	80	248	ohv	JAP
			1	79	101	496	ohv	Sturmey-Archer
Imperia	Ulster	D	1	70	88	346	ohv	Python
	Grand Sport		1	85	88	498	ohv	Python
	Sport		1	80	94	498	ohv	MAG
	Berggeist		1	90	94	598	ioe	MAG
	Rheingold		1	70	88	676	ohv	JAP
James	C 10	GB	1	57.5	67	172	2	Villiers
	C 4		1	73.5	83.5	348	ohv	own
	C3		1	85	88	498	ohv	Python
	C 2		2 V	64	77.5	497	ohv	own
Jawa	CS		1	58	65	173	2	Lic. Villiers
			1	63	80	246	2	Lic. DKW
			1	84	90	499	ohv	Lic. Wanderer
Keller	O 1	CH	1	79	81	397	sv	own
Koehler-Escoffier	KG 35	F	1	72	85	347	ohv	MAG
	K 50		1	80	99	498	ohc	own
Levis	Z	GB	1	67	70	247	2	own
	A 2		1	70	90	346	ohv	own
Magnat-Debon	LMP	F	1	57	68	174	2	own
	MOSSE		1	59	90	246	ohv	own

Make	Model	Country	Cyl.	Bore	Stroke	cc	Type	Engine
Magnat-Debon	CSS	F	1	85.5	85	490	ohv	JAP
Mammut	2 T	D	1	61	67	196	2	Villiers
	4 T		1	56.3	79	198	sv	Blackburne
MAS	119 L	I	1	60	61.5	173.8	ohv	own
	125/3		1	85	61.5	348	ohv	own
Matchless	R 7	GB	1	62.5	80	246	sv	own
	D		1	69	93	347	sv	own
	C/S		1	85.5	85.5	495	ohv	own
	X/3		2 V	85.5	85.5	990	sv	own
	S. Arrow		2 V	54	86	398	sv	own
	S. Hawk		4 V	50.8	73	593	ohc	own
Miller-Balsamo	Erretre	I	1	57	67	172	ohv	own
	TT-Replica		1	85	88	498	ohv	Python
La Mondiale	LT	B	1	75	68	308	2	own
	ZS		1	75	79	349	2	own
	GS		1	70	90	346	ohv	JAP
	GSSS		1	85.7	85	490	ohv	JAP
Monet-Goyon	AT	F	1	67	70	247	2	Villiers
			1	72	85	348	ioe	MAG
			1	82	94	498	ohv	MAG
Montgomery		GB	1	62.5	80	248	ohv	JAP
			1	70	90	348	ohv	JAP
			1	85.7	85	490	sv	JAP
			2 V	70	88	676	sv	JAP
Moser	STD	CH	1	60	61	174	ohv	own
			1	74	81	348	ohv	own
			1	79	100	498	ohv	own
			1	85	106	598	ohv	own
Motobécane	B1	F	1	46	60	99.6	2	own
(Motoconfort)	B2		1	56	70	172	2	own
	B4		1	70	90	346	ohv	own
	B7		4	54	81.7	749	ohc	own
	B 75		4	54	54.5	499	ohc	own
Moto Guzzi		I	1	68	68	248	ohc	own
			1	88	82	499	ioe	own
			1	88	82	499	ohc	own
Motosacoche	316	CH	1	72	85	347	ioe	own (MAG)
	317		1	72	85	347	ohv	own (MAG)
	417		1	82	94	498	sv	own (MAG)
	714		2 V	72	91	746	ioe	own (MAG)
MT	H 29	A	1	79	70	342	2	Villiers
	N.O.		1	85.7	85	490	sv	JAP
	TSP 4		1	79	101	496	ohv	Sturmey-Archer
	2 29 B		2 V	70	97	746	sv	JAP
New Hudson	31	GB	1	70	90	346	sv	own
	33		1	70	90	346	ohv	own
	3		1	79.5	100	496	ohv	own
			1	83.5	100	547	sv	own
New Imperial	Leinster	GB	1	62.5	80	248	ohv	own
	10 Prince		1	70	90	348	ohv	own
	11 Prince		1	86	86	499	ohv	own
Norton	JE	GB	1	71	88	348	ohv	own
	CJ		1	71	88	348	ohc	own
	16H		1	79	100	490	sv	own
	18		1	79	100	490	ohv	own
	CS		1	79	100	490	ohc	own
	19		1	79	120	588	ohv	own
	Big Four		1	82	120	633	sv	own
NSU	Pony	D	1	45	40	63	2	own
	175Z		1	59	64	174	2	own
	201 Z		1	63	64	198	2	own
	251 TS		1	63	80	247	ioe	own
	351 TS		1	71	88	346	ohv	own
	501 TS		1	80	99	494	sv	own
	500 SS		1	80	99	494	ohc	own
OEC		GB	1	70	90	346	sv	JAP
			1	85.7	85	490	ohv	JAP
	Flying Squad		2 V	80	90	994	ohv	JAP
OK-Supreme	N	GB	1	85.7	85	490	sv	JAP
	A		1	70	64.5	248	ohc	own
	M		2 V	70	97	749	sv	JAP
Peugeot	P 109	F	1	54	76	174	sv	own
	P 107		1	72	85	348	sv	own
	P 105		1	72	85	348	ohv	own
P&M-Panther	50	GB	1	84	90	498	ohv	own
	90 Redwing		1	79	100	490	ohv	own
	25		1	65	70	247	2	Villiers
Praga	350	CS	1	70	90	346	ohc	own
	500		1	84	90	499	ohc	own
Premier	A 1	CS	1	70	70	269	2	Villiers
	S2		1	71	88	346	sv	own
	S3		1	85	88	499	sv	own
	SL		1	75.5	110	494	ohv	own
	S6		2 V	76	82	744	sv	own
Puch	250	A	1	45 x 2	78	248	2	own
	500Z		2	45 x 2	78	496	2	own
Radco	L	GB	1	55	62	147	2	Villiers
		P	1	67	70	247	2	own
Raleigh MO		GB	1	65.6	88	298	sv	own-S.A.
	MT		1	71	88	348	ohv	own-S.A.
	MH		1	79	101	496	ohv	own-S.A.
Ready		B	1	70	90	346	sv	JAP
			1	85.7	85	490	ohv	JAP
Rene-Gillet	H	F	1	70	90	346	sv	own
	G		2 V	70	97.7	749	sv	own
	J		2 V	80	97.7	981	sv	own
Rhony'X	VM	F	1	46	60	100	2	own
	H3		1	70	90	346	sv	own
	H51		1	83	90	490	sv	own
RMW	200	D	1	62	66	198	2	own
			1	71	88	348	sv	Sturmey-Archer
			1	82	96	498	ioe	MAG
			1	82	96	496	ohv	MAG
Royal-Enfield	C	GB	1	70	90	346	sv	own
	CO		1	70	90	346	ohv	own
	HA		1	85.5	85	498	sv	own
	JA		1	85.5	85	498	ohv	own
	H		1	80.5	99.25	570	sv	own
	K		2 V	85.5	85	976	sv	own
Rudge-Whitworth	250	GB	1	62.5	81	249	ohv	own
	350		1	70	90.5	349	ohv	own
	500 Spec.		1	85	88	499	ohv	own
Sarolea	A	B	1	75	79	347	sv	own
	S		1	80.5	97	494	ohv	own
Schliha		D	1	69.3	70	193	2	own
			1	82.4	86	349	2	own
			1	102.5	86	498	2	own
Schüttoff	200	D	1	60	68	192	2	DKW
			1	74	68	296	2	DKW
			1	72	85	346	ohv	own
			1	80	99	494	sv	own
			1	80	99	494	ohv	own
Scott	Squirrel	GB	1	73	71.4	298	2	own
	Fl. Squirell		2	68.25	68.25	498	2	own
	Fl. Squirell		2	74.6	68.25	596	2	own
	TT Replica		2	66.6	71.4	498	2	own
	TT Replica		2	73	71.4	596	2	own
SMW	S IV	D	1	61	67	196	2	Villiers
	S III		1	81	96.8	498	ohv	Blackburne
Soyer	500 Block	F	1	80	91	498	ohc	own
	500 S Sport		1	80	91	498	ohc	own
Standard	DS 250	D	1	62.5	80	249	ohv	own

Standard	CT 350	D	1	72	84	342	ioe	MAG
	CS 500		1	82	94	498	ohv	MAG
	Rennsport		1	82	94	498	ohv	MAG
	BT 1000		2 V	82	94	997	ioe	MAG
Stock	Extra		1	55	50	119	2	own
	Kardan 200		1	66	58	197	2	own
	GR 300		1	74	68	292	2	own
Sunbeam	10	GB	1	74	80	344	ohv	own
	Lion Longstroke		1	77	105.5	492	sv	own
	9 (90) TT		1	80	98	493	ohv	own
Super-X	Touring	USA	2 V	76	83	752	ioe	own
Terrot	LPP	F	1	57	68	174	2	own
	FST		1	67	70	247	2	own
	OSSE		1	59	90	246	ohv	own
	NSSL		1	85.5	85	490	ohv	JAP
	V		2 V	70	88	676	sv	JAP
Titan	Spezial	A	1	75	77	340	2	own
	500		1	81	96.8	498	sv	Blackburne
Train	M-5	F	1	64	54	173	2	own
			1	76	76	344	ohv	own
Triumph	X	GB	1	59.5	62.5	74	2	own
	WO		1	63	80	249	ohv	own
	WL		1	72	85.5	348	sv	own
	NT		1	84	89	493	ohv	own
	ND		1	84	99	548	sv	own
Triumph (TWN)	SK 200	D	1	59	72	197	2	own
	T 350		1	72	85	346	ioe	MAG
	SST 500		1	82	94	498	ohv	MAG
Triumph (TWN)	RR	D	V 2	72	91	741	ioe	MAG
Universal		CH	1	70	90	348	sv	JAP
			1	85.7	85	490	ohv	JAP
UT		D	1	60	68	193	2	Bark
			1	70	90	348	ohv	JAP
			1	85.7	104	599	ohv	JAP
Velocette	GTP	GB	1	63	80	249	2	own
	KTP		1	74	81	348	ohc	own
	KTT		1	74	81	348	ohc	own
Victoria	KR 20	D	1	60	88	248	sv	Sturmey-Archer
	KR 35		1	71	87	348	ohv	Sturmey-Archer
	KR 50		1	79	101	492	ohv	Sturmey-Archer
	KR 6		2 F	77	64	596	ohv	own
Wimmer	GG 25	D	1	67	71	247	ohv	own
	GG 50		1	84	90	499	sv	Bark
Wolf	Utility	GB	1	61	67	196	2	Villiers
Württembergia	BL 200	D	1	56.3	79	196	sv	Blackburne
	SS 350		1	71	88	348	ohv	Blackburne
	RL 600		1	85	105	596	sv	Blackburne
Zündapp	S 200		1	60	70	198	2	own
	S 300		1	68	82.5	298	2	own
	S 500		1	85	88	499	ohv	Python

THE POST-WAR PERIOD

MARQUE	MODEL	COUNTRY	CYL	BORE	STROKE	CC	2/4-STROKE	ENGINE	BHP
Adler	M 100	D	1	50	50	98	2	own	3.8
	M 150		1	54	59	147	2	own	8.4
	M 250		2	54	54	247	2	own	16
Aermacchi	125	I	1F	52	58	123	2	own	5
Aero-Caproni	Capriolo	I	1	47	43	75	ohv	own	3.5
AJS	16 M	GB	1	69	93	347	ohv	own	15.2
	18		1	82.5	93	498	ohv	own	21.1
	7R Boys Racer		1	75.b	78	349	ohc	own	30
Alpino	Sport	I	1	53.5	55	123	2	own	6.5
Ardie	BD 175	D	1	60	61	172	2	own	9
	B 252		1	66	72	244	2	own	13
Aeriel	NG	GB	1	72	85	347	ohv	own	14.2
	VG		1	81.8	95	497	ohv	own	22
	VH Red Hunter		1	81.8	95	497	ohv	own	24.6
	VB		1	86.4	102	598	sv	own	15.5
	4G Square Four		4 Sq	65 x 4	75	997	ohv	own	34.5
Astoria	Sport	I	1	56	60	148	2	own	6.3
B (Motobi)	115	I	1	52	54	115	2	own	5.2
	200	I	2 F	48	54	196	2	own	9
Bauer		D	1	68	68	246	ohv	own	16
Benelli	Sport Leoncino	I	1	54	54	123	2	own	6.5
	Leonessa		2	53	56	247	ohv	own	16
Beta	Sport	I	1	57	62	158	2	own	7.5
Bianchi	Freccia Celeste	I	1	52	58	123	2	own	7.5
BMW	R 25/2	D	1	68	68	245	ohv	own	12
	R 51/3		2	68	68	494	ohv	own	24
	R 67/2		2	72	73	590	ohv	own	28
	R 68		2	72	73	590	ohv	own	35
Bonvicini	BM 160	I	1	58	66	174	2	Ilo	6.5
Borghi	Olympia	I	1	52	58	123	2	BSA	5.5
BSA	C 10	GB	1	63	80	249	sv	own	8
	C 11		1	63	80	249	ohv	own	11
	B 31		1	71	88	348	ohv	own	17
	B 33		Z	85	88	499	ohv	own	23
	M 20		1	82	94	496	sv	own	13
	M 21		1	82	112	591	sv	own	15
	M 33		1	95	88	499	ohv	own	23
	A 7		2	66	72.6	498	ohv	own	27.4
	A 10 GF		2	70	84	646	ohv	own	35.5
Bücker	TZ 200	D	1	62	66	198	2	Ilo	11
	Ilona II		2	52	58	246	2	Ilo	15.1
Carnielli	75	I	1	46	44	73	2	Vittoria	3
Ceccato		I	1	54	54	123	2	own	5.5
Cimatti	SS	I	1	57	62	158	2	own	7
CM		I	1	52	58	123	2	own	4.5
		I	2	52	58	246	2	own	8.5
Condor	25 De Luxe	CH	1	63	72	225	2	Villiers	10
	Racer		2	58	66	348	2	own	14
	580 Ralye		2 F	70	75.2	577	sv	own	20
	750 Touriste		2 F	78	78	748	sv	own	25
Cotton	Vulcan	GB	1	79	72	197	2	Villiers	7.6
	Herald		2	50	63.5	249	2	Villiers	8.5
	Messenger		2	57	63.5	324	2	Villiers	—
CZ		CS	1	52	58	124	2	own	5.6
			1	57	58	148	2	own	6.5
			1	60	61	173	2	own	6.5
			1	65	75	247	2	own	9
Delta Gnom	Luxus	A	1	52	58	123	2	Rotax	5.8
DKW	RT 125	D	1	52	58	123	2	own	4.75
	RT 200		1	62	64	192	2	own	8.5
	RT 250		1	70	64	244	2	own	11.5
	RT 350		2 F	62	58	348	2	own	18
Douglas	Standard Mk. III	GB	2 F	60.8	60	348	ohv	own	20
Dot	200 SCH	GB	1	59	72	197	2	Villiers	7.6
	250 SCH		1	66	72	246	2	Villiers	8.5
Dürkopp	MD 150	D	1	53	60	150	2	own	7.5
	MD 200		1	61	64	198	2	own	10.2
Ducati	48	I	1	39	40	48	ohv	own	1.5
EMW	R 35/3	DDR	1	72	84	340	ohv	own	14
Excelsior	Autobyk	GB	1	50	50	98	2	Brockhouse	2.2
Excelsior	Consort	GB	1	47	57	98	2	Villiers	2.8
	Condor		1	50	62	123	2	Villiers	5
	Courier		1	55	62	148	2	Villiers	6.5

THE POST-WAR PERIOD

MARQUE	MODEL	COUNTRY	CYL	BORE	STROKE	CC	2/4-STROKE	ENGINE	BHP
Excelsior	Roadsmaster	GB	1	59	72	197	2	Villiers	8.5
	Talisman		2	50	62	244	2	Villiers	12.8
Express	SL 107	D	1	48	54	98	2	Sachs	3.1
	Radex 200		1	62	66	197	2	Ilo	11.2
	Radex 252	D	2	52	58	244	2	Ilo	15.1
FBM	Gabbiano	I	1 F	52	58	122	2	own	4.75
FB-Mondial	200	I	1	62	66	198	ohc	own	12
Ferrari	Tourismo	I	1	54	54	124	2	own	6
FN	22	B	1	45 x 2	55	173	2	BP	8.3
	13250		1	63	80	249	ohv	own	11
	13350		1	74	80	344	sv	own	10
	13350		1	74	80	344	ohv	own	13
	13450		1	84.5	80	444	ohv	own	18
	20		2	63	80	498	ohc	own	22
Franchi		I	1	57	58	147	2	Sachs	6.5
Francis-Barnett	66	GB	1	50	62	122	2	Villiers	5
	62		1	59	72	197	2	Villiers	8.4
	68		1	63	72	225	2	Villiers	9.7
	80		1	66	73	249	2	Villiers	12.8
Fusi	250	I	1	68	68	248	ohc	own	13
Galbusera	Lusso	I	1	57	58	147	2	Sachs	6
Ganna	Sport	I	1	40 x 2	59.6	148	2	Puch	6.5
Gilera	150 S	I	1	60	54	152	ohv	own	6.5
	Nettuno S		1	68	68	248	ohv	own	14
	B 300		2	60	54	306	ohv	own	13
	Saturno		1	84	90	498	ohv	own	22
Gillet (Herstal)	150 S	B	1	55	60	143	2	own	6.5
	175 S		1	57	68	172	2	own	8
	200 Belgica		1	61	68	194	2	own	9
	250 S		1	65	72	248	2	own	9
	250 Milan		1	65	72	248	ohv	own	11
	300 S		1	70	76	292	ohv	own	13
	500 S		1	77	105	488	ohv	own	17
Gitan	Turbine	I	1	52	58	158	ohv	own	7.5
Giricke	200 S	D	1	62	66	198	2	Ilo	11
Greeves	20 DB	GB	1	59	72	197	2	Villiers	9
	25 DC		2	50	63.6	240	2	Villiers	13.2
Guazzoni	150 SS	I	1	56	62	148	2	own	8
	250 T		1	68	68	246	2	own	9
Harley-Davidson	XLH	USA	2 V	76	97	833	ohv	own	
	FLF		2 V	87.3	100.8	1213	ohv	own	
Hecker	K 175	D	1	58	66	173	2	Ilo	8.5
	K 250 Z		2	52	58	246	2	Ilo	15.1
Hercules	313	D	1	57	58	147	2	Sachs	6.5
	315		1	65	75	248	2	Ilo	11.2
Hoffman	250	D	1	65	75	248	2	Ilo	12.8
	Gouverneur		2 F	47	58	248	ohv	own	13.4
Horex	Regina	D	1	69	91.5	342	ohv	Columbus	19
	Regina		1	74.5	91.5	399	ohv	Columbus	21.2
Honda	Benly C 92	JAP	1	44	41	124	ohc	own	11.5
	Dream C72		2	54	54	247	ohc	own	20
Husqvarna	30	S	1	55	50	120	2	own	6
	281		1	60	61.5	174	2	own	7
Iso	200	I	1	44 x 2	64	199	2	own	10.5
Itom	Alba MT 34	I	1	39	40	48	2	own	0.7
Ifa	BK 350	DDR	2 F	58	65	343	2	own	15
James	Captain	GB	1	59	72.8	199	2	Villiers	9
	Commando		1	66	72.8	249	2	Villiers	12.8
Jawa	250	CS	1	65	75	248	2	own	9
	350		2	58	65	348	2	own	12
	500		2	65	73.6	498	ohc	own	26
Kreidler	K 50	D	1	38	44	50	2	own	2.2
KTM	R 100	A	1	48	54	98	2	Rotax	3
	125 T		1	54	54	123	2	Rotax	6.1
Laverda	75 Sport	I	1	46	45	75	ohv	own	3.2
Leprotto	Tourismo	I	1	46 x 2	60	198	2	own	10.5
Maico	Fanal	D	1	61	59.5	174	2	own	9.2
	M 200 T		1	65	59.5	197	2	own	11
	M 250 S		1	67	70	246	2	own	13.2
	Taifun		2	61	59.5	348	2	own	18.2
	Taifun		2	65	59.5	394	2	own	21.2
Mammut	257 S	D	1	57	58	147	2	own	6.5
Mars	Stella	D	1	58	62	174	2	Sachs	9.5
MAS	Zenith	I	1	62	57.5	174	ohv	own	7.5
Matchless	G3L	GB	1	69	93	347	ohv	own	16.6
	G80		1	82.5	93	498	ohv	own	23.5
	G9		2	66	72.8	498	ohv	own	30
Miller Balsamo	175 Sport	I	1	58	66	174	2	own	6.5
	250 Jupiter		1	62.5	81	249	ohv	own	16
Mival	125S	I	1	52	58	123	2	own	6
MM	AS	I	1	64	77	247	ohc	Sachs	
	CT		1	76	77	349	ohc	own	
Monark	M88B	S	1	57	58	148	2	Sachs	6.5
	M550		2	52	58	244	2	Ilo	15.1
Morini	125 Sport	I	1	52	58	123	2	own	7.5
Motobecane	D45S	F	1	51	60	122	sv	own	4.3
	Z54C		1	52	58	124	ohv	own	5.4
	Z2C		1	56	71	174	ohv	own	8.5
	L4C		2 V	56	71	348	ohv	own	
Moto Guzzi	65	I	1	42	46	65	2	own	2
	Galetto		1	62	53	158	ohv	own	5
	Airone Tour		1 F	70	64	249	ohv	own	9.5
	Falcone		1 F	88	82	498	ohv	own	23
Motom	Delfino	I	1	62	54	158	ohv	own	7.5
MV Agusta	125 T	I	1	53	56	123	2	own	6
	150 S		1	56	60	149	2	own	8
	500 Sport		4	54	54	497	ohc	own	45
Norton	16H	GB	1	79	100	490	sv	own	12
	18		1	79	100	490	ohv	own	20
	Intern. 40		1	71	88	348	ohc	own	24
	Intern.30		1	79	100	490	ohc	own	29.5
	Manx 40		1	71	88	348	ohc	own	27
	Manx 30		1	79.6	100	499	ohc	own	33
NSU	Fox	D	1	50	50	98	ohv	own	5.2
	2 T Fox		1	52	58	123	2	own	5.4
	2 T Lux	D	1	62	66	197	2	own	8.6
	Max		1	69	66	247	ohc	own	17
	Consul		1	80	99	497	ohv	own	22
Omea	125 C	I	1	56.5	50	124	2	own	5.4
Orix	175 GS	I	1	66	58	173	2	Ilo	8.6
Panther (P&M)	60	GB	1	60	88	248	ohv	own	11
	70		1	71	88	348	ohv	own	18
	100		1	87	100	499	ohv	own	26
Panther	KS 175	D	1	58	62	173	2	Sachs	9
Parilla	125 Sport	I	1	54	54	124	2	own	7
	250 Boxer		1	65	75	249	2	own	9
	Fox		1	59.8	62	174	ohv	own	9
	Fox SS		1	59.8	62	174	ohc	own	12
	Veltro Twin		2	62	58	349	ohv	own	16
Peugeot	55 TA	F	1	51	60	124	2	own	4.5
	176 GS		1	60	60	174	2	own	10
	256 TC4		2	51	60	248	2	own	13
Puch	125 SVS	A	1	38 x 2	55	124	2	own	8
	175 SVS		1	42 x 2	62	172	2	own	12.3
	250 SGS		1	45 x 2	78	248	2	own	16.5
Rabeneick	F 250/1	D	1	65	75	247	2	Ilo	12.8
Rondine	SS	I	1	53	56	124	2	own	5.8
Royal Enfield	Re 2	GB	1	53.8	55	123	2	own	4.5

MARQUE	MODEL	COUNTRY	CYL	BORE	STROKE	CC	2/4-STROKE	ENGINE	BHP
Royal Enfield	Ensign	GB	1	56	60	148	2	own	8
	Clipper		1	64	77	248	ohv	own	11.2
	Bullet		1	70	90	348	ohv	own	18.3
	Bullet		1	84	90	498	ohv	own	25.4
	500 Twin		2	64	77	496	ohv	own	25.4
	Meteor		2	70	90	692	ohv	own	36.5
Rumi	Sport	I	2 F	42	45	124	2	own	8.5
RWC	T 98	A	1	48	54	98	2	Rotax	2.3
Sarolea	Carena	B	1	60	70	198	2	own	7.5
Sarolea	Vedette	I	1	75	79	349	ohv	own	15
	Continental		1	75	90	398	sv	own	10.5
	Atlantic		2	63	80	498	ohv	own	26
	Atlantic Major		2	70	78	599	ohc	own	30
Sitta	250	D	2	52	58	244	2	Ilo	15
Sparta	125	NL	1	50	60	122	2	Villiers	5
	250		1	67	70	247	2	Villiers	10.3
Sunbeam	S7 & S8	GB	2	70	63.5	487	ohc	own	25.4
Taurus	B8	I	1	65	60	199	ohv	own	13.8
Terrot	ETD	F	1	52	58	123	ohv	own	5.5
	OSSD		1	68	68	247	ohv	own	11
	RGST		1	84	90	499	ohv	own	22
Thunder	Twin	I	2	43	44	127	ohv	own	5.5
Tornax	K 125 H	D	1	52	58	123	2	Ilo	5.9
	KTV200		1	62	66	197	2	Ilo	11
	Z250		2	52	58	244	2	Ilo	15.1
Triumph (TWN)	BDG125	D	1	35.5 x 2	62	123	2	own	6.5
	BDG250		1	45 x 2	78	246	2	own	11
	Boss		1	53 x 2	78	344	2	own	16
Triumph	T 15 Terrier	GB	1	51	58.5	149	ohv	own	8
	T 20 Tiger Cub		1	63	64	199	ohv	own	10
	T 5 Speed Twin		2	63	80	498	ohv	own	27
	T 100 Tiger		2	63	80	498	ohv	own	34
	T 6 Thunderbird		2	71	82	649	ohv	own	34
	T 110 Tiger		2	71	82	649	ohv	own	42
Universal	Junior	CH	1	67	70	247	ohv	own	14
	Meteor		2 F	72	71	578	ohv	own	30
UT	KTN125	D	1	52	58	123	2	Ilo	5.9
	TS250		1	65	75	248	2	Ilo	12.8
Velocette	Le II	GB	2 F	50	49	198	sv	own	8
	MAC		1	68	96	349	ohv	own	14.3
	KSS Mk II		1	74	81	348	ohc	own	
	MSS		1	86	86	499	ohv	own	39
Victoria	Bifix	D	1	51	60	123	2	own	5
	KR25		1	67	70	247	2	own	10.5
	KR26 Aero		1	67	70	247	2	own	14
	Bergmeister-Sport		2 V	64	54	345	hc	own	21
Vincent HRD	Comet	GB	1	84	90	499	hc	own	28.4
	Rapide		2 V	84	90	998	hc	own	45
	Black Shadow		2 V	84	90	998	hc	own	55
	Black Lightning		2 V	84	90	998	hc	own	70
Zündapp	Norma Luxus	D	1	60	70	198	2	own	8.3
	Elastic 200		1	60	70	198	2	own	9.5
	Elastic 250		1	67	70	236	2	own	13
	KS601 Sport		2 F	75	85	597	ohv	own	32

The 1960s and 1970s

MARQUE	MODEL	COUNTRY	CYL	BORE	STROKE	CC	2/4-STROKE	ENGINE	BHP
Ancillotti	Cross	I	1	40	39.5	49	2	Sachs	11
	Cross		1	54	54	123	2	Sachs	24
	Cross		1	71.5	61	245	2	Sachs	32
Aspes	Cross	I	1	54	54	123	2	own	24
	Hopi		1	54	54	123	2	own	21
Avello	Nebraska	E	1	38	43	49	2	Puch	5
	Cobra		1	48	39.7	72	2	Puch	10
Benelli	125	I	1	56	49	120	2	own	15.4
	125 Enduro		1	56	49	120	2	own	15.4
	125 2C		2	52.5	44	124	2	own	16
	250 2C		2	56	47	232	2	own	30
	250 Quattro		4	44	38	231	4 ohc	own	26.6
	500 Quattro		4	56	50.6	498	4 ohc	own	55
	750 Sei		6	56	50.6	748	4 ohc	own	75
Beta	125 SG	I	1	54	54	124	2	own	20
	250 GS		1	70	64.5	249	2	own	34
	250 CR		1	70	64.5	249	2	own	36
BMW	R60/7	D	2	73.5	70.6	599	4 ohv	own	40
	R75/7		2	82	70.6	745	4 ohv	own	50
	R100/7		2	94	70.6	980	4 ohv	own	60
	R100S		2	94	70.6	980	4 ohv	own	65
Bultaco	Mercurio GT 175	E	1	61.15	60	176.2	2	own	12.5
	Metralla GT250		1	72	60	244	2	own	22.7
	Alpina 250		1	71	60	237.6	2	own	14.1
	Alpina 350		1	83.2	60	326	2	own	21.6
Bultaco	Sherpa Trials	B	1	54.2	51.5	119	2	own	9.12
	Sherpa Trials		1	71	60	237	2	own	14.1
	Sherpa Trials		1	83.2	60	326	2	own	18.5
	Pursang MC		1	51.5	60	124	2	own	24.5
	Pursang MC	E	1	72	60	244	2	own	34.3
	Pursang MC		1	85	64	363	2	own	40.2
CCM	MC 500	GB	1	84	90	498	4 ohv	own	45
CZ	125	CS	1	52	58	123	2	own	11
	175		1	58	65	172	2	own	15
	175 Enduro		1	62	57	172	2	own	16
	250 Enduro		1	70	64	246	2	own	20
	250 Twin		2	52	58	246	2	own	17
	350 Twin		2	58	64	343	2	own	21
	Moto Cross 125		1	55	52	123	2	own	21
	Moto Cross 250		1	70	64	246	2	own	34
	Moto Cross 400		1	82	72	381	2	own	42
DKW	MC125	D	1	54	54	122	2	Sachs	24
	GS250		1	71.5	61	245	2	Sachs	32
Dniepr	M 10	USSR	2	78	68	649	4 ohv	own	34
Ducati	125 ISDT	I	1	54	54	123.7	2	own	22
	350 GTL		2	71.8	43.2	349.6	4 ohc	own	27
	500 GTL		2	78	52	496	4 ohc	own	40
	500 S Desmo		2	78	52	496	4 ohc	own	50
	750 Super Sport		2 V	80	74.4	748	4 ohc	own	68
	GT860		2 V	86	74.4	864	4 ohc	own	65
	900 Super Sport		2 V	86	74.4	864	4 ohc	own	72
Fantic	Caballero Reg.	I	1	55	52	123.5	2	own	21.5
	Caballero Cross	I	1	55	52	123.5	2	own	21.6
Garelli	50 RSL Electr.	I	1	40	39.5	49.6	2	own	6.3
Gilera	150 Strada	I	1	60	54	152.6	4 ohv	own	14.2
Gori	Codice 50	I	1	40	39.5	49	2	Sachs	6.5
	Moto Cross		1	54	54	123	2	Sachs	22
	Competizione		1	71.5	61	245	2	Sachs	33
Greeves	250 MX	GB	1	70	64	246	2	own	28.5
	380 MX		1	82	72	380	2	own	44
Harley-Davidson	SX 125	USA	1	56	50	123	2	own	12
	SX175		1	61	59.6	174	2	own	17
	SX250		1	71.8	59.6	243	2	own	20
	SS250		1	71.8	59.6	243	2	own	19
	XLH (XLCH)		2 V	80	97	975	4 ohv	own	65
	FX (FXE)		2 V	87.3	100.8	1207	4 ohv	own	66
	Electra Glide		2 V	87.3	100.8	1207	4 ohv	own	66
Hercules	K 50 Sprint	D	1	38	44	49	2	Sachs	6.25
	K50 Ultra		1	38	44	49	2	Sachs	6.25
	K125S		1	54	54	122	2	Sachs	17
	125 GS		1	54	54	122	2	Sachs	22

The 1960s and 1970s

MARQUE	MODEL	COUNTRY	CYL	BORE	STROKE	CC	2/4-STROKE	ENGINE	BHP
Hercules	175 GS	D	1	60	61	173	2	Sachs	26
	250 GS		1	71.5	61	245	2	Sachs	32
	Wankel		3 Chamber			294		Sachs	27
Honda	ST 70 (Dax)	J	1	47	41.4	72	4 ohc	own	5.2
	CB125S		1	56.5	49.5	124	4 ohc	own	14
	CB125 disc		2	44	41	124	4 ohc	own	15
	CB200 disc		2	55.5	41	198	4 ohc	own	17
	CJ250 T		2	56	50.6	249	4 ohc	own	27
	CJ360 T		2	67	50.6	356	4 ohc	own	34
	CB500 T		2	70	64.8	498	4 dohc	own	42
	CB400		4	51	50	408	4 ohc	own	37
	CB500		4	56	50.6	499	4 ohc	own	48
	CB550		4	58.5	50.6	539	4 ohc	own	50
	CB750		4	61	63	736	4 ohc	own	63
	GL1000 Gold Wing		4 F	72	61.4	999	4 ohc	own	82
	TL125 S		1	56.5	49.5	124	4 ohc	own	9
	CR125 Elsinore		1	56	50	123	2	own	24
Indian	ME125	USA	1	55	52	123.5	2	own	19
Jawa	23	CS	1	38	44	49.9	2	own	4
	634		2	58	65	343	2	own	26
	GS175		1	62	57.5	174	2	own	22.5
	GS250		1	70	64	246	2	own	28.5
	GS350		1	78	72	344	2	own	35
	GS370		1	80	72	362	2	own	36
Kawasaki	KH125	J	1	56	506	124	2	own	
	KX125 M/C		1	56	50.6	124	2	own	22
	KX250 M/C		1	40	64.9	249	2	own	34
	KX400 M/C		1	82	76	401	2	own	42
	KE125		1	56	50.6	124	2	own	13
	KT250 Trials		1	69.5	64.9	246	2	own	16
Kawasak	KH250	J	3	45	52.3	249	2	own	28
	KH400		3	57	52.3	400	2	own	40
	KH500		3	60	58.8	498	2	own	52
	City Bike		1	46	44	73	2	own	4.2
	Z200		1			198	4 ohc	own	
	Z400		2	64	62	398	4 ohc	own	36
	Z750		2	78	78	746	4 oho	own	51
	Z650		4	62	54	652	4 2 x ohc	own	64
	Z1000		4	70	66	1015	4 2 x ohc	own	85
Kreidler	Florett RSL	D	1	40	39.7	49.8	2	own	6.25
KTM	GP50 RS Comet	A	1	38	44	49	2	Sachs	6.25
	GP125 RS Comet		1	54	54	122	2	Sachs	17
	MC125		1	54	54	124	2	Sachs	26
	MC250 x GS 250		1	71	62	246	2	own	34
	MC400 x GS 400		1	81	69	356	2	own	42
	GS125		1	54	54	124	2	own	24
	GS175		1	63.5	54	172	2	own	27
Laverda	H125TR	I	1	55	52	124	2	own	24
	H250 Tr		1	68	68	247	2	own	27
	500 Twin		2	72	61	497	4 2 x ohc	own	46
	750 SF 3		2	80	74	744	4 ohc	own	50
	1000		3	75	74	980	4 2 x ohc	own	78
Maico	MD50	D	1	38	44	49	2	own	6.3
	MD125		1	54	54	124	2	own	16
	MD250		1	76	54	245	2	own	27
	GS125		1	54	54	124	2	own	21
	GS250		1	67	70	247	2	own	36
	GS400		1	77	83	386	2	own	43
	GS 50		1	82	83	438	2	own	47
Malanca	125 E2 C	I	2	43	43	124	2	own	15
	125 E2 C Sport		2	43	43	124	2	own	18
	150GT		2	46	46	149	2	own	20
Mondial	Touring	I	1	55	52	123	2	own	9
	Regolarit†		1	54	54	124	2	own	12
Montesa	Enduro 250	E	1	70	64	246.3	2	own	27
	Cota 123		1	54	54	123	2	own	13
	Cota 247		1	72.5	60	247	2	own	20
Montesa	Cappra 125 Reg.	E	1	54	54	123	2	own	24
	Cappra 250 VB		1	70	64	246	2	own	36
Morbidelli	Competizione	I	2	44	41	124.6	2	own	35
Morini	Corsarino ZZ50	I	1	41	37	49	4 ohv	own	4.5
	125 T		1	59	45	123	4 ohv	own	14
	3 1/2 V		2 V	62	57	344	4 ohv	own	35
	3 1/2 Sport VS		2 V	62	67	344	4 ohv	own	30
Motobecane	125 LT	F	2	43	43	125	2	own	16
	350		3	53	52.8	349.5	2	own	38
Moto Guzzi	250 TS	I	2	56	47	231	2	own	25
	350 GTS		4	50	44	345	4 ohc	own	38
	400 GTS		4	50	51	397	4 ohc	own	40
	Falcone Sahara		1	88	82	499	4 ohc	own	27
	750T		2 V	82	70	748	4 ohv	own	70
	850T3		2 V	73	78	844	4 ohv	own	68
	850T3 California		2 V	73	78	844	4 ohv	own	68
	V1000 Convert		2 V	88	78	949	4 ohv	own	71
	850 Le Mans		2 V	73	78	844	4 ohv	own	81
Mototrans-Ducati	350 Road	E	1	76	75	340	4 ohc	own	28
Münch-4	1200 TSS-E	D	4	78.5	66.5	1278	4 ohc	NSU	104
MV Agusta	125 Sport	I	1	53	56	123.5	4 ohv	own	12
	350 Sport		2	63	56	349	4 ohv	own	35
	800S		4	67	56	790	4 2 x ohc	own	82
	900S		4	70	58	893	4 2 x ohc	own	95
MZ	150TS	DDR	1	56	58	143	2	own	11.5
	250TS		1	69	65	249	2	own	19
Norton	Commando	GB	2	77	89	828	4 ohv	own	51
Ossa	250 S.Pion	E	1	72	60	244	2	own	27
	350 S.Pion.		1	77	65	302	2	own	30
	GS 250 Desert		1	72	60	244	2	own	32
	350 MAR Trial		1	77	65	302	2	own	18
Planeta (Jupiter)	Sport	SU	1	76	75	355	2	own	32
Puch	M50 Jet	A	1	40	39.7	49	2	own	6.25
	M125 GS		1	54	54	124	2	Rotax	23
	M175 GS		1	62	57.5	174	2	Rotax	28
	M250 GS		1	74	57.5	247	2	Rotax	32
	MC250 Replica		1	70	64	246	2	Puch	43.5
	MC50 Super		1	40	39.7	49	2	Puch	11.2
Rickmann	Kawasaki CR	GB	4	66	66	903	4 ohc	Kawa	82
Sanglas	400F	E	1	82	79	422	4 ohv	own	24
	500S		1	89.5	79	496	4 ohv	own	27
Seeley	Honda-750	GB	4	61	63	736	4 ohc	Honda	67
Simonini	Long Range R	I	1	54	54	123	2	Sachs	21
	HR Cross		1	54	54	123	2	Sachs	24
Suzuki	TS125	J	1	56	50	123	2	own	13
	TS250		1	70	64	246	2	own	18.7
	RM125		1	56	50	123	2	own	21
	RM250		1	67	70	247	2	own	36
	RM350		1	77	80	372	2	own	42
	GT125		2	43	43	124	2	own	14.2
	GT185		2	49	49	184	2	own	15
	GT250		2	54	54	247	2	own	26
	GT380		3	54	54	371	2	own	33
	GT500		2	70	64	429	2	own	38
	GT550		3	61	62	539	2	own	48
	GT750		3	70	64	738	2	own	63
	RE 5 Rotary					497	Ro.	Wankel	63
	GS400		2	65	60	398	4 2 x ohc	own	36
	GS750		4	65	56.4	738	4 2 x ohc	own	63
SWM	Silver Vase	I	1	40	39.7	49	2	Sachs	10
	Cross		1	40	39.7	49	2	Sachs	11
	Silver Vase		1	48	54	97	2	Sachs	19.5

MARQUE	MODEL	COUNTRY	CYL	BORE	STROKE	CC	2/4-STROKE	ENGINE	BHP
SWM	Silver Vase	I	1	54	54	123	2	Sachs	24
	Silver Vase		1	60	61	173	2	Sachs	28
	Silver Vase		1	72	61	248	2	Sachs	34
	Silver Vase		1	73	61	255	2	Sachs	35
Testi	Easy Raider	I	1	52	55	123	2	Minarelli	9
	Corsa 2000		1	52	55	123	2	Minarelli	16
Triumph	Bonneville	GB	2	76	82	744	4 ohv	own	53
	Trident		3	67	70	741	4 ohv	own	64
Villa	Enduro 125 F	I	1	54	54	123	2	Morini	16
	Reg. + Cross		1	54	54	123	2	Morini	22
	Reg. + Cross		1	85	78	442	2	own	42
Voskhod	175	SU	1	62	58	174	2	own	10.5
WSK	M 06 B3	PI	1	52	58	123	2	own	7.3
	M 21 W2		1	61	59.5	174	2	own	14
Yamaha	RD 50 DX	J	1	40	39.7	49	2	own	6.26
	RS100DX		1	52	45.6	97	2	own	10.5
	RD200		2	52	46	195	2	own	22
	RD250		2	52	54	247	2	own	27
	RD400		2	64	62	398	2	own	43
	YZ125		1	56	50	123	2	own	24
	YZ250 motocross		1	70	64	246	2	own	34
	YZ400 motocross		1	85	70	397	2	own	41
	TZ250 racer		2	54	54	247	2	own	46
	TZ350 racer		2	64	54	347	2	own	54
	XT500		1	87	84	499	4 ohc	own	27
	XS500		2	73	59.6	498	4 2 x ohc	own	48.5
	XS650		2	75	74	653	4 ohc	own	51
	XS750		3	68	68.6	748	4 2 x ohc	own	60
	TZ750 racer		4	66.4	54	747	2	own	90
Zündapp	KS50 Sport	D	1	39	41.8	49.9	2	own	6.25
	KS50 Super-Sport		1	39	41.8	49.9	2	own	6.25
	KS50 W/c		1	39	41.8	49.9	2	own	6.25
	KS125 Sport		1	54	54	123	2	own	17
	KS175		1	62	54	163	2	own	17
	KS350		2	62	57	344	2	own	27
	GS125		1	54	54	123	2	own	18

The 1980s

MARQUE	MODEL	COUNTRY	CYL	BORE	STROKE	CC	2/4-STROKE	ENGINE	BHP
Accossato	Cross-Unitrac	I	1	54	54	124	2	own	31
Ancillotti	CH 125	I	1	54	54	124	2	own	24.5
Aspes	Yuma monoscocca	I	1	54	53.8	124	2	own	17
Bajaj	Chetak	IND	1	57	57	145	2	own	6.3
Benelli	125 T	I	2	42.5	44	124	2	own	18
	Sport		2	42.5	44	124	2	own	18
	250 2CE		2	56	47	231.4	2	own	32
	124		2	45.5	38	123.5	4 ohc	own	16
	304		4	44	38	231.1	4 ohc	own	27
	354 T (Sport)		4	50	44	346	4 ohv	own	27
	654 Sport		4	60	53.4	605	4 ohc	own	50
	900 Sei		6	60	53.4	906	4 ohc	own	80
Bimota	HB2	I	4	64.5	69	901.8	4 dohc	Honda	95
	SB3		4	70	64.8	997	4 dohc	Suzuki	90
	KB2		4	58	52.4	553.8	4 dohc	Kawasaki	54
	KB1		4	70	66	1015	4 dohc	Kawasaki	81
BMW	R45	D	2	70	61.5	473	4 ohv	own	35
	R65 (LS)		2	82	61.5	650	4 ohv	own	50
	R80 G/S		2	84.8	70.6	797	4 ohv	own	50
	R100		2	94	70.6	980	4 ohv	own	67
	R100 (CS, RT, RS)		2	94	70.6	980	4 ohv	own	70
BSA	Tracker 125/6	GB	1	56	50	123	2	—	—
	Tracker 175/6		1	66	50	171	2	—	—
Bultaco	Sherpa T125	E	1	54.2	51.5	119	2	own	10
	Sherpa T200		1	61	60	175	2	own	10
	Sherpa T250 (Alpina)		1	71	60	238	2	own	10
	Sherpa T350		1	83.2	60	326	2	own	17
	Alpina 350		1	83.2	64	348	2	own	17
	Frontera 250 GS		1	70	64	246	2	own	17
	Frontera 370 GS		1	85	64	363	2	own	27
Cagiva	SST 125 I		1	56	50.6	123	2	own	10
	SST250/Chopper		1	72	59.6	243	2	own	10
	SST350/Chopper		1	80	68	325	2	own	27
	SX125 (RX 125)		1	56	50.6	124	2	own	17
	SX250		1	72	59.6	243	2	own	17
	SX350		1	80	68	325	2	own	27
	RX250		1	72	81	249	2	own	15
Can-Am	125	CDN	1	54	54	123	2	Rotax	—
	175		1	62	57.5	173	2	Rotax	—
	250		1	72	61	248	2	Rotax	—
	400		1	84	72	399	2	Rotax	—
	Sonic 500		1	89	79.4	494	4 ohc	Rotax	40
Dnjepr	MT 12	USSR	2	78	68	650	4 ohv	own	37
Ducati	Pantah 350 XL	I	2	66	51	349	4 ohc/desmo	own	40
	Pantah 600 TL		2	80	58	583	4 ohc/desmo	own	58
	900 S2		2	86	74.4	863.9	4 ohc/desmo	own	70
Egli	CBX	CH	6	64.5	53.4	1047	4 dohc	Honda	100
	CBX		6	67	53.4	1129	4 ohc	Honda	113
Enfield	Bullet 350 S/L	IND	1	70	90	346	4 ohv	own	17
Fantic	RSX 80	I	1	47.5	45	79.7	2	own	6.5
	Trial 80 Exp.		1	47.5	42	74.4	2	own	8
	Cross-Comp.		1	47.5	45	79.74	2	own	17.5
	RSX 125		1	55.2	52	124.4	2	own	16
	Strada 125		1	55.2	52	124.4	2	own	18.6
	Trial 125		1	55.2	52	124.4	2	own	12
	Trial 200		1	62	52	156.9	2	own	14.5
	Trial 240 Prof.		1	69	56.5	212	2	own	18
Gilera	TG1 (GR1)	I	1	57	48	122	2	own	14.5
	T4		1	66	58	198	4 ohv	own	17
Godier-Genoud	1000 GG 03	F	4	69.4	66	998	4 dohc	Kawasaki	102
	750 GG 07		4	66	54	738	4 dohc	Kawasaki	75
Harley-Davidson	Sportster/Roadster USA		2	81	96.8	998	4 ohv	own	55
	Other models (FXE, FXR, FXRS, FXS, FXWG, FXB-Sturgis, FLH, FLHC, FLT, FLTC)		2	88.8	108	1338	4 ohv	own	67
Hercules	K125	D	1	54	54	122	2	Sachs	12.5
Hesketh	V1000	GB	2	95	70	992.3	4 ohc	own	—
Honda	CR80R	J	1	49.5	41.4	79	2	own	—
	CR124R		1	55.5	50.7	122	2	own	—
	CR250R		1	66	72	246	2	own	—
	CR480R		1	89	76	472	2	own	—
	MTX80		1	45	49.5	78.7	2	own	8.4
	CB125 Twin		2	44	41	124	4 ohc	own	10
	CB250 N E.-Sport		2	62	41.4	245	4 ohc	own	17
	CB250 RS		1	74	57.8	249	4 ohc	own	17
	CL250 S		1	74	57.8	249	4 ohc	own	17
	VT250 F		2	60	44	248	4 dohc	own	35
	XL250 S (R)		1	74	57.8	249	4 ohc	own	17
	CB400N		2	70.5	50.6	395	4 ohc	own	*ff*
	CM400T		2	70.5	50.6	395	4 ohc	own	27
	FT500		1	89	80	498	4 ohc	own	27
	CB500		4	56	50.6	498	4 ohc	own	48
	CX500 (CX 500 Euro, C)		2	78	52	497	4 ohv	own	27
	CX500 Turbo		2	78	52	497	4 ohv (T)	own	82
	GL500DX Silver Wing		2	78	52	497	4 ohv	own	27
	XL500R (XL 500 S)		1	89	80	498	4 ohc	own	27
	XR500R		1	89	80	498	4 ohc	own	35
	CBX550F (F II)		4	59.2	52	572	4 dohc	own	60
	CB650 (650 C, 650 SC)		4	59.8	55.8	626	4 ohc	own	50

The 1980s

MARQUE	MODEL	COUNTRY	CYL	BORE	STROKE	CC	2/4-STROKE	ENGINE	BHP
Honda	CB750K (C, F, F 2)	J	4	62	62	748	4 dohc	own	79
	VF750 Custom (Sport)		4	70	48.6	748	4 dohc	own	81.6
	CB900F (CB 900 F2)		4	64.5	69	901	4 dohc	own	95
	CBX1000 Pro Link		6	64.5	53.4	1047	4 dohc	own	100
	CB1100 R (F)		4	70	69	1062	4 dohc	own	115
	GL1100 Interstate (flat)		4	75	61.4	1085	4 ohc	own	83
Horex	Rebell 80 N	D	1	46	48	79.8	2	Sachs	8.1
	Rebell 80 T (TC, L)		1	46	48	79.8	2	Sachs	8.5
	80 TR		1	46	48	79.8	2	Sachs	7
Husqvarna	125 WR	S	1	55	52	123	2	own	15
	250 WR		1	68.5	64.5	240	2	own	16
	Military Automatic		1	69.5	64.5	245	2	own	24
	420 A E Automatic		1	86	71	412	2	own	17
Ish	Planeta	USSR	1	76	75	346	2	own	20
	Jupiter		2	—	—	347	2	own	27
Italjet	Casual 350	I	1	83.7	60	329	2	own	26
Jawa (Cezet)	350	CS	2	58	65	343.4	2	own	18
Kawasaki	KE125	J	1	56	50.6	123	2	own	10
	KX125		1	56	50.6	123	2	own	32
	KE175 (KDX175)		1	62.5	57	173	2	own	17
	Z250J	J	2	55	52.4	248	4 ohc	own	17
	Z250A		2	55	52.4	248	4 ohc	own	27
	Z250C (Z250LTD)		1	70	64	246	4 ohc	own	17
	KL250 (KLX250)		1	70	64	246	4 ohc	own	17
	KX250		1	70	64 9	249	2	own	42.5
	Z400J		4	52	47	399	4 dohc	own	27
	Z440H (Z440 LTD)		2	67.5	62	443	4 ohc	own	27
	Z550 LTD (Z550 B)		4	58	52.4	553	4 dohc	own	50
	GPZ550		4	58	52.4	553	4 dohc	own	62
	Z650F		4	62	54	647	4 dohc	own	67
	Z750 LTD		2	78	78	745	4 dohc	own	49
	Z750 LTD		4	66	54	738	4 dohc	own	74
	Z750		4	66	54	738	4 dohc	own	77
	GT750		4	66	54	738	4 dohc	own	78
	GPzZ750		4	66	54	738	4 dohc	own	80
	GPz750 Turbo		4	66	54	738	4 dohc	own	110
	Z1000J		4	69.4	66	998	4 dohc	own	98
	Z1000 LTD		4	69.4	66	998	4 dohc	own	95
	Z1100ST		4	72.5	66	1089	4 dohc	own	97
	GPz1100 FI		4	72.5	66	1089	4 dohc	own	100
	Z1300		6	62	71	1277	4 dohc	own	99
Kramer	ER125	D	1	54	54	124	2	own	10
	EX125		1	54	54	124	2	own	30
	ER250 (Gritti Rep.)		1	72	61	248	2	own	17
	EX250		1	72	61	248	2	own	42
	ER500		1	84	72	406	2	own	27
	EX500		1	84	73	406	2	own	50
KTM	GS125	A	1	54	54	124	2	own	10
	GS250		1	76	54	246	2	own	17
	GS420		1	85	54	420	2	own	17
	GS500		1	89	81	503.5	4 ohc	Rotax	45
Laverda	125 SLZ Custom	I	1	54	54	1236	2	Zündapp	16.5
	500 (500SFC)		2	72	61	497	4 dohc	own	45
	1000 Jota (RGS1000)		3	75	74	981	4 dohc	own	85
	1200 TS		3	80	74	1116	4 dohc	own	86
Maico	MD250 wk	D	1	76	54	245	2	own	27
	MC250 (GSE240)		1	67	70	247	2	own	40
	MC400 (GSE400)		1	77	83	386	2	own	47
	MC490 (GSE490)		1	86.5	83	488	2	own	53
Malaguti	Cavalone	I	1	47	46	79.8	2	Franco Morini	7
Malanca	E2C Sport	I	2	43	43	124	2	own	17
	E2C Sport w/c		2	43	43	124	2	own	24
MF	650 R	F	2	77	70	652	4	Citroen	52
Montesa	Cota 123	E	1	54	54	123.7	2	own	7
	Cota 200		1	64	54	173.7	2	own	10
	Cota 248		1	69	64	239.3	2	own	12
	Trail 348		1	83.4	64	349.4	2	own	16
	Enduro 360 H7		1	83.4	64	349.4	2	own	27
Morini	125 T	I	1	59	45	123	4 ohv	own	9
	Amex 250 J		2	59	44	240	4 ohv	own	23
	3 1/2 Sport (V)		2	62	57	344	4 ohv	own	27
	500 T/S		2	69	64	479	4 ohv	own	42
	500 Camel		2	69	64	479	4 ohv	own	38
	500 Turbo		2	69	64	479	4 ohv	own	75
Motobecane	Enduro 80	F	1	43	48	78	2	own	7.4
	125 LT 3		2	43	43	124.8	2	own	16
Motobi	253	I	4	44	38	231	4 ohc	own	26
Moto Guzzi	V35 II (Imola, 35C)	I	2	66	50.6	346.2	4 ohv	own	35
	V50 III (Monza, 50C)		2	74	57	490.3	4 ohv	own	49
	V65 (V65 SP)		2	80	64	643	4 ohv	own	52
	850 T4		2	83	78	844	4 ohv	own	68.5
	850 Le Mans III		2	85	78	844	4 ohv	own	76
	V 1000 Convert (G5, California II, SP)		2	88	78	949	4 ohv	own	61
	V1000 Le Mans II		2	88	78	949	4 ohv	own	82
MZ	123	DDR	1	52	58	123	2	own	10
	ETZ250		1	69	65	243	2	own	17
Ossa	250 Desert	E	1	72	60	244	2	own	16
	T250 Copa		1	72	60	244	2	own	27
Peugeot	TXE125	F	1	57	48	123	2	own	14
Planeta	Sport 350	USSR	1	76	75	346	2	own	32
Puch	GS80 W	A	1	50	40	78.5	2	own	21
	GS125 FS		1	54	54	123.7	2	Rotax	29
	GS250 F3		1	72	61	248.4	2	Rotax	38
	GS366 F3		1	84	66	365.8	2	Rotax	40
	GS504 F4 T UHS		1	90	79	502.6	4 ohc	Rotax	45
	MC 250 UHS		1	72	61	248.4	2	Rotax	40
	MC 500 UHS		1	91	72	468.3	2	Rotax	47
Sanglas	400Y	E	2	69	52.4	391	4 ohv	Yamaha	27
	500 S2		1	85.5	79	496	4 ohv	own	27
Suzuki	DR125 S	J	1	57	48.8	124	4 ohv	own	9.5
	GSX250 E		1	60	44.2	249	4 dohc	own	17
	GN250 E		1	72	61.2	249	4 ohc	own	17
	DR250		1	72	61.2	249	4 ohc	own	17
	GN400TD (400L)		1	88	65.2	396	4 ohc	own	27
	GS400T (GSX400 L & E)		2	65	60	395	4 dohc	own	27
	GSX400F Katana		4	53	45.2	394	4 dohc	own	42
	GS450L (GS450T)		2	71	56.6	448	4 dohc	own	42
	DR500S		1	88	82	495	4 ohc	own	27
	GS550T (GS550M Katana)		4	56	55.8	543	4 dohc	own	50
	GS650G Katana		4	62	55.8	665	4 dohc	own	73
	GS750E		4	67	53	742	4 dohc	own	80
	GSX750S Katana		4	67	53	742	4 dohc	own	82
	GSX1100E		4	72	66	1074	4 dohc	own	100
	Bimota SB 3D		4	70	64.8	986	4 dohc	Suzuki	90
SWM	XN500 Enduro	I	1	89	81	502.3	4 ohc	Rotax	45
	RS125 TL (RS-GS, GTS)		1	54	54	124	2	own	10
	RS175 GS		1	62	57.5	174	2	own	15
	RS250 GS		1	72	61	248	2	own	15
	RS320 TL		1	76	61	277	2	own	15
	RS280 GS		1	76	61	277	2	own	25
	RS370 GS		1	84	71	393	2	own	17
Tornax	TS80	D	1	47	46	79.8	2	F. Morini	7
	RX80 Enduro		1	47	46	79.8	2	F. Morini	7
Triumph	TR6 Thunderbird	GB	2	76	71.5	649	4 ohv-twin	own	42
	TR7 RV Tiger		2	76	82	744	4 ohv-twin	own	46
	TR7 Tiger Trial		2	76	82	744	4 ohv-twin	own	42
	T140 Bonneville		2	76	82	744	4 ohv-twin	own	49
WSK	125 KOS	PL	1	52	58	123	2	own	7.3

The 1980s

MARQUE	MODEL	COUNTRY	CYL	BORE	STROKE	CC	2/4-STROKE	ENGINE	BHP
WSK	175 Perkoz	PL	1	61	59.5	174	2	own	14
Yamaha	DT125 LC	J	1	56	50	123	2	own	16.2
	DT175 MX		1	66	50	169	2	own	16
	SR350 Spec.		1	73.5	56.5	238	4 ohc	own	17
	RD250		2	54	54	248	2	own	27
Yamaha	DT250 MX		1	70	64	244	2	own	16
	XT250		1	75	56.5	249	4 ohc	own	17
	RD350		2	64	54	347	2	own	46
	XS400 (XS 400 Spec.)		2	69	52.4	386	4 ohc	own	27
	SR500 G/S (XT 500)		1	87	84	499	4 ohc	own	27
	XJ550		4	57	51.8	528	4 dohc	own	50
	XZ550 LC		2	80	55	552	4 dohc	own	50
	XJ650		4	63	52.4	653	4 dohc	own	50
	XJ650 Turbo		4	65	52.4	653	4 dohc	own	85
	XS650		2	75	74	653	4 ohc	own	50
	XS650 Special		2	75	74	657	4 ohc	own	48
	XJ750 Seca		4	65	56.4	748	4 dohc	own	81
	XV750 Special		2	83	69.2	749	4 ohc	own	50
	XS850		3	71.5	68.6	826	4 ohc	own	79
	TR1		2	95	69.2	981	4 ohc	own	69
	XS1100 (XS1100S)		4	71.5	68.6	1101	4 dohc	own	95
Zündapp	KS175	D	1	62	54	163	2	own	18

The 1990s

MARQUE	MODEL	COUNTRY	CYL	BORE	STROKE	CC	2/4-STROKE	ENGINE	BHP
Aprilia	AF1	Italy	1	54	54.5	124.7	2	own	12
	RS125	Italy	1	54	54.5	124.8	2	own	12
	Pegaso 125	Italy	1	54	54.5	124.7	2	own	13
	RS250	Italy	2	56	50.6	249	2	own	65
	Tuareg 600	Italy	1	94	81	562.12	ohc	own	45
	Pegaso 650	Italy	1	100	83	651.8	ohc	own	50
	Moto 6.5	Italy	1	100	82.7	649	ohc	own	45
BMW	F650 Funduro	Germany	1	100	83	652	dohc	own	47
	K75	Germany	3	67	70	740	dohc	own	74
	R80	Germany	2	84.8	70.6	798	ohv	own	49
	R80 G/S	Germany	2	84.8	70.6	798	ohv	own	48
	R850 R	Germany	2	87.8	70.5	848	ohv	own	70
	R100 R	Germany	2	94	70.6	980	ohv	own	59
	R100 RS	Germany	2	94	70.6	980	ohv	own	69
	R100 GS	Germany	2	94	70.6	980	ohv	own	59
	K100	Germany	4	67	70	987	dohc	own	89
	K100 RS	Germany	4	67	70	987	dohc	own	89
	K100 LT	Germany	4	67	70	987	dohc	own	
	K1	Germany	4	67	40	987	dohc	own	99
	R1100 R	Germany	2	99	70.5	1085	ohv	own	79
	R1100 RS	Germany	2	99	70.5	1085	ohv	own	89
	R1100 GS	Germany	2	99	70.5	1085	ohv	own	79
	K1100 RS	Germany	4	70.5	70	1092	dohc	own	99
	K1100 LT	Germany	4	70.5	70	1092	dohc	own	99
	R1200 C	Germany	2	70.5	75	1170			
	K1200RS	Germany	4	70.5	75	1171	dohc	own	
BSA	125 Tracker	UK	1	56	50	125	2	own	12
Buell	M2 Cyclone	USA	2	88.8	96.8	1203		Harley	93
	S1 Lightning	USA	2	88.8	96.8	1203		Harley	
Cagiva	Roadster 125	Italy	1	56	50.6	124.6	2	own	12
	Super City 125	Italy	1	56	50.6	124	2	own	12
	Mito	Italy	1	56	50.6	124	2	own	12
	River 600	Italy	1	102	73.6	601.4	ohc	own	34
	Canyon 600	Italy	1	102	73.6	601.4	ohc	own	34
	Elefant 750	Italy	2	88	61.5	748	ohc	own	60
	Elefant 900	Italy	2	92	68	904	ohc	own	68
	Gran Canyon 900	Italy	2	92	64	904	ohc	own	
Ducati	400SS	Italy	2	70.5	51	398	ohc	own	42
	600 Monster	Italy	2	80	58	583	ohc	own	53
	600SS	Italy	2	80	58	583	ohc	own	53
	750 Paso	Italy	2	88	61.5	748	ohc	own	73
	750SS	Italy	2	88	61.5	748	ohc	own	66
	750 Monster	Italy	2	88	61.5	748	ohc	own	98
	748	Italy	2	88	61.5	748	dohc	own	98
	851 Strada	Italy	2	92	64	851	dohc	own	100
	851SP	Italy	2	94	64	888	dohc	own	103 115
	900SS	Italy	2	92	68	904	ohc	own	73
	900 Monster	Italy	2	92	68	904	ohc	own	80
	906 Paso	Italy	2	92	68	904	ohc	own	90
	907iE	Italy	2	92	68	904	ohc	own	90
	916	Italy	2	94	66	916	dohc	own	112-114
	916 SP	Italy	2	94	66	916	dohc	own	
	ST4	Italy	2	94	66	916	dohc	own	
	ST2	Italy	2	94	68	944		own	83
	996 Biposto	Italy	2	98	66	996	dohc	own	
Easy Rider	JH 125L Trail Blazer	China	1	56.5	49.5	124	ohc		
Enfield	Bullet 350 Standard	India	1	70	90	346	ohv	own	18
	Bullet 500 Standard	India	1	84	90	499	ohv	own	22
Gilera	Saturno	Italy	1	92	74	491	dohc	own	45
	Nordwest	Italy	1	98	74	558	dohc	own	53
Harley-Davidson	XLH Sportster	US	2	76.2	96.8	883	ohv	own	
	XL53C Sportster Custom	US	2	76.2	96.8	883	ohv	own	
	XLH 1200 Sportster	US	2	88.8	96.8	1200	ohv	own	64
	FXR Superglide	US	2	88.8	108	1340	ohv	own	69
	FXRS Convertible	US	2	88.8	108	1340	ohv	own	69
	FXD Dyna Super Glide	US	2	88.8	108	1340	ohv	own	69
	FXDL Dyna Low Rider	US	2	88.8	108	1340	ohv	own	69
	FXDWG Dyna Wlde Glide	US	2	88.8	108	1340	ohv	own	69
	FXST Softail	US	2	88.8	108	1340	ohv	own	69
	FXSTB Softail Nightg Train	US	2	88.8	108	1340	ohv	own	69
	FXSTSB Bad Boy	US	2	88.8	108	1340	ohv	own	69
	FLSTC Softail Heritage Classic	US	2	88.8	108	1340	ohv	own	69
	FLSTS Heritage S/T Springer	US	2	88.8	108	1340	ohv	own	69
	FLSTF Fat Boy	US	2	88.8	108	1340	ohv	own	69
	FLHR Electra Glide Road King	US	2	88.8	108	1340	ohv	own	69
	FLHTC-U Ultra Classic Electra Glide	US	2	88.8	108	1340	ohv	own	69
Honda	C90 Cub	Japan	1	47	49.5	85	ohc	own	8
	H100	Japan	1	50	49.5	99	2	own	11
	CA125 Rebel	Japan	2	44	41	124	ohc	own	11
	CG125	Japan	1	56.5	49.5	124	ohc	own	11
	NSR125F	Japan	1	56	50.6	124	2	own	12
	MTX125 Trail	Japan	1	56	50.6	124	2	own	12
	CD250	Japan	2	53	53	233	2	own	16
	CN250	Japan	1	72	60	244	ohc	own	
	CB Two Fifty	Japan	2	53	53	233	ohc	own	21
	CMX250 Rebel	Japan	2	53	53	233	ohc	own	21
	VFR400R3 (NC30)	Japan	4	55	42	399	dohc	own	63
	CB450DX	Japan	2	75	50.6	447	ohc	own	43
	CB500	Japan	2	73	59.6	499	dohc	own	57
	Revere	Japan	2	75	66	583.1	ohc	own	50
	Transalp	Japan	2	75	66	583.1	ohc	own	50
	CB600SF Hornet	Japan	4	65	45.2	599	dohc	own	
	CBR600F	Japan	4	63	48	598	dohc	own	100
	VT600 Shadow	Japan	2	75	66	583	ohc	own	39
	NTV650	Japan	2	79	66	647	ohc	own	55
	NT650 Deauville	Japan	2	79	66	647	Sohc	own	57
	Dominator	Japan	1	100	82	644	ohc	own	44

The 1990s

MARQUE	MODEL	COUNTRY	CYL	BORE	STROKE	CC	2/4-STROKE	ENGINE	BHP
Homda	CB750F2	Japan	4	67	53	747	dohc	own	73
	VFR750	Japan	4	70	48.6	748	dohc	own	100-104
	RC30	Japan	4	70	48.6	748	dohc	own	112
	RC45	Japan	4	72	46	749.2	dohc	own	118
	VF750C	Japan	4	70	48.6	748	dohc	own	88
	VT750C	Japan	2	79	76	745	Sohc	own	
	Africa Twin	Japan	2	81	72	742	ohc	own	59-62
	VFR800	Japan	4	72	48	781	dohc	own	104
	CBR900RR Fireblade	Japan	4	70	58	919	dohc	own	128
	VTR1000	Japan	2	98	66	996	dohc	own	108
	CB1000	Japan	4	77	53.6	998	dohc	own	98
	CBR1000F	Japan	4	77	53.6	998	dohc	own	125
	XL1000 Varadero	Japan	2	98	66	996	dohc	own	94
	CBR1100XX Blackbird	Japan	4	79	58	1137	dohc	own	164
	ST1100	Japan	4	73	64.8	1084	dohc	own	99
	F6C Valkyrie	Japan	6	71	64	1520	sohc	own	99
	GL1500 Gold Wing	Japan	6	71	64	1520	sohc	own	99
Jawa	350 De Luxe	Czech	2	8	65	343.5	2		28
	500R Special	Czech	1	89	179	494	ohc	Rotax	32
Kawasaki	KH100	Japan	1	49.5	51.8	99	2	own	11
	KE100	Japan	1	49.5	51.8	99	2	own	
	KMX125	Japan	1	54	54.4	124	2	own	
	KDX125	Japan	1	56	50.6	124	2	own	12
	KMX200	Japan	1	67	54.4	191	2	own	
	Z250T Scorpion	Japan	2	55	52.4	248	2	own	33
	GPX250R	Japan	2	62	41.2	248	dohc	own	
	EL250	Japan	2	61	41.2	248	dohc	own	36
	KR1-S	Japan	2	56	50.6	249	2	own	59
	GPz305	Japan	2	61	52.4	306	ohc	own	36
	ZXR400	Japan	4	57	39	398	ohc	own	64
	ER500	Japan	2	74	58	498	dohc	own	
	GPZ500S	Japan	2	74	58	498	dohc	own	
	KLE500	Japan	2	74	58	498	dohc	own	48
	GT550	Japan	4	58	52.4	553	dohc	own	55
	Zephyr 550	Japan	4	58	52.4	553	dohc	own	49
	GPZ550	Japan	4	58	52.4	553	dohc	own	64
	GPZ600R	Japan	4	60	52.4	599	dohc	own	76
	ZZ-R600	Japan	4	64	46.6	599	dohc	own	97-99
	ZX-6R Ninja	Japan	4	66	43.8	599	dohc	own	99
	GT750	Japan	4	66	54	738	dohc	own	77
	Zephyr 750	Japan	4	66	54	738	dohc	own	71
	GPX750R	Japan	4	68	51.5	748	dohc	own	
	ZXR750	Japan	4	68	51.5	748	dohc	own	107
	ZX-7R Ninja	Japan	4	73	44.7	748	dohc	own	123
	VN800	Japan	2	88	66.2	805	dohc	own	54
	GPZ900R	Japan	4	72.5	55	908	dohc	own	107
	ZX-9R Ninja	Japan	4	73	53.7	899	dohc	own	123
	ZX10	Japan	4	74	58	997	dohc	own	
	GTR1000	Japan	4	74	58	997	dohc	own	91
	Zephyr 1100	Japan	4	73.5	62.6	1062	dohc	own	90
	ZRX1100	Japan	4	76	58	1052	dohc	own	
	GPZ1100S	Japan	4	76	58	1052	dohc	own	123
	ZZ-R 1100	Japan	4	76	58	1052	dohc	own	123
	Z1300	Japan	6	62	71	1286	dohc	own	128
	VN1500	Japan	2	102	90	1470	dohc	own	60-71
KTM	Duke 620	Japan	1	101	76	609			
LAVERDA	668 Sport	Italy	2	78.5	69	668	dohc	own	
	750S	Italy	2	83	69	748	dohc	own	85
MORINI	Dart 350	Italy	2	62	57	344	ohv	own	34
	Kanguro	Italy	2	62	57	344	ohv	own	33
	New York	Italy	2	71	64	507	ohv	own	42
	Excalibur	Italy	2	71	64	507	ohv	own	42
MOTO GUZZI	V65 GT	Italy	2	80	64	643	ohv	own	52
	750 Strada	Italy	2	80	74	744	ohv	own	48
	750 Nevada NT	Italy	2	80	74	744	ohv	own	48
	750 Targa	Italy	2	80	74	744	ohv	own	52
	Mille GT	Italy	2	88	78	949	ohv	own	65
	Le Mans	Italy	2	88	78	949	ohv	own	82
	Spada III	Italy	2	88	78	949	ohv	own	71
	California III	Italy	2	88	78	949	ohv	own	65
	Daytona	Italy	2	90	78	992	ohc	own	95
	1100 Sport	Italy	2	92	80	1064	ohv	own	90
	1100 California EV	Italy	2	92	80	1064	ohv	own	
M7	ETZ 125 Luxus	Germany	1	52	58	123	2	own	11
	ETZ 250 Luxus	Germany	1	69	65	243	2	own	20
	ETZ 301 Luxus	Germany	1	69	65	291	2	own	23
	Skorpion Sport	Germany	1	00	84	660	ohc	own	48
NEVAL	Soviet	Russia	2	68	78	649	ohv		32
NORTON	Commander	UK	Twin Chamber Rotary			588		own	86
	F1 Sport	UK	Twin Chamber Rotary			588		own	95
SUZUKI	GP100	Japan	1	50	50	98	2	own	12
	GS125E	Japan	1	57	48.8	124	ohc	own	12
	RG125 Gamma	Japan	1	56	50	123	2	own	
	TS125X Trail	Japan	1	56	50.6	124	2	own	12
	GN250	Japan	1	73	61.2	249	ohc	own	22
	RGV250	Japan	2	56	50.6	249	2	own	59-62
SUZUKI	DR350	Japan	1	79	71.2	349	ohc	own	30
	GSF400 Bandit	Japan	4	53	45.2	398	dohc	own	54
	GS500E	Japan	2	74	56.6	487	dohc	own	52
	GSF600 Bandit	Japan	4	62	48.7	599	dohc	own	80
	GSX600F	Japan	4	62.6	48.7	599	dohc	own	
	RF600R	Japan	4	65	45.2	600	dohc	own	100
	GSX-R600	Japan	4	65.5	44.5	600	dohc	own	
	LS650 Savage	Japan	1	94	94	652	ohc	own	
	DR650SE	Japan	1	100	82	644	ohc	own	
	XF650 Freewind	Japan	1	100	82	644	ohc	own	
	GSX750F	Japan	4	73	44.7	748	dohc	own	106
	GSX-R750	Japan	4	72	46	749	dohc	own	129
	DR800 Dr Big	Japan	1	105	90	779	ohc	own	53
	VS800 Intruder	Japan	2	83	74.4	805	ohc	own	60
	RF900R	Japan	4	73	56	937	dohc	own	125
	TL1000S	Japan	2	98	66	996	dohc	own	
	TL1000R	Japan	2	98	66	996	dohc	own	
	GSX1100G	Japan	2	78	59	1127	dohc	own	100
	GSX1100F	Japan	4	78	59	1127	dohc	own	125
	GSX-R1100	Japan	4	78	59	1127	dohc	own	125
	GSF1200 Bandit	Japan	4	79	59	1157	dohc	own	96
	VS1400GL Intruder	Japan	2	94	98	1360	ohc	own	71
	VL1500	Japan	2	96	101	965	ohc	own	
TRIUMPH	Trident 750	UK	3	76	55	749	dohc	own	96
	Thunderbird 900	UK	3	76	55	885	dohc	own	69
TRIUMPH	Trident 900	UK	3	76	65	885	dohc	own	97
	T509 Speed Triple	UK	3	76	65	885	dohc	own	
	Trophy	UK	3	76	65	885	dohc	own	97
	Tiger 900	UK	3	76	65	885	dohc	own	84
	Sprint ST	UK	3	79	65	955	dohc	own	
	Daytona 955i	UK	3	79	65	955	dohc	own	
	Daytona 1200	UK	4	76	65	1180	dohc	own	147
	Trophy 1200	UK	4	76	65	1180	dohc	own	107-123
YAMAHA	RXS100	Japan	1	50	50	98	2	own	12
	SR125 Custom	Japan	1	57	48.8	124	ohc	own	12
	TZR125R	Japan	1	56	50.7	124	2	own	12
	DT125R	Japan	1	56	50.7	124	2	own	
	YP250 Majesty	Japan	1	69	66.8	249	ohc	own	20
	TZR250	Japan	2	56.4	50	249	2	own	50
	TDR250	Japan	2	56.4	50	249	2	own	50
	RD350F	Japan	2	64	54	347	2	own	63
	FZR400RR	Japan	4	56	40.5	399	dohc	own	60
	XV535	Japan	2	76	59	535	ohc	own	46

The 1990s

MARQUE	MODEL	COUNTRY	CYL	BORE	STROKE	CC	2/4-STROKE	ENGINE	BHP
Yamaha	XJ600S Diversion	Japan	4	58.5	55.7	598.8	dohc	own	60
	FZS600Fazer	Japan	4	62	49.6	599	dohc	own	
	FZR600 Genesis	Japan	4	59	54.8	599	dohc	own	91
	YZF600R Thunder Cat	Japan	4	62	49.6	599	dohc	own	100
	YZF-R6	Japan	4	65.5	44.5	599	dohc	own	
	XT600E	Japan	4	95	84	595	ohc	own	43
	XVS650 Dragstar	Japan	2	81	63	649	ohc	own	
	SZR660	Japan	2	100	84	659	ohc	own	48
	YTZ660 Tenere	Japan	2	100	84	659	ohc	own	48
	FZ750 Genesis	Japan	4	68	51.6	749	dohc	own	100
	FZR750R (OWO1)	Japan	4	72	46	749	dohc	own	120
	YZF750R	Japan	4	72	46	749	dohc	own	125
	XTZ750 Super Tenere	Japan	2	87	63	749	dohc	own	70
	TRX850	Japan	2	89.5	67.5	849	dohc	own	80
	TDM850	Japan	2	89.5	67.5	849	dohc	own	70-77
	XJ900F	Japan	4	68.5	60.5	891	dohc	own	92-98
	XJ900S Diversion	Japan	4	68.5	60.5	891	dohc	own	89
	FZR1000R EXUP	Japan	4	75.5	56	1002	dohc	own	
	YZF1000R Thunder Ace	Japan	4	75.5	56	1002	dohc	own	145
	YZF-R1	Japan	4	74	58	998	dohc	own	
	GTS1000	Japan	4	75.5	56	1002	dohc	own	101
	XV1100SE	Japan	2	95	75	1063	ohc	own	62
	FJ1200	Japan	4	77	63.8	1188	dohc	own	125
	VMX1200 (V-Max)	Japan	4	76	66	1198	dohc	own	95
	XV1600 Wild Star	Japan	2	95	113	1600		own	

GLOSSARY

ABS
Anti-lock braking systems
AC
Alternating current (as produced by an alternator)
Acceleration
Rate of change of speed, commonly expressed in terms of standing-start quarter mile times
Accelerator
Mechanism for controlling engine speed, commonly called the throttle or twistgrip on motorcycles
Accelerator pump
Carburetor feature which enriches the fuel/air mixture when the throttle is opened quickly
ACU
Auto Cycle Union, UK sports governing body, founded in 1903 as the Auto Cycle Club
Aerodynamics
The science of gas flow over solid objects, in motorcycles of air over the machine and rider
Air-cooling
The removal of heat from an engine by air passing directly over it, a process helped by metal cooling fins on the outside of the engine
Airbox
A pre-chamber of still air feeding the engine, surprisingly important for performance. Often contains the air filter
Air filter
A screen, usually of paper or oiled rubber foam, for keeping dust out of an engine
Alternator
The electricity generator on most motorcycles, producing alternating current (AC) which must be rectified to direct current (DC)
Alpha angle
Throttle position parameter on some types of fuel injection
Amal
Make of slide carburetor, now seen only on classic machines
Ambient
Prevailing atmospheric conditions, such as temperature and pressure, which some fuel injection systems monitor
Ammeter
Instrument which measures electrical current flow
Anti-dive
Term used for systems in telescopic forks which reduced or slowed compression under braking, usually activated by the brakes' hydraulic systems. Strictly not anti-dive, but dive reduction
Austenitic
High-grade steel used for four-stroke valves
Automatic transmission
'Gear-less' drive between engine and rear wheel, favored on commuter machines, in which some sort of fluid drive or variable belt system transmits power
Automatic inlet valve
Early type of valve in which the 'suction' of the piston opens and closes the inlet valve
Automatic tensioner
Spring-loaded self-adjusting tensioner, usually used on cam chains or belts
Bacon slicer
1. Outside engine flywheel (such as on several Moto Guzzi singles); 2. extra cooling disc sometimes fitted to drum brakes
Balance shaft
Rotating shaft within engine with counterweights designed to reduce engine vibration
Bastard
Type of file
bdc
Bottom dead centre: point at which the piston is at the lowest point of its travel (opposite of top dead center)
Beaded-edge tyres
Early tyre in which a hard edge (the 'bead') located into a channel on the wheel rim
Bellmouth
Trumpet-shaped tube designed to improve air-flow into a carburetor
Belt drive
Flexible toothed belt which takes the drive to the rear wheel (e.g. modern Harleys) or drives the camshafts (Ducati), or other components such as superchargers. Many early machines used a crude leather belt for the final drive
Bevel drive
Pair of gears which turn a drive from one shaft to another through an angle, usually 90 degrees. Once common in cam drives (Manx Norton, Ducati), now used in some shaft final drives (eg shaft driven transverse fours)
bhp
Brake horsepower, the horsepower developed by an engine, so called because it is measured on a water or electrical brake dynamometer
Bias-belted
Tyre construction with two or more fabric belts at different angles, effectively a half-way house between cross-ply and radial construction
Big bore
The fitting of a larger piston to increase engine displacement
Big end
The 'eye' in the lower end of a connecting rod and its associated crankshaft journal
Bore
1. The diameter of the cylinder in which the piston travels; 2. to machine a bore
Black box
Slang name given to any electronic system (usually in a sealed 'box') controlling ignition timing or full engine management
Blow-down
In a two-stroke, interval between exhaust port and transfer port opening
BMEP
Brake Mean Effective Pressure, a measure of the mean thrust on the piston crown
Borrani
Italian make of alloy wheel rim
Bosch
German manufacturer of auto-electrical equipment
Bum-stop
Type of seat with a hump to prevent the rider sliding back under hard acceleration
Butterfly
Rotating disc acting as a throttle valve in some carburetors and most fuel injection inlets
Caliper
Disc brake component in which one or more pistons press friction pads against the disc rotor
Cam
Projection on a rotating shaft which transmits movement to another component
Camshaft
Shaft, usually with several cam 'lobes' which control the opening of valves, either directly or via some intervening mechanism
Cantilever suspension
A now little-used term for monoshock rear suspension (without a rising rate linkage)
Capacity
The displacement of an engine, a function of bore, stroke and number of cylinders (3.142 x (half bore diameter, squared) x stroke x No of cylinders)
Carbon-carbon
Sintered carbon, used as both a disc rotor and pad material in exotic racing brakes
Carbon fibre
Very strong, light composite of fine filaments of carbon, woven and bonded in a matrix (e.g. epoxy resin)
Carburettor
Device, usually working on the Venturi principle, for mixing fuel and air in the correct quantities for combustion
Cardan shaft
The final drive shaft (usually splined) in shaft driven motorcycles
Cable
On a motorcycle, usually a 'Bowden cable' with a stiff outer and flexible steel inner which transmits linear movement (e.g. clutch cable) or rotation (speedometer cable)
Carillo
Californian maker of very high quality racing parts, esp con rods
Castor
See 'rake'
cc
Cubic centimetres, the most common unit for measuring engine displacement (1 cubic inch = 16.4cc)
Centre of gravity
Point at which the whole mass of an object or objects (eg motorcycle or motorcycle and rider combined) can be considered to act
Ceramic
Inorganic material (related to pottery) sometimes used in modern engines because of its extreme hardness and low thermal conductivity
Chain
Series of side-plates and rollers used to transmit drive from sprocket to sprocket, such as cam drives or chain final drive
Charge
Used of combustion, it refers to the incoming fuel/air mixture; 2. of a motorcycle's electrical system, it relates to the alternator or generator's output; 3. to replenish a partially or fullly drained battery
Choke
Refers both to the carburetor's venturi (or fuel injector body bore), and to any mechanism for enrichening the fuel/air mixture for cold starts
Chopper
Custom machine, typically with hugely extended forks and 'Easy Rider' styling
Classic
Loose, often debated, expression for 'collectible' models
Clocks
Slang for instruments: speedometer, tachometer, etc
Clip-ons
Two-piece handlebars which clamp to each fork leg, usually for a low, racer-like riding position
Clutch
Device for controlling the transmission of power from engine to gearbox, usually by means of friction plates
Coil
Electrical windings which turn a low-voltage current into the high voltage required by the spark plugs
Combustion chamber
The space (usually in the cylinder head) above the piston at top dead center in which combustion begins. Its precise shape is crucial to engine efficiency
Compression damping
In suspension systems, the mechanism (usually hydraulic) which controls the rate at which the wheel reacts to bumps as the suspension compresses
Compression ratio
The ratio of maximum cylinder and combustion chamber volume at bdc to that at tdc, usually in the range 7:1 to 14:1
Configuration
The layout of an engine , e.g. V-twin, transverse four, etc
Connecting rod/Con rod
The metal rod which joins the piston to the crankshaft
Contact breaker 'Points'
Pairs of mechanically-controlled electrical contacts which, with high-tension coils, create the current for the spark plug at a specific time
Crankcase
Commonly separates into two halves, the cases (usually aluminum) in which the crankshaft (and usually the gearbox on modern machines) are located
Crankshaft
Iron or steel shaft (one-piece or 'pressed up') which turns the up-and-down motion of the pistons into rotation.
Cross-ply
Tyres having fabric layers with cords running across the tire from one side to the other, as opposed to radial tires
Cush drive
Device for reducing shock loadings in a transmission, usually comprising rubber blocks in a vaned chamber in the rear hub
CV
Constant Vacuum, Constant Velocity Carburetor in which the choke is controlled by depression rather than a direct mechanism such as in a slide-type carburetor
Cylinder
The usually cylindrical chamber (Honda's NR750 had oval cylinders) in which the piston travels
Cylinder head
The 'crown' of an engine. In two-strokes it is little more than an inverted metal dish with a spark plug; in four-strokes it contains the valves, and often the camshafts
Damper
Device for slowing the movement of components relative to each other. Usually hydraulic, but friction dampers were once common
DC
Direct current, as used by most motorcycle electrical components
Deltabox
Term used by Yamaha to describe its twin spar aluminium frames
Desmodromic
Valve system in which a cam rather than a spring controls the closing of the valve, as well as the opening, such as on many Ducatis
Diesel/Compression ignition engine
Engine where combustion is initiated by cylinder pressure, rather than a spark. Heavy and low in power, so rare on motorcycles
Dirt bike
Any motorcycle designed for off-road use, such as a motocrosser
Disc brake
Brake in which pads of friction material are squeezed against a spinning rotor
Disc valve
Type of valve using a rotating disc with a window to control flow, sometimes seen on two-stroke inlet ports
Dog
Engagement device, usually used of the side projections on a motorcycle gear wheel which lock it to an adjacent gear
Drag
Resistance of air to a moving body, usually expressed in terms of drag coefficient, CD. Drag also occurs with engine components moving through oil
Drag racing
Sprint-type racing, usually over a measured quarter mile
Drum brake
Brake in which 'shoes' of friction material are moved radially against the inside of a cylinder (the drum)
Dry sump
Type of four-stroke engine in which the lubricating oil is contained in a separate tank rather than within the crankcases
Dry weight
The weight of a motorcycle without fuel (and sometimes oil, water, and battery acid)
Dual-CBS
Complex braking system used by Honda to link front and rear brake calipers
Duplex
Literally, 'double'. Used of frame design and double-row chains, etc
Dural
Duralumin: a high-grade aluminum alloy common in motorcycle fabrications
Dwell
The duration of a process. Typically used of the length (in time)of an ignition spark, or the time (in degrees of crankshaft rotation) for which a valve or contact breaker is held at a certain degree of lift
Dynamo
Simple device for converting rotation of a shaft into electricity, used only on early motorcycles
Dynamometer
Often abbreviated to 'dyno'. Instrument for measuring engine torque (from which power can be calculated). 'Rolling road' dynos are more convenient and common than the more accurate fixed water brake systems
Dyno
See dynamometer
EFI
Electronic fuel injection
Enduro
Off-road motorcycle racing over an 'unseen' course
Engine braking
The braking effect of an engine when the throttle is closed, caused mainly by pumping effects
Engine management system
Sophisticated computer-driven engine control systems, controling ignition timing, fuel injection and other variables
ET Ignition
Energy Transfer ignition
Excess (insurance)
First part of a claim met by insured person rather than insurer
Exhaust
1. The pipes and silencers which conduct spent combustion gases away from an engine; 2. the gases themselves
Expansion
The characteristic of almost all materials to grow larger as they are heated. Different materials have different coefficients of expansion which must be considered closely in engine design
Expansion Chamber
Bulbous portion of two-stroke exhaust system, designed to maximise exhaust pressure-pulses and so improve engine efficiency
Extractor
Puller for separating components
EXUP
Yamaha term for valve in exhaust system which opens secondary chamber and changes effective volume of exhaust system, improving engine power characteristics
Face cam
Cam whose operational surface is on its face rather than circumference
Fade
Lose effectiveness, especially of overheated brakes
Featherbed
Legendary Norton frame, designed by the McCandless brothers, introduced 1950
Feeler gauge
Metal strip of precise thickness used to measure fine clearances
Fender
American expression for 'mudguard'
Fettle
To work on something, especially mechanical. Can be anything from smoothing rough edges to getting running again
Filament
Thin wire in light bulb which glows when passing current
Filler
Inert, usually adhesive compound used for bodywork repairs
FIM
Federation Internationale Motorcycliste, the world governing body for motorcycle sport
Fin/finning
Cooling extensions, on cylinder, crankcase, brake drums and some electrical components
Fir cone valve cap
Screw-in finned valve covers on early side-valve engines
Fishtail silencer
Silencer with flattened, wedge-shaped end portion
Flame front
The leading edge of the flame advancing through the combustion chamber: the mixture does not explode, but burns
Flanged wheel rim
Rim with projecting edge to secure tyre bead
Flangeless wheel rim
More common type of rim without flange
Flathead
Cylinder head offering flat combustion chamber face, such as many sidevalves and 'Heron' head ohv (Morini)
Flat slide carburetor
Carburetor in which slide is flat rather than cylindrical. More common in race applications than on road bikes
Flat-top piston
Piston with flat or nearly flat combustion face, common in two-strokes
Flat twin
'Boxer' engine layout with two cylinders opposed at 180 degrees, e.g. BMW, Douglas
Float
Buoyant object in carburetor used to actuate a petrol cut-off valve
Float chamber
Vented chamber housing float. Can be part of carburetor or sited remotely
Fully floating
Usually applied to brake drums or calipers tied to the frame rather than a suspension member. Also applies to a brake disk rotor loosely mounted on its internal carrier
Float needle
Needle-shaped part of a carburetor's fuel cut-off valve
Flooding
1. Deliberately over-riding the fuel cut-off valve to promote a rich mixture for cold starts; 2. inadvertently causing a too-rich mixture so that the spark plug 'wets' and the engine won't start
Flow bench
Forced-air rig used to assess the ability of an engine to flow fuel/air mixture
Flow meter
Instrument for measuring the rate of fuel flow in an engine, used in conjunction with a dynamometer
Fluff
Term used when an engine dies, or runs erratically due to over-rich mixture
Flux
1. Substance used in welding and soldering to prevent oxidation 2.Changing magnetic field in e.g. an alternator

Flywheel
Rotating mass, commonly in crankshaft assembly, used to store energy and smooth power delivery

Flywheel clutch
Clutch mounted on the crankshaft rather than on the layshaft, e.g. Yamaha TD1, MZ TS250

Flywheel magneto
Magneto mounted directly on the crankshaft, rather than driven remotely

Fontana
Prized Italian make of drum brake

Footboard
Flat board used instead of footrests on some cruiser machines

Footchange
Gearchange mechanism operated by foot (early bikes were hand-change)

Foot-pound
Unit of work: the raising of one pound vertically through one foot. Should be written as ft.lb. Mathematically the same as lb.ft, but convention uses the latter to signify a measure of torque

Footrest
Fixed or hinged rest for the rider or passenger's foot

Forced induction
Engine using a supercharger or turbocharger

Forecar
Bath-chair attachment replacing the front wheel and forks on some vintage motorcycles

Forging
Component hammered or pressed from hot metal, usually superior to equivalent cast component

Four-stroke
Engine operating on the Otto cycle (named after its inventor, Dr Nicholas Otto), where the power stroke occurs every fourth stroke (two rotations of the crankshaft)

Free play
Clearance in a mechanism, such as at the clutch cable

Freeze fitting
Shrinking parts by extreme cooling prior to making an interference fit

Fuel injection
Positive metering and introduction of fuel by mechanical or electro-mechanical means, now often integrated into comprehensive electronic engine management systems

Full bore
Flat out or maximum speed

Full bump
Suspension at maximum compression

Gaiter
Flexible protective shroud, usually around a suspension unit or control linkage

Gap
Space between two elements, esp contact breaker points or spark plug electrodes

Gasket
Sealing between two joint faces. May be of paper, metal, composite or plastic

Gas tight
Seal or joint which is impervious to gas, used especially of cylinder head to barrel face

Gas welding
Joining materials by heating with burning gases, usually oxygen and acetylene

Gauge
Measuring device; measure of thickness

Gear tooth
Projection on a gear designed to mesh with a complementary indent on a matching gear

Gear ratio
Ratio of turning speeds of a pair of gears, or the aggregate ratio of a train of gears

Gel coat
Thin, uppermost coat used in glass-fibre lamination to give a smooth finish, with or without colour

Girder fork
Front suspension comprising rigid beams, movement being allowed by links at the steering head

Girdraulic
Vincent's proprietory form of girder forks employing light alloy blades and hydraulic damping

Gland
Joint, usually in a pipe, with either jointing material or a preformed seal

Glass fibre
Fine strands of spun glass, usually pressed or woven into sheet and treated with a chemically-setting resin

GP
1. Grand Prix 2. Type of Amal racing carburetor

Grand Prix
Blue-riband motorcycle road racing competition, began in France in 1913 but was not incorporated into a world championship until 1949

Grass track racing
Specialist off-road bike racing on an oval grass circuit

Grease
Stabilised mixture of a metallic soap and a lubricating oil

Grinding paste
Abrasive compound of carborundum powder and oil, used to bed-in valves and mating surfaces

Grommet
Doughnut-shaped item, usually rubber, preventing chafing of control and electrical cables passing through a hole

Ground clearance
The distance between the lowest sprung point of a motorcycle and the ground

Ground joint
Face joint made by lapping two surfaces together

Gudgeon pin ('wrist pin' in USA)
Hard steel tube linking the piston to the small-end

Guide
Component that directs, aligns or positions another, e.g. valve guide

Gusset
Piece used to strengthen any open structure, such as steering head assembly

Gyroscopic precession
The effect in which gyroscopic forces give a rotating wheel both a self-centering effect and the capacity for counter-steering

Hairpin spring
Commonly a valve spring, hairpin-shaped but often with coils at the closed end

Half time pinion
Crankshaft gear or sprocket sized to drive ignition or camshaft at half engine speed

Halogen bulb
Light bulb using one of the halogen family of gases, e.g. iodine, to increase light output

Handlebars
Projections from the steering column used for mounting controls and steering by the hands

Harden
To toughen, usually by heat, mechanical or chemical process

Head angle
Angle of the steering axis with reference to the horizontal (castor angle) or vertical (trail angle)

Head steady
Tie-bar between cylinder head and frame

Heat sink
Mass (usually metallic) used to absorb heat away from another component (e.g. brake, rectifier) until it can be shed

Helical gears
Gears having spiral or part-spiral meshing faces

Helicoil
Brand name for a type of threaded female insert, used in aluminum alloy to repair or strengthen a fastening

Hemi head
Hemispherical cylinder head, favored in some older engines, in which the combustion chamber is roughly half a sphere

Heron head
Type of cylinder head in which combustion chamber is formed in the piston rather than the head itself, e.g. Morini

High tensile
Material, commonly steel, of high 'stretch' strength

High tension
'HT', the high-voltage secondary phase in an ignition system

Hill climb
Standing-start speed competition over a twisting uphill course

Honing
Achieving a fine finish to precise size by abrasion, typically in rebored cylinders

Horizontally opposed
Engine layout with pairs of cylinders opposed at 180 degrees, e.g. BMW 'Boxer', Honda Gold Wing

Hose
Any flexible pipe, commonly hydraulic brake lines

Hot spot
Area of a combustion chamber which gets too hot, causing pre-ignition. Often caused by incandescent carbon deposits

Hot tube ignition
Primitive ignition system in which a platinum tube is heated by spirit burner

H-section
Shaped like a letter 'H' in cross-section, e.g. con-rod

HT leads
High tension cables, from coil to spark plug or coil to distributor to spark plug

Hub
Centre part of a wheel

Hub centre steering
Steering system in which the axis of wheel movement lies within the wheel hub

Hugger
1. Lightweight, racing-style rear fender which moves up and down with the wheel 2. Low slung Harley-Davidson models

Hunting
Erratic tickover, often caused by incorrect carburation

Hydraulic
Mechanism using the flow or pressure of a liquid through valves and orifices, such as with motorcycle brakes and suspension dampers

Hydrometer
Instrument for measuring specific gravity of a liquid, e.g. to test state of charge of a battery

Hygrometer
Instrument for measuring humidity, such as to calculate jetting for racing engines

Hygroscopic
Substance which attracts water, such as (most) brake fluids

Hysteresis
Literally, lag. Of tire rubber, high-hysteresis compounds (invented by Avon) have less internal bounce and more grip

Ice racing
Racing on oval ice tracks with speedway-like machines fitted with metal-spiked tyres

Idiot light
Slang expression for an instrument warning light

Idler gear
Gear interposed between two others to avoid using overlarge working gears

Ignition advance
Extent to which the ignition spark precedes TDC, necessary because combustion is not instantaneous but takes a finite time

Import, grey
Motorcycle imported into a country which does not officially import that model

Import, parallel
Motorcycle which is imported in direct competition with official imports

Index mark
Vehicle identification number (VIN) or registration number 2. Reference point for adjustment, e.g. of wheel alignment or ignition timing

Induction
Drawing-in of fuel/air to an engine, although correctly it is mainly pushed in by atmospheric pressure

Inertia
The tendency of all things to carry on moving in the same direction once started. Everything in an engine – the pistons, even the air in the carburetor – has inertia

Injector
Pressurized nozzle for squirting fuel or oil into an engine

Inlet
Place of entry, as in inlet valve, inlet tract

Instant gasket
Plasticized glue-like substance, sometimes hardening, for sealing joint faces

Instrument
Device which measures or controls a function

Intake
See inlet

Integral
Belonging to a complete whole

Inter
'Between', as in inter-cooler

Internal combustion engine
Any heat engine in which energy is developed in the engine cylinder and not in a separate chamber

Inverted forks
'Upside down' telescopic forks, in which the sliders are at the top rather than the bottom. Theoretically stiffer than conventional forks, and with less unsprung weight

IOE
Inlet Over Exhaust – engine with overhead inlet valve and side exhaust valve

ISDT
Former name of the ISDE, the International Six Day Enduro (Trial), an international team off-road endurance event

Isle of Man
Island in the Irish Sea which first allowed motorcycle road races in 1905 and has hosted the motorcycle TT since 1907

Isochronous
Occurring at the same time, e.g. two-stroke induction and exhaust phases

Isolastic
Proprietory name for the rubber-mounted engine/swingarm system on the Norton Commando

Jompot
Slang for the fat rear dampers of 1950s AJS and Matchless machines

Jet
An orifice, usually of precise size through which fuel passes

Jet needle
Tapered needle in a carburetor which rises and falls to vary fuel flow at medium throttle openings

Jig
Cradle used to manufacture or check the dimensions of an assembly such as a motorcycle frame

Jointing compound
Material applied to joint faces to assist sealing

Journal
Accurately machined portion of a shaft on which a bearing (e.g. big end) engages

Jubilee clip
Originally a brand of hose clip, the title is now generic

Kadency Effect
Using pressure waves to enhance cylinder filling and scavenging

Keihin
Japanese brand of carburetor

Kevlar
A synthetic (para-Aramid) fibre with enormous tensile strength, used in exotic motorcycle components and protective clothing (including bullet-proof vests)

Kick back
Brief but often fierce reverse rotation of an engine during starting

Kickstarter
Foot-operated crank for starting an engine

Kilowatt
kW, now becoming the standard ISO measure of horsepower.1kW equals 1.3596PS or 1.341bhp

Kneeler
Usually a low-profile sidecar outfit in which the rider kneels; more rarely special solos such as the 1953 Norton kneeler

Knee slider
Slippery attachment to racing leathers allowing the rider to drag his inside knee on the ground in corners

Knurling
Machine tool rolling process for cross-hatching components

Laminar flow
The tendency of fluids near a solid surface to 'stick' with the surface and lubricate the movement of fluids farther away. The principle relates to mixture in an inlet tract, motorcycle aerodynamics and high pressure oil lubrication properties

Lap
1. Complete circuit of racetrack 2. Bed-in by lapping with abrasive compound

Latent heat
Heat needed to change a solid to liquid or liquid to gas

Lathe
Machine tool with rotating workpiece and fixed cutter

Layshaft
Gearbox shaft parallel to the mainshaft in a direct gearbox, carrying the laygears

Leaded
Gasoline bearing tetra-ethyl lead, an anti-knock compound and neuro-toxin

Leading link
Form of front suspension using a pivoted link with the wheel spindle in front of the pivot

Leading shoe
In a drum brake, the brake shoe with its actuating cam at its leading edge

Leaf spring
Suspension spring comprising one or more narrow strips of spring steel

Lean
Ingoing fuel/air charge which has too little fuel

Lean-out
Make mixture more lean; extent to which the steering head leans away from the vertical in a sidecar outfit

Level plug
Plug, usually screw-in, which marks the desired upper level of fluid in a chamber

Lever
Handle for achieving a mechanical advantage, typically a brake or clutch lever

Lift
Amount something is raised, e.g. a valve off its seat

Light alloy
Loose expression for a multitude of aluminum alloys

Liner
Detachable insert, commonly a steel cylinder liner in an alloy barrel

Linkage
Typically an articulated joint, such as in a gearchange mechanism

Lobe
Raised part of a cam

Lock
1. (Maximum) steering deflection 2. Key-operated security device to prevent unauthorised removal

Locking wire/lockwire
Strong, usually stainless steel wire used for securing items against loosening

Locknut
Nut tightened hard against another to prevent loosening

Lock stop
Abutment to the steering gear limiting amount of steering lock

Lock washer
Washer with anti-loosening feature

Lockwire pliers
Special pliers with jaws capable of locking onto and twisting lockwire

Loctite
Proprietory liquid used for securing threads, bearings, etc

Long reach
Term for a spark plug of 3/4in (19mm) reach

Long stroke
Undersquare engine, in which the stroke exceeds the bore

Lubricant
Any substance interposed between rubbing surfaces to reduce friction

Magdyno
Unit combining a magneto and dynamo in a common housing

Magic box
Anything electrical which you don't understand. See black box

Magnesium
Metal, 36 per cent lighter than aluminum, expensively used for some motorcycle castings

Magneto
Ignition spark generator requiring no external electrical power source

Main bearing
Any principal bearing, but usually those carrying the crankshaft

Main jet
The principle fuel jet in a carburetor

Mains
Crankshaft main bearings

Mainshaft
Principle shaft, usually in gearbox

Manifold
Branched system conducting mixture to, or exhaust from, an engine

Marque
Alternative term for make or manufacturer of motorcycle

Marshal
Safety official at race meeting

Master cylinder
Reservoir and pump at the operator end of a hydraulic system

Maudes Trophy
ACU trophy infrequently awarded for feats of unusual machine endurance

Megaphone
(Coloquially called 'megga'). Outward tapering four-stroke exhaust chamber capable of increasing power and power spread

Metalastik
Flexible bush acting as both pivot and vibration insulation

Mikuni
Japanese carburetor manufacturer, began by making Amals under licence

Mixture
Ingoing fuel/air charge

MON
Motor octane number, arrived at by a more severe test than RON and more relevant for racing purpoes

Monobloc
1. Amal carburetor with float bowl and mixing chamber formed in one casting. 2. Any such carburetor

Monograde oil
Oil with a viscosity defined by a single SAE number

Monoshock
Rear suspension system employing a single shock absorber, strictly a Yamaha trade name

Moped
Pedal-assisted motorcycle, with engine less than 50cc

Motocross
Off-road circuit racing, formerly called scrambles

Motocross des Nations
Annual international team motocross championship

Mudguard
(Fender) Shroud designed to prevent road dirt being flung from wheels onto machine and rider

Multigrade oil
Oil with viscosity characteristics encompassing two or more SAE numbers

Multi-rate
A spring which changes length unequally for different increments of load

Needle roller
A bearing roller very much longer than its diameter

Negative earth
Connecting the negative battery terminal to earth

NGK
Nippon Geika Kaisha, Japanese spark plug manufacturer

Nikasil
Proprietory process for applying a thin, hard coating to alloy cylinder bores

Nimonic
Nickel-rich iron alloy favored for exhaust valves

Nipple
Boss with a hole in it for admitting grease

Nitriding
Process for hardening steel

Nitro
Nitro-methane, an oxygen-rich fuel of low calorific value

Non-unit
Engine layout in which the powerplant and transmission are separate units

Normally-aspirated
Engine charged by atmospheric pressure, rather than forced induction

Nyloc
Nut with a nylon insert which resists loosening through vibration

Nylocable
Bowden cable with 'self-lubricating' nylon inner sheath

Observed section
Part of a trials course in which penalties can be incurred

Observer
Official stationed at observed section to monitor competitors' performance

Octane rating
Measure of the knock resistance of fuel, higher numbers being more knock resistant. Usually given as average of MON and RON

Odometer
Mileage recorder, usually part of speedometer

OHC
Overhead camshaft

OHV
Overhead valve

Oil
Natural or synthetic fluid with good lubricating properties

Oil bath
Protective oil reservoir into which a component dips

Oil cooling
Where oil is used to collect engine heat and transport it to cooling surfaces. Although all engines are partially oil cooled, Suzuki's GSX-R series has taken this to extreme lengths

Oil cooler
A radiator containing engine oil rather than water

Oil pump
Mechanical device for pressurizing oil in an engine

Oil seal
Lipped, semi-elastic oil barrier on a shaft

Oil thrower
Shaped ring or plate designed to throw oil away from a particular site

O-ring
Rubber sealing ring, typically in oil feeds

O-ring chain
Final drive chain using O-rings to seal in grease

Otto Cycle
The four-stroke cycle

Outside flywheel
Flywheel carried outside the crankcases, where it can have a larger diameter and thus more effective with less weight

Overlap
Time when the inlet and exhaust valves are simultaneously open

Over-square
Engine in which the bore is greater than the stroke, as in most modern engines

Pannier
Component hanging down either side of a motorcycle, as in luggage bags or fuel tanks

Patent
Protection granted by the state to an inventor

Pattern parts
Replacement parts not authorized by the original manufacturer

Pawl
Catch meshing with a ratchet wheel

Peak
Highest point, as of cam lobe, power output, revs

Peak revs
Maximum safe revs for a particular engine

Penetration
1. Consistency of a grease 2. Infiltration of a freeing agent 3. Depth of a weld

Pent roof
An efficient combustion chamber form in multi-valve heads, shaped like a pitched roof

Petroil
Gasoline and oil mixture used in some two-stroke engines

Petroleum jelly
Waxy petroleum product used to protect battery terminals, eg 'Vaseline'

Phased piston
Large 'supercharging' piston in such as in DKW and early EMC racers

Phillips
Proprietary form of crosshead screw, often wrongly used generically

Phosphor-bronze
Copper/tin alloy with excellent bearing qualities, often used for small-end bushes

Piggy-back
Often used of the pressurized gas reservoir attached to a modern suspension unit

Pigtail
Short length of conducting wire connected to a pickup brush

Pilgrim
Simple type of double-ended pump using a single plunger to supply and scavenge

Pillion
1. Seat behind the rider 2. Person on it

Pilot jet
Auxilliary jet in a carburetor which governs fuel flow at small throttle openings

Pilot light
Small, low-wattage bulb; parking light

Pinking
Metallic tinkling noise produced by pre-ignition

Piston
Moving plunger in a cylinder, accepting or delivering thrust

Piston ring
Springy metal hoops in groove on a piston, designed to promote gas seal or scrape oil from bore

Piston slap
Audible contact of piston skirt against cylinder bore, worse in cold or worn bores

Pitch
Distance between two repeating characteristics, such as rollers on a chain or teeth on a gear

Pinchbolt
Bolt pinching two elements of a part together, such as on a fork yoke

Plain bearings
Bearings surfaces which are flat and depend on a thin film of oil (supplied at pressure) to keep them apart (such as some big-ends and mains)

Plating
Electrolytic deposition of a metal onto a dissimilar material for protective or cosmetic purposes

Plug cap
Spark plug cover acting as protection, HT conductor and often radio suppressor

Pocketing
Valves sunk into the cylinder head by repeated hammering effect, to the detriment of performance

Polarity
Positive or negative, as of electrical connections

Polycarbonate
Lightweight, resilient plastic used for crash helmets

Pop rivet
Deformable metal pin used for joining two components

Poppet valve
Reciprocating valve (as in cylinder head), essentially a disk on a stick

Popping back
Spitting back through the carburetor

Porous
Material allowing the passage of fluids. Often this is unwanted, as in porous castings which allow oil to pass through

Port
Any opening, now commonly applied to two-stroke's cylinder windows and their associated tracts

Positive earth
Electrical system in which the battery's positive terminal connected to earth

Pot
Slang for cylinder

Power
The rate of work, as measured in horsepower; more loosely, an engine's peak power output

Power band
The range of rpm in which an engine is making useful power or the bulk of its power

Power-slide
Cornering with deliberate power-induced wheelspin, as in speedway

Power valve
Two-stroke exhaust mechanism which alters the height (and thus duration) of the exhaust valve, usually known by manufacturers' trade names

Pre-ignition
Spontaneous combustion of the fuel/air mix before sparking

Pre-load
Compression applied to a spring in installation. It has no bearing on the spring's rate

Pre-'65
Class of trials and motocross competition for machines built before 1965

Pressure gauge
Instrument for measuring air or oil pressure

Pre-unit
Description of a layout with seperate engine and gearbox, but of a model type which later had them in unit

Primary chain
Chain transmitting drive from crankshaft to gearbox

Primary gears
Gear train transmitting drive from crankshaft to gearbox

Progressive rate
Spring compressing at a rate which decreases with load

Projector
Type of headlight which uses small diameter lens (similar to a slide projector's) to focus the light beam

Prop-stand
Retractable side-stand

PS
Widely-used German measure of horsepower (equivalent to French'cv'). 100PS equals 98.6bhp

PTFE
Poly-tetra-fluoro-ethylene, a low-friction plastic often used for bearing bushes

Pudding-basin
Early, abbreviated form of crash helmet, cork-lined with leather temple protection

Pulling power
Slang term for an engine's ability to work under heavy load at low rpm

Push rod
Metal rod used to transmit motion, such as from cam follower to rocker arm or in a clutch mechanism

Quench
To cool; used of metal treatments, and combustion chambers in which a large area of metal is in close contact with combustion gases, restraining pre-ignition

Quietening ramp
Gradual slope between base circle of a cam and the lobe proper

Radial tires
Tires where plies run across from one bead to the other at 90 degrees to the wheel rim. An additional belt runs around the circumference of the tire

Radial valves
Multiple valves 'radiating' from the centre of the cylinder head or combustion chamber rather than in parallel pairs

Radiator
Device for dissipating heat through a large surface area, usually used for engine oil or coolant

Rake
Effective slope of the front forks relative to the vertical. Subtracted from 90 gives the castor figure. Also called head angle, although confusingly, so is castor

Ram Air
Name trademarked by Kawasaki, now used generically, to describe the use of forward-facing air-scoops to pressurize an air box. At least as much benefit is gained because the air at the front of a bike is the coolest, and therefore most dense

Ramp cam
Cam fitted with quietening ramps

Reamer
Fluted tool used to cut a hole to an exact final size

Rear wheel steering
Steering a motorcycle by deliberately drifting the rear wheel

Rebore
Machine a cylinder to accept an oversize piston

Rebound damping
The damping which resists the spring's tendency to recoil after compressing. Also called extension damping

Reciprocating
Moving backwards and forwards along a single path, such as a piston

Rectifier
Electrical device passing current in one direction only, thus converting AC to DC

Recoil
The bouncing back of a spring to its unloaded position

Reed valve
A 'flapper' valve in a two-stroke's induction system, comprising flexible plates housed in a reed cage

Reflector
1. Polished bowl of a light unit 2. Passive safety reflector in rear light units 3. Element in some exhaust systems designed to maximise exhaust wave harmonics

Regulator
Electronic component which maintains the desired voltage, sometimes 'voltage control unit'

Rev counter
Tachometer: instrument for measuring the rotational speed (rpm) of an engine

Reverse cone
Extension to some megaphone silencers having a steep taper in the opposite direction to the megaphone

Riffler
Small fine-toothed file, especially used in porting work

Rich (mixture)
Fuel/air mixture with excess fuel

Rim
Edge of a wheel carrying the tire

Ring gear
In engines with a longitudinal crankshaft, the gear around the flywheel engaging with the starter motor

Ring pegs
Small metal locaters preventing piston rings from rotating, esp in two-strokes

Rising rate
Suspension in which linkages cause the rate of movement to increase as wheel travel increases

Rocker
Pivoting arm translating rotational cam action into linear valve movement

Rockerbox
Closed compartment housing the rocker gear

Rocking couple
Lateral rocking motion set up in some types of multi-cylinder crankshaft

Roller bearing
Bearing having cylindrical rollers rather than balls

RON
Research octane number

Rotary
Spinning, rather than reciprocating. Usually applied to Wankel engines

Rotary valve
Rotating, rather than piston-port or poppet valve, which opens and closes gas passageways as it spins

rpm
Revs per minute, the rotational speed of a shaft or engine

Rumble
Low-pitched noise emitted, especially, by worn crankshafts

Running on
Phenomenon of an engine continuing to run after the ignition has been switched off, usually due to local hot spots

Run-out
Out-of-true of a shaft or wheel

SAE
1. Society of Automotive Engineers, USA 2. standards established by it

Sand racing
Racing on beaches, often on speedway-type courses

Sand casting
Metal component made by pouring molten metal into pre-formed sand mould

Scavenge
Clear away, especially of exhaust gases from a combustion chamber

Schnurle Loop
Two-stroke scavenging process in which transfer ports direct gases up and away from the open exhaust port, propelling exhaust gases ahead of them

Schraeder
Design of tire valve core, also used for air suspension

Scraper
1. Tool for scraping 2. Piston ring designed to clear oil from bores

Sealed beam
Light unit with lens, filament and reflector in one piece

Security bolt
Clamped rubber pad designed to prevent creep of tires running at low pressure

Seizure
Binding together of inadequately lubricated or heat-expanded parts, esp pistons in bores

Selector fork
Fork-shaped prong, controlled by a cam-plate or -drum, able to slide gearbox pinions and thus change gear

Serrated
Toothed, as in a serrated or 'Shakeproof' washer

Set screw
Bolt threaded almost to its head, with no plain shank

Shim
Tough metal insert of known thickness used to achieve desired clearance

Shock absorber
Device for smoothing transmission impulses; also applied less correctly but more frequently to suspension dampers

Shorrock
Brand of rotary, vane-type supercharger

Short reach
Spark plug hole of half-inch depth

Short stroke
Markedly oversquare engine

Shot blasting
Bombardment of parts to de-scale or work-harden them. Bead blasting is similar but less destructive

Shuttle valve
Valve free to move to and fro, often found in telescopic forks

Siamese
Two pipes joined into one, esp of exhaust

Sidevalve (sv)
Engine with valvegear at the side and below the combustion chamber, rather than above

Sidewall
The part of a tire between the tread and the bead

Silencer (Muffler, USA)
Portion of an exhaust system concerned with reducing its noise, now very sophisticated to meet modern noise limits

Silentbloc
Proprietary part made from rubber block bonded to metal

Silver solder
Solder with high silver content giving much stronger joint than ordinary tin solder

Simmonds nut
Precursor of the nyloc nut, with fibre anti-loosening insert

SOHC
Single overhead camshaft

Single leading shoe (SLS)
Drum brake with one actuating cam, and hence one leading and one trailing shoe

Sintered
Formed by heat and pressure, usually of metallic powders

Skimming
Removing thin layer metal to achieve a flat or straight surface, e.g. of cylinder head face

Skirt
Hanging portion, particularly of the piston below the gudgeon pin

Slave cylinder
The end of a hydraulic system remote from the operator

Slick
Treadless racing tire

Slickshift
1950s Triumph gearchange mechanism which automatically disengages the clutch. Not to be confused with the modern racing mechanism which cuts the ignition momentarily between gearchanges

Slide
Moving piston in a slide carburetor which both opens the venturi and governs the flow of fuel through the main jet

Slider
The moving lower part of a telescopic fork leg

Slipper piston
Piston with its skirt cut away to reduce weight and friction

Slipper tensioner
Tensioning device employing a synthetic blade, typically on a cam drive chain

Slip ring
Rotating part of a magneto on which the brushes bear

Sludge
Accumulation of oil-insoluble material in an engine, sometimes centrifuged into a sludge trap

Small end
Bearing on a con rod through which passes the gudgeon pin, sometimes called 'little end'

Snail cam
Chain adjustment eccentric

Socket
1. Cylindrical spanner fitted with a positive square drive 2. Female electrical connector

Socket head screw
Fastener with a recessed head taking hexagonal 'Allen key'

Sodium-filled valve
Hollow valve containing sodium which melts at working temperature, aiding heat transfer to the cooler end of the valve

Solder
Tin alloy of low melting point, typically used to join electrical components

Solenoid
Electrical device using a magnetic field to move a soft iron core and engage a mechanism

Spark arrestor
Silencer component designed to reduce fire risks from some off-road motorcycles

Spark erosion
Process for discreet removal of hard components from softer ones by bombardment with high tension sparks

Spark plug
Device for arcing HT current across two electrodes to initiate combustion

Spectacle head
Cylinder head with iron element comprising valve seats and spark plug boss, onto which is cast a skull of light alloy

Speedometer
Instrument for measuring speed

Spigot
Protrusion, e.g. of cylinder liner into crankcase mouth

Spindle
Fixed rod about which another part turns, e.g. wheel spindle

Spine
Backbone, esp of spine-type frame

Splayed head
Four-stroke twin-cylinder head with widely splayed inletand/or exhaust valves

Spline
Grooved shaft allowing longitudinal but not radial movement of a complementary part

Split single
Two-stroke engine with two pistons sharing a common combustion chamber

Spring
Anything which deforms to permit movement and recoils elastically

Spring washer
Spring steel washer of interrupted circle, designed to prevent loosening

Sprung hub
50s Triumph suspension with the springing located within the rear hub

Square four
Cylinder layout using two crankshafts to place four parallel cylinders at the corners of a square; Ariel Square Four

Squat
Extent to which the rear suspension of most motorcycles sags under power. 'Anti-squat' are designed-in features intended to reduce this

Squish band
Area of cylinder head almost touched by the piston at TDC, promoting quenching and turbulence of combustion gases

Stainless
Corrosion-resistant steel, often non-magnetic, having some 25 per cent of alloyed metals such as chromium

Stall
Stop an engine by overloading it

Stanchion
Rigid structural member; in telescopic forks, the static tube clamped by the yokes

Steering damper
Friction or oil-damped device for combatting uncontrolled steering movement

Steering head
The section of fame into which the front forks engage

Stiction
Static friction' – initial resistance to movement esp in suspension systems

Stinger
Relatively narrow-bore pipe to the rear of two-stroke exhaust systems, important in exhaust resonance control

Stoichiometric ratio
Theoretical air:fuel ratio for perfect combustion at molecular level, 15:1 by weight

Straight (oil)
Mineral grade oil without additives, and thus monograde

Stroboscope
Instrument using an intermittent bright light to 'freeze' rotating markers and so determine ignition timing

Stroke
Linear travel of any component, esp a piston in a bore

Stoppie
Monowheeling on the front wheel under extreme braking

Stud
Threaded rod

Subframe
Framework secondary to the main frame, usually at the rear of a motorcycle

Sump
Oil reservoir, below or integral with the crankcase, in 'wet sump' engines

Supercharger
Mechanically-driven air pump for used in forced induction engines, now rarely used

Suppressor
Electrical resistance in a spark plug to suppress TV and radio interference

Swan neck
S-shaped tube linking sidecar to motorcycle

Swarf
Scrap metal from machining processes

Swept volume
The volume covered by a piston's travel, cylinder displacement

SWG
Standard Wire Gauge, a measuring convention in which smaller numbers refer to thicker wire

Swinging arm, swingarm
Pivoting rear suspension member carrying the wheel at its free end. More accurately called a swinging fork unless single-sided

Synthetic
Substance such as oil or paint based on artificial rather than organic materials. Synthetic oils can be finely tuned to their desired purpose and offer greater performance and longevity

Tab washer
Washer with one or more tabs capable of being bent to secure a nut

Tachometer
Rev counter

Tank rail
Frame tube on which sits the gasoline tank

Tank-slapper
Violent lock-to-lock handlebar and wheel movement of a moving motorcycle

Taper
A narrowing, especially of a shaft onto which another component is pressed

Taper roller
Tapered roller bearing, adjustable and able to take loads radially and axially, such as at the steering head

Tappet
Part interposed between cam and valve or pushrod, often with provision for valve clearance adjustment

Tappet clearance
The free play allowed at a cold tappet to allow for thermal expansion

TDC
Top Dead Centre, the highest position reached by the piston, opposite of BDC

Telescopic
Paired tubes, one able to slide within the other, as in telescopic forks

Terminal
A battery post to which connections are made

Thackaray washer
Spring washer with three coils

Thermal efficiency
Ratio of an engine's output to the potential energy of the fuel it consumes

Thermo-syphon
Water-cooling system using convection rather than a pump

Thermostat
'Switch' responding to temperature, typically one which opens a valve in a water-cooling system

Throttle
A variable restriction in, usually, a carburetor; the twistgrip

Thrust bearing
Bearing whose working face takes up the thrust and any rubbing action of associated shaft

Thrust washer
Washer which ditto

Timing
1. The opening and closing points of valves, and of spark occurrence, expressed in degrees of crankshaft rotation or distance from TDC 2. Adjusting the same

Timing cover
Access cover to the valve timing mechanism

Timing gears
Gears driving the valvegear and/or ignition

Titanium
Strong, grey metal, 43 per cent lighter than steel, used in exotic motorcycle applications

Toe-in
Extent to which the path of a sidecar wheel converges with that of the motorcycle

Tolerances
Allowable variations in manufacturing dimensions

Tooth
Meshing projection on a sprocket, gear or rack

Torque
The twisting force exerted by the crankshaft. Horsepower is a measure of torque multiplied by engine rpm

Torque converter
A fluid coupling using oil and rotating vanes in some automatic transmission systems

Total loss
System of lubrication, usually in two-strokes, in which the oil is lost after delivery to the working surfaces; racing ignition systems with a battery but no charging system

Tract
Passageway in an engine, as in 'inlet tract'

Traction control
Electronic system which reduces power to the driven wheel in the event of wheelspin. Rare on motorcycles - fitted to Honda ST1100 Pan European

Trail
The distance the steering axis, extended to the ground, lies in front of the tire's contact patch. Its effect is to make the bike run straight when upright, but to turn the bike in the direction of lean when cranked over

Trailing link
Form of front suspension using a pivoting link with the wheel spindle behind the pivot

Trailing shoe
Brake shoe with a cam at its trailing edge

Transmission
The general term for the drive train from crankshaft to final drive, including clutch and gearbox

Tread
Part of a tire intended to clear water from the road

Trial
Motorcycle competition over off-road hazards in which penalty points are incurred by a rider putting his feet down, falling or failing a section

Trickle charge
Slow charge given to a battery

Tri-axis
Name given by Yamaha to its gearbox design where one shaft is positioned above the other, to reduce engine length. First used on YZF-R1

Trigonic
Triangular-section race tires developed by Dunlop in the 60s

Triplex chain
Chain with three parallel rows of rollers

Trumpet
Inlet tube (bellmouth), typically applied to fuel injection applications

Tubeless
Tire needing no inner tube

Tungsten
Rare metal used as alloy with tough steels and as filament in conventional light bulb

Turbocharger
A forced air pump, broadly similar to a supercharger, but driven at very high speed by exhaust gases, rather than mechanically

Turbulence
Agitation in a fluid, especially of inlet charge, where it can promote combustion

Twistgrip
Rotary throttle control on the right handlebar

Twin leading shoe (2LS)
A brake with two actuating cams and hence two leading shoes

Under-square
Engine with stroke greater than the bore

Unit construction
Engine in which the powerplant and transmission are formed in one integrated unit

Universal joint (UJ)
The double knuckle joint in shaft drive which allows play in the driven shaft to permit suspension movement

Unleaded
Gasoline devoid of tetra-ethyl-lead, deriving its anti-knock capability from other ingredients

Unsprung weight
That part of the wheels, brakes and suspension which lies the road side of the springs

V-twin
Twin-cylinder engine having its cylinder axes arranged in a 'V' formation, both big-ends usually sharing a common crankpin

Valve
Any device for regulating flow

Valve bounce
Destructive condition where a poppet valve is travelling faster than its spring can control it

Valve gear
The timing gear, cam(s), pushrods, rockers, valves and associated parts in a four-stroke engine

Valve lift
The distance a poppet valve is raised from its seat

Valve lifter
Mechanical device, sometime automatic, for reducing compression during starting of a four stroke single

Valve seat
Insert of harder material into an aluminum cylinder head on which the poppet valve sits when closed

Venturi
A narrowing in a gas passage, esp in a carburetor

Venturi principle
The basis on which carburetors work: gas moving through a narrowing creates a partial vacuum able to lift fluid (fuel) into the venturi

Vernier
Precision measuring device comprising parallel-jawed sliding caliper

Veteran
Any motorcycle made before 1915

Viney bones
Rubber bands cut from old inner tubes, named after trials ace Hugh Viney

Vintage
Any machine made before 1931

Viscosity
Runniness, indicated by SAE number. Higher number denotes more viscous

Volumetric efficiency
Ratio of the actual mass of charge drawn into an engine to that which the cylinder could hold at atmospheric pressure. Can exceed unity in racing engines

Vulcanising
Hot curing of rubber

Wankel
Rotary engine invented by Felix Wankel, operating on four-stroke cycle but without reciprocating parts

Washer
Disk, usually of metal, placed under a nut or bolt head to prevent scouring, loosening or to seal

Water-cooling, liquid cooling
Transmission of heat from an engine to atmosphere via a liquid intermediary and radiator

Watt
Unit of electrical 'volume' - volts times amperes

W-clip
'W'-shaped clip securing headlamp unit to shell

Weave
Term used to describe unwanted side to side movement of a motorcycle, usually at high speed, often during cornering.

Weight distribution
Ratio of a vehicle's weight which bears on the front and rear wheels respectively

Weller tensioner
Self-adjusting spring-loaded blade tensioner, such as used on camchains

Weld
Join materials by melting

Werner Position
1. The usual site for a modern motorcycle engine in a frame 2. The name of two brothers who first put one there in 1897

Wet liner
Cylinder liner which bears directly against the cooling liquid

Wet sump
Engine in which the oil is carried in a well below the crankcase, rather than in a remote tank

Wheel
Any circular object rotating on an axle at its center

Wheelbase
The distance between front and rear wheel spindles

Wheelie
Mono-wheeling on the rear wheel under power

White metal
Applied to various alloys of a whitish colour, typically used in plain bearings for its soft surface

Whitworth
Type of thread of coarse pitch

Winding
Coil of wire around a core in a solenoid or generator

Wire-wound piston
Vintage piston with split skirt wrapped in coils of steel wire, eliminating differential expansion with an iron bore

Woodruff key
Half-moon-shaped piece of hard steel locating a component by keyways onto a shaft

Worm gear
A uni-directional gear set in which a gear-wheel messes with a screw-type thread, such as in speedometer drives, some shaft final drives (eg Sunbeam)

Wrist pin
1. Secondary big end pin in such as radial and some V-twin and split single engines 2. Gudgeon pin (USA)

Y-alloy
Hiduminium, a brand of light alloy which casts well and retains strength at high temperatures

Yoke
Component connecting two or more others, esp fork yoke

Zener diode
Voltage regulator commonly allowing excess voltage to leak to an associated finned heat sink

Zinc
Grey metal used in galvanizing

Zoller
A Vane-type supercharger